Exporting:
From Start
to Finance

Exporting: From Start to Finance

L. Fargo Wells

Karin B. Dulat

Third Edition

McGraw-Hill

New York   San Francisco   Washington, D.C.   Auckland   Bogotá
Caracas   Lisbon   London   Madrid   Mexico City   Milan
Montreal   New Delhi   San Juan   Singapore
Sydney   Tokyo   Toronto

Library of Congress Cataloging-in-Publication Data

Wells, L. Fargo.
    Exporting : from start to finance / L. Fargo Wells, Karin B.
Dulat. — 3rd ed.
       p.   cm.
    Includes bibliographical references (p.   ) and index.
    ISBN 0-07-069300-5 (alk. paper)
    1. Export marketing—United States—Handbooks, manuals, etc.
I. Dulat, Karin B. II. Title.
HF1416.5.W45   1996
658.8'48'0973—dc20   95-44388
                                          CIP

McGraw-Hill

A Division of The McGraw-Hill Companies

ISBN 0-07-069300-5

The sponsoring editor for this book was David Conti, the editing supervisor was Paul R. Sobel, and the production supervisor was Donald F. Schmidt. It was set in Garamond by Estelita F. Green of McGraw-Hill's Professional Book Group composition unit.

Printed and bound by R. R. Donnelley & Sons Company.

This publication is designed to provide accurate and authoritative information in regard to the subject matter covered. It is sold with the understanding that the publisher is not engaged in rendering legal, accounting, or other professional service. If legal advice or other expert assistance is required, the services of a competent professional person should be sought.

      —from a declaration of principles jointly adopted by a committee of the American Bar Association and a committee of publishers.

McGraw-Hill books are available at special quantity discounts to use as premiums and sales promotions, or for use in corporate training programs. For more information, please write to the Director of Special Sales, McGraw-Hill, 11 West 19th Street, New York, NY 10011. Or contact your local bookstore.

This book is printed on recycled, acid-free paper containing a minimum of 50% recycled, de-inked fiber.

Dedicated to overcoming America's trade imbalance—and to our export colleagues for their patience and essential contribution

Contents

Part 7. Government Programs for Export Assistance

Preface

The export/import business has a romantic sound that is irresistible to many of us—rather like an adult career dream. For many thousands, it has proven to be an achievable dream either as an exciting career or as a relatively easy route for starting their own business. It is both challenging and exciting, offering an endless chain of new experiences and opportunities. Few things, however, are as profitable or as enjoyable as they should be—unless we are enjoying the level of success we set for ourselves. This is rarely the case unless we know what we are doing and understand all of our options. This book was written to provide the knowledge needed to maneuver through today's trading problems and to confidently plan tomorrow's export strategies to reach those goals.

Although I spent many years in exporting—during the 1970s with their abundant opportunities and then suffered through the lean 1980s—it has only been in the last few years that I have realized how broad the spectrum of export alternatives really is—alternative export methods and structures, avenues for selling and contracting, means of financing, and the multiple sources for export assistance. Adding to that personal experience, I learned from my involvement with the financial and operational problems of a wide range of exporters, manufacturers, and other businessmen in the course of starting up and administering the California Export Finance Office (CEFO), of California's Trade and Commerce Agency.

In the capacity of (CEFO) director, I was afforded a rare insight into export and manufacturing businesses. It was a challenge to my associates and me to help many of these firms take advantage of better financial practices and funding techniques, and to convince them to acquire or hire the export know-how that is necessary to successfully and profitably compete overseas. Unless firms have a major stake in exporting, or a keenly interested international or banking advisor, they are unlikely to have exposure to country risk analysis information and specific country practices or perils. The consequence is usually either an overstated or understated assessment of the risks associated with a particular foreign involvement or credit. Unfortunately, just as often the risk comes from within, as a result of our own government's regulations. Of added concern is the fact that the export projects are often large, and frequently the transaction being undertaken represents at least several times the net worth of the company that is involved.

These observations let me perceive the need for a comprehensive book on all phases of exporting and financing, and finding that it did not then exist was the incentive to fill that gap. We decided to provide the most comprehensive review possible of the choices, the sources of assistance, and the parameters of exporting, written from the exporter's standpoint. This resolve was reinforced by a personal desire to provide today's exporters with a book that would have enlarged my personal horizon and enhanced and accelerated my export career when I first entered this exciting field 20 years ago. The result would have been more profit for less investment in money, time, and energy.

This book provides the export "know-how" that is necessary right from the start; the options and means of financing and developing a successful export venture; and information on where to obtain additional assistance in all aspects along the way. It is addressed to the person who is responsible for export in an existing manufacturing business, but it is equally targeted at the independent exporter who feels that there is more to learn about the craft—and who doesn't? It is a complete course in exporting, whether it is to be self-taught while learning on the job, or used as a textbook in a college classroom. Furthermore, it should be included in any company's export library as a reference book for procedures, facts, and methods.

We are pleased that *Exporting: From Start to Finance* has been so widely accepted and used as a cornerstone by so many businesses and academic institutions, even though subsequently other good books have appeared on the scene. Consequently, we have taken special care that this third edition be reviewed and rewritten chapter by chapter. The result has been a near total revision, representing the vast changes in programs, regulations, practices, communications and computers with their databases that have occurred since the book was first published in 1989. Our only, but unavoidable, regret is that the forces for change in the 104th Congress of 1995 have not yet been resolved between the two houses or with the administration, as this edition is prepared for printing. Fortunately, we have an understanding of the legislative versions of the changes affecting international trade as passed each by the House of Representatives and by the Senate. Consequently we can anticipate most of the probable changes in the federal agencies or departments involved. The very real possibility of the elimination of the Department of Commerce presents a particular problem, even though most of the programs discussed in this book would be moved, probably to the U.S. Trade Representative. Many of these changes and their probable impact are pointed out in the portions of text to which they apply. We have also included an "Update" page in the front of Part 7 that will be inserted just before printing to provide the latest information as to where and how to find the relative programs even though the names and addresses might have changed. In spite of this complication. We believe it to be a better, more accurate representation of the export universe and that it will continue to inspire a few of our readers to look into the deeper commitment and wider opportunities that exporting requires and offers, and perhaps assist in speeding the readers' ultimate success.

L. Fargo Wells

Introduction

Exporting: From Start to Finance is about the business of exporting. Its purpose is to transform good ideas or desirable products into a slice of the global market share. In this third edition, you will find the basic body of knowledge and mechanics that are needed to successfully undertake or explore every avenue of exporting. Throughout the book, many sources of information are provided to enable you to pursue any particular area in still greater depth. The exporting information that is needed can be found in this text, whether you anticipate becoming involved as an entrepreneurial export trader, desire to expand a business through foreign sales, or simply want to improve the operations of an existing export department. The chance for success in any of these endeavors is excellent in light of America's continued expansion in export sales.

This book describes the essentials as well as the parameters of exporting. The emphasis in the book's title on "finance" stems from our discovery of how frequently a successful export effort is unnecessarily blocked or frustrated by financial problems arising from accumulating foreign receivables or the additional working capital required to handle the extra large sales that exporting can generate. Otherwise sophisticated business people regularly overlook the opportunities that "trade finance" in skilled hands can provide to solve such problems, as well as the many special sources of financial assistance that are available exclusively to exporters. A heightened interest in offering export finance by banks and non-bank lending institutions, combined with a lower priced dollar make this an even more attractive opportunity.

The book first addresses the company that has decided to make an export effort or to take its present export efforts more seriously, and then looks at the entrepreneurial third-party exporter. Obviously, in each case the beginning is different. In the first chapter, the question is how much potential the company's products have and how many corporate resources can be devoted to the export process; in the second chapter, the opportunities, skills, and type of products are highlighted. The next chapter deals with the basic tools that can be used in exporting and setting up physical and informational facilities specifically for export. This is a topic where even established businesses will find some useful hints.

A discussion of the various means and channels of export serves to define the subject, its techniques, and its boundaries, as well as an introduction of the basics. The final chapter in Part 1 explains the ramifications of the legal and tax advantages the United States government offers to exporters and their companies. These considerations would probably come much later in the real chain of events; however, in theory, and possibly in fact, it is a logical first consideration for an export operation.

Part 2 covers the second step for everyone—marketing. This includes analyzing how and if a given product fits into a particular foreign market, and how to set up distribution and promotion thereafter. Chapter 13, "International Bid Opportunities,' details very under utilized sources of business for export trading and management companies, manufacturers, and some contractors.

Part 3, "Trading Blocs and Investment Strategies," discusses the European Union, Central and Eastern Europe, Asia, and the Americas, and is a review of the vital areas of geo-economic cohesiveness, where a region should be viewed in a strategic sense as opposed to merely a collection of "target" countries. Some form of investment beyond marketing costs should be considered to secure long-term market share. Special attention was given to this section in view of the emerging National Export Strategy and its emphasis on "Big Emerging Markets."

Part 4, "Export Operations," is important to both the marketing and sales departments, since failure to understand selling terms and conditions, including credit risks and how to minimize them, can make a company's export business a waste of time and money. In no other field must all the functions of doing business interlock more than in foreign sales.

Part 5, "Staying Out of Trouble," is a guide to assist in avoiding problems and litigation by understanding the regulations that control exporting and how to plan for them. It is pleasing to note that government and its national export strategy seem to be trying to minimize unnecessary handicaps imposed by regulations of an earlier era.

Part 6 addresses the specialized areas of export financing, with some important information on general finance and banking relations in any business. This is an area in which there is often a serious deficiency in otherwise successful companies. Here too, the outlook is brighter with a more aggressive U.S. Export-Import Bank and, internationally speaking, a less timid banking industry.

Part 7 describes, in easy to understand language, the working details of all the government assistance programs that are available to every exporter even as they are in the process of change. These details of those changes have not been overlooked, and the update proceeding Part 7, provides the latest directions of change as 1995 and the congressional calendar draws to a close.

Finally, a wealth of references and information on exporting are provided in the extensive appendixes, entitled "Sources of Information" which have been updated and reorganized for easier use. Important in every business, such references and information are a special key to exporting, and one of the best ways to stay ahead of the competition. Some practical sample contracts, intended only as a starting point for developing agreements for the exporter's special needs, can also be found in the appendixes.

The authors have assured the book's high level of accuracy and authoritativeness by having each section extensively reviewed for errors, omissions, and suggestions by widely respected professionals in their particular area of expertise, but humbled by the experience of finding errors or omissions where none were known to be, we apologize in advance for those still lurking within. We also urge careful checking with experts and authorities and the Trade Information Center, mentioned throughout the book. It has never been more apparent that changes occur rapidly in the business of international trade.

Acknowledgments

The contribution of the following people and their special skills and professional knowledge has enhanced the value and usefulness of this book and has greatly eased the task of its writing. In some cases, their encouragement and help was the very fuel that kept the fires burning. The authors offer them our sincere gratitude. We have included some names in memorium, who are no longer with us, of their inestimable assistance with the first and second edition.

Richard Barovick, Publisher
International Business Affairs Corp.
on Federal support agencies

Robert DeMartini, Vice President
The Meridian Group
on trade shows and overseas promotions

Michael R. Doram, Attorney-at-Law
on intellectual property rights

Stanley W. Epstein, Owner
American Export Trading Co.
on export management and trading companies

William Filbert, Owner
International Diversified Technologies
on export administration regulations

Irene Fisher, Director (ret)
California Export Finance Office
Office of International Trade, SBA
on small business export support servies

Hugh Grigsby, V.P., Trade Finance
Bank of America (ret)
on trade finance

Endy Hoffman, President
International Insurance Associates
on credit and transportation insurance

John R. Liebman, Attorney-at-Law
Tuttle & Taylor
on antiboycott and foreign corrupt practices

Lou Munoz, Vice President (ret)
Far East Bank
on letters of credit

William Norman, Attorney-at-Law
Ord & Norman
on foreign sales corporations

James R. Phillips, Director (ret)
European Trade and Investment Office
on trading blocs under construction in the new Europe

James Schill (ret)
U.S. Agency for International Development
on AID bid opportunities

Donald F. Schmoll, Acting Director
Export Import Bank of the U.S., Los Angeles Regional Office
on the U.S. Export-Import Bank

L. Stroh, Publisher & Editor
The Exporter magazine
on export statistics

In Memorium
Carl Scanlon
Fred Hoffman
for their kind assistance with the first edition

We also wish to acknowledge the many excellent articles on general export information in *Trade Finance, Export Today, The Exporter, Business America, International Business, Journal of Commerce* and *The Los Angeles Times.*

1

Organizing for Export

1

Exporting
Makes Sense

In 1991, when the first edition of this book was written, the decline of the dollar to realistic levels was already making it a much more opportune time to begin exporting than it had been throughout most of the 1980s. Now, in the 1990s, the dollar has moved from being merely more competitive vis-à-vis the currencies of our most important trading partners to a bargain price typified by having crashed the 100-yen-per-$1 barrier. During the relatively brief time between the first and the third editions of this book, the United States has moved through a recession to almost effective full employment in early 1995, even though economic growth dampened by mid-year workers and consumers continue to feel anxious about their security and their futures. Despite complaints that many newly created jobs are in the lower-paid segments of the service sector, it is generally conceded that export-generated jobs tend to be in the higher wage ranges. In view of the starring role enjoyed by export growth during this period, that is wonderful news.

New trading spheres are being formed and realignments continue to develop in the older groupings. Even with an export growth rate surpassing that of most other countries, we are engaged in unprecedented levels of global competition for our own domestic markets. In spite of these conflicting trends, the importance of exports to the economy is underscored by the fact that, in recent years, total exports have accounted for roughly 40 percent of the growth in the merchandise sector of the U.S. gross domestic product (GDP) and for 58 percent of the growth in the service sector. On average over the last seven years, exports have grown twice as fast as the U.S. economy. In 1993 exports of goods and services totaled $640 billion. Of this total, $465 billion consisted of goods in the

3

following three categories: manufactured goods, 84 percent; extractables such as coal, gas, and oil, 7 percent; and agricultural products, 7 percent. The balance of exports consisted of services valued at $174 billion (roughly one-fourth of total exports).[1]

In the immediate term, export success can be seen as an outstanding job generator, and in the longer run, it provides an added benefit as an anticyclical damper for business ups and downs. At one time, participation in international trade, besides being a cure for the economic problems brought on by the trade deficit, was a lever for expansion of U.S. businesses and exports. Now it is safe to add that for a substantial percentage of U.S. businesses, failure to engage in international trade and seek export markets is a threat to future growth and possibly even viability. Consider the handicap you accept for your company's growth if you overlook current export opportunities—especially in the light of the key role that exports play in our GNP figures and the ongoing assault on market share being waged by our overseas competitors.

This book deals primarily with export-related specifics. It is designed to help you reach a conclusion about the export potential of your particular business after reviewing all the factors involved—the advantages and problems, risks and benefits. As you weigh your options, I hope you will also consider the economic rationale for export in the framework of our national priorities as a continuing economic power, the dramatic global forces at work in the 1990s, and the amazing pace of change in trade activities. Think of the passage of NAFTA and its dramatic consequences. Even Mexico's financial and political upheaval in 1995 and the short-term problems it has engendered have helped set the stage for a major step forward for the Western Hemisphere. Consider the implementation of GATT, which alone will create enormous growth in world trade, to say nothing of the new or expanded free trade areas being considered by the Pacific Rim and Latin American nations. The Uruguay round of GATT puts special focus on opportunities for third-world countries to share in the growth of international trade. This fact, besides having an enormous political and economic impact, means vast new markets for the U.S. exporter.

As James Flanigan stated in the September 1, 1993 edition of the *Los Angeles Times,* "Growth in world trade has been slowing for years…as the economies of Western Europe, Japan and the United States have reached something of a saturation point and are taking in each other's washing. New markets have to be developed in the less developed regions of Latin America, parts of Asia, Russia and Eastern Europe, the Middle East and Africa." Many of these areas are already on the move and their populations have increased. Today, global population is about 2.5 billion, but depending on which statistics are used, that population in the year 2025 will be between 7.8 billion and 9.5 billion. The bulk of this population growth will be in Asia, Latin America, and Africa, where 86 percent of the world's people will reside. This is where much of the United States' and world's investment capital and savings are flowing—to provide the capital for construction and manufacture of the new infrastructure needs and product requirements of these emerging countries and their markets.

In terms of national priorities, even though statistics indicate a continued major growth in exports, our trade deficit problems still exist and our global share of the world's trade has been trending consistently downward from more than 16 percent to the 12–13 percent range of today.

Export growth must continue to be a national priority in view of the outlook for rapidly expanding world trade that will affect our separate businesses, our personal fortunes, and our job security. This export priority is recognized at virtually every level of government and in a wide variety of export support programs. Hopefully, the political sea change of 1995 will not fulfill its initial isolationist promises. It is regrettable that the federal government does not allow for a more logical allocation of funding between agricultural export support, which is very high relative to its share of total exports, and support for the promotion and export development of manufactured goods, which is low by this or any other comparison. Nonetheless, there is a very large range of federal help and service available to exporters of every kind, even after the current budget cutbacks. There is also a growing amount of help available at the state, county, and city level, all of which will be addressed in detail in Part 6 as well as throughout the book. The newly emerging market and global forces will be discussed in Part 2, under marketing.

Some would say that the world market represents the possibility of quadrupling a business's existing domestic market. For most businesspeople, however, a more realistic excitement comes with the discovery that their company has a viable product for export and can gain a meaningful market share in a newly found foreign market, whatever the increase may mean to its total sales. While naturally most export demand is for current proven products, the demand is often for products that are otherwise facing obsolescence in the domestic market. It can also happen that onetime export best-sellers to a particular country reverse themselves and become prime net export commodities of that same former net importer. (Rice is a good example; certain high-tech products are another.)

Exporting in many countries is a basic and fundamental part of doing business to achieve economy of scale, to reach wealthier markets, and because of the proximity of so many borders. While American attitudes on foreign commerce are slowly changing, it is still true that, in light of our huge domestic market, the decision to export remains optional, and is usually driven by one of the following factors:

1. **Demand.** The company has a successful domestic product but may receive occasional orders from overseas, or it is already actively exporting to a limited extent and could increase sales with a minimum of effort if the product were exposed to additional markets.

2. **Supply.** The company makes a conscious decision to establish an aggressive export department and expand its sales by acquiring a presence and market share in specific markets abroad.

3. **Entrepreneurship.** An individual or a trading company seeks to create a new business by selling products overseas that are manufactured or provided by others. These are referred to as third-party or independent exporters

and Export Management Companies (EMCs) or Export Trading Companies (ETCs).

Obstacles to Exporting

Products that sell well in the domestic market are successful because they fill a need or create a desire and are promoted with good initial marketing strategies and appropriate follow-up. Success in exporting is no different. However, because of the differences in culture, weather, income level, transportation, and education, the same standards that are used in domestic marketing cannot be applied to other countries. Just recognizing this is often the most difficult hurdle to overcome in establishing a successful export effort.

On the bright side, the current administration and congress agree on the need for eliminating unnecessary obstacles. The best example of this is in the complete revamping of the much-maligned export controls and validated licensing. In less than one year, comparing the fourth quarter of 1993 to the third quarter of 1994, the value of goods requiring special export licenses dropped from $6.1 billion to $1.9 billion—a dramatic reduction even prior to the new procedures effective in 1996.

There are other obstacles to overcome, however, such as different rules for arranging payment terms and extending credit; additional, or at least separate, operational details that are not normally a consideration in domestic business; and different methods of financing that can offer opportunities as well as complications. The problem most often faced by entrepreneurial third-party exporters is that of financing, although this is a problem that they share with many other businesses and manufacturers. The domestic manufacturer expects to treat the exporter as a domestic account and requires payment terms accordingly. The overseas importer wants allowances and longer terms on both the cost of the product and the freight in order to establish the product, and in many cases, to distribute and receive payment from the overseas end user before remitting to the exporter. This book addresses all of these concerns, details, and opportunities.

Making the Export Decision

Many companies have long felt that exporting was only for large firms— defense manufacturers, aircraft companies, and agricultural commodities dealers. And, in a sense, that feeling has been justified by the commonly quoted government statistic that about 250 companies are responsible for 80 percent of our exports. However, on rechecking this statistic, *The Exporter* magazine, in cooperation with the Department of Commerce, has found that there are approximately 105,000 exporters, of which 2000 companies (fewer than 2 percent of U.S. companies) handle 82.5 percent of total U.S. exports. As illustrated in Figure 1-1 this group of 2000 is made up of what *The Exporter* terms "most

EXPORTERS AND THEIR EXPORTS

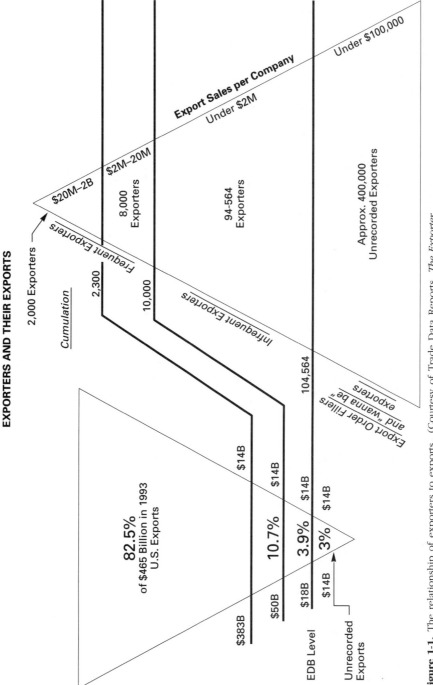

Figure 1-1. The relationship of exporters to exports.. (Courtesy of Trade Data Reports, *The Exporter,* N.Y.)

frequent" exporters, averaging more than 1300 export shipments per year, which, together with another 8000 "frequent" exporters, averaging more than 120 exports per year and shipping 11 percent of U.S. exports, make up over 93 percent of America's export activity. The estimated 95,000 remaining exporters share a mere four percent of all exports. Of the 105,000 exporters, approximately 40,000 are manufacturers, and the remainder are export traders, wholesalers, and service providers.

These more understandable figures should serve to beckon and encourage the new-to-export firm. It is estimated there are at least 25,000 nonexporting companies with export-worthy products. A good portion of those 25,000 are small and midsize businesses, each of which has a chance to dramatically improve its performance through exports, to say nothing of similar opportunities available to the 105,000 "infrequent" exporters whose export sales growth has averaged 15 percent each year since 1990. In fact, the surge of export volume in manufactured goods beginning in late 1987 has been fueled by these thousands of small and midsize companies. That the smaller firms have failed to achieve a greater share of exports is not because they cannot export, but because so many have not attempted to export, have not developed any export plans or strategy, or simply wrongly think it is too much trouble and a game for large firms only. There are a thousand stories to prove the error of that thinking.

The Exporter magazine's figures have focused the efforts of the United States Department of Commerce to help existing less-than-frequent and infrequent exporters sell more. While reinforcing the fact that a major portion of United States exports are handled by large firms making many smaller shipments ($5000 to $50,000) and some large shipments, it also highlights the excellent opportunity that exists for smaller firms and/or infrequent exporters. *The Exporter* magazine in an editorial[2] points out that small businesses with fewer than 20 employees tend to outperform large companies with more than 500 employees in the same industrial category (SIC) on the basis of sales per employee by as much as six to one. In only three of the top 20 manufacturing industries (tobacco, petroleum, and wood products) do large companies outsell small companies on this basis. The two best performers—apparel and textiles— regularly suffer severe import competition. In apparel, the companies with fewer than 20 employees sold $23,333 per employee, while the large companies averaged only $3,517. Average per-employee sales of apparel by small manufacturers in fact exceeded the national average of $17,981 for all categories of companies of any size. The rule held true even in high-capitalization industries like transportation, which includes export giants such as Boeing.

There are innumerable opportunities for businesses of all sizes and entrepreneurs of many different persuasions to be successful in exporting and to help sustain this country's global economic growth at the same time. The United States needs continued increases in its exports to continue to reduce its burdensome trade deficit, and in the long-term, serious exporting must be done by more than a minority of American corporations to achieve volume and diversity and ensure that we achieve and maintain a fair balance of trade. It must become a profitable pursuit and way of life for American business in general. This country's deficit problem and our attitudes on international trade cannot be solved by the sale of wheat and Boeing 747s alone.

The decision to export is a major one for any company, regardless of its size and product range. It requires a genuine commitment by management in terms of assigning personnel as well as funds to make exporting profitable. Therefore, it should not be done for the wrong reasons, such as, "Let's export the surplus production we can't sell on the domestic market" or, "The domestic price is low at the moment; let's export until prices firm up" or, "Let's get into export so we can travel overseas and write off the expenses." On-again, off-again export efforts undertaken for inappropriate reasons like these have, in the past, diminished our image abroad. And, to the extent that similar thinking persists, they will continue to waste resources that could be better directed to sound export strategies or at least to improving domestic efficiency. If you want to establish a successful export department, you should plan on making many export shipments, even if some of them are quite small. It is all right to look for some big transactions, but success, profit, and economy of scale demand a steady stream of exports.

The Pros and Cons of Exporting

To be successful, any worthwhile export effort requires the same ingredients as domestic business: a firm commitment, a realistic budget, time, patience, and a systematic, informed approach. What follows are some key points to consider before making a final decision.

The Advantages of Exporting Your Product

- The added sales volume should lower production costs.

- Lower production costs and increased sales will increase overall profitability.

- Opportunities for overseas licensing can be sought.

- Advanced technical methods used abroad may be discovered.

- New markets may increase product life cycles.

- Research and development costs can be amortized.

- Some risks can be reduced through diversified markets.

- Market diversity will flatten business cycles as a slowing trend in one market is offset by advances in another market.

- New markets yield ideas for new innovations.

The Disadvantages of Exporting Your Product

- Management will need to devote substantial time to assist in the start-up procedures and decisions.

- Key personnel might have to be diverted from domestic responsibilities.

- Additional plant facilities may be needed.

- Catalogs and brochures may need to be translated.

- The product will probably need to be modified to meet foreign market specifications.

- Credit terms may need to be extended because of competition, local custom, and transit time.

- Claims must be dealt with at great distance with little opportunity for examination.

- Claims may be higher because of transportation and duty costs.

The Adaptability of Your Product to Foreign Markets

- Does it require changes or adaptations to conform with safety, quality, and/or technical standards in other countries?

- Do the modifications that are required outweigh the benefits to be gained?

- Does the quality of the product compare to those that are presently in foreign markets?

- Once the cost of transportation, duties, and selling overseas is added to the product, will it still be competitive?

The Adaptability of Your Company, Staff, and Facilities to the Export Trade

- How committed is your company to exporting, recognizing that it is a major investment in time and resources that might not pay off for months or even years?

- If your company is presently operating to capacity, with sales either steady or growing, is it possible to enlarge both staff and facilities to meet the demand of additional overseas sales?

- Is management sufficiently committed to the idea of international trade and global marketing to make the investment necessary to provide continuous availability of the product overseas?

- Is the personnel who will be affected by and involved in the exporting process in full agreement with the plan to export and willing to cooperate fully?

Getting Your Company Ready to Enter the Export Market

When organizing your own in-house export department, plan to develop the personnel to handle export affairs, either from within or through outside recruitment. Determine the degree of training and special schooling that will be necessary so that your chosen staff can properly handle export transactions. Also determine the cost of this retraining in terms of absence from present duties and tuition fees.

The export manager selected might go by any number of titles, but it is common wisdom that this person should report directly to the top executives. To be successful, the position of export manager usually must be considered a full-time job and be removed from the domestic sales effort. The export manager should not report to the domestic sales manager, the obvious reason being that a domestic sales manager will favor the company's domestic salespeople and representatives and possibly even resent the travel that may be necessary to do the job the export manager has to do. Supervision by a marketing vice president is more appropriate.

You should be prepared to assign appropriate personnel and spend some time studying the problem to develop an overall marketing and operational strategy from within the company. A working knowledge of the following chapters will help you understand the problems and judge the performance of those you have retained.

As an alternative to your own in-house export department, you might wish to consider some of the alternative approaches to exporting, including substitutes for an export effort, a topic discussed in detail in Chapter 4. As overseas markets have become more sophisticated and the problems of dealing with them more complex, domestic intermediary alternatives to in-house departments can be more cost effective, at least initially. It is one of the tasks of this book to help you make such decisions.

Exporting: Good for You and for the Country

The long-term outlook for continued growth in exports remains bright, especially in view of GATT and NAFTA, even though no one knows how we can catch up altogether with America's tremendous appetite for imports. Secretary of Commerce Ron Brown states as part of the well-conceived National Export Strategy Report to Congress in October 1994,[3] prepared by the interagency Trade Promotion and Coordinating Committee (TPCC) that exports of goods and services doubled from 1986 through 1993 to $640 billion dollars annually, and that by the year 2000, this figure is expected to exceed $1 trillion. In 1994, exports comprised 21 percent of goods produced in the United States, compared to a mere 13 percent in 1983. Exports create jobs—about 20 per $1 million of manufactured goods, according to the Department of Commerce—accounting for more than 10.5 million jobs in 1992. The TPCC's National Export Strategy Report estimates that jobs supported by goods exports paid 13 percent more than the average wage. In addition to manufacturing, the export of services creates much more than merely low-paying jobs; it also creates millions of highly paid professional-level jobs.

"Productivity" was the buzzword of the late 1980s, and productivity was pursued with a vengeance. Let us hope that the accompanying downsizing is now largely completed and that we can enjoy its fruits while replacing many of the jobs that were lost. To do so, we need to increase the export sales of products whose greater competitiveness was achieved by downsizing. In the second half of this decade we need to achieve increased export productivity, based on our much-improved domestic productivity, rather than on any further reliance on a devalued dollar that diminishes our buying power even as it helps our export statistics.

A World of Opportunities

If a U.S. product sells successfully in the U.S. market, it will probably also sell overseas in markets where similar needs and conditions exist. Such products may need little or no modification, especially if the product is unique and has advantages that are hard to duplicate abroad. Even if a product is no longer selling well in the United States because of competition from more technically advanced products, good export markets may still exist because of the time lag in less advanced countries. Third-World countries may not yet require the latest in technology and may have a demand for U.S. products that are older, less expensive, and not as sophisticated.

The following facts emphasize the fundamental role that exports play in our business economy. Despite dramatic improvements in the level of U.S. merchandise exports from a low of 5.3 percent of our GDP in 1986 to an estimated 7.5 percent of our GDP in 1992, we still compare unfavorably with our principal trading partners. By comparison, exports as a percentage of GDP in Germany for 1992 were 21.9 percent; Canada, 22.6 percent; the United Kingdom, 18.8 percent; and Japan, 9.2 percent. That translates into the fact that numerous small businesses in those countries are doing a lot of profitable exporting, directly or indirectly, and it should be an indication of our own tremendous potential. These countries' most successful businesses place much emphasis on market share, a concept that U.S. business originated. However, they have carried it a step further and sought a more significant market share, not just for their own country, but for each appropriate, targeted foreign market. As yet, such focused thinking and planning have not become a fundamental part of the export mindset of most American businesses.

Endnotes

1. *Business America,* April 1994.
2. *The Exporter,* Editorial, November 1992 pp. 2–3.
3. Ronald H. Brown, Secretary of Commerce and Chairman, Trade Promotion Coordinating Committee, *National Export Strategy* Report to Congress, October 1994.

2

Getting Started

This chapter is addressed to every hardy and optimistic entrepreneur determined to get into international trade. It is not always an easy goal, but it can be exhilarating and fun. It also has many moments of routine dullness and high frustration. Consider your options carefully.

The New-to-Export Entrepreneur

There are many companies nationwide that are content with the success of their product on the domestic market and do not want to get involved in the additional personnel, paperwork, and details that exporting necessarily entails. This presents an ideal opportunity for the new-to-export entrepreneur who is seeking to start a business. Such an entrepreneur might have a particular product in mind for which a need exists overseas or might have close ties to, and intimate knowledge of, a particular overseas market.

With today's innovations in communication, this entrepreneur need not be tied to a particular location, and once the office is equipped and in operation, the additional investment is minimal. Some feel that exporting can be done with little or no cash. While it has been done, reasonable equity, as well as a lot of time and travel, are usually required to make a serious marketing effort overseas. Lack of export experience at the beginning can be somewhat offset by product and market knowledge, willingness to study, and an eagerness to learn.

The commonplace idea that international trade and travel would be "terrific" is no basis for seeking work in foreign trade, much less for starting a business. Neither is an idea that because of a specific ethnic heritage, it will be easy to start a trading company. On the other hand, facility in a second language is a real plus. So is product knowledge and a well-founded understanding of the needs and problems of a region of the world.

Interest, Skill, and Location

If, in spite of these caveats, you, the entrepreneur, still feel you are ready and have what it takes to start a business as an independent exporter, what next? In the event that a particular area of product knowledge is not what gave you the impetus to attempt export marketing, the array of possible export products on which to focus may seem to present a difficult and even overwhelming choice. In attempting to select a logical and effective range of products, you might find it helpful to ask yourself these three questions: (1) What are your special interests? (2) What are your special skills? (3) What does your location offer? The next section will help in answering some of these key questions.

What Are Your Special Interests?

Your interests could refer to a special product or an entire product line. It is easier to learn about a field if you have a special interest in it. Most important, your creative ability to sell is greatly enhanced if you have intimate knowledge of the product and have confidence in it. Many of our entrepreneurial exporters tend to begin with consumer products. While there are many other areas (see Key Export Products and Destinations, pp. 16–19), consumer goods are usually readily available and are used here as an example.

If your interest is golf, it will be easier to contact manufacturers and learn the specification of their golf clubs because you know something about the sport. And because you already know something about golf and golf equipment, it will be easier to convince the manufacturer to take the time to explain the details you need to know to sell its golf products overseas.

The same applies if your interest is in fashion, which can involve all kinds of export possibilities from apparel to cosmetics and jewelry. If you have always been interested in cars, there is a wide variety of car accessories and car-care products, many of which have export potential. The gardening enthusiast will find interest in everything from seeds to gardening gadgets to plants themselves. Dogs and cats are highly prized and pampered companions in many countries of the world, and the United States is a leader in finding new ways to treat, cure, and spoil pets—with a better-tasting dog biscuit, a new flea collar or spray, vitamins, medications, and softer beds.

There are always new equestrian products on the market if you are involved with horses. Racing and showing are popular in many countries of the world, and the upkeep of horses is a large industry, constantly looking for the newest in medication and equipment. Assorted track items and riding apparel are of great interest to people who can afford their own horse.

There are also many export-related products associated with cooking: herbs, spices, pot holders, place mats, kitchen towels, pots and pans, dishes, glassware, and cookbooks, as well as an endless variety of kitchen gadgets. The fitness craze is catching on in many countries, and there is interest in items from jumping ropes to inversion boots, as well as the big body-building machines and most items in between.

There are real and would-be artists all over the world always interested in aids to improve their creations. This can include the newest paints and brushes available, new cleaning fluids, and any of the countless items seen in art supply and hobby shops, including books and posters.

Outdoor activities, such as hiking, camping, skiing, surfing, boating, fishing, climbing, bicycling, jogging, and swimming, offer many products for export. Consider the potential not only for the actual equipment involved in the different sports, but also for the related apparel and accessories. An area ready-made for moving from consumer to commerce is computers, because of the ever-multiplying number of computer buffs.

What Are Your Special Skills?

Let's assume that you have worked in the automotive industry for many years. During that time you have made many contacts with various suppliers of parts, tools, accessories, and so on, and you have an intimate knowledge of the automotive industry. This combination will help you find items that have export potential.

Consider the export possibility of a particular product your company produces and whose function you are totally familiar with. If you are, or have been, employed in the medical field, you would probably know how to find out about the newest in medical equipment or supplies, which is a viable category for export and in great demand in most countries. If you have experience in working with agricultural commodities, there is a wide variety of export functions, from direct export to export broker or consultant/buyer for importers, in various countries. There is demand overseas not only for crops and commodities that are grown in the United States, but for plants and seeds and the expertise to grow them.

Consultation and technical services are gaining an increasing share of the export market, along with the more traditional export of goods and products. Professions in, or even special knowledge of, a particular field can be marketed overseas in areas such as telecommunication, environmental services, educational services, architecture and engineering, management services, information services, transportation services, water and sanitation services, agricultural and rural development, urban development, tourism, population science, nutrition, energy sciences, and construction.

You might also obtain valuable assistance and information from relatives or friends who are living in countries with export potential and who are in a position to know needs or buyers. Personal and detailed knowledge of a market, combined with language fluency, can be the cornerstone of a successful business. It could be a market where, for some reason, you have achieved a useful understanding of how things are done and how life is lived. Your American competitors at this point still tend to be very provincial and inclined to pay little attention to foreign customs, language, and lifestyle. Therefore, you might have a major advantage in this area.

Best of all is a combination of market knowledge and special product knowledge, preferably in a little-understood specialty with strong demand. The field does not have to be large. A good example is that of a businessman who used his knowledge of theatrical lighting to get him started in export. He combined that knowledge with his fluency in Spanish and specialized in Latin America. Thus a narrow field, in an area that offered relatively small export potential, became the foundation of a successful business because of:

- *Specialization*—therefore minimal competition

- *Demand*—an industry's need for American technology or product availability

- *Knowledge*—product, language, and culture

What Does Your Location Offer?

Check with your local Chamber of Commerce and learn about the largest industries in your area. Consider local products that you feel have export potential. Attend exhibits and trade shows and look for items that are of interest to you for export. Go to your local library and look up the *Thomas Register,* which has two sections that could aid in your search for manufacturers of your chosen products. One section to consult is "Products and Services," which you should check when you need a product or service and want to find out what is available and who can supply it. This section gives the addresses and a brief description of companies, listed under more than 50,000 separate product and service headings.

The other section is the "Company Profiles," which should be used if you want to learn more about a company. It lists addresses and phone numbers of more than 135,000 American companies. Some of the listings include asset ratings, names of executives, and an indication of whether or not the company exports.

Take this opportunity to investigate many manufacturers that make either the same or similar products. Try to deal with well-established, competitive companies that are leaders in their field. It is hard to convince a foreign buyer to import a product that is not yet fully accepted in this country. Evidence of American national media advertising is a convincing sales tool for overseas buyers.

Check for other products to export that will complement the item you have chosen. For example, if you are exporting skin-care items, you might find a cosmetic line to add to it, since the same importer would probably handle both types of merchandise. Or, if you have decided to export ladies lingerie, you might add a line of exercise apparel, such as leotards, leg warmers, and so on. Any foreign buyer interested in computers would presumably be a potential buyer not only for computer accessories, but also for supplies, computer furniture, and, of course, software.

Key Export Products and Destinations

In any one country, one customer buying one profitable export product may be a best customer to any one firm. Nevertheless, the following breakdown of leading United States customers for total goods by country will provide an interesting perspective. You might easily name many of the countries on the list as being among our top customers in 1994, but you might be surprised at their actual order in terms of dollar amounts.

1. Canada $114.4 billion
2. Japan   53.5
3. Mexico   50.8
4. United Kingdom   26.8
5. Germany   19.20
6. South Korea   18.0
7. Taiwan   17.1
8. France   13.6
9. Netherlands   13.6
10. Singapore   13.0

Canada's predominance in U.S. exports is often not recognized because it is accomplished with so little fanfare and, since it is so close, the shipments scarcely seem to be exports. Our exports to Canada in 1994 ($114.4 billion) amounted to over twice our exports to Japan ($53.5 billion), a ratio more or less typical of the last few years. The amount of our exports to Japan is roughly similar to that of our exports to Mexico ($50.8) consistently our third-largest customer since 1985—and bound to grow rapidly in importance with the advent of the NAFTA agreement in spite of Mexico's current problems. Several other substantial changes have occurred since 1989, such as Taiwan and Korea overtaking France, and Singapore becoming one of our top 10 export customers. Closely following it are Hong Kong, Belgium/Luxembourg, China, and Australia. Recently Asian countries have been increasingly replacing European countries on the list of leading country customers. Many U.S. customers' imports roughly doubled between 1986 and 1994, but Mexico quadrupled and many Asian countries tripled.

Even though most countries, the United States included, have what they call their "traditional" export products; because of the extraordinarily wide range of agricultural and manufactured products and even raw materials, the mix of leading U.S. export products changes more than those in most countries. This becomes still more pronounced because of U.S. leadership in technology, the advent of new inventions and industrial developments, and our many lifestyle innovations. Overseas markets also reflect shifts in comparative advantages and changes in international political and economic activities or relationships. Naturally, the persistently declining value of the U.S. dollar also plays an important role in the overseas demand and the competitiveness of our products, especially where consumer items are concerned. Analyzing Bureau of Census 1994 statistics for goods exported world-wide based on the United Nations Standard International Trade Classifications (SITC) results in the following list of the top 30

U.S. dollar value export product classifications out of 265 SITC product classifications. The list is long enough to extend to the level of wheat and corn which puts these two primary agricultural exports in a comparable value context or relationship with our far more dominant manufacturing sector. The natural resource export sector is smaller still. For example, the U.S. exports about the same amount of cotton textile fibers as coal, of which we have vast quantities.

Compared to 5 years earlier there are some marked differences. Pulp and waste paper dropped from a rank of 14th to 34th. Maize and wheat dropped

Top 30 U.S. Export Products for 1994 Categorized by SITC Code to Three Digits

Rank	SITC #	Product(s)	$ Export Value in Billions
1	792	Aircraft & assoc. equip.	$30.380
2	776	Electronic parts (e.g., thermionic, cold cathode, photocathode valves, etc.)	26.459
3	784	Parts & accessories of motor vehicles	22.275
4	752	Auto. data processing mach. & units thereof	20.415
5	781	Motor cars and other motor vehicles	16.873
6	764	Telecommunication equip., N.E.S. & parts	14.799
7	759	Parts, etc. for office mach. & units thereof	14.013
8	874	Measuring/checking/analyzing inst., N.E.S.	11.710
9	713	Int. combustion piston engines & parts, N.E.S.	8.400
10	714	Engines & motors, nonelectric & parts	8.333
11	770	Electrical mach. & apparatus, N.E.S.	8.274
12	772	Elec, apparatus for switch., protectg. circ.	7.294
13	723	Civil engineer & contractors' plant & equip.	7.088
14	728	Machry, etc. specialized for particular ind.	6.694
15	898	Musical inst. & parts, records, tapes, etc.	6.263
16	971	Gold, nonmonetary (exc. ores & concentrates)	5.722
17	122	Tobacco, mfg.	5.421
18	641	Paper and paperboard	5.036
19	741	Heating and cooling equipment & parts	5.012
20	743	Pumps, air or other gas compressors & fans	4.696
21	222	Oil seeds	4.688
22	782	Motor veh, for trnspt of gds & spec. purpose	4.375
23	872	Instr. & appls. for medical/dental purposes	4.311
24	598	Miscellaneous chemical products, N.E.S.*	4.212
25	044	Maize	4.197
26	699	Manufactures of base metal, N.E.S.†	4.154
27	892	Printed matter	4.086
28	041	Wheat	4.059
29	334	Oil (not crude) from petrol & bitum minerals	4.032
30	891	Arms and ammunition	4.018

*SITC 598, "Miscellaneous chemical products" includes products as diverse as chemical elements and compounds, chemicals doped to use in electronics, chemical preparations, diagnostic or laboratory reagents, catalysts, etc.

†SITC 699, "Manufactures of base metal" includes products from hinges to padlocks to car springs, forged and stamped iron, steel chains, aluminaum casting, to knitting needles.

NOTE: Extracted from Bureau of Census Report FT925.

from 10th and 11th respectively to 25th and 28th. Telecommunications equipment rose from 9th place to 6th and electrical machinery and apparatus rose from 15th to 11th place. Few categories stayed exactly the same but aircraft and associated equipment continued its total dominance. The real secret, of course, is guessing what the changes will be in the next five years.

As you can see, manufactured consumer goods do not make up a large portion of the top 30 categories in the context of retail selling, except for musical instruments and motor cars, and increasingly, the consumer side of the huge computer industry. Buried in the statistics, however, are billions and billions of dollars of everyday products even though they do not dominate as a single category. This would include products as diverse as fresh and dried fruits and nut exports of over $3.5 billion; made-up textile articles and floor coverings of $1.5 billion; glassware of over $500 million; tools of $1.5 billion; household equipment of $2.4 billion; furniture $3.3 billion; men's or boys' coats and jackets, $1.6 billion; baby carriages, toys, and games of $3.4 billion. The list goes on to include jeans, bath and kitchen accessories, exercise equipment, lingerie, skin and hair care products, sporting goods and towels and sheets, to name some of the perennial favorites not defined at the 3 digit level. A tiny fraction of any of these multimillion- and billion-dollar categories or dozens of similar categories can make a very substantial export business and offers a world of opportunity.

3

The Tools of Trade

For companies and individuals not yet fully acquainted with export operations (however familiar they are with business practices in general and domestic operations in particular), this chapter offers a basic introduction to the "tools of trade": export terminology, equipment, procedures, administrative backup, and essential sources of information.

If you are not only the new-to-export entrepreneur addressed in Chapter 2, but are also new to business, consider a visit to your Small Business Administration (SBA) office. SBA has many excellent books on business, information on necessary licensing, and a consulting program called Service Corps of Retired Executives (SCORE) that utilizes retired executives.

What You Need to Know

Some office procedures apply to overseas trade in particular, such as the terminology used in letters, the calculations necessary for making offers, and the system used to keep track of quotations and transactions.

Correspondence

In international business, even more than in domestic business, it is important that you write clear and concise business letters. Of course, you should not use idioms, slang, jokes, or obscure cultural references, since they are often difficult to translate and may be misunderstood. Many firms prefer to correspond on a "company to company" basis only and do not indicate a person's name in a letter. It is best to address your letter to the company, and if you want to include a person's name, write "Attn:" below the company name. To avoid confusion, it is also important to spell out the name of the month, since it is customary in most other countries to indicate the day first and then the month. (For example, a date of 7/12 would most often mean December 7 in other countries.)

Answer all letters within a few days of receipt, even if your reply is negative, remembering that overseas mail is slower but that the overseas customer's patience does not expand accordingly. It is good business practice to be prompt. A courteous reply might keep the door open for future contact and business. Lack of courtesy has consistently been one of the biggest complaints by foreign business people dealing with American businesses.

It can be an enormous advantage if you are able to correspond with the overseas customers in their native language; however, use caution, even if you are quite fluent. Business terminology is often difficult to translate, and misunderstandings can be costly. Take advantage of the fact that English is used almost universally in business. If you decide to correspond in a foreign language, make it a practice to attach the English translation, or at least a rough summary, to both incoming and outgoing material before filing it. This translation enables people who do not understand a foreign language to quickly understand the background of a transaction during routine reviews of files or documents. Professional outside translation is always available, but it is usually too expensive to be used on a regular basis. If a particular correspondence calls for a translation, always send with it the original English version. This permits the overseas customer to verify any questions that may arise about the translation, and also makes it clear that such translations are not your standard practice.

Measures and Calculations

It is essential to know how to convert the measurements and weights used in the United States into the more commonly used metric form. This is easy enough for linear measurements, but can become tricky when you are involved with area (square) or cubic measurement metric conversions. (See Appendix M for a complete table on measurement conversion.) Become practiced in this if you are not naturally handy with math, and in any case, always visually recheck the calculation to be sure it meets requirements of reason and good sense. Mistakes can be costly.

It's especially important to know how to calculate the cubic measurements of any carton or article: measure in inches and then multiply length by width and then multiply that total by depth or height. Divide the total by 1728 to get to cubic feet (cft.). For many applications, this number will need to be converted to cubic meters. The cube is very important when you need to calculate how many cartons will fit on a pallet, or how many boxes fit into a container, or what the air or ocean rates will be. Such calculations are mostly based on metric measurements or volume rather than on weight.

Shipping Weights

When making export shipments, you will be dealing with three weights: *net weight,* which is the weight of the product without packing; *tare weight,* which usually refers to the weight of the container but also refers to the packing material without the product; and *gross weight,* which includes both the weight of the product and its packaging.

Postage

Your local post office has information on rates for mailing overseas broken down into first class, printed matter, air and sea parcel post, as well as information on insuring your packages and size limitations. Request charts and publications regarding these rates from your post office and be sure to keep them up-to-date. Note that increases and changes for international mail are not always effective on the same date as changes in domestic mail. Sending sample packages will become a way of life, so make sure that the proper parcel post customs forms and tags are attached to your package and that they are filled out correctly. For packages that weigh four pounds or less, you only need a universal customs sticker, U.S. postal Form 2976. For larger packages, use Form 2966A. Keep a supply of these forms on hand and fill them out with a typewriter whenever possible, both to save time at the post office and to make sure all copies are legible.

The post office also offers express mail service, which is very expedient and inexpensive for urgent mail or for firms without a telex. This express mail service is not available to all countries. Do not use stamps that indicate airmail on anything that you want to send surface, and be sure to indicate airmail on all letters and packages intended for air shipment. Failure to do so can delay mail for several weeks and waste postage. Because postage will become an important component of your overhead, consider every savings possible. For example, send your letter with the offer and description of your product via first-class airmail, but send samples and catalogs via air printed matter. Be sure to mention in your letter the specific item you are sending under separate cover so that your correspondent is alerted to its contents and purpose.

Samples

Whether you bill your customer for samples or send them free of charge, you must include an invoice for customs purposes with the samples. To make customs clearance easier and less expensive for your customer, the invoice should clearly state "Value for Customs Purposes Only—No Commercial Value." The price per item should reflect the net price. Deduct any discount you offer; do not show your regular price on the invoice; and on the bottom line, indicate a discount (50 percent discount, for example), as the customer will have to pay duty on the highest value shown—in this case, on your regular price before the discount. Air or surface parcel post, using the proper forms supplied by the post office as mentioned above, are the most cost effective methods of shipping samples and the most expedient for customs clearance. If shipped by air or ocean carriers, fees to clear a $5 sample may run as high as $100.

Couriers

For urgent overseas packages or letters, there are private courier companies that will pick up from and deliver to your office. These couriers include DHL Worldwide Express, Emery Worldwide, Federal Express, Purolator Courier, United Parcel Service, and TNT Skypak, all of which are listed in your telephone directory under delivery service. Not all courier services have direct service to all countries, but all will have areas of special emphasis. Their qualifications also will depend on whether you seek "next day," "second day," or "soonest" delivery.

Geography

Study the world map and get to know the cities with major airports, as well as the seaports for each country. This knowledge is necessary when you get freight rates from either steamship lines or airlines. To determine postage, you will need to know the various island groups in the Caribbean and the countries in Central America, because first-class postage to these places is less than to the rest of the world. Do all you can to brush up on your geography. One opportunity to do so will present itself as you read Chapters 14 through 17. Keep a good world map handy and refer to it often as you read these chapters about the development of the world's trading blocs.

Budget

A separate budget, strictly and specifically for the company's export division or department, is needed, since it will contain items that are unfamiliar to the firm's regular domestic operation and since the cost of some of these items may be quite out of line with domestic costs. The budget should include income projections as well as an expense side. As with the overall budget, the income side may contain some unfamiliar figures as well. John R. Jagoe, in his *Export Sales and Marketing Manual,* provides an exhaustive analysis of both export pricing and export expense and income budgets. In export pricing, this manual provides formats for marginal pricing and for pricing, considering duplicated domestic costs. It also introduces the factors to consider with respect to the constraints on gross margin that are placed on the exporter as a result of the type of overseas distribution system selected. The market entry conditions will, of course, play their part in determining to what degree the firm will have to "buy" its initial market share.

On the expense side of the budget, funds must be made available for necessary market research, which will save expenses that would otherwise be wasted on unproductive efforts. There will also be higher postage and communication costs, to say nothing of sample and sample shipping costs, production costs for overseas directed brochures and labels, translation costs, and other similar start-up costs. Special allowances will have to be made for overseas travel and transportation (consult a good travel agency that specializes in commercial foreign travel), for publications, for legal costs for overseas agreements, perhaps for some consultant time, and for a myriad of similar details.

Above all, do not forget personnel. Specific human resources must be assigned or procured so that the export effort is not a second-rate attempt. Avoid confusing the work of a serious export department, well on its way to becoming an important profit center, with the pickup export sales that merely happen to come along. Sometimes casual export sales, made without knowledgeable consideration of what they are doing to future market shares, opportunities, and intellectual property rights, can add substantially to the ultimate budget of a serious export program. It is much better to face up to both initial and permanent expenses in the beginning, so that all resources can be allocated in a fashion that assures a profitable export operation in the long run.

Bookkeeping

Bookkeeping is a field that people starting a new business often ignore. When first setting up your export venture, attempt to keep account of your sales on a transaction-by-transaction basis, the better to understand your time and operational costs from procurement of your product, to agent commission, to bank charges and interest. This is even a good idea for more sophisticated firms. With computers in all areas of accounting these days, good bookkeeping and transactional analysis should be no problem, because there are so many excellent software programs for small businesses and exporters.

Because your export business might begin with each transaction so carefully observed and with so much paperwork attached, you might feel that normal cash and bookkeeping safeguards are not important. However, as more work is delegated and many transactions are taking place simultaneously, cash flow can quickly become substantial and open up a surprising number of avenues for wasted money and even dishonesty. Big accounting firms have moderately priced pamphlets on accounting and cash flow analysis. Again, the Small Business Administration (SBA) is a prime source for materials and counseling.

Filing

Another issue often postponed and overlooked is a proper filing system. A system that enables you to find the companies, countries, or individuals that you have contacted is essential for later follow-up. A good basic system is to start with a file for each country. As you have more correspondence, make separate files for each company and keep them in alphabetical order in a country file. Also set up a separate alphabetical system for your domestic suppliers and contacts. When writing letters, always make two copies, keeping one copy in the appropriate country or company file and the other in chronological order in a reader file. This is insurance against misfiling and allows easy and quick reference, since most companies will refer to the date of your letter when replying.

For exporters, the tickler file is as important as it is in a domestic business. Make extra copies of a letter or project that needs to be followed up by a certain time and insert it in the file that is marked with a certain day or month. File any mailing lists you buy or develop yourself in the appropriate country file, with notations as to the most recent date used, what was offered, and so forth. If you export several industrial or consumer categories, it is essential to develop both industry-specific and country-specific, (or at least region-specific) lists as well. In addition to files concerning export, your regular office files for paid bills, taxes, banking records, insurance, and office equipment should be in separate but logical order for easy reference and access.

Administrative Skills

Upgrading administrative skills represents an ongoing challenge. Of course, it takes more than basic knowledge to run a business successfully. Knowing how to manage the business is crucial for a new owner. It's obvious businesses fail because of lack of sales but few realize how often they fail because of sales growing too fast, not to mention careless control of operating expenses, lack of organization, poor bookkeeping, and poor cash management, all of which are deficiencies compounded by rapid growth. Because the entrepreneurial spirit is so often sales- or product-oriented, it is commonplace for a new business to fail because the competence level of the owner does not keep pace with increasing sales. A constant upgrading of administrative and financial skills—through reading, seminars, adult education, and a willingness to seek and take good advice—are the only cures for this major cause of business failures, export or otherwise.

Essential Equipment

Besides the obvious telephone, answering machine, typewriter, desk, and accessories, your export business will demand other important items of equipment. The following are some of the principal items to consider.

Computers

Computers are virtually essential today, even for the very small office. Almost any personal computer with a good printer will assist greatly when making large-scale mailings, setting up price lists and contracts, and performing bookkeeping and documentary applications. Consideration should be given, however, to stretching the budget somewhat to be able to utilize the increasing number of excellent software programs written especially for exporting—from order receipt through shipping and collection (even including the translation of correspondence). Some are very sophisticated and designed to interface on-line with your freight forwarder. It's probably even more important to have the capacity to take advantage of the increasing number of databases and informational services providing information from country research, sales leads, and trade statistics to tariffs—all available to any exporter who has a computer equipped with a modem (14400 baud rate suggested) and communication software plus a CD-ROM reader. The CD-ROM represents another revolution in terms of virtually making entire

libraries of trade databases readily available to every exporter at a very afford-
able price. The computer is also essential to one of the newest revolutions in
business and of particular interest to international trade—Electronic Data
Interchange (EDI). EDI relates to the "paperless society," and to exporters it
means moving transport documents and financial documents more quickly and
surely thus providing faster cash flow and better service. EDI promises increased
efficiency in the movement of both goods and money. (This is discussed in more
detail in Chapter 26.)

Telex Equipment

Not long ago, some form of access to telex equipment was important for just
about every export or import operation. A few years before that, a firm could
not have operated affectively without it. Today, it is safe to say that unless the
telex is being used to deal in certain parts of the world having inferior telephone service, there may be no need for it at all. In fact, many companies dealing primarily with regions having a fairly good communication system, have
stopped their telex service altogether. The facsimile (fax) has replaced the telex
for most operations with a better, faster, less expensive, and more convenient
product for the average application.

While there are still some situations in which the telex remains a useful tool
for international trade, the fax and computer definitely take precedence. Unless
and until some definite need arises, therefore, the telex can be left off your list.
Even if the use of a telex is called for, it is easier to buy the software and a
modem for the computer to get connected with a telex carrier or service
provider than to purchase a telex yourself. The U.S. telex carriers (Western
Union, MCI, TRT/FTCC) and the discounters (Swift Global, ICI, Syscom, Tel-
Mac) offer a store-and-forward service that saves dedicating another telephone
line for telex operations. With store-and-forward, incoming messages remain in
a mailbox in the carrier's computer until they are retrieved at a convenient time,
and outgoing messages are bundled for most economical transmission by the
telex service.

If communication with countries having poor telephone service is important,
the telex can and should be considered an alternative means of communication.
This may be true of parts of Russia and Eastern Europe, and it is also true, to
some extent, beyond the central cities of such less-developed countries, as
China, India, Pakistan, and some countries in Africa. Keep in mind that each
year millions are spent in improving telecommunications around the world, so
that such conditions may prove merely temporary. If you need to experiment
with telex communication, check the Yellow Pages, under the heading
Teletypewriter Transmission Service.

Facsimile

As we have already indicated, a facsimile (fax), formerly a luxury for a start-up
business, is today a virtual necessity. For business purposes, a fax should have

at least a 9600 baud terminal, permitting a typical one-page letter to transmit in less than one minute. A very desirable, but added cost feature, is a sheet feeder and paper cutter for inbound faxes. Still more expensive fax machines represent a major improvement by using a laser jet printer to print the incoming fax on plain paper rather than on the conventional thermal paper, which is difficult to write on and fades with time.

Most fax users have a dedicated telephone line servicing their fax terminal. If this seems impractical because of cost and because the machine is only used very infrequently, a fax switch can be installed that permits use of the same telephone line for both voice and fax. The switch senses an incoming fax and activates the fax terminal, or senses a voice and allows the usual ring. Careful checking before installing such a switch is advisable, since some of them create a pause or a click before ringing that can discourage a caller. Some new fax machines have a built-in switch, but so far many have proved unreliable. If at all possible, this is an economy that is better avoided.

Photocopy Machine

A plain paper copy machine of good quality, even though it may be small, is essential equipment because you will need to make copies of price lists, documents, and countless other materials. The photocopy machine will also serve as your in-house printing shop for small jobs or documents.

Scale

To save time at the post office, it's a good idea to have an accurate scale. In fact, it's helpful to have two scales: a small one for your letters and printed matter weighing up to 16 ounces, and another, larger one for small packages enclosing samples and catalogs. Postal scales with a digital readout of weight and required postage are excellent and very handy, but remain relatively expensive.

World Map

Every export-oriented office should have a large, detailed, and up-to-date map. A world atlas is also very useful.

Sources of Information

In the course of this book, virtually all sources of information and government help for exporters will be covered in some detail. The following is a quick overview of some of the most common sources, most of which will be dealt with at much greater length in later chapters.

In export, as in any other business, it's important to become part of a business community to exchange information, become aware of changes in trends, and learn about new international trade developments, either in casual meetings or specifically targeted seminars. In most smaller communities, this would begin with the local Chamber of Commerce, economic development offices, trade associations, and county agricultural offices. Also keep in contact with the District Office of the International Trade Administration (ITA) and its U.S. Foreign and Commercial Service (US&FCS) departments of the U.S. Department of Commerce (DOC) in your particular district, plus world trade clubs or associations formed by exporters in key cities. Check with the National Association of Export Companies, P.O. Box 1330, Murray Hill Station, New York, New York 10156, or the Export Managers Association of Southern California, 110 East Ninth Street, #A–761, Los Angeles, California 90079, for the nearest export trading association. Other large cities, like Chicago, Dallas, Houston, and Miami also have export trade associations, so check with the local chambers of commerce. Attend trade shows relating to your field, both in the United States and abroad, if possible. It is vital to keep abreast of new developments, new export possibilities, and new customers and their needs.

Read the financial section of your daily paper to stay informed as to the value of the dollar relative to the currencies of your overseas customers and keep up-to-date on other international events that may have an economic impact on your business and your export opportunities. As an example, even though you are paid in U.S. dollars, your customers will appreciate your awareness of any fluctuation in its value and about the effect this may have on their own sales efforts. Often overseas importers complain about the lack of understanding and consideration by American suppliers regarding their operational and marketing problems. If your local paper lacks sufficient international and economic news, subscribe to a major regional newspaper or to the *Journal of Commerce,* which is especially oriented to international trade, DOC trade leads, and shipping.

There are many publications available (see Appendix L) to keep you informed about the export business in general, as well as about certain aspects of exporting in particular. Gathering and evaluating current information is an essential part of any ongoing business, especially in exporting.

Counseling Sources

Many firms and individuals hesitate to get involved in export because they fear that unforeseen complications and difficulties, combined with their own lack of experience, will make success doubtful, if not impossible. These hesitant firms are especially concerned about the possibility of encountering significant and unmanageable financial risks abroad. They also worry that they will be cheated in their contacts with foreign businesspeople. They conclude that it's simply easier to expand their share of our enormous domestic market.

The truth is, however, that exporting is not nearly as difficult as it sounds, if you just get on with it and properly utilize the many sources for help available. If you are trading with countries that have a well-developed commercial code, for instance, you will find that there are no more rogues abroad than at home. They might have a different version of prompt payment or other commercial customs, but there are good worldwide sources for obtaining information on your customer and his or her credit (which are later detailed in Chapter 25).

Most firms doing open-account business abroad with people they know or have properly investigated experience no greater losses than they do at home. Aside from commercial information, exporting is almost unique in terms of the vast amount of advice and assistance available from many different sources, often at a minimal cost.

U.S. Department of Commerce

The Department of Commerce (DOC) is your initial source of advice and assistance and should be the starting point for any novice exporter or new-to-export company. The organization within the DOC dealing with exports is the International Trade Administration (ITA). The ITA has four principal divisions, each with a variety of services and functions, but the touchstone for access to most of their activities is the local district office of the U.S. and Foreign Commercial Service (US&FCS). The US&FCS has 47 district offices and 22 branch offices located in major cities throughout the United States and Puerto Rico. These offices in turn are in direct contact with the US&FCS foreign offices and staff in 69 countries.

The district offices also provide excellent basic export orientation seminars and participate in and support more advanced or specialized seminars, often in cooperation with the SBA. Before attending such a seminar, purchase *A Basic Guide to Exporting,* published by the DOC and sold at a modest price through the Government Printing Office or bookstores. For more information on the DOC, see Chapter 42 or call the Trade Information Center (TIC) at 800/USA-TRADE for general information, contacts, telephone numbers, and addresses for all federal export support agencies.

U.S. Export Assistance Centers

In 1994 four of these U.S. Export Assistance Centers (USEACs) were established experimentally and were successful enough that 11 more are planned to open during 1995. The concept was to provide one-stop counseling from most of the federal agencies available for export and export finance support. They draw on the resources of the SBA, the DOC and its US&FCS district offices, and Eximbank, and in a limited number of centers have U.S. Agency for International Development (AID) personnel on hand. Personnel from the first three of these organizations are permanently on staff in the USEACs and are also supposed to be informed about the other agencies not directly represented (such as OPIC, AID, and individual state programs). Information and some counseling are immediately available, together with references to the individual agencies, depending on your needs. If one of the USEACs is nearby, you should find it a more useful and accessible source of help for new-to-export firms. It remains to be seen how much in-depth information the USEACs will be able to give on the spot and/or how much they will assume a referral function. But if such a center is accessible to you, it represents a logical and potentially very helpful first stop. (See Chapter 42.)

Small Business Development Centers (SBDCs)

The Small Business Development Centers (SBDCs) share some of the start-up help characteristics of the USEACs in terms of being in existence to help any start-up or very young company. In most of the SBDCs this does not depend on any special interest in the international aspects of the business. SBDCs typically provide counseling and give some assistance in handling market research, legal roadblocks or options, and some direction for financing. They are a function of, and are supervised by, their SBA district office, although often jointly managed and partially financed by the state's trade or small business office, together with a sponsoring organization. Each will offer varying degrees of export expertise through its counselors, depending on the emphasis of the sponsor and the geographical proximity of major trade-related ports. There are several SBDCs in the Los Angeles area, for example. One of them, together with its suboffice in Oxnard, is devoted entirely to assisting small business export development. Check with your nearest SBA office to locate the various SBDCs in your area and the one most likely to help you with export problems. (See Chapter 44.)

Small Business Administration

Export counseling services are also offered through the Small Business Administration (SBA) by those members of the Service Corps of Retired Executives (SCORE) and the Active Corps of Executives (ACE) who also happen to be knowledgeable regarding international trade. All the dedicated individuals in SCORE and ACE have years of practical experience in business, and those with knowledge of export as well are especially happy to give trade advice to small firms. SBA is placing renewed emphasis on supporting small business export development through counseling, finance, export market research, and they interface with ITA's services throughout the USEACs we have mentioned in addition to their work with export oriented SBDCs. (See Chapter 35 and Chapter 44 for more on the SBA. Related help from the Agency for International Development (AID) is covered in Chapter 13.)

U.S. Department of Agriculture

If you are involved in agricultural exports, the Foreign Agricultural Service (FAS) performs a similar function for the U.S Department of Agriculture (USDA) as the U.S. and FCS does for the DOC. FAS is one of your best counseling resources as is your nearest U.S. Department of Agriculture (USDA) office. In addition to marketing and research assistance from FAS, USDA offers financing and price-competitiveness-support programs. (A complete overview of the USDA, its programs, and organization is provided in Chapter 43.)

State and City Agencies

There is a substantial list of cities, counties, and states with programs for supporting their own exporters. These agencies range from direct lending programs that support any business being directed through certain ports, to loan guarantee and insurance programs, to basic counseling. (See Chapter 44 for more details on these nonfederal programs and how to contact them.)

Local associations, trade organizations, chambers of commerce, trade associations, and world trade centers all offer programs and seminars with advice and information for the new-to-export firm or individual. They can also give you advice concerning private consultants. Check the Yellow Pages under "Business and Trade Associations." Unfortunately, these associations tend to be concentrated in the larger cities. Recently, however, country agricultural organizations, universities, and colleges have begun developing assistance programs and courses aimed at exporters. As an example, in California there are a number of community colleges offering export counseling away from urban centers through a program called Centers for International Trade Development (CITD). These can offer excellent one-on-one counseling, plus student-intern-based research. Many states have similar programs under other names.

International Trade Consultants and Market Research Organizations

Once you have obtained a good working knowledge of your export possibilities from these relatively inexpensive sources, you might consider the professional services of a consultant. Depending on the specialty, the consultant can simply provide basic advice on export management, planning, and marketing, or become further involved with hands-on assistance in all phases of your export program. Don't overlook your avenues for financial advice. A good international trade finance consultant might point out financial support opportunities that would never occur to you. (See Chapter 37.) To locate trade consultants, look under "Export Consultants" in the Yellow Pages of any large city.

Most of these organizations and options are discussed in detail in Part 7 of this book, as well as where appropriate within specific chapters. Market research consultants are discussed in more detail in Chapter 7.

4

Exporting Through a Domestic Intermediary

There are many ways to enter the global market if your product is domestically well established and you are ready to invest meaningful funds, personnel, and time. One category of entry is domestic intermediaries, which in themselves come in many forms.

In Chapter 1 we provided some clues and qualities for measurement as to an organization's readiness to export. (The US&FCS Trade Specialists even have something called the Computerized Export Qualifier Program to assess export readiness. However, if you honestly and objectively answered the issue we raised in Chapter 1 concerning making the export decision, you have a pretty good idea of your particular readiness and commitment.) If your investigation turns up a minimal level of commitment and resources, you may decide to consider a domestic intermediary, at least initially or for a portion of the potential world areas. This is not to say that a marginal situation is the only justification for considering an intermediary. Even indirect exporting, with an export trading firm to provide hands-on management, is not effortless and will require some attention and planning on your part.

The export trading or management companies are high on the list when it comes to choosing domestic intermediaries. The independent entrepreneur discussed in Chapter 2, however, might be the one contacting you to handle your export affairs, or one of several other types of specialized independent or third-party exporters.

The Role of the Independent Exporter

The independent, or third-party, exporter is statistically rather silent, but is a very important exporter nevertheless. Most independent exporters are known as Export Management Companies (EMCs) and Export Trading Companies (ETCs). The available data vary regarding exactly how many EMCs/ETCs there are and what percentage of American exports these independent exporters account for within the merchandise exports figure. A common guess, however, is from 6 to 8 percent. According to government statistics, of the approximately 41,000 firms that have exported (and that are wholesalers rather than manufacturers or other intermediaries), only about 5000 intermediaries derive more than 50 percent of their sales from exports. The Commerce Department was recently quoted to the effect that there were about 2000 trading companies, but those of real substance with staff and travel budgets are much fewer. The confusing and contradictory statement also comes from a DOC study of 1987 statistics stating that "trade intermediaries" accounted for 37 percent of the nation's exporters. On the face of it, this is an impossible figure because a more recent analysis of exporters by size and frequency showed that the top 1000 exporters in the United States accounted for 78 percent of total U.S. exports and that the median dollar value of their export sales was about $50 million, a figure that almost no trade intermediary comes close to reaching, because they are primarily smaller businesses. The explanation is that the DOC study apparently included the subsidiary corporations utilized by the Fortune 500 companies to function as their export and/or international trade companies, often as "Foreign Sales Corporations" for tax purposes. Thus the captive and subsidiary corporation handling exports for corporate giant 3M would have been counted as a "trade intermediary" even though it is actually a completely different entity from what we are discussing here.

Many people maintain that independent exporters could and should account for much more of our exports, as they do in many other countries, especially in Japan. In most countries where exporting is part of the lifeblood of commercial and national existence, the independent export manager or trading company is an important element in maintaining a trade balance. As our trade deficits have climbed and the need to encourage more companies to export aggressively has been recognized, export trading companies have become a viable alternative.

Independent exporters have the advantage of selecting products that have appeal in certain countries for which they have an affinity. These exporters can sell several products that complement each other and thus save on container load shipments in a way that would not be possible with only one product. There are also occasions in which products have only seasonal appeal, which the exporter can replace with products for each season. These factors contribute to the opportunity for economy of scale that is a critical component of export success. Certainly EMCs/ETCs can be the key to a successful effort by a small business to profitably engage in global marketing.

Because of the potential impact of EMCs and ETCs on this country's expansion of its exports, this section will expand beyond what would be required to merely describe their function as an export effort. The subject receives further attention in the section on finding, selecting, and negotiating with an EMC or ETC in Chapter 9. (This section would also merit careful study by any EMC/ETC staff member or prospective EMC/ETC.)

Stanley Epstein, former president of the National Federation of Export Associations as well as an export management and trading company owner and industry leader, makes an interesting case for the EMC/ETC. In tracing the history of American independent exporters, Epstein feels that this nation's lack of emphasis on exporting stems from the post-World War II economic rehabilitation era. Many agree that the restoration-aid concept of the Marshall Plan, however laudatory and successful, seems to have fixed forever in our minds the role of the United States as an economic benefactor. As a result, we developed an idea that the United States would always provide the most technology, dominate in the production of most specialized goods and services such as transportation and aerospace, provide consulting services to all, and feed the world. And for a while we nearly did. Today, however, many of these countries we helped rebuild are our creditors.

During much of the last 40 years, U.S. exports have been taken for granted. They have not received the same kind of priority attention—an integral element of the nation's economic equation—that is accorded them in most other countries as a matter of course. It is not surprising, therefore, that during this period, the important role of the independent exporter has not flourished in the United States as it has in other countries. The economy of scale, which is so important in global marketing efforts and which the export trading company can offer in abundance to small and midsize businesses, has never had a chance to develop. In nearly every other part of the world, export is looked on as a nation's lifeblood, and the independent exporter or trading company is seen as an integral part of this equation.

Now, finally, the nation as a whole is realizing that our unique benefactor status has dissolved, and that, just as we have been lecturing to so many other nations, we must pay for our imports with our export earnings. As our trade deficit began to develop in 1971, the government increased its verbiage, though not its budget, to encourage small and midsize companies to export their products. Too often, what time and funding has been available has not been properly targeted to the companies with the greatest need and potential for export success. Besides existing small and midsize organizations making products with export potential, these companies include existing and functional independent EMCs and ETCs. The latter, almost by definition, must be highly leveraged if their slim margins are to permit a satisfactory return on investment, and they often need some support to develop adequate financial strength. In recent years the DOC has consciously started to target both these categories, leaving small companies that are simply exploring the idea of export and individuals that would someday like to be EMC/ETC to the SBA programs. This is probably a practical approach. An all-out effort has yet to be made to encourage nonexporting manufacturers to seek the help of qualified independent exporters in waging an aggressive export effort.

The Export Management Company

By definition, an EMC represents various complementary, or at least noncompetitive, manufacturers with whom it has an agreement for a given time period. The EMC may either be compensated on a commission basis or may purchase and take legal title to the merchandise that it sells. Whatever the financial arrangement, the objective of an EMC is to function as the manufacturer's export sales department. In this capacity, the EMC works out an overall market strategy in certain agreed-upon areas. This includes utilizing or expanding the EMC's existing network or seeking new distributors or sales representatives.

Therefore, the EMC must maintain as close a contact as possible with its clients—perhaps an even closer relationship than that with its overseas distributors. With a key client, depending on the product and the nature of the overseas prospects, it can be advantageous to correspond on the letterhead and use the business card format of the client supplier. This can help in some situations to diminish any hesitancy on the part of buyers to purchase through a third party, because they have fears about having an indirect or short-term relationship with the manufacturer. In other situations, in which the prospective buyer knows and regularly deals with the EMC, this clearly would not be a problem.

Depending on the length of the contract and the type of relationship, there can be limits in the marketing area. The EMC may not be able to afford long-range strategies, for instance, and the manufacturer is not likely to have the patience for them. By the same token, EMCs and their clients seldom enjoy any advantage from their relationship until after 6 to 12 months of effort. Therefore, it should certainly not be a short-term relationship and should not be entered into lightly by either party.

To be as competitive as possible, the manufacturer's price to the EMC must be determined by adding the necessary overhead costs and margins to the manufacturer's cost of goods sold. In practice, EMCs usually negotiate the best price possible by convincing the manufacturer that the EMC is now bearing the costs of selling and advertising, as well as the credit risks and financial costs.

There is disagreement as to whether it is more common for the EMC to take title to the goods or accept a commission. Either method is acceptable. Often the reason a manufacturer enters into an agreement with an EMC is so that export sales can be treated as if they were domestic transactions. This is not the case if the manufacturer must evaluate and accept foreign credit risks, whether open account or documentary. Foreign buyer risk is an area in which an EMC should develop special skills and learn how to minimize and control these risks.

The assumption by the EMC of the additional cost and loss potential of taking title, however, clearly increases the margin that the EMC must achieve.

Conversely though, the manufacturer might be the party desiring to maintain control with respect to pricing and suitable customers. In that scenario the EMC would not take title and would leave the credit decisions to the manufacturer. The EMC would then receive a commission, possibly combined with a base retainer, as opposed to a gross profit on sales.

Going one step further, the EMC can also function as the overseas distributor or wholesaler and therefore might be responsible for carrying inventory as well as receivables. The problem with such a scenario is that, excluding those circumstances in which stock is actually carried, a typical margin for the EMC is about 15 percent. This seldom allows a fair net profit if the EMC really undertakes the selling responsibilities it claims to undertake, to say nothing of after-sales service. Therefore, short of providing larger margins or commissions, unless excellent economy of scale savings can be made or the sales function can be minimized, profitability is a problem. In fact, economy of scale has forced many successful export companies to focus on related products in those regions of the world in which they have already developed the necessary network.

The fine line an export company must walk, as an EMC or ETC, is that of balancing focus and diversification. Focus is necessary in order to utilize specialized knowledge, contacts, and networks in an effort to achieve economy of scale. Diversification is necessary to protect against possible rapid economic or political changes in one country and to take advantage of the differing impact of business cycles on various products.

The Export Trading Company

The ETC has the same functions and many of the same problems as an EMC except for a diminished client relationship (which is countered by greater freedom of action). The ETC's business is typically demand-driven and conducted on a transaction-by-transaction or ad hoc basis.

The ETC concept implies that there be less responsibility or no responsibility on the part of the ETC toward the supplier or buyer. Each transaction is a separate entity, even though the ETC's activities usually find cohesiveness and scale through specialization in terms of product categories, customer profiles, geographic area, or a combination of these factors. Although no obligations are professed to the supplier or the importer by the ETC, few relationships are successful without a broad level of confidence. There is, therefore, a natural tendency to repeat business and develop continuing transactions with the same ETC. Quite often foreign tender bid offerings are the vehicles that determine the source used, and in other typical cases provide a sourcing or buying office function for a group of steady overseas clients within an industry or product grouping.

The ETC is even more likely to take title to the goods than an EMC, except if a very large transaction or countertrade arrangement is involved. In the case of the very few remaining trading companies owned by banks, a financial capability for individual transactions exceeding $250,000 is most often a primary reason for existence. An ETC would not carry stock or perform after-sales service and would probably not provide a continuing sales effort. Rather, it provides more of a sourcing function for both buyer and seller. Countertrade should fit naturally into the scope of a large ETC.

Federal legislation, known as the Export Trading Company Act, permits export trading companies to apply for an Export Trade Certificate of Review through the Department of Commerce. This provides the ETC with immunity from prosecution for activities that might otherwise be in violation of antitrust regulations.

This legislation permits banks to be financially involved in ETCs and created a rash of bank-owned trading companies. When passing this act, Congress was looking at the highly successful, bank-related Japanese trading companies as a role model. Very few bank-owned ETCs have survived as active trading companies because the banking mentality for risk avoidance did not mix well with the trading mentality. There are only a few exceptions, while others have remained in business primarily for documentary purposes and are trading companies in name only.

EMC/ETC Hybrids

In actual practice, many EMCs and other types of third-party exporters evolve into a combination EMC/ETC, accepting different levels of responsibility for various products and client companies. They seek, or at least accept, single-transaction opportunities, the largest of which help to achieve economies of scale and hopefully improve profits through marginal utility. Such exporters may function as an ETC as opportunities arise and then subsequently find that some of the supply sources offer sufficient new and continuing sales potential to develop into an EMC relationship. There is no harm in this format for the manufacturer using such an EMC/ETC, as long as both understand each other and share similar objectives.

Characteristics of EMCs/ETCs

As a result of research undertaken by the National Federation of Export Associations (NFEA), Richard Barovick prepared a *Trading Company Sourcebook* from which the following information about EMCs/ETCs was extracted in the July 13, 1992, issue of *Business America* magazine:

> Most such companies are small, employing from 2 to 50 people. Based on a 1989 survey, over 60 percent reported six or fewer employees, and 15 percent reported 21 or more. Approximately one-third reported volumes of under $1 million, another third from $1 million to $5 million, and 11 percent grossing from $10 to $50 million. The very large firms tend to be good product and commodity firms, a few well in excess of $100 million. While most

are individually owned by entrepreneurs, some are owned by food giants or other large companies to handle their own products together with other related or subproducts. Quite often the EMC/ETC operators' skills are based on earlier experience with the corporate export departments; and less often from work for other export intermediaries. Certainly the profiles of the trading companies contrast with those of Europe and Japan, which are often large and involve both import and export.[1]

The Pros and Cons of Using EMCs/ETCs

There are, of course, both advantages and disadvantages to using an EMC or an ETC. Credit should be given to the research done by several large accounting firms that have taken great interest in export in general and EMCs/ETCs in particular. An excellent case in point is the article by Catharine H. Findiesen of Coopers & Lybrand in Washington, D.C., which addresses most of these considerations:[2]

The Advantages of Using an EMC/ETC

- Faster entry into the overseas market in terms of first recorded sales
- Better focus on exporting, because most firms give priority to their domestic problems
- Lower out-of-pocket expenses
- An opportunity to study the methods and potential of exporting
- Expertise in dealing with the special details involved in exporting, as well as its strategies

The Potential Disadvantages of Using an EMC/ETC

- Loss of control of the export strategies and quality control of after-sales service
- Competition from the EMC's/ETC's other products
- Reluctance on the part of some foreign buyers to deal with a third-party intermediary
- Some added costs, and/or higher selling prices because of gross profit margin requirements of the EMC/ETC, unless economies of scale can be used to offset this factor
- The possibility of the EMC/ETC neglecting the client's product in favor of other products that might be more profitable or easier to sell

The challenge of negotiating a sound working relationship with an EMC/ETC is discussed in Chapter 9.

Import-Export Trading Companies

Another hybrid exporter develops from the natural tendency of companies that are involved in international trade to pursue both import and export activities. If this can be done without diverting too much attention away from primary activities, it is commendable. As major external factors beyond the trader's control such as the dollar's value or government policies, wax and wane, the relative profitability of importing and exporting changes. Independent exporters considering such a move, however, should keep in mind that a variety of skills, different financing schemes, and new networks are necessary for success.

Other Intermediaries

Various other intermediaries are no less important than EMCs/ETCs, but they are more specialized and concentrated within special product areas or modes of operation.

U.S. Military Post Exchange and Commissary Sales Agents

Many firms have discovered the overseas military market through someone in their domestic sales organization who was familiar with the methods and practices of selling to the U.S. military buying organizations. It probably does not occur to them that they are exporting, although today most firms engaging in this business must handle both the domestic and the overseas portions as one business. The business is declining as a result of defense cutbacks, but this market probably continues to have potential for the exporter with the type of consumer product it requires. Unless an EMC/ETC has a special department for this purpose, however, it would in most cases be more efficient to engage a qualified firm specializing in this business. These firms have well-established contacts and friendships that can pave the way through what can be a tiresome and involved process, requiring regular follow-up. They can also give you an idea of your product's potential in this specialized market.

A number of the largest military representatives are members of the Armed Forces Marketing Council (955 L'Enfant Plaza North, Washington, D.C. 20024). To study the market more directly, there are public and private publications you can request or to which you can subscribe. These include *Vendor Facts,* from the Army and Air Force Exchange Service, Red Bird Plaza, Dallas, Texas 75222; *Exchange and Commissary News,* P.O. Box 788, Lynbrook, New York 11563; and *Military Market,* 475 School Street, Washington, D.C. 20024.

International Buying Offices

International buying offices come in many forms. The best known are buying offices for large overseas retailers. They might be domestic buying offices serving American department and specialty stores with a separate department for their international trade, or they might specialize in international trade only. Others serve only one major overseas retailer who owns and operates the office, sometimes in conjunction with other activities in this country. International buying offices are mostly useful for selling consumer goods, but it is difficult to develop an ongoing export trade with them. International buying offices are best to test new items, although from time to time, major stores will plan U.S. fairs. If you have the right kind of merchandise, these fairs can represent major opportunities for both overseas sales and market entry. In most cases, the buying office will take full credit responsibility and have the merchandise billed to it, marked for a certain store's attention. Take normal domestic credit precautions concerning the buying office itself and do not rely on the famous store name for whom your goods were purchased. The DOC maintains a fairly complete list of these United States–based international buying offices.

Project Buying Offices

Some project buying offices might be set up on a temporary basis by the prime contractor for a major overseas project for which a wide variety of products, entirely unrelated to the prime contractor, must be purchased. While these channels do not really represent exporting, they can serve to instill enthusiasm and understanding for the potential and give an idea of who might be interested in your product and in what countries. It is a very meaningful business for the right kind of firm.

See Chapter 13 for more details on how to pursue this business. The DOC maintains a list of overseas project managers, such as the Bechtel Group, Dravo Corp., Kiewit Constructions Group, and Morrison Knudsen Corp.

Piggyback Marketing

Piggyback marketing occurs more often by accident than design. It can develop when a company involved in overseas selling needs to provide other goods or services to complement the product, such as accessories or certain follow-up services. These are provided by a third party utilizing the exporting firm's channels, structure, and supervision. It can also be the opposite of the previously mentioned project buying office in that it represents an active effort by subcontractors to find business through prime contractors, as emphasized in Chapter 13.

Export Merchants or Remarketers

Export merchants or remarketers order for their own specifications and usually under their own label in order to develop overseas business that they can count on remaining exclusive to their private purposes. This is often a separate activity of an otherwise conventional EMC. The problem is that the manufacturer will most likely never learn where the merchandise is being shipped. The reason for our even mentioning it here is to caution you that it could interfere with your present direct export activities or those of an EMC who represents you. It is worthwhile to find some means of tracking the territories the remarketer's goods are reaching if you are dealing with them.

Endnotes

1. Barovick, Richard, *Trading Company Sourcebook,* International Business Affairs Corp., 4938 Hampdon Lane, #364, Bethesda, Maryland 20814.

2. Findiesen, Catharine H., "Guidelines for Choosing and Using an Export Trading Company," based on remarks to the State of Tennessee Matchmaker Conference, Nashville, Tennessee, May 25, 1983.

5

Entering the Overseas Market

Direct involvement in the overseas export or marketing process naturally requires a higher degree of commitment and attention. Three principal categories of market involvement are discussed in this chapter. The first, *direct exporting selling,* means setting up at least a limited export organization and establishing sales contacts with overseas agents and other interested parties. The second, *indirect market entry,* does not refer to the physical shipment of the product, but rather to the know-how involved, as in the case of licensing and franchising. The third, *corporate presence,* means a corporate commitment and is not normally considered until substantial effort has first been expended on testing the market.

Direct Export Selling

Depending on human and financial resources, direct sales can accelerate your export sales volume in the long run even though a well matched EMC/ETC may get faster initial results. Such success, however, is very dependent on the attention level your firm can give to the project for an extended period of time. One of the most obvious advantages of selling directly and doing it yourself is that you begin to develop personal relationships overseas from the beginning. Even if you decide to sell directly to certain overseas markets, you still have the option of using an export manager in other parts of the world and a consultant to assist you and help organize your timetable in the direct area.

You have several options when considering direct sales channels: a representative/agent; a distributor/importer; overseas retailers; central trade offices like China's; and general trading companies like Japan's.

Representative/Agent

The terms *representative* or *agent* are used to describe a person or firm selling and taking orders without being directly responsible for the payment, no matter how great the responsibilities might otherwise be. A representative might handle one or several similar lines of merchandise and sell them by showing customers catalogues and samples that are prepared by the supplier or manufacturer. In most countries the representative will have the same role as in domestic business, and may well be carrying both local lines and import lines. You will often find a big difference in the representative's attitude on commissions if your product is in competition with local sources. This has some merit because you will probably pay commission based on FOB (free on board) prices, but the retailer or end user has to add tariff, freight, and import costs to your FOB price, and therefore your FOB-based commission represents a substantially smaller percentage of the actual wholesale value.

A typical commission for a representative ranges from 3 percent to 15 percent or more, depending on the product and the size of a typical order. This commission is usually included in the prices furnished to your representative and is payable to the representative at fixed intervals following shipment or payment. Because representatives do not buy for their own account, it is your responsibility to check the credit of the overseas firms and arrange payment terms with them after you have received the order. The representative can be a great help in credit decisions. However, you must always remember that the primary concern of salespeople the world over, is to make the sale. Depending on the product, size of average sale, representatives' relationship to their customers, access to credit information, and the influence you allow them to have as to acceptable customers, some will agree to their commission being contingent on payment. A representative will definitely want a binding agreement from you as to territory, exclusivity, and term.

Legal advisors strongly recommend avoiding use of the term *agent* in favor of the term *representative* or almost any other substitute term, such as *appointee*. The word *agent,* in varying degrees and depending on the country, apparently implies a greater authority to contract on your behalf, which carries fairly broad legal responsibilities in some countries. The greater the representative's responsibility for independent activity and scheduling without instruction from the supplier in the course of selling the supplier's product, the clearer it is that the representative has little or no contracting authority; and the less likely it is that a foreign government might claim the right to tax the supplier on any foreign revenues or profits resulting from the supplier's overseas business activity. Since there is a possibility that you are potentially compounding your problems by use of the term *agent,* by all means use alternatives unless there is a very good reason to do otherwise and you are sure of the consequences. In any case, there is also much greater protection for agents or representatives in many foreign countries than in the United States in respect to termination, with or without justification, as well as in other areas of the relationship. These subjects come up again in connection with the discussion of finding and developing agreements with representatives in Chapter 9.

Distributor/Importer

In contrast to representatives, *distributors* might also be called *jobbers, dealers,* or *wholesalers,* but they will always be the party responsible for payment of the product that is exported. While they will probably be assigned sales goals or quotas, just as representatives would, their first responsibility is to buy and to pay, which includes the tasks relative to clearing the goods through customs. A distribution arrangement is excellent if your product and brand are well known, or are otherwise valuable enough for the importer to make this commitment and remain eager to fulfill it. Import distributors are sometimes known to take on lines that they then neglect, thinking that at least it keeps the product away from their competition. Distributors usually buy for their own account, sometimes maintaining inventories in their own warehouses, but some only place orders against their customer's firm orders. The distributor must be investigated to be sure adequate facilities and personnel exist, especially if your product requires maintenance or spare parts. Exclusivity for a certain territory and a certain period of time is normally a necessity. See Chapter 9 for details on distributor relationships.

Overseas Retailers

Sales to foreign stores are usually limited to consumer goods and may be sold at a lower price because no agent commission is involved. This can create competition for your own agent when you ultimately see the need for one. If possible, sell to the retailer at a price that will permit you to pay an agent in the future. While store owners want the lower cost, they also often do not like losing the service of the agent who places the order for them, follows it up, and takes care of any claims.

China's and Other Nation's Central Trade Offices

In the case of the few remaining controlled market economies, importing is sometimes governed by central trade or buying offices. Today, these are subject to the rapid changes taking place in such areas. Chief among these is China, by far the largest remaining controlled, or semicontrolled, economy. The other major fully controlled market economy as of early 1995 is North Korea, but thanks to the utter authoritarian domination of the country, the economy is small—one-tenth the size of South Korea. Even so, businesspeople from many nations, especially South Korea, are beginning to see it as a potential market.

China's trade and buying offices, which are most often called Foreign Trade Corporations, tend to be divided into industry groups that may buy for the whole country or, increasingly, for smaller, regional, or provincial groups, as part of a reform agenda item in the name of less bureaucracy. Increasingly, factories and entrepreneurs within the capitalistic enterprise zones have been allowed to circumvent the oversight of the central offices (see Chapter 15), but even these zones remain subject to control through the banking system as a result of the necessity for approval of import letters of credit. In the case of central control, some of the Chinese trade organizations tend to do most of the negotiation and the final contracting, but an end-user group, such as a factory unit, is likely to have trade office representatives involved as well. It often happens that time is spent negotiating with lower level officials only to find that the ministry involved is opposed. Sometimes the reverse is true, and the factory level turns out not to be interested, even though the assumption was that the sale was being accomplished at a much higher level. If at all possible, it is best to make sure everyone involved agrees and stays with the transaction and marketing effort from headquarters out to the field or the reverse.

Japan's and Other Nations' General Trading Companies

Japanese general trading companies, called "Sogo Shoshas," are indigenous to Japan and are the driving force behind Japan's internal and external trade. There are nine major trading companies, including Mitsubishi, Marubeni, Mitsui, and many smaller specialized trading companies (senmonshosha). Though seldom a channel for ongoing relationships, they are perfect for single sales and can give newcomers some valuable experience in cracking the Japanese market and preparing for future dealings with Japan. Sales to Sogo Shoshas might almost be considered sales through domestic intermediaries if they were handled through one of their American offices.

All nine major Japanese trading companies have offices in American cities and around the world that you can visit. The problem is that, if it is interested, the trading company will probably have to forward the sample to Japan to reach the specialist in charge. The trading companies also can be approached directly on one of your visits to Japan. They are definitely worth considering. With luck, you can have an excellent customer in Japan, but you risk wasting a great deal of your time while they are deciding. See Appendix H for the addresses of headquarters of the major Japanese trading companies and the cities in which they have offices. The Japan External Trade Organization (JETRO) can be very helpful to exporters who want to do their market research from their home base. JETRO (see Appendix G for address) has received a mandate in recent years to assist American exporters in view of Japan's shared concern about the trade deficit.

The major trading companies from the "Four Tigers" of Southeast Asia—Korea, Taiwan, Singapore, and Hong Kong—also have offices in the United States, though to a lesser extent than do Japan's trading companies.

Indirect Market Entry

If direct export selling is impractical or undesirable, there are alternatives in the form of licensing, franchising, or contract manufacturing. These alternatives enable you to profit from overseas markets without needing to get involved in direct export. These forms of market entry, however, also require substantial diligence and attention, even if somewhat less time and personnel.

Licensing

Licensing is considered an indirect entry because a version of your product is placed in the foreign market without your actually having to ship it there. Finding and working with a successful licensor, however, is not a passive exercise. On the contrary, it takes careful planning, supervision, and follow-through to produce a successful licensing program.

A license usually involves one or all of the following:

- Technology and know-how
- Design
- Trademark, logo, name

A *license* is a contract to provide all or part of the licensor's trademarks, patents, designs, copyrights, and know-how. This contract should clearly spell out what is being licensed and under what terms. The licensor receives compensation in the form of a royalty that may be a fixed dollar sum, a percentage of sales results or, more often, a combination of the two. Under what circumstances licensing will be successful depends on factors such as the ease of obtaining accurate reports and enforcing future royalty payments. These, in turn, are governed by factors such as the future dependence of the licensee on continuing assistance, as in the case of a design license. Many of the big six American accounting firms have offices in various countries and can be called on to assist you by means of audits for enforcement purposes if your license agreement permits such examinations.

A license commonly calls for advance minimum royalties against a percentage-based royalty. A typical agreement used for licensing apparel designs and trademarks may be found in Appendix R. This agreement has been the basis for a fair understanding in many cases but can easily be drawn to be much more demanding. The general format may help you understand what is involved as you are giving the concept further consideration. Legal, and probably accounting, advice is important, and the assistance of an international trade consultant should be considered. In the case of technology transfer, the varieties are limitless, as are the complicating considerations. Therefore, an agreement must be customized to each situation. Licensing can be necessary as a means of entering some markets that otherwise could not be entered because of tariff and/or nontariff barriers. As with a domestic license, the success or failure of a foreign license depends to a large degree on the human equation and on the integrity of both parties entering into the agreement.

Before licensing negotiations are undertaken, the licensor should check on restrictions or regulations that are imposed by the licensee's government, which often must approve a license agreement before it is valid. A majority of countries impose imputed income taxes on the licensor and require the withholding of income taxes from royalty payments before remittance to the licensor. Some countries have limitations on the key components in the license agreement, especially as to the percentage of royalty. Others, including Japan and a number of countries in Latin America, have very specific rules as to what terms are acceptable in technology transfer agreements. Have your attorney check whether this will come up in negotiations to make sure that the prospective licensee is stating a fact rather than using it as negotiating wedge.

Licensing should be regarded as an option that permits a company to enter a foreign market more quickly, but it usually does not produce the revenue that is potentially available from direct selling or successful overseas operations. On the other hand, licensing involves few financial risks if you have a well-drawn license. Many companies have found it very profitable.

One clear disadvantage is the possibility of losing control of your product and thereby creating a future competitor. Also, there is always the problem of getting your know-how back at the end of the license contract. A key element for keeping a license profitable and interesting to the licensee is the creation of new designs and technology on a frequent basis. Be certain your agreement gives you adequate protection from the overseas licensee against having your own technology or design used to compete with you in territories where you are selling directly.

For all these reasons, it is important to negotiate a substantial disclosure fee to be paid up front. Most international attorneys recommend that this fee be as much as 50 percent of the total consideration, because the licensor must part with its know-how or technology at the beginning of the agreement, and it is therefore not equitable to permit all of the licensing income to depend on future royalties. Substantial advance payment ensures a vital interest on the part of the licensee.

A major plus from a well-drawn and harmonious license agreement is that many companies have found they can learn much from their licensees, including ways to improve the original product. There are many books and publications on drafting and negotiating foreign licenses, franchises, and joint ventures. At least some can be found in any major library. The following checklist courtesy of, and adapted from, the *Management Export Information Manual,* prepared by Richard E. Sherwood and Walter R. Thiel with contributions from many members of the Southern California District Export Council and published by the Council,[1] may be helpful in preliminary negotiations.

License Contract Checklist

1. Performance is the keystone of license contracts. Take your time in finding the licensee.

2. The span of the contract should be fixed but provide intermediate escape points in case of poor performance options to renew if and when performance is good.

3. Specify the national law governing the contract. You might want both parties to execute your contract in the United States.

4. Semantics may be a problem. Specify an official language for the contract. Clarify the meaning of any terms open to misinterpretation. For technical products, you might want your own glossary of translated terms.

5. Provide for allocation of taxes during the life of the agreement and upon its termination.

6. Observe, and require that your licensee observe, all foreign government tax and administrative regulations.

7. Safeguard your patents and trademarks before you start to negotiate.

8. Use your own trademark if you can. You might want to do the manufacturing yourself at a later date. Consider this and similar goals and fit your licensing arrangement into long-range planning.

9. Specify who will take judicial and administrative action to protect property rights, and who is to bear the costs.

10. Provide for review of changes in designs, techniques, parts, or procedures. Someone in the home office should be clearly responsible for keeping technical communication free of misunderstandings between you and the licensee.

11. Ensure that the right to assign or sublicense is exclusively yours.

12. Keep informed on any de facto sublicensing assignment of responsibility by your licensee to others through subcontracts.

13. Watch carefully to catch defaults before they occur. Waivers of conditions can undermine the strength of the contract.

14. Make sure you are getting the substance, not the shell, of your patents if you have to recapture them.

15. Guard your know-how. Consider substantial liquidated damages if nondisclosure requirements are violated.

16. Provide for careful indoctrination of know-how and reciprocal exchange of information on new developments.

17. Supplying know-how may involve key personnel. Avoid tight travel and personnel schedules.

18. Don't brainwash your licensee by insisting on complete adherence to your own systems. Foreign needs may not involve close tolerance in quality of American customers.

19. Be aware that exclusive rights may limit your sales and profits and may violate antitrust laws.

20. Leave the door open for amendments that will help counter new legal or trade factors.

21. Insert a reciprocal force majeure clause.

22. Leave the door open for renegotiation or rearrangements of the license in case common markets or changes in common markets occur.

23. Let opportunity, not geography, shape sales boundaries.

24. Encourage, but watch out for any antitrust aspects of, compelling the use of components, replacement parts, and accessories produced by or bought by you.

25. Arrange disclosure fees as advance royalties. You may be able to take advantage of treaties to generate high foreign source income at low foreign tax rates.

26. Be aware that royalties might be transitory; stock participation can yield more permanent values.

27. Be sure a minimum yield is payable on a sliding percentage royalty scale and that nonpayment or unsatisfactory performance gives you the right to cancel.

28. Reserve the right to cancel if you cannot get the cash in American dollars or a satisfactory equivalent.

29. Look into United States government guarantees.

30. Be aware that adequate protection means adequate inspection.

31. Remember that interim production and sales reports are important; the right to independent audit is a safeguard.

32. Watch for financial danger signals; bail out before bankruptcy.

33. Be sure to negate any warranties not specifically given by you. The warranty you or your licensee give today could haunt you in court tomorrow.

34. Monitor your licensee's advertising because it can misrepresent your product and damage your name.

35. Consider providing arbitration as an alternative to court if you cannot reconcile your differences.

36. Consider momentum if you have to cancel. Provide adequate notice for termination and look out for damages payable because of abusive termination under foreign law.

37. Be careful of restrictive covenants.

38. Examine all prospective or existing licenses in light of American and foreign antitrust laws.

Franchising

Franchising in the United States accounts for more than 35 percent of total U.S. retail sales, according to an article by James W. Wolfe in the June 1992, issue of

Export Today.[2] This percentage was composed of more than 2500 franchisors operating over 542,000 franchises with over 18,500 new franchises opened in 1991. This rate of increase has slowed somewhat in recent years but is being replaced today by international expansion. The expansion is occurring in nearly every world region from Europe to Asia to Latin America. Franchisors have been very successful in Hungary, and China is hot. The U.S. Agency for International Development, [Center for Trade and Investment Services (CTIS)] has a program to provide foreign investors in U.S. franchises loan guarantees to assist them in borrowing from local private lending sources. You will find McDonald's hamburgers on the Ginza in Tokyo, 7-11 stores in France, and ICEE cones on the beaches of Australia. All that has been said of licensing can apply to franchising, except that most foreign franchising is done by companies for whom franchising is also the primary domestic objective. The most popular franchises have been in the area of business products and services, restaurant chains, nonfood retailers, and food retailers.

Canada has been especially prosperous for franchisers because of its proximity. Japan, Europe, Australia, and the balance of Asia, respectively, follow Canada in franchise development. In Asia, including Japan, it is reported that most franchisers hope to find a master license to handle all of the sublicensing, presumably to aid in overcoming the cultural and language barriers. In 1994 *International Business* reported that Brazil had become the third-ranking country, behind the United States and Japan, for goods sold through franchise outlets, with even faster growth expected during the remainder of the decade. There is also a great concentration of franchises in the United Kingdom, numbering more than 2500.

Many items in the checklist on licensing and joint venture should also be considered relative to franchising as well as to virtually any type of overseas alliance.

Contract Manufacturing

Contract manufacturing refers to entering into a contract with a foreign manufacturer to produce your product in a region to which you would otherwise have exported, and/or as a possible means of achieving an improved competitive stance in the U.S. domestic market at the same time. This indirect form of market entry can help you gain a market share through competitive prices, while maintaining full control of the product quality. It is an especially simple form of entry in those situations where the contractor is already manufacturing for your domestic market. A prime issue, however, might be how much know-how it is necessary to give the foreign firm to make contracting possible.

On this and related issues Ralph J. Gilbert of Baker & McKenzie's Chicago office makes a number of points in a paper entitled "Fundamental Choices for a Company Entering the World Market,"[3] concerning the disadvantages of a foreign contract manufacturing operation which are:

- lack of direct quality control over the product line
- vulnerability to the risk of foreign work stoppage and access to products

■ the inherent risk in disclosing the company's valuable technology and know-how to a third party who may not protect it, or ultimately might itself use the technology to manufacture a competing product

In other situations, contract manufacturing can be the first step in setting up subsidiary operations abroad, for while it is a method of indirect exporting, it does not address the crucial matter of establishing distribution and sales channels. This next step can be considered independently, which also brings into consideration the possibility of a subsidiary Foreign Sales Corporation (FSC) as discussed in Chapter 6, or as a joint venture or alliance with the contract manufacturer selected, depending on the contractor's marketing and distribution facilities, as is subsequently discussed in this chapter.

A Corporate Presence

Not long ago, the company interested in joint ventures or subsidiaries was the exception and would have had legions of attorneys and specialists in the United States as well as abroad to advise it. While this is still true to a degree, the increased level of involvement with a corporate presence on the part of many small companies is nothing short of astounding. An Ernst & Young International Trade Advisory Service survey taken of small and midsize exporters in the Baltimore-Washington area (see Figure 5-1) indicates that 45 percent of the exporters surveyed gave the establishment of foreign subsidiaries as their primary method of selling overseas. The second choice was the use of foreign distributors, followed by involvement in joint ventures. In last place were manufacturer's rep-

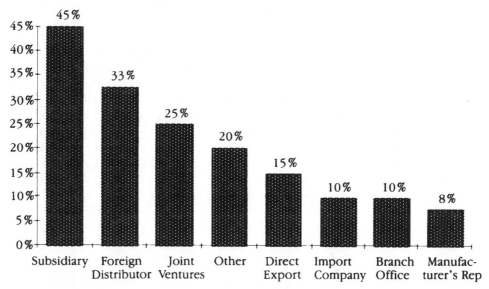

Figure 5-1. The relationship of exporters to exports.

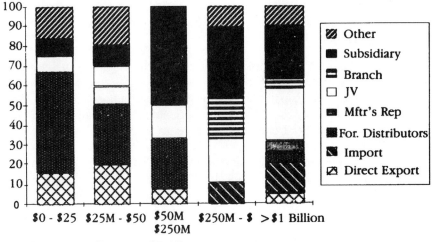

Figure 5-2. Types of business relationships.

resentatives. Figure 5-2 breaks this down by size of company, indicating that few if any in the survey became involved in joint ventures until their volume exceeded $25 million. Yet those same companies do not hesitate to form subsidiaries, which have become the most popular of all forms of overseas business for those in the more-than-$50 million range. For the smaller firms with exports of less than $25 million, foreign distributors are by far preferred and exceed the manufacturer's-representative format by almost 10 to 1. There are many forms of corporate presence, and we will highlight a few of the most popular. Whenever a corporate presence decision is made and whatever form it takes, it requires a great deal of careful planning and the services of a competent attorney—in most cases, one with a counterpart in the host country.

The strategies relative to international trade and foreign corporate investment are of interest to an increasingly broad range of firms, and these strategies are altered in each case by a growing number of trade blocs and free trade agreements. For this reason, Part 3 of this book covers overseas investments and strategic planning by trade blocs. As an example, the great flood of American jobs that were to transfer to Canada because of the original Canadian Free Trade Agreement (now known as NAFTA since Mexico became part of it) actually worked in reverse. Many companies found that with tariffs and trade barriers removed, there was no longer justification for separate manufacturing facilities in Canada, so these facilities were shut down and changed over to distribution facilities. In Mexico many U.S. distribution strategies are likewise changing because of NAFTA. This will no doubt result in expanded facilities there to accommodate the vastly increased market, and in some cases, to take advantage of lower labor costs.

Joint Venture and Coventure

Joint ventures are usually a partnership between an American firm and a foreign counterpart in the host country, each with a common commercial objective.

Each partner in the venture makes a significant contribution to it in the form of varying proportions of money, technical skill, and local knowledge. You not only expand your knowledge and resources, but also spread the risk and establish a distribution network through your foreign partner. Perhaps best of all, you may gain valuable insight into your new market and the tastes of its customers. There are other advantages to a corporate presence, such as competitiveness, not only concerning your foreign competition, but also your domestic competition. There is also the possibility of using the host country's export enhancement or financing facilities, which you might find are sometimes more aggressive than their American equivalents. (See the United States Government financing programs discussed in Part 7.)

Although normally subject to taxation in some way, various forms of income tax advantages or waivers are frequently offered by the host countries, together with other combinations of tax incentives covering tariffs, sales tax, and property tax. The greatest potential disadvantage in a joint venture is that, in many countries, the foreign partner cannot exceed a 49 percent interest in the venture. This appears to threaten your managerial control, but many companies have worked out arrangements whereby, even with that rule in effect, the strategic management control effectively continues to stay with the American partner. They claim that if the relationship is right, it need not be a major problem.

To quote further from Ralph J. Gilbert's paper for Baker & McKenzie:

> A U.S. company, however, should always endeavor to preserve a significant management role in the joint venture company, even if it has only a minority interest. This can be accomplished by providing in the joint venture agreement and in the joint venture company's articles of incorporation for a qualified majority in specified major corporate decisions. Assume, e.g., that the U.S. company holds a 40% interest in the joint venture company and appoints two members of a five man Board of Directors. Assume further that the joint venture agreement and articles of incorporation specify a 66 2/3% of the shareholders or at least four Board members must agree to 15 enumerated corporate actions. Though a minority shareholder, the U.S. company effectively will retain a veto power (or negative control) over these enumerated company actions, such as borrowing money or making capital investments above a certain dollar limit, hiring staff, opening new branches, making bids, expanding sales into new territories, etc. The U.S. company's interests will be fully protected.[4]

The quasigovernmental group called International Executive Service Corps (IESC) (see Appendix J) is engaged by the Agency for International Development (AID) to provide worldwide support in developing countries for a range of business development services including the creation of joint ventures and coventures. It originally represented one means of helping third-world countries develop sound and competitive industries to raise their standard of living. In the last few years, the primary objective of helping poorer nations become more competitive has reversed itself, and now the IESC introduces U.S. companies to their foreign counterparts to help American firms remain competitive, both here and abroad, through cheaper manufacturing and resource costs.

Of course, the initial goal of assisting poorer nations is still being served, and in the 20-plus years since IESC was founded, more than 10,000 third-world projects have been completed utilizing more than 9000 retired executives.

The IESC distinguishes between joint and coventures. In a *joint venture,* both parties make significant direct investments into the new venture. In a *coventure,* the emphasis is on the partners cooperating in terms of production and marketing, using existing facilities or resources with less emphasis on new equity. The IESC successfully created many such ventures through utilization of their corps of retired executives and consultants. They point out that the joint venture idea works very well for both small and midsize companies and often provides many operating advantages to enhance both profit and market share in the United States as well as in the foreign country.

The volunteer aspect makes the IESC program especially opportune for the small company that does not wish to make the up front investment that is necessary to explore this approach with an appropriate international consulting firm. IESC will do advance consultation in the United States to assure feasibility before it or the prospective joint venturer becomes fully engaged in advanced plans. IESC's assistance is accomplished through volunteers and at a very modest cost: out-of-pocket expenses plus administrative costs. Study the following checklist for additional items to be aware of.

Following is an additional checklist adapted from the *Management Export Information Manual,* courtesy of the Southern California District Export Office.[5]

Joint Ventures Checklist

1. Consider carefully American tax aspects of your participation. American tax rules will be used to characterize your investment for American tax purposes, notwithstanding foreign law.

2. Obtain your foreign counsel. Get the foreign counsel involved as early as possible.

3. Consider carefully the laws of the host country concerning your proposed operation.

   ▪ Know the host country rules limiting investment in any form. You may be limited to a minority position in any joint venture and will have to carefully consider problems that are raised by loss of control.

   ▪ Check special restrictions applicable to your product and operation. For example, are there limitations on foreign ownership, occupation, or use of real property?

   ▪ Check work permit and other restrictions that limit the number and percentage of American employees that can be used in your project.

   ▪ Get advance clearance, where possible, of necessary imports and permission necessary to remit to the United States.

   ▪ Check favorable provisions of foreign law or administrative practice. Sometimes host country tax relief is available that might make the difference between profit and loss.

4. Consider carefully applicable American law and export licensing regulations, particularly regarding licensing for export of defense-oriented items and limitations on outflow of American dollars.

5. Be aware that buying into an established foreign operation is easy but may mask risks of past practice.

6. Check out ways to spread the risk.

7. Use local sources—banks, accounting firms, the Department of Commerce, your local attorney—to acquire necessary expertise in special problems within the host country.

8. Investigate the possibility of bringing in the local government as a partner in the venture.

9. Study the following carefully when considering either equity or nonequity ventures:
   - Agency agreements
   - Franchise and brand-use agreements
   - Management, training, and technical-service agreements
   - Construction and job-performance agreements
   - Licensing, patents, trademarks, know-how, technical assistance, and research results

10. Become knowledgeable about the following when considering either a statutory entity or contract:
    - Cumulative voting
    - Voting trust
    - Unanimous shareholder consent for certain actions
    - Flexible quorum requirements
    - Dissolution of deadlock

11. Consider how control of the venture can be maintained.

12. Consider voting control.

13. Learn all you can about the following control techniques and devices:
    - Term of venture
    - Applicable law
    - Voting mechanism in varying situations
    - Restrictions on transfer of ownership interests
    - Procedures for approving contracts and settling disputes between the venture and its participants

14. Obtain qualified legal assistance in drawing the management contract.

15. Seek and consider limitations favoring the American venturer.

16. Study the level of control necessary to assure successful operation of the venture.

17. Consider what must be done for protection of the investment and property rights.

18. Consider the legal ramifications in selection of governing law.

19. Select location and governing body for arbitration provisions.

Wholly Owned Subsidiaries and Branches

As with a joint venture, a subsidiary makes you "one of them," in terms of both benefits and regulations, including taxes. However, in the case of taxes, a distinction is sometimes made between branches and subsidiaries. Your subsidiary employees thoroughly understand the market for which they are constructing your product, and you will be accepted as part of the marketplace, just as in the case of a joint venture. You will probably also enjoy similar access to the national export financing facilities as you would have under joint venture rules. Unlike the case of a joint venture, however, your company will enjoy sole control of all decisions concerning marketing and production. Its technologies, patents, trademarks, and know-how have the maximum protection available under the host country's laws.

Adapting from Ralph J. Gilbert's paper, he has this to say about wholly owned subsidiaries:

> [They are] usually located in countries offering labor savings, tax and capital incentives, and in some cases proximity to major markets. The following examples are illustrative: Under a tax incentive program which continues until December 31, 2000, in Ireland, all Irish manufacturing companies (foreign owned or otherwise) are subject to a flat 10 percent rate of tax. Under a previous incentive program, profits on the manufacture and export of products were totally exempt from Irish tax for a period of 15 years. Ireland further offers capital grants and financing incentives to investors. Because Ireland is within the EU, the manufactured products have duty-free access to Western European markets.
>
> Singapore offers 5- to 10-year tax holidays for companies that are manufacturing approved "pioneer" products. The incentive program scheme is administered by the Economic Development Board, which, like the Irish Development Authority, is a flexible and highly responsible government body with offices in most of the major commercial cities in North America, Europe, and Asia. Our own neighbor to the South, Mexico, has had in place in various incarnations its "Maquiladora" program over the past 27 years....In Brazil, the Manaus Free Trade Zone as of 1988 boasts 390 foreign companies with projected aggregate sales of $4.1 billion....
>
> Finally, options are available in the Caribbean. The Caribbean Basin Economic Recovery Act eliminates duties on almost all products entering the United States from many beneficiary countries in the Caribbean for a 12-year period. Fully-loaded labor rates [were as of 1988] estimated to be $6/hour, versus U.S. rates of $23–$27 per hour. Section 936 of the U.S. Internal Revenue Code provides U.S. tax exemption with respect to qualifying manufacturing income of U.S. corporations operating in Puerto Rico and possessions of the United States other than the Virgin Islands. The government of Puerto Rico complements Section 936 by granting tax exemptions of up to 90 percent for income of approved enterprises for periods of 10 to 25 years. Since Puerto Rico is within the U.S. customs zone, the company's Puerto Rican–made products further enjoy duty-free access to the U.S. market.[6]

The February 1994, issue of *International Business* contained a cover story study by Carla Kruytbosch regarding the choice places in the world to consider for owned or jointly owned manufacturing facilities.[7] In the industrialized world the first choice among the top ten as ranked by a wide variety of factors was the United Kingdom, chiefly because of relatively low labor costs for Europe, good incentives, less regulation, and the fact that the United Kingdom itself is an excellent market. The countries ranking below it were France, Canada, Japan, Ireland, Australia, Germany, Spain, and Portugal (in that order). Although U.S. investment in the developed countries had slowed to a rate of about $80 billion dollars in 1992, the rate of investment in the emerging companies was growing at a fast pace of about $48 billion per year in the same year. The greatest recipients of U.S. investment are developed countries in the European Union. After that group come the emerging nations of Asia, Latin America, and Eastern Europe (in that order). The number-one country for such investment, as ranked by *International Business,* is China, with considerable help from its 10- to 12-percent gains in GDP growth and the promise of a huge quantitative market growing rapidly in buying power. China is followed in IB rankings by Mexico, Russia, Brazil, the Czech Republic, India, Poland, Venezuela, Hungary, and the Philippines. The leader in the high-tech area is India, with a burgeoning industry of its own in this field. Brazil's ranking is somewhat surprising in view of its political difficulties and import barriers, but it is a huge market with a reputation for good treatment of investors and abundant natural resources.

Of course there are disadvantages to being governed by the laws and customs of the foreign host country. To determine the net advantages, you need competent legal and tax advice concerning the country under consideration. A subsidiary may or may not enjoy favored treatment in terms of taxation, but unlike a branch, it will be taxed based on host country rules. No taxes would be due to the U.S. government until profits or dividends are repatriated. A corporate branch of an American corporation is treated simply as an extension of the domestic operation. Exact details might vary and should be thoroughly reviewed by an accountant.

If the prime purpose of a subsidiary is to provide for warehousing and distribution, one cost-saving option, taken by some experienced companies like General Electric, is public warehousing. This vehicle can also assist by providing the logistics for intramarket transportation from the warehouse. Jerry Leatham, president of the American Warehousemen's Association (AWA) in Chicago says his group can help find reliable warehouses around the world, especially in the new Europe, where warehousing is becoming very appropriate.

Alliances

As the European Union matures, fueling interest in a corporate presence there, and as the trading blocs in Asia and Latin America develop, strategic alliances are more and more being created, reported on, and studied. An interesting early article appeared in the April 1990 issue of *Export Today* by Robert P. Lynch, president of the Warren Company, a consulting firm that specializes in joint ventures. He describes *alliances* as a deliberately loose term used to acknowledge that, besides the formalized joint venture or subsidiary, there are alternative strategic alliances. Even though consummated by a written contract, an alliance does not "result in the creation of an independent business organization." Rather, it might represent a minority equity stake, distribution or trading agreements with features for mutual product development, cross-licensing or production, and technology-sharing agreements. In other words, an alliance is much more than a simple buy-sell relationship involving mutuality that would include "tight operating linkages with cross-training, product development coordination, long-term contracts based on quality—not just price—and customer feedback mechanisms." The result of the alliance is a "mutual vested interest in each other's growth" with strong high-level management contact. Of course, this could also be a recipe for a successful joint venture; but the point is, a form of presence can be achieved with a less entangling formal agreement.[8]

In his article, Lynch makes some excellent points regarding the characteristics of a good partner and a well-structured alliance that could apply with equal force to most of the corporate presence arrangements we have discussed. *A good partner* is one that has something unique and valuable to offer, shares your company's strategic objectives, can perform as promised, and provides market leadership. *A well-structured alliance* is one with clarity of purpose, shared operating style (or one that is readily adaptable), similar financial goals, and good support from top management.[9]

International Business, in its September 1993 survey of internationally oriented business, reported that alliances were of interest to almost 60 percent of the respondents, with the objective being to help them keep a competitive edge, both here and abroad. Many of the respondents represented small to midsize companies that saw alliances as a cost-conscious answer to alternative foreign investment approaches that require large amounts of capital up front. In the same vein, today's rapid technological change rate sharply reduces the life cycle of so many products today that "small and mid-sized companies don't have the luxury of slowly developing a foreign market anymore."[10]

Endnotes

1. Adapted from: *Management Export Information Manual,* published by the Southern California District Export Council, Los Angeles, California, circa 1969, based on voluntary contributions of the Council members and prepared by Richard E. Sherwood and Walter R. Thiel.

2. "Is There an Overseas Franchise in Your Future?" by James A. Wolfe, *Export Today,* June 1992 issue.

3. "Fundamental Choices for a Company Entering the World Market," a paper by Ralph J. Gilbert of Baker & McKenzie, Attorneys at Law, Chicago, Illinois, June 1988.

4. Gilbert, p. 90.

5. Adapted from: *Management Export Information Manual,* pp. 85–88.

6. Gilbert, p. 90.

7. Carla Kruytbosch, "Where in the World to Make It," *International Business,* February 1994 issue.

8. Robert Porter Lynch, "Expanding Exports Through Alliances," *Export Today,* March/April 1990 issue.

9. Ibid.

10. Survey: "What's in Store for 1994," *International Business,* September 1993 issue.

6

Privileged Export Companies/ Special Business Formats

The first unique business format for exporters only was established by the Webb-Pomerene Act, which was passed early in this century and provided exemptions for trade associations from antitrust laws and regulations. This was followed, in 1971, by the Domestic International Sales Corporation (DISC) for the purpose of offering exporters tax advantages. This, in turn, has been supplanted since 1984 by the law creating the Foreign Sales Corporation (FSC). The latter was set up to overcome objections by the signatories of the General Agreement on Tariffs and Trade (GATT).

Still another development occurred as the necessity of improving our export climate became apparent in the 1980s. In 1982 this resulted in passage of a law known as the Export Trading Company Act. One of the purposes of this act was to provide an improvement in antitrust exemption over the Webb-Pomerene Act. Another was to provide the tools to create a stronger economic instrument in the form of a bank-owned or bank-supported export trading company. All these special formats have had a positive effect on the U.S. export climate, but, for the most part, much less of a one than lawmakers anticipated.

When establishing your own business format or corporation, consider all possibilities, even if it means establishing a second corporation to transact the export sales. Given the right situation and sufficient volume, the cost of a second corporation for export can be easily offset with tax savings or marketing advantages. Although some restrictions apply, excess funds from retained earnings can be put to good use with careful planning. Information about the rights, duties, and legal requirements for establishing any of the business forms described in this section can be obtained from your DOC district office. This is an area that should also be discussed with an accountant or attorney.

Webb-Pomerene Act Associations

Even though the Webb-Pomerene Act is more than 60 years old, many of the early Webb-Pomerene Associations still exist today. Almost all are trade associations of one kind or another, and the great majority are agriculture associations, including some of today's largest agriculture cooperatives. The sole purpose of being a Webb-Pomerene Association is to attain exclusion from antitrust provisions. As such, it may negotiate prices and terms of sale, buy members' products for resale abroad, and arrange transportation. These associations function much like export management companies for their members and may use government financing facilities, such as Eximbank, or become FSCs themselves for tax purposes. Webb-Pomerene Associations need not necessarily be incorporated and are extremely simple and inexpensive to set up. Their legal shield, in terms of their antitrust protection, is well established through court cases but is not as comprehensive as the protection found in the Export Trading Act. Many organizations that were initially expected to request Export Trading Company Act certificates of review held back in the beginning, remaining Webb-Pomerene Act Associations while the Export Trading Act was tested and eventually found favorable.

Export Trading Company Act Businesses

The Export Trading Company Act was passed in 1982 with high expectations. Some people even thought that the United States would soon have its own version of the famous Japanese Sogo Shoshas as a result of banks being permitted to be financially involved in trade activities, and the act's antitrust exclusion features. While this is not happening, and most bank-related ETCs created under the act have abandoned the effort or retrenched, the ETC act continues to be a useful tool for some businesses or groups in the antitrust area. Roughly 5000 firms, represented directly or through associations, consortiums, joint ventures, and trading companies, are shielded from a variety of actions otherwise subject to antitrust regulations or penalties and are exempt by virtue of the Export Trade Certificate of Review.

The ETC act covers four basic areas, or titles.

- *Title I* establishes the Office of Export Trading Company Affairs in the DOC (see Chapter 42). The purpose of the office is to administer the antitrust export trade certificate of review program, promote formation of ETCs, and facilitate contact between the producers of goods and services and export intermediaries of all kinds.

- *Title II* permits financial institutions and bank holding companies to invest in, or own outright, ETCs, which are subject to Federal Reserve approval. Such an ETC must be exclusively engaged in international trade or related activities and must derive 50 percent of its revenue from exporting.

- *Title III* contains the principal benefit of the act. It provides antitrust protection covering the export of services and goods for all types of business institutions. This is a broader exclusion than is found in the Webb-Pomerene Act. Exporters do not have to form a new entity or corporation to seek this protection, and any exporter may apply. Activities certified under reviewed and approved protection have included price fixing, exclusive dealer arrangements, customer and territorial allocations, and the exchange of business information. These activities are not allowed to affect competition in the United States.

- *Title IV* further clarifies the jurisdictional reach of the Sherman Antitrust Act and the Federal Trade Commission Act, which make up the primary federal antitrust regulations. The clarifying and easing provisions of Title IV automatically extend to all exporters, and do not require application and qualification as do Titles II and III. For a better understanding of U.S. antitrust restrictions, besides reading Title IV, check the Justice Department's guideline book, *Antitrust Enforcement Guidelines for International Operations* (1988). (See also Chapter 34.)

The DOC feels that misunderstandings and lack of awareness have caused the ETC Act to have less than anticipated use. One of the misunderstandings is the impression that companies must form an export trading company to receive the benefits of the act. Actually, existing proprietorships, partnerships, corporations, and associations are eligible to receive antitrust protection. In addition, there has been some initial hesitation by associations because of concern as to whether the courts would sustain or overrule the antitrust certificates that were issued. Only one litigation has occurred concerning the antitrust provisions, but that case was resolved so favorably by the Third Circuit Court of Appeals that it has encouraged some former Webb-Pomerene Act Associations to seek Export Trading Company Act certification. The ETC act is therefore seeing increasing utilization from agricultural and other trade associations. The lack of awareness stems from ignorance as to what antitrust restrictions do apply to export endeavors and how competitors could combine to compete with the foreign consortiums that so often outbid us. American exporters might want to consider more consortiums and other possibilities in order to better match our foreign competition. This is a step beyond the cooperative marketing efforts of the closely knit trade and agricultural associations.

Some very substantial benefits can result from obtaining a certificate of review. It is an excellent way to band together for negotiating strength with transportation companies, foreign buying consortiums, and other services that are required by the group. Bigger is usually better if administered so that action is not inhibited. This can help in terms of sharing costs and risks, entirely apart from facilitating a coordinated pricing structure. Among the 155 organizations that represent some 5000 individual firms certified to confer, plan, bid and negotiate as a group there have been a variety of cases in which a certification has proved effective in resolving a difficulty. In one case, the certification helped a trade group negotiate removal of a nontariff trade barrier in Japan that had been in place for years. In another, an energy consortium successfully used the antitrust protection to bid on some major projects.

Finally, banks are resisting the restrictions under Title II of the act. They claim that the requirement that 50 percent of revenue must come from exports is much too severe, and that it is made worse by the exclusion of third-country transactions plus other financial restraints. Some of these problems have already been addressed and improved thanks to the 1988 Omnibus Trade Bill, which attempted to strengthen the role of ETCs. But the basic mindset and risk aversion among bankers will continue to be a natural and severe limitation on the number of successful bank trading companies. If, however, banks can be encouraged to invest in ETCs but leave the management to genuine trading mentalities, the combination in the long run may enhance our export competitiveness. The trade bill affords bank ETCs great latitude as to export versus import revenue during a two- to four-year period and prohibits the Federal Reserve from "over-regulations" concerning bank ETC leveraging and inventory size. More information can be obtained on these issues from the Office of Export Trading Company Affairs, DOC, Washington, D.C.

Foreign Sales Corporations

Foreign Sales Corporations (FSCs) were created to provide a tax incentive for exporters under the Deficit Reduction Act of 1984, and the Domestic International Sales Corporations (DISCs), originated in 1971, were modified at that time to provide for an annual interest charge (i.e., the IC-DISC). The motivation for the change was the objection from our trading partners that the old DISCs were an illegal tax subsidy under the terms of GATT. The new FSC law was drafted to circumvent these problems. Congress provided a onetime exemption for the tax that would have been levied on the accumulated DISC income when all existing DISCs were terminated on December 31, 1984. The conversion options were to simply drop the DISC, or convert to: a regular Foreign Sales Corporation; a small Foreign Sales Corporation; a shared Foreign Sales Corporation; or an interest charge–Domestic International Sales Corporation (IC-DISC). These same options continue to be available today to any exporter of U.S. products.

An FSC provides 15 to 32 percent permanent tax savings on income from export of U.S.-produced goods. An IC-DISC permits tax deferral on export-related income by paying interest on the deferred amount. The small FSC and IC-DISC are easier to set up, and they provide tax benefits for export sales of up to $5 million to $10 million, respectively. The FSC or small FSC may be shared by several companies. An FSC provides limited benefits if it has as its primary shareholders individuals or S corporations.

The tax regulations and details are complex, and the following is intended to give you a basic understanding of the various plans, as well as an idea of the tax savings. Naturally, if you find them of interest, it will be essential to discuss the possibilities with your tax advisor.

Regular Foreign Sales Corporations

General Incorporation Requirements. A Foreign Sales Corporation (FSC) is a company incorporated offshore in a qualified foreign country or possession by an independent merchant or broker; by a grower, processor, extractor, or manufacturing parent; or by a business group with common export interests. A valid corporate election with shareholder consent must be made to become an FSC, and certain requirements of incorporation, management form, operations, and record keeping must be met. The most important of these requirements are as follows:

- Must incorporate and maintain an office in a possession of the United States (American Samoa, U.S. Virgin Islands, Guam, or Northern Marianas), or in a foreign country that has an exchange-of-information agreement with the United States and is approved for this purpose by the IRS. To date, the U.S. Virgin Islands and Barbados have been the preferred locations because they have the most accessible and the best-developed infrastructures. A directory of professional FSC management companies in the Virgin Islands may be obtained by writing to: The Lieutenant Governor, P.O. Box 4501, Charlotte Amalie, St. Thomas, Virgin Islands 00801. The place of incorporation and the office need not be the same, but the same qualification rules apply to each.

- Must have no more than 25 shareholders.

- Must not have preferred stock (common stock only).

- Must maintain corporate books of account, including invoices or statements of account in the foreign country or possession. Duplicate copies of certain accounting and tax records must also be kept in the United States.

- Must have at least one member of the board of directors who is other than a United States resident.

- Must maintain the same taxable year as that of the principal shareholder.

- Must not be a member of a controlled group of corporations in which a DISC is a member.

- Must file an election to be treated as an FSC.

Foreign Management Requirements. FSCs other than "small FSCs" must meet additional foreign presence tests in order to generate qualified income:

- All meetings of shareholders and directors must be held outside the United States.

- The principal bank account must be maintained in a qualified country or possession, though not necessarily the same as that of incorporation, but rather where the office is located. It may be a minimal bank account in terms of balances carried.

■ All dividends paid in cash, as well as officers' and directors' salaries, must be disbursed from this principal foreign bank account.

In practice, many of the costs, which these rules could create, might be minimized or eliminated by means of proxies and the use of agents. (See Figure 6-1.)

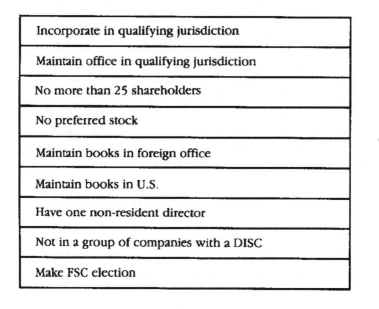

Incorporate in qualifying jurisdiction
Maintain office in qualifying jurisdiction
No more than 25 shareholders
No preferred stock
Maintain books in foreign office
Maintain books in U.S.
Have one non-resident director
Not in a group of companies with a DISC
Make FSC election

● *Must meet all 9 requirements*

Foreign Management Requirements

for FSC's other than "small FSC's"

Shareholders' and directors' meetings held outside U.S.
Principal bank account in qualifying jurisdiction
Pay legal and accounting fees, directors' and officers' salaries and dividends out of principal bank account

● *Must meet all requirements*

Figure 6-1. FSC requirements.

Foreign Economic Process Requirements.   Foreign presence for FSCs other than "small FSCs," also requires that certain economic activity on each transaction or group of transactions must be met, based on the following two tests:

1. The sales activity test requires the FSC or its agents to participate outside the United States in at least one or more of these activities:

    ■ Solicitation (other than advertising)
    ■ Negotiation
    ■ Making the contract

    Communication with customers by the foreign office of the FSC in reference to the sales made will usually meet one or both tests for solicitation and negotiation. Many FSCs have their foreign offices send a standardized letter of solicitation to their regular customers. The test for making the contract can be easily met at minimal cost through standing instructions to accept offers or confirm acceptances by telex or telecopy from outside the United States.

2. The foreign direct costs test requires that a certain portion of the direct costs actually incurred in connection with the sale in the following five activities are costs incurred by the FSC outside the United States:

    ■ Advertising and sales promotion
    ■ Processing orders and arranging delivery
    ■ Transportation (costs outside the United States)
    ■ Billing and collection
    ■ Assumption of credit risk

On an annual basis the FSC may choose to meet the foreign direct cost activity requirements by incurring abroad, directly or through agents, 50 percent of the attributable total "direct cost" of all five categories, insofar as they were engaged in, or 85 percent of the total "direct cost" of any two of the five categories. The test is applied transaction by transaction (or by group of transactions) so you can pick and choose as to the 50-percent or 85-percent test. If a given activity did not create costs, that category is not to be taken into account in meeting the test.

The definition of incurring costs abroad does not necessarily mean the costs must literally be incurred abroad. For example, advertising costs will be considered incurred abroad even if paid in the United States if the advertising is aimed at a market outside the United States. Also, transportation costs are measured by mileage inside and outside the United States—not by actual cost—during the time the FSC is responsible for the shipment. Thus, there is an incentive for CIF (not C&F) and delivered-at-destination pricing, in which case all transportation costs can usually be taken as foreign. (See Figure 6-2 for an overview of Foreign Economic Process Requirements.)

An attempt is being made to administer the law in such a way as to make it as easy as possible to comply. Therefore, most of the requirements mentioned might be economically satisfied through use of agents, appropriate contractual

FSC REQUIREMENTS
Foreign Economic Process Requirements

1. Foreign Sales Activity Test

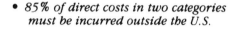

Solicitation	Negotiation	Making of a Contract

- *Only one activity needs to be performed outside the U.S*

2. Foreign Direct Cost Test

Advertising & Sales Promotion
Assumption of Credit Risk
Transportation
Order Processing & Arranging for Delivery
Billing & Collection

- *85% of direct costs in two categories must be incurred outside the U.S.*

or

- *50% of direct costs in all categories must be incurred outside the U.S.*

Figure 6-2. FSC foreign economic process requirements.

provisions, and the grouping of transactions. By means of grouping, not all individual transactions will need to qualify. This must not be interpreted to mean that noncompliance will be overlooked.

Qualified Export Transactions. Besides the corporate and operational requirements of an FSC, certain restrictions apply to transactions to qualify for FSC benefits. Qualified transactions involve exportation for foreign use of export property meaning property manufactured, produced, grown, or extracted in the United States by an entity other than an FSC, with the exception of a few limited classes of property which do not qualify. No more than 50 percent of the export property's fair market value may have been imported. A special election is avoidable when U.S. components are processed outside the United States and then imported for further U.S. manufacturing.

Such a qualified transaction might involve the sale, exchange, lease, or rental of export property, and commissions or revenues earned from the performance of services related to these activities. Engineering and architectural services related to foreign construction also qualify. The FSC might be involved in the transactions as a principal or as a commission agent. All such qualified revenues are called foreign trading gross receipts (FTGR). If an FSC earns at least 50 percent of its gross income from exports as just described, it might also receive earnings considered as FTGR from export management services (including such services as export market studies and prospect contacts) performed for unrelated FSCs and DISCs.

Establishing Allowable FSC Income. Income earned by the FSC may be generated as a principal (buy/sell FSC) or as a commission agent (commission FSC).

FSCs with a related supplier should use the commission structure. FSCs with related suppliers, or those functioning as a subsidiary of a trading company, must calculate their combined taxable income (CTI). CTI is the foreign sales or FTGR less related cost of goods and expenses incurred jointly by the FSC and its related supplier. In any case, the taxable income of both types of FSCs is determined by either: (1) the arm's-length method; or (2) one of the administrative pricing rules methods, consisting of the 23 percent of CTI method, or the 1.83 percent of sales method.

1. *The arm's-length method* allows the FSC to earn an amount of income equal to the income that would have been earned by the FSC if it had conducted business with unrelated parties. It may therefore be closely scrutinized and challenged by the IRS. Usually, arm's-length pricing does not allow the FSC to earn significant income from a related U.S. exporter (related supplier) unless the FSC is a fully operational sales company and actual costs are readily determinable.

2. *Administrative pricing rules* are used when the FSC is related to the supplier in an effort to determine the transfer costs, or cost of goods, of the sale, and, therefore, of the portion of export income the IRS agrees can be allocated to the FSC. Two administrative pricing rules methods include:

   - *The 23 percent of income method.* Under this method, 23 percent of the CTI of the FSC and related supplier will be considered the FSC's taxable income.
   - *The 1.83 percent of sales method.* Under this administrative method, the FSC is deemed to derive profit equal to 1.83 percent of the FTGR. However, the FSC's taxable income, calculated under this method, may not result in income more than twice the amount (46 percent of CTI) derived by using the 23 percent of income method. This rule is usually most advantageous for the low-profit-margin supplier.

FSC Taxation Procedures, Rates, and Benefits.   If the taxable income of the FSC is determined under the arm's-length method, 30 percent of the FSC income is exempt if the FSC is owned by corporate shareholders, and 32 percent is exempt if the FSC is otherwise owned. If taxable income is determined under the 1.83 percent of sales or 23 percent of CTI administrative methods, the exemption is 15/23 (approximately 65 percent) if the FSC is owned by corporate shareholders, and 16/23 (approximately 70 percent) if the FSC is owned by noncorporate shareholders.

When using administrative pricing rules, the remaining nonexempt income is taxed as any U.S. corporate profit is taxed. If arm's-length pricing is used, the nonexempt portion is taxed as if earned by a foreign corporation, and thus may escape taxation entirely until it is distributed to shareholders.

The effect of the FSC tax exemption and the rules determining FSC income is to produce a tax savings of approximately 15 to 30 percent on the income related to the foreign sale of U.S. goods for FSCs using the administration pricing rules, and tax savings of approximately 30 percent or 32 percent of the profits earned by an arm's-length FSC.

Because the FSC is presumably incorporated in a jurisdiction with little or no income tax levy, the FSC's income is subject only to this diminished U.S. income tax. Many states have not conformed to the federal provisions and will subject the income of the FSC to full tax or allocate its income to its supplier. The American corporate shareholder in an FSC gains a 100-percent-FSC-dividends-received deduction whether the income was attributable to tax exempt or non-tax exempt FSC income, and so is taxed only at the FSC level. (In the case of arm's-length pricing, only tax exempt income receives this treatment.) Noncorporate shareholders receive no such deduction of FSC distributions, which is why an FSC is of much less interest to individuals or S corporations.

Whether an FSC is beneficial will depend on a comparison of the tax savings with the increased administrative costs associated with an FSC. Proper planning, however, can greatly diminish the cost of establishing and operating an FSC and maximize the export profits that are eligible for FSC benefits. For someone interested in a complete review of FSC management techniques, we suggest the *FSC Owner's Manual*.[1]

Small Foreign Sales Corporations

As an alternative to the regular FSC, the small FSC is intended to permit the smaller exporter to gain FSC benefits while being exempt from the added cost and details of the foreign management or foreign economic process requirements. FSC tax benefits may apply to no more than $5 million in export sales, even though the firm's export sales may be higher. The exemption from these management and economic process requirements will save substantial FSC-related costs and detailed compliance, even though the initial incorporation and formation requirements still must be met. If the administrative pricing rules are used, the FSC, under contract with a related supplier, must meet the sales activity tests and foreign direct cost activities test, but in this case, those activities need not be performed outside the United States. In other respects, the small FSC is treated the same as any other FSC in terms of requirements and taxation. Taxpayers can choose their most profitable sales to qualify for small FSC treatment.

The FSC/DISC Tax Association advises that a company with foreign sales of around $1 million and a gross margin, for tax purposes, of 20 percent may find a small FSC attractive. The savings would be approximately 15 percent of the $200,000 taxable income, or $30,000. They estimate the start-up costs for a small FSC to be a minimum of $2000, although related professional consulting and compliance fees will bring this cost nearer to $6500. The yearly maintenance costs can be kept under $2000 if no significant additional professional services are required. Even allowing for start-up costs of $10,000, the annual savings in the first year would approximate $20,000. The association indicates that companies with export software can easily adapt the software to perform FSC record-keeping requirements without much difficulty.

Shared Foreign Sales Corporations

Another alternative to a regular FSC of your own is a shared FSC, whereby exporters can take advantage of sharing the overhead costs of an FSC, thereby reducing any extra foreign costs and fixed overhead. States, regions, and cities are forming shared FSCs to help their business communities gain all possible incentives and advantages for export. Trade associations, banks, accountants, shippers, and others can sponsor and/or promote shared FSCs.

Twenty-five or fewer unrelated exporters can own and operate an FSC, each owning a separate class of stock and running its own export business. One major accounting firm, Price Waterhouse, estimates that companies with export sales of $300,000 and a 20 percent margin—or an equivalent combination—should consider a shared FSC. Conceivably, such a shared FSC may also qualify as a shared small FSC composed of three to five exporters if the combined annual foreign sales of the group totals $5 million or less. In a shared FSC, the other shareholders do not become involved in each others' internal business, do not know who the other participants' customers are, and are not at risk for one another's debts. The same is true of the sponsoring agency when there is one. Typically, if it were a state-sponsored shared FSC, the state might pay the start-up costs, with or without future amortizing charges for such costs, and have the participants share the administrative, banking, accounting, and legal costs of running the shared FSC.

All of the big six, as well as most of the regional accounting firms and many internationally oriented law firms, are aware of this concept and will be happy to provide further advice. They will also be able to inform you of the various FSC management companies that have sprung up. In some cases these are formed as a partnership of interested accountants and attorneys and in other cases, by bank holding companies. You may wish to write to the FSC/DISC-Tax Association, P.O. Box 748, FDR Station, New York, New York 10150 for a copy of the *FSC Annual Directory.* The FSC/DISC Tax Association is an organization of more than 800 foreign sales corporations and their professional advisors in the fields of law, accounting, and management, plus software providers.

Delaware has entered the business of assisting exporters from any state to establish shared FSCs, small or regular. The first shared FSC was organized by Delaware in early 1988 and started with five member firms. The state introduces exporters to shared FSCs that are being established and contracts with Price Waterhouse and its FSC management subsidiary for program administration utilizing Price Waterhouse's overseas affiliates. Delaware also uses Chase Trade, Inc. and the Chase Manhattan Bank for electronic fund transfers. Under this program, the start-up costs are $500 plus the greater of $2500 or one-tenth of 1 percent of the exporter's gross receipts from exports for the first year of operation. Future annual costs are estimated to be similar. Other organizations, public and private, including states and world trade centers, are following suit.

The Delaware-sponsored program provides a typical example of actual use of a shared FSC that may serve to clarify the operation. An exporter conducts its export sales transaction in the usual fashion. After receiving payment, it is necessary to sweep these funds into and then back out of the shared FSC electronically. At the end of the year the exporter may pay a commission of 23 percent to the FSC and receive in return a dividend of the same amount, less any tax due. About 65 percent of the shared FSC's income will be exempt from federal taxes, and 35 percent will be taxable in the shared FSC. When distributed back to the exporter, it will be tax-free in the hands of the exporter. Thus, approximately 15 percent of those export profits (65 percent of 23 percent) will not be taxable, either to the shared FSC or to the exporting corporation, nor will they be subject to further U.S. taxation. The following is an illustration of such a commission FSC owned by a corporation, without taking into account state taxes.

	With FSC	Without FSC
Export Profits		
Commission to FSC (23%)	$100,000	$100,000
	(23,000)	
Taxable income	$ 77,000	$100,000
Parent company's federal tax (34%)**	$ 26,180*	$ 34,000*
FSC:		
Commission income	$ 23,000	
Exempt portion (15/23)	$ 15,000	
Taxable income	$ 8,000	
Federal tax (34%)	$ 2,720	
Total taxes	$ 28,900	$ 34,000
TAXES SAVED	$ 5,100	

*Some states follow the federal FSC rules, creating an advantage on state taxes as well.

**The maximum marginal tax rate for firms with a taxable export income under $10 million.

Interest Charge–Domestic International Sales Corporation

While most exporters believe an FSC to be the better strategy, an IC-DISC is another alternative. The IC-DISC provides an opportunity for tax saving to smaller firms in lieu of forming an FSC or any other offshore corporation. The benefits, however, are limited to a tax deferral on a maximum of $10 million of the firm's annual sales and involve tax deferral rather than partial exemption as in the case of FSCs. It closely resembles the former DISC and was primarily structured for smaller firms that had been DISCs under the old law.

Before determining if an IC-DISC is best for you, consider the requirements for DISC eligibility. The most notable of those requirements is that 95 percent of the gross receipts must be qualified export receipts, and 95 percent of the assets reflected on the annual statement must be qualified export assets, such as inventory, foreign receivables, and assets used to generate qualified export receipts. This is a major qualification for a firm that wants to conduct both import and export operations and would therefore be forced to have two corporations.

The new IC-DISC has greater tax deferrals, 16/17 or approximately 47 percent to 94 percent of the income attributable to qualified export receipts up to $10 million (100 percent if the IC-DISC is owned by noncorporate shareholders), provided the DISC reinvests its tax-deferred earnings in qualified export assets. The regulations provide that the IC-DISC may earn income equal to 50 percent of combined taxable income or 4 percent of qualified export receipts. The result is a tax deferral of from 47 percent to 94 percent after the 47 percent reduction in the case of corporate shareholders. The name *interest charge–DISC* stems from the interest charged to the DISC shareholders on the tax they did not have to pay on the undistributed and untaxed income. This interest is levied on the tax savings created by the difference between the tax paid on what is termed the deemed distribution and the tax the shareholders would have paid had all the DISC income been, in fact, distributed.

A key advantage of the IC-DISC is the favorable rate used for this interest charge, which is based on treasury bill rates, and is well below normal borrowing rates for small businesses. In effect, this rule permits borrowing from the treasury at very advantageous rates. The interest is paid at the time the tax would have been due. Under current law, interest paid by an individual shareholder may not be deductible. Therefore, to the extent that cash flow is a large factor, the IC-DISC may be useful, because the deferred tax less the interest charge from an IC-DISC—at least in the early years—will be roughly three times greater than the permanent tax savings of a small FSC. An exporter may not have an FSC and an IC-DISC at the same time. An IC-DISC that is owned proportionately by the shareholders of a company with a regular dividend policy, in contrast to the IC-DISC as a subsidiary of the parent, is a particularly good use of that vehicle.

Endnote

1. William K. Norman, *The FSC Owner's Manual—A Compliance Manual for the Owner and Manager of a U.S. Virgin Islands Large FSC,* 1995, 1901 Avenue of the Stars, Los Angeles, CA.

2

Export Marketing and Strategy

7

Assessing and Researching Export Potential

Before investing the necessary time and capital to launch a product overseas, you should examine its export potential, based on the same or similar commodities being sold overseas. A first step is to visit the DOC's district office and talk to your trade specialist at the U.S. and Foreign Commercial Service (US&FCS), where he or she will help you find worldwide statistics and information on products or services similar to yours that have been exported or imported: where, when, and how much. To obtain this kind of information, however, you need to know the statistical codes for several basic classification systems pertaining to your product.

Statistically Classifying Your Product

There are four basic classification schedules for market research, all of which are used to comply with customs or census reports.

1. U.S. Standard Industrial Classification (SIC Number)
2. Schedule B Number (Harmonized System)
3. Harmonized Tariff Schedules of the U.S. Annotated (HTSUSA)
4. Standard Industrial Trade Classification–Revision 3 (SITC)

These classifications were changed or modified in 1988, when our trading partners converted to the Harmonized System (HS). Unfortunately, the United States did not convert, as it originally intended to do, because legislative authority to do so was delayed pending finalization of the Omnibus Trade Bill, which was not passed until August 1988, making the HS effective in the United States only as of January 1, 1989. During 1988, the rest of the world worked with one system and the United States with another. This fact continues to make world trading figures difficult to compare during that period.

The Harmonized System

It is worth explaining the relatively new Harmonized Description and Coding System at the outset because it bears on finding the correct code and understanding how accurately it represents your product relative to the overall product range. It is now a nearly universally accepted classification system—more often referred to as the Harmonized System (HS). It has been the dream of researchers, statisticians, freight forwarders, transportation, and customs tariff specialists for decades. The HS was years in development under the auspices of the Customs Cooperation Council (CCC) in Brussels. This is the same international technical body previously responsible for the CCC Nomenclature (CCCN) and the Brussels Tariff Nomenclature (BTN), which until now have been the basis for most tariff structures and comparisons.

The HS is organized into 21 sections according to materials and industry. It begins with animals and agricultural crops, progresses through successive industries of increasing economic activity or complexity, and ends with Miscellaneous and Works of Art and Antiques as the twentieth and twenty-first sections. The sections, whose Roman numbers do not comprise part of the HS tariff or "B" number, are broken down into chapters that are arranged so that each successive chapter covers a more highly processed or more technical product insofar as practical, as do the subheadings within the chapter. In all, there are 97 chapters with more than 5000 headings at the internationally harmonized level. See Figure 7-1 for a description of the 21 basic sections plus the 22nd section for special classifications.

Products are classified under a ten-digit system. The first two digits indicate the chapter, the second two, the heading, and the third two, the subheading. The United States uses the last two digits for its own statistical purposes.

The HS is a hierarchical system because there is nothing classifiable at the successive two-, four-, and six-digit levels that is not included in the root, or prior level. It is intended that all products that have the same essential character share headings. In cases of confusion, first use the most specific description. If that fails, fall back on the essential character determination. In classifying, the new system places greater emphasis on the state in which a product or process would be traded or sold than on the technical stage of its processing.

The HS was intended to serve as a universally accepted product nomenclature for worldwide use in customs valuation, import and export statistics, and all

The Harmonized System of Tariff Nomenclature

SECTION:

I Live Animals; Animal Products

II Vegetable Products

III Animal or Vegetable Fats & Oils and Their Cleavage Products; Prepared Edible Fats; Animal or Vegetable Waxes

IV Prepared Foodstuffs; Beverages, Spirits, and Vinegar; Tobacco and Manufactured Tobacco Substitutes

V Mineral Products

VI Products of the Chemical or Allied Industries

VIII Raw Hides and Skins, Leather, Furskins and Articles Thereof; Saddlery and Harness; Travel Goods, Handbags and Similar Containers; Articles of Animal Gut (Other than Silkworm Gut)

IX Wood and Articles of Wood; Wood Charcoal; Cork and Articles of Cork; Manufacture of Straw, or Esparto, or of Other Plaiting Materials; Basketware and Wickerwork

X Pulp of Wood or of Other Fibrous Cellulostic Material; Waste and Scrap Paper or Paperboard; Paper & Paperboard and Articles Thereof

XI Textiles & Textile Articles

XII Footwear, Headgear, Umbrellas, Sun Umbrellas, Walking Sticks, Seatsticks, Whips, Riding Crops and Parts Thereof; Prepared Feathers and Articles Made Therewith: Artificial Flowers; Articles of Human Hair

XIII Articles of Stone, Plaster, Cement, Asbestos, Mica or Similar Materials; Ceramic Products; Glass and Glasswares

XIV Natural or Cultured Pearls, Precious or Semiprecious Stones, Precious Metals, Metals Clad with Precious Metal and Articles Thereof; Imitation Jewelry; Coin

XV Base Metals and Articles of Base Metal

XVI Machinery & Mechanical Appliances; Electrical Equipment; Parts Thereof; Sound Recorders & Reproducers, Television Image and Sound Recorders & Reproducers and Parts & Accessories of Such

XVII Vehicles, Aircraft, Vessels, and Associated Transport Equipment

XVIII Optical, Photographic, Cinematographic, Measuring, Checking, Precision, Medical or Surgical Instruments and Apparatus; Clocks/Watches; Musical Instruments; Parts & Accessories Thereof

XIX Arms & Ammunition; Parts & Accessories

XX Miscellaneous Manufactured Articles

XXI Works of Art, Collectors' Pieces and Antiques

XXII Special Classification Provisions; Temporary Legislation; Temporary Modifications Proclaimed Pursuant to Trade Agreements Legislation; Additional Import Restrictions Proclaimed Pursuant to of the Agricultural Adjustment Act, as Amended

Figure 7-1. Harmonized system.

forms of freight tariff schedules. It has been accepted on these terms, and as such will save everyone in the business of international trade and transportation a great deal of effort and confusion. The Harmonized System makes it much easier to analyze trade data and makes for better use of electronic data processing.

Each of the U.S. schedules will continue to have unique characteristics. The two schedules, HTSUSA and Schedule B, are expanded in a different fashion through additional four-digit levels for statistical purposes, and they only have a

56 percent concordance at the ten-digit level, even though it is a 100 percent concordance at the six-digit level. In the case of the other two schedules, they are modified for easier comparison, but remain essentially different in terms of numbers, logic, and purpose. Table 7-1 represents a sample page from Section X ("Pulp of wood and other fibrous cellulosic material;"...); Chapter 49 (Printed books, newspapers, pictures, and other material of printing industry, manuscripts, typescripts, and plans."); Heading #4901 covering "Printed books, brochures and leaflets, and similar printed matter," to help you understand how the Schedule B Commodity Classification System works.

The application of these new HS codes worldwide has many implications. It makes the import/export process more compatible to computerization; it permits an easier comparison of import and export statistics; and it affects exporters and their import customers in terms of duties to be levied. For example, the HS requires textile and apparel articles of two or more fibers to be classified according to the component of chief weight. The old rule called for classification by chief value, which resulted in quite a different tariff. The HS also makes customs and export licensing enforcement easier. Here is how the HS impacts commodity classification of interest to international trade:

U.S. Standard Industrial Classification (SIC Number)

Although the SIC number is not used for export documentation purposes, it is one of the classification systems by which you must identify your product for market research purposes. This is the classification code used to identify the articles of our domestic production and manufactured products for economic statistic purposes. SIC is also the classification code most commonly used for domestic market research purposes, and yet, in its modified, post-harmonization version, it relates well enough to Schedule B and HTSUSA to be one of the nomenclatures used by DOC and US&FCS to relate to our U.S. imports and exports. This number can be found in the *Standard Industrial Classification Manual* published by the Bureau of Census and available in the reference section of most libraries. It, as well as all the other schedules and documents discussed in this chapter, may be purchased from the government bookstore located in most major cities or at bookstores with large business and reference book sections. The Bureau of Census revised the SIC code to be as comparable as possible to the new HS, but the two do differ. HTS and Schedule B classifications are summarized in approximately 450 four-digit SIC-based import codes and 450 export codes.

Schedule B Number (HS)

The second classification system necessary for export is the Schedule B, which, in its harmonized form, is a ten-digit number composed of about 8000 commodity classes. The first six digits are identical to the HS system and to the import

Table 7-1. Classification of Exports—Section X, Chapter 49

Sched. B no. and headings	Chk dgt	Commodity description	Unit of quantity
4901		Printed books, brochures, leaflets and similar printed matter, whether or not in single sheets:	
4901.10.0000	0	In single sheets, whether or not folded	kg
4901.91		Other: Dictionaries and encyclopedias, and serial installments thereof:	
4901.91.0020	8	Dictionaries (including thesauruses)	No.
4901.91.0040	4	Encyclopedias	No.
4901.99		Other:	
4901.99.0010	2	Textbooks	No.
4901.99.0020	0	Bound newspapers, journals and periodicals provided for in note 3 of this chapter	No.
4901.99.0030	8	Directories	No.
		Other:	
4901.99.0040	6	Bibles, testaments, prayer books and other religious books	No.
4901.99.0050	3	Technical, scientific and professional books	No.
4901.99.0055	8	Art and pictorial books	No.
		Other:	
4901.99.0070	9	Hardbound books	No.
4901.99.0075	4	Rack size paperbound books	No.
		Other:	
4901.99.0091	4	Containing not more than 4 pages each (excluding covers)	No.
4901.99.0092	3	Containing 5 or more pages each, but not more than 48 pages each (excluding covers)	No.
4901.99.0093	2	Containing 49 or more pages each (excluding covers)	No.

tariff schedule, HTSUSA. The Schedule B number is used to report exports on the Shipper's Export Declaration and therefore has been, and continues to be, the classification number used to properly complete the Shipper's Letter of Instruction. You can obtain the appropriate number code with the help of a foreign freight forwarder or by visiting one of the district office libraries of the DOC. The Schedule B classification manual can be purchased from the Superintendent of Documents.

If the product is difficult or impossible to locate in one of the categories, send it with a product specification sheet to the Foreign Trade Division, Bureau of Census, DOC, Washington, D.C. 20232, for a determination of the correct Schedule B number. Alternatively, you may obtain assistance by calling the "help" desk at Census: 301/457-3484.

Harmonized Tariff Schedules of the United States Annotated (HTSUSA)

The Harmonized Tariff Schedule (HTSUSA) is a very important classification code in terms of overall U.S. trade statistics, and certainly in terms of any import activity you might conduct. This code contains the numbers that are necessary for reporting imported products. With the implementation of the HS, HTSUA became a ten-digit number, with the first six digits based on the HS and the remaining four used for additional statistical detail. While the pre-harmonization tariff schedule contained 15,000 commodity classes, the new HTSUA contains more than 10,000 classes. It is comparable to the Schedule B number through the first six digits, but thereafter is increasingly different through eight and then ten digits. Exporters are permitted to use the new HTSUA on the Shipper's Export Declaration in place of the Schedule B number for an indefinite period of time. The reverse is not true: the new Schedule B number cannot be used on the import forms. If you need help, the same addresses or telephone numbers can help with HTSUA as well.

Standard International Trade Classification (SITC)-Revision 3

The Standard International Trade Classification (SITC) was devised, and is primarily used, by the United Nations to compile and report trade information and statistics among all nations. It is based on broad categories for general economic analysis of external trade between nations. Typically, the processing stage is emphasized over the nature of the materials from which the goods were made. The most current revision, Revision 3, was designed to bring the SITC as closely in line with the HS as practical. Complete comparability was not considered desirable because of the two different purposes and concepts.

A First Step in Determining Product Potential

With your commodity codes established, you are ready to begin the export process. One of the easiest and least-expensive methods currently available to research the export history of a potential product (or at least a similar product) are the CD-ROMS available by subscription or the most current monthly disk from the National Trade Data Bank (NTDB) of the DOC, using the HS Schedule B numbers of HTSUSA codes for imports. The NTDB is a huge and very useful collection of data from many federal agencies. (It will be discussed in greater detail in the next chapter, on target country research, as well as in Chapter 42, covering all DOC facilities, and mentioned repeatedly throughout the book.) In addition to a multiple encyclopedic assortment of over 100,000 documents, magazines, and databases, the NTDB includes the Bureau of Census export and import statistics by commodity and country, detailed to ten-digit harmonized codes as above. At $40 per current month's updated disk or $360 annually, it's a bargain, both in information and convenience, if you have the necessary CD-ROM reader. For more information on the NTDB call the all-purpose Trade

Information Services (TIC) at 800/USA-TRADE (800/872-8723). You will also encounter this number frequently relative to a broad spectrum of federal export support services. Alternatively, contact your nearest DOC District Office.

A good source of detailed HS import/export statistical information, including shipping method, customs district, and more, is the CD-ROM disks from the Bureau of Census report: CDIM/____ for imports and CDEX/____ for exports. These reports take the form of annual summaries for any given year (available by placing the last two digits of the year desired after CDEX/____). They are also available by each quarter or month. For a more historical approach, they can be obtained as a five-year history (by ordering as CDEX/90-94, for example). These statistics are prepared by the Census Bureau, but can be obtained through Trade Data Services, at 301/457-2242.

Until the introduction of the CD-ROM, only printed commodity code reports were available to research the export history of your product and comparable products to the various countries. With the increasing use of the CD-ROM for commodity sales research, a number of the printed reports have been discontinued. This includes the Foreign Trade (FT)247 for imports and FT447 for exports which were ten-digit HS codes annual reports. The CDIM/ and CDIX/ discs mentioned above are the only replacements. The printed trade volume reports appropriate for researching trade volume for the exporter's purposes are available from Trade Data Services or the GPO. They are:

- *FT900 U.S. Merchandise Trade by SITC Codes and SIC Codes.* This is a monthly report, plus annual-to-date for general trade analysis by commodity groups and selected countries. It is published about 45 days following the month covered. Trade is presented in a number of different exhibits and fashions but because of the SITC/SIC code base "selected" exhibits, it is not as useful to the exporter in analyzing a specific commodity quantity and value shipped to specified countries.

- *FT925 Exports, General Imports, and Imports for Consumption.* This is a monthly report by subscription based on SITC 3 digit codes, by commodity, by country.

- *FT947 Exports and General Imports,* six-digit HS commodity by country. This report does not report quantities, only total value, and only annual. If the commodity detail to six digits is sufficient, it provides a good picture of which countries are buying meaningful quantities of that six-digit Schedule B or HTSUSA commodity group and how much and from which countries U.S. traders are importing in turn. The information is provided by FAS dollar value for exports and customs value basis as well as CIF value for imports for each country and product. See Table 7-1 for a sample page.

- *EM545 U.S. Exports of Domestic and Foreign Merchandise,* based on Schedule B ten-digit commodity codes. This is a monthly, customized, computer-generated report sold on a subscription basis at a cost based on units of 1 to 10 commodity classifications for exports by country and by customs district of exportation showing quantities and FAS value for the current month and year to date. It is intended to be used for closely tracking very specific situations. A comparable report is available for imports. The minimum current price for statistics on 1 to 10 commodity numbers, covering all countries and all U.S. customs districts, is $160 for 12 months.

All of the above reports are available from the same Trade Data Services mentioned above, but they will no longer be available from the GPO, except for the FT925 monthly reports, although TDS will provide the annual report. For more detailed regions of origin there is a database called MISER compiled by the University of Massachusetts, which can be found on the NTDB disks. Previously, no state could be sure how much it was manufacturing for export, as opposed to merely being a conduit through its ports for goods made in other states and vice versa. Of course, limits on this definition of origin are imposed by the need to ensure privacy when statistical numbers become so small that they reveal commercial information attributable to just one or two firms in an area.

CD-ROM discs have the advantage of monthly updating and therefore are always at least as recent as the information can be processed. Although the CDEX/ and CDIM/ series are expensive, costing $150 each to purchase, an economical alternative is to study the CD-ROM information available at one of the more than 900 Federal Depository Libraries (many located in universities) throughout the United States where you can make a print from particular areas or screens of special interest. CD-ROM reports can also be accessed through various international trade centers and other export support centers. For more information on the Census Bureau reports, or to order, contact Trade Data Services, Bureau of the Census, Washington, D.C. 20233; phone 301/457-2242 or call 800/USA-TRADE. If only a very limited amount of data is needed, you might have it faxed to you for a modest fee by calling the TDS number.

In spite of the cost, the increasing value and convenience of having at least some of the proliferating databases readily at hand is why we mentioned the growing importance of a CD-ROM reader as part of your computer setup in Chapter 3.

A shortcut, however, and a free one at that, is offered by the Small Business Administration's (SBA) Automated Trade Locator Assistance System (SBAatlas). It is also a product-specific and country-specific report which ranks the top 35 import and export markets for a particular product or service. The country report identifies the top 20 products most frequently traded in a specified market. Contact your nearest SBA district office or a Small Business Development Center (SBDC), or call 800/U ASK-SBA.

Additional sources of information and background by country are provided in Chapter 8 on researching target countries. For a more complete discussion of statistical research, you might want to read the *Guide to Foreign Trade Statistics,* available from the government bookstores or the GPO, but also to be found on the ubiquitous NTDB disk.[1]

Using and Compiling Export/Import Statistics

When analyzing reports obtained through various classification codes, it's important to decide what should be ignored or discarded as well as where to focus. In the case of some products in certain countries, the figures can be very misleading because of the considerable offshore manufacturing activity by U.S. manufacturers. For example, a very small Central American country might be reported as importing major quantities of U.S. lingerie. A little investigation into the equivalent U.S. import statistic will show that the lingerie is virtually all cut parts, shipped to contractors in that country for sewing, subsequently returned to the United States, and statistically reflected as an import from Central America. Another example might be the export of very large amounts of certain goods (relative to the size of the population), to a Panamanian free port. The reality is that most of these goods are intended for reexport to other countries in Central and South America. Some of the import statistics help by indicating the "Imports for Consumption" as opposed to "General Imports"—the former being imports received into bonded warehouses or foreign trade zones. This is true in the case of FT947, FT247, and the CDIM reports.

Another pitfall in statistical analysis occurs when the product you propose to export is not sufficiently defined by the ten-digit HS. In this event it is necessary to extrapolate by checking the broader definition to determine that at least this general type of product is being imported by a given country or region, and let the remainder of your country research reinforce any tentative assumptions necessary.

Initial Research

Finding out what countries are importing how much of your product by using only the commodity statistic may not always be the answer. Your product may be so new that the answer can only be found through customer profiles or country characteristics. A first step in developing your statistics and other research requirements should be to establish a contact with a trade specialist in the DOC district office and to develop a rapport and a cooperative relationship with that person. In recent years, district offices have become very understaffed, and experienced trade specialists are not always available. However, when an experienced specialist is available, he or she can be of real help by suggesting current and useful reports or statistics that the DOC or others have prepared on a country or region.

The trade specialist may know of other reports and where to find them. Many times research or consulting firms will prepare a custom report to meet general demand. Sometimes one of their clients may agree to subsequently make a special report available to the public to reduce costs by sharing. Prepared reports can cost anywhere from $50 to $2000. Colleges and universities are another source, either for the reports themselves or information as to their availability. Universities often encourage their international graduate students to do private research papers for business, and in some cases this form of custom research can be excellent and much less expensive. An important source for finding prepared studies is *Findex: The Directory of Market Research Reports, Studies and Surveys*. The Findex address can be found in Appendix K. Their directory purports to have more than 10,000 report titles, both domestic and foreign. It can be found in larger libraries.

Even in the early stages of your research you should start following the ITA Trade Opportunities Program (TOP). Although you may not be ready to follow up on its leads, you will get an idea of the trend—a bit like watching the classified advertisements before you get ready to buy or sell. TOP leads are available through DOC or private on-line services and the Economic Bulletin Board (EBB) at DOC (or call 800/USA-TRADE).

The Customized Sales Survey

The Customized Sales Survey (CSS) is a customized service, available through the DOC district office, that provides American manufacturers with key information about a specific product in selected countries. The use of this service will be premature unless the product cannot be defined statistically with trade figures or the county target research described in the next chapter has been quite definitive as well as positive. If one or two countries are obvious and strong possibilities, it may help you choose between them as well as highlighting various future targets and product modification decisions. The US&FCS foreign staff in the subject country will help determine marketing facts about the product, including sales potential in a given foreign market, competition and availability of comparable products, distribution channels, and competitive pricing. This information should enable you to compare your product to others on the market and assess its export potential. The time required for its completion, as well as its thoroughness and accuracy, depends somewhat on available embassy staff and their dedication at the time. Considering the price of on-site custom research and surveys, you should have a good idea about your target countries, since even a mediocre effort could represent a good savings at a price of from $800 to $3500 per country. The CSS is available in selected countries, including Australia, Brazil, Canada, Colombia, France, Germany, India, Indonesia, Italy, Korea, Mexico, the Philippines, Saudi Arabia, Singapore, and the United Kingdom. The DOC is adding to this list as it finds the resources and the need.

Professional Research

There could be several reasons why you might want to use assistance data resources other than those offered by the US&FCS. One reason is the lack of accessibility. Conducting private, academic, or even independent research is time-consuming, but there are many professional sources and materials available to a prospective exporter, and often at a reasonable cost. To consider professional help depends somewhat on the export initiation budget and on the depth and complexity of the planned export project. There are several options in addition to the least expensive method of seeking private and academic catalogs of existing reports and surveys that were mentioned in the reference to "Initial Research." One option is using a firm that specializes in accessing a wide variety of domestic and foreign lists and sources for business and credit information by region. Typically, a relatively simple agent or distributor search through private overseas contacts for one smaller country might cost $200 to $300. The average cost of a credit report is $150, but can reach $300 depending on the world region. An overseas market study for a limited product and region can reach $10,000, as compared to a cost of $2000 to $5000 if conducted on domestic reports.

Another option is to retain a consulting firm that specializes in international trade or one of the big six accounting firms with offices in the overseas area of interest. They have many services available, but the cost is considerably higher, with a comparable market survey running $50,000 to $100,000. Law firms with a strong international department are not normally used for market development, but possibly for market research with future investment, joint ventures, or even formal distribution agreements in mind. These can range from international law firms, like Baker & McKenzie, that have law offices in most of the centers of trade around the world, to much smaller firms that have close contact with companies doing international business and partners or associates who make a specialty of certain key trade areas. (Several such firms are listed in the acknowledgments at the beginning of this book.)

If the export sales potential provided by a consulting firm is sufficient, the time and labor savings may offset the cost, and probably affords a chance to obtain more focused information. The conservative answer might be to do the preliminary investigation with in-house staff and to limit any professional research to the most likely areas of activity. The best of the export and trade consultants or overseas market research firms may be difficult to find in the Yellow Pages; a large chamber of commerce and/or an international trade association may be a better source of references.

Case Study: Shube's Export Adventure

The 1992 October, November, and December issues of *The Exporter* magazine published a very illustrative case history of product export potential statistical analysis, market and product research, and distribution strategy and personnel. Permission was given both by *The Exporter* and by the marketing executive Mike Mercurio, the participating executive from Global Business Access, Ltd., a consulting firm in Washington, D.C., to reprint excerpts from the series here and in Chapters 8 and 9 to provide concrete illustrations of the strategies and tools discussed. The manufacturer utilizing Global Business to expand its export program is Shube's Manufacturing, an Albuquerque, New Mexico, maker of silver jewelry and pewter giftware including native American jewelry.

Following is a brief summary of how Mike Mercurio proceeded:

> The first stop on Global's market research trail was the computerized National Trade Data Base (NTDB). Reading from the CD-ROM Mike selected

its Bureau of Census merchandise trade export statistics and found, under "jewelry and parts thereof," "silver" (HS code 7113-1100-00), data on U.S. exports in that category, by country, from 1987 through April 1992.

The report showed that while the U.S. is not a huge exporter of silver jewelry, it does make significant shipments—$34 million worth in 1991. As expected, U.S. jewelry finds a ready market in affluent Western countries like Germany, Canada, and the U.K. but the report also showed the Japanese were buying over half of the U.S. exports and that the Netherlands Antilles (Curacao and Aruba) was the second largest market ($3.3 million).

The Japanese are inveterate gift givers, spending twice as much on jewelry per capita as Americans and four times as much as anyone else. In the case of Netherlands Antilles, as a popular tourist destination just off the north coast of South America it attract shoppers from many countries, as well as a stream of cruise ships because of their free port status and reputation for selling quality goods at low prices. It appeared that Asia, with a special focus on Japan, is probably the place to be; even though strong sales might also be possible in the much closer Caribbean area.

Checking further, Mike went into the market research section of the NTDB and retrieved recent reports on the jewelry market in the U.K., Germany, Japan, Italy, Switzerland and Australia. He also visited the DOC in Washington and the Japan Export Trade Organization (JETRO) where he was lucky to find a recently contracted report on the Asian jewelry market. The report was particularly useful because it described the markup percentages that U.S. sellers should expect as their products move through Japan's notoriously costly distributions system. Among other documents the center had on Japan was a list of best prospects for American companies, which included jewelry. An important jewelry trade association was also very helpful and suggested key trade shows that the firm might attend overseas.

The basics about Shube's were readily apparent: the firm had met all the prerequisites for a strong move into exporting—domestic sales approaching $10 million, roughly 240 employees, sound finances and, most impressive, a strong growth pattern. Mr. Shube decided to make the export move and to administer and spearhead it personally. He appointed one of his best employees, Doug Lopez, as the export sales manager and provided him competent staff to back up his international efforts to be sure of priority handling for international orders and correspondence while the international sales manager was traveling.

Global made a few key suggestions—and encouraged Shube's to focus on Asia, which they did. Mike also recommended they: (1) Use the trip to get to know prospective distributors, with an ultimate aim of finding one exclusive distributor in the key Asian countries scheduled for a visit; (2) Expect to make several trips before deciding on an exclusive distributor; (3) Set a price structure which will allow Shube's to upgrade packaging, share promotional expenses, and absorb part of the cost of an anticipated dollar rise against the yen; (4) Get a full explanation of how prospective distributors intend to market the product and what the markup will be at every stage of the distribution process. In fact, in the Shube's distribution setup in Japan as it actually worked out, the retail price was eight times the landed price. Under the right circumstances, a markup of four times the landed price should be possible. More of Shube's export adventure will be recited in Chapter 8.

Product Preparation

Even if you have a large line of products available and suitable for export, you may want to concentrate on just one key portion of that line in the beginning. Given a choice, select those products that have a proven track record or status in this country and that can be sold overseas with minimum modification.

Having assessed the product's export potential in various overseas markets, do everything possible to determine what, if any, modification is required to sell your product successfully. Often the reason that changes are required lies in government regulations—many of which are, in fact, nontariff trade barriers. The passage of GATT will rapidly minimize tariffs and some nontariff barriers, such as unnecessarily strict labeling and packaging requirements and excessive safety or other specifications. Nontariff barriers will be slower in coming down. Sometimes barriers can be overcome not so much by edict or legislation as by administrative interpretation fostered by compromise and cooperation. A starting point for becoming familiar with the regulations in the various countries might be to checking with your own potential customers. If, however, you are completely new to the international markets, an ITA Industry Officer and/or a Country Desk Officer (see Chapter 42) can be of help, provided you have preselected a few countries. The NTDB already mentioned includes excellent information on trade barriers from the U.S. Trade Representative's office, as does the *International Business Practices* DOC publication.[2]

If you are interested in exporting agricultural products, the Foreign Agricultural Service (FAS) has very active services showing where a commodity is sold, who is buying, at what price, and in what quantity. The Agriculture Trade and Marketing Center, which is related to the National Agricultural Library and the AGRICOLA on-line database, assists exporters by determining if product labels and ingredients comply with legal requirements in targeted foreign markets and supplying other similar market-preparation information and activity. The *Country Commercial Guides* found in the NTDB, for which FAS overseas staff also provides input, include current updates of a specific country's labeling and packaging requirements for food products. It's especially crucial to know phytosanitary rules in the country of import before you ship any agricultural products. These requirements change, and it is best not to rely solely on the USDA inspector but to get updated information from the USDA office as well as your overseas customer. If the statement is not absolutely correct, your shipment may be allowed to rot on a foreign wharf or be destroyed at your expense. The same is true of canned and other packaged foods, in terms of labeling and possibly contents, although time is not so critical with these products.

Your research may be less centralized for nonagricultural products. To start with, ask your international freight forwarder to check for special product documentary requirements in the BNA shipping manual (*BNA International Trade Reporter Export Shipping Manual,* published by the Bureau of National Affairs, Inc., 1231 25th Street N.W., Washington, D.C. 20037). This manual, which is continually updated, is a prime source used by many freight forwarders or in-house export departments for country information on everything from postal requirements and rates to import documentation requirements and tariff structure. Next, check with the DOC Country Desk Officer in Washington, D.C., about the particular country in which you are interested.

Modifications to a product may be necessary because of geographic and climatic conditions. For example, high humidity may affect the product, not only during transit but in actual use as well. Consider cultural and religious customs, not only in regard to the product itself, but also in regard to the packaging and catalogs. An example is the case of selling lingerie and related items in Saudi Arabia, where illustrations of the products being worn are objectionable even though the product itself is accepted.

Some consumer goods may also have to be relabeled to correspond to the smaller sizes of the consumer, as in the case of apparel and toys for Japan. Labels on garments and most other items should indicate exact contents, washing and other care instructions if applicable, and the country of origin. Color consideration is a factor for both product and packaging because some colors have negative or derogatory meanings in various cultures—as do "lucky" or "unlucky" numbers. Size, compactness, and shape have a powerful influence in high-density, crowded countries. A secondary use for the package or container itself can also be a strong sales incentive.

Translate your literature, instructions, and the description on the package, if at all possible. Be specific with labels and product information regarding contents and the net and gross weight of each unit. Provide this information in local language and standards of measure. In some countries this may be delayed until after the test market phase, but even when not a requirement, it should eventually be done if the product is to achieve its full market potential.

If the cost for these adaptations and modifications was not considered initially, careful analysis is in order now to make sure that these costs do not make export of the product too expensive or unprofitable. Most demands for product changes or packaging can be verified through research of either the laws or customs of your target country. Do not rely entirely on your foreign distributor or agent unless the agent is paying for all, or a good part, of the modifications. It is easy for agents to suggest modifications as the line of least resistance. If possible, always test the product first, since agents may request unnecessary changes from you, either to suit their purpose or because of unfounded personal preference.

Use great care when it comes to changing the name of your product or translating it into the appropriate language (which is usually unnecessary). Some countries are very brand-conscious and want the foreign label name or look, even though instructions for use must be in their language.

With respect to freight charges, try to construct the product so that it can be shipped in condensed form, such as "kd" (knocked down) or unassembled. Undue bulk or a tendency to a high percentage of breakage in transit presents serious problems that must be resolved. The demand for installation, warranties, and servicing will vary from country to country and should be appraised carefully to see if this important cost factor is necessary or if alternative solutions are available. If problems arise only in certain markets, concentrate first on those that require little or no change and return to the more difficult markets once you are better established and have more export experience.

Don't overlook electrical standards that are different from country to country and could possibly make adaptation too expensive. This concerns electrical codes as well as voltages and hertz. Most of the world's electric systems are based on 220V, 50 Hz. The almost-universal metric system, which the United States has neglected or ignored, can play another important role in the adaptation of your product and must be considered if tools or parts are needed to operate or repair your product. For assistance in this area, the DOC has its National Institute for Standards and Technology (NIST), including an Office of Metric Programs. Much of this information is in the NTDB or you can call the TIC for your best contact.

Foreign product standards and certification requirements affect about half of U.S. exports. For information regarding product standards and specifications for specific countries or regions, a central point of contact is the National Center for Standards and Certification Information at 301/975-4040. NIST has hotlines for GATT standards that apply to the many GATT members worldwide and another hotline for the European Community's efforts at standardization through its European Normalization Committees (ENC). Alternatively, check with the ITA's Single Internal Market 1992 Information Service (SIMIS). Call the TIC for current numbers. (See also Chapter 42.)

International Organization for Standardization (ISO) 9000

There is another major factor for consideration regarding future exporting, one that is currently impacting about $45 billion of U.S. exports (especially those to the European Community). This factor is the ISO 9000 standards for quality manufacturing and service and the related certification and monitoring systems, originally undertaken by the European Union but now involving roughly 100 nations. Many nations are promoting adoption of this generic family of standards and quality control systems including the United States, which is represented in the Organization by the American National Standards Institute (ANSI). Its promoters insist that aggressive pursuit and follow-through of ISO 9000 principles results in significant savings that build themselves into the corporate structure and its ongoing profits. There is much debate, however, about the ISO 9000 in many quarters, including companies within the EU, and even more from those outside the EU who fear it will become a form of legal trade barrier. Of greatest concern among many is the need to go through a lengthy and expensive process of certification, the cost of which is apparently at least $25,000 to $35,000 for a midsize company when fully accounted for, and can be much more. Even its most ardent supporters admit that the program has fallen short of its promise to produce international quality assurance that can replace all other similar or related standards. The fact is that the United States has probably had less control over the process than it should have had in view of its global manufacturing impact, but more than some quarters would have you believe. The entire world will benefit from a final satisfactory outcome, and it will ultimately be a process, not a document. The United States, including our Defense Department, one of the biggest customers of all, is currently involved in the ISO 9000 process.

Although certification is a burden on companies large and small, the burden is especially heavy in financial terms for very small manufacturers. At this time, a lack of certification will not necessarily prohibit you from selling to the EU. Nonetheless, it is a growing disadvantage to lack certification. If your competition is certified, then circumstances are clearly against you. The application of ISO 9000 will inevitably spread to many countries outside the EU, so it is not a subject to ignore, even if your firm is strictly a domestic manufacturing or service company, because the standards, intended to result in more consistent customer satisfaction, will eventually impact U.S. business as well. Make sure you are up-to-date on this issue, even if you are a service provider, especially if you are contemplating selling to Europe. There are many consultants on this subject who not only advise on the matter, but can also take an active role in your certification process. For general information, call DOC's Trade Information Center (800/USA-TRADE) for the department's current best reports and sources of information on ISO 9000. They can also give you the best current EU addresses here and abroad to contact on the subject. The key source for initial contact would be: National Center for Standards and Certification (NCSC), TRF Building, Room A-163, Gaithersburg, Maryland 20899; phone 301/975-4040; fax 301/926-1559 or the American National Standards Institute, 11 West 42nd Street, New York, New York; phone 212/642-4900; fax 212/302-1286.

A Final Word

While remaining objective, do not let the nay-sayers have full control. Many would-be experts have said, "This will sell" and, "That won't sell" with great certainty. Yet experience has shown any number of times that the consumer remains quite unpredictable and is full of surprises if offered the right bait. Furthermore, while much has been said on a number of questions and problems for any one product in a particular region, it is not nearly so cumbersome or difficult as it might seem from this perspective. Just begin.

Endnotes

1. *Guide to Foreign Trade Statistics,* U.S. Department of Commerce, Superintendent of Documents, U.S. Government Printing Office, Washington, D.C. 20402.

2. *International Business Practices,* published by the U.S. Department of Commerce in cooperation with Federal Express Corporation. Distributed at no charge by the U.S. Department of Commerce.

8

Researching Target Countries

Once you establish the export potential of a product and decide that the product adaptations necessary for export purposes are practical, the orderly process of selecting overseas markets should begin. Don't even think of selling worldwide. Begin instead with an objective analysis of a few countries that are: (1) importing meaningful quantities of similar or substitutable products; (2) easy to deal with in terms of language and customs; (3) safe in terms of political and economic stability; and (4) reasonably industrialized. Hopefully they will also be good markets for U.S. exports in general, which will make them areas in which you can obtain maximum public and private export information and help. Don't necessarily choose the largest or most complex markets, such as Japan, for example, where start-up can be difficult or expensive. With the confidence generated by success in your chosen countries and a growing background of experience to guide you, the next steps will be at minimum risk.

The Principles of Target Selection

In selecting target countries, consider each of these points:

- Product demand and suitability
- Political and economic stability
- Industrial development level
- Country purchasing potential for economy of scale
- Import barriers

- Demographics
- Culture (including religion and leisure habits)
- Legal system and commercial practices
- Language and climate
- Ease of access
- Overall degree of trading difficulty
- Availability of foreign exchange
- Geography relative to regional management

Selection Strategies

First, analyze the components of country statistics thoroughly to determine that, aside from the economic conditions of the country and its average per capita income, the distribution of wealth indicates that a sufficient percentage of the population will be potential customers. You can't sell to empty pockets, even with a product of great utility or exceptional price. The very narrow customer base in many less-developed countries, no matter how wealthy that small base might be, could make the development effort less than worthwhile in terms of quantity and export value.

Avoid countries with an erratic import history. They might just have obtained a large foreign aid program or face tighter import restrictions or have a lack of foreign exchange. Besides determining that a particular country probably contains a market niche for your product, study the product itself to be sure it is in an acceptable price and quality range. You might consider a certain country because your product is not readily available there, but obviously the target market must have both the need for it and the ability to pay. You need to research the lifestyle of the target population to avoid finding yourself trying to sell lawn mowers to apartment dwellers.

Besides studying the economic and trade background, you should research the culture, customs, and business practices of your key target countries. Don't wait until you're about to make your first trip. There are two excellent books that can provide background on this subject. One, by Roger Axtell of the experienced multinational, Parker Pen, is called *Do's and Taboos Around the World*.[1] The other is a more recent book, *Going International* by Lewis Griggs and Lennie Copeland.[2] You'll find additional sources listed in Appendix K.

It's also important to consider the law of the land. This will affect you in product liability suits, relations with your representatives and employees in that country, and the cost of doing business. Some businesses are more prone to legal problems or employee and representative difficulties than others. The law of the land also bears on your ability to maintain your trade secrets and other intellectual property rights, such as trademarks and patents. The DOC publication, *International Business Practices*,[3] offers some good suggestions on that subject.

The American executive is fortunate to speak English, a language that allows him or her to travel and sell just about anywhere. The disadvantage is that this good fortune has probably made us more inattentive to learning foreign languages than any other advanced nation. But the fact remains that English-speaking people can be found in virtually every country, and in many nations it is a common language of business. This facility with our language ranges from complete fluency, as in Sweden, where almost any department store salesclerk speaks flawless English, to the more typical case of Japan, where most people in business speak English well enough to get by. The tragic folly inherent in the latter example is that there are thousands of Japanese in this country selling to us in good English every day and only a few hundred Americans selling to the Japanese in Japanese. This is one of the factors contributing to our trade deficit. Nevertheless, it is rare to find a country in which it is impossible to do business because there is a language barrier. Of course, American firms with salespeople who can speak the native language are usually more successful. For this reason, language capabilities in your organization should be considered a strong plus.

Climate is another factor to consider beyond the obvious issue of comfort. It can have a major effect on how your product works. Consider a country's cold, heat, and humidity in regard to the shelf life of your product. Climate can force you to make important product adaptations or, more frequently, packaging changes.

Even after eliminating many countries as lacking potential for a variety of reasons, the list of remaining target countries may still be too large to begin your export efforts. The following points should be reviewed again when trying to reduce that list further:

- It is easier to sell to countries with which the United States regularly trades, especially if they have been importing meaningful amounts of your type of product.

- The largest of those countries may be the most difficult and expensive targets. You may wish to wait until you have gained experience and can better judge your costs and results.

- As a counterpoint, it can take almost as much effort and time to gain a market share in a very small country as it does in a much larger market. Considering these two points, it may be best to avoid both extremes.

- The more sophisticated the consumer, the more demanding the marketplace.

Practical Considerations in the Selection Process

When examining specific markets, look at the top 20 or 25 American export markets but remember that numbers alone tell only part of the story. Your resources, products, and abilities have an equal say in determining the best targets (subject always to product demand, of course). Canada is by far our largest customer. You may wish to treat Canada, as many companies do, as a special category in view of its location and the ease of dealing with it. Some firms use export management firms to handle their exports to every country except Canada, with which their own domestic sales force deals directly.

Japan buys twice as much as any other Asian country, but it remains one of our most difficult markets. If you do approach this market, the Japanese External Trade Organization (JETRO) (see Appendix H) can be of great assistance and is very sincere in doing what it can to help balance the trade deficit. From the information JETRO provides, you might think selling in Japan would be easy, but it isn't, regardless of whether your product faces direct or indirect trade barriers.

Far behind Japan come South Korea and Taiwan, both with a vested interest in reducing their trade deficits with the United States. Both are long-term growth markets, as are Singapore and Hong Kong. In Europe, Great Britain and Germany are the leading markets, but it is often easier to sell in England than in the more demanding Germany. The Netherlands is another great market in a small package. Although not as high on the list in terms of total purchases as some of the other European nations, the Scandinavian countries in general are easy to deal with and are the favorite customers of many firms. Language is rarely a problem, and the consumer seems to share many American characteristics. France remains a difficult consumer goods market, although overall it is now our seventh-largest market and recently pulled ahead of the Netherlands. The French are also enthusiastic European Union (EU) supporters.

Unfortunately, one of our most traditional and profitable markets, Latin America, for many years had grave foreign exchange problems (see Chapter 16), although this problem has been easing with many enjoying a great burst of economic activity and reform. Mexico continues to be a major market for the United States as our third-largest customer and fastest-growing export customer even prior to the completion of NAFTA. Unfortunately, Mexco's new president suffered a serious internal misstep at the end of 1994, and a severe monetary panic and devaluation followed. It remains to be seen how much this episode will damage the substantial promise and fulfillment NAFTA seemed to be offering. Currently, the U.S. Department of Commerce considers Argentina and Brazil to be promising markets. Even though South American sales have fallen, they are now growing again, and exporters who are specialists in goods that South Americans really need are increasing sales steadily by concentrating on the Latin countries. Latin America seems to become more stable as it becomes more democratic, but the political stability of any target country should be a prime consideration. Serious political instability is a good reason to delete a country from your target list. With the exception of South Africa, sub-Saharan Africa has always been a most difficult place for most exporters to make money. On the other hand, except for the Yugoslav war zone, Central and Eastern Europe are now a very promising part of the world. Firms that really understand the region are doing well in the face of many unstable circumstances. But the novice should beware (see Chapter 15).

Geographic Considerations

Remember that you are going to have to travel to the countries you select, and that you may ultimately need to employ managers for some regions. There is a fine international marketing book that makes an excellent analysis of world regions for both travel and regional management purposes. It is Erik Wicklund's *International Marketing—Making Exports Pay Off.*[4]

It is too costly, both in terms of time and money, to take a trip around the world to visit a few unrelated countries in which to begin your overseas operations, except in the unlikely case that they are major endeavors meriting separate trips. The essence of Wicklund's writing on this subject is that you must distinguish between the centralized and decentralized countries. The latter will require several stops within the country if you are trying to establish your product countrywide, which it is usually best to do. The decentralized countries include Canada, Germany, Italy, the Netherlands, Spain, Sweden, Switzerland, Brazil, Columbia, Australia, New Zealand, Japan, India, Turkey, Saudi Arabia, the United Arab Emirates, Nigeria, and South Africa. It is not the size of the country but its centers of commerce that determines the degree of centralization. (With today's air travel, it is generally the trip to the airport and the hotel that make for a complicated and expensive itinerary, not the number of miles flown.) As Wickland writes: "Among the most centralized countries, countries where a visit to a single city may be sufficient are: France, England, Norway, Denmark, Finland, Greece, Austria, Portugal, Egypt, Mexico, Argentina, Chile, Venezuela, South Korea, Thailand, Indonesia, Malaysia, Singapore, Taiwan, and the Philippines."

As a practical issue, it makes a lot of sense to cluster targets. You can start several clusters at one time, but try to have enough business in one part of the world to make a single trip worthwhile. That cluster can ultimately be administered by a single regional manager. Australia, for example, is an ideal target, but consider the trip required to get there! If Australia does seem to be a good target, then by all means try to include New Zealand as part of the package. You might then also see what can be developed in Singapore and Southeast Asia.

The special knowledge you may have of a certain country or region can be an important factor. Certainly the continuing success of many exporters is built on their having an intimate knowledge of the country to which they are exporting. For example, an exporter might succeed because of his or her prior experience with adapting the physical size and proportions of various products to the needs of an Asian population, or because he or she was aware that certain colors have a negative connotaton in some countries. With careful planning and effort, however, you can obtain and benefit from the same information without such prior knowledge.

Besides the two books already mentioned, other excellent sources of help with cultural aspects of international business are as follows:

- *Snowdown International Protocol, Inc.,* New York, offers training in cross-cultural communications and international business practices.

- *The Business Council for International Understanding,* American University, Washington, D.C., uses members of the diplomatic corps to help train interested parties in cultural awareness.

- *The David M. Kennedy Center for International Studies,* Brigham Young University, Provo, Utah, produces *Culture Grams* on the customs, manners, and lifestyles of more than 100 countries.

- *Going International, Inc.,* San Francisco, California, is a private consulting firm focusing on cross-cultural training and information.

- *The International Society of Intercultural Education, Training and Research,* Washington, D.C., affiliated with Georgetown University, is an association of professionals devoted to intercultural understanding.

For reference books on this subject, see Appendix K.

Sources for Research and Information

The International Trade Administration (ITA) of the DOC, and especially ITA's U.S. and Foreign Commercial Service (US&FCS) are the primary and most readily accessible sources for a wide variety of country information on markets, economics, demographics, industrial practices, and trade practices for all but agricultural exports. The Department of Agriculture (USDA) and its Foreign Agricultural Service (FAS) perform similar services and research for the agricultural industry. (The Department of Agriculture and its FAS programs will be described in detail in Chapter 43.)

Thanks to recent interagency efforts by the USDA and others under the leadership of the DOC, there is an increasing wealth of statistics, reports, information, and other assistance available through the ITA's district offices and the new U.S. Export Assistance Centers (USEACs).

The vast amount of current information available from the NTDB's CD-ROM has already been mentioned relative to statistical information in Chapter 7 and will be featured in Chapter 42 on the Department of Commerce. The CD-ROM is proving to be extremely useful, current, and accessible if you have the required CD-ROM reader or access to one of the more than 900 federal depository libraries and a knack for computerized databases. Lacking the latter, you can still be helped in one of the DOC district offices, a U.S. Export Assistance Center (USEAC), or one of the many parallel sources utilizing DOC and Bureau of Census information and statistics.

There are several steps you can take to determine what country information is currently available and how many sources of information you really need or can absorb. First, obtain the most recent edition of the DOC's *Basic Guide to Exporting* (very modestly priced in the $10 range) and the Small Business Association's newest free export publication, *Breaking into the Trade Game.* Together, the two guides provide an excellent summary of government services and serve as handy address and telephone references. Keep them by your side as you read this book and study them in connection with what you find in these chapters.

The Small Business Association offices have their own international departments as well as representatives at the various USEACs. At such locations, SBA staff stand ready to provide assistance to individuals and firms that are really new to export. This permits the Department of Commerce trade specialists to spend more time with firms that already clearly have an export potential or current export activity.

After this preliminary screening of information and availabilities, you should go to the SBA or DOC district offices or to one of the USEACs and ask a trade specialist about the availability, cost, and purpose of the most appropriate programs and information you need. There is an overwhelming amount of services, agencies, offices, hotlines, and data that can be brought to bear on your subject. If you'd like to find out just how much is available, look over the free booklet, *Export Programs: A Business Directory of U.S. Government Services,* summarizing all international trade-oriented services for research, marketing, and financing. It is distributed by the GPO and by the Trade Information Center (at 1-800/USA-TRADE). For a more in-depth look at government resources for international trade, review William A. Delphos's *Inside Washington,* a highly regarded book providing every conceivable resource and the key publications and databases.[4]

Besides the resource list mentioned in the *Export Programs* booklet, both the *Basic Guide to Exporting* and *Breaking into the Trade Game* list the primary-target country research publications and sources the government provides and their current cost. However, because of the vast compendium of foreign statistics and information now in the DOC's National Trade Data Bank CD-ROM facility, it has not surprisingly become the current favorite for general research. The CD-ROM includes the equivalent of three encyclopedias and contains over 100,000 documents. The annual subscription for monthly disks is fairly expensive ($360), but in any given month you can obtain this complete storehouse of data on the current month's updated disk for $40. The NTDB disks include publications as well as trade data. They offer a computerized version of the *Basic Guide to Exporting,* as well as many of the ITA publications mentioned in this book. Among the latter is the DOC's newest and best country and industry market research tool, the Country Commercial Guide. These guides are a result of the TPCC's effort to eliminate overlapping efforts and make export support services more readily accessible as part of the information revolution. The guides include and expand on eight former separate reports and are now complete for over 100 of our trading partners, with in-depth studies of up to 200 pages each. The portion of particular interest to you can be downloaded and printed out on your computer's printer. The guides will be updated at least annually, so they should be your first and basic research tool. (See Chapter 42 for additional details on the NTDB, contact the 800/USA-TRADE number, or order directly by calling 202/482-1986.)

Listed below are summaries of some of the other key publications, reports, and sources available for your target country research, in addition to the export volume statistics by commodity and country reviewed in the previous chapter. Your trade specialist may be able to give you guidance as to which might serve you best. With two exceptions, they are all public sector sources because the private sector resources are too diversified and numerous to consider here. In each case, the supplying agency is indicated, and if the details are provided elsewhere in this book, the chapter location is given in parenthesis. Any of them could be discussed in detail with TIC personnel on the 800/USA-TRADE line:

- *Country Consumer Market Research,* Center for International Research, Bureau of Census. Published with public/private funding that compiles current information on demographic and economic developments in key countries throughout the world, including projections of future developments in both areas.

- *International Business Practices, International Trade Administration.* (See chapters 7, 8, 9, and 42.) A very important publication that details the individual practices relating to trade for 117 countries. It covers business organizations, exporting, foreign investment, intellectual property rights, taxation, regulatory agencies, and useful contacts.

- International Economic Policy country desk officers, International Trade Administration. (See Chapter 42.) Country desk officers are available by phone or in person to discuss most of the individual countries with whom the United States has active trade.

- Trade Development industry officers, International Trade Administration. (See Chapter 42.) Trade Development's industry officers are specialists working with their industry to expand its exports. They identify export opportunities for their particular industry worldwide, arrange trade fairs, and provide individual counseling.

- Customized Sales Survey, International Trade Administration. (See Chapters 8, 9, and 42.) This is a custom-tailored research service to provide firms with specific information on marketing and foreign representation to determine overall marketability in terms of price, trade barriers, competition, and distribution practices.

- Regional Business Centers, International Trade Administration. (See Chapter 42.) These specialized ITA centers aid in determining business opportunities under special circumstances for specific world regions, including Russia, the Newly Independent States (NIS), Central Europe, Japan, Latin America and the Caribbean, Mexico, Canada, and the Pacific Basin.

- Country Studies, International Trade Administration. These are complete books, available in a range of costs, providing detailed information on everything from the economy to the history and lifestyles of selected countries.

- Agricultural Trade and Market Information Center, Foreign Agricultural Service. (See Chapters 7 and 43.) This unit of the National Agricultural Library is a service to assist exporters in locating relevant research material.

- Economic Research Service, Foreign Agricultural Service. (See Chapter 42.) This valuable service provides in-depth economic analysis of agricultural economies and foreign trade policies, demand, and demographics.

- *World Bank Atlas,* the World Bank. Together with its International Monetary Fund (IMF) and International Development Association (IDA), the World Bank produces many reports on a worldwide basis. The bank's address is 1818 H Street NW, Washington, D.C., 20433; phone 202/473-0385.

- *Maps 'n' Facts* by Broderbund. Unlike the services or publications listed above, this is a private sector database in the form of an atlas. Some US&FCS trade specialists maintain that it is widely used in the DOC district offices. It is on CD-ROM with sound and can be purchased for under $50 from your computer software retailer. *Maps 'n' Facts* includes detailed information (including demographics) for business research, and it is reported to be relatively user-friendly. It is likely to be one of the resources a trade specialist would utilize if you were to go to him or her for one-on-one counseling regarding country facts and background.

- *Findex: The Directory of Market Research Reports, Studies, and Surveys.* This is another private sector source of information previously mentioned in Chapter 7 relative to Initial Research.

Making the Most of Your Assistance

DOC Trade specialists or market researchers can combine government and DOC sources of information and statistics with information prepared by the United Nations, the World Bank, the International Monetary Fund (IMF), and the Organization for Economic Cooperation and Development (OECD). There is an enormous selection of material (much of it repetitive) out there, and the process of sorting it out, learning how to use it effectively, and making sure it is up-to-date and remains that way can be extremely time-consuming. As a result, the business of intern-generated market research is booming. Many exporters today are already taking advantage of professional services, even though the cost is naturally greater. Whether you work independently or engage help, you must be careful not to let the process begin to overwhelm the objective. Study no more research than what you actually need to know. A trade specialist or professional can be of assistance on this point. So can your own experience after you have studied one country or a smaller region. In any case, whether independently or with help, it is important that you do at least some research on the proposed target countries and perhaps talk it over with the DOC Washington desk officer in the International Economic Policy unit of ITA. After that, apply your own judgment and common sense.

Putting It All Together

If you have the opportunity to visit Washington, D.C., during or after your research and consideration of target countries, by all means do so. A visit to the appropriate DOC country desk officer in Washington will be very useful, even though you may have spoken to the country specialist by phone. The Trade Information Center (at 800/USA-TRADE (800/872-8723, fax 202/482-4473) is worth some time in person as well. In addition, you might also wish to speak to some of the people who prepare the export statistics at the Census Bureau or Department of Commerce in order to obtain their input on the exact implications of the various facts and statistics. In some situations it is a good idea to visit the Washington embassy of your target country to speak with its trade representative or use its reference library and telephone books. However, keep in mind that the embassy staff is there to aid their country's exports, not their imports. The exceptions are some of our major trading partners in Asia with whom the United States has a large trade deficit, and who take a somewhat different attitude, out of political necessity.

If you are closer to the West Coast, you can visit the consulates in Los Angeles or San Francisco where most countries are represented as well. A good many countries also have consulates in other major cities, such as Chicago or Dallas, and they, too, have reference libraries.

While not necessary, or even always possible, it is useful to attend an appropriate trade fair in the area *before* making a final decision on target countries. This will give you a feel for the people you will be dealing with and the level of their interest in your product. (See Chapter 12 on "Trade Fairs.")

This chapter can best be summed up with a continuation of the second installment of the case history detailing Shube's Manufacturing export expansion. As earlier, in Chapter 7, the report is adapted from an article in *The Exporter* magazine.[6] It is based on an account of the operation by Mike Mercurio of Global Business Access.

Shube's Export Adventure, Part 2

Mike Mercurio had analyzed trade data on U.S. jewelry exports, read a raft of market research reports and done what he could to assist Doug Lopez, Shube's international sales manager, in preparing for the trip he was about to take to Asia. In the course of this Global expanded its initial conclusions on target markets and representative or distributor policies and strategies.

(1) Beginning with their longer range conclusions concerning target countries, Global suggested: (a) The initial target should be Japan together with any secondary market opportunities in readily accessible Asian countries that could be visited on the same trip. Based on market research, Global found that Japan buys about half of all silver jewelry exported from the U.S. on a per capita basis. It takes patience and resources to properly service the Japanese market, but Shube's can do it. They already have some experience with marketing and trade show activity in Japan, and the export sales manager, Doug Lopez, is familiar with the country and speaks some

Japanese. (b) Many European markets would be receptive to Shube's lines as the export project progresses, but the company should not try to do everything at once. Germany is the best place to start for it is the largest economy on continent with the highest GNP per capita, no significant trade barriers, a low 3% customs duty, and Germans are less chauvinistic in their choice of jewelry than the French or Italians. Great Britain's drawback is their hallmarking requirement for silver products, which can be dealt with, but one need not start with this market. (c) The Netherlands Antilles islands of Curacao and Aruba buy almost as much jewelry from the U.S. as Germany, and can eventually be explored as an independent opportunity without concern for marketing to other areas of Latin America because of their ready access and the ease of exporting in a free port situation.

(2) Global reiterated the importance of aiming for exclusive distributors in each country considering the style and brand name nature of the Shube product. It is more cost efficient for exporters to deal with one large customer in each country than many small ones. For this reason alone, Global emphasized the care with which exclusive representatives should be chosen, and the importance of developing a true sense of partnership. Confidence in a representative should be such that he or she provides advice on a host of issues—including product adaptation to local market demands. Overseas distributors generally prefer a close "joint venture" type relationship, including frequent personal contact. Mutual commitment is easier to establish in the case of exclusive relationships, but this still requires patience for such relationships are built slowly.

(3) At the financial level Global suggested Shube's Manufacturing should share market development costs with a satisfactory distributor or representative and accept some of the financial risk of the distributor's efforts to expand sales providing they can jointly agree on market promotion activity and costs. The downside of not granting exclusivity is that the distributor, or even a representative, may feel that it must take a very high markup to protect itself against its time and effort spent in a short term relationship, with resulting lower than potential sales for the manufacturer.

(4) Set the price structure at levels that allow for market development expenses and a degree of exchange rate fluctuation. Global recommends that Shube's sell to their overseas distributors at prices equivalent to their wholesale prices, less 20 percent.

(5) With improved packaging, Shube's product can compete in more prestigious outlets overseas.

(6) Shube's should increase its number of international marketing representatives from one to two. It is perfectly reasonable for Shube's to aspire to doing half its business overseas, but in order to do that, 50 percent of its resources must be oriented toward serving these markets.

(7) Shube's should consider the introduction of products specially designed for [its] overseas markets.

Endnotes

1. Roger Axtell, *Do's and Taboos Around the World,* John Wiley and Sons, New York.
2. Griggs and Copeland, *Going International,* New American Library, New York, 1985.

3. *International Business Practices,* U.S. Department of Commerce in cooperation with Federal Express, U.S. Government Printing Office, Washington, DC 20402, 1993.

4. Erik Wicklund, *International Marketing—Making Exports Pay Off,* McGraw-Hill, New York.

5. William A. Delphos, *Inside Washington,* Venture Publishing, Washington, DC, 1992.

6. Michael Mercurio and the *The Exporter* magazine staff, "Expanding Global Sales," October, November, December 1992 issues of *The Exporter* magazine; summarized here by special permission of the magazine.

9

Establishing Channels of Distribution

No matter how carefully you've thought out your strategies of targeting, market research, and product preparation, they will be of minimal value until you find the best people or organizations to represent or distribute your product. The first real step in making the sale—finding the right export marketing company (EMC)/export trading company (ETC), representative, distributor, or licensee— can be more important than the promotional effort that follows. If an export consultant, market research firm, or overseas marketing consultant is to be retained, the consultant or researcher should suggest or assist in the research for key names of potential representatives and/or distributors in the various countries. The support you get from the International Trade Administration (ITA), the Foreign Agricultural Service (FAS), and other agencies can be of great assistance. Nonetheless, a good deal of effort, ingenuity, initiative, instincts, and probably travel, will also be required on your part.

Exporting through an EMC/ETC

Your very first consideration must be to determine whether you will use direct or indirect exporting methods. (See Chapters 4 and 5.) If indirect exporting through an intermediary is most appropriate for you, an EMC or ETC is the most frequent choice. For convenience, EMCs and ETCs will be referred to collectively as EMCs/ETCs. To recap, the advantages and disadvantages offered by an EMC/ETC to the exporter are as follows:

Advantages

- Probably faster market entry

- A more consistent focus on exporting

- Lower out-of-pocket expenses

- An opportunity to learn

- Expertise in export details and strategy

Disadvantages

- Loss of control

- Competition from other products

- Buyer reluctance to deal with third-party intermediaries

- Added costs and/or higher selling prices

- Neglect of your product in favor of others

You need to weigh these advantages and disadvantages, seeking maximum benefit at minimum risk, when considering the qualifications of various EMCs/ETCs. Above all, establish goals that both you and the EMC/ETC clearly understand. Far too many firms have executed contracts with EMCs/ETCs on nothing more than a "What can we lose if they sell something?" attitude. You *can* lose your reputation in the international market, and you *can* lose integrity as far as the export community is concerned. You could also add one more black mark to America's reputation for not being very concerned about our foreign trade commitments and responsibilities.

Finding interested and qualified EMCs/ETCs will take a certain amount of care and time. Speak to the international department of your bank, the local district office of the DOC, local and international world trade organizations, and the international department of your chamber of commerce. Try the same media you would use to find a first-class salesman or consultant, such as an advertisement in your regional newspaper business section, the *Wall Street Journal,* the *Journal of Commerce,* or other business publications that are distributed in your area. While an EMC/ETC near you may be convenient, don't let the firm's geographical location in the United States overshadow other qualifications.

The newest DOC aid in this search is an annual publication called *The Export Yellow Pages*. It is a national classified directory that lists names, addresses, and products or services of more than 18,000 firms offering export services (including banks and financial services), export trading and management companies, technical services, producers, and manufacturers. The directory has special sections for the environmental and the high-technology industries, which are listed alphabetically by type of firm (i.e., producers, trading companies, export services, technical services) and then indexed by product classification. *The Export*

Yellow Pages is available at no charge through the DOC district offices and is updated annually. The most recent export intermediary dictionary available is NEXCO's Registry of Export Intermediaries, 1996–1997 edition, containing over 4500 names.[2] A detailed description focused on export management and trading companies only the *Trading Company Sourcebook* by Richard Barovick.[1]

It can be difficult to select the best EMC/ETC for you from among the applicants or lists. Don't hesitate to ask for references, including bank and client references, plus detailed credentials in the form of company history, personnel, and present activities. It is no secret—and not ordinarily a problem—that EMC/ETC are typically highly leveraged business firms because they have little need for a large asset base. This makes their reputation, good credit history, and payment record doubly important, however.

Visit the EMCs/ETCs office and meet the staff. Is the company large enough? Is it organized in a fashion that will work for you and your product? Does its staff have sufficient technical knowledge to do the job? While not absolutely necessary, it is also a plus if the office has its own export freight-forwarding personnel and if the staff processes or reviews their own documents before negotiating or banking. Depending on your global focus, foreign language capabilities can also be a major advantage.

Ask questions about overseas activity in terms of travel schedules and frequency. How many agents does the company deal with and where are they located? Does the office have full-time or salaried staff overseas? Only the largest will normally have the latter. If you're in favor of a certain company because it is especially strong in a product category or works in an area of the world that interests you, ask for evidence of this specialization. If you like the EMC/ETC because it covers a large part of the world, ask for proof that it really has that experience and expertise.

However broad the EMC's territory professes to be, you don't need to give it the whole world as a territory, or even a large part of it. You may wish to use several different firms that have the best performance record in certain parts of the world, or possibly retain certain areas for yourself. These, however, must all be rational decisions not casual choices based on miscellaneous inquiries you've received. And they should be implemented with solid plans of action that have a logical relation to world areas as discussed in Chapter 8. An EMC/ETC must be able to take a sales trip to any one of the world regions and not run into competition just across the border. For example, it would probably be counterproductive for the sales organization and the manufacturer alike to split the European Union among more than three EMCs/ETCs, unless the EU continues to expand. Internal EU regulations also bear upon exclusivity provisions within the EU. It is also important that everyone, including in-house salespeople, use the same price list. It is as easy to create chaos in overseas markets as it is in the domestic marketplace.

Look for an organization that is capable of handling the immediate efforts required to launch your product, and one that has the flexibility to expand its product knowledge, territorial contacts, staff, and network. Remember that it is not always in your interest to consider only the largest EMC/ETC. You want a firm to which your business is important and for which your product presents a special opportunity. Unless your company is quite large and your product is fairly dominant in its field, your interests may get lost in the larger operation.

EMCs and ETCs have been spoken of as if they were one, but there are distinctions. If an EMC seems closest to filling your needs, you should focus on such considerations as the compatibility of your product with other products that are sold by that EMC, possible synergistic effects or conflict as a result of such a combination, and the degree of exclusivity required from the EMC to accomplish your ends. If, on the other hand, you favor the ETC concept, the financial strength of a large ETC may be a deciding factor, because it will enable it to handle larger transactions than you could otherwise consider. Other factors, such as an ETC's involvement in countertrade expertise, may also deserve your consideration—especially if countries with weak currencies form an important segment of your target countries. (Review the comments on EMCs and ETCs in Chapter 4.)

Creating a Sound Working Agreement with an EMC/ETC

A well-tested and equitable sample contract between an EMC and a manufacturer is included in Appendix P. Obviously, this contract will not fit all conditions, such as those involving after-sales service or those in which there are other complicating or technical details unique to a particular product.

The most important understanding is the spirit of clear and mutual intent. A written agreement, however, is necessary to assure the EMC/ETC that it really does have a client relationship if that is the intent. The document is also there to remind both parties of what they originally agreed to (but if it must be referred to frequently, the relationship is doomed).

The agreement should cover at least these points:

- Duration and termination
- Territory and exclusivity
- Rights to overseas PX and commissary sales
- Performance standards for both exporter and manufacturer
- Export pricing policies
- Payment terms
- Transfer of title
- Delivery schedules
- Market development expense
- Compensation or commissions
- Product liability

Most EMCs/ETCs hesitate to undertake an agreement for less than one year because of the time required to develop overseas markets. They usually are more prepared to promote the product if it is for the more typical term of three years. In the case of very short contracts or trial contracts with no term, it's advisable to use some performance standard that automatically provides for an agreeable term when those standards are met. In such circumstances, the manufacturer should be prepared to undertake a good part of the development expense. Goals demanding fast sales results can be very counterproductive for the long-run country market development of a product. These goals can lead to decisions permitting distribution by the wrong parties, or by too many parties, resulting in what the Japanese call a "disorderly market."

If EMCs/ETCs are to take title rather than be commissioned, the manufacturer can help enhance their creditworthiness by cooperating on especially large transactions through various financial devices, such as letter of credit assignments or transfers. This is not an issue of contract, but of mutual cooperation. The effort, strategy, ethics, and methods of the EMC/ETC, as well as your inter-relationship, usually have more to do with overall success than initial sales goals.

Remember, the EMC/ETC is also observing your ability to deliver a quality product on time, your willingness to cooperate, train, and in general to provide the tools any good salesperson or regional manager would need. Your mutual openness and willingness to work together as a unit will determine the nature of the relationship more than the agreement you sign. Of course, there are many trade-offs in your EMC/ETC relationship, the importance of which depends on your level of interest in the export process. Trade-offs include willingness on the part of the EMC/ETC to accept your participation in return for knowledge of customers and policies; and confidence on your part to enter into an agreement of sufficient strength and duration to make it practical for the EMC/ETC to permit such a high level of involvement on your part.

Pursuing Other Domestic Channels

If you do not wish to use an EMC/ETC, but want to confine your export sales efforts to domestic channels, you might consider one of the following:

- PX sales agents
- International buying offices
- Project buying offices
- Export merchants
- Piggyback marketing

Sufficient information is provided in Chapter 4 to enable you to pursue those options.

Making Your Own Overseas Connection

Although there is a substantial difference and clear distinction between *representatives* (sometimes called agents or appointees) and *distributors/importers* (who may also be called dealers, jobbers, wholesalers, or sometimes even retailers) for the purposes of this chapter, foreign distributors and representatives will be considered as one and referred to collectively as *representatives*. Representatives or distributors as a group must be distinguished from overseas retailers or end users, although during the actual business of finding one or the other, it is often difficult to distinguish between them. Good search lists and programs often make the distinction for you, and you should by all means note or specify the distinctions they offer. But don't count on their necessarily being accurate, many such contacts are multifunctional.

Representation of any kind in a foreign country is much like a marriage—often much easier to enter into than to leave. Termination can be expensive and time-consuming and will delay market entry. If you have little confidence in the prospective distributor, sell directly to retailers or other end users while waiting for the right representative and a better understanding of the territory. If you have had little experience in the territory or with exporting, this may be the best solution for the time being.

Searching for Prospective Representatives

The export services, mailing lists, and assistance provided by DOC/ITA and its US&FCS unit are often underused, especially by new-to-export businesses. While getting assistance and information from the DOC has always been a frustrating process, the current direct computer communication between district offices, Washington, D.C., and overseas posts is making the department's information more current and effective. The new TIC facility, with its easy-access phone number, 800/USA-TRADE, has eased much of the frustration and made your work and search easier.

The Foreign Agricultural Service (FAS) administers export affairs for the U.S. Department of Agriculture (USDA) in a fashion similar to ITA/US&FCS for DOC. It also has a worldwide network of attachés and counselors who gather and access information on world agriculture production and trade. (See Chapter 43 for complete details.) At FAS the initial point of contact for market information and trade contacts within FAS for assistance is through the U.S. Trade Assistance and Promotion Office (TAPO), (phone 202/720-7420 or fax 202/690-4374). There are three primary services to assist food and agricultural exporters with trade contacts through their AgExport Connections.

Following are some of the many and useful tools designed to help you find overseas customers or representatives by means of direct mail. Many have already been mentioned in other contexts.

The DOC's Agent/Distributor Service.   This important DOC service can minimize or even eliminate multiple mailings in your search from the home office for a representative. (All the other tools we will be describing are basically a means of obtaining *unscreened* names of potential candidates.) If your product consists of 51 percent or more U.S.A.–made content, the DOC will send your product literature to the US&FCS post in the countries you specify. The US&FCS commercial officer will conduct a search and prepare a report identifying up to six foreign prospects that have examined your product literature and have expressed interest in representing you. When it works, this is a fine service at a reasonable price. If the Agent/Distributor Service (A/DS) cannot provide appropriate and qualified names, the US&FCS will refund your money, but you may need to ask for it. Keep in mind that there is a wide range of service quality from the US&FCS leads, since aside from the availability of qualified prospects and product interest, everything depends on the dedication and size of the foreign staff at any given time.

While A/DS can sometimes be frustratingly slow—and even provides poor results at times—you should not be discouraged from mining this source for potential leads at the current price of $250. The cost is double what it was a few years ago, and in fact, we notice a very rapid increase in most of the DOC cost-recovery fees, many nearly tripling over a ten-year period. A decade ago, many DOC fees were surely underpriced, but it's apparent that the situation is being corrected—understandably so, in view of the agency budgetary problems. Even now, however, when the service is performed "as advertised," the prices are still very modest compared to private sector costs, and even when compared to doing the mailings on your own, given the cost of direct mail.

Lists for Direct Mail and Fax Contact. The comments here concerning direct mail and mailing lists are focused on a search for representatives. Some of the direct-mail techniques suggested in Chapter 12 can be adapted for the representative search as well.

Foreign Traders Index (FTI) and Export Contact List Service. DOC has a list of over 55,000 prospects in its file of foreign firms known to be interested in importing U.S. products. The complete list is part of each two-disk edition of the NTDB, targeted by commodity classification, and it identifies manufacturers, agents, retailers, and service firms, listing their address, product/service interest, year established, and other data. In its computerized database form, it is supposed to be much more current and accurate than similar predecessor lists. Contact the Trade Data Services Branch at 301/764-4811, or call 800/USA-TRADE. The Export Contact List Service is a hard-copy customized retrieval version of the FTI. Contact your trade specialist at the nearest district office. In the past, the FTI lists were one of the weakest of the US&FCS services because of the difficulty of keeping the lists current and because many of the firms included were not qualified. A 2 percent return was considered a good result from a mailing relying on these names. The DOC now believes that the advent of computer links for the US&FCS domestic offices, overseas offices, and Washington offices has greatly added to the value of these lists and that the customized handling of custom lists makes them more useful and accurate than the FTI.

Trade Opportunities Program (TOP). This DOC program already alluded to in Chapter 7 disseminates all trade leads received by the DOC daily and for the prior week. It has continued to improve and become more timely. Trade leads are published daily in the *Journal of Commerce* and in other public and private publications. These leads are also available electronically to CompuServe database subscribers and through the DOC's Economic Bulletin Board (EBB). (Contact 202/482-1986 for more information.) The most recent leads can also be retrieved directly onto your fax at a charge of 65 cents per minute. The faster dissemination has made TOP more effective. Selected leads are also published in *Commerce Business Daily* and in a number of regional or industry publications nationwide. As with so many industries, the DOC is relying more and more on computers to provide data to its users, and has phased out some of its older, more familiar programs. CompuServe and Dialog data banks also have a number of DOC databases.

FAS Trade Leads.   Furnished by the AgExport Connection, these leads consist of inquiries that come in daily from the 80 FAS overseas offices. They are available on electronic bulletin boards, the *Journal of Commerce,* and by fax.

FAS Foreign Buyer Lists.   These lists provide a customized retrieval from an agricultural database of over 20,000 foreign firms, with their specific commodity interests listed by country.

Sources for a More Targeted Approach

Trade Associations and Publications.   By checking with appropriate domestic trade associations—which sometimes receive requests from foreign representatives either directly or from their counterpart organizations in the target country—you may find very qualified contacts already interested in your category of product. Trade associations are often restricted to professional salespeople and executives in a given product area. *Trade Directories of the World,* by Croner Publications Inc., provides an encyclopedic body of information on such associations.[4] Trade publications, often sponsored or published by trade associations, are an excellent source for many industries. Sometimes these publications have a designated column in which you can list inquiries regarding representation or distribution, domestic or foreign, and often at no cost. The advantage of using such sources is that they are more likely to put you in touch with established professionals rather than with "budding entrepreneurs" who are merely enchanted with foreign trade and "ready to try anything."

Banking and Shipping Contacts.   Banks are once again interested in developing their international departments, and some can be of real assistance through their international departments and corresponding overseas banks. They can provide leads before you travel and act as your office—sometimes even offering secretarial help and translators—while you are visiting. Banks can be invaluable in helping you with a few key telephone calls. Other options include steamship lines, airlines, and freight forwarders that maintain offices throughout the world and that can get inquiries from their overseas offices or find an outlet for your product. They are often able to tell you what countries are interested in your type of product based on their own experience.

State, City, and Port Assistance.   Check to see what services your state provides. The majority of states offer considerable help and many have overseas offices at their disposal in selected countries. Some major American cities and port authorities provide excellent help; take the time to do the research. The ports of New York/New Jersey, Virginia, and Massachusetts all have forms of ETCs. (See also Chapter 44.)

Chambers of Commerce.   The chambers of commerce in the larger cities or metropolitan areas throughout the United States have an international division and promote foreign trade for their communities in various forms. They send and receive newsletters, in addition to organizing events for overseas visitors that might affect and promote trade. They occasionally receive requests from abroad as a result.

Binational Chambers of Commerce.   These chambers usually concentrate on trade between two specific countries. (The German/American Chamber of Commerce is one example.) Some of the larger states even have country/state chambers of commerce, such as the Canada/California Chamber of Commerce. These binational chambers of commerce are playing an active role in many trade functions, from certifying documents to assisting with trade inquiries. Because they often have a counterpart in the foreign country, they can be of help in providing information about potential overseas importers.

American Chambers of Commerce Abroad.   These organizations are located in about 40 foreign countries (see Appendix B). Their members are firms and individuals from America and various host nations who share an interest in promoting trade and a better understanding between the United States and the host countries. They will usually respond to inquiries from any American firm; however, for more detailed service, they will charge a fee to nonmembers. An American chambers of commerce will have current information about trade opportunities in the host country, as well as knowledge about competition, market share, general trade activities, and local practices. In some situations, the chamber of commerce can be a very useful place to visit on your travels.

Printed Media, Magazines, and Bulletins

Commercial News USA.   This publication is put out ten times a year by the US&FCS and promotes American products to overseas markets through distribution by U.S. embassies and consular posts around the world to 110,000 potential buyers and representatives. It is a very inexpensive way both to test worldwide for the areas of greatest initial interest and to indicate that you are searching for representation.

Showcase USA.   This is a commercial magazine intended to accomplish a purpose similar to *Commercial News,* in which your advertisement can also advise of your search. For more details, see the media section in Chapter 12.

Buyer Alert.   This is a weekly overseas newsletter mailed out by FAS to introduce American food and agricultural products to foreign buyers at no charge to the exporter.

Foreign Trade Association Newsletters and Publications.   Just as these organizations can be used to obtain qualified and highly targeted names, they can also be used to run classified or display advertisements for representatives.

Making the Most of Foreign Travel

Foreign Buyer Program.   This program enables you to take advantage of someone else's foreign travel. The DOC selects special domestic trade shows throughout the United States for industries with high export potential and encourages foreign buyers to attend the shows by promoting them through American embassies and trade-related overseas publications. Trade specialists also attend the shows and work closely with the exhibiting American firms, helping them meet the overseas visitors and providing counseling and assistance for the comfort of both parties. The foreign buyer you meet at such a show is as likely to be a qualified representative or distributor/importer as a direct customer. Don't limit yourself to using such shows only when seeking direct customers. Contact Export Promotion Services at 202/482-0481. (See also Chapter 12.)

Trade Shows.   Attend trade fairs in your region and talk to the sales people of allied but noncompeting lines, even though you are not exhibiting. It is much cheaper to attend as a visitor. Such fairs can give you a chance to learn before you leap and an opportunity to contact good local or regional representation.

Matchmaker Events.   Like trade missions, matchmaker events are staged in various overseas cities by ITA with the limited objectives of matching new-to-export firms with overseas representatives and furthering joint-ventures and/or licensing. Contact your DOC district office to obtain US&FCS current plans that fit into your travel schedule and are appropriate for your needs. Evaluate these events relative to the criteria for other trade shows, missions, and catalog shows sponsored the by the ITA, state, and private organizations. (See Chapter 12.)

Overseas US&FCS.   The commercial attaché or the US&FCS officer stationed at the U.S. embassy or trade consulate in the target country may be able to assist you in locating interested firms while you are visiting, especially if they are advised in advance of your visit and you have a reasonable stopover planned.

Overseas Telephone Books.   We mention these last for good reason, because they are something of a last resort. But in the course of your travels the various means of locating qualified prospective representatives for future evaluation are limited only by your ingenuity and networking ability. One fairly common practice is to look in the telephone directories in the various key cities of your target countries. While this is very questionable as a primary method, it is clearly an option frequently used, judging from the number of battered classified telephone books in the hotels of many countries. Actually, telephone books may serve their best purpose, not so much for seeking representation, as for locating specific types of retail customers, if that is your objective. Telephone books are often difficult to come by until you have personally arrived in the country, which is too late for advance references. A contact in a target country can obtain such telephone books for you. A cheaper way, especially considering postage, is to request a photocopy of the pages containing the appropriate listings from the local foreign trade specialist or perhaps from a secretary in that country's American chamber of commerce. In some major commercial cities you will find special English-language classified telephone books for business travelers.

Interviewing Prospective Representatives Abroad

You may receive many replies from potential representatives in answer to your mailings and other inquiries, but you must be able to concentrate on the most promising contacts. Time and money restrictions will probably make it quite impossible to visit them all personally, and, as noted, the investigative reports are costly enough that you will need to narrow the field. With some experience and ingenuity, you will improve your skills for this initial evaluation, which will be subject to different rules in different countries and regions of the world.

Assuming that you have decided on a trip to meet and investigate your potential representatives and possibly to locate additional alternatives, here are a few tips.

First, advise your contacts of your plans to visit, but do not divulge all the details of your itinerary. This can give you some breathing space. If you are met at the airport by a prospective representative, or if you allow many other major arrangements to be made for you, it can be very difficult to arrange free time for other interviews and appointments. The representative who meets you may end up getting the appointment virtually by default. Be assured that this is much harder to avoid or control than it would be in the United States. The issue of arrival, meeting, and advance arrangements by unknown representatives poses a special problem in some of the Middle Eastern countries, such as the United Arab Emirates, where you cannot enter on a regular visa *unless* someone meets you and sponsors your visit.

It is also uncomfortable to decline your sponsor's bid for representation. If it must be done, it is better to do so after your departure. Under these circumstances, you must summon your most diplomatic and cautious posture and work things out as best you can. The readiness of people to meet in your hotel lobby is a saving grace in this instance, and it is often a good idea for strictly preliminary meetings. Afterward, you can arrange to see the candidate's place of business, which will naturally have a major bearing on your final decision. Incidentally, having *World Trader Data Report* (WTDR) and/or a credit report in hand for the first interview is a big help in asking the right questions.

During your visit, it is wise to discuss your best prospects with the commercial officer at the U.S. embassy. There is little the embassy staff can do for you via correspondence, either before or after your trip, other than providing formalized responses such as *World Traders Data Reports* or putting you in touch with the Agent/Distributor Service (A/DS). While you're in the country, the embassy staff may be able to give you firsthand information about a certain company or representative or make some calls for you. Above all, don't rush your decision. Setting up a new representative takes time and money—perhaps more than it would for a domestic territory—and it can be much more difficult to terminate. If at all possible, defer your final decision until you return to your home office and can analyze all you have learned on your trip.

Evaluating Prospective Representatives

World Traders Data Report and Commercial Credit Reports.   The exporter has several tools to help him preview the qualifications of a representative. Two of these are the DOC *World Traders Data Report* and, of course, the overseas credit report, both of which are discussed again in Chapter 25. The WTDR is an especially useful tool in determining a prospective representative's eligibility because of its emphasis on background, years established, number of employees, and product handled. Although less expensive than most credit reports, it is still costly if many must be ordered for the sorting-out process. Your DOC district office can request this report by fax or modem directly from its overseas post at a current cost of $100. However, to avoid spending too much on too many, try to make some early eliminations.

Company Letterheads.   Letterheads offer many clues for sizing up a new contact. You can get a sense of the representative's professionalism from the design. The letterhead may or may not tell you much about the office's locale. In this regard, it's important to take local conditions into account. For example, in some countries, especially the Middle East and parts of Latin America, there are no numbered street systems, so businesses are forced to rely entirely on post office box addresses. The letterhead is also likely to indicate the level of the office's communication facilities, which is an important practical matter in terms of your ability to stay in touch with your representative. Look to see whether the prospect is relying on its own private communication equipment or whether it is utilizing public facilities. Again, in some Third-World countries, use of public facilities is a necessity for everyone except the government and the oldest and largest private firms. Don't put much store in a cable name address or telex because they tend not to be used and are meaningless today.

The letterhead may provide the name of the principals, the firm's capital, and its founding date, as well as its bank name and account number. The letterhead will also tell you whether the firm is incorporated by showing such letters as LTD, A.G., S.A., A.B., or K.K., depending on the country. Larger companies will show their branch offices and often list logos or brand names of foreign firms and manufacturers they represent.

Let the information on the letterhead create the impression it was intended to create, and then—think again. Remember that some disreputable companies seem to have a letterhead and business card for every purpose. The very existence of a long list of companies represented, covering everything from A to Z, is in itself a warning that either this is not true or that the firm has too many product responsibilities. Of course, this would not apply to some world-class trading companies that have many employees and divisions, but these you would generally know of, or could quickly learn about. Even then, more often than not, you might get better service from a smaller, specialized, management-owned firm that is less subject to radical changes in service resulting from personnel shifts. (An exception may be the situation in which your representative needs a heavy investment in financial resources and facilities for after-sales service.)

Be sure to respond to all correspondence as quickly and as concisely as possible, but with sufficient facts and brochures to stimulate interest and make the exchange meaningful to both parties. Remember, it is as much your job to sell yourself and your product as it is the representative's job to sell its service—perhaps more so, if your message is to reach the best. On the other hand, within limits, play for time to be sure you have done all that is possible to make the proper contacts. When responding, ask the important questions. Why does the firm want your line or product if it is already representing so many excellent firms in the field? Which of these products are exclusive and which are not? Are they willing to give you names and permission to check references, and if not, why not? Don't be dazzled by names, titles, or other references that seem exotic to you, including connections to a royal family.

Shube's Export Adventure, Part 3

Before proceeding further with this process, it will help to illustrate its reality by completing the story of Mike Mercurio's efforts through his firm, Global Access Ltd. of Washington, D.C., as reported in the January 1993 issue of *The Exporter* magazine to help Shube's Manufacturing of Albuquerque expand the exports of its line of silver jeweler and pewter giftware.

After studying the target countries, developing a basic strategy and agreeing that Japan was the best of the target markets, Shube's requested Global Access to focus on helping them find a qualified distributor for this large but difficult marketing region. Mike again turned to JETRO, the Japanese External Trade Organization, which was originally set up to promote Japanese exports. In view of today's troublesome trade deficits, it also helps foreign companies sell in Japan. Through a search, JETRO provided the names of three potential distributors and the name of the party to contact. In addition, Mike asked Shube's to employ the DOC Agent/Distributor Service (described in this chapter and Chapter 42) for Japan at a cost of $250. Shube's rushed out 15 copies of the catalogs and sales literature needed by the US&FCS office in Japan and thereafter phoned the Japanese national who would be handling the survey. Shube's found him to be knowledgeable of the jeweler sector and its appropriate commercial contacts in Japan. The two remained in periodic contact, and about six weeks later Shube's was presented with a list of five companies that had shown a "medium" interest in the silver jeweler portion of the company's line. In this case, the Japanese national with US&FCS felt Shube's should select three firms to gain some firsthand experience in Japan and to negotiate with each firm before deciding on one exclusive distributor. All three Japanese companies employed between 7 and 25 employees and had sales of between $4 and $16 million.

Global asked Shube's to send a sample selection without charge to the interested companies to get feedback from their customers as to design, quality, and prices. Global felt that this would assure the deliberative and consultive decision-making process the Japanese prefer. They also encouraged Shube's to display its best and key products with new, high-quality packaging designed especially for Asian sales. This had the advantage of proving to the prospective Japanese customers that Shube's was taking the long view of its market development.

Shube's director of international sales, Doug Lopez, thereafter visited Japan with appointments to see all the distributors on the final list. All were well aware of the jeweler's line and time could be taken to develop the beginning of personal and trusting relationships. On his return, the final sample lines were prepared and the agreements drawn up. A relatively small but aggressive company, Shube's could look forward to good long-term business in Japan and the start of a meaningful international market share.

Making the Final Selection

To make your representative selection as sound as possible, consider sending a courteously worded but purposeful questionnaire. This should be simple, covering only the facts and background concerning the representative and perhaps asking for a business plan or suggestions for your product and how it would relate to the representative's present offerings. A request for the company's projections for the first year or two is a good idea. Include the following information in your request:

- Names of owners and the managing director

- Date established

- Banking and trade references

- Size of the firm's turnover and number of employees

- Size of sales force

- Product categories

- Firms represented (and whether exclusive or non-exclusive)

- Office and branch locations

- Warehousing and service facilities

- Territory regularly served

- Primary category of customer

Answers to your questionnaire will quickly reduce the size of your candidate list. The good representatives will be especially interested and responsive if you can provide them with similar background information on your own firm, as well as with detailed product information. If you have already targeted a certain firm, but have received no reply, don't hesitate to write again, or better yet, try a telex or FAX contact. If you feel sure there is no language barrier, a telephone call can also be extremely effective.

If the territory is important to your overall strategic plans, it is always a sound investment to visit final prospects in their own countries and, circumstances permitting, it can be very helpful to have them return a visit to your own plant before making the final decision. At the least, it is wise to defer a final choice until you can visit the prospects on their own turf. It is also wise, unless you are absolutely convinced of the qualities of the representative, to minimize the territory of exclusivity. It is no more possible for them to do a first-class job of personal representation throughout the geographically larger countries of the world than it would be in the United States. If a decision must be made without a personal visit, put it on a clearly stated trial basis for a short period, with a definite ending and no automatic renewals, or at least with clearly stated minimum sales to renew depending on the laws of the country. DOC's *International Business Practices* (see Appendix K), is an excellent country-by-country reference for this purpose.

Drawing Up the Agreement

After finding the right representative or distributor, the first step to gaining full cooperation is to agree on a contract so that the representative will feel fully involved and know you mean what you say, even if it is only on a trial basis. A handshake and your assurance that no contract is necessary is unlikely to motivate or create confidence in the new association. If a trial period is to be utilized even after a personal visit, note the conditions mentioned above relative to such an agreement, and in any case check the country practices and laws relative to agents and distributors through your attorney and/or in the *International Business Practices* book. A recital of the major conditions to be included in the permanent contract can forestall objections to the trial agreement.

If cost and availability make it feasible, by all means consult an attorney. Be sure the attorney or an overseas correspondent of the attorney has a working knowledge of international law and has access to the agency and commercial laws of the country in question. Even with an attorney and your preliminary check with the DOC *International Business Practices* book, it is wise to call the appropriate country desk in the International Economic Policy section of the DOC (see Appendix A), and ask about the primary difficulties regularly experienced with representative or distributorship agreements in the specified country. Broadly speaking, the areas in which you should take special note are Latin America, Europe, and the Middle East. The major developed trading countries of Asia offer relatively few problems.

Whether dealing with a representative or distributor, your understanding should be clearly stated in a reasonably formal written agreement. If the budget is limited and the agreement need not be too formal, you will probably save some money by drawing it up yourself and then requesting your attorney's review and suggestions. At least get the basic business agreement together in words that both parties clearly understand, and then let the attorneys formalize it. You may wish to discuss points you want to negotiate first with your own attorney, but thereafter it will save considerable cost not to involve the attorney while the prime parties thrash an agreement out. Furthermore, it often leads to a better understanding by the contracting parties. Briefly stated, the following points should be covered:

- Careful description of the product.
- The territory—which might be an area surrounding a major city, a country, or several countries.

- Exclusivity conditions.

- If commission is involved, the cost basis that may readily be calculated by both parties, such as FCA, CIF, or ex factory value and timing of periodic payments. Both points must be stipulated.

- Allowance for price changes, with a specific time for notice.

- Nontransferability of assigned rights.

- Barring of any dealing with the competition or revealing confidential information to same. (If applicable.)

- Responsibilities concerning advertising, inventory, and maintenance facilities. These must be clearly spelled out.

- Locale of jurisdiction governing the agreement.

- Term of the agreement and specific conditions for renewal or termination.

Contract provisions, which are subject to frequent change—especially to change by mutual agreement or stipulation within the contract period—are better stated in an appendix or attachment than within the body of the contract. This would include such items as pricing, perhaps even territory, if the territory is likely to expand, requires a great deal of description and minimum annual sales volume, if the contract entails other conditions that must be met before the representative/distributor can exercise the renewal clause. Changes can be made by initialing the new attachment, provided that the complexity of the basic contract is kept to a minimum. If a firm has a number of contracts, the variables in each can be readily found.

John H. Norton, a speaker and writer on international trade as well as a consultant for Business International Corp., with offices at 530 Broadway, San Diego, CA 92101, suggests with much validity that there are many items that should not be included in a representative/distributor agreement. Keep in mind, for instance, that they are seldom maintained by legal sanctions, certainly not at a price acceptable to most small and midsize companies. Norton correctly describes them as similar to "treaties between nations—they continue to be honored to the extent that they benefit both parties."[5] Agreements fail because of inadequate market research, the inability of at least one of the parties to perform, or because market demand shifts. Only a relatively few fail because of bad faith. The ability of the agreement to overcome these problems is limited. This does not imply that there should be no agreement or that it should be drawn carelessly or taken lightly, but it does indicate that spelling out each and every detail is of little consequence to the ultimate success of the venture. What is important is to set realistic goals based on market size and to rationally determine a share of that market. This is best done in writing in order to facilitate termination if necessary and to ensure that the two parties share and mutually understand an achievable goal in an atmosphere of good will and joint purpose. We subscribe to Mr. Norton's premise that contracts can be unnecessarily long and even serve to wreck what might otherwise be a good deal for all.

Therefore, as possible clauses are considered, think as hard about the possibility of "no need" as "need," and avoid putting in clauses merely for the sake of their existence in a format or model contract.

Today every writer on the subject of representative/distributor agreements stresses the increasing problems surrounding termination. About 65 countries have enacted laws to protect their buyers, distributors, and agents, and this is one subject that should never be ignored. Each writer on the subject includes cautionary tales, and Belgium figures in so many of them that a recent writer even referred to termination troubles as the "Belgium trap." The country has extremely tough rules and compounds the problem by differing from normal practice in giving its distributors more protection than its representatives. Laws and attitudes change, therefore, the safest course is to consult an attorney and/or independently research private and government sources. Because the European Union (EU) represents so many sales territories, it's important to be aware of the recent EU *Directive on Independent Commercial Agents (86/653EC)* covering one of Western Europe's most protective agent laws in the world. A chilling clause states a "definite term agreement which is renewed by both parties after expiration of its initial term is deemed to be indefinite." Therefore, not only is a definite term important, it also indicates that subsequent, automatic renewals should surely be avoided. Other language in the directive makes it advisable to avoid clauses that require a distributor to establish and communicate customer lists or market-share information compiled by a distributor. Such provisions are taken to imply a degree of control that is associated with an agency relationship.

Evergreen clauses should be avoided because, if they permit automatic renewal without changes in the contract, they make termination very difficult and the inevitable compensation much higher when there *is* any kind of agency protection under the law. In addition to changes in definite terms, any contract or attachment should be changed from time to time to avoid an implied automatic renewal and, therefore, an indefinite term. Various legal just-cause reasons for termination should be clear and in writing, based on measurable objectives that appear to be commercially reasonable in the context of that country and the market. John Masterson, Jr., chief counsel for the International Commercial Transactions office of the DOC, suggests another good rule to consider: "The longer advance notice of termination or nonrenewal in the contract, the greater the exporter's chances of avoiding substantial compensation obligations."[6]

It bears repeating that the use of the word *agent* is discouraged by attorneys because of the authority an agency relationship implies and the widely varying interpretation of that authority from country to country and among the various legal codes. *Representative* is preferred, and some experts, believing that even this is too broad, suggest *appointee*.

In general, governments are much more protective of their agents or representatives than they are of their distributors (with the notable exception of Belgium, already mentioned). Many courts will insist on compensation being paid to the representative for loss of income and on reimbursement for the cost of establishing the territory in the event of "unjust" termination, even at the end of a contract period. Penalties for cancellation may be imposed for what in the United States might be considered good cause. These comments highlight some of the chief problems and the importance of research and legal advice. It might be well to review the distribution agreements section of Chapter 34 that relates to antitrust laws.

To provide a starting point for discussion with your legal advisor, there is a distributor agreement in Appendix Q we developed over a period of time initially stemming from a model distributed by the DOC many years ago. Note that it was never used for a distributorship that required extensive after-sale servicing or highly technical products but otherwise it functioned quite satisfactorily for many relationships. Some attorneys would consider it already too long (keep in mind our comment above about clauses for the sake of clauses); other attorneys might feel there are many issues it fails to cover. To adapt it to an agreement for representation instead of distribution, the agreement does require deletion of certain key responsibilities and a few wording adjustments. In some cases, you might simplify it even further. Keep in mind, however, that representatives or distributors cannot waive rights relative to local law that concerns termination, either knowingly or unknowingly, by terms of the agreement or by the U.S. company's choice of state law in most cases. This foreign law exposure is often overlooked.

For a more comprehensive agreement and mention of additional concerns, you may want to look over the "International Sales Agreement" in *Export/Import Procedures and Documentation,* by Thomas E. Johnson, an international attorney associated with the Baker & McKenzie law firm.[7] Johnson's comprehensive book examines all documents relevant to import and export and contains an excellent discussion of possible clauses, together with sticking points between seller and buyer and suggested compromises. For instance, on pricing, Johnson explains that it is impossible in some countries to restrict the minimum resale price, while the maximum price can be controlled. This can be of importance in prohibiting the distributor from overpricing the product. Another consideration in pricing is the possibility that exchange-rate fluctuations will make it possible for the distributor in one country to create a gray market in competition with distributors in another country which has a less favorable exchange. Therefore, you may wish to retain the right to adjust the export price within certain exchange-rate boundaries if the distributor does not make corresponding adjustments of the resale price. With regard to exclusivity and territory, it may not be possible to prohibit a distributor from selling in other markets (especially in the EU), but you can prohibit it from establishing warehouses or sales outlets outside the territory.

Another issue not addressed elsewhere concerns the need in some countries for government approval. If this is required, it should be stated that the agreement does not become effective until after government review. Elimination of minimum purchases, for instance, may make the manufacturer or EMC/ETC desire to renegotiate the entire contract, including its term. Johnson also suggests that the right to appoint subdistributors should be subject to approval or even denied because of possible loss of direct contact and control. He further suggests going beyond making it clear that intellectual property rights, such as patents or trademarks, are not granted with a statement that the representative agrees to take no steps to register them or otherwise interfere with the ownership rights of the seller.[8]

Regarding agents, Johnson recommends that commissions be made payable only through direct wire transfer to the agent's bank in his or her country to avoid any violation of that country's foreign exchange control or tax laws. He also suggests having the agent recognize the existence of the U.S. Foreign Corrupt Practices Act and agree not to make any payments that might violate its provisions.[9] (See Chapter 33.) For those wishing to be sure their own attorney that is fully informed on agency or distributor contracts or who feel they must do them themselves, two very definitive and extensive works were published in 1993 by ICC Publishing, Inc. (related to the International Chamber of Commerce) named *ICC Model Commercial Agency Contract* and *The ICC Model Distributorship Contract,* at a price of $85 and $39.95, respectively.[10]

As a final note to the legal aspects of foreign distribution, you might wish to use a program called Export Legal Assistance Network (ELAN). This is a SBA nationwide network of attorneys with experience in international trade who are willing to provide free initial consultations to small business exporters. They will not prepare a contract for you, but they may discuss with you the agreement you are proposing, the special pitfalls you face, or any general, export-related legal problems you have. Call 202/778-3030 or 800/U-ASK-SBA for the nearest district office.

Foreign Retailers and Other End Users

If your interest is in selling to retailers directly—especially to the larger retailers in a particular country—there are books available describing the department stores of the world and some of the major specialty stores. These books contain complete information as to size, management, headquarters and branches, merchandise range, names of department heads, and a great deal more. For information on European retailers, the most current of these books is *Directory of European Retailers.*[11] A new edition is published every two years. Your DOC district office also keeps a list of the department stores around the world that are actively importing and those that might be planning specific American promotions.

There are limitations in selling directly to retailers, including follow-up difficulties. Because store buyers' assignments are subject to change and there is frequent personnel turnover, you may often lose prime contacts. However, with good catalogs and occasional visits to keep acquainted, this avenue can be moderately successful. Note: You will have difficulties later if you decide to use a representative and have failed to quote prices to the retailers that permit an agent's commission or distributor's margin.

Any arrangements for direct selling to end users overseas is outside the realm of this book. It would entail a highly unusual and unique arrangement that would not be of interest to most exporters. Home selling is as effective in many foreign countries as it is here. Some airport shops and duty-free operations do very well selling to the foreign tourists homeward bound. Products for sale include everything from the standard duty-free products known to all travelers, to special meat cuts and bargain-priced rice in ten-kilogram bags for the Japanese.

Endnotes

1. *The Export Yellow Pages,* William A. Delphos of Venture Publishing, N.A., 1995, published in cooperation with the U.S. Department of Commerce.

2. Registry of Export Intermediaries, 1996, National Association of Export Companies (NEXCO) and SPC Marketing Co., P.O. Box 364, Northport, NY 11768.

3. Richard Barovick, *Trading Company Sourcebook,* International Business Affairs Corp., 4938 Hampden Lane, Suite 364, Bethesda, MD 20814.

4. *Trade Directories of the World,* Croner Publications, Inc., 211-03 Jamaica Avenue, Queens Village, New York, NY 11428.

5. John Norton, "What *Not* to Put in a Distributor Agreement," *World Trade,* Fall issue 1988.

6. John T. Masterson, Jr., "Drafting International Distributorship and Sales Agreements," *Business America,* November 21, 1988.

7. Thomas E. Johnson, *Export/Import Procedures and Documentation,* 2nd edition, AMACOM, Saranac Lake, NY, 1995.

8. Johnson, ibid.

9. Johnson, ibid.

10. *ICC Model Commercial Agency Contract* and *ICC Model Distributorship Contract,* ICC Publishing, Inc., New York, NY, 1993.

11. *Directory of European Retailers,* Newman Books, 33 Vauxhall Bridge Rd., London, SW1 V2SS, England, biannually.

10

Selling Services

Much of the information in this book applies to exporters of services as well as to exporters of manufactured goods and agricultural commodities. There are some differences, however, that deserve special attention in terms of exporting services. The services sector is the fastest-growing sector of the economy. It is expanding so rapidly as a percentage of our gross domestic product (GDP), that services are now responsible for roughly 75 percent of nonfarm private employment (almost 68 million jobs). It's no wonder that the United States is the world's leading producer and exporter of services, accounting, at $3.4 trillion in 1993, for more than half of the nation's GDP. Even though service exports have more than doubled since 1987—reaching $173 billion in 1993—service exports have still attained only a fraction of their potential, according to the Trade Promotion Coordinating Committee's National Export Strategy Report to the U.S. Congress in October of 1994.

While the service sector accounts for some of our lowest-paying jobs, it also includes many of our most highly compensated positions, such as doctors, lawyers, and football or baseball players. As analyzed by the DOC, the top ten service exports in rounded numbers are as follows:

Tourism	$54.0
Transportation	40.0
Financial services	11.0
Education and training	6.5
Business	6.0
Telecommunications	3.3
Equipment (including installation)	3.0
Entertainment	2.8
Information	2.6
Healthcare	0.7

As part of our overall balance of payments account, private business service exports are less dominant than are services in the domestic economy, but they are skyrocketing as a segment of our exports. In 1993 services were over 25 percent of the total U.S. merchandise exports as a percentage of Gross National Product (2.7 percent versus 7.3 percent in goods exports), or over one-third the dollar value of goods. Exports are very much a plus factor in our international trade balance. Services are the one area in which the U.S. has a substantial trade surplus. Service exports are an elusive statistic, but were estimated to be in the range of $80 billion in 1987, $120 billion in 1990, and an estimated $174 billion in 1993. These numbers represent only business-related, private sector services, which include consulting and professional services, but not investment income.

Regardless of a number of government trade barriers that confront our export services sector, services remain highly competitive exports. They tend to go into the most sophisticated of the world markets, even though the engineering and design category of services are in great demand for Third-World infrastructure projects. The primary U.S. markets are the European Union, at $52.4 billion in 1992 (representing a 16 percent increase since 1991), Japan at $25.6 billion, and Canada at $17.6 billion. The National Export Strategy, however, anticipates significant growth for service exports in Asia, Latin America, and Eastern Europe. While the Mexico crisis will temporarily slow the growth in Latin America, franchising has already made giant strides in the last three to four years in that area.

Many future merchandise exports are created by professional services statistically described as "unaffiliated services." This design and consulting category accounts for more than 20 percent of business services and encompasses engineering, architecture, and planning, plus many other technical consultants, and ultimately has an important multiplier effect on exports of American manufactured goods. One-third of the total private business services category is represented by travel and transportation. Most of the balance is made up of licensing fees, copyrights, and royalties, which account for about 10 percent of services.

Federal Assistance

Department of Commerce

Service exports have a separate section in the DOC/ITA organization chart. But considering the very substantial value that they represent in dollars and as a percent of total exports, services probably deserve far more than the budget and staff allocated to them. In fairness, however, there are a number of offices and agencies that also directly support consultants and contractors as part of their overall program. The name of the primary office is Service Industries and Finance (202/482-5261), which is within the same Trade Development unit that provides many other functions for services exports as well. (See Chapter 42.) Within the Office of Service Industries (which appears to have been recently downsized) there are two divisions:

1. *Information, Entertainment and Professional Services Division.* This division includes entertainment services, data processing and electronic databases, advertising, direct marketing, franchising, professional services, statistical services, and education and training services.

2. *Transport and Health Care Division.* This division includes health care services, land transportation, aviation, retailing and wholesaling, and environmental services.

Within the Office of Finance there are also two divisions:

1. *Trade and Project Finance Division.* This division relates to Eximbank and multilateral aid programs.

2. *Financial Services and Countertrade Division.* This division includes insurance, banking, mutual funds, investment banks, commercial banks, countertrade operations, venture capital groups, lease financing, factoring, and forfaiting services.

The Office of Service Industries and Finance is planning a realignment of these divisions and responsibilities that was not finalized at the time of this writing. However, the above will provide a general idea of the office activities and staff orientation in these divisions. One of the first priorities of the staff is to counsel exporters concerning existing opportunities, techniques, and strategies, as well as to provide help in suggesting the best network, publications, or channels for finding and pursuing available opportunities and leads.

According to the National Export Strategy Report, the federal government's Trade Promotion Coordinating Committee (TPCC), through an interagency effort led by DOC, has mounted one of the most ambitious strategic plans in all the industry divisions in services. This includes continuing support to remove barriers beyond GATT and NAFTA through negotiation and a focus on market expansion, both in the traditional markets and in the emerging Asian and Latin markets. Significantly, it also includes specific efforts on an industry-by-industry basis in information technologies, air transport, entertainment, insurance and other financial services, including mutual funds. At this writing, missions are planned or completed in China, South Africa, Brazil, and Argentina. There is a special sectoral focus on such energy services as safety, design engineering, training, conservation, technical support, and similar services. This effort is being led by the Department of Energy and the Environmental Protection Agency. Tourism is being considered for special study, and improved statistical analysis of the export services is being sought. There really is a major emphasis on interagency cooperation as part of the strategy.

The DOC might also be of help through the ITA Trade Development unit's Office of International Major Projects (although this has recently been downsized) and the Office of Environmental Technology (if you are in the technology field). The District Offices could be still another source of help for leads once you inform an alert trade specialist of the services you are offering.

Trade Development Agency

A related but specialized entity outside the DOC is the Trade and Development Agency (TDA) which funds Technical Assistance Grants to bring U.S. technical assistance to bear on a variety of projects and feasibility studies. Before a feasibility study is authorized, the agency often hires a technically qualified consultant to visit the country, discuss the plan with the project sponsors, and define the study's work program, or Definitional Mission. Even though TDA will accept suggestions for initiating studies, feasibility studies must be approved by the host country, which then hires the U.S. contractor and pays with TDA funds. TDA also makes trust funds and grants available to the major multidevelopment banks to finance consultancies and feasibility studies. The agency's participation typically is in the range of $150,000 to $750,000. (Its activities are discussed again in Chapter 13.)

Help from MDBs

Be sure to contact the Multilateral Development Bank Operations (MDBO) office in the DOC. It has US&FCS officers stationed in the World Bank and the other MDBs who can help advise you about current and future MDB projects worldwide and how to do business with MDBs, and can guide you to on-line electronic project information relating to consultant opportunities. This might include the Technical Assistance Trust Funds for developing countries available to U.S. consultants. Call TIC at 800/USA-TRADE for details, contacts, and phone numbers of the various staff desks. (See also chapters 13 and 42.)

World Bank

The World Bank, a large user of technical assistance, operates a consulting availabilities facility. Its database is called DACON (DAta on CONsultants) and the facility can be contacted at 1818 H Street, NW, Washington, D.C. 20433 or reached by fax at 202/334-0003 to obtain a DACON registration kit at no cost. The World Bank makes DACON available to most other MDBs, which also have many consultancies, so that registration there will also register you with many other multilateral banks. DACON will only accept registration from consulting firms with at least five permanent professional staff, although registration is not necessary to be eligible for selection. Individual consultants seeking to sign up may forward a resume or CV to the World Bank's Recruitment Division at the above address. It no longer provides consultant roster forms to individuals, but instead utilizes a staff panel to review each individual's qualification for inclusion in its register. Consultants are selected on the basis of experience, skills, and quality of proposal rather than on the basis of cost. The World Bank urges consultants to obtain a free copy of the bank's *Use of Consultants by World Bank Borrowers and by the World Bank as Executing Agency* and *Guide to International Business Opportunities*. These can be obtained directly from the bank or from the DOC/US&FCS Multilateral Development Bank Operations (MDBO) in Washington, D.C.

Most of the major MDBs have similar guideline publications. For example, the Inter-American Development Bank publishes a booklet called *Business Opportunities for Consulting Firms.* Consulting is called Technical Assistance by the MDBs and is a very important part of their activity. As an operational component of the World Bank, it amounted to $2.2 billion in 1993. Of that amount, $1.9 billion funded project components, while $300 million was for 22 free-standing technical assistance projects. U.S. consultants obtained by far the greatest share of this in both number of contracts awarded and total value.

Agency for International Development

A ready-made source for standing offers of a particular service to less developed countries is the Agency for International Development (AID). (It is discussed in context in Chapter 13.) AID encourages registration in the Consultant Registry Information System (ACRIS) for professional and technical services, which are often required for AID-financed projects. ACRIS is a computerized database listing U.S. firms and individuals and their technical service capabilities. The intent is to match them with appropriate AID projects relative to offering and bid opportunities. The same opportunities are announced in the *Commerce Business Daily,* a DOC publication.

Special Considerations

The search for opportunities to provide a particular service overseas depends less on statistical analysis and channels of distribution than on networking and on tracking appropriate projects as they develop. There is no ten-digit classification system for services and little relationship between the problems of establishing a financial service, such as a bank, and offering custom software design or bidding on a construction or engineering project. If you wish to review a comprehensive listing of service industries and consultants to help you identify and name your own service offering, you might want to look at the *Annual Survey of Current Business,* put out by the DOC's Bureau of Economic Analysis and available in any of the 900 Federal Depository Libraries. It gives a detailed listing of services exported and the dollar volume of activity, which may provide an idea of the potential for your service.

As mentioned in Chapter 7, service companies are not excluded from ISO 9000 problems and rewards, which can definitely impact a firm's acceptance as a service provider in Europe and elsewhere. In an article in the March 1995 issue of *Export Today,* Barry Lynn reports that service providers ranging from freight forwarders to engineering firms have reported some surprisingly favorable results for performance and profit after putting themselves through the ISO 9000 standards process.[1]

Not everything can be accomplished through the various government offices and agencies. Many service providers will find it necessary to market their services directly after identifying a lead. There are clear differences in techniques and problems in marketing services abroad. Most services are harder to sell than products are by means of letters, brochures, and other forms of nonpersonal communication because they are intangible. They are also much more difficult to standardize as to quality, or even quantity, which is evidenced by the wide range of estimated figures as to total annual volume. These differences underscore the necessity for more personal contact and communication. Service providers often have only themselves to sell, and generally within a fairly narrow time frame. While this is also true in domestic markets, the problems of travel and verbal communication are obviously compounded in the case of working overseas. A certain amount of country and culture research can pay off very handsomely in terms of correctly framing the service offered, determining its use, and making the actual presentation of the personal service.

There is another important and troublesome difference between exporting products and exporting services: financing. Because there is no tangible merchandise for the lender to secure or to inspect in the event of a dispute, it's more difficult for the service provider to obtain financing. The uncertainty of the overseas buyer in terms of assured performance after, as well as prior to, performance means a far greater likelihood that performance bonds and elaborate inspection procedures will be demanded. The service provider in turn often needs protection in the form of downpayments, which can give rise to requests by the buyer for advance payment bank guarantees. For these reasons progress payments, as well as performance and payment triggers, are especially useful in drawing the contract. Look into the U.S. Export-Import Bank's and SBA's Working Capital Guarantee and other programs (described in Chapters 39 and 40). Also look into possibilities for financial support through your state's export finance support program (discussed in Chapter 44).

Endnote

1. Barry Lynn, "Service Companies Go ISO," *Export Today,* March 1995.

11

Overseas Travel

With your target markets selected and correspondence under way—and perhaps even a few key representatives or buyers in place—it is time for a trip. A serious effort at international marketing cannot be made without travel any more than you could establish a market share in this country without visiting your customers and understanding the marketplace. As a matter of fact, this observation is probably even more valid overseas. Whether you are an independent exporter or the person selected to start your company's export program, at this stage of your marketing efforts it's time to plan a trip if these efforts are to fulfill their purpose and potential. It's an investment that simply must be made. Thorough advance market research and initial communication with key prospective representatives or buyers will maximize the effectiveness of any trip as well as minimize its costs. Again, the excellent books, *Do's and Taboos around the World* and *Going International,* on cultures and business practices, mentioned in Chapter 8, are suggested background reading.

Planning the Visit

Any overseas trip has to be planned well in advance and properly organized to be successful. Otherwise it can become an expensive form of frustration and exhaustion. Since the target countries have already been selected and organized by world market areas, it should only be necessary to decide when to travel, taking into consideration local holidays, vacation time (for example, France is practically closed during the month of August), and religious holidays (doing business during the month of Ramadan is out of the question in any Moslem country, just as the week from Christmas to New Year is in Western countries). Request a copy of "World Commercial Holidays," published yearly in *Business America,* from your DOC district office for more detailed information.

Holidays, weather, and similar considerations can be dealt with more easily if you have grouped the countries as discussed in Chapter 8. The optimum time to be away on any given trip will vary with your traveling experience, the extent of your duties in the home office, and the pace of your trip. Assuming a fair load of other duties in the home office and a tough travel agenda, two and a half to three weeks is optimum. Some experienced travelers will stay as long as seven to eight weeks, but you can be sure they have a place to hang their hat for a week or so in the course of the journey. More than six or seven weeks away (and much less than that for most people) will leave you feeling completely out of touch with what is going on at home. With an extended itinerary and a busy agenda, it will be months before you can effectively travel overseas again, even though you should plan on a regular pattern of trips each year.

Apart from jet lag, foreign travel is much harder on the human system than domestic travel, even though the initial exhilaration of such travel may mask this fact. You can come home with too many notes, too much to follow up on, and too much time already elapsed between your promises and your performance. Furthermore, after a certain period of time, your perceptions tend to become blurred, with everything tending to look good or bad, black or white. For many people, the amount of time needed to recover fully from such a trip will be about equal to the length of the trip itself.

One of the first concerns for the trip should be your passport, which must be valid for the duration of your trip. In addition, many countries require a visa that must be obtained through the foreign country's embassy or consulate in the United States. Be sure to apply for these documents well in advance of your departure date. Obtaining a visa from some countries, especially those in the Middle East, can be a difficult and time-consuming process. There are specialized visa services that may be able to speed things up and they are often a wise investment. The United Arab Emirates and Kuwait, for example, not only require that a "host" from that country invite you, but also meet you and vouch for you during your stay. Arranging for this alone can require weeks. In most countries requiring a visa, you have the choice of applying for a tourist visa or a business visa. Most seasoned business travelers will advise you to apply for a tourist visa, even though you will have briefcases and sample cases with you. Only if you plan to physically sell or transfer goods, earn money, or undertake similar activities is it prudent to request a business visa. The tourist visa is more easily obtained and customs officials seem to feel less compelled to give you a difficult time.

Time Factors

Allow enough time to correspond with the people you want to see in each country and make as many of your appointments as possible prior to your departure. Confirm both your airline and hotel reservations in advance and advise your contacts of the hotel in which you are staying and the date of your arrival, so they can advise you of any unforeseen changes. If you agree to be met at the plane, you run the risk of being ensnared for the remainder of your visit, giving you limited ability to make other contacts. There are other cases, however, in which being met may be both wise and appropriate.

When setting up advance appointments, it is usually best to make only two firm appointments in the morning and two in the afternoon, using any free time between meetings for additional appointments, research, or to make telephone contact for meetings the following day. Because of the many differences in customs, including language and transportation, each contact will take more time than a similar arrangement or meeting back home. The cultural differences are challenging enough; don't complicate them further by making your prospects feel that they are being rushed (translation: "hustled").

Getting ready for a fairly complex international trip can be the biggest challenge in your secretary's career, to say nothing of your own. A separate agenda and log, prepared in advance for each city of destination, is a very helpful tool. Include in the log each advance appointment, subject, telephone number, address, name, code reference to prior key correspondence, and so forth. Leave room in the log for a few cue words to indicate the result of the meetings and whatever follow-up is required. Also, indicate the name, telephone number, and address of parties that you did not make appointments with but that you might want to contact once you arrive, and leave similar blanks for the complete surprises. This log is no substitute for the detailed write-up, summary, and analysis at the end of your trip, but it will keep you on track while in the foreign city, and provide cues for your upcoming efforts. Take what opportunities you have to make notes of your reactions, promises, and strategies. Your memory will not be as good as you think it will be after a host of additional meetings and the passage of even a few days.

Be sure to leave free time for new appointments or follow-up appointments. This free time should total between 25 and 50 percent of the time specified for your advance appointments, depending on how well organized you are in advance. Never think that your plans are so well laid that no time for additional appointments needs to be reserved unless you are on a routine goodwill tour of established accounts or representatives. Unplanned meetings can come about through referrals by embassy officials or even through some of your initial contacts who may suggest another company more suitable for your product line.

The reason for leaving free time is not only that these unplanned meetings are often your most valuable leads but also because some of your advance appointments may need a second visit for any number of reasons. Speaking of unscheduled time, one very good use of it is suggested by Stuart Mechlin in the July/August 1993 issue of *Export Today*.[1] His slogan is "Shop Till You Drop." He believes that shopping can improve sales by leading to a better understanding of how the country really works. It can amount to serious market research and help identify business opportunities, because shopping allows you to become like everyone else: a customer. You gain a better understanding of the "real" economy and how prices are arrived at, as in the case of haggling. It can also give you insights into quality standards and the infrastructures of distribution and transportation. If you are accompanied by your host, going shopping can also serve as an opportunity to build a relationship. If nothing else, what you finally purchase will be a good conversation starter with others at future meetings. Last but not least, going shopping eliminates the need for last-minute souvenir hunting at the airport.

Still another reason for allowing extra time is the possibility that you may have to make a major itinerary change, especially if your travel plans call for several world areas. Between uncooperative travel bureaus, relatively limited flight schedules (often not daily), and the difficulty of juggling hotel and plane reservations, arrangements for such a change of plans can easily take a full day. Quite apart from time, however, digressing from your original transportation package can be very costly. You may discover that the cost of flying back to Stockholm from Copenhagen, for example, represents a big percentage of your original entire round trip, multistop, international air ticket. It is encouraging to learn, however, that as this is written, European airfares are getting less expensive as some of the former national airlines become more competitive through privatization or semiprivatization.

Another complicating factor in setting up your itinerary and advance plans—as well as in changing them—is the variety of business hours and business days in various countries. As an example, businesses in Middle Eastern countries are closed on Fridays. Although it is diminishing, the siesta still lives on in hot countries (definitely this does not apply only to Latin America). Check for duration of lunch hours in other countries—they can range from 30 minutes to four hours.

Jetting around from country to country and region to region can provide the opportunity to work virtually seven days a week. Don't take it! Considering the high cost of travel, your conscience might encourage such a seven-day-week schedule, but here, as in no other situation, you need a day of rest. Even if you are a workaholic, you need a day to take stock of the situation, to make notes and summarize, and to orientate yourself—to say nothing of doing a little sightseeing for relaxation and the chance to get a feel for the nature of the county and people you are selling to.

Samples

Some of your most challenging times while traveling can be caused by your samples, especially if they are heavy or bulky. Organize your samples so that they are easy to carry and demonstrate. If you have an extensive assortment of valuable commercial samples or professional equipment, apply for a carnet, especially if you are traveling on a business visa. A *carnet* allows you to take material to the more than 30 countries that are members of the ATA Carnet System for a temporary period of time without paying duty. You will be required to put up cash equivalent, a bond or letter of credit as guaranty for 40 percent of the value of the samples in most cases to cover duties that would be due in case you do not return to the United States with the samples. Before your departure, be sure your carnet is officially executed by United States

Customs and the goods examined and cleared by customs at the point of export to avoid penalties and delays on your return. Read the instructions on your carnet carefully.

On the other hand, if you are traveling on a tourist visa and your samples are easily recognized as samples and are of little value, it might be best to simply declare them as samples. Occasionally, it may be necessary to mutilate them or in some way render them useless for resale. This is most likely to be the case in parts of Latin America and possibly Africa. This alternative can save considerable time at customs, since customs officers' handling the carnet and comparing it with the samples can cause additional delay. You may choose to have a carnet available but use it only when really necessary. It is best to experiment for yourself initially while being prepared for the worst. The value of the carnet depends on the nature and resale value of your samples and what countries you are visiting, as well as on the kind of visa you are using. For information about ATA carnets and countries that are part of the carnet system, contact the U.S. Council of International Business, 1212 Avenue of the Americas, New York, New York 10036; or call 1-800/ATA-2900 for number for branch offices of the Council whose business is selling bonds for ATA carnets. You may also wish to speak to the nearest U.S. Customs office on this subject.

Before finalizing your plans, you might wish to contact the country desk officer at the DOC in Washington about any current special conditions in the country that you are about to visit. Then contact the foreign commercial officer in the countries you wish to visit (see Appendix A) and advise him or her of your travel plans and needs. If possible, contact such officers when your plans are firm and advise them exactly when, and in what way, you will require their assistance.

The commercial officer in the American Embassy or Consulate can be of considerable assistance to you by arranging introductions and briefings, and in some cases, even providing office space and related services for a modest fee. But do not expect this person to have done much on your behalf prior to your arrival. Unfortunately, many business travelers who have advised embassy staff of their plans in advance end up changing their plans without notice. Some simply fail to visit the embassy as promised. Therefore, make this one of your first stops when you arrive. Commercial officers and their foreign national staff can be extremely helpful if you give them a chance and some of your time once you are in the country.

Travel Tips

Stay in first-class business hotels, since they are usually less expensive than the luxury hotels. Staying in better hotels will pay off in most cases, especially if you are new to the area. Many hotels have business service centers that can help you with communications, translators, secretaries, fax and telex machines, and general business information above and beyond the excellent assistance a good concierge can provide. You might want to suggest initial meetings in the hotel lobby to save time in large cities or in cities that are difficult to get around. You are in much better command of any situation in such a hotel, which probably caters to English-speaking guests, than in one where you might have language difficulties getting any kind of service. In addition, since both you and your appointment share a bit in the prestige of the surroundings, your contact will often suggest a lobby visit in a first-class hotel.

Even though it is easier to make telephone contact to reconfirm meetings or establish new ones from your room, hotel telephone service is usually not as efficient as in the United States, and business customs and practices are quite different. Frustration abounds for American businesspeople trying to make calls that don't go through to people who cannot understand them. Plan ahead and be prepared to get help from the hotel operator, the embassy, or a translator.

It is usually best to change money at the airport of entry. In most countries it is about the best rate you will get, and not much different from what you would obtain if you were to take the extra time to find a bank in the center of the city. The airport rate is almost always much better than the hotel rate. An alternative for the well-organized traveler is to obtain, before stateside departure, one of the standard coin and currency packets from a currency exchange firm that contains just about enough currency to get you to your hotel and into the room, in case you arrive late or the lines at the exchange kiosk are very long.

As you leave the airport for your hotel, try to find the transportation information stand, but at all cost, skip the taxies that hound you before you ever approach the taxi stand. Their rates are usually much higher than those of the regular cabs at the stand—in some cases, three to four times as high, including those later to be found in front of first-class hotels. Get the driver to agree on the price in advance. In some countries, such as Saudi Arabia, these drivers might even have the hotel employees so intimidated that they fail to tell you that such cabs will cost double or more, depending on how gullible you look.

Finally, no matter how adventurous you consider yourself to be as a vacationing globe-trotter, control yourself when you are traveling professionally. The stakes are higher, the risks are greater, and the results can be less than stimulating. There is nothing that says you can't have an interesting and enjoyable time on the trip, but "going native" with local transportation, local little inns, and local rental cars is really not advisable on a business trip. If you must try them out, do so in your spare time.

Negotiation Techniques and Adaptation to the Culture

If you are new to the territory, brush up on your original target country research. Recall the basic facts about the country and the industry associated with your product in that country. Since it is always good practice to be informed and considerate, also remember the local courtesies and social practices. Libraries and bookstores have many books on the practices and customs of most countries and/or regions. (A number of these books are listed in

Appendix K.) For a quick, in-flight review, the "Culture Grams," developed by Brigham State University's Center for International Trade, offer excellent information. They cover more than 100 countries in separate leaflets and are inexpensive. Edward T. Hall's classic article "The Silent Language of Overseas Business," written in 1960, is still valid.[2]

Whatever the country, once you meet your prospective customer, let that person set the tone. Refrain from smoking until invited to do so. Use last names and don't ask personal questions until you are sure a less formal approach is desired. Subjects considered "too personal" include chitchat about the wife and children. This is a topic that is simply not discussed in many countries until you are well acquainted—if ever. It follows that there is no need to discuss your own personal life, if for no other reason than that it is embarrassing to your guest not to respond in kind. If there is a language barrier, convey sincerity and let your product speak for itself. If in doubt, tend to be formal, but not stiff.

Cultural Negotiating Styles

Besides the importance of attempting to adapt your social habits and business practices to the country you are visiting, there will be additional peculiarities and techniques to keep in mind relative to negotiating the deal. For help along these lines, there are many books on negotiating techniques. (You'll find a number of these books listed in Appendix K.) John Norton packs a lot of common sense on the subject of cross-cultural negotiation into a recent bulletin, which offers the chance to reflect on your individual negotiating style. Mr. Norton suggests:

> Consider the following cultural differences: The tolerance of silence in a conversation, the importance of cleanliness, orderliness and punctuality, the amount of trust or suspicion toward strangers, respect for age and gender, the number of inches at which the presence of another person becomes uncomfortable, the value of time, the relative trust placed in institutions versus individuals, the meaning of eye contact, competition versus consensus, the precise meaning of certain gestures, and the nature and use of humor. All of us receive a notion of what is right behavior very early in life, about the same time as we acquire our native language. These attitudes are so deeply held as to be almost inherited. They interfere with the transmission of what is apparently rational information such as goals, agendas, procedures and promises.
>
> One cannot let these concerns overwhelm one's confidence, but a little thought when reading of the culture may permit adjustments to be made that will minimize errors. Some traits that may need to be adjusted arise because Americans in general are intolerant of silence; are open-hearted and trusting, but put strong emphasis on winning; are legalistic, moralistic, individualistic, and impatient. They tend to disagree openly among themselves in front of the other side. Knowledge of these characteristics is very helpful to foreign negotiators. A number of bad agreements have been made by Americans in a hurry at the end of a trip. Knowledge of one's own culture as seen from abroad can help Americans protect themselves. American naivete can also be a mask.

During actual negotiations overseas, we recommend that you become as self-conscious of your style as you are of your tennis or golf game—enough to improve your game but not to interfere with it.[3]

There are so many principles, details, and nuances that could be considered that it would be folly to hope to digest them all and presumptuous to pretend here that we can do more than mention just a few of the most important. (This is best proven by the length of the reading list we have provided.) Nevertheless, just to give you some idea of the variety and complexity of the subject, below is a list of basics adapted from an article by Kerry Pechter in the March 1992 issue of *International Business:*

- Germans bargain like Americans. They stress clarity, precision and literal interpretation of contracts. They will pursue their self-interests, maximize their advantages, concede as little as possible, and hide their hole card. It's ok to bring your lawyer with you. The above also applies to the Swiss.

- Japanese seek flexible relationships. Don't expect snap decisions; they must retreat, confer, and reach a consensus. Nods don't necessarily signal agreement. Leave your lawyer at home.

- Koreans negotiate with Americans from a position of strength. Compared to the Japanese, they have a straightforward, American negotiating style. Koreans respect status: in Seoul, hire a chauffeur and emphasize your link with Fortune 100 companies.

- Latin Americans establish specific positions and bargain hard; but they communicate through hints, nonverbal clues, and intermediaries. Pay close attention to the location and mood of the meeting. Choosing the right restaurant or wine can speak louder than words.

- Britons speak the same language as Americans, but the similarity stops there. Citizens of the U.K. resent aggressive, direct demands. Sensitive issues should be broached over an informal dinner or through intermediaries. Don't "micronegotiate." Get the big picture right, and the details will fall into place.

- Russians have been taught by history to be inscrutable, stolid, and skeptical. Then Communism crushed their entrepreneurial instincts. Basic concepts such as risk need to be explained. Capitalism remains slightly shameful, so stress the social benefits of a deal. Establish trust, and the details will follow.[4]

The best tactic is to study what you can, when you can, with attention to logical priorities based on the importance of the deal and the immediacy of the need. You will probably never get it all just right unless you live in the country. Simply be aware of some of the most crucial blunders and know that the other side is probably thinking and reacting along quite a different line than you are. They may be expressing pleasure and displeasure in ways that are almost the opposite of your own. Knowing that will make for better business and improved relationships.

Successful Cross-Cultural Negotiation

Quite apart from cultural and political nuances, in order to create a solid business relationship, you should enter into negotiations with some preconceived and fundamental concepts and issues, from which there should be no departure. These should be discussed with those responsible in your firm before the trip abroad or before foreign visitors arrive. The following is a good start for putting those basics into shape as set forth in *Going Global: Strategies and Techniques for New Multinationals* by Business International Corporation.[5]

> Preparation is the key to successful international negotiations. Before sitting down at the bargaining table, you should know your industry, company, products or services, export and import regulations affecting your products, and as much as possible (including financial information) about the company or customers with whom you are dealing. Arrange for an interpreter if the other party does not understand or speak your language fluently. Give the interpreter appropriate background material before the meeting, such as company literature that will familiarize him or her with product names, technical jargon, and so forth. Also, brief the interpreter on your objectives, technical issues to be discussed, and other matters likely to come up at the meeting.
>
> Basic negotiating skills are transferable to all cultures and countries. Here are some general guidelines:
>
> - Establish the least you will accept (your "walk-away" point) before starting negotiations.
> - Always have at least two people on your team—one to talk and one to listen and take detailed notes. Write up the notes after each session, and have the participants compare them at the next meeting. Although this can be time-consuming, it is essential when a series of small agreements are being reached or points are being conceded that lead up to the overall agreement.
> - Volunteer to draft the agreements. It is always advisable to be the one who does this; the other participants then react and respond with revisions. (Since drafting means hours of extra work after the negotiating sessions, the other side is usually willing to let you do it.)
> - Be careful not to make one small concession after another so that in the end you have given up too much. Consider the various requests and look them over at the end of the day in light of the entire package.
> - Be ready with delaying tactics if the negotiations reach a difficult point. (For example, announce that you must check with your technical people at the home office.)
> - Leave enough time. Do not set strict deadlines that can hurt your position.
> - Remember that the aim of negotiations is to work out a deal that is best for everybody.[6]

Follow-Up

The first few days and weeks following your return from a trip are vital to the overall success of your travel objectives. A speedy follow-up will not only reinforce the good impressions made on your trip, it will also impress your contacts as to your sincerity and efficiency. The agenda and log of the city-by-city contact list, with notes for purpose and results, will be very helpful. What seemed crystal clear during a particular meeting will look quite different to you in your own office two or three weeks after the meeting.

Because there is so much to do and catch up with on your return, it is a real advantage if you can make rough drafts of some of your planned correspondence while still en route. You will be clearer on what was done and said, and it will save precious time on your return. This can be done by mailing dictation tapes back to the office; better yet, you can send your handwritten drafts by fax or modem. On a long trip these might even be utilized by a trusted colleague back home to send a preliminary note assuring them of your interest and advising they will be hearing in detail from you soon. Incorporating at least part of your trip notes into a draft letter form will not only help focus your thoughts on the meeting, but also keep your trip narrative as brief as possible. If notes are too copious or too hard to read, you may never read them on your return home.

As a seller of U.S. products, you may encounter ready-made interest and a predisposition toward confidence in your product—or at least in some product areas. But you may also encounter concern about our country's lack of commitment to export. Overseas customers and representatives have suffered many times as a result of this deficiency. Evidence of a positive commitment on your part—through a show of genuine interest, immediate follow-up, and the presence of a master export distribution plan can do a lot to dispel such concern and boost the confidence factor.

Follow-through includes thank-yous even when nothing concrete was agreed on, as well as taking care of your commitments and promises. But in the larger scheme of things, follow-through is what really proves your commitment to the international marketplace. It probably takes a domestic salesperson who has been left out in the territory too long with too little support to fully sympathize with the overseas representative or distributor who can't seem to get a reply to inquiries, much less discuss a problem in person.

Distances, other languages, and different modes of operation all contribute to the isolation felt by your overseas representatives, and you need to go out of your way to compensate for this problem. If it is possible, bring them to your plant or your supplier's plant on occasion. By all means make sure these representatives can count on regularly scheduled visits from you or other appropriate parties. This is true even when your representative, distributor, or customer is a native of the region and has other affairs or products to attend to. It's essential to keep in touch, which is much easier with today's multiplicity of communication systems. Because communication technology *is* so available, however, failure to stay in touch can create more resentment than in the past when doing so was more difficult.

Some consideration should be given to regional managers in terms of commitment and strategy. Naturally, having regional managers depends on potential volume and the number of countries and regions of the world in which your firm is involved. But assuming that you are involved in multiple regions, the possibility of regional managers should be considered as one means of achieving constant contact and supervision of the territory, and keeping both representatives and customers in touch and well served. It is doubtful that one export manager can supervise the problems at home *and* visit the foreign territories long enough, or often enough, to express the kind of commitment needed to succeed against worldwide competition.

Erik Wicklund, author of *International Marketing,* strongly urges the use of such regional managers. Furthermore, assuming that Americans are employed overseas, he reasons that in the long run it may be cheaper to base them in the United States than in the various regions.[7] The exception might be in cases where managers indigenous to the region are used. Unless the product is highly specialized and both it and the firm are somewhat prestigious, it can be difficult to gain the full loyalty and understanding of local staff.[7]

Endnotes

1. Stuart Mechlin, "Shop Till You Drop Pays When Doing Business Overseas," *Export Today,* July/August 1993.

2. Edward T. Hall, "The Silent Language of Overseas Business," *Harvard Business Review,* May/June issue, 1960.

3. John Norton, "Cross-Cultural Negotiating," *World Trade* magazine, February/March 1990.

4. Kerry Pechter, "Can We Make a Deal?," International Business, March 1992.

5. *Going Global: Strategies and Techniques for New Multinationals,* Business International Corporation, 215 Park Avenue South, New York, NY 10003.

6. *Going Global: Strategies and Techniques for New Multinationals,* published by Business International Corporation and written by a team effort in cooperation with many contributors in the field, 1992.

7. Erik Wicklund, *International Marketing—Making Exports Pay Off,* McGraw-Hill, New York, NY.

12

Overseas Promotion

The advertising effort begins with your first overseas letter in search of representatives, distributors, or retailers, as you introduce your company and product to explore your target market. In that initial act, you are starting to establish your image. Remember this as you draft your letter and decide on enclosures. Your image is further reinforced during the course of your introductory trip, through your actions and conduct, perhaps even by your choice of hotel; certainly by the way you follow up on your travels and your succeeding promotional efforts, including advertising and trade events.

Direct Mail

The most common means of advertising for smaller exporters, or until a market is established, is through correspondence and brochures—in other words, through direct mail. While in many parts of the world it is sufficient to use your American brochures, it is better to translate the essential material. Even though your professional or business audience may be able to read English, translation into the local language is evidence that you are serious. Suppose you spoke a little French—how much time would you spend trying to read a form letter or brochure in French? And in many cases, the language of a brochure is harder to translate than most prose.

To see what the competition is doing and how your type of product is advertised overseas, ask your distributor or other foreign contacts to send you newspapers and magazines covering your product field. Also, work with your distributors or representatives concerning user-instruction translation, training manuals, and other key material.

You might be sending out direct-mail letters and brochures long before you have distributors or representatives, and even if you already have a few, the success of the direct-mail campaign will depend on your source and quality of mailing lists. This was mentioned in Chapter 9, but bears repeating and enlarging in the context of more general, broader-based promotion. The careful development and acquisition of mailing lists is a key step to export success or failure.

Leads from foreign readers of domestic trade and technical journals in which your product appears editorially or in advertisements is naturally one of the very best sources for direct mail follow-up. By the same token, should there be fairly product-specific domestic publications, it might be possible to buy or rent their foreign subscriber lists. Lists also can be gleaned from importer directories, foreign visitor listings of domestic trade shows, visitor lists from overseas American pavilions, classified telephone directories, and your own American trade association (including foreign associate memberships). Mailing lists can be purchased from private companies' lists covering all types of customers—retailers, wholesalers, and other end users, including representatives and distributors—by product.

Land Grant of Land Grant + Company is an export marketing consultant and international direct-mail specialist in Brooklyn, New York, and current president of the National Association of Export Companies (NEXCO). Grant writes a continuing series on what he terms "BtB IDM" (an acronym for business-to-business international direct mail) that expands and reinforces comments concerning direct mail. His thoughts on international direct mail naturally include the premise that the foundation of a successful direct-mail campaign is the renting or finding of properly targeted and profiled mailing lists.[1]

Demographic segmentation by age, income, occupation, and similar criteria are important. For demographic segmentation to mean anything, one must first do the research and achieve an understanding of the geography and cultures of the target country. Grant explains that, with the word processing and related electronic technologies available today, personalized and/or "rifle shot" overseas direct mail campaigns can be a low-cost method of export marketing on a per-sale basis, especially if your product is a big ticket item.[2]

The trick is to find the owners of the right lists. One source is a specialist list broker or agent who is in the business of renting or selling lists which may have been compiled from original research to meet prior requests or which can be prepared specifically for your own use. Some lists are very large and broad but sufficiently broken down into criteria so that they can be segmented to fit very precise profiling definitions. Lists that have been successfully used before have the advantage of having passed the test.[2]

If list development interests you, Mr. Grant suggests a tool with the intriguing name: trade tripod. The tripod he has in mind is made up of trade publications, trade associations, and trade shows. Use this basic business cluster to take advantage of efforts already expended by any of the three that parallels your own interests.

The first leg of the tripod is trade publications. Any large business library reference room will have the resources (databases, catalogs, directories, etc.) you need, and the librarian can help you. Writers of articles in trade publications that focus on your product category can be contacted for still more specialized information, connections, and resources. The trade journal publishers themselves are a rich lode of carefully screened names, and these lists are often for sale or rent. Because English is the primary language of business throughout the world, there are few areas and publications that are inaccessible without interpreters.[3]

Trade associations for your industry are the second leg of the tripod. Many have their own specialized libraries, replete with names of people and membership lists, but you may have to invest in joining some of them to gain access. *Trade shows,* the third leg of the tripod, can yield the richest rewards if the shows include, as most important ones do, visitor centers and lists of prior attendees and exhibitors. The show directory and catalog alone can be a gold mine. If the DOC has certified a foreign trade show, such lists from prior shows will be available, as will foreign visitor lists for major domestic shows, sometimes conveniently available on floppy disks. Some of these lists can be obtained without even attending the show, although attendance as a visitor at least is always an advantage. Make note of the principal speakers and seminar leaders. Mr. Grant's final suggestion is that, besides searching in your own industry, you should do some exploring of publications in the direct mail industry while you are at the library. The industry has its own trade publications, shows, and associations, and your research may turn up some ideas to make your task faster and easier.[4]

In addition to these sources, there are all the facilities of the US&FCS described in Chapter 9 and summarized again in Chapter 42. To recap, these facilities include the Foreign Traders Index (FTI), the Export Contact List Service, and the TOP trade leads, which are available through printed sources as well as by fax or modem on the Economic Bulletin Board. Chapter 9 also describes the FAS facilities of the Department of Agriculture, with their highly targeted buyer and commodity database. The FTI lists provide considerable company information to permit such screening if you take the time to consider the information. In addition there are the numerous private lists available from a variety of sources and with varying degrees of verification and profiling as suggested by Mr. Grant.

The very targeted services mentioned in Chapter 9, such as the World Traders Data Reports (WTDR) and the Agent/Distributor Service (ADS), are too expensive for general direct-mail promotion lists, and are for use after a prime prospect is found or when seeking a specific representative.

Media Advertising

Should you seek broader exposure than direct mail can provide, publications prepared in the United States can be a cost-effective and relatively inexpensive means of getting started or supplementing direct mail. Set up a reasonable budget based on your projections and your pocketbook, just as you would do in going after a market share in a new American territory. After the budget is estimated, check the costs, which can vary widely. In the beginning, your budget will probably be somewhat limited, so you might first experiment with the lowest-cost media.

Government-Supported Advertising Media

The U.S. Department of Commerce (DOC) publication, *Commercial News USA,* is an example of government-supported advertising and is described in Chapter 9. This publication offers a relatively low-cost means to experiment with display advertising and editorial advertising. It is definitely one of the best of the US&FCS promotion programs, and the rapid rise in its cost proves it. Just two or three years ago, the minimum ad was under $200, but in 1995 it has climbed to $395. Some of the US&FCS overseas offices have begun to produce their own publications for their specific territories to supplement *Commercial News USA.* Other publications are produced by port authorities and state- or city-sponsored promotional organizations that also provide an opportunity for free or low-cost advertising to all the new-to-export companies to gain a foothold in international marketing.

Commercial Publications

Many American trade publications and technical journals are regularly read all over the world and represent relatively good advertising buys in some cases. One journal publisher, who specializes in overseas markets, is Johnston International Publishing, 25 Northwest Point Boulevard, Suite 800, Elk Grove Village, Illinois 60007; phone 708/427-9512. It has two publications targeted for overseas readers: *Export* and *Automobile and Truck International.* Both publications are printed in both English and Spanish.

Another magazine designed for American exporters and overseas buyers, is *Showcase USA,* published in the United States by Sell Overseas America. It is a bimonthly magazine sent to all U.S. embassies and foreign posts as well as to regular overseas subscribers. Many exporters have reported excellent success with this type of advertising. For details and rates for *Showcase USA,* contact Sell Overseas America, 2500 Truck Boulevard, Redondo Beach, California 90278.

Foreign Media

Your opportunity for limited-cost cooperative overseas advertising will depend on who your customer is. Distributors selling complementary product lines may want to include your advertising in their own program and will ask you for an advertising allowance. An overseas retailer may include your product in its catalog or other advertising campaign. An alternative could be to support these retailers by providing some of your domestic advertising material, layouts, and camera-ready copy and leave initial advertising costs to them.

To otherwise save on costs for your start-up overseas advertising budget, consider advertising in foreign trade publications to gain access to retailers, representatives, and importers. A good source for these, also previously mentioned in Chapter 9, is the *Trade Directories of the World,* published by Croner Publications, Inc.[5]

For trade publication advertising and certainly for the more costly general advertising, an advertising agency is probably the safest way to proceed. Consider an agency operating in your target country, one that is completely familiar with the market and helps analyze all media available. Some local agencies might be associated with a large American advertising agency; however, use care that the American associate shares only the commission but not the attention to your account. Obtain names of overseas advertising agencies from the International Advertising Association, Inc., 475 Fifth Avenue, New York, New York 10017. Also check the annual international issue of *Advertising Age* for references.

In an article in the February 1992 issue of *International Business,* David J. Morrow writes that several small companies needing foreign publicity press releases on a limited budget have used a company called Industrial News Service, based in Stockholm, Sweden, with great success, gaining releases in about 60 top European trade magazines at a modest cost.[6] Another company reported about 20 clippings from European trade magazines at a cost of $5000. Several companies report a good rate of inquiries from these releases and expect costs of from $2000 to $8000 per project, but the catch is that the negotiated fee must be paid, regardless of the number of resulting clips, if any. The service firms mentioned in the article include INS, with offices in Stone Ridge, New York; Bacon's Information Inc. in Chicago; and the IR Service Bureau in New York City. It would be worth checking into these.

If you have overseas contacts, let them assist you in making the final decision on which agency to recruit. The media best suited to your product in other countries might differ from those you are using in the United States. In countries with high illiteracy, consider advertising on radio or television. In some countries, however, such media do not even carry advertising. In addition to publications, outdoor advertising can reach a wide audience and direct-mail consumer marketing can also be successful.

Review any copy and layout carefully and, if possible, get input from several local people as to its effectiveness and comprehensibility. Some of the worst horror stories about mistakes American firms make in selling overseas have resulted from disastrous double meanings or translations that are much too literal. You have surely seen or heard examples of such mistakes as a result of foreign advertising efforts in this country.

Depending on the printing process used and the material available in the country in which you are advertising, the quality of reproduction may not be what you are used to. In some cases, however, notably Japan, it may be superior. Any basic photography and layout material you provide will possibly improve that quality. In the case of cooperative advertising, besides requesting and approving copy, layouts, and storyboards, you should also require tearsheets or other proof of publication, just as you would in this country.

Trade Fairs, Trade Missions, and Catalog Exhibitions

There are several levels of international events and organized trips that vary in impact, preparation, and expense.

Industry-Organized Domestic Fairs and Exhibitions

Almost every major industry in this country has its own organization, such as the National Sporting Goods Association, the American Electronic Association, and the National Restaurant Association. These organizations set up annual or semiannual exhibits in this country and sometimes abroad, which are attended by potential customers from around the world. This is an excellent opportunity to make new and worthwhile export contacts, and even though it is a domestic event, it should not be overlooked as part of your overall export effort.

Unfortunately, many firms are represented at these shows by strictly domestic salespeople who ignore foreign contacts. As any manufacturer knows, it can be difficult enough to assure all domestic customers good service if they happen to be outside the salesperson's immediate territory. Salespeople and even corporate executives, orientated solely to domestic business, all too often dismiss inquiries from foreigners and throw away the business cards left at the company's booth year after year. Finally, an unusually aggressive foreign buyer successfully presses the company to sell to them, and suddenly the American firm realizes how many opportunities have been wasted in the past.

Government-Sponsored or Certified Events

To find out about catalog shows, trade missions, fairs, and exhibitions set up by the DOC in any of your target countries, call the TIC number we have mentioned so often, 800/USA-TRADE, to find the best contact for you, depending on the kind of show and your target countries. If your product falls into one of the seven major industry sectors that is covered by the Trade Development Office, you might wish to contact your particular specialist in Washington, D.C., who will also know about most other promotions and programs in that particular industry in any foreign country. (See Appendixes D and E.)

Catalog Shows

Catalog shows are mentioned first, not because they are the best, but because these events are a bargain-priced international marketing tool. They may therefore represent an inexpensive first approach to direct overseas marketing. The DOC organizes a limited number each year for specific products in key foreign cities in a region. Each participant provides a supply of catalogs. An independent party, selected from the industry's trade group, or a qualified trade specialist, is retained to answer basic questions from attendees and report interested buyers or representatives to the participants at the end of the show. The catalog show gives the participant a lot of exposure for the cost, but your fate is in disinterested hands and you are showing your catalogs impartially, side by side with possibly ill-matched competitors.

The success of catalog shows is largely determined by the support given by the overseas post. They are usually successful in less-sophisticated markets and in places where the opportunity to actually see new products is rare. Catalog shows can be a good lead generator for direct-mail programs. While some shows produce little or no direct sales results, once in a while a catalog show can be the start of some very good business.

Trade Missions and Matchmakers

Also inexpensive and uncomplicated are the trade missions, which are more specialized events, usually organized by the DOC and FAS, but sometimes by your state's business development or commerce office as well as industry and trade groups. Trade missions organized by the DOC usually include about 12 participants in a single product category and cover several countries in a geographic region. The total cost, including travel, ranges from about $3000 to $6000, which is much less than an important trade fair.

The DOC puts in a lot of advance work in terms of scheduling, arrangements, and publicity, and in that sense you get your money's worth. Unfortunately, offers for participation are often extended to firms without too much regard to qualifications. Another problem is that you are solely dependent on the prospective representative's or buyer's response to the DOC publicity. In contrast, an established trade fair for which you know about how many and what kind of buyers will be attending is far more predictable. There is often a fairly high ratio of curious consumers that are of little or negative value at trade missions.

Trade missions are probably best used for getting the feel of a new market and perhaps for making a tentative start. DOC matchmaker events, mentioned in Chapter 9, have created interest recently and are specifically organized to find representatives or joint venture and licensee partners. Trade missions or matchmaker events also may be useful as a crash introductory course in exporting for key executives in a firm that is just becoming interested in exporting.

The International Trade Fair

The full-scale trade fair is the most important promotion event for many exporting companies. It is also the most expensive, whether the DOC is involved or not. The decision to participate in a trade fair should be an integral part of your overall marketing plan and be subject to the considerations already discussed concerning product adaptation, country targets, travel plans, and followthrough. The fact that the DOC has chosen not to make it one of its certified or sponsored fairs should definitely not be the deciding factor, although it's a plus if the DOC is involved. The DOC's decision not to involve itself in a specific trade fair can be the result of time, staff, or budget limitations or of the fact that an insufficient number of American firms have shown interest in it.

Many of the comments on trade shows that follow can be adapted on a lesser scale to the decisions and efforts already discussed in respect to trade missions and catalog shows. The trade fair can be viewed as an opportunity to make a final decision on extending your market to additional target countries, as well as a primary means of marketing to a given region. Even done on a modest basis, however, trade fairs are expensive, and can easily range from $10,000 to $25,000 or more. Costs can be held to a minimum by joint participation in DOC-sponsored U.S. pavilions or in shared state booths. Besides cutting costs, the pavilions can be of great aid and comfort to first-time exhibitors. The Department of Agriculture's FAS also organizes or participates in fairs for specialty-crop and high-value agriculture products. There are both federal and state programs, including outright grants from FAS. Often, matching funds from state economic development or agriculture departments can be used to defray trade fair costs.

To keep the cost of such events in perspective, The McGraw-Hill Laboratory of Advertising Report #8018.3 quotes the following costs in the late 1980s for a business-to-business sales call in Europe. The average was $640.13, with a range from $128.18 in Ireland to $1439.62 in Denmark, with Germany near the median. The average number of calls required to close a sale was six. (Although these figures are fairly recent, dollar value fluctuations create an undefined distortion quite apart from increases created by inflation.) The study was based on a survey of 699 sales executives from ten European countries.

Trade fairs provide an excellent market research opportunity to look over your competition and talk to other people in the industry. For this reason, it is useful to visit an important show as a visitor attendee before full-market entry. This will serve as a prime research tool and a reinforcement of your overall marketing plans, and the result will be a greatly enhanced knowledge of your new market territory.

Selecting the Right Event.   First decide on your target countries, then see where and when trade fairs are scheduled. Trade fair availability might modify your goals but should not control them. Select fairs that are right for you in terms of product, territory, and cost.

There is no advantage in investing in the largest and most expensive fairs that bring buyers from around the world unless you are capable of serving a reasonable percentage of the prospects that visit your booth. It might be better to find a less expensive regional fair in which you can pay more attention to all contacts, and in which your product will be more easily found and perhaps have a little less competition. Also consider your objectives and the nature of the event itself. Trade shows in Europe tend to be major buying and selling events. In Japan there is much less actual business done, and the emphasis is on meeting people in the industry. Therefore, look into the effect that the cultural differences will have on the show's objectives. The Japanese External Trade Organization (JETRO) has published a book entitled *How to Succeed in Trade*

Shows and Exhibitions in Japan. Contact one of the JETRO offices listed in Appendix H for your copy.

When seeking assistance from the ITA desk officers or trade specialists as to which fairs to attend, keep in mind that the DOC might be trying very hard to fill up a pavilion, and therefore might not be entirely objective. The same applies to your state or your trade group.

Do some of your own research and ask questions of those in charge. There are books published periodically that list trade shows and fairs worldwide for just about all products. Some are distributed by the various industries, some by the DOC, and others are issued as a courtesy by the trade offices of the various nations. The latter can be found by calling the consulate of the countries in question. There are also commercial publications covering all industries in all countries. Lufthansa German Airlines has in the past offered at no cost an annual *Calendar of Events for Trade Fairs and Exhibitions* that covers most of the world. Ask questions within your industry about the fair's general reputation, past participants, and sponsors. Other good sources for trade fair research and similar events are the *Country Marketing Plans* and information on previous shows which can be obtained from the involved US&FCS foreign offices.

The decision to participate in a trade fair must be made well in advance because deadlines for final commitments typically run from six months to one year, and the later you commit, the less desirable your booth assignment will be. Get postshow reports and all other information possible about the fair from its organizers. Many shows will have an American representative located in this country who can be very helpful. Find out if DOC or your state or trade group intends to be involved. As mentioned, this can substantially reduce the booth costs, to say nothing of easing your way into this form of marketing if you have not already practiced it domestically.

If the show is held seasonally, determine which is the best season for the first-time attendee. This can make a big difference because of buyer reluctance to start with a new resource in the lesser season. Learn who will be showing, what countries will be represented (by sellers and buyers), entertainment practices, hotels, preshow and postshow activities, facilities, availability of translators, and possible competing events within the industry.

Planning for the Fair.   Once you have selected a trade fair, set up your budget, determine your objectives, and plan your preshow promotional program. In preparing your budget, consider what you must allow for entertainment in the booth. This can run from a few goodies to very elaborate efforts. Avoid being stampeded into large expenditures here, even though you hear that some exhibitors do make costly investments. As a new participant you will attract some special interest anyway, and you have no prior reputation to maintain. You should, however, allow for some entertainment costs during and after the show, and hope that by then you really do have justification for entertaining.

Consider also the cost and need for translators. Even though most of your visitors will speak English, it is a courtesy that will make you friends and help visitors feel more comfortable if they can turn for help to a combination hostess-translator. DOC shows often try to have such roving translators as part of your package cost.

Another cost element is booth decoration and furnishings, which are estimated to equal the rental costs of the booth itself. Shared American or state pavilion participation often helps on this score as well. As a smaller company, you have an advantage because, except for the jumbo booths, you can project a corporate image that compares favorably with those of much larger companies if your booth is well designed. One means of helping you gain an oversized image is a brief video presentation of your product line designed for trade fair use. The appropriate language is readily dubbed in and it is a proven tool used by small firms as well as large. A number of firms specialize in preparation of these videos at a reasonable cost.

In terms of objectives, your purpose might be to find a representative or distributor, to make direct sales, to better understand your market, or a combination of all of these. A lot of representative/supplier negotiations occur during such shows, and sometimes the knowledge and contacts of a prospective representative are put on a trial basis at fairs. If this is attempted, be certain a very competent and experienced person from your company is in attendance at all times.

The promotional effort for a particular fair should be started several months in advance. This is usually done by direct mail, but some shows offer media opportunities to reach the attendees. If the budget is limited, go for the direct contact first. The trade fair promoters can provide the names of attendees at previous shows. These can be the best contacts, but for a really big show you will have to have some means of sorting out the names, since the total list may be too large. Check your own prior contacts and the DOC or private lists. Consider translating your basic brochure into the appropriate languages if you have not done so before this event.

Part of the promotional effort might be a preshow press conference if you have a unique new product or some other newsworthy item. Even if you cannot arrange a press conference at the fair, you may be able to get an advance story into your own trade press or technical journals that have a large overseas subscriber list.

Sometimes technical symposiums are conducted simultaneously with fairs featuring high-tech products. Papers are presented and new techniques and products are discussed by experts. Your participation in this part of a trade fair can be the key to a new product launch, an opportunity for free publicity, and/or recognition in subsequent trade journal publications. Major fairs receive intensive trade press coverage.

If you are thinking of making the show part of a larger overseas trip, be careful not to arrive at the show already tired and with used or abused samples. It is better to plan any additional traveling for after the show. Regarding samples, check for an official show freight forwarder, as this is usually the best way to get your samples safely through customs and to the show on time.

Carefully check all requirements regarding export licensing, customs, and carnet details. Make certain that you are at the show on time, which means early enough to be sure that your booth is well set up, that the samples are displayed properly, and that you have time for any show briefings and press conferences. Have your exhibit staffed at all times and see that you and your staff give every appearance of being attentive and alert. Anything less can be counterproductive to your image in the new market before thousands of potential buyers. It is also a good time to take a look at your competition, so try to have someone who can replace you at the booth at least part of the time. Have business cards on hand in appropriate languages, or on the back side in case the language does not use our alphabet. Include your fax and telex numbers if you have them. If you do not at least have your own fax (with a dedicated phone line) make arrangements with a local fax service in any large city, which can be found in the Yellow Pages under Fax Transmission Service.

Even if you are determined to only quote FOB in your normal export affairs, have accurate CIF estimates on hand for the principal overseas ports to which you would expect buyers to request shipment. And, of course, if any product modifications are being considered, now is the time to know what effect they will have on delivery and price.

Follow-Up.   Plan to stay in the vicinity of the trade fair after the show for a day or two for follow-up calls or meetings. If the show is expected to draw from a large area, cover that area during the remainder of your trip. There will never be a better opportunity to make your investment in the trade fair pay off.

All the rules for follow-up to your trips discussed in Chapter 11 apply here as well. In the case of trade fairs, follow-up can be complicated somewhat by the numerous business cards you'll be left with. Even though they will not all merit individual correspondence, do send some kind of a mailing piece that will remind them of you, and most important, tell them how to reach you.

Endnotes

1. Land Grant, "International Direct Mail," a three-part series of monographs published in the February, September, November 1993 issues of the *Exporter* magazine.

2. Grant, ibid.

3. Land Grant, "International Direct Mail," the fourth of a four-part series of monographs, of which the fourth is not yet published, but summarized here courtesy of Mr. Grant.

4. Grant, ibid.

5. *Trade Directories of the World,* Croner Publications, Inc., 211-03 Jamaica Avenue, Queens Village, New York, NY 11428, published periodically.

6. David J. Morrow, "Need Ink Abroad?," *International Business,* February 1992.

13

International Bid Opportunities

This chapter is intended to alert small and midsize exporting manufacturers and service companies to opportunities available by bidding on international projects. This area of business is woefully overlooked by almost all U.S. businesses except the industrial giants and a handful of major engineering and consulting firms that have made it one of the core sectors of their business. Yet there are many opportunities for the small but alert manufacturer and service provider, especially today, when international projects are smaller but more numerous and often very technologically oriented. Some small businessmen are already at work in this untilled field and making fine profits as a result. One reason many other small firms fail to get involved is the amount of advance tracking and effort required where international bids are concerned. But more often, it is simply lack of awareness of the opportunities provided by the World Bank; by the multilateral development banks (MDBs); by the U.S. Agency for International Development (AID); by the United Nations; and by other sources of assistance. Some of these agencies and MDBs offer an American bidder a built-in advantage, but U.S. firms on the whole are handing a huge piece of business, along with the wealth and employment that accompany it, to competitor nations.

Multilateral Development Banks

A multilateral development bank (MDB) is part development agency and part bank. An MDB promotes long-term stable economic growth in developing nations, by lending funds to those nations. It takes responsibility for sound financial decisions and oversight relative to such development loans and the management of the MDB's assets. Because a variety of nations contribute funds to MDBs and are involved in MDB programs, MDBs are said to be *multilateral*. MDBs create abundant and readily available opportunities for U.S. firms to do business with less-developed countries (LDCs) without the currency and credit risks that are otherwise encountered. Although the DOC is making it a high priority to increase its outreach in this area via the relatively new Office of Multilateral Development Bank Operations in US&FCS, there is still insufficient concentration on MDB opportunities by American exporters. What interest there is tends to focus on the East Coast. As of mid-1994, according to Treasury figures, MDBs had awarded some $2.83 billion worth of contracts (probably only a fraction of the true total) in the United States over "the last several years." New York state was number one with $493 million from 220 contracts, closely followed by Texas at $474 million, Illinois with $244 million, Colorado $205 million, and finally California (the first-ranked in gross state product) in fifth place, with $205 million from 147 contracts. California's foreign project management firms helped its fifth-place showing, but when the state's role as the dominant economic power in the nation and the largest U.S. export state is considered, it clearly highlights how the activity level declines as one moves from east to west. California's place among the Pacific Rim nations did make it the leader in terms of Asian Development Bank (ADB) procurement. In a 1994 report entitled *The Multilateral Development Banks: Increasing U.S. Exports and Creating U.S. Jobs,* then-Secretary of the Treasury Lloyd Bentson stated that no more than 40 percent of the disbursements made to U.S. firms was captured for the report year.[1] There is now an effort to start tracking MDB contracts state by state as we realize what an enormous potential impact MDBs could have on the U.S. economy and how much more business could be achieved if U.S. firms better understood the MDB process and the opportunities it represents.

Today, smaller companies and service providers should be especially alert as the MDBs' emphasis—and that of the U.S. Agency for International Development (AID) and the U.S. Trade and Development Agency (TDA)—shifts from huge infrastructure projects to projects more concerned with communications, technology, health, alternative forms of energy, and the environment. This means smaller—but more—infrastructure projects with an increased demand for small business technology and technical consultants. Included are import substitution projects through local production process technologies and export promotion by means of trading companies, national export banks, and foreign buyer insurance agencies. In all, the MDBs are making commitments of roughly $45 billion each to 150 developing countries around the world, according to the Treasury report, an amount far beyond the capacity of any single donor or bank, including the World Bank or the United States government.

Bid Qualifications and Participation

Companies such as Bechtel and General Electric depend on projects that are financed by MDBs, but they must seek a wide variety of subcontractor bids because of the diversity and complexity of such projects. Even though you might be a third, fourth, or even lower level subcontractor or exporter, depending on the product, there is literally a world of opportunity awaiting you if you are qualified and interested. This is especially true of projects for which a U.S. firm may enjoy a "home court" advantage over foreign competition—as, for example, when AID is assisting a project or when the TDA has financed the feasibility study, thereby providing a preference or an outright requirement for a firm of U.S. origin. The United States also enjoys a considerable influence in World Bank projects because of the bank's location in Washington, D.C., and because of the very substantial U.S. investment in the bank.

The same is true if the project is being cofinanced or supported by the U.S. Eximbank or the Overseas Private Investment Corporation (OPIC). In fact, projects are increasingly being cofinanced among several of these agencies plus an MDB. Don't ignore, however, the many other projects that do not enjoy this special advantage but which might be equally suitable, depending on the product and the special qualifications of the company. To illustrate the matter of special qualifications, take a hospital project in an African country. The country, for political or cofinancing reasons, may have an overall preference for England, France, or Germany. However, as a manufacturer or distributor of high-tech hospital equipment, you may have an inside track for that subcontract by virtue of American preeminence in this area. The same could be said for pumps, spare parts, telecommunications, or design and consulting.

It is important, however, to understand that this is an extremely competitive business and, with rare exceptions, should not be considered as an underlying base for most company's export efforts. Rather, it should be looked on as an adjunct, or additional business to improve your company's total marketing and sales effort. In most cases, the originating bidder must be prepared to provide bid bonds in the range of 2 to 5 percent and subsequently, if successful, performance bonds in the range of 5 to 10 percent, or even 15 percent on occasion. If an advance payment is involved, it will usually be necessary to put up a bank guarantee that is roughly equal to the down payment you are to receive. Refer to Chapter 22 for more information on standby letters of credit that are required for such bonds or guarantees.

According to a 1986 U.S. Chamber of Commerce report, *How U.S. Firms Can Boost Exports Through Overseas Development Projects,* professional advisors and participants in the MDB bidding arena feel that the major reason American businesses don't do better is their failure to identify future projects early and thereafter to pursue them vigorously.[2] What success the United States has enjoyed from MDB projects awarded to date has been largely because of U.S. success in consulting contracts.

Even worse than American companies' inadequate tracking of forthcoming projects, or their delayed involvement when they do become aware of such opportunities, is the simple fact that the vast majority of American management knows little or nothing about the subject. A case in point is the fact that many American businesses mistakenly believe that bids are awarded by officials in the

MDB countries, rather than by the host country. This basic misunderstanding automatically leads to improper follow-up and completely unnecessary procedural problems. The traditionally strong areas for MDB financed business include: energy, transportation, industrial equipment, agriculture, education, and telecommunications.

More recently the following areas have become important: investment and financial services, auditing, municipal development, health, water and sewage, environment, housing and tourism.

Our major competitors for this business are Japan, Germany, and the United Kingdom. The U.S. Chamber of Commerce found several factors in its surveys that seemed to account for the lack of a more active pursuit of the MDB business on the part of American business management. These were:

- Ignorance, even among relatively sophisticated businesses, of the "hows and whys" of MDB business.

- A perception that the MDB bidding process is unfair. This is not true in general, although it is true that in some situations there is adverse preference.

- Fear of excessive bureaucracy and red tape. This objection is not without some justification, but it is also largely attributable to the disinclination of Americans to become involved in export endeavors of any kind.

- Concern that MDB specifications are vague or otherwise poorly drawn. This, of course, depends on who did the engineering and consulting.

- Concern that MDB standards sacrifice quality.

- Concern that other nations offer better financing to Third-World buyers. This used to have some justification. However, recent basic revisions in Eximbank, AID, and TDA policies should correct some of the imbalance. Further revisions are being sought to improve the U.S. trade posture and the balance of payments.

- Concern that MDB financial requirements and American banks' lending policies are too strict. Banking requirements, once a problem, are becoming much less so as American banks become interested again in trade finance and, in particular, as they begin to adapt to the increasing use and demand for bid and performance bonds, most of which require or can only be met with standby letters of credit and, in some cases, with letters of guarantee.

The MDB Project Cycle

The problem of early identification can be solved in a number of ways, depending on the time available and the exporter's dedication. First, it's important to understand the typical project cycle to pinpoint when an opportunity exists. As detailed by the World Bank, the cycle phases (which are similar for all the MDBs) are: identification, preparation, appraisal, negotiations and board presentation, implementation and supervision, and evaluation.

Identification.   It's important to identify and make a determination of high-priority projects. At least in the case of the World Bank, priority in recent years has shifted from the basic infrastructure (e.g., roads, railways, power) and industry emphasis to include agriculture and rural development, urban services such as water supply and sanitation, various small-scale enterprises, and health and nutrition. These areas represent an emphasis on what is known as structural adjustment lending (as opposed to project lending) and present improved opportunities to new, and sometimes smaller, bid seekers, as well as to consultants.

In addition to priority and need, creditworthiness, feasibility, sector objectives, and private sector involvement are considered. It requires a minimum of 12 months and an average of 27 months from this identification stage to project approval, which is the conclusion of the fourth stage, negotiations. The World Bank, as well as most other MDBs, first formally identifies a project when it is listed in the Monthly Operational Summary (MOS), which is part of the overall World Bank Information Services–International Business Opportunities Service. Even at this early stage it should be of interest to consulting firms.

Preparation.   Preparation is normally a one- to two-year process during which the project briefs are prepared and technical and financial plans are developed. It is the key stage for the serious pursuer of bid opportunities to note projects of special interest. This is equally true for the subcontractor, who can begin to identify likely prime contractors. Strategic planning and contractor preparation starts here, and failure to do this is said to be the American bidders' main shortcoming. This is the opportune time for engineering and consulting contracts, which may be the first bids let, and which are not only valuable in their own right, but provide, in terms of their specifications, great advantages to the country of origin and, of course, to a particular bidder. While preliminary environmental and demographic studies usually have been made in the prior phase, this is also a period for determining the environmental impact and similar studies.

Appraisal.   Appraisal is the phase during which the MDB staff makes a comprehensive review of all aspects of the project. The staff checks for soundness of design, engineering, cost estimates, and procurement arrangements and makes sure that the institutions are in place to conduct the construction phase and the ongoing operational phase. Then the staff rechecks the cost benefits and economic impact, as well as a financial appraisal, considering all available fund sources to be sure of meeting costs, principal, and interest repayments. Appraisal reports often contain useful exporter information. This is the prime time for initial identification by contractors and suppliers.

Negotiations and Board Presentation.   Board presentation is the conclusion of the preliminary stage and represents the final negotiations between the MDB and the borrower regarding the loan agreement as to interest, repayment terms, and so on. Thereafter, the project loan agreements are approved and signed. At this point, projects are dropped from the World Bank's monthly operating survey (MOS).

Further information is available to subscribers of the World Bank's *International Business Opportunities Service*. Similar publications by the other MDBs will come in the form of the bank's technical data sheets and general and specific procurement notices.

Implementation and Supervision. The project should be under way a few months after approval and signing. The procurement process is conducted under rules largely laid out in the loan agreement, and the bank continues to oversee the procurement process to ensure that its guidelines are followed. These guidelines usually include international competitive bidding for the project and various consulting services. Of course, where possible, the MDB encourages using contractors and services from the borrowing country. Therefore, while these are often limited, be prepared for the multilateral banks to give preference to domestic contractors, consultants, and suppliers. For large projects, expect a prequalification process to limit the number of bidders. This is to everyone's advantage. As a subcontractor, you will be much less handicapped than a prime contractor in terms of preferred countries of origin.

Evaluation. Evaluation is purely a bank function for its own learning process and has impact primarily on the identification of future projects.

Payment Cycle

Where MDBs are concerned, suppliers of both services and goods are paid in one of three ways:

1. Directly by the borrower, who will then be reimbursed by the MDB on the borrower's application for withdrawal.

2. Directly by the MDB on behalf of the borrower, when so requested in the borrower's application for withdrawal.

3. Indirectly by the borrower, who may arrange a letter of credit with a commercial bank in the supplier's country when the borrower makes an application for Special Commitment from the MDB. The bank then provides the commercial bank nominated with a Special Commitment to provide protection to the issuing bank for its letter of credit commitment.

The Five Principal Multilateral Development Banks

There are well over 30 development banks, and some could be of interest to exporters as a source of financing to their customers, even though they are not necessarily multilateral. China even started the State Development Bank of China in late 1994. There are European investment banks, Nordic investment banks, an Australia development bank, Arab, East African, West African, Andean, OPEC, and Caribbean development banks (the latter especially interesting to Caribbean Initiative suppliers). A complete list of such banks is available from the World Bank and the OMBD. The five MDBs universally considered the major multilateral development banks are: the World Bank, the Inter-American Development Bank (IDB), the Asia Development Bank (ADB), the African Development Bank (AfDB), and the European Bank for Reconstruction and Development (EBRD).

The World Bank.   This is the largest of the MDBs for the very reason its name implies: it operates worldwide and is owned by more than 140 member governments, including the United States, which makes a heavy financial contribution. Check the World Bank's publication, *Guidelines for Procurement Under World Bank and IDA Credits.* Its financial support extends worldwide, with Asia slightly in the lead, followed by Latin America. While it may be addressed as one unit, the bank functions as separate divisions, although only IBRD and IDA represent direct procurement opportunities:

■ The International Bank for Reconstruction and Development (IBRD). The IBRD is the largest division of the World Bank and provides most of its assistance to creditworthy, middle-income developing nations. Most of its funds are raised through bond sales in the international capital markets. It is now proposing to cofinance, with government export agencies, the extension of medium- to long-term credit to private firms that want to import capital goods, spare parts, and services in third-world nations.

■ The International Development Association (IDA). The IDA member of the World Bank family helps the poorest of the poor countries. Terms can be up to 50 years at little or no interest. It is funded by government contributions and shares staff with the IBRD.

■ The International Finance Corporation (IFC). The IFC is the arm of the World Bank that makes both equity investments and loans in the private or mixed sectors without government guarantees. While the IFC is important indirectly as a potential project financing source for private sector projects, it does not offer direct bidding opportunities, as do the other MDBs.

■ The Multilateral Investment Guarantee Agency (MIGA). The MIGA investment affiliate of the World Bank became active in 1989. MIGA's purpose is to guarantee private investments against political risk, much as OPIC does for the United States. Therefore, MIGA does not directly offer any bid or procurement opportunities. Its objective is to encourage capital inflow to the third world. Some of the regional MDBs have commenced similar schemes.

The Inter-American Development Bank (IDB).   The IDB is a regional MDB serving all of Latin America.

The Asian Development Bank (ADB).   The ADB is a regional MDB serving most of Asia.

The African Development Bank (AfDB). The AfDB is a regional MDB intended to finance both foreign and intra-African trade. Its present focus is largely short term and attempts to offset the reluctance of commercial banks worldwide to finance African business, including bid and performance bonds.

The European Bank for Reconstruction and Development (EBRD). One of the newest of the MDBs, the FBRD was established especially to assist the Eastern European nations that have so recently been freed of the Soviet yoke, as well as the European Newly Independent States (NIS). The EBRD was also an important player in assisting the assimilation the former East Germany by the Federal Republic of Germany.

More details and a listing of some of the publications and addresses for these banks is provided later in this chapter but it might be best to establish your most appropriate contacts through the TIC and talk to the US&FCS liaison office at the appropriate MDB. Further details will also be found in the NTDB.

How to Participate in MDB Opportunities

To participate in this major international market with its lucrative opportunities, a small business should focus its research on the MDBs, their publications, private sector publications, and DOC facilities to identify new projects and their status. But remember, it is the responsible agency within the borrowing country that provides the bid details. In many cases, it prequalifies the bidders (in a process also called shortlisting) and otherwise makes all contracting and supervisory decisions (under some general supervision by the MDB). The exception occurs when you are selling only as a supplier to a contractor or subcontractor who might be either domestic or foreign. This is the alternative to direct bidding, but you must still track the likely projects to know whom to contact when you read of the contracts being let.

Don't overlook the opportunities for individual sales listed in the Notices for Specific Goods. These will be found in the *UN's Development Business* or as part of the World Bank's International Business Opportunities Service or its equivalent at the other MDBs. These opportunities might include anything from a drainage ditch to a forklift truck and are apart from any general project bid. It may be possible for you to make an educated guess as to the most likely successful bidders and proceed with your sales presentations and catalog distribution ahead of the bidding. With luck, you may realize the advantage of having your parts or product specified within the contractor's bid when such specification procedures are not prohibited, making it likely that if the contractor's bid is accepted, your product will be included. Of course, the same principle applies, only more so, if you can work far enough ahead to get your product specified during the engineering phase.

In any event, you must make your move no later than the time when the MDB loan is authorized at the end of the negotiation stage—and preferably sooner. Once the project contract awards have been made, you are only dealing with the leavings. Nevertheless, you should study the notices of contract awards to see who received them in order to provide you with clues as to where to concentrate your future efforts. In all this searching, tracking, and bidding, don't forget that the basic elements of successful salesmanship still apply. Avoid just sending your catalog—present it! Make contact with the project officials and sell both your qualifications and your integrity. Personal contact in this arena is as important as anywhere else in the business world. You might need to search for a local agent for a project in which you have a special interest.

Sources of Information and Help

The primary sources of information are the DOC, private publications, and the MDBs themselves, and are briefly described below:

The DOC's Multilateral Development Bank Operations (MDBO). The MDBO is now part of the same US&FCS unit of ITA that you work with in your DOC district office. With at least one US&FCS officer as a liaison in the five largest MDBs, this is the most direct point of contact if you know which bank or banks you wish to pursue, either directly, or through the district office. For a more generalized approach, try the MDBO office itself. The MDBO can provide direct input from its MDB liaison officers on specific projects, advise of current and future projects worldwide, provide guidance and advocacy to pursue the business, and offer on-line information. (See also Chapter 42.)

The DOC's Office of International Major Projects (OIMP). This used to be the DOC's lead office for interfacing with MDBs. Today its role seems a bit more uncertain, but it is there, nevertheless, to help in many of the same ways as the MDBO office. When you need information, you'd do well to make this one of the places you check to see what help you can find.

The National Trade Data Bank (NTDB). NTDB's *International Financial Assistance* is the newest avenue for information on the MBDs. The multipurpose National Trade Data Bank added MDB information in 1995 where it can quickly be accessed from your computer's CD-ROM reader. This makes the NTDB disc a very inexpensive tool for any business seriously interested in MDB business.

Development Business (DB). *DB* is a United Nations publication distributed every two weeks. *Development Business* carries the Monthly Operating Summary (MOS) for the World Bank and the Inter-American Development Bank on an alternating-issue basis. This is a primary trade paper of the industry and provides general news coverage of various projects, third-world countries, projects under consideration, and contract awards.

DB also carries procurement notices from all the other MDBs and other agencies as well. This includes the notices for specific goods, which offer excellent opportunities for specific products on which companies can bid without being involved in a project of any kind. It is also available in a computerized Scan-a-Bid version.

The DACON Information Center. Consulting firms should list information about their services with the DACON Information Center at the World Bank. This is a computerized data center, described in more detail in Chapter 10, that the other MDBs and Third-World nations share to locate firms with specific capabilities and to invite their participation in bidding.

The International Business Opportunities Service. International Business Opportunities Service is the complete World Bank information service. It consists of five principal sources of information:

1. *The Monthly Operational Summary (MOS)* provides key information that should be studied to obtain early notification. It provides continuously updated information concerning the project cycle until approval, after which it appears in other portions of the service. Detailed project information and administrative contacts are included. This advance information is particularly important for consulting firms. The MOS can be subscribed to separately for substantially less.

2. *Technical data sheets* provide details on what items will be purchased, including consulting and procurement arrangements. They are printed immediately after loan approval and amount to about 200 pages per year in weekly mailings.

3. *General procurement notices* normally appear even before the loan has been approved and describe the project in broad terms with the various components required. They provide contractors and suppliers with general information to determine whether the project should be pursued further. Any prequalification requirements of the bidding firm are described, such as experience or financial strength.

4. *Specific procurement notices* appear subsequently with details of the items or equipment to be purchased in a particular contract, together with advice as to when bidding documents are available and when bids are due. These notices are published twice a month and, if you are interested, you should request either the general or specific notice from the administering agency and ask to be sent bidding documents and advice of the fees and other details. Bidding documents are not mailed automatically, but must be requested.

5. *Notices of contract awards,* advising of all major contracts let, are published twice a month. These notices can be of particular interest to potential subcontractors.

The Practical Guide to the Development Bank Business. This manual, available for $185, describes MDB procurement arrangements and includes sections specifically written for small and midsize exporters. It is published by Development Bank Associates, 1901 Pennsylvania Avenue NW, Washington, D.C. 20006.

The Development Bank Business Market. This 460-page reference guide, available for $375, cross-references over 40 sectors. It is published by Development Bank Associates, 1901 Pennsylvania Avenue NW, Washington, D.C. 20006.

To obtain information on the other MDBs listed in Appendix I, it is best to contact them or the US&FCS liaison officer directly. You can obtain the number from the TIC. The general breakdown of progressive information and the titles of their publications are essentially the same for all the MDBs.

Following are some additional suggestions for bringing you and your company up to speed on MDB opportunities and procedures:

- Attend World Bank seminars and other conferences at which bank officials speak about MDB procurement.

- Talk to your trade associations and related organizations with general knowledge about the MDBs or international projects.

- Talk to your contact at MDBO or OIMP about which of the private firms that track the MDB market would be best for your needs and particular situation.

- Develop an active network of overseas agents who can track government plans, survey local bid notices, and monitor trade publications.

- Track upcoming bids with your own resources, in addition to using the DOC offices mentioned. Your starting point should be the NTDB CD-ROM discs. From there you can graduate to the key publications already mentioned: the MDBs themselves, including others in an area of the world in which you are especially active; and the best private sources suggested. (See Appendix I for MDB addresses.)

- Review more technical sources of information, such as the procurement and consulting guidelines prepared by the development banks themselves, samples of which can be obtained from the World Bank's Informational and Public Affairs Office and the other MDBs.

- Contact the US&FCS liaison officers at the banks or the MDBO staff to resolve problems with bidding.

For all these suggestions you will find the Trade Information Center and the referenced DOC offices most helpful with the necessary names, addresses, and telephone contacts.

MDB Support for Bank Lines of Credit and Negotiated Contracts

Until now we have been focusing on project and other international bidding opportunities related to the World Bank and the regional MDBs. While somewhat at odds with the title of this chapter, your own customers can prove a valuable resource in terms of obtaining lines of credit to purchase your company's products or negotiated contracts without any bidding process at all. The

World Bank and many of the MDBs, including some of the smaller banks not mentioned here in detail, offer lines of credit (LOC) for small and midsize companies as well as larger firms. The trick is to find a line of credit available when you are still negotiating or selling so that prospective customers can accept it as a selling point and as a means of demonstrating your ability to pay when considering your offer. While few firms recognize the opportunities inherent via the development banks, fewer still recognize lines of credit as source of funding and for closing a deal. The U.S. Eximbank has a similar LOC program which involves "bundling." It is the buyer that must apply for lines of credit and each bank may have slightly different rules and criteria, but the total dollars available represent very substantial sums.

The situation is not quite so clear concerning directly negotiated contracts. The World Bank permits financing such contracts when they are extensions of existing contracts and when they involve proprietary requirements or specific projects where the contracts are relatively small. The World Bank idea of a "small" contract—say $100,000—may be quite different from your concept, so the opportunities may be greater than you would first suspect. To locate this financing check with the development banks involved, have your customer investigate through his or her own government agencies, and talk to the DOC Office of Multilateral Development Bank Operations.

Agency for International Development

The Agency for International Development (AID) administers American foreign aid programs throughout the world to less developed countries (LDCs), in close cooperation with the State Department. The objectives, levels, and means of providing such aid are often a contentious issue between any given administration and its State Department, the right and left aisles of Congress, and nearly everyone else.

Prior to the Clinton Administration, AID's stated primary purposes had evolved as:

1. Promoting economic and political stability

2. Encouraging creditworthy trading and investment partners, not only for economic and commercial purposes, but also to ensure a supply of strategic resources for defense and the basic U.S. economy

3. Reducing poverty and hunger for humanitarian considerations

The Clinton Administration altered the emphasis somewhat, restating the purpose as promoting "sustainable development," characterized as "continued economic and social progress" based on the principles of improved quality of life, stewardship of resources, broad-based political and economic participation, and effective public institutions capable of functioning without external support. The focus of sustainable development was organized in four areas consisting of the environment, health and population, democracy, and economic growth. The broad oversight of this concept is borne by a major bureau of AID named the Bureau for Global Programs, Field Support, and Research (GFR), intended to be the repository of technical expertise for the agency as a whole. GFR, in turn, is subdivided into five centers based on the four focus areas mentioned above, plus a Center for Human Capacity Development. The Center for Economic Growth absorbed whatever carryover activities remained of the former Bureau for Private Enterprise (PRE) of pre-1992 AID. Regardless of any political assessments, this is a tall order and contradicts the past trend demanding a clear benefit and job-creation potential to be blended with America's humanitarian efforts and foreign aid dollars.

U.S foreign aid experience began with the hugely successful Marshall Plan after World War II. In 1961 AID was organized to coordinate what had become a variety of foreign assistance programs. During its first two decades, most of AID's foreign aid policies were for democratization and humanitarian needs and largely focused on the needs of the very poor. Although some projects were very successful, there were many failures. Increasingly, the emphasis shifted from purely humanitarian or massive infrastructure projects to market-driven structural readjustments intended to impact the entire population of the country in an attempt to achieve sustained growth just as was explained above, relative to the multilateral development bank programs. Democratization continues to be one of AID's primary goals and it can claim many successes, just as it can with the parallel objective of improved U.S. export markets in developing countries. This can be demonstrated in terms of the substantial percentage growth of U.S. exports in those same countries.

Traditionally, AID has quite understandably given American suppliers preference, with some 70 percent of American bilateral economic assistance typically being spent on American goods and services. For this reason, exporters should become familiar with the opportunities offered by this program. Although AID has in the past been accused of being too inclined to a philosophy of aid to Third-World countries first and American business only incidentally, it has over time changed its position of aid versus trade, especially in terms of investment opportunities. In recent years it has attempted to structure its projects to leave a legacy of better trade links for American business after AID diminishes or ceases its activity in a country as it graduates from an LDC status as in the case of South Korea. It remains to be seen if this can be achieved while at the same time obliging the rather isolationist and much more conservative 104th U.S. Congress. Besides budget reduction, there is clearly much less inclination to provide foreign aid of any kind. But the tests of U.S. job expansion and economic interest will presumably be applied with a heavy hand, regardless of who is in the White House.

Until 1992 the underlying strategies that AID had been emphasizing in its U.S. economic assistance program were economic reforms, free market values, structural readjustment, and technology transfer. This assistance was, and still is, provided in three main categories. The first two consist of development assistance in the form of loans (with grants occasionally being provided in lieu of loans where the economic problems justify such largesse) and economic support funds to promote economic and political stability. The third category of assistance consists of portions of the Department of Agriculture's concessional food assistance programs, operated in conjunction with the Commodity Credit Corporation (CCC) and administered by AID. These include Titles II and III of the Food for Peace (PL 480) program, plus two other lesser-known food programs: Food for Progress, a support program for countries trying to expand free enterprise, and 416(b) which provides for donations of CCC surplus food. In addition, some AID funds are used in connection with the U.S. Export-Import Bank's lending in the form of mixed credit. Mixed credit refers to blending a grant element in the form of economic aid with the loan for a project to reduce the apparent interest cost of the loan and otherwise enhance its payback terms. It is then known as a "tied aid" facility.

Recent administrations have increasingly stressed close adherence to State Department policy concerning priority for Third-World countries attempting to democratize and achieve a free-market economy. The Clinton administration's 1992–1994 shift in the direction of a greater AID focus on humanitarian issues, population growth, poverty, health care, and the environment does not appear to be altogether viable, and the 104th Congress of 1995 may well be in a position to reverse that trend. More than ever, there will be a tendency to stress the private sector role in the delivery system for aid or projects, as well as in the host-country financing and ownership of AID projects. AID must help poor countries improve their standards of living and still hew to the new political line if it expects to survive in recognizable form. The Clinton administration, however, should be credited with successfully making major cuts in staff and payroll, including such moves as the elimination of AID foreign missions that are no longer required or that are being abandoned as hopeless.

It should also be noted that in terms of the total aid provided to less-developed and needy countries by all developed countries, U.S. aid expenditures have dropped from an unsustainable 50 percent of worldwide funding in the 1950s and 1960s to about 17 percent in 1993. U.S. aid now represents only half of 1 percent of the federal budget, and compared to other developed nations, the U.S. budget represents the smallest percentage of GNP of any developed nation in terms of aid and overseas development assistance. Therefore, any future changes should be made to improve AID's productivity in terms of all its objectives, including increased export business opportunities, not to reduce net real dollars compared to present expenditures.

Even in a more self-serving mode and confining itself to its most successful and proven activities, the agency can do many good deeds as it supports American business and creates jobs. It should be remembered that the acknowledged success of the postwar Marshall Plan was in large part due to its efforts to encourage the impoverished and war-torn countries it was assisting to trade with each other as well as with the U.S., thereby generating regional economic growth, which in turn helped speed the reconstruction of many countries. This was one of the means that provided the leveraged and dramatic economic growth that helped stimulate America's own great postwar economy. To strike the right balance between doing good and seeking a payback is a difficult challenge, but with ingenuity and finesse it is not necessarily at odds with free-market concepts and priorities.

AID Outreach Programs

AID is not the easiest export vehicle for small businesses to ride into the international arena, and doing business in the Third World is not easy for a firm of any size, but for self-preservation and sound political reasons, AID is currently doing its best to be user-friendly to this segment of the economy. If small businesses utilize the special tools and advantages AID provides, however, they will find that the agency can be useful, both in the sale of goods for export and in the service and consulting sector.

Center for Trade and Investment Services (CTIS).   One very highly publicized development intended to ease the path for companies seeking to do business with AID and its Third-World clients was the creation of the Center for Trade and Investment Services (CTIS). This unit is a subcenter within the Center for Economic Growth, which is one of the five prime centers previously AID's Bureau for Global Programs, Field Support, and Research (GFR). The CTIS center in Washington was established as a central point of contact for free-of-charge inquiries about business opportunities in AID-assisted countries. It is staffed by regional analysts specializing in Asia, Latin America and the Caribbean, the Near East, Eastern Europe, and the Newly Independent States. Call 800-872-4348 for information on specific business opportunities, as well as for counseling on small-business contracting and procurement via AID. It also develops world-sector-specific guides to AID programs. In cooperation with DOC, SBA, Eximbank, and OPIC, the center provides information on all of AID's programs and attempts to coordinate personnel and relevant programs to guide the new-to-market exporter through the bureaucratic maze. It intends to help especially in cases where there is an opportunity in the 40 or so countries of the 80 in which AID is active that have an AID mission but no US&FCS personnel. Contact CTIS directly at 800/874-4348 or TIC at 800/USA-TRADE. CTIS can also be reached by fax or by modem on the Internet: CTIS@USAID.GOV.

Environmental Technology Network for Asia (ETNA)/U.S.–Asia Environmental Partnership (USAEP).   ETNA is operated by CTIS and matches environmental trade leads from USAEP technology representatives in nine Asian countries with appropriate firms registered with ETNA's database. The leads are passed by fax broadcast within 48 hours of being received from USAEP. (See also Chapter 42.)

Procurement Information Access System (PIAS).   PIAS is a means of obtaining an early alert of AID-financed procurement opportunities. It makes use of the DOC's Economic Bulletin Board to provide contractors with advance details of future AID activities, contracts, grants, and cooperative agreements over $100,000.

This advance information system is designed to fill the information gap between the *Congressional Presentation* and the notices in the *Commerce Business Daily*. The information contained in PIAS is updated on a quarterly basis. Since it forecasts activities as well advising on plans as they firm up, it can also be considered a marketing tool for planning, the strategy to use in marketing a firm's special capabilities to AID. Subscribers may gain access through the DOC's Economic Bulletin Board at a cost of $35 per year, which includes two free hours of connect time plus a nominal usage charge. It is also hoped that it will be available on Internet in the foreseeable future. For details on subscribing, check with DOC at 202/377-1986 or TIC for further information.

AID Management Bureau, Office of Administrative Service. The information support services of this group distribute on a subscription basis AID's Directive Resource CD, a CD-ROM disc containing the complete AID handbook services, including *Procurement Policy, Host Country Contracting, Grants, Federal Acquisition Regulation (FAR), AID Procurement Regulation,* and more. Access to these documents is essential for anyone doing business with AID. The subscription charges are $55 per disc or $130 for a subscription to four consecutively issued discs.

Center for Development Information and Evaluation (CDIE). CDIE of AID also distributes on a subscription basis a CD-ROM disc containing the complete AID document and databases and the full text of selected AID reports and publications.

Commerce Business Daily (CBD). Although this is a multipurpose federal publication designed to announce activities of interest to firms doing business with the government in many areas both domestic and foreign, it is a key GPO publication for tracking AID opportunities. It contains a daily list of all U.S. government invitations for bids (IFBs), requests for proposals (RFPs), contract awards, subcontracting leads, sales of surplus property, and foreign business opportunities, including those through AID. The Federal Acquisition Regulations require all federal agencies to synopsize in the *CBD* any contract actions and award expected to exceed $25,000, or $10,000 for noncompetitive requirements.

AID Procurement Information Bulletin (PIB). *PIBs* are targeted to small and minority firms and announce informal, negotiated procurement by the public and private sector covering trade opportunities and general procurement. (See Figure 13-1.)

Internet. AID is making large amounts of contracting information available on Internet via E-mail, an FTP site, and Gopher. To access all this information, use the following addresses: for E-mail—procure@info.usaid.gov; for FTP—ftp .info.usaid.gov; for gopher—gopher.info.usaid.gov. Contact AID information or TIC for more information and access details.

Issued by the Agency for International Development

A.I.D. Procurement Information Bulletin   Trade Information for U.S. Suppliers

	P.I. BULLETIN NO.
	88-45
	DATE
	August 12, 1988
	M/L
	Entire Mailing List

Office of Small and Disadvantaged Business Utilization/Minority Resource Center

Washington, DC 20523
Area Code 703 875-1590

ITEM ONE   - LABORATORY EQUIPMENT; GLASSWARE & MISCELLANEOUS SUPPLIES/EQUIPMENT . . . . SUDAN
ITEM TWO   - PRIVATE SECTOR TRADE OPPORTUNITY . . . . PAKISTAN

****

Item 1

Country: Sudan
Authority: C.I.P. Grant 650-K-608B
Source/Origin: A.I.D. Geographic Code 941 (Selected Free World)
RTO/IFB No.:   SUDAN/MOH/88-002
Purchaser: Ministry of Health, Sudan

Bid Deadline: September 27, 1988, at 11:00 AM at the Embassy of the Republic of Sudan, Office of Economic Counsellor, 2210 Massachusetts Ave., N.W., Washington, D.C. 20008

Commodities: LABORATORY EQUIPMENT; GLASSWARE; MISCELLANEOUS SUPPLIES/ EQUIPMENT including:

Group A - Laboratory Equipment including microscopes; centrifuges; incubators; air ovens; water baths; auto claves; water stills; various types of balances; haemoglobinometers; photometric cuvettes; and instrument sterilizers - 27 line items

Group B - Glassware including various aspirator bottles; beakers; flasks, microscope slides; test tubes; measuring cylinders; hydrometers; thermometers; perti dishes; and various pipettes - 41 line items

Group C - Miscellaneous supplies/equipment including anaerobic jars; various test tube racks; various brushes aspirator bottles; various laboratory refuse bins; gloves; tissue paper; pipettes; inoculation loops; microlitre tips, heaters; measures; blenders; circulation pumps; blood suspension mixers; cartons; disposable syringes and needles; wood applicators; dispensers; vacuum vessels; filter papers; funnels Ph meters; calculators; relays and fire extinguishers - 77 line items

NOTE: Beginning August 12, 1988, interested suppliers may obtain a single copy of the Request for Technical Offers/Invitation for Bid (RTO/IFB), by written request to the Agency for International Development, Office of Procurement, Commodity Support Division, Room 1422, SA-14, Washington, D.C. 20523. Requests must be accompanied by three (3) self-addressed mailing labels. Please refer to RTO/IFB No. SUDAN/MOH/88-002 when requesting tender documents, and insure that your complete business address, telephone number, and telex/cable number are included with the request.

****

Item 2

The following is a Private Sector Trade Opportunity published for the information of U.S. suppliers.

1. The U.S. Agency for International Development (U.S.A.I.D.) and the Government of Liberia (GOL) plan to make funds available to Liberian businesses in October, 1988. To assist small scale Liberian importers, USAID/Liberia will make available to them expressions of interest from U.S. Suppliers of the following commodities:

1. Chain saw
2. Rice and coffee mills and grinders (0.5 to 2 tons per hour)
3. Vegetable and grain seeds
4. Agricultural tractors
5. Sugar cane crushers (small scale)
6. Hand tractors
7. Pick-up trucks
8. Trucks (up to eight tons)
9. Carpentry tools
10. Generators (3 to 30 kva)

Financing is not yet available for these commodities, and there is a chance that the program will not receive additional funds; these are private sector transactions, and no formal bid documents will be issued; USAID/Liberia's role will be limited to passing on any information received from suppliers to prospective importers.

Authorized source/origin of the goods is U.S. Only. Interested suppliers should write to Commodity Management Office, USAID/Econ, APO, New York 09155. Suppliers are encouraged to provide as much information as possible on the commodities, including approximate prices, catalogues, and descriptive literature.

*********************   *************

Figure 13-1. Copy of SBC bulletin for AID.

Office of Small and Disadvantaged Business Utilization/Minority Resource Center (OSDBU/MRC). Despite its name, AID considers OSDBU/MRC to be the initial contact point for all businesses for obtaining one-on-one detailed information on AID-generated export opportunities and for receiving notice of bid and contract invitations. This specifically includes disadvantaged businesses comprised of socially and economically disadvantaged owners and workers, including women-owned firms and certain other organizations and colleges or universities with a high percentage of ethnic minority enrollment. The office largely exists as an advocate for small businesses and disadvantaged enterprises and ensures their consideration as sources for procurement of goods and services financed by AID. OSDBU/MRC also coordinates the agency's implementation of the Disadvantaged Enterprises Program (formerly referred to as the Gray Amendment). The introduction of CTIS and the Economic Bulletin Board (PIAS), hotlines, and other tools, however, clearly lessens its duties of assisting the general business population. It distributes at no cost the very useful *Guide to Doing Business with the Agency for International Development,* and may be contacted directly for copies of this book oriented to the smaller business. It sponsors seminars and conferences, acts as an information clearinghouse, and works closely with SBA's 8(a) program involvement. Finally, it administers the Consultant Registry Information System (ACRIS), mentioned in Chapter 10 in connection with exporting consultant and other personal services.

The Consultant Registry Information System (ACRIS). This is a computerized database for profiles of providers of technical and professional services that might be needed on future AID-financed projects. It lists American firms and individuals, especially smaller firms, and details their capabilities and services for the purpose of having them matched up by its Washington staff or field mission personnel with appropriate AID projects or acquisition needs. Registration is voluntary, but consultants are encouraged to register with the OSDBU/MRC.

Business Development Services (BDS). On a grant basis under the BDS program, AID engages the resources of the private sector volunteer-staffed by the International Executive Service Corps (IESC), to support business development services in developing countries and emerging democracies. BDS activities are designed to assist smaller overseas businesses to improve their future opportunities through technology transfer and joint ventures or through coventures with U.S. firms to the mutual advantage of both. AID also engages the Small Business Foundation of America and the National Association of State Development Agencies to assist IESC in matching small businesses in developing countries with U.S. counterparts. (IESC's activities relative to joint ventures are described in Chapter 5.)

International Executive Service Corps (IESC). Nearly 13,000 men and women, both retired and employed, are registered to share their skills and experience around the world as needed on a volunteer, expense-paid basis. To date this has included over 16,000 projects in 120 countries. The IESC focus is on technical and managerial training, technology and business access, and business research for firms in developing countries. It has helped in virtually every commercial field, with machinery and agriculture being the two largest classifications. IESC's success record and reputation are excellent. It can be contacted through AID or directly at its headquarters in Stamford Harbor Park, P.O. Box 10005, Stamford, Connecticut, 06904.

Participating in AID Commodity Bids

If you are interested in the possibility of working with AID, your fist step should be to procure *The Guide for Doing Business with AID* from the GPO or AID's OSDBU/MRC. Below are some highlights from the guide to help you decide whether to pursue these opportunities. There are two primary ways in which American exporters can participate in AID programs for commodity purchases (the term *commodities* as used here includes equipment, material, foods, supplies— everything except services and consulting, which are dealt with separately).

First is the **Commodity Import Program (CIP)**, in which AID provides U.S. dollars through loans or grants to host countries (in which case they are responsible for negotiating the contract) in order to finance a wide variety of products that can help keep that country's economy moving or meet urgent needs, including foreign exchange availability. CIP funds are allocated by the foreign host government to both its own agencies (public sector) and/or the private sector to make purchases of needed commodities. The purchases must be negotiated, signed, and paid for by the host country according to AID's regulations, which the exporter new to AID should study. Part of the regulations refer to allowed sources of origin of the commodities to be purchased. Sometimes the commodities must be of U.S. origin; in other situations they may be purchased from any one of the selected free-world country-approved lists. Public sector procurement may be made on a bid basis, and if over $100,000, is announced first through the Procurement Information Access System (PIAS) (already described) and shortly thereafter in *Commerce Business Daily*. Alternatively, if it is a negotiated procurement, it is announced through an *AID Procurement Information Bulletin* (*PIB*). Private sector procurement is advised in a similar fashion, but the offerings and negotiations are conducted through regular commercial trade channels. The only difference in procedure from typical business transactions that would be apparent to the exporter is that AID confirms the letter of credit. To further assist American exporters in learning about these private sector opportunities, AID provides lists of importers by commodity categories in the AID-recipient countries, providing special opportunities to alert suppliers and manufacturers.

The second means of participation is through **AID-financed contracts for projects**. This means that AID arranges loans or grants through the public sector of host country to finance specific projects, facilities, or undertakings. Such contracts are also subject to host-country contracting regulations, and AID mission officers must review the RFP and the subsequent stages of such contracts. The contracts can be for construction of irrigation facilities, equipment for rural health care networks, or supplying small farmers with appropriate tools and machinery. Commodities purchased as part of this program, sometimes in conjunction with MDBs, are called project procurement. Here again are many opportunities for component sales for exporters not capable of handling an entire project. Such AID-financed projects are advertised in *Development Business* (referred to in the section on MDBs and through the other sources of AID information already described).

Just as in the case of the MDBs, under both types of programs AID is not ordinarily the buyer, except for some supplies and services. Both the public and private sectors of the AID-recipient countries typically buy directly from American firms, whether by means of a bidding process or through negotiations. Since AID's objective is to make a positive contribution to the development of less-developed countries in accordance with current U.S. policies and laws, certain items are not eligible for AID financing, such as unsafe or ineffective products, goods that are entirely luxurious or frivolous, surplus or used items, items for military use, surveillance equipment of micro-miniature design for audio surveillance activities, weather-modification equipment, and commodities for support of police and other law enforcement activities. There are other AID terms and conditions that change with the category and size of the transaction, which will be readily apparent to any reader investigating these bid opportunities further.

To determine whether your product qualifies for commodity eligibility, check the *AID Commodity Eligibility Listing,* published according to Schedule B numbers, which is available from the Agency for International Development (AID), the Office of Small and Disadvantaged Business, Utilization/Minority Resource Center (OSDBU/MRC). Or, in a fashion truer to the decade, review the AID CD-ROM, which is updated quarterly explaining all AID regulations.

If your product falls into an eligible AID category, you can obtain a mailing list application from the AID office or from USAID, Commodity Management Division, Office of Procurement. After the application is submitted, you will receive, free of charge, AID *Procurement Information Bulletins* (PIBs) allowing a lead time of 30 to 60 days, which include descriptions of the desired commodities. The PIBs are prepared by AID's Office of Small and Disadvantaged Business Utilization/Minority Resource Center (OSDBU/MRC), but they are intended for all U.S. businesses. Procurement information is also advised in the DOC *Commerce Business Daily* publication up to one week earlier than the PIB publication date.

AID Acquisition or Procurement of Services

Service companies, such as research, architect/engineering, consulting, and construction firms, that are interested in bidding on AID financed projects should register in the AID Consultant Registry Information System (ACRIS). The professional and technical services required for most AID-financed projects are also announced by PIAS and in the *Commerce Business Daily.* Firms providing technical services will find ACRIS (previously described) a helpful tool for participation in AID technical service (noncommodity) contracts. Do not, however, rely entirely on ACRIS, but do your own research.

Some of the frequently sought-after services include: telecommunications, environmental services, education services, architecture and engineering, management services, information services, transportation services, water and sanitation services, agricultural and rural development, urban development, tourism, population science, nutrition, energy sciences, and construction.

All of the above are considered nonpersonal services. (AID considers personal services to be those in which an employer/employee relationship exists. Personal services will not be considered here.) If the scope of work for nonpersonal service is $25,000 or less, the opportunity need only be posted on the bulletin board in AID's procurement office for ten days (this appears to be a literal fact, so that an insider group that can check this board weekly sees opportunities not available elsewhere) and the entire procurement process may take only three or four weeks to complete. If the scope of the work is under $10,000, AID may limit itself to contacting a minimum of three qualified individuals and the process can be completed very quickly. The two last-named procedures point up the potential value of networking as well as being listed on the ACRIS register. (See Chapter 10 on selling services.)

Acquisition Activities for AID Direct Contracts

This area of activity is not relative to this book on export, but nevertheless represents a profitable range of opportunities to firms otherwise familiar and active with AID that should be examined. It can apply to services and products needed by AID for use within this country or for goods and services which will be utilized overseas directly by AID rather than through the normal host country channels. Such arrangements are subject to Federal Acquisition Regulations (FAR) and are advertised in *Commerce Business Daily* if the goods or services exceed $25,000.

Getting Paid

AID has a wide range of regulations governing technical assistance, construction services procurement, commodity procurement involving the recipient foreign country, and the American exporter wishing to receive payment from AID-related funds. For example, foreign content is restricted and products or components not from the free world are forbidden. AID also requires that 50 percent of the gross tonnage be shipped on U.S. flag vessels if available, unless a waiver is obtained for cause. Payments are usually made by the buyer with an irrevocable letter of credit confirmed through AID. Two or three special AID forms are often included in the documentation requirements. Form AID-11, which is an application for approval of commodity eligibility, assures AID that product or commodity requirements are met under the CIP transaction. This form must be approved before shipping. Form 282 is the supplier certification and invoice and contract abstract for CIP transactions; and Form 1450.4 is the comparable form for project procurement.

Small Business Administration's Role in AID

The Small Business Administration (SBA) has an 8(a) program to assist small businesses owned by socially or economically disadvantaged individuals, including those wishing to participate in AID-financed programs. In the case of AID, this activity is conducted through AID's OSDBU/MRC. This office, which acts as a clearinghouse and counselor for American businesses and academic organizations, is also the advocate for encouraging participation by small and disadvantaged businesses in AID-fostered opportunities. In this capacity it coordinates AID's implementation of the 1984 Gray Amendment to the Foreign Assistance Act. This amendment provides for a set-aside of 10 percent of AID's development assistance funds for socially and economically disadvantaged firms. For the purpose of this amendment, firms owned by women were added to the socially disadvantaged category that was historically occupied by Black, Hispanic, Native, and Asian Pacific Americans.

The 8(a) program permits the SBA to contract with any federal agency on a noncompetitive basis to provide goods and services. SBA, in turn, subcontracts with approved 8(a) businesses for the performance of the contract and ensures that the selected firm has the capability to perform and does perform the specific job requirements.

Financial assistance to 8(a) contractors is available in the form of counseling and professional guidance in management, as well as loans, advance payments, and business development expenses. Companies may also be eligible to receive assistance for bonding, when necessary, to perform on government contracts. Participation in this program is limited to a maximum term of five years, with one possible extension. Firms must submit a business plan showing adequate business experience and demonstrate sufficient potential for completing the program before they are accepted. For further information and how to apply, contact your regional office of the SBA.

Trade and Development Agency

The Trade and Development Agency (TDA) was formerly a program operating as part of an umbrella agency in tandem with AID and OPIC. Today, even though it is the smallest of all the federal agencies, it is highly regarded and has increased funding and responsibilities because it is now the only agency providing feasibility study grants for overseas projects. TDA continues to cooperate closely with AID and OPIC however, for they are both focused on serving the Third World, although with TDA's dual mandate providing feasibility study grants in both developing and middle-income countries, they also work closely with Eximbank. TDA is a member of the TPCC interagency group that is attempting to maximize the impact of the U.S. export support dollar and implement the National Export Strategy.

The TDA provides the grants to the foreign country sponsor on condition that it contract with a U.S. firm. While the host country receives substantial benefits from the grants, the economic objective for the United States is to create jobs as the result of increased exports of U.S. goods and services to these countries stemming from the TDA study's technical advice and the availability of U.S. origin equipment and systems that might be incorporated into the resulting project itself. Such suggestions are often taken, although the host country is not required to give the final project to U.S. contractors or suppliers. Historically, since its establishment in 1980, the TDA has been associated with $5.3 billion in U.S. exports, which is 25 times its accumulated expenditures.

The majority of the TDA's funds are used for feasibility studies for public sector projects in which the host government plays a major role in developing, selecting, and monitoring the work. Recently the TDA has extended its work with large engineering and construction firms to include manufacturers. It has done this by funding visits by foreign procurement officials to U.S. manufacturing facilities, further reinforcing and expanding U.S. business opportunities. Activities cover a wide range of development sectors, including energy development, food production, minerals development, industry, transportation, communication, and technical training.

The TDA defines *project* as a major industrial or infrastructure priority of a developing country, whether undertaken by the public sector or the private sector, in which U.S. companies are involved as joint venture partners. Such projects can range from airports in Indonesia, to telecommunication networks in Tunisia, to a health care system in Tatarstan. The agency learns of viable projects from government agencies such as US&FCS, as well as from the public and private sectors of foreign companies and from U.S. suppliers and contractors. The TDA attempts to narrow the potential projects to those that fit certain criteria, including:

1. *Priority.* Projects must be developmental priorities of the host country and therefore likely to be implemented. The TDA must receive a formal request from the host government, and the U.S. embassy must endorse the TDA's involvement in the proposed project.

2. *Export potential.* Projects must present an opportunity for substantial sales of U.S. goods and services many times the cost of the studies.

3. *Financing availability.* There must be assurances that untied financing for project implementation will be available and that procurement will therefore be open to U.S. firms.

4. *Strong competition.* It must appear that U.S. companies will face strong competition from foreign companies that would likely receive subsidies or other support from their governments.

As a first step, the TDA suggests that a Definitional Mission be funded by a smaller grant to determine whether the project should be funded and that a consultation be arranged with the project sponsor to define the work program for the feasibility study. If sufficient information is already available or the project is quite small and straightforward, a Desk Study may be conducted in place of a mission. The TDA looks to small businesses and service providers to perform these tasks to gain an opportunity or foothold in the country for future work and sales of their own. The TDA also makes available grants for consultancies and feasibility studies arranged by the World Bank and the regional MDBs for projects under their respective consideration. Other countries who are equally anxious that their constituencies not be discriminated against by U.S. specifications. So they, too, offer such grants, leading to competition as to who will be the feasibility study grantor.

If the TDA approves a feasibility study proposal, planning assistance is available through a grant to a developing country to finance a study, on the condition that it agrees the study will be performed by a U.S. firm, competitively selected. The grant for a typical study ranges from $150,000 to $750,000 and averages $320,000. If the study is the result of a private U.S. firm's suggestion, the firm is expected to share half the cost of the study with the TDP. In some circumstances, however, studies may be undertaken through a grant provided to the host country when the country is in the process of selecting a contractor and when a U.S. bidding firm risks losing the project to foreign competition due to assistance from its government. Only friendly countries, as determined by the Department of State, and developing countries planning to allocate substantial resources for procurement of foreign goods and services are eligible.

U.S. firms are encouraged to submit information about possible projects to: U.S. Trade and Development Program, Room 309, SA 16, Washington, D.C. 20523; phone 703/875-4357.

The TDA sponsors some reverse trade missions and conferences to familiarize foreign decision makers with U.S. goods and services and to give them an opportunity to meet U.S. suppliers. The TDA funds occasional trade-related training grants to let personnel in a foreign country receive the technical and managerial training necessary to operate a U.S.–implemented finished project. The TDA also funds technical assistance grants on an as-needed basis to respond to problems when the required expertise is unavailable in a country where a U.S.–led project has been established.

To track TDA activities and opportunities, watch for its Requests for Proposals (RFP) in *Commerce Business Daily* or call for on-line computer-related information or subscription information on its *TDA Bi-Weekly* and its *TDA Early Bird* publications. TIC can provide the numbers. There is a TDA hotline, which is 703/875-7447.

United Nations

The many subgroups and advisory groups of the United Nations (UN) collectively represent a very important global customer. These groups represent the world's greatest collection of alphabet soup, and the largest customer of all is UNICEF (United Nations International Children's Educational Fund). This is not to ignore such enormous organizations as FAO (Food and Agriculture

Organization), UNESCO (UN Educational, Scientific, and Cultural Organization), WHO (World Health Organization)—to say nothing of IMCO, WMO, ITU, ILO, UNFPA, ICAO, IAEA, and so forth. The important thing is to know how to reach these agencies after determining who might be interested in purchasing what you have, or can, provide. The first step in this process is to write to: United Nations Development Program, Interagency Procurement Services, 54-56 rue de Montbrillant, CH-1202 Geneva 10, Switzerland.

Ask for the free publication *General Business Guide to the United Nations System*. It is a well-organized publication, explaining the procurement needs for the entire UN system and how to go about presenting your own products. One of the means of obtaining business from this worldwide complex of customers is to present your products, catalogs, and prices so that the agencies understand what you wish to sell. If such products are required, you will then be in line to receive notification of a request for bids or quotations.

Naturally, your ingenuity and creativity can enhance your opportunity to profit from this business. This would again include some of the techniques discussed relative to the MDBs, such as encouraging your overseas representatives in the key city of the organization or on the scene of a project to keep in touch with the proper authorities. Your own visit to the procurement officers of the appropriate organizations in New York City or elsewhere would, of course, be very useful. Many exporters, manufacturers, and consultants have had excellent success in achieving a share of this business without any special "in," just common sense, diligence, and patience.

If you are a consultant interested in UN business, register your facilities with the World Bank DACON Information Center, 1818 H Street, NW, Washington, D.C. 20433, which serves as the computerized data center for the UN's consulting availabilities as well. Above all, an effort to make personal contact to understand the conditions, needs, and requirements will distinguish you from the hundreds of others who are also interested in bidding.

Foreign Military Sales (FMS) and the Defense Security Assistance Agency (DSAA)

Military sales are largely excluded in discussions of the programs or agencies designed to assist the exporter in export market research, development, and financing. Even though it is asked much less in today's environment, the question still arises: Where does someone wishing to sell defense and military equipment, an important segment of our economy, go for help?

Because so many of the players in this area of exports are large firms already fully involved, this question is a matter of importance to only a narrow group of exporters or manufacturers. Therefore no attempt to summarize the fairly complex procedures will be made here. However, for those not informed, but interested, it comes under the heading of Foreign Military Sales (FMS), and if U.S. federal funds are being used to assist the foreign country, it will be administered through the Defense Security Assistance Agency (DSAA).

Many of the procurement, certification, and payment procedures of DSAA resemble those of AID. If DSAA is involved, that agency will control many aspects of the pricing and other sales details. The Department of Defense (DOD) and the Department of State's (DOS) Office of Munitions Control also will be involved as to export licensing and other matters, as mentioned at the beginning of Chapter 31.

Complete coverage of the subject of procurement and payment process for FMS orders through DSAA can be found in two publications by DOD. *Security Assistance Management Manual,* Publication No. DOD 5105.38M (a fairly expensive 900-page how-to book on procurement practices relative to FMS); and *The FMS Financial Management Manual,* Publication No. DOD 7290.3M (a 600-page book on getting paid and financing FMS). Both books are available from DISAM, Building 125, Area B, Wright Patterson Air Force Base, Ohio 45433. Call TIC for contact information.

Endnotes

1. *The Multilateral Development Banks: Increasing U.S. Exports and Creating U.S. Jobs,* Department of the Treasury, 1994.

2. *How U.S. Firms Can Boost Exports Through Overseas Development Project,* U.S. Chamber of Commerce, Task Force on International Economic Policy and the Bretton Woods Committee, October 1986.

3

Trading Blocs and Investment Strategies

14

The European Union

Today's European Union (EU) was originally called the European Economic Community (EEC) and was often informally referred to as the Common Market. It was composed of only six nations: the Netherlands, Belgium, and Luxembourg (the trio that comprised the original Benelux common market), plus West Germany, Italy, and France. Its activities were largely a matter of curiosity and passing interest to the average American exporter. The addition of the United Kingdom and the Commonwealth was a major step forward, although Britain has often been at odds with the other EU members.

As the EEC grew and strengthened, it came to be known as the European Community (EC), and in 1985, a White Paper by the EC Commission proposed completion of the internal market by 1992. This goal, often referred to thereafter as EC '92, was made official under the Single European Act in 1986, but its realization was viewed by many as unlikely, except possibly as a threat to free trade. Very few anticipated the dynamic revival of Europe it would create.

Before 1988, many pundits could speak only of the glorious opportunities to be offered by the Pacific Rim, while considering most of Europe (with the possible exception of Germany) as having its commercial strength eroded by a host of problems, including excess social welfare and minimal competitiveness. In fact, few in the business community took their eyes off the Pacific Rim long enough to discuss the subject of EC '92 with any urgency until well into 1988.

The EC Commission and its parliament may have somewhat diluted their underlying support with the binding ties built into the Treaty of Maastricht (signed in 1992 and effective as of 1993), especially in regard to their proposal to adopt a common European Currency Unit (the ECU). Nonetheless, the movement is eminently successful overall in terms of achieving the greater part of the goals the EU set for itself in the EC Commission's 1985 White Paper. Interestingly, the 1992 goals have had their primary impact on the world of commerce and politics, where the EU concept has more support than it has with the general public. Federalism that reaches into everyday life, such as the imposition of a new currency, requires more popular support. But many people still believe that the ECU currency will be a reality by the end of the decade.

The European Community indicated its more binding nature by renaming itself the European Union (EU) in 1993, and it is being taken very seriously both by its members and by the world as a whole. Some see it as a marvelous commercial opportunity, others as a grave threat. Most of the European nations see it as something they cannot afford to be outside of. This is evidenced by the fact that as of 1995 the EU consists of 15 nations. Besides the United Kingdom, Spain, Portugal, Greece, Ireland, and Denmark all joined the EU, followed in 1995 by three members of the former European Free Trade Association (EFTA), Austria, Sweden, and Finland. It should not go unnoticed that although it did not change the count, the unification of East and West Germany substantially changed the population and potential economic might of the EU. This list leaves only the western European nations of Switzerland, Liechtenstein, and Norway out of the EU. Together with Iceland, they are all that remains of EFTA, except for Switzerland, which continues to be an undecided EU applicant.

Objectives and Strategies

The founders of the European Union had as their overriding aim to unite Europe in hopes of avoiding future European wars. But in addition, they were guided by a powerful economic concern. The best and largest businesses of Europe were motivated to pursue an economic community concept because, without the benefit of unrestricted access to all of Europe, too few of them were gaining the strength needed for world-class competition. Ready access to such a huge market was necessary to permit more of them to aggressively compete with the giant companies of Asia and the United States. These businesses perceived that there were three major barriers in what was their more-restricted home market:

1. Physical barriers at customs that prevented free movement of goods and people
2. Technical barriers created by multiple standards and quality tests
3. Fiscal barriers in the form of widely varying rates of value added taxes (VAT) and excise duties

These barriers conspired to prevent European businesses from gaining the economies of scale and the strategic advantages necessary to deal freely and economically with the very large European marketplace. The EU did well in quickly abolishing intra-EU tariffs and quotas following the 1957 Treaty of Rome that established the European Union. Nonetheless, it was a surprise to everyone that so many diverse nations could continue to move in unison to create so many radical changes as quickly and surely as they did under the Single European Act. How well they will fare with the Treaty of Maastricht's further objectives remains to be seen, but the development of the EU is an ongoing process that will continue long after the year 2000, both in terms of structure and in terms of membership.

It should be understood that the primary goal of the EU is not to be a political "United States of Europe" or to abandon the very substantial ethnic and cultural differences that characterize the member nations. The most far-reaching goal is probably the single currency or European Currency Unit (ECU), and it will be a hotly contested issue for years to come. The objective of a single currency is called Stage III of the Maastricht Treaty and is to be achieved through creation of a European Central Bank in 1997 at the earliest or by 1999 at the latest. Although the issue is far from settled, it is still amazing that it would even be seriously considered so soon. It is quite conceivable that the ECU, which already exists, will at least become the primary currency for intra-EU trade and for settling many foreign balances in a foreseeable future. Giving up sovereign or national rights and privileges will be something else again, and remains an unlikely possibility.

It is clear that the EU is likely to continue to grow. As many as eight to ten nations of Central and Eastern Europe are interested in joining (Hungary and Poland have applications pending), in addition to Turkey, Malta, and Cyprus in the Mediterranean. Several of these could be considered for entry as early as the year 2000 or even earlier, if the Union can afford to have them. Adding less-developed nations is, and will be, a burden to the EU economy until each new member is fully integrated and its economy improves. In fact, the addition of East Germany, which was a burden to Germany alone, probably nevertheless slowed the entire European Union's progress toward its goals because Germany had to delay its progress while digesting this very large bite, called by some the world's most expensive "leveraged buy-out."

Turkey has applied for membership, but has been refused for the time being because of Turkish agricultural subsidies. It has reapplied, but its acceptance remains debatable because of the burden that would be created by its admission, unless this and other problems can be resolved, as most expect they ultimately will. The EU population now exceeds 370 million, compared to 255 million in the United States, which has a land area three times as large. The EU gross domestic product (GDP) in 1994 was $6.9 trillion, about 10 percent higher than that of the U.S. Because of the economic enhancement created by the efficiencies and competitiveness derived from the EU plan, its GNP growth is expected to outpace that of the United States in the immediate future. In 1994, the EU was our second-best customer, with its purchases of goods from the U.S. reaching $108 billion—far exceeding all but Canada's at $114 billion. The $108 billion in goods exports to the EU in 1994 was more than double that of American exports to Japan. As a whole, our EU trade is a relatively balanced trade, without large deficits on either side, and it continues to grow.

The U.S. is better positioned to take advantage of this trade than are many of the individual EU countries themselves, because of our economies of scale and experience in marketing to a large and diverse market. However, this will not last forever because the removal of the above-mentioned barriers, together with other enhancements, permits keener competition within Europe and greater economies of scale for its aggressive companies. EU firms are catching up fast as their business environment becomes almost as open as our own in the United States.

In view of these developments, any misconceptions as to the Pacific Rim being the only growth market for U.S. exports in the future or notions about Europe being a poor market for American exports should be readily dispelled. In fact, even as the EU threatens us with greater competition, it also beckons us as an enormous opportunity that will be more accessible than ever before. The questions a business should ask itself are: How is the European Union changing and developing? and What are the best ways and means to reach it as a single, yet diversified market?

Evidence of the myriad ways in which the European Union is evolving and will continue to change and develop is contained in the hundreds of directives formulated by the European Commission, the administrative body of the EU. The commission in turn proposes the directives to the European Parliament, and on the parliament's favorable review, each is submitted to the Council of Ministers, where a majority is required for most directives to become EU law. The fact that only a majority is required is significant evidence of progress and general desire. Details of the directives are readily available from the commission offices in Washington, D.C. The following list of categories for the directives provides an idea of how comprehensive the EU structuring is, with additional categories still under discussion:

- Harmonized standards, testing, and certification, for home and personal products, food, cosmetics, telecommunications, and construction equipment
- Harmonized packing, labeling, and processing requirements
- Harmonized regulations pertaining to the health industry, including marketing regulations
- Harmonized government procurement regulations
- Harmonized regulations for services, including banking, broadcasting, finance, and credit cards
- Liberalized capital movements
- Harmonized consumer protection regulations
- Harmonized laws on corporate law and behavior, including trademarks, mergers, and bankruptcy proceedings
- Harmonized VAT and excise taxes
- Harmonized product liability laws

- Harmonized veterinary and phytosanitary controls
- Eliminated and/or simplified national transit documents and procedures for intra-EU trade, including customs formalities and the Single Administrative Document (SAD)
- Established rules for the free movement of labor and professions

The issues concerning standards, a key part of the single-market objective and strategy, are the responsibility of the European Committee for Standardization, which became a vital force in the 1992 EU goals and in the ISO (International Organization for Standardization), an acronym worth remembering. ISO is comprised of the national standards institutions in about 100 countries, including our own American National Standards Institution (ANSI). The EU is the key contributor to the ISO 9000 standards for quality manufacturing and service discussed in Chapter 7. The issues and problems concerning technical standards have been among the EU's most vexing, but good progress has been made. Any firm seriously planning on doing business in the EU should be aware of these quality standards and the possibility of the ISO 9000 certification process.

We should never lose sight of the fact that the overriding objective of the EU members is to improve the competitiveness and stature of their businesses, not just within the European Union, but on a global basis. To want to reach this goal while maintaining an open commercial society (as opposed to a "Fortress Europe") is natural, since there is little value in improving global competitiveness within a trade protectionist world.

Market Characteristics

The European market is described as one of changing demographics, with an increasing number of working spouses, smaller households, declining school dropouts, more elderly people, and people with more time and money for travel and leisure. A guidebook entitled *Europe 1992: Implications for California Business,* prepared in cooperation with the California State World Trade Commission and its European Trade and Investment Office in London by the KPMG Peat Marwick accounting firm, provides a wide variety of information on the EU and strategies for doing business there. This guidebook states that such a market profile means that "small- and medium-sized businesses with innovative or high-quality products will be able to penetrate this larger, more affluent market more readily."[1]

A factor in this improved access for smaller business is the revolution that Europe is experiencing in the expanded reach of its broadcast media. In the past, broadcast media has been tightly controlled, but as a result of the EC '92 White Paper, satellite transmission has been made freer from government regulation and accessible to households throughout Europe. Such "pan-European media networks will make it much easier to cost-effectively 'reach' consumers," according to KPMG Peat Marwick.[2] It is also noteworthy that English is the most often used language in pan-European broadcasts. Caution: This universality of English, however, does not spill over to English units of measure. *Metric is a must!*

The fact that English is spoken in commerce does not mean that Europe will cease to be a diverse assortment of languages, cultures, and market preferences. In fact, as countries are added to the EU, it will become a more, not less, diverse market. Therefore, the mere presence of open borders and common regulations should not lead to the assumption that the entire EU is viable for a given product or firm, no matter how well it may be matched to any one country. The product and the company resources must still dictate the focus of the marketing. Market research, country by country, remains as important as it always was in determining market strategy. It is simply that there are now more and better options for small businesses to reach all the present 15 countries. For the foreseeable future, the EU will be thought of as Western Europe, even though Greece extends further East than Albania. Should Turkey eventually join, the EU border will lie on a line east of Moscow in Asia Minor.

In the course of country market research, it might be useful to take the line of least resistance whenever possible. In other words, in the case of Europe, this means remembering that Germany is by far the largest market, but that while the United Kingdom is only fourth-largest, it is compact, English-speaking, and has the reputation of being the most susceptible to the purchase of American goods. In this regard, Germany, Italy, Holland, Ireland, and Belgium follow closely, with France usually being the least eager to purchase U.S. merchandise unless technology demands it. Another item of research that should be factored into this equation is the far less expensive, faster, and more convenient intra-EU distribution logistics that will be available to a central warehouse location.

Part of a market research program should probably be participation in an appropriate trade show. (This subject is dealt with in depth in Chapter 12.) Since in Europe the trade show really is a place to do business and write orders, the attendee should be prepared. There is also a good opportunity to deal with distributors and businesses from all over Europe on a one-on-one basis, which means getting a real feeling for potential buyers as opposed to working only with "lookers" who are far from deciding on a firm order.

If there is any urgency in getting EU trade started because of the rapid pace of development of the EU, you should seriously consider market consultants in order to speed up the process. Many are available. Chambers of commerce in Europe are said to play a broad role, and may be a good place to seek references for service firms or even to identify potential business partners or alliances.

An interesting consideration was raised by Yves G. Aureille in an article for *Export Today*. He wrote that the realization of a single European market has led large European groups to revise their corporate strategies in terms of their range of business activities. They are moving away from a national conglomerate's approach, involving several sectors of industrial or commercial activity, and toward becoming relatively specialized transactional firms. They may also be seeking a strong partner or alliance in a second or third country to speed the process of reaching a multinational dimension.[3]

Any U.S. firm should think about both strength through specialization and taking on a European partner to improve its ability to compete and develop quick responses. Going into partnership is certainly cheaper than buying entry into Europe, as many large firms are doing, and a partnership demands much less in terms of available human resources.

Considering an EU Investment

In addition to direct export, all the various business formats, including mergers, acquisitions, and joint ventures should be studied when thinking about entering or expanding in Europe. Traditionally, smaller companies have settled for licensing arrangements or distributor/agent arrangements, but many experts are now predicting that these will not be enough in a sharper, more competitive environment. This may or may not be true, depending on the licensee, the distributor, or the partner and, naturally, on the product and its competition. Much the same is true for timing. If a firm has export potential, the changing face of Europe and the goals that the EU has imposed on itself inevitably imply that a time frame exists for present and future competition in this arena. But, as with all decisions, the mere existence of a real or imagined deadline should not shape the decision itself. Once the time frame has dissolved, the European market will still be there and available, even though the factors going into a delayed decision may well be altered. In any case, there may be a substantial potential for expansion pending an informed decision that surely should not be lost by default.

Expanding into Europe is not a step to take out of fear that this is the last chance. If there is reason for involvement, it should be the result of rational analysis and a conviction that at least some cost elements, such as manufacturing, assembly, distribution, marketing, research, or administration will be diminished and that market share can thereby be enlarged. Only if that's the conclusion can a firm expect the added benefits that should be available because of its presence in the community and its acceptance there. It is most unlikely that this last factor alone could justify such an investment of resources unless foreseeable developments clearly provide other incentives.

This should not be taken to mean that a presence in the EC is a precondition for exporting to Europe. Many firms will simply do a fine job of marketing and make a profit doing so. Whatever the ultimate shape and form of the EU, Europe is in the process of creating the largest single market in the world for U.S. exports, and we, in turn, are their largest market. Everything will become easier with one set of standards, documents, regulations, and so on—even though each country must still be addressed as an individual market as well as part of the EU. In many cases, it may well prove that a company should invest first in good distribution facilities, using existing U.S. manufacturing facilities to full capacity before further investing in factories or other facilities abroad. If on-site manufacturing of the European product or its components becomes a factor, the conceivable development of a European sun belt, as pointed out by the

California State World Trade Commission report, might be worth considering.[4] The tendency of high-tech firms to gravitate toward good weather, would point to the sunny climes of Spain, Portugal, and Greece—countries that also offer the least expensive labor costs.

For some firms or individuals undertaking export efforts for the first time or expanding a current modest effort with a European presence, a fixation on creating a joint venture or subsidiary could be absolutely wrong. Waiting for just the right initial partner under the right conditions, can extend the start date for expanding overseas trade too far into the future and, in the process, let too large an investment in human resources and unconsummated sales accumulate. It can also be an excuse for doing nothing. It is universally agreed that a mistake to avoid at all costs is undertaking a joint venture or any kind of a partnership arrangement without a solid basis for confidence in the foreign partner. It follows that the safest way to gain such confidence is by working together in some form before sealing the relationship in the form of a partnership. Ingenuity and circumstances will dictate the most appropriate type of partnership, but the most obvious route to it in many circumstances is a distribution agreement or cooperation on a single project.

Overall, it's wise to take a cautious approach toward planning your presence in the EU. It's as likely that you'll be shut out of the European market forever by not undertaking a joint venture right away as that the United States will suddenly ban all imports. Prematurely tying up scarce capital, or taking on inappropriate partners in a hasty decision-making process are but two of many good reasons for not rushing into a joint venture or any other kind of association.

Sources of Help and Information

If you would like general information on the European market, contact the Public Inquiries office of the European Commission Delegation at 2300 M Street NW, Washington, D.C. 20037. On the U.S. side there is an Office of European Union Affairs, Department of Commerce, Room 3036, 14th and Constitution Avenue NW, Washington, D.C. 20230. It appears, however, that the information that office has available is distributed primarily by means of the National Trade Data Bank CD-ROMs and the Country Commercial Guides. There is also a DOC European Union Hotline at 301/921-4164 for fax retrieval of specific subjects, such as information regarding new product standards.

Endnotes

1. *Europe 1992: Implications for California Businesses, A Guidebook,* prepared by KPMG Peat Marwick for the California State World Trade Commission and the California European Trade and Investment Office, 1989.
2. KPMG Peat Marwick, ibid.
3. Yves G. Aureille, "Corporate Strategies for EC '92," *Export Today,* May/June 1990.
4. KPMG Peat Marwick, ibid.

15

Central/Eastern Europe

Central Europe

Enormous changes have taken place in less than five years in Central Europe, which for our purposes includes Albania, Bulgaria, the Czech Republic, Slovakia, Hungary, Poland, Romania, and the war-torn remnants of the former Yugoslavia—Slovenia, Croatia, Bosnia-Herzegovina, Macedonia and rump Yugoslavia (Serb-dominated). After a breathtaking series of events, the vast region once termed the Communist Eastern Bloc has been completely dismantled and reborn as a group of fledgling market economies—democracies at best and destitute or warring anarchies at worst. But for all the initial enthusiasm these events initially evoked among those engaged in international trade, many now believe that what has taken place is merely a resumption, after a half-century hiatus, of the "balkanization" that characterized the region after the breakup of the old Hapsburg Empire. It is difficult, even several years after the astounding and sudden collapse of Communism, to reach any but the most limited and short-term conclusions about much of the region, particularly as war still rages in most of former Yugoslavia, with the ever present possibility of it spreading. Little has yet come to rest long enough for us to feel assured that anything other than change itself will be permanent, or what further alternatives will be chosen. An exception to this may be the countries of Poland, the Czech Republic, Slovakia, and Hungary, but they, too, are subject to powerful political shifts to the right or left.

One irreversible fact, however—aside from it being apparent that Central Europe is a growing and substantial export market—is that there will be no return to COMECON, the political mechanism that once dominated the

Communist world. At its peak, COMECON accounted for 30 percent of the world's industrial output. Besides the Eastern European republics of the former USSR—which was composed of Russia plus its many multiethnic republics stretching across Europe and Asia to the Pacific—COMECON included most of the states of Central Europe, as well as Cuba, Mongolia, and Vietnam. Albania was once a member, and Yugoslavia long held observer status. As of 1991, the COMECOM countries attempted a transition to a group called the Organization of International Economic Cooperation, trying to preserve as much as possible of their former economic relationship as their economies moved toward world prices and convertible currencies. That attempt has been largely abandoned, and at best Central Europe—plus possibly pieces of Eastern Europe—will evolve into an essentially European group, with the majority of its members already in an associate relationship with the EU. These countries share a strong desire to leave their loose association and join the EU as fully fledged members. The EU is entering into such associate arrangements, termed Trade and Cooperation Agreements with Eastern European Countries, as a transitional aid. These agreements are intended to form the groundwork for a coherent basis of political, economic, financial, and cultural association. The isolation of most of these nations is clearly over, and it can only be hoped that the ethnic cleansing process will spread no further and that differences will be resolved peacefully in the future without further damage to the economy.

It is important to many of the central European nations to be called and thought of by the Western world as Central Europe, rather than being grouped under the former Cold War categorization of "East" versus "West." This attitude has forced the U.S. State Department to reconsider its terminology, just as traders and investors are doing. In 1994 the State Department was proposing to segment Europe for nomenclature purposes into: (1) Western Europe as we commonly think of it today; (2) the three newly independent Baltic states of Estonia, Latvia, and Lithuania, together with the Scandinavian nations, as Baltic-Nordic Europe; (3) Poland, the Czech Republic, Slovakia, Hungary, and Romania as North-Central Europe; (4) the former nations of Yugoslavia, plus Bulgaria and Albania, as South-Central Europe; and (5) Russia, plus the remaining Newly Independent States as far east as the Urals, more or less as Eastern Europe. The last-named category was to include Belarus, Ukraine, and Moldova, but it was unclear what would be the proposed status of the Caucasian states of Georgia, Armenia, and Azerbaijan, which appear to be a logical extension. The final outcome of this exercise was uncertain at the time of this writing. The new categories reflect the Central European states' strong desire to be distinguished from Eastern Europe, and their economic interest in becoming part of the EU someday. Each grouping has a different history, culture, and economy, as well as a very different potential transition rate to a free market.

Economic, Political, and Cultural Problems

The path to democracy for Central Europe and the Baltic states has neither been unanimous nor on a consistent and straightforward line. In a number of countries, including Poland and Hungary in 1993 and Romania and Bulgaria before that, power has reverted to people who were key players in the former Communist regimes. The same process has also occurred in Lithuania, in the Baltics, and in Ukraine and Belarus in Eastern Europe, and if the former East Germany were not now part of greater Germany, it would probably have occurred there as well.

In spite of these political developments, the countries involved continue to absorb increasing amounts of goods, and foreign investment continues to pour into them. The lion's share, however, has gone to the North-Central region of the Czech Republic, Slovakia, Hungary, and Poland, plus, of course, eastern Germany, is a region that has experienced dynamic economic growth in recent years and is now a rapidly expanding U.S. export market. This North-Central and Baltic European nations were struggling to adopt market reforms even during the Communist era. The South-Central European countries' less promising economic performance has traditionally been aggravated by the generally poorer conditions of southeastern Europe, typified by the economic woes of Bulgaria and Romania.

Czechoslovakia, Poland, and Hungary appear to be in the best shape by comparison, in part because they enjoyed a head start by signing the Central European Free Trade Agreement (CEFTA) as early as 1991. This agreement commits the signatories to eliminate all internal tariffs on nonagricultural goods by 1998. Since Slovakia broke away from Czechoslovakia, currently the most dynamic economy in Central Europe, it has not done as well as the Czech Republic, but it is still seen as being one of the better potential trading opportunities in Central Europe. These same countries also lead in privatization. In fact, Hungary was reported to have more than 4500 private companies as early as 1990, and its banking system seems to have been in the process of aligning itself with Western principles well before the Communist overthrow. This fact may account to some degree for Hungary's receiving the greatest influx of foreign capital since 1990. Poland leads in economic growth, but only after suffering very harsh reform policies. These have, however, been adhered to with remarkable tenacity. There remains considerable protectionism in Poland, in the form of tariffs and other obstacles to trade, but it is tending to diminish rather than grow. The U.S. Trade Promotion Coordinating Council (TPCC) includes Poland on its target list of Big Emerging Markets (BEMs) and considers it to be the single-most important market in Central or Eastern Europe. What has been especially noteworthy in the case of Poland has been that even though their radical economic reform medicine included privatization of their large industries, the many small businesses and budding entrepreneurs have become the driving force in Poland's economic recovery. Watch for similar entrepreneurial leadership in many countries in this region. With a population of 38 million and a GDP of $85 billion, as well as a strategic location, it is the largest U.S. trading partner in the region and a customer for a broad range of products. Exporters can look for special help in marketing to Poland as a result.

All the Central European countries except Albania have individually signed association agreements with the EU. This is supposed to lead to a nearly duty-free trade, except in the agricultural area, after 1995. Bulgaria is described by most experts as too desperate for serious targeting at this time. Little external private investment has entered the country, because surviving elements of the former Communist regime appear to feel it threatens the local industries. Romania offers more promise, even though it was the last of the European Communist nations to fall and has one of the worst of Central Europe's infrastructures. Its first reform government failed and the successor regimes have not shown a fondness for radical reforms. Nevertheless, some privatization has gone forward, with many well established private enterprises reported, and it has enjoyed some conservative but sensible economic policies. Albania is the most backward country in the region and, as noted, is the only country of Central Europe that has failed to sign an association agreement with the EU.

Keep in mind that all the nations of this region have a strong reason for offering EU countries better access to their markets than any nation outside Europe. They desperately want to be part of the EU and will do whatever is necessary to foster that objective. But in the long run the fact remains that all of them are also members of GATT. When the finally completed Uruguay Round is ratified by all the participants, there will probably be a lowering of tariffs for Europeans and non-Europeans alike.

Because of the historically unprecedented unification of the two Germanys, export and investment prospects in the former East Germany require a different approach from that for the Central European countries. Economically speaking, the reunified Germany now has a foot in both Western and Central Europe, considering its eastern borders and former relationships, which makes Germany a very different entity, both as an export customer and as a global competitor. The unification created five new German states plus Berlin, namely: Mecklenburg-Vorpommern, Saxony-Anhalt, Thuringia, Saxony, and Brandenburg. Some of the problems that will not be resolved for some time in Central and Eastern Europe were instantly resolved in the former East Germany, such as membership in the EU, well-defined intellectual property rights, appropriate bilateral trade agreements, well-established financial channels, and a hard currency. These issues, major problems for many of the former East Germany's neighbors, were among many trade problems solved at the stroke of a pen when reunification occurred.

While eastern Germany has experienced some disillusionment along with some employment and production problems, there is little doubt about its rapid growth during this decade, according to the country desk at the Department of Commerce and others. The only question is how fast. The privatizing stage was completed with surprising speed by the Trusteeship Agency (Treuhandanstalt), which included technology transfers and licensing agreements. The successfully privatized eastern German firms surely have some advantage over many of their Central European competitors, but even so, with a new labor and entrepreneurial climate, new attitudes, and infrastructures that need to be developed, the now private sector enterprises of eastern Germany will be almost as hard-pressed as those in most other former Communist states as they attempt to establish themselves and become profitable, creditworthy businesses. Given EU standards, it will require difficult adjustments before eastern Germany's products can be allowed to enter the EU market.

The former East Germans will no doubt do a lot of their trading with their new countrymen and buy their services internally, but despite Germany's emerging role as the world's largest exporter of manufactured goods, it is also a major importer. Many sales and enterprise opportunities will abound for U.S. exporters, regardless of the built-in advantage for the former West Germans. Many U.S. products and services are highly admired in this part of Europe, and it would be as foolish to give up this market as it would be to ignore the established western German market.

For firms selling appropriate products and having adequate know-how and staying power, the region as a whole represents substantial potential for both direct exports and joint ventures, depending on the country and the current availability of foreign exchange or acceptable countertrade options. The former roadblocks that existed in obtaining validated licenses should largely vanish. Export licensing problems are, or have been, sharply diminished throughout Central and Eastern Europe, except for the core list of sophisticated super-computer technology or high-tech military products, but the continuing political crises in the region may slow this process. Nevertheless, for the average firm without a special situation or reason for undertaking activities in this part of the world, there are far more compatible areas in the world to begin to build an international trade.

Entrepreneurial Challenges

The *Journal of Commerce* reported in September of 1990 on a nearly textbook example of smart and perfectly targeted entrepreneurship that still applies. Peter Fried, a Hungarian who fled to America and who runs an Entre computer store franchise formed a company named Donosphere. He gained the Hungarian franchise right from the parent company of his own franchise and, in turn, acquired two former Hungarian state-owned companies with existing staff and facilities to serve as the basis for a series of Entre outlets. Part of the $1 million needed for start-up came from U.S. investors and $500,000 came from the Hungarian-American Enterprise Fund, one of several sources of funding available for investment in that area, and from a U.S. government-sponsored non-profit entity to promote bilateral trade. Donosphere intends to import and sell American-brand computers through distributors under a licensing arrangement rather than a franchising plan because Hungary has no franchise law. It is a textbook example because the principal has a special qualification in terms of his cultural and ethnic background and because he is selling a badly needed product that is imported but that represents an investment in the country, utilizing existing facilities. The Entre franchise will enjoy a further advantage because of this ability to sell part of the product in local currency since it will have host-country operational costs.

Of course there will be demand for imports that can be satisfied with less-targeted solutions, and often demand will have little rational justification in view of the more serious needs of the country. As Michael Tomezyk related in an article for *Export Today* in June 1990, "these countries need can opener factories more than they need can openers."[1] But even though the need is for capital goods and medical equipment, there will be demand for Levis and Nikes and many other sophisticated consumer goods. A backward commercial infrastructure should not be confused with a lack of sophisticated tastes or limited education.

One problem with imports of consumer goods that can less readily be solved with ingenuity or foreign exchange is the issue of distribution and transportation infrastructure. Even though the demand is there, and some say that almost anything can be sold if you can carry it on your own truck, it is quite another thing to realize the product's potential because the distribution system is still weak and what infrastructure there is overburdened. To a greater or lesser degree throughout Central and Eastern Europe, there are allocation and priority problems caused by there suddenly being too much freedom of choice—both politically and economically—for people who have to some degree lost the ability and will to choose. These problems are bound to be compounded by the disequilibriums created by neighboring wars.

At the present time, caution is still advised in appointing distributors from either Central or Eastern Europe. Good distributors are few in number, as most have not had free-market experience for more than a generation. In many cases it might be more productive to use an Austrian intermediary. As in the financial areas of forfaiting and countertrading, the Austrians have maintained serious commercial relationships throughout the years, so that a network is in place, composed of regular practitioners who are skilled in commerce and who have long been dependent on the eastern portions of Europe for at least part of their livelihood. Whatever the choice, changes in distribution can be difficult and expensive and should be carefully investigated.

Long-Term Strategies

For those who have the means, it will probably be a more successful and profitable long-term strategy to identify and organize facilities in the region to manufacture products or parts for export to the United States or Third World countries. Certainly the American businessperson is welcomed for such endeavors. Hungary, the Czechs, and Slovakia have clearly expressed to our various state and federal officers in Europe that they are eager for U.S. investment before they are swallowed up or dominated by Germany, economically. Japan is also pursuing the Central and Eastern Europe opportunities with its usual aggressiveness and willingness to invest and take losses initially for the long-term benefit.

The reasoning behind a joint venture, investment, or contract manufacturing strategy is to establish a profitable presence now, when a relatively small investment can leverage many jobs and permit Central European businesses to develop hard currency in sufficient quantities to become more fruitful customers down the road. While these countries need imports, they must export for both jobs and cash; therefore, countertrade should always be seen as a possible alternative to conventional trading in this area. However, some traders suggest buyback commitments as more productive and easier to implement than countertrade arrangements. (See a further discussion of countertrade in Chapter 38.)

One category of exporting that is in great demand is technology transfer, whether performed as a licensing agreement or resulting from the product itself. Here, as in most developing countries, including those of Asia, middle-level technology is of the greatest value. This is typified by such product areas as telecommunication, factory automation, computers and software, conservation and pollution-control products, and robotics of many kinds, particularly for electronic assembly. In Hungary, agribusiness-related technology and products continue to be in great demand. All these products are ideal candidates for plans involving some elements of technology transfer, manufacturing, and investment within the country, combined with exports to the country. In regard to technology transfer and licensing, it should be noted that the intellectual property rights status has been a shambles in Central and Eastern Europe, and those involved in transferring will benefit from the emphasis placed on this subject in the now completed Uruguay Round of GATT.

The format for doing business in Central Europe deserves some special thought, and one such format is the joint venture. It clearly has merit, but perhaps less so than in Western Europe and should be very carefully thought out. Unless the U.S. firm is skilled in working with joint ventures, is confident of the future, and has an understanding of the labor force and its present badly diminished work ethic, as well as the other socio-economic problems in both Central and Eastern Europe, there may be safer and more prudent ways to proceed. The American joint venture partner must be of sufficient financial strength to suffer the burden of long delays in expatriating joint venture profits. One option, if finding a management partner is an issue but the labor force seems acceptable, is to seek a good buyout opportunity and operate the plant with U.S. management. By this means one can also indirectly, and perhaps with more security, transfer much precious technology that will be repaid in extra profits rather than in contract fees.

Still another alternative to the joint venture is the strategic alliance. This increasingly popular, but loosely defined, form of business association for smaller firms or firms who want to test the waters before taking the big plunge, can be especially appropriate in an area surrounded by so many uncertainties. It is a less formal relationship, based on synergisms, that has enjoyed some success and is discussed in Chapter 5. One suggestion for a modified initial level of activity that might be accomplished within the first phase of such a strategic alliance, is having an OEM manufacture for the U.S. firm, which the flexible and open-ended arrangement of a strategic alliance would permit. If a joint venture is being sought, a Western European partner with experience and interest in Central and Eastern Europe may be a better solution. Someone in Germany or Austria should be among those candidates.

When assessing the wisdom of adding manufacturing or importing to a firm's overall international strategy, special opportunities, some quite transitory and created by the radical political shifts, must be considered, as well as the completely different cultural and economic environment. For example, it has been observed that there is unlikely to be a replay of capitalizing on large cost savings on labor-intensive products. Today the people of this region are not eager to work with their hands, and so technology must play an important role. It might be important to note such differences as the fact that Czechs are often excellent engineers and tend to have the best machinery, while Serbs are among the most divisive, ethnically speaking, and historically have had lesser skills. Jim Phillips, former director of California's European Office, advises us that "history and visits in the region tell me that East Germans will play a large part in South-Central Europe's development [when the hostilities cease] and will provide the engineering skills that are now lacking."

If U.S. product liability or environmental rulings are an issue, the new EU Harmonized Products Liability laws and environmental restrictions should be studied. The results could add or subtract points from the decision process, because there is a reasonable likelihood that at least parts of Central Europe will eventually adopt EU regulations or acquire them as a result of EU admission. In terms of import quotas, it is likely that there will be an advantage over the more restrictive quotas of Southeast Asia. Another production factor to consider is the very dramatic decline in Russia's defense budget compared to its USSR predecessor, which has meant that many plants formerly making technical equipment and parts for the Russian military are now available and desperate for civilian business. In most other areas of manufacturing as well, the former Soviet Union, once Central and Eastern Europe's largest customer, no longer has the buying power.

Eastern Europe

Having referred to Central Europe's recent history as "a breathtaking series of events," it is difficult to find another superlative phrase to introduce the volatile subject of Eastern Europe, comprised of Russia and the Newly Independent States (NIS)—or Commonwealth of Independent States (CIS), as the Russian government would prefer to have us call it. The appellation "Newly Independent States" might also be used to include the Baltic states, but we have already included them in the Baltic-Nordic subregion of Europe, along with the Scandinavian nations.

Somewhat less than one-third of Russia lies west of the Ural Mountains and forms most of Eastern Europe. Western, or "European," Russia is quite different from eastern Russia and the whole of the Russian Federation, ranging as it does from the Atlantic to the Pacific. It is also very much in a transitional and uncertain state. For both reasons, it seems fair to address Russia within the context of both Europe and Asia. Eastern Europe as considered here consists of the Russian Federation and the NIS states of Belarus, Ukraine, Moldava, Georgia, Armenia, and Azerbaijan. Considering its frantic pace of change, the entire region, like the former Yugoslavia, is probably a subject more suited to a monthly magazine than it is to a book. We know that dramatic changes are occurring and that nevertheless there are, and will continue to be, excellent trade opportunities in the region. Of the NIS states included in Eastern Europe, Russia, at $2.6 billion, represented about 86 percent of the total U.S. exports to the region in 1994 and nearly half the total exports to Central and Eastern Europe combined. The overall pattern has been one of rapid growth. A market of this magnitude and growth rate cannot be overlooked, in spite of its inherent difficulties. As cataclysmic and fluid as South-Central Europe is, Russia and the NIS seem to be even more so. The non-European portion of the Russian Federation, geographically speaking, lies in Central Asia and the Siberian portion of Asia, which will be taken up again in the discussion of Asia.

Special Problems

Many of the comments made about Central Europe also apply to Eastern Europe as well, but often with a slightly different slant. As an example, countertrade is important here, but an extra difficulty arises with the Russian Federation and the NIS because, aside from their extractables, little of their manufactured product except for caviar and vodka is saleable to the rest of the world. Also, in view of domestic shortages, even products that might be acceptable are not available for export, thereby making even countertrade quite difficult. At least the better trading candidates in Central Europe have a far larger range of desirable goods, such as the already noted Hungarian software.

The difficult conditions in regard to transportation, distribution, and warehousing in Central Europe have already been described, but in parts of Russia these vital infrastructures are close to nonexistent. However, don't let such shortcomings obscure the fact that Russians are a highly educated and intellectually oriented people, with a high percentage of graduate degrees among them. They will quickly learn the skills of management in a free market economy and black marketeers will evolve into capitalistic entrepreneurs in great numbers.

There are many anomalies in the region and to a prospective trader or investor, the mere vastness and complexity of the country not to mention the bureaucracy, can be overwhelming. This may remain an obstacle for some time to come, reform notwithstanding. However, as Austria offers a reliable entry into Central Europe, so does Finland to the Baltic states and Russia. There is nevertheless a fast-growing export trade, and our European and Japanese competitors seem to be working with greater diligence to take advantage of the current, more hospitable environment to build trade infrastructures for the future than are our Yankee traders. It clearly requires patience and resourcefulness. The up-to-the-minute "hotlines" and fax services, such as BISNIS and EEBIC Flash, can be a great help in such a fluid environment.

There are some outstanding success stories that are at least as interesting as McDonald's well-documented success story. Overall, the market's needs in Russia are similar to those of the rest of Eastern Europe. They include commercial electronics, communications equipment, consumer goods of all kinds, and products for Russia's seriously deficient health industry. In many categories the country's needs are greater than those of Eastern Europe; this applies to the well-documented shortage of transportation infrastructure and indeed, to the entire food industry, which together create the debacle of often losing 40 percent of annual Russian farm production.

According to Zak Karamally, export manager for Texas Instruments, more than 80 percent of Russians would be considered poor by Western standards, whereas Hungary, Czechoslovakia, and former East Germany enjoy a large middle class.[2] With limited incomes, few bank accounts, no credit facilities, and the problems of establishing a consumer distribution infrastructure, the task of developing large-scale consumer demand is formidable, but it will happen one day. Today, the region's consumer economy depends heavily on the exchange of labor and services on a person-to-person basis.

Whether or not you are prepared to engage in countertrade is a question you must be prepared to answer fully and rationally before you begin your marketing efforts, for the request will surely be made even though much trade goes forward under conventional terms. If the answer to a countertrade request is a firm "No," it may as well be phrased adeptly and graciously. If the answer is "Yes" or "Maybe," then you must know in advance what products could conceivably be dealt with this way, and/or what specific countertrade brokers could handle the traded product, together with the various costs and fees involved. The costs should be built into the price quotations, since discounts can always be provided for cash. As already indicated, countertrade presents difficulties in terms of quality standards, if manufactured goods are involved. A further difficulty has been introduced by restrictions on barter deals because of the foreign exchange problems caused by trading goods that could otherwise earn Russia hard currency. If rules are put into place to control this, more joint ventures will be formed as an alternative because of exemptions that apply to joint ventures with foreign partners.

A very active international firm in the toy manufacturing industry has reported that it has found serious work-ethic and productivity problems among the population of Moscow and most of the interior of western Russia. By contrast, it has found a different attitude, in terms of both ambition and workmanship, in the northern, more Scandinavian areas such as Leningrad and, to some extent, in the Ukraine and Georgia as well. The Ukraine especially has been held up as more driven to economic reforms. In contrast, in the former Baltic republics, in cities such as Riga, where everyone seems to agree that the attitude is entirely different. There, the workforce can remember a more independent, capitalistic time, unlike the Russians, who were dominated first by the monarchy and subsequently by Communism. However, such generalizations can be unfair because, as in all societies, there have developed many different kinds of people. Even in Moscow there are individuals with a natural entrepreneurial instinct as well as those habituated to doing a minimal amount of work in the government service.

When trading with Russia, there is an extra dimension of difficulty in financial partnerships of any kind that needs to be considered: the lack of experience in independent business undertakings and the absence of management expertise and effective accounting procedures, especially cost accounting. The same can be said of laws and regulations pertaining to a freely conducted business. In the last few years, however, a substantial business class is emerging but finding that the bureaucracy is their greatest obstacle or even their enemy.

In spite of the problems, substantial business can be done. Most consider the long-term potential of the huge Eastern European market to be greater than that in the rest of Central Europe, but it is definitely not for the "quick-trippers," and both human and financial resources must be available for a long-term effort. This does not mean that everyone determined to do business in the region needs to be thinking in terms of some form of joint venture or strategic alliance. While it is clear that joint ventures are a good tool for a real presence, other companies can be found doing business on a smaller scale without an alliance of any kind, but operating with the kind of on-site care previously mentioned. The up-front cost of establishing a joint venture, or even a lesser working arrangement, can be very high, and it would be an unnecessarily dangerous mission, financially speaking, for many companies.

Assessing the Future

Central and Eastern Europe are introduced in Part 3 only because of their current and future impact on the EU rather than as a prospective major trade bloc in global terms. Much of Eastern Europe and possibly some part of Central Europe not absorbed by the EU but desirous of increased foreign investment could become part of a free trade area, possibly within the framework of the Commonwealth of Independent States that Russia envisions, in some sort of concert with the EU as cooperating entities or associates. It is expected that many of the Central European nations may eventually join the EU, but there is much restructuring and economic improvement to be done before this can occur. This sort of compromise arrangement could be made in the not-too-distant future, providing an orderly transformation to a reasonably democratic and capitalistic society takes place.

In view of the dramatic events of recent years and the earlier economic history of the region, Central/Eastern Europe has to be included as a vital link in the European equation. Here the labor is not nearly as cheap as it is in Southeast Asia or Latin America, and although the work ethic may be diminished in some areas, there is infrastructure, a manufacturing history, ready markets, and many other factors that are very promising. The region deserves a careful look and is very germane to any overall decisions concerning Europe, even though it obviously includes some special risks beyond those already recited in the case of the EU—currency risks being not the least among the added risk. The opportunities are very real, but the need for patience and trader skills is even greater. When the experts are asked how soon "normal trade practices," by our definition, can be expected in much of this part of Europe, the answer is no more than a guess, but the guess is another few years for the best and most adaptive countries, such as Hungary or Czechoslovakia, and another decade for some of the least. Many people hoped that the new millennium would see Central Europe well settled, but the continuing war in the Balkans leaves those anticipations in a very uncertain and precarious state.

Sources of Help and Information

There are a number of agencies that can provide information to any firm interested in doing business in the region, especially when at least some element of foreign investment exists. Call the DOC's Eastern Europe Business and Information Center (EEBIC) at 202/482-5745 (see address in Appendix A or check with 800/USA-TRADE) or the Business Information Service for the Newly Independent States (BISNIS) at 202/482-3145. Both have fax menus. Through the National Technical Information Service (NTIS), a catalog is available providing country information for export or for investment in each country. Also available are industry-specific reports, as well as reports on foreign economic trends and the legal climate. EEBIC also publishes an *Eastern Europe Business Bulletin*. Both of these services provide specific opportunities in the form of service and merchandise needs or joint ventures possibilities.

Financially, there are many special or temporary sources of support. Chief among them are the Polish-American, Czech and Slovak-American, Bulgarian-American, Hungarian-American and Baltic-American Enterprise Funds. All are designed to promote the development of the private sectors in those countries. For more information, call the Eastern Europe Business and Information Center. These various funds are for disbursement under a wide variety of terms and conditions, some as loans and others as grants. Also, besides the World Bank, the European Bank for Reconstruction and Development (EBRD) is a major player. (Both are described further in Chapter 13 in the discussion of multilateral development banks.)

The usual export finance support agencies of the U.S. government, such as Eximbank, have specially targeted programs for Central and Eastern Europe in addition to their regular menu. Eximbank's foreign credit insurance programs also go to special lengths to provide coverage. The Overseas Private Investment Corporation (OPIC) and the Trade and Development Agency (TDA) can also be of special help in the region. For more information on such sources, see the appropriate agency chapters in Part 7 of this book. The Agency for International Development (AID), discussed in Chapter 13, has special interests here as well.

Endnotes

1. Michael Tomezyk, "Eastern Europe: Selling to the New Markets," *Export Today*, May/June 1990.
2. Zak Karamally, "The New Frontier: Is It Time to Trade with the Bear?," *Export Today*, March/April 1990.

16

Asia

Asia's fastest-growing trade bloc lies along its eastern Pacific rim. In Southeast Asia it is made up of Singapore, Indonesia, Thailand, and Malaysia. And in East Asia, it is comprised of South Korea, the three Chinas (the PRC, Taiwan, and Hong Kong), and Japan. This is the heart of an area about which economist James Flanigan, in his *Los Angeles Times* column, made the statement that within this decade, 100 million Asian households outside of Japan will attain middle-class incomes and consumer tastes to match. While that statement may require a little refining, in terms of the economic definition of "middle class" in America versus "middle class" in Asia, it seems safe to say that very soon there will be a far greater number of households with significant purchasing power in that part of the world than in the United States. Yet, in spite of this reality, U.S. business has been relatively slow to become fully engaged in Asia. If Americans do not take greater advantage of the potential for manufacturing and selling in this dynamic consumer market, they will be helping Japan to further increase its dominance in the area. The United States is clearly losing ground and is no longer the number-one foreign investor in Asia; it has been succeeded by Japan. Some analysts, however, predict that Japan will eventually find its economic role somewhat diminished within this trading bloc, especially as China's economic reforms advance and U.S. investment in the area increases. A professor at Japan's Tokai University is quoted as saying that Korea will overtake Japan by the year 2010, although this seems to be an exaggeration.

The Big Emerging Market Strategy

The TPCC's National Export Strategy calls for a Big Emerging Market (BEM) export and investment target program. Eight of the twelve nations named in the overall BEM program are in Asia and five of those eight form this chapter's East

Asian focus. Together, the southeastern ASEAN countries, plus the three Chinas and South Korea, purchased U.S. exports in 1994 in an amount roughly equal to total U.S. exports to all of Latin America. If exports to Japan are included, the combined total of $141.2 billion substantially exceeds our total export of goods to the newly enlarged 15-nation EU by over $33 billion. The comparable GNP totals for these countries and their projected growth rates over the next 20 years are even more dramatic.

India and Turkey are also targeted BEM markets, but they do not belong to the portion of Asia under discussion here as a present or potential trading bloc or blocs. The DOC and other related agencies are establishing bilateral forums for each BEM area, opening freestanding U.S. Commercial Centers, expanding travel budgets to strengthen commercial ties, and crafting long-term export strategies for each country. The Chinese Economic Area, or CEA, has a GDP growth rate among the fastest in the world and is undertaking the highest dollar value of infrastructure projects. Indonesia is expected to grow at 7 percent annually throughout the decade and is in great need of infrastructure projects. It is also a major source for extractable resources with a central position in the ASEAN. India was chosen as a BEM by the DOC because this historically diffi-cult business environment has awakened and is moving toward a more open, market-oriented system whose U.S. imports rose by 44 percent in 1993 to $2.8 billion. India has a huge population of 900 million, but more important, the population now includes a consumer class of 100 million and has a highly developed industrial base (twelfth-largest), with a workforce and entrepreneurs readily adaptable by training and instinct to work with advanced technology.

South Korea is our eighth-largest trading partner, but in the past, it has been seen as a relatively difficult destination for the export of goods and services and foreign investment. However, since President Kim's election in 1993, it has been actively seeking foreign investment, including retailing. President Kim has promised the U.S. that South Korea will adhere to a five-year plan for liberalizing the country's foreign trade policies, so that this already solid export market of 44 million, with its rapidly growing GDP per capita income and its large infrastruc-ture needs will offer the potential for rapid expansion and development.

Asia's Need for Infrastructure: An Opportunity for All

There has never been such a worldwide need for infrastructure, a fact that pre-sents a golden opportunity for exports and investment companies large and small. This is a major reason for the stock market strength of internationally ori-ented companies like Caterpillar and General Electric, but the opportunity extends to subcontractor companies and services such as engineers and consul-tants. The March 1995 issue of *International Business* quoted, "Public Works Financing International," a Westfield, New Jersey, newsletter, stating that there are $480 billion worth of projects in 33 countries in the public or private devel-opment pipeline. The World Bank estimates that the developing world will spend $200 billion of this enormous sum on infrastructure development in 1995 alone. While *International Business* lists major projects scheduled for both Central and Eastern Europe—the largest being Russia's $40 billion telephone system—another 65 percent of such projects are located in Asia. In China five of the world's 20 largest infrastructure projects are under way, and there is also one in Hong Kong and one in Taiwan. The largest of China's projects is a $20 billion project for the Suzhou Industrial Township; the second-largest is the controversial Gorges Dam. In Hong Kong the Chek Lap Kok Airport has a price tag of $20 billion. The principal focus of infrastructure development has been in the areas of telecommunication, power generation and distribution, gas distribution, railroads, highways, and water.[1]

One major force behind infrastructure development is thought to be the rapidly increasing use of privatized projects. This solves many of the problems and concerns created by political uncertainties, because foreign investors and developers, having a stake in the project, offer a stronger guarantee of getting the projected return on investment, and therefore payment. A second incentive is that developing nations need to attract investment, and they know that inadequate infrastructure is one of the primary obstacles to attracting investment. This trend places a special burden and importance on organizations such as OPIC and the private sector side of the larger multilateral development bank guarantee activities. Among the latter are the International Finance Corporation (IFC) of the World Bank for loans and equity financing in collaboration with other investors, and the World Bank's Multilateral Investment Guarantee Agency (MIGA), which covers foreign investors against losses caused by noncommercial risks such as war, expropriation, breech of contract, or currency transfer with guarantees similar to those of OPIC.[2]

The World Bank estimates that 20 percent of Indonesia's development budget will be for transport and communications equipment. This is already happening: the government has installed hundreds of thousand of new telephone lines and still has not caught up with demand. Similar situations apply to Thailand's roads and ports, South Korea's power grid, and China's roads and railroads. Southeast Asia and China require technological help for their vast array of badly needed infrastructure projects and do not want it all to come from Japan.

If your company is an investor in Southeast or East Asia, it will be easier to capture a share of these vast projects as an economic participant and financial partner of the bloc. Southeast and East Asia clearly deserve careful study as a region more than simply as part of a country-by-country targeting process. The decision to get involved in trade with this most dynamic of all regions need not be made on an either-or basis and may complement market plans in other strategic regions. The number of options will depend on the product, resources, and extent of commitment. That United States business investment has lagged in the huge Asian market is highlighted by the fact that U.S. investment in Asian markets is less than 25 percent of our investment in Europe, a smaller market. Even smaller companies should consider raw material and labor procurement decisions, along with manufacturing and marketing decisions, on a global, rather than a national basis. This will open up new profit opportunities to many businesses and add sinew to our country's global economic muscle. America, and its business and industry, must not leave the rapidly developing Asian trade bloc to be presided over by Japan or China, alone or in combination. Successful entry into Southeast and/or East Asia can favorably impact a company's options and maneuverability and will also expand America's geopolitical options.

Southeast Asia

A large portion of Southeast Asia is bound together as a group of countries called the Association of Southeast Asian Nations (ASEAN). The ASEAN members are Thailand, Malaysia, Indonesia, the Philippines, Singapore, and Brunei. The first three of these, Thailand, Malaysia, and Indonesia, are nicknamed the "Dragons," because they are working fiercely and successfully to grow in economic stature. The Philippines could soon be among the Dragons, but for now the country continues its struggle to achieve necessary political and economic stability and an enlarged middle class for sustained growth. Brunei is simply very rich and doesn't need to work. Although an ASEAN country, the city-state of Singapore is more advanced and is considered to be one of the four "Tigers." The other three Tigers, all in East Asia, are Hong Kong, Korea, and Taiwan.

The ASEAN group represents a market of over 300 million people, and in combination with the Tigers of East Asia, emerges as a strong trade bloc that does not want to be dominated or even entirely led by Japan. Australia and New Zealand are very non-Asian in character and this is presumably the primary reason that these two, the southernmost countries of the Pacific Rim, are not presently part of this trade bloc. Logic would have it that their future lies with East Asia more than with America and England, for whom they have such a natural affinity. To date, this natural mating of economic interests has not really occurred. It seems very likely to happen someday, however, and the Australians are wisely encouraging their youth to become students of Asian languages and cultures. In the meantime, Australia and New Zealand have created a free-trade agreement of their own.

The Dragons are not by any means limited to providing low-cost labor to the other members of this ultimate Asian trade bloc, nor to the rest of the world. The same industrious, largely English-speaking, literate, and well-educated labor force is available to the Western industrial nations of the world, although without the advantage of such proximity. Indonesia, Malaysia, Thailand, and other nations of the area have long understood the importance of foreign investment to growth in other developing nations. They do not believe that they can reach their full potential by their own efforts as readily as did Japan, Taiwan, and South Korea. Therefore, like Eastern Europe, they will be looking for that most important quid pro quo of trade: investment in exchange for highly competitive labor and the opportunity to enrich their economies and standards of living. In the meantime, the wealth of the four Tigers is growing to such a degree that they have, or will soon, become consumer-driven economies assuring future consumption of a growing range of Southeast Asian industrial products and thus increasingly able to provide the Dragons external investment.

Some highlights on this vital and strategic area might help us understand just how dynamic it is. Singapore, according to DOC statistics, far outstrips its Southeast Asian neighbors in both total and incremental U.S. foreign direct investment. Indonesia is second; it is also Southeast Asia's second-most populous nation, with 190 million people, but trading can be more difficult there because the country is composed of many ethnic and religious groups. Indonesia has a GNP growth rate of 7 percent annually and actively seeks external investment. This is one of DOC's Big Emerging Market (BEM) targets, and as such it already has a new U.S. DOC commercial center in Jakarta designed to support American efforts there. Thailand lays claim to being the current most dynamic trade prospect. It has a homogeneous population of 60 million and a GNP growth rate exceeding 8 percent. Thailand, like all the Dragons, is encouraging high-tech industries and has in place favorable legislation. Thailand has received the third-largest share of total U.S. investment as well as the third-highest rate of increase in investment over the last ten years, followed by Malaysia and the Philippines respectively. Thailand has a growing middle class whose sophisticated lifestyle requires quality consumer goods, including telecommunications equipment.

Malaysia has had an 8 percent GNP growth rate over eight years, although this may now be slowing. It is becoming a showplace of Asia's growing new middle class. In Kuala Lumpur, for example, two giant office tower buildings, taller than the Sears Tower in Chicago, are under construction and should be completed in 1966. The political climate is relatively stable. Malaysia's average manufacturing wage is less than one-third of the comparable wage in Taiwan and it is already one of the world's largest producers of semiconductors. Of course, continued success will drive up these wages, but countries like Vietnam, Myanmar (Burma), Laos, and Cambodia will then be in line to take up the slack on the lower end of the wage scale.

Vietnam has started to develop at an almost hectic pace, especially since the U.S. boycott was lifted in 1994. The United States had to allow open trade with the country to avoid doing irreparable damage by omission to U.S. businesses, to whom the area is important. Vietnam is a likely candidate to become part of ASEAN in the foreseeable future as the seventh member. Even Cambodia, Laos, and Myanmar are enjoying some activity in spite of Myanmar's poor record on human rights. It is still premature for many exporters to become active in Vietnam, but it is by far the best bet of the four countries mentioned. Concentrate for now on the Dragons and on Singapore, the Southeast Asian Tiger.

A Department of Commerce (DOC) survey indicated that to the extent that some investment is made to take advantage of opportunities in Southeast Asia, it can be profitable. The average annual return on investments in Singapore in 1989 was 31.2 percent and in Malaysia, 28.8 percent. For South Korea the return of investment was 17.9 percent; for Hong Kong, 23.6 percent; for Taiwan, 22.2 percent; and for Japan, 14.1 percent. These figures can be compared to a 15.2 percent annual return for total U.S. investments abroad.

United States exports to ASEAN nations have jumped from $7.5 billion to about $30 billion in the last ten years, and imports have soared from $15.6 billion to almost $60 billion. Even so, U.S. exports lag far behind those of Japan, and U.S. direct investment accounts for just 10 percent of the region's total external investment—and that investment was largely centered in Singapore, according to a report on the ASEAN marketplace in the March 1995 issue of *International Business*.[3] Western businesses cannot afford to leave this area largely to nurturing by East Asia. It is no longer valid to view the region chiefly as a low-cost labor resource. Today it is one of the most vibrant areas of the world for trade—buying, selling, manufacturing, and investment.

East Asia

East Asia truly is an area in transition as the People's Republic of China (PRC) increasingly asserts itself economically and prepares to absorb Hong Kong, one of the great commercial hubs of the world, as a Chinese province in 1997. It also increasingly appears that China and Taiwan will reach some sort of rapprochement so that what the DOC refers to as the Chinese Economic Area (CEA) and what others call Greater China, will really be just that. Based on 1994 export sales of $37.8 billion, the CEA would become our fifth-largest market, behind only Canada ($114.4), the European Union ($107.8), Japan ($53.5), and Mexico ($50.8). In addition to the three Chinas, which include two of the Tigers—Taiwan and Hong Kong—East Asia includes a third Tiger, South Korea, and of course Japan.

The Four Tigers

The four Tigers—Singapore, Hong Kong, South Korea, and Taiwan—represent economic miracles. They all started as less-developed countries (LDCs) with nothing but cheap labor to offer and rose through diligence, hard work, and savings to become economic dynamos. We've already discussed Singapore, the one Tiger located in Southeast Asia. This leaves South Korea as the single Tiger of East Asia that will definitely never be part of the CEC, or Greater China. Koreans have quite a different culture and history from Japan and even from China combined with bitter memories of past hostilities, but there is the real probability that eventually the two Koreas will become one, and surely the end result will more closely resemble the South than the North. South Korea is one of our largest export customers (currently number six), and it has a strong and growing economy that will be enhanced by the liberalization of trade and foreign investment rules under President Kim Young-san.

The next Tiger is Taiwan, which is decidedly a maturing economy and our seventh-largest export customer. The United States has a substantial, negative trade imbalance with Taiwan. A more important issue is that our diplomatic and trade relations are improving again, even as the Taiwan/PRC relationship improves and the two seek some form of union or common bond. Unfortunately, as all this develops, the United States' relationship with China seems to deteriorate although it is our conviction that the necessities of trade will overcome the problems. The emergence of a CEA therefore is now seen as very real possibility as 1997 approaches and the fourth Tiger, Hong Kong, starts to close the Chinese circle. Furthermore, while mainland China as a whole is far more than a Tiger, the enterprise zones of China might certainly be viewed as such, which is why China proposed an initial Chinese union in 1992 on just such face-saving terms. Imagine the opportunity and the challenge such a union presents to world trade.

The ease and freedom of doing business in Hong Kong is legendary and scarcely needs to be expanded on here, except to repeat that it is now one of the most popular doorways to mainland China. Its importance in that respect can only increase exponentially as the day of reverting to China's direct dominion in 1997 begins to be calculated in months. For many smaller companies with a base in Hong Kong, the opportunity is especially real and profitable deals are very achievable. Hong Kong is not the only entry point for smaller businesses, however, as some small businesses have had excellent results with exporting and joint ventures in Chinese industrial enclaves such as the Hainan Island. With relationships as they are today, even Taiwan can serve the same purpose, while at the same time functioning as a very major market and trading partner whose relations are warming, not only with the United States, but also with the rest of the world. If a China strategy for a particular business is ever to be formulated, now is the time to do it.

The Monsters

There are special creatures that effect multiple trade blocs and all the world's trade, but that do not now, and perhaps never will, fit neatly within any one trade bloc. These Monsters are: the United States, the Russian Federation, Japan, and China. Each has a large gross national product (GNP); each is an important trade factor in multiple world regions or trade blocs; and most possess great landmass and natural resources or some combination of these properties.

All four of the Monsters are too large in their own way to play a cooperative intraregional role within trade bloc development. This is not to say that their trade with any given trade bloc is not vital. In fact, the Monster may be the key to the bloc, but it may play a somewhat stand-apart role, and it is probably involved in a similar way with more than one trade bloc. The Monster title helps us understand world trade and regional trade blocs better in terms of their special position as both outside and central to the trade blocs in question. It is often easier to discuss the nature of trade and investment opportunities in different world regions by excluding these Monsters from the statistics for the region. One reason is that their physical size (except in the case of Japan's relatively small landmass), market potential, and/or GNP distort statistics such as growth rates for the smaller or less-developed nations in the area. Two of the Monsters were formerly called superpowers, but with the changing world order and emerging geo-economic regionalism, "Monster" seems a more apt title to be used in an economic sense.

The People's Republic of China (PRC)

It is especially difficult to know what to do about China relative to its future with Hong Kong and Taiwan. It may well be that in terms of international trade, many businesses will deal with it in pieces or parts—that is, as one of various economic or enterprise zones, possibly with Hong Kong as a superzone and entry point and Taiwan as a sort of separate entity, depending on what it and mainland China finally decide.

China is a huge market. By the UN's reckoning, it is already the world's second-biggest economy in terms of purchasing power; at 8.2 percent, it was forecast to be the fastest-growing economy in the world by DRI/McGraw-Hill during the period 1993–1998; and it was chosen by Ernst & Young as the number-one emerging market in the world. Thus it cannot be ignored. But for such a major economic and military power, China is backward in many areas, both geographically speaking and politically. It is monolithic in some ways, yet there is a clear dichotomy between the natural entrepreneurial and trading instincts of its people (proved by the 15 to 20 million private enterprises now operating in China, with 10 million more expected by the year 2000) and the willingness of a majority of its people to retain China's conservative and authoritarian brand of Communism. In its present ideological isolation, China does not want to be part of any bloc, except what it sees as its own—Hong Kong, Taiwan, and the Chinese mainland. It knows, however, that it must interface economically and technologically with many nations.

Foreign investment is one of the driving forces in China's economic zones and one of the primary reasons for their existence. The government concentrates foreign investment in these zones and not only permits it, but actively seeks it. The enterprise zones of China will have an effect on the country far beyond their size or population. These enclaves, all located in the southern part of China and best exemplified by Guangdong, Fujian, Guangxi, and Hainan Island, permit economic activities to take place in a very entrepreneurial fashion with a minimum of central control. Here, in the south, the new China will ultimately be reborn, whether the conservatives like it or not, out of economic necessity and consumer demand, but with as-yet-undetermined levels of violent struggle.

The economy is expanding at an astounding rate and very fashionable and upscale consumer products are selling well, as are the computer-related products one would expect to be in demand. Yet marketing to mainland China remains a venture subject to many sovereign decisions and influences, both at the time of market entry and at any time thereafter. Deeply embedded corruption adds greatly to the cost of doing business in mainland China. It will be some time, if ever, before anyone can count on user demand to maintain, much less increase, a business. The term "market share" is simply not appropriate in this special situation. It has often been demonstrated how quickly political events alter ideological attitudes, which in turn effect trade—sometimes for the worse as in the case of the Tiananmen Square incident—but events have proven that China is very unlikely to lose its most favored nation (MFN) status because of the realities of trade as mentioned earlier.

China is a growing trade opportunity for the United States in spite of the political fluctuations and economic problems caused by its frequent foreign exchange shortages. The downward spike in China business following the Tiananmen Square episode is proving to be just that, a brief interlude, as the planned, long-term increase in business continues and export sales rise again. With China's tendency to do business with small and midsize firms, the China market should be of special interest to many U.S. entrepreneurs. However, the market is an immature one, and for many, the wisest course may well be the commonly used alternative of selling to China through Hong Kong, with Singapore and Taiwan increasingly becoming additional choices. In order to do business in China, it is helpful to have a good contact, preferably a Chinese agent, to help negotiate with the particular foreign trade corporation involved. Such corporations often contact U.S. firms whose technology they desire, and they are fairly prompt about responding to direct inquiries. The Chinese are trying to establish both government and quasigovernmental agencies in the United States to facilitate this, sometimes with uncertain results. It is clear, however, that the projects inside the country, as opposed to those in the special enclaves, have now been brought under somewhat more centralized control.

Some Chinese organizations are in place now and offer advice on their needs and help channel information. The National Council for United States–China Trade, 1818 North Street NW, Suite 500, Washington, D.C. 20036, is one of the key U.S. organizations involved in giving information, advice, and counseling to U.S. businesses involved in Chinese trade and investments. It is a private, non-profit, member-supported group with offices in Beijing as well as in Washington, D.C. The China United Trading Corporation Ltd., located at One World Trade Center, Suite 3333, New York, New York, 10048, is strictly a Chinese organization that does what its name implies. It can also provide the names and addresses of the appropriate Chinese export corporations and industry groups, as well as information about trade fairs to which an invitation is required. Both are excellent initial contacts.

The Chinese organize, or permit to be organized, a large number of trade fairs in China each year. In recent years there have been on the order of 50 trade fairs in the Jiangsu province alone, mostly held in Shanghai, even though many were temporarily cancelled after Tiananmen. The schedules for new events are again increasing. The mainland Chinese are doing substantial business with a number of very small U.S. firms. This is especially true in the high-tech area, but there is also trade in other areas, such as low- to medium-technology production machinery, software, and medical equipment. The demand for consumer goods, especially appliances, is also growing. The emphasis on small business makes one suspect that, since technology transfer is usually the vital element in this business, there is a key reason for doing so much of it with small businesses. It could be because small businesses are so pleased with the opportunity to complete the sale and make the immediate profit that they do not negotiate for licensing income from the intellectual property that they are providing in the course of the sale. If the Chinese were to approach a major

high-tech firm for similar deals, often turnkey projects, they would find themselves in just such licensing and sales negotiations. This is intended, not so
much as a warning, but as something to consider when negotiating a contract,
and to highlight a technique that the Chinese are using for entering the modern
world they had dropped so far behind.

It is very important to consult a well-informed person before going to China,
and definitely before concluding a deal. There are certain contract clauses that
have appeared as a pattern and which they have used successfully just by
implying that their preprinted contracts are the norm if a firm wishes to deal
with China. However, this is not true, and experienced China negotiators are
every day concluding deals without "standard clauses." Some stipulations can
make it very difficult to make a profit on a transaction and, even more important, to finance it. A few of the problems most commonly encountered when
dealing with the Chinese are these:

- Deferring the opening of the export letter of credit until just prior to shipment.

- Demand for Chinese arbitration.

- Unduly favorable post-shipment or post-completion inspection privileges.

- Large performance bonds and long warranties.

- Contracts lacking triggers to force action on the part of either party to perform. (Such a trigger would be a specified response from them to a request
  by you to complete the required inspections thus denying them an opportunity for continued "strategic" delays.)

Although the rigidity of the 1970s and early 1980s has receded, there are certain characteristics often mentioned by those who have had substantial dealings
with the Chinese. One of the most common is a very literal translation of the
contract or order. As a result, the exporter had better be sure that if it calls for
1000 bolts, there are exactly 1000, no more and no less. This means that your
packing list is very important. Also, there is often a problem in obtaining qualified Chinese labor to fulfill the terms of a training contract in China. Some U.S.
firms have trained a Chinese crew, only to return to find that they have all been
replaced, and by workers who have been given little or no training.

The tightness of China's foreign exchange situation makes the Chinese try to
maintain sufficient control to delay opening or paying if foreign exchange is
especially tight at the time or a plant is not quite completed to accept the equipment that has been manufactured for it. These problems should be kept in mind
and a certain level of caution maintained when dealing with the Chinese, even
when you are favored with a letter of credit. They are tough negotiators, but
their reputation is good and there have been few reports of unbusinesslike conduct or dishonest dealing; however, there have sometimes been payment delays.

Chinese culture, while surely different from our own, is probably more readily bridged than the Japanese culture. China's need to acquire technology is as

great today as Japan's was many years ago. The Chinese market has enormous potential for companies that are aggressive and in a position to provide appropriate products. It is a challenging opportunity that requires certain precautions and expertise, plus great patience, to keep it profitable and free of excessive risks and difficulties. For some firms, China could offer far greater business opportunities than Japan.

The challenge in China is to make each transaction stand on its own by concentrating on careful and patient negotiation for a fair deal without excessive risk and obtaining a fair return for time, product, and technology. The loss-leader approach does not work; it just makes the next contract more difficult to negotiate. The Chinese want the machinery and technology to meet their own new consumer demands and technological needs, so that they, in turn, can export to the world.

Japan

Japan, another Monster, is unique in being geographically small and yet extremely powerful in terms of both its economy and its worldwide trade. It is an unparalleled demonstration of how a nation poor on resources can become very wealthy and successful by virtue of hard work and unanimity of purpose—to say nothing of more than a little hard-core mercantilism. Japan's world trade is greatly enhanced by that awesome tool, its global trading companies, or *sogo shoshas,* so singular to Japan. They are unique, not only for their worldwide presence through hundreds of offices and commercial and industrial agreements, but also for the closely interwoven, world-class financial institutions that are a key element of each one. In view of this global business network, Japan is unlikely to become focused on any single trade bloc. Japan's trade pacts and approach to trade diplomacy provide ample evidence of this.

A lesson to be learned by internationally inclined businesses in the United States is that, among the many good global business strategies practiced by the Japanese, none more clearly defines their acumen than the care they take to see that imports follow investments into the host country. More so than in most countries, investments are not permitted to be an end in themselves, but serve to aid the investing company's continued export growth. This cannot be said, however, without pointing out that they have come full circle so that some investments are now being used to export back to Japan. This is typified by the very substantial Japanese investment in automotive assembly plants in the United States. Their failing real estate investments and speculations notwithstanding.

Most experienced exporters would agree that in the past, even though they spoke of selling to Japan, there was some question about whether anything was ever truly *sold* to the Japanese. There is a strong suspicion that they only bought what they liked, wanted, or needed, and that the sales effort was simply a formality that they patiently endured. Many who have worked a good deal with the Japanese feel that a wider cultural gap exists between the Japanese and the rest of the world, than is true of any other developed nation, including China. Assuming this to be true, it seems sensible to seek more creative means of bridging that gap than simply going on trying to sell goods and services to Japan in the traditional American way. Moreover, if we find it difficult to do business in Japan today, picture how difficult America must have looked to the Japanese 30 years ago. All the Westernization that has occurred in those years should make the present business climate in Japan far easier for us to understand than our own culture was for them to grasp as they pioneered their products here in those early days. This should inspire us to try harder to learn their ways and to do business their way.

It often appears that frustration with non–tariff barriers and things we cannot do in Japan, results in overemphasis on the negative, causing much of the U.S. business community to go on failing to understand American marketing problems in Japan, especially when compared to European efforts. In the period from late 1985 to late 1987, the yen almost doubled in value against the dollar but increased only modestly against the European currencies. Yet in 1987, it was European sales that surged from 35 percent to almost 50 percent in Japan, while American sales rose only around 10 percent. While this has improved somewhat, it underscores the lack of resolve on the part of U.S. manufacturers and exporters as a whole. What will happen in the last half of this decade, given the dramatic devaluation of the dollar against the yen? It certainly can no longer be said that the value of the yen impedes trade. Leading business analysts feel that a major cause of this development is the lack of the seller's local presence in Japan, a country where it seems to be especially essential. With only a few exceptions, export selling has relied almost entirely on Japanese businessmen for distribution. Realizing the limitations of this approach, many of the more aggressive U.S. firms have studied the Japanese systems and established their own distribution networks, using Japanese to make them compatible, even though different. An example of such is the success of Toys "R" Us in establishing its own retail outlets. Even if this approach is not practical for smaller U.S. businesses, the fact remains that there is a genuine and major reformation of the Japanese retail structure that will allow much more access to the Japanese consumer through traditional retailers than was ever thought possible a few years ago.

Entirely apart from adapting to Japanese needs and requirements, a major quality hurdle must be overcome, even while facing the admittedly difficult non-tariff barriers. These barriers can be tough, but they are not always insurmountable. Many barriers are removed each year by skillful maneuvering or negotiations on the part of such aggressive U.S. businesses as Coca-Cola, McDonald's, the Campbell Soup Company, Johnson & Johnson, IBM, and Texas Instruments. These and other firms have learned to step around barriers. In 1987 the Japanese themselves, under pressure from the serious U.S. trade deficit, reduced the average tariff level on mined and manufactured goods to 2 percent, as compared to about 4.5 percent for the United States and the EU in terms of tariff averages. The tougher Clinton Administration trade policies vis à vis Japan are well advised for specific sectors if intelligently followed up by business and government policies, as will be the impact of the GATT agreement. But for many product sectors it should not be forgotten that they have no application at all and for many industries there are no barriers. As an example, whereas Coca-Cola sells 310 eight-ounce drinks per capita in the U.S. and 49 worldwide, it sells 133 in Japan, compared to 274 in Australia, 6 in Indonesia, and 3 in China. McDonald's has a similar record, based on thousands of people per restaurant. Some of the greatest government-to-government differences that are aired so regularly in the press only affect a small minority of the individual businesses that might be involved in export. An example is the fact that Japan is one of our largest agriculture customers, though it is Japan's refusal to import rice that makes the headlines.

For a quality product, the three most basic principles required for success in selling in Japan could be applied to almost any export marketing effort. They are:

1. A successful product and marketing track record in the U.S. market and a willingness to transfer it overseas

2. The cultivation of an appropriate infrastructure and network of contacts in Japan similar to those in the United States

3. The development of cross-cultural communication skills to make the Japanese comfortable in dealing with a U.S. firm

Because of its high profile and size, many exporters seem to look at Asia and see only Japan. Some consultants specializing in Japanese marketing feel that Japan is the latchkey for opening the door to all of Asia. Others feel that Japan is not necessarily the best place to begin export efforts. If, however, it is necessary to undertake initial international marketing efforts with the kind of challenge Japan represents, make use of all the advice and creative thinking available to find the right approach with patience and consistency. The Japan External Trade Organization (JETRO) seems to be making serious efforts to assist U.S. exporters and, in cooperation with Japan Export-Import Bank, has established a preshipment guaranteed lending program. One thing that can certainly be said for the Japanese market is that there is no necessity for countertrade, buyback contracts, or many of the other complications facing the exporter in some of the other countries under consideration. Nor is investment as necessary as it is in some other countries to make modest inroads in the Japanese market, and surely there is no shortage of foreign exchange. Yet Japan's own strategy has relied on investment in the United States and elsewhere, and the Japanese seem to know better than anyone how to make an investment in a country yield large increases in the Japanese export volume to that country as well as achieving a good return on investment.

The Russian Federation

This segment of the Asian story is included primarily for the sake of completing a picture and could have as easily been titled Northeast Asia, for the region of Far Eastern Siberian more or less comprises all of the northeastern quadrant of Asia. Russia has already been discussed relative to Eastern Europe, but in the

Monster context, it should be thought of in its federated form. This includes many states and ethnic groups, spanning the two continents of Eurasia from the Atlantic to the Pacific. As a faded superpower, the western portion of Russia impacts Europe as part of Eastern Europe, together with the European portion of the Newly Independent States. East of the Ural Mountains, on the Asian side of Eurasia, the Russian economy takes on more relevance to those of China and Japan and the Asian Dragons and Tigers.

The Russian Federation alone is a nation containing the world's largest populated landmass and covers a vast variety of geography spread across 13 time zones, ethnic origins, and cultures, all of which remain quite unassimilated. The 15 republics contain over 100 ethnic groups and 100 languages. As such, Russia's land and people stretch from the west, where the nation borders on Scandinavia and the states of Central Europe, eastward to a sea whose shore is but a few hundred miles from Japan and indeed, our own Alaskan Pacific shores. The ongoing opportunities for trade and investment in Russia, and in any part of the Commonwealth of Independent States (CIS) should that become a reality, have already been discussed relative to the Eastern European trade.

Possessing yet unexploited riches, Russia, adjoining two of the world's most affluent markets—Japan in the East and the EU in the West—together with a rapidly developing China containing the world's largest population to the south, is the perfect Monster. In the eastern portion of Siberia live 7.2 million people in an area that is said to contain almost half the world's natural resources. Russia shares with China two major problems that are severely hindering both of these Monsters—namely a bureaucratic political system uncertain of its future leadership and inadequate transportation and communication. A step toward correcting the transportation inadequacy was the linkup in 1992 of Russia's rail line from Western Europe to China's railway, which will have a long-term impact on economic development and trade. The new rail line stretches from Russia's eastern seaboard at Lianyungang through northern Xinjiang to the Soviet border. It is called the Iron-Silk Road and is 1300 miles shorter than the Trans-Siberian route. The world's largest infrastructure project is the $40 billion telephone system in Russia. Russia has hardly begun to solve its many problems, and it will be difficult to determine its ultimate general direction until after the regular elections in 1996. There is clearly a threat of a crackdown from the right, together with insurrections from other states of the federation such as Chechnya's rebellion. In the long run Russia has much to offer, both as a marketplace and as a supplier. However, it probably cannot afford to become part of any bloc and furthermore, like the other Monsters, it would be a "nine-hundred pound gorilla."

No attempt will be made here to comment further on Siberia or the NIS states of Central Asia. These are areas that might be explored by businesses that have good reason to do so and possess the necessary preexisting knowledge or experience, combined with adequate time and financial resources. One of the BEMs, Turkey, is suggested by some as a good doorway to Central Asia. It is for some, and may well become for many, a market or area with great potential.

For the uninitiated or those lacking a highly specific purpose, Central Asia is not an area that one would expect to undertake in the early stages of even the most ambitious of export strategies. For the reader of this book, there are greener pastures.

Investing in Asia

Investment and participation will be a key in taking full advantage of the business potential in Asia, and especially in Southeast Asia. For real success everywhere it will require a strategy that entails more than merely shipping and selling to importers. Middle- or larger-sized U.S. businesses will need to increase their investment in the region to bring, at least in part, their own distribution systems to Asia. It is not just for the industrial giants to utilize the available labor pool, as the typically very small garment manufacturing businesses of America found out many years ago. The difference today is that a business can do so in such a way as to become part of this developing and promising trade bloc and profit from the entrée that some form of investment beyond marketing costs provides for sales within the bloc. The offshore manufacturing problems seem less objectionable when, in addition to sharpening a firm's overall competitive position, they also provide an expansion of the total sales opportunity.

Endnotes

1. Dave Savona, "Remaking the Globe," *International Business,* March 1995.

2. Savona, ibid.

3. Frank Gibney, "Unscrambling the Asean Marketplace," *International Business,* March 1995.

17

The Americas

The Western Hemisphere in which we live received relatively little attention from U.S. exporters in recent years, until the public discussion of the U.S.–Canadian Free Trade Agreement (CFTA) in 1989 followed by outright rancorous debate over the follow-on North American Free Trade Agreement (NAFTA) that drew Mexico into the partnership in 1994. Prior to the brouhaha over NAFTA, the relative inattention given Latin America as a whole was due to the major losses our financial institutions and exporters sustained in Latin America in the 1980s. Before that, most of Latin America was a profitable cornerstone of U.S. international trade, in the 1970s and before. As for Canada, it has long been taken for granted by smaller U.S. businesses and EMCs/ETCs, since it has been so often treated as merely a northern extension of domestic marketing policies, usually to the detriment of their total sales potential. Larger U.S. firms were more likely to treat Canada with the respect it deserved as our largest trading partner and a major consumer market. However, first CFTA and then NAFTA have changed our view of our nearest neighbors forever.

NAFTA

CFTA, the free trade agreement with Canada, is now expanded by the agreement of the initial partners, Canada and the United States, to extend the principals of tariff elimination and "national treatment" to a three-way agreement with Mexico. The basic concept of national treatment in general rests on each country treating imported goods, most services offered, and business investments originating from one of the three partner countries, in the same manner as the receiving country treats goods of domestic origin in terms of regulations and restrictions. Therefore, each country can have its own rules and regulations, but they will be applied universally among the three partners.

Tariffs were largely eliminated between Canada and the United States at the outset of the CFTA in 1989, with the remainder being reduced 20 percent each year over five years, or 10 percent per year over ten years, and all U.S.–Canadian tariffs destined to vanish at the end of 1998. A mechanism was provided between these two countries for faster elimination of many tariffs by mutual agreement, because faster tariff reductions proved to be popular. Surprisingly, in the first two years, 700 such applications were made. The few dispute settlement procedures have so far mostly involved agriculture and animal products. Neither the substance nor the pace of the earlier tariff reductions negotiated between Canada and the United States has been affected by the reduction schedules for Mexican tariffs in NAFTA. U.S. tariffs on imports from Mexico average around 4 percent, and Mexican tariffs average around 10 percent. Some tariff reductions went into effect with the NAFTA agreement, with the remainder to be phased in, as in the case of CFTA, but over a 10- to 15-year period. As with the Canadian agreement, the parties can petition each other to speed up selected tariff reductions if mutually agreeable. Present and future tariff reductions in both Canada and Mexico apply only to goods that qualify under the Rules of Origin, which include goods entirely made or produced by one of the three countries, or at least a certain minimum-permitted percentage of production value or components added to foreign raw materials. It is an interesting sidelight that the NAFTA agreement is the first international treaty in history to include principles governing the treatment of labor, which was done as a result of concern over the low cost and benefits of Mexican labor.

The stir caused by the debate over NAFTA was rather astounding when one considers that (1) it was all about free trade with a nation whose economy is one-twentieth the size of the U.S economy; (2) only about 5 percent of our total imports come from Mexico; and (3) a significant portion of that 5 percent of our imports consists of oil and therefore has no impact on U.S. jobs. It was hard to conceive that given these numbers any damaging "flood" of low-cost Mexican imports could present a critical economic problem or potential job losses. As for U.S. jobs lost due to plant relocations, the concerns seemed to ignore the fact that most manufacturers seeking low-cost labor had already moved to Mexico or Asia, and the small tariff differential would not create a mass movement of jobs anyway, especially considering the long-established and successful maquiladora program.

What no one anticipated (and it is somewhat surprising that no one did) was the astonishing problem with Mexico's peso, which when combined with a sudden, massive growth of nonproductive consumer imports from the United States, led to a severe devaluation of the peso and a consequent downturn in the Mexican economy in early 1995. Mexico's pent-up demand for U.S. goods and equipment (which is where 70 percent of Mexico's imports come from, in contrast to the Mexico's 5 percent share of U.S. imports) and the resulting outflow of foreign exchange placed Mexico in a real crisis. The situation might have triggered even greater problems if the United States had not moved to rescue the peso. The incident will slow the successful fulfillment of NAFTA but will not ruin it, especially if the Mexican government and its people can continue to suffer through the necessary reforms. Adding to the crisis is the fact that some of the offsetting inflow of investment capital from the United States to Mexico did not occur on schedule because of concern over the peso. If anything, the merit of NAFTA and free trade in general was enhanced, and the folly of controlled currencies was proven by the actual events of the day. Most economists expect the problem to be ironed out in something like two to five years. But they predict that a recovery will already be under way in 1996 to the point that the economic advantages to business, employment, and living standards will begin to be perceived. With a little bit of luck we believe this will be the scenario, barring the advent of any serious and damaging political crisis, of course, which is always possible. Even by mid-1995, however, there were already signs that capital investment was increasing, along with a rapid growth in exports. On the same note, it was interesting to learn that CFTA had already had a positive impact in the case of Canada, where the free flow of goods across the border had resulted in increased jobs in the United States. This welcome news was due partly to increased trade, but also to the fact that U.S. businesses were beginning to close their small, less-efficient manufacturing plants in Canada as they discovered that there was no longer a need to produce there to gain a market share, and that low-cost, low-employment distribution centers were all they really needed.

It is constantly overlooked that today the United States is the world's most open market as well as the world's largest exporter. The strides made in the late 1980s and 1990s to increase U.S. productivity have been very successful in meeting that challenge. Therefore, any general lowering of tariffs from GATT, or NAFTA, and whatever follow-on agreements take place will favor the United States more than most other nations. Although we can be sure that many more reactions and counteractions relative to NAFTA will take place—with results often quite different from those anticipated—it is important to remember that NAFTA is a trading bloc that is 12 percent larger than the EU in terms of population and roughly 25 percent larger in terms of GNP. The United States is as much a part of the equation for the trading bloc of the Americas as Japan is for Asia, and it is also a badly needed catalyst for the ultimate development of a strong and healthy trade area for the whole Western Hemisphere. The United States should continue to take a leading role in putting together a North/South coalition of trading partners, especially now that NAFTA is a reality, but in today's political climate, this role may prove to be more difficult to assume than first anticipated.

NAFTA Information Sources

Updated information and administrative interpretations on rules of origin and product by product tariffs and regulations basis may be obtained by means of the National Trade Data Base CD-ROMs so frequently referred to in this book. There is also a fax retrieval system from the DOC Office of NAFTA, reached by phone at 202/482-4464. Option #1 of Amerifax provides information on Canada and Mexico and the NAFTA agreement, the main menu being #0101. Document #5000 contains information on making the NAFTA rules of origin determination;

document #6000 contains information on the Mexican tariff schedule; and document #7000, the Canadian tariff schedule. The same system provides information on Latin America and the Caribbean through Amerifax option #2. For a list of documents on this region, request document #0100. If the numbers change or there is a problem, call 1-800/USA-TRADE for the most current sources to meet your particular needs.

Canada

Although Canada is the largest trading partner of the United States by far (in fact, the United States and Canada are the world's two largest trading partners, with a bilateral trade in 1994 of over $243 billion), Canada is nevertheless relatively dull reading for a book on export. Selling in Canada, with the exception of Quebec, is very similar to marketing to another region of the United States. It has similar laws, procedures, mores, and ethics but—more often than would be expected—different customer preferences. The few export-oriented challenges that did exist have mostly been dismantled as a result of CFTA. Just before CFTA became effective, 90 percent of U.S./Canada trade was either duty-free or attracted tariffs of less than 5 percent. Thanks to CFTA, these tariffs were cut roughly in half at the outset, and today no market anywhere in the world is as open and free as the Canada/U.S. market.

The Canadian Free Trade Agreement created a sharp contrast to U.S./Canada trade in the late 1970s, when severe import quotas were placed on products such as apparel and textiles, so that in terms of certain consumer goods industries, something close to a trade war was in process. Just before the CFTA went into effect, the textile and apparel industries were highly protected by tariffs in the range of 15 percent to 35 percent, even though the former quota system had been eliminated. Under the CFTA agreement, U.S. exports to Canada increased from $71.6 billion in 1988 to $114.4 billion in 1994—an increase of 60 percent. The 1994 exports to Canada were more than double those to Japan, our second-largest trading partner, and even exceeded U.S. exports to the new 15 EU countries by 6 percent. It is predictable that trade with Canada will continue to improve under NAFTA at a robust pace.

Regional Strategic Implications

The mere fact that Canada has long been our largest trading partner and export customer should persuade almost any firm with the slightest interest in increasing its market to undertake an export program there. It may well represent an immediate increase in the potential market of 10 percent, which is roughly the Canadian percentage of the U.S. population, unless the export product is one on which a higher-than-normal tariff remains, or there is an overabundance of the product or commodity in Canada. Of course, if the product is for consumers and is of a nature that would be affected by culture, the question of the product's acceptance by the nation's French-speaking population (one-third of the Canadian market) can be a major determinant as to total potential market share.

On the other hand, a U.S. firm's proximity to the nearest provinces of Canada could actually mean a freight or lifestyle advantage over other areas of the U.S. market. It should also be noted that 80 percent of the Canadian population lives within 100 miles of the U.S. border. These observations are a reminder that it is an error to look at any foreign market as monolithic.

Information on business opportunities may be obtained from the addresses below by requesting placement on appropriate source or bidding lists. For these and other details, contact the DOC through your local US&FCS district office or the Office of Canada, Room 3033, U.S. Department of Commerce, Washington, D.C. 20230. The nearest Canadian trade office or commercial consulate can be of great assistance to firms seeking an alliance partner in Canada if they promise investment or jobs in that country. For research reports and personalized information, check with the privately funded Conference Board of Canada, Inc., 845 Third Avenue, New York, New York 10022; 212/759-0900.

The very reasons that make Canada an easy entry-level export effort render it uninteresting to some export trading or management firms. Export firms are essentially service providers, and there is little service to provide in a market so closely corresponding to the United States. Most manufacturers will handle the export work to Canada by themselves. Even those not interested in export may be selling through their own salesmen or distributors to that country.

Canada is of great importance in terms of its place within the North American free-trade region and—looking farther south—in terms of North America's relationship to Central and South America. Because of its geographical location, the United States is a necessary land bridge and economic link between Canada and Mexico and between Canada and the Latin American nations south of Mexico. The United States is also the single-largest customer of most countries in Latin America and by far the largest market for both Mexico and Canada.

Mexico

Clearly Mexico's financial and political problems are not as close to resolution as once imagined, but it would be reckless to ignore the growing trade and investment opportunities in Mexico in spite of the problems of 1995. Most experts on the region expect at least the economic problems, if not the political ones, to be relatively short term. By mid-1995 a shift has become noticeable as Mexico's infrastructure needs begin to be met with capital equipment purchases and as U.S. investors that had been delaying their proposed capital investments start moving back in. Mexican exports have begun to grow because of the peso devaluation—and exports are an absolutely necessary ingredient to a recovery. Mexico is America's third-largest trading partner. It is a major customer to whom we exported $50.8 billion in 1994, within $2.6 billion of what we ship to our second-largest customer, Japan. Furthermore, Mexico will remain in this rank, even for the difficult year of 1995, for in 1994 exports to Mexico were nearly twice those of our fourth-ranked and next-best customer, the United Kingdom. Equally important is the fact that we share a 2000-mile border with Mexico. This nation, approaching 90 million people, has been making good progress. The many positive developments that occurred in a span of just four or five years as a result of President Salinas' reforms were heartening—especially after more than a decade of crisis characterized by personal discontent and a growing demoralization in almost every sector of the business community. President Carlos Salinas de Gotari deserves credit for instituting many programs to encourage reform, and it is truly unfortunate that he apparently attempted to make them appear more than they were and failed to take the traditional devaluation step as his term ended. The violence that accompanied the presidential succession made things still worse, of course, but the succession that actually took place may be triggering a series of events that will have long-term benefits for democracy and social reform.

The Political and Economic Climate

There is no question that the Mexican political system is not yet fully representative, despite the fact that many reforms have taken place. Nonetheless, it does seem apparent that further advances are occurring with surprising speed. The key questions are if and when the continuing civil unrest will become civil violence, as occurred in the case of Chiapas, and to what extent President Zedillo can maintain control. There is a feeling among many that, in view of Mexico's volatile political history and nature, any political reform should go forward slowly if order and economic growth are to be maintained.

Great progress has been made, in any case. By 1991 Mexico's budget deficit had been cut dramatically, with massive reductions in public sector spending. Inflation was cut from 160 percent in 1987 to under 20 percent in 1989, and even though it increased to 30 percent in 1990, it declined again and is expected to run at 21 percent in 1995. Non-oil exports increased sharply, driven by the private sector, and today oil represents only 11 percent of total expanded exports, compared to 80 percent in 1982. The largest share of the increase in non-oil exports has come from the automotive industry as a result of heavy investment by the United States and Japan in this area. Privatization has taken place at an amazing pace as thousands of businesses, from banks to transport companies, have gone private.

Average import duties dropped to under 10 percent, where 100 percent was once commonplace and many goods were simply prohibited. Investment opportunities have opened up to the extent that some claim that two-thirds of Mexico's GDP of $234 billion is available for outright purchase by investors. To prove that it is sincere, the administration has imposed a rule on its foreign investment officials that a definitive response must be provided to foreign inquiries within 45 days. All of this occurred before NAFTA and GATT which will assure still further strides toward an economy free to grow and improve living standards for all.

Although the selection of Mexico by the TPCC as one of three Big Emerging Markets in Latin America was quite logical in 1993, its status as such in 1995 may be diminished. There are, however, many reasons to think 1996 can reconfirm its BEM status. Informed sources, ranging from exporters active in the area to the Inter-American Development Bank to Salomon Brothers in New York, expect a small growth in the GDP even in 1995, with a consensus speaking of a growth rate just above 4 percent in 1996, combined with the peso stabilizing in the range of 5 or 6 to the dollar. Anyone's predictions are suspect in the present unstable political climate, however, with the PRI party taking some major defeats and the fortunes of the PAN party on the rise.

The severe and sudden peso devaluation hurt many investors, foreign and Mexican alike. Exporters of consumer goods to Mexico were particularly hard hit, especially stores such as Wal-Mart that had been planning major expansions. Consumption levels within the country will no doubt decline dramatically, but overall exports to Mexico continue to grow. It is regrettable that many short-term negative developments will probably be emphasized at this time as a result of the problems in 1995, which will give ammunition to the anti-NAFTA forces both here and in Mexico. Two such negative developments will be (1) more U.S. plants moving to Mexico to take advantage of the still-lower labor cost created by the exchange rate; and (2) more social distress in Mexico, exacerbated by the current unemployment rate. It will be necessary for enlightened leadership on both sides of the border to hold the free trade gains during a difficult, however mercifully short, readjustment period.

The Maquiladoras

Maquiladoras preceded this reform, but very possibly helped lead the way to what has happened in terms of opening up Mexico for investment and manufacturing. The maquilas will continue to exist during the phase-out period until until the year 2001 and it is possible existing plants may be "grandfathered" into an extended life if so desired, depending on the extent of duties remaining. In any case presumably they will not play as vital a role as before NAFTA since tariffs have already dropped so dramatically and will be levied after 2001 on only about 10 to 15 percent of all commodities—and even then at a very modest rate. At that point, however, still more benefits will bestow upon the Maquilas such as the restrictions on selling within Mexico and other restrictions dissolve.

Maquiladora plants are usually partly or wholly foreign-owned by corporate nationals of countries that have concluded a treaty with Mexico to be a maquiladora partner. The maquiladora company imports on a duty-free basis the foreign manufacturer's work-in-process or raw materials for assembly or manufacture in Mexico, having posted a bond or by other arrangements assuring that the goods will subsequently be exported. The finished product or enhanced work-in-process is then exported back to the country of origin, paying duty on its return only on the value added and any components not originating in the foreign manufacturer's country. It may also be exported from Mexico directly to a third country as is the case with many maquiladora shipments to the United States that are not of U.S. ownership. In this case, the third country's tariffs apply.

The Mexican maquiladora plant may be wholly owned by the foreign company but is subject to Mexican law in all respects. Alternatively, it may be a Mexican company acting as a subcontractor for the foreign client, or a more closely controlled relationship, called the "shelter" program that diminishes the Mexican political risk exposure substantially as opposed to the fully owned approach. The program was once strictly for the border areas, but now has spread throughout the country even though the greatest concentration is in the Baja California area near Tijuana. The next greatest concentration is in Ciudad Juarez, across from El Paso, Texas. In 1992 there were about 1800 plants and 437,000 employees involved, more than double the number in 1985.

Maquiladora activities encompass a wide range of industries, but with special emphasis in electronic equipment and in transportation, mostly in automotive accessories and assembly. There has also been significant activity in textiles, furniture, tools, chemicals, and foodstuffs. Originally begun primarily for U.S. manufacturers in very low-tech assembly processes, such as apparel sewing, the maquiladora program has become internationalized, with plants owned by nationals from Canada, Japan, Germany, France, Hong Kong, South Korea, and Taiwan utilizing greatly escalated technology. The majority of the assembly and manufacturing processes from whatever national origin are to produce products for the U.S. market. The program has become a dynamic stimulus for the Mexican economy in terms of jobs, foreign exchange, and new investment.

Whether called the Maquiladora program or attributed to NAFTA, as tariffs no longer impact the process of moving goods across the border for added value from utilizing Mexican labor, to the extent low-cost labor must be used for competitive reasons, it makes more sense to use and develop Mexican labor and create Mexican jobs than to create Taiwanese and Korean jobs. It creates easily accessible markets for U.S. manufacturers who will have a permanent competitive edge in those markets and will provide relief to our current border and immigration problems. In the longer term this should also improve Mexican living standards, which will benefit the United States, since such a large disparity in per capita income between the two countries and thus diminishing current sources of friction and causes of immigration. As a natural market and assembly center today and as the potential linchpin for the America's trading bloc of the next decade, Mexico deserves careful attention from the standpoint of market and investment strategy.

Latin America

Until the oil crisis brought about the massive debt problems of the early 1980s, Latin America had long been the key export target for many American corporations and businesses including trading companies of all sizes. This was not surprising in view of the fact that this is a region in our own hemisphere with over 350 million people. Although foreign exchange was a problem even in the 1980s and business often had to be done in a rather irregular fashion, the countries of Latin America were among the United States' best and most reliable customers.

During much of the 1980s, many exporters simply ignored the region because of the difficulties—and, in many cases, the sheer impossibility—of doing business. Many exporters who maintained solid contacts in the area continued to do business in a wide range of products, with the determining factor often being just how badly the sovereign government felt the prospective import was needed. The net result of the overall falling away of U.S. business in the region during the 1980s has been that our trading infrastructure there has deteriorated badly and now needs to be rebuilt almost from scratch, in terms of distributors, agents, and subsidiaries or joint ventures.

An Improving Outlook

There are rapidly rising demands and needs in South America today, in terms of both infrastructure and consumer goods. Trade and opportunity even look bright in Central America after decades of civil war. The stabilizing effects of widespread democratization and privatization have led to dramatic improvements in economic outlook and market demand throughout most of South America, with import restrictions rapidly diminishing. It is not surprising that many political and economic observers are pointing out how much more attention U.S. businesses have given the emerging countries of Eastern Europe, with all their political and economic troubles, than they have to the more favorable political and economic developments in South America, where the United States has so much more at stake. For example, in 1994, U.S. exports to South and Central America totaled $35.6 billion (to say nothing of $50.8 billion to Mexico), 2.5 times those of five years earlier, compared to about $5 billion in Central and Eastern Europe (the U.S.S.R. included). To understand the magnitude of the economic changes under way, current exporters might find it instructive to look into the comparative sales records of companies that were active in Latin America in the 1950s, 1960s, and 1970s.

Politically, the changes are almost as dramatic as the economic statistics in terms of free elections and fewer governments dominated by the military. In fact, for the first time in history, all 12 sovereign nations of South America are governed by popularly elected governments (French Guiana is still governed by France). Economically, the changes are at least as dramatic as the political turnaround. Crisis after crisis has been resolved as Latin policies have changed to restructure debt, privatize, and adopt monetary and fiscal policies to contain inflation. Some of the changes have been voluntary, some brought about by political upheaval, and some forced by the International Monetary Fund as part of debt restructuring plans. The combination of the movement toward freer trade (including lower tariffs), less restrictive import licensing, and a general realization that protectionism has done nothing to strengthen Latin economies, adds to the promise of a resurgence of the region to its former status as a Very Important Trading partner. This optimism is reinforced because so many Latin countries seem to be facing up to the necessity of economic reforms no matter how painful.

Stimulated by these developments, an increasing number of free trade agreements have been created, some with the long-range objective of joining the NAFTA process. Chile, as one of the most open Latin-American economies with high labor and environmental standards, was first in line to be invited to join the NAFTA partners. When the invitation was made official at the Summit of the Americas in Miami in December of 1994, the term "The Four Amigos" was coined, and almost at once the "queue of South American NAFTA applicants began to form at the podium steps," according to John Mooney, editor of *Export Today*.[1] Unfortunately, the subsequent collapse of the peso in Mexico dramatically changed the politics of free trade in the Americas, and little, at best, is likely to occur until after the U.S. presidential elections of 1996. Even thereafter developments will depend on many factors, including the predominance of the present highly vocal and powerful neoisolationists. Although it seems incomprehensible, there are many who would insist the United States stay entirely removed from trade blocs even in the face of growing trade regionalism throughout the world. The U.S. has an excellent opportunity to broker to its own advantage a hemispheric trade bloc that would offer both economic opportunity and more stable geographic neighbors, representing better export markets as a result of greater per capita incomes. Such a trade bloc would also provide trump cards to play, if necessary, to counter any possible protectionism from the growing European and Asiatic trading blocs. Such protectionism seems to be the very sin that some of the new political leadership is proposing.

Trade Regionalism in Latin America

Before discussing the present trading blocs of Latin America, it should be noted that historically a fundamental problem of intra–Latin American free trade agreements has been a narrow range of traditional exports, which resulted in a lack of complementary or synergistic trade opportunities. As the southern economies become more diversified and sophisticated, however, this inherent problem is starting to resolve itself, often thanks to foreign investments made for the manufacture of nontraditional products. Such problems can also be eased if the Americas continue to become more of an economic partnership. It will be easier to negotiate trade problems in Latin America by negotiating with trading blocs or regions than by negotiating with 19 individual Central and South American countries to say nothing of the numerous countries and territories of the Caribbean.

Mercosur.   By far the most important trade bloc in Latin America today is the Southern Common Market, known as Mercosur and sometimes referred to as the Southern Cone group. Mercosur currently includes Argentina, Brazil, Paraguay, and Uruguay. It was formed in 1986 and has had an up-and-down history, but became a reality as of January 1995 when tariffs were abolished among the four members. It represents a combined population of nearly 200 million (larger than Europe) and includes South America's two most productive economies, Brazil and Argentina. Brazil has come to enjoy unusual success in the short period since July 1994 when its new economic plan, including open trade, was introduced and inflation fell to a fraction of its former rate almost overnight. Both retail sales and manufacturing output are booming, and tariffs have dropped by two-thirds. Argentina has been one of the three fastest-growing economies in the world even though it has seen a recession in 1995. It was the newfound strength of both Argentina and Brazil that suddenly made Mercosur a real factor. Mercosur is already negotiating with other countries and free-trade groups to extend free trade across the continent, with agreements looking toward the formation of a Southern Free Trade Area (SAFTA). Mercosur has invited Bolivia, which is now a member of the Andean Pact group, to join its members, and it would welcome Chile, the original hard-core free trader of South America. Chile represents the wild card in the South American deck. Besides its invitation to join NAFTA, it has an excellent location and good timing on its side, permitting it to coolly observe developments before committing to any trade alliance, while meantime establishing a number of bilateral pacts.

Since Mercosur began lowering tariffs in 1991, trade among the four countries has expanded from $2.7 billion to about $12 billion, and foreign investment has increased as rapidly as one would expect. Unfortunately, a serious step backward was taken when Brazil felt forced to raise some of its external tariffs as an emergency response to economic problems created by Mexico's peso devaluation. Most exports feel the damage can be repaired. Its combined GDP in 1994 was estimated to be nearly $1 trillion. The partners all currently enjoy a high level of political and economic harmony and have established a common external tariff structure, making Mercosur the only major customs union outside the EU. Mercosur has the long-range goal of becoming, over time, a community similar to the EU. There are no solid plans in place at this time, but Mercosur has begun special tariff negotiations with the EU. As evidence of how fast international trade conditions can shift, just four years ago Mercosur's ambitious goals were regarded as unrealizable. Mercosur has made a major contribution to the health of its members but, in turn, Mercosur's strength stems from the largely productive and literate workforce of these countries. Today it appears to be a regional bloc of sufficient size and cohesiveness to become a major contributor to former President Bush's vision of a hemispheric trade zone.

The Andean Pact.   The second-most important trade bloc in Latin America is the Andean Pact group, formed in 1969 but currently struggling for a variety of reasons. The pact includes Venezuela, Columbia, Ecuador, Peru, and Bolivia. It has a combined population of 100 million (slightly larger than Mexico's and half the size of Mercosur's) and a GNP of $165 billion. With a goal of achieving free trade by 1997, the group seemed to be doing fairly well in the early 1990s, but its long-term problems grew worse as two of its members, Peru and Ecuador, let their long-term border problems break into open hostilities. The pact's more serious current problem is that its largest member, Venezuela, is again in a financial crisis and proving to be the sick man of South America. Columbia, however, is attracting substantial foreign investment as the most-developed member, and Peru is undergoing a total change for the better with the Senderoso terrorists out of the way and vast economic reforms successfully in process. The Andean Pact has encouraged a number of bilateral free-trade agreements in the area, producing beneficial results like the one that tripled trade between Columbia and Venezuela in the three-year period from 1990 to 1993.

The Latin American Integration Association.   The original Latin organization for free trade was the Latin American Integration Association (ALADI), established in 1980. It included the ten largest economies of South America, plus Mexico, but excluded Central America. It has done little as a free-trade association, but it does serve as an umbrella organization to assist in organizing bilateral and multilateral agreements for reciprocal preferential tariff rates in the region. There are about 15 such agreements, one of the most important of which is the triliteral free-trade pact known as the Group of Three, signed in 1994 between Mexico, Columbia, and Venezuela and intended to phase out tariffs among them over a ten-year period.

Other Groups.   The Central American Common Market (CACM) (which excludes Panama) has been in existence since the early 1960s and might be added to the Latin free-trade groups. It once offered real promise; however, hostilities and other problems in the area have diminished its importance substantially. It was never considered a common market as such, but rather an enhanced trade arrangement. It is currently being restructured. The Caribbean Community (Caricom) covers the English-speaking portion of the Caribbean area, plus Guyana and Belize. It has assumed some real importance in the area, especially relative to the U.S. Caribbean Basin Initiative. Caricom has developed a common external tariff and formed a special counsel to seek investment and joint ventures from Europe, as well as to target European markets and create trade pacts. Similarly, CARIBCAN is a trade preference pact between Canada and the Commonwealth Caribbean States and the Lomé Convention which came into being in 1990 offering duty-free access to the European Union from developing countries in Africa, the Caribbean, and the Pacific. It is clear that trade blocs and trade pacts do not necessarily stand still, and they create trade channels that can easily bypass isolationist or protectionist nations.

Reassessing the Future

When this chapter was first put together for the second edition of our book in 1991, much of it was written in the future tense. At that time, we could only assume that NAFTA would come about; Columbia was thought to be a lawless state; the Senderoso terrorists had brought Peru close to anarchy; Venezuela was booming; and Brazil—along with many another Latin American nation—was in a state of hyperinflation. Today, inflation is Venezuela's problem. Brazil and Argentina are experiencing growth and investment inflows, as are Columbia, Chile, and Peru. The lesson to be learned is that conditions in the region can change far more rapidly than one would imagine, but that the potential for major economic improvement is there or already exists. South America now realizes how desperately it needs investment inflow and, in the main, is prepared to make reforms to see that happen. Although today the United States alone buys 44 percent of Latin American production, those countries are quite willing and able to redirect that flow toward either the European trade blocs or to Asia. Chile's largest trading partner, for instance, is Japan.

Once, the question was whether a U.S. business should institute or rebuild relationships in the region so that when and if Latin American trade fully reactivated, the company's structure for distribution and trade would be in place to take full advantage of the Latin American market. The question now is how a U.S. business can become involved in Latin America as a business, with what kind or form of investment, with which trade bloc or blocs, and so on. There are obvious risks in terms of how quickly the fortunes of any given nation can turn, but this risk can be somewhat mitigated by operating within the growing trade blocs and thereby hedging the changing fortunes of any one specific country. For many firms, this may include the possibility of a physical presence, realizing that this area comprises one of the giant markets of the world in terms of both consumers and industrial customers. It is a market that is relatively close to home, within our time zones, and with customers who have always looked to the United States as their key supplier. The alternative is to lose this market to Japanese and European firms, who in the meantime have become well established in Latin America and are now threatening to overtake us there. The best evidence of this threat is the cars on the streets of South America. Not so many years ago, at a time when auto parts and accessories and after-sales equipment were a large and profitable export business in Latin America, the cars were almost entirely of U.S. origin. No longer. Now they are mostly Japanese and European.

Financing is becoming less a part of the Latin problem as the U.S. banking community once again becomes interested in trade finance in general and Latin America in particular. Through the U.S. Export-Import Bank, guarantees and credit insurance can be obtained for a majority of the Latin countries. The Overseas Private Investment Corporation (OPIC) provides guarantees and insurance to encourage private U.S. investment in Latin America. It is regrettable that OPIC is still unable to provide that service in the case of Mexico for lack of reaching a special agreement to make that possible. (Eximbank is fully explained in Chapter 40 and OPIC in Chapter 41.) Financial support is also available through the World Bank, the Inter-American Development Bank, and the Caribbean Development Bank. (See Chapter 13.)

Although there will always be surprises, some of them sudden and intense, Latin America could be the most strategic of all the world's major trade blocs. And a major trade bloc it will be, whether as part of NAFTA, in tandem with NAFTA, or in competition with a future SAFTA. Had it not been for the crisis in Mexico and the recent change in the tenor of Congress in the direction of neoisolationism, the chances for NAFTA becoming hemispheric were far more possible than most would have expected. This result may still come about as the pendulum swings back and forth. It clearly represents both a challenge and an opportunity, and it is a region in which the United States is already a dominant or at least a major player. In the Andean Pact countries 36 percent of the imports are from the United States; in the Group of Three, 62 percent; in Mercosur, 23 percent; and in NAFTA, 80 percent.

Any firm engaged in trade in the Americas has to make a careful reassessment of the need for investment and a corporate presence in Latin America, just as in the case of the European and Southeast Asian trade blocs. In fact, such investments for the benefit of international trade and improvements in the economies of less-advantaged countries may be a prerequisite to successful market-share development, even as they make a small contribution to world peace. But the decisions concerning the Americas are not unrelated to the other major trade areas of the world, as we shall see.

A Global Viewpoint

As new alliances, blocs, and trading relationships develop around the globe, new corporate tools and structures are quickening change, driven by the ever-increasing intensity of competition that requires the exchange and purchase of new technologies, better market position, and increased economy of scale. Production alliances and economic treaties among nations that are sharing economically strategic landmasses will make it more difficult for the outsider, while facilitating competitiveness for the member. Competitiveness naturally includes low labor costs, and as the EU turns to labor from the Newly Independent States (NIS) and Asia and Japan and the Tigers use more Southeast Asian labor, competitiveness may force North America to look to Mexican and other Latin labor unless current U.S. productivity growth can be maintained. But as has been demonstrated, labor, given time, tends to generate a better standard of living for the laborers and their country. This enables that community to become a better consumer in its own right. Growing complaints in this country that cheap Latin labor will cost American jobs ignores the rates available from other low-cost areas and more importantly overlooks the fact that improved U.S. GNP and economic well-being comes not from dislocation of some low-paying jobs in which retraining can and should be accomplished, but from an enhanced economic base of more competitive and sophisticated production. This represents a boost up the development ladder for both parties or, as economist Flanigan puts it: "Cars are not made where labor is cheapest, but where production is most efficiently organized."

Even if developments permit worldwide free trade to continue its four-decade advance, there will be a continuing trend toward regional trade blocs for economy of scale and shared resources. These blocs will include both skilled and cheap-labor countries, and the countries inside a bloc or region will want preferential treatment over those outside the bloc. This observation does not imply that trade blocs are bad, even though few economists presume that alone, or in a struggle with each other, they will foster the levels of trade that global free trade creates. In spite of trade blocs, there will always be trade between the nonmember countries and the various blocs, as in the case of the European Union and the United States. But nations within free-trade blocs have a trade and industrial synergism enhanced by few trade limitations and therefore they tend to favor trade among themselves. The optimum situation would be that intrabloc advantages would be slight and not at undue expense to those nations in other blocs.

While new and better products and services will always be in demand, whether in markets at home or abroad, it bears repeating once more that almost any company should be prepared for more aggressive competition in the U.S. market from overseas competition. A company is likely to find its domestic competitors well entrenched in the best foreign markets when it finally does go abroad. The EU and other trade blocs will become increasingly adept at matching or beating our best as they take advantage of less expensive labor within their respective trade blocs to lower costs and, in turn, use the expanded home market of that bloc to gain economy of scale. This fosters more product and market research and reduced costs and results in keener, more aggressive competition worldwide as well as here at home.

An issue of greater concern to the entire world is the possibility of increasing friction among ethnic, language, and cultural groups, even as the importance of national borders and clashes between economic ideologies diminishes. The re-balkanization of the Balkans, the ethnic-originated clashes in the Russian Federation, and the conflict between Islamic fundamentalism and other forms of religion are excellent examples. Former Secretary of State George Shultz, now a professor in Stanford's Graduate School of Business states, "Today, ideas, information, pollution, and drugs go across borders, and governments can't do much about it. Borders mean less, but the idea of national governments and ethnic identity is more important than ever." Also of Stanford, Jerry Meier of its Graduate School of Business makes another point when he states that business may be, in fact, the most truly "global arena" today. What is unprecedented may not be the level of international transactions, but the way in which they are completed. As a result of technological advances, Meier observes, "The geographical location of decision making has become immaterial, the management of international functions has been facilitated, and international transaction costs have decreased. One result is that a growing number of corporations, large and small, are undertaking worldwide operations. Products can easily be financed in France, designed in California, manufactured in Korea, and marketed in Brazil."

As trade becomes freer, prosperity increases and expands the income of the poorer countries participating in it. The net result is to diminish the possibility of cultural conflicts becoming military conflicts.

Endnotes

1. Editorial by publisher John Mooney, *Export Today,* January 1995.

4

Export Operations

18

Components of an Export Quotation

Once overseas contacts are established and you are in touch with representatives and customers, inquiries should start coming in for your product. This means making quotations and making sure they are accurate and successful. It also means you are pricing your product competitively but profitably.

Pricing Your Product

As a manufacturer you already know production costs and have determined your profit objectives. As an export management company (EMC) or an export trading company (ETC), your minimum margin must probably be around 12 to 15 percent or higher, depending on the extent of the responsibilities you have accepted for the product beyond marketing and shipping, such as financing and credit. There still remains a large variance in terms of appropriate margins, and therefore prices, depending on a host of factors that apply to manufacturers and third-party exporters alike. Some examples might include, but are not limited to:

- Time sensitivity of price, keeping in mind the longer time cycle of export sales
- Anticipated volume and its incremental effect
- Availability of supplies or components
- Anticipated major complications in filling the order
- Payment terms, including special risks and/or the costs of covering those risks

- Extra export selling and export administration costs
- Special product modification costs

The temptation to make it on volume in export trading activities is very strong for any EMC/ETC. Therefore, understanding true costs and necessary profit margins is very important. It has been said of entrepreneurial exporters that the first sale establishes the addiction, and each sale thereafter is a fix.

By definition, the EMC/ETC has already a highly leveraged investment relative to sales and profit, and fixed or capital costs are, or should be, low. If an EMC/ETC considers reducing its normal margin percentages to take advantage of a large potential profit, it should do so only because of easy procurement of the item, quick turnaround, minimal shipping challenges, low banking and financial costs, and a small credit risk exposure. More often than not, the big deals contain few or none of these elements. In the case of the manufacturer, the equivalent of "making it on volume" thinking might be to utilize the theory of marginal cost or contributory profit in computing the selling price. Some firms, in fact, use this approach for their export pricing, but doing so usually has certain short-term implications that contradict a sound, long-term export policy.

When establishing the price for your product, take careful note of direct costs that must be factored in when computing your bid or selling price. In addition to freight, handling, and insurance, check with your forwarder and review the items on the quotation worksheet (Figure 18-1) for the many smaller charges such as wharfage or dock charges, handling, documentation and legalization fees, inspection fees, courier charges, and the harbor maintenance fee (.125 percent of FAS value). Don't forget to include items such as agent commissions and, in some cases, even bank charges. The latter is especially important in the case of small shipments covered by letters of credit that create extraordinary collection costs. Proper allocation and accounting of direct sales costs versus ongoing general expenses also make it easier to prepare business plans, sales projections, and cashflow projections. If pricing for export seems to be a problem, the *Export Sales and Marketing Manual,* by John R. Jagoe, makes a detailed analysis of this subject[1] (see also Appendix K).

Shipping Rates, Costs, and Savings

Assuming you are willing to quote something other than ex-works (factory), the first step is to calculate freight costs. Before you can determine accurate air-freight or ocean freight costs, you need to know the exact weight and dimension of your product when it is packed and ready for shipment.

Packing Costs

Adequate packing is a must, but excessive or unnecessarily heavy packaging should be avoided because it will add to the final cost. When deciding on the type of packaging, consider ease of handling as well as breakage, moisture damage, and pilferage opportunities en route. One often-overlooked detail is

```
ORDER/REF. NO. _____     NAME _____     DATE _____

PRODUCT INFORMATION
Product _____          Schedule B No. _____
No. of units _____        Dimension _____ x _____ x _____
Units per master ctn ____        Cubic Measure _____ sq. in.
Net weight _____lbs _____kg       (per unit)     _____ sq. ft.
Gross weight _____lbs_____kg                      _____ m²
Volume Weight (air)_____        Total measure _____


                 #####################################


PRODUCT COST/CHARGES                          EST.COST   SELL
Price per unit _____ x units _____  Total  _____  _____
Profit/Margin                                          _____
Sales/Agent commission                        _____  _____
Export packing, container or truck loading    _____  _____
Financing cost, including L/C bank fees        _____  _____
Consular invoice, export license, notary      _____  _____
* TOTAL FCA SELLER'S PLACE OF BUSINESS                 _____

PORT CHARGES
Unloading (heavy lift)                        _____  _____
Freight forwarding charges                    _____  _____
Inland freight to _____                     _____  _____
Harbor Maintenance fee (.125% of FAS value)   _____  _____
* TOTAL FOB PORT or TOTAL FCA MAIN CARRIER             _____

FREIGHT CHARGES     CARRIER _____
Based on ___ weight ___ measure; ocean ___ air ___
Rate quoted _____ date _____
Terminal charge _____ minimum _____ Amount       _____
* TOTAL CFR PORT OF DESTINATION                        _____

INSURANCE
Type of Coverage _____
Basis _____ Rate _____ Amount            _____
War Risk @ $_____ rate per $100                       _____
* TOTAL CIF PORT OF DESTINATION                        _____
                                                       ========
```

* the application of charges under the various INCOTERMS is only
approximate and typical, and not intended to be definitional.

Figure 18-1. Export quotation worksheet.

that most shipments are put on pallets for ease of maneuvering with forklifts, and the added weight and dimension of the pallet, as with all other packaging refinements adding weight and measure, must be included in your calculation. The added bulk of the pallets can represent an important percentage of total freight costs. A good packaging specialist can save money, not only in terms of freight costs, but also in terms of breakage claims and pilferage. Your freight forwarder can make suggestions of export packers or you can request a list of export packers from the Packaging Institute, 342 Madison Avenue, New York,

New York 10017. (Also look under Ports of the World in Appendix K for shipping references.)

Inland Freight or Cartage

Inland freight may involve nothing more than delivering your goods on pallets via a cartage company to the airline or the harbor, or it may involve complex routing problems created by oversize loads for shipment on trucks, rails, or a combination thereof. When compared to domestic freight rates, ocean rates usually seem like a bargain, especially on competitive ocean routes.

Airfreight

Charges for airfreight can vary widely depending on the tariff classification, the competitiveness of the route, the availability of space, and the willingness of the forwarder to share negotiated rates and commissions. When either the forwarder or the airline gives you a price per pound or kilogram, be sure to base your calculation on both actual weight and volume weight and see which produces the greater revenue for the airline, because this is the price they will charge you. To arrive at the volume weight, take the total cubic inches of the product and divide by 166. The result is the volumetric weight and is multiplied by the quoted airfreight rate per pound to determine freight cost. Should the actual weight exceed the volume weight, the higher weight will prevail as the basis for freight cost. For air shipments, the most commonly used containers are LD1 containers, with an internal volume of 164 cubic feet; the LD3, with 150 cubic feet; and the LD7, with 343 cubic feet. There is also the pallet and net, which is simply a pallet similar to the floor of an LD7 on which packages are stacked and then covered and strapped with a net. The usable volume is usually about 370 cubic feet. Some airlines have a container rate to certain destinations with a maximum allowable weight. When deciding on ocean freight versus airfreight (which is more expensive on the face of it), consider the possibility that the time gained by getting the product to the destination quickly—and therefore possibly sold or utilized quickly—may offset this added expense. This is especially important for high-priced items or time-critical merchandise and in cases where pilferage is a consideration.

Ocean Freight

Ocean freight rates are obtained from the steamship line or a forwarder. These are usually based on weight or measure (revenue ton)—whichever produces the greater revenue. Rates are usually quoted per kilogram or metric ton (1000 kilograms, which is equal to 2204.6 pounds) or occasionally in "long ton" of 2240 pounds; or per cubic meter or cubic 40 feet (measure ton). In some cases, prices are quoted on a per unit or per piece basis, as in the case of oranges, which are packed in a standard carton accepted by the industry. In both cases, terminal charges and minimum bill of lading costs apply. Depending on the commodity, some steamship lines also offer flat rates per container, which usually produce a more advantageous rate.

Ocean Containers.   Standard carrier containers are provided by the steamship carriers at a flat rate. Most common ocean containers are either 20-foot containers holding approximately 1000 cubic feet or 40-foot containers with approximately twice as much space. The maximum weight of any container of whatever cube is generally 44,000 pounds to permit legal hauling on public roads. While 20-foot containers remain popular and necessary, ocean carriers are increasingly emphasizing 40-foot containers. SeaLand offers 35-foot containers, largely as reefers, but has no 20-foot containers, while APL now offers 45-foot containers in addition to 20-foot and 40-foot sizes. Check with the appropriate carrier for exact dimensions and weight limits so that you can accurately determine how many cartons or items will fit into each type of container. Even among so-called 20-foot and 40-foot containers there are differences; some carriers offer high-cube containers that have additional capacity through increased height. The correct container can make a vast difference in shipping economy. Truckers usually charge similar flat rates for hauling any of the ocean containers, whether 20-foot or 40-foot.

NVOCC Carriers.   An important means of saving on ocean freight costs in the case of less-than-container-load (LCL) lots is shipment via NVOCCs (nonvessel operating common carriers). These are companies that buy space wholesale on vessels and resell it at their own rates. NVOCCs have altered the ocean freight pricing structures and competition factors. However, sometimes NVOCCs accept a full container from a single shipper, contrary to their basic function as consolidators. They usually do this because they have contracted for more container loads with a carrier than they can fill and therefore need to use more space quickly. The result can mean big savings for the exporter. Since these companies often specialize in certain routes, it may take some time to find the carriers that work for your shipments. Don't count solely on your ocean freight forwarder to determine the best route and rate because there may be conflicting interests or simply a lack of time. If an NVOCC is handling the shipment, it may be able to serve as the forwarder as well. In fact, many forwarding companies own their own NVOCC operation.

NVOCCs can offer large savings if you are shipping LCL, but be sure to check the NVOCCs' reliability even though they must now be bonded, because fierce competition resulted in a number of unstable operations. Also, be sure that the NVOCC can provide you with a bill of lading showing that it is acting as agent for an ocean carrier. This document must be usable within the terms and requirements of most letters of credit for an ocean bill of lading. The alternative is to request that your letter of credit states that "NVOCC bills of lading"—or "house bills of lading," in the case of air freight—are acceptable. Some letters of credit are drawn to permit such bills anyway, but unless you are certain that is the case, be sure to make the request.

Multimodal Transport

Today, besides airfreight or ocean freight and the other forms of domestic transportation, you must consider the increasingly used combination of transport modes, called *multimodal* or *intermodal,* shipping. This is an umbrella term, referring to use of at least two modes of transportation in moving goods from origin to destination. *Multimodal,* however, specifically utilizes what was once called a combined transport bill of lading. Renamed the *multimodal transport document* by the International Chamber of Commerce in the new Uniform Customs and Practices code, the document is understood to apply to the process of loading and/or unloading at an inland point and proceeding from there by rail, truck, or inland waterway to an ocean port and then continuing abroad by ocean vessel. The document can even cover a continuation of the voyage to an inland point after unloading at the foreign port, which in itself would be multimodal. Parenthetically, such a shipping itinerary avoids the Panama Canal, which saves a meaningful measure of shipping time. The availability of the multimodal transport document has brought about or necessitated many changes in the format and procedures for letters of credit. *Multimodal transport document* is not, however, the term used in the case of the more common mini land-bridge or land-bridge systems, in which ocean carriers provide an onboard ocean bill of lading for a container which the ocean carrier arranges to put on a rail car at an ocean port for transport across the continent, and which is then loaded onto a vessel for an ocean voyage, or vice versa. It may also be called a land-bridge, or micro land-bridge, shipment under the same circumstances, if the voyage begins or ends at an inland city and continues to or from the ocean port of export or import (inland point international, or IPI). The land-bridge concept has been in common use for some time and is regularly covered with a single ocean bill of lading.

Multimodal strategies, together with the land-bridge concepts, continue to revolutionize intercontinental shipping in terms of cost as well as speed. Because they are still a growth area of the transportation market, intermodal quotations can sometimes reduce shipping rates or shipping times far beyond what could be expected from efficiency savings. This is because intermodal shipping is free of some regulations and carrier treaties and its proponents are eager to increase their market share. It need not always be complex and applies to airfreight as well. Intermodal shipping can be as simple as using trucks from origin to international airport and again from the destination airport to the city of delivery overseas and they can certainly result in substantial savings.

Shipping Conferences

There are conference carriers and nonconference carriers. The *conference carriers* are a group of carriers that have established common freight rates on a certain route. You will be asked to sign a conference contract for a certain period of time to get a contract rate. This contract, however, forces the exporter to ship exclusively on conference vessels to their areas of the world so that you can't take advantage of the lower rates that nonconference carriers offer if they are competing on the same route. Many conferences have been disbanded, and they are less of a power today in the current, more competitive and deregulated, climate. Naturally, this has also forced the conferences to become more competitive themselves, and therefore some continue to survive.

Shippers' Associations

A *shippers' association* is a group of shippers that consolidates the freight of their members to obtain volume transportation rates or service contracts. Check with other exporters in your field, especially with firms frequently shipping to one or more common destinations, regarding the possibility of an existing shippers' association. Local cartage operators or traffic management trade associations may also be helpful in your quest. Associations are effective in both domestic and overseas shipping and using one can result in major savings if it is a so-called rate negotiator association. The Shipping Act of 1984 requires ocean carrier conferences to negotiate with shippers' associations and provides antitrust immunity to the conferences for certain rate-setting agreements. The Shipping Act does not provide antitrust protection to shippers' associations for concerted action by its members. Under the Export Trading Company act, an export consortium or established shippers' association can minimize or eliminate this risk by obtaining a certificate of review covering activities performed in the course of exporting.

Shipping Terms, Terms of Sale, and International Trade Terms

The titles, *shipping terms, terms of sale,* or *international trade terms* are all used interchangeably in international trade to describe the various combinations of respective duties and liabilities of the buyer and seller. These terms are of vital importance in order to avoid misunderstandings and disputes. While there is no official agreement among nations, the trade terms as defined in the Incoterms, initially introduced by the International Chamber of Commerce in 1936 and several times updated, are widely accepted around the world. Some businesses, usually domestic, continue to quote terms as if the world were still using the 1941 *Revised American Foreign Trade Definitions,* in which almost every term was one of about six versions beginning with the prefix "FOB." But today's variety of transportation modes no longer permits that. For all international shipments, Incoterms should be used for clarity and for your own protection.

The updating to match changing documentary and shipping practices is a major advantage of Incoterms, and the last codification became effective in July of 1990. The prior 1980 revision included new terms to accommodate the growing use of multimodal transportation, which has an important bearing on when the transfer of risk occurs. The 1990 changes were primarily to further accommodate this trend and the rapid growth of document handling through Electronic Data Interchange (EDI).

When considering shipping terms, keep in mind that besides expressing who is to carry the burden of certain shipping and insurance costs, the terms are also intended to be an abbreviated contract to indicate both transfer of risk and, at least in some cases, passage of title (a different legal definition and issue than transfer of risk), unless specific contractual statements changing or modifying a defined Incoterm are put forth. Incoterms also carefully spell out the obligations of both the buyer and seller. Keep in mind that merchandise that has been lost or damaged before reaching the buyer or prior to payment may be very much the seller's property, regardless of the niceties of Incoterms, depending on pragmatic factors such as the existence and perfect execution of a letter of credit.

In this context, especially in view of the recent changes, bear in mind that many overseas buyers are not aware of the multiple ramifications of shipping terms and think only in terms of who pays the freight. It is therefore wise to not only be informed yourself, but also to advise the buyer under some pretext of quoting at least the essential elements of the shipping terms without sounding condescending or unnecessarily technical or legalistic. This is especially true in the case of very large transactions, new customers, or a change in terms customarily used.

A Guide to Incoterms provides a detailed analysis of the terms and is published by ICC Publishing Corp., at a cost of $24 (Appendix K).[2] Analytical descriptions of Incoterms may also be found in manuals at the library, your international banking department, or the Department of Commerce (DOC)/ITA.

Because of the importance and value of the 1990 Incoterms, a recognized author and lecturer on exporting, Frank Reynolds, has published an interesting book entitled *Incoterms for Americans*.[3] The ICC committee that drafted the new terms was essentially European in makeup. Reynolds's book meets a definite need in reanalyzing the committee's definitions from an American shipper's perspective. Among other things, Reynolds recommends that U.S. exporters use FCA terms instead of following the longstanding practice of using FOB terms for almost any place, whether it be on the buyer's or the seller's side of the transaction, a practice that is really not acceptable today. It is necessary, however, to understand the seller's responsibilities under FCA terms and exactly when the transfer of risk occurs. FCA can be used to indicate that goods are free of added cost at any named point from the factory to the main carrier's ocean or air U.S. terminal. This is far more accurate than FOB terms, except when FOB terms are used precisely as Incoterms describes and intends they be used, that is, FOB Port of Shipment. Consider this as you study the terms below, and if you experience some confusion, consider getting *Incoterms for Americans* for supplemental reading. But whatever you do, use the proper term for your own protection as well as for reasons of good customer relations and understanding.

Highlights of the Current (1990) Incoterms

Following are highlights of ICC description of the 1990 Incoterms as found in detail in *A Guide to Incoterms,* an excellent reference item to have in your export library.[4] The new version encourages an exporter to think of shipping terms in four groups, designated by the first letter in the shipping term name or acronym. The words enclosed in brackets [ ] after the Group headings E, F, D, and C are words added by the author for clarification:

Group E   [Little or no accommodation by seller]

EXW   **EX W**orks [factory] (named place)
Goods available only at seller's own premises, to be picked up and
*loaded on a conveyance or "stuffed" into the container at the buyer's
expense,* with all export arrangements being the buyer's responsibility
except for whatever assistance in this endeavor is requested by the
buyer. It is very difficult for the overseas buyer to arrange shipment or
understand the final cost under these terms in most cases.

Group F   [Main carriage not paid, but seller is responsible for, and at risk, until
delivery to carrier]

FCA   **F**ree [in the hands of] **CA**rrier (named place)
A new term used to avoid the confusion and inaccuracy caused by the
former, little-used terms and by the numerous and careless versions of
FOB terms, especially FOB Airport, which is no longer acceptable. FOB
is now reserved for its original purpose, a term for waterborne vessel
shipments only. The original attempt to replace such FOB terms in 1980
by Freight/Carriage Paid to is abandoned. *Thus, FCA is the shipping
term to use in the case of overland shipments, shipments by air carrier,
or when the shipper is told to use a consolidator unable to provide a
negotiable bill of lading.* FCA terms define the seller's responsibility to
be discharged and the transport risks to transfer when the carrier or a
buyer's named freight forwarder or a carrier's agent takes charge of the
goods, as at an airport. These terms have nothing to do with freight
being loaded on board the plane or whatever other conveyance may be
contemplated by the buyer. As noted earlier, these terms should replace
many Americans' misuse of FOB Factory and FOB Airport, plus countless others. They also better reflect modern shipping practices in more
instances than not, such as when one really wants to be done with the
goods after delivery to a buyer's freight forwarder.

FAS   **F**ree **A**longside **S**hip (named port of shipment)
*For waterborne shipments only. The price is to include only charges
required to deliver the goods alongside the vessel.* The buyer, rather than
the seller (as in FOB), must clear the goods for export and pay to have
them loaded on board and bear any risks of loss during these procedures. This long standing term is less used today except in certain
trades and product types because of the many special types of loading
and containerization now available, and also because under this term
the continuing mobility of the goods being exported is interrupted,
exposing them to added hazards. In general, it is best to avoid use of
this term unless there is good reason.

FOB   **F**ree **O**n **B**oard (named port(s) of shipment)
This term also is *restricted to waterborne shipments.* It is a very ancient
term, but one of the most frequently used and now once again means
exactly what it says. The issues of seller's and buyer's responsibilities
are very well defined. *The seller's responsibilities end and the risks transfer when the goods "cross the ship's rails."* The seller accepts all responsibility for export arrangements, subject to the requests of the buyer. For

this reason, the buyer will often find it acceptable to name several alternate ports, "any U.S. East (West) Coast port," or even "any U.S. port" to aid the seller in finding the first, fastest, or cheapest combination of overland and marine transportation. This term is usually the closest to the point of origin that letters of credit call for because the bill of lading is the preferred prime instrument for negotiating a letter. The buyer's bank will discourage inland terms that require truck bills of lading or dock receipts and other such less verifiable and nonnegotiable documents.

Group C   [Main carriage paid by seller but without risk of loss after shipment or delivery]

CFR   **C**ost [of merchandise] and **FR**eight (named port of destination)
For waterborne freight only. This term for a widely used quotation basis replaces the former C&F term and has the same meaning, in that *the price quotation adds the freight charges to the cost of the merchandise.* The freight charges include loading and export documentation or other incidental costs required to carry the goods to the port of the buyer's destination country. While the costs are therefore higher, *the transfer of risk is the same as in the FOB quote,* in that it still changes as the goods cross the ship's rails at the port of origin, *not* the port of destination.

CIF   **C**ost, **I**nsurance, and **F**reight (port of destination)
For waterborne freight only. This widely used term is identical in meaning and designation to what it always was. The price quotation adds the cost of insurance as well as freight to the CFR price of the goods, making the shipper responsible for obtaining the minimal or basic insurance unless an underlying contract specifies a requirement to obtain broader coverage. In any event, the insurance policy becomes one of the documents required for collection.

CPT   **C**arriage [all shipping costs] **P**aid **T**o (named place of destination)
This is another new term and its distinction is similar to that of FCA compared to FOB in the F Group of terms. The quotation *can apply to any form of carriage:* air, water, overland or multimodal. *The seller is obliged to clear the goods for export and pay shipping costs for the goods' arrival at a named point* suitable to the buyer, such as an airport or some port or terminal at which the buyer (or agent or carrier) can receive the goods. The *transfer of risk or loss, however, occurs when the seller hands the goods over to a suitable carrier or agent* of the carrier as in the FCA term.

CIP   **C**arriage and **I**nsurance **P**aid To (named destination)
The same term as CPT above, except that *insurance costs are added* with the same stipulations and transfer of risk point that applied to the addition of insurance to the related CFR term to create the CIF term.

Group D   [Seller pays all freight and bears all risk until arrival of the goods at named destination]

DAF   **D**elivered **A**t **F**rontier (named place)
The goods are to be delivered to the border according to a certain time frame, but before customs or duties are paid.

DES   **D**elivered **Ex S**hip (named port of destination)
The goods are made available on board the ship in buyer's port before unloading.

DEQ   **D**elivered **Ex Q**uay (named port of destination)
The goods are made available on the buyer's dock, cleared for importation, duty paid. Therefore, the exporter is responsible for obtaining the import license.

DDU   **D**elivered **D**uty **U**npaid (named place of destination)
This is relative to a foreign inland delivery, but before costs or risk of customs formalities or payment of duty.

DDP   **D**elivered **D**uty **P**aid (named place of destination)
Exporter has entire responsibility for all costs, risks, and duties until delivered into buyer's hands in buyer's country.

All D Group terms share the concept that *the seller pays all costs to place the goods at the disposal of the buyer at a named point* and bears all risks of loss until they are at the buyer's disposal—"disposal" presumably being more cleanly defined in the underlying contract. The terms are seldom used except in the case of a project, usually one requiring installation and/or other duties requiring the seller to have employees or agents at the named place. Otherwise, it is probably an unwise or needlessly difficult shipping term for the seller to accept.

The organization of the terms into four basic groups helps exporters to recall them more readily. It is also helpful to relate the terms to the manner of shipping to which they apply. Therefore, we list them here in that context:

- For any mode of transport, including multimodal, these terms apply:
  EXW Ex Works (…named place)
  FCA Free Carrier (…named place)
  CPT Carriage Paid To (…named place of destination)
  CIP Carriage and Insurance Paid To (…named place of destination)
  DAF Delivered At Frontier (…named place)
  DDU Delivered Duty Unpaid (…named place of destination)
  DDP Delivered Duty Paid (…named place of destination)

- For air transport, use **FCA** Free Carrier (…named place)

- For rail transport, use **FCA** Free Carrier (…named place)

- For sea and inland waterway transport, these terms apply:
  FAS Free Alongside Ship (…named port of shipment)
  FOB Free On Board (…named port of shipment)
  CFR Cost and Freight (…named port of destination)
  CIF Cost, Insurance, and Freight (…named port of destination)
  DES Delivered Ex Ship (…named port of destination)
  DEQ Delivered Ex Quay (…named port of destination)

Some believe that the FOB contract is a delivery contract and that the CIF contract is a shipment contract, but the Group C terms are the same as the Group F terms in that the seller fulfills the contract in the country of dispatch. The Group C terms differ from all other groups, however, in that the risk for loss or damage passes after shipment even though the seller must arrange and pay for the main carriage. It is for this reason that ICC recommends against adding obligations of the seller to the Group C and F terms, such as some landed cost, which can lead to misunderstandings, since the additional obligations occur after the seller is relieved of risks. Specifically, ICC recommends that the seller use terms "which do not attach the handing over of goods for carriage to shipment 'on board,' namely FCA, CPT or CIP instead of FOB, CFR and CIF." The strongest reason for this is that today goods are usually delivered by the seller well before the goods are taken on board. Competition or industry practice may demand otherwise, however.

Making the Most of Your Quotation Research

In the beginning you might quote FCA or FOB only. CFR and CIF quotations are more time-consuming, especially if you are making offers to many destinations. There is also the risk of dollar loss if you miscalculate the cubic measurements or any other factor. Keep in mind that while CFR and CIF offers may create risk of loss to the inexperienced, they offer an opportunity for profit to the knowledgeable exporter and a chance for extra profit when you find an especially good freight offer, such as from an NVOCC or nonconference carrier. It is in your best interests, as well as your customers', to spend extra time and effort to obtain the most advantageous freight rates and not leave it all up to your forwarder. CIF terms are usually preferred by the buyer, and using them when offering your product may give you the competitive edge.

Make a separate file for all information pertaining to your quotations, such as how much the pallet adds to the cubic measurement and how the goods were packed to arrive at the measurement and weight. Also, keep notes in this file on the various carriers, their routing, and special conditions. Getting the details together for an accurate quotation is a time-consuming and often expensive task, especially if long distance telephone costs are involved. All information and cost factors should be saved as reference for future quotations. Your computer can be a great help in making export quotations, and there are many fine software programs available for that purpose. If you send your quotations in the form of a price list, your personal computer can quickly adapt the price list to individual customers. To be sure that all costs are included in a quotation and that margins are as you planned them, use a worksheet similar to the one shown in Figure 18-1.

Other Costs and Risks to Consider

Once merchandise and freight costs are established, there are a number of additional charges that must be added to create your ultimate export price, depending on your flexibility as to shipping terms. Customarily, it's best to have several basic export quotations on hand: an FCA or FOB port quotation for the coast nearest you or possibly both costs; and CIF quotations for the major ports in your target countries. In most cases, it's difficult to prepare competitive CIF quotations unless you base them on the assumption of full container loads; or weight of more than 660 pounds, or LD3 container loads, in the case of air shipments. Therefore, if it is practical to sell your product in container lots, the CIF price should be mentioned in your quotation as a supplement to the basic FCA or FOB price, but with the provision that prices are based on a specific container load or minimum weight or cube.

The FOB quotation, according to Incoterm definitions, includes all costs that can be anticipated, but none that are peculiar to a particular buyer or country or those relative to obtaining a bill of lading for the buyer. Even though the seller is responsible for providing certain services, these services are at the buyer's expense. Among these expenses, according to the definition, are many of the forwarder's charges. However, it is common practice for the exporter to pay the forwarder's costs, and it may well be in your interest to get the goods safely on board and obtain appropriate documents, including a bill of lading, for a letter of credit negotiation. The exception occurs when the buyer has specified a forwarder, but the FCA is the better quote in most cases. Special fees, such as fees for certification and legalization, as well as consular fees, can be substantial, depending on the country you ship to, and can be added to the invoice of an FOB quotation unless you have a letter of credit that does not permit this procedure. In that case, you would need to absorb such fees or bill them separately.

An important factor, both in terms of cost and potential risk exposure, is the insurance cost that is part of a CIF quotation. There can be real danger in quoting CFR (formerly C&F) as compared to CIF. Making a CFR quotation implies that the buyer/importer will take out insurance on the shipment. However, there is the risk that the buyer will fail to properly insure the shipment, even though in theory it is the buyer who bears the risk of loss once the goods clear the ship's rails and the tackle is released.

If there is a claim that is not covered by insurance, you can have a problem even though title has technically passed on to the buyer, because the buyer quickly loses interest in paying for damaged or destroyed merchandise. Even a letter of credit may not protect you, because you must obtain a clean bill of lading to negotiate the letter of credit, and in the event of the loss of the bill of lading, discrepancies in the letter of credit may be difficult to negotiate. An inexpensive solution is to take out contingency insurance or an FOB sales endorsement on your marine policy, which applies only in the event the buyer's coverage is missing or inadequate. This also should be discussed with the freight forwarder, who can usually provide this coverage if you do not have your own marine insurance broker. (These and other insurance problems will be discussed in more detail under the subject of marine insurance in Chapter 25.)

Terms of payment are another cost factor that must be considered when making a final export quotation. Even if you intend to be very firm on payment terms to minimize credit risks, it does not need to be emphasized as part of your initial offering. It will put off some potential customers and is better discussed after both interest in the product is established and something is known of the customer's creditworthiness. Nevertheless, the terms under which you are selling are part of the final cost variable and therefore affect the quotation. Check the "Factors to Consider Before Setting Payment Terms" in Chapter 19, Table 19-1.

Your credit risks increase from zero for shipments paid for in advance (assuming that you wait until the check or draft has cleared and has been credited to your account) to the other extreme if you are extending open credit to a buyer in an unstable country short on foreign exchange. Since payment in advance is not ordinarily practical, letters of credit are the exporter's safest and most acceptable terms, even though open account transactions, on a selective basis, are far more commonplace than is generally realized.

While cash in advance may be a negative cost, letters of credit under perfect conditions will cost only about one-tenth to one-eighth of a percent to negotiate, plus usually some additional flat fees. Collection costs, however, can rise rapidly because of discrepancy charges, amendment charges, and other minimum fees on smaller transactions. These additional charges can balloon the collection costs and should be kept in mind when quoting your price if you plan to insist on a letter of credit. As you get into documentary collection terms, the fees are much less, but credit insurance costs become a factor. Documents against payment (D/P) will be less expensive to insure than documents against acceptance (D/A), and open account is the most expensive to insure, but the least expensive operationally.

One additional payment term carrying very special risks—but also with possible rewards—is that of accepting payment in other than U.S. dollars. This is called a currency exchange risk. It is not an insurable risk as such, but it is one that can be "hedged," which amounts to the same thing, for the risk can be nullified at a precalculated cost. (See Chapter 25.)

Other cost considerations are purely financial and predictable, such as the costs of carrying the financing for whatever the average terms might be. For operational and financing details of payment terms, see Chapter 19, Chapter 20, and Chapter 23.

A Pro Forma Invoice: The Ultimate Quotation

Although it is not always used, providing a pro forma invoice is a highly recommended procedure, and if one is appropriate or requested, send a pro forma invoice to the overseas customer as soon as there is a clear understanding on both sides as to the content of the shipment and the shipping and payment terms. Type the invoice on your letterhead or regular commercial invoice and clearly state that it is a pro forma invoice. Include details such as exact quantity, unit and total price; payment terms, including letter of credit details if one is involved; a clear description; net and gross weight; and packing and shipping charges in accordance with the terms of sale. The better an understanding the buyer has as to the primary four aspects of a sales agreement, at what price, quantity and quality, as well as under what terms and conditions, the less likely it is that there will be future problems or misgivings. If no exact shipment date is agreed upon, it should be tied to other required documents, such as within a certain number of days from receipt of an order acknowledgment or, best of all, from receipt of the letter of credit. To prevent misunderstandings, indicate currency nomenclature (i.e., dollars), and be specific in all details. At the least, the pro forma should contain sufficient details to enable the buyer to open a letter of credit.

Since the pro forma invoice can be held to constitute an offer, specify a time limit for validity to preclude future litigation. Others will state "Prices are subject to change without notice," but a date certain is preferred for the sake of all concerned unless prices are exceptionally volatile. The pro forma invoice should enable the importer to calculate all costs, including duty.

If your staff is not familiar with the mechanics of export quotations, freight arrangements, document preparation and collection, some training may well be in order. There is an excellent training course available called *Developing Skills for International Trade*[5] with full details and clear examples. The text accompanies a workbook for practice and hands-on application together with an instructor's answer book for the workbook assignments.

Endnotes

1. John R. Jagoe, *Export Sales and Marketing Manual,* Export USA Publications, Minneapolis, MN, 1992.

2. *A Guide to Incoterms,* ICC Publishing Corp., New York, NY, 1990.

3. *Incoterms for Americans,* by Frank Reynolds, International Projects, Inc., P.O. Box 397, Holland, Ohio, 1993.

4. *Guide to Incoterms,* ibid.

5. *Developing Skills for International Trade,* by JuDee Benton, Team Export, Merced, CA, 1992.

19

Methods of
Payment

When considering the extension of credit to overseas customers, you must consider at least these four factors:

1. Country stability (political and currency)
2. Customer creditworthiness
3. Competition
4. Exporter's financial resources

Woven through all four of these factors are the qualitative and quantitative considerations of size, terms, and complexity of the transaction. A little research and conversation with your banker will resolve the factor of country stability. Customer creditworthiness is something that can be fairly well determined, although at greater cost in terms of both time and money than in a domestic business. If you decide, after considering the risks, that the rewards make it worth going ahead with the transaction, study Chapter 25 to see what can be done to minimize the risks. The third factor, competition, is purely a function of what others are doing relative to your own degree of aggressiveness. In considering this, think not only about your competition in this country, but about what the rest of the world is offering. Your own financial resources will, to a large degree, determine how flexible you can afford to be with your terms of payment. These will also be tempered by transaction size and frequency as well as by customer turnover.

The most common terms of payment, in order of risk are: payment in advance/cash in advance (CIA); irrevocable letter of credit (ILC); documentary collection against payment or acceptance; open account; minimum guarantee; and consignment.

Payment in Advance/Cash in Advance

Payment in advance/cash in advance (CIA) is the exporter's most advantageous method of payment, since it eliminates all concerns about collection and allows the exporter advance use of the money. Except in the case of sample orders and a few other special circumstances, however, most overseas importers understandably insist on better terms and assurance that they will receive what they ordered as well as better cash utilization, just as you would as a domestic or overseas buyer. Foreign exchange restrictions or political instability may present other roadblocks. Perhaps equally important, a request for payment in advance may be considered insulting in the eyes of a creditworthy importer to whom doing business across borders is routine. In the case of sample orders from prospective customers, it's a good idea to ask for money in advance for the actual sample and then compromise that with an offer to ship postage-paid. This will eliminate some of the companies that seem to conduct a business based on free samples, especially in some African countries. You'll need to reconsider this position, however, if the request comes from an established firm in a stable country, for example.

Irrevocable Letter of Credit

The next safest term is an irrevocable letter of credit (ILC), assuming that it *is* irrevocable, as most are. There are many forms and variations on letters of credit. There are also degrees of credit risk—such as *confirmed* as opposed to *unconfirmed*—to say nothing of factors such as the relative strength of the issuing bank and the country's stability. Indeed, ILCs constitute a complete subject on their own. For now it is enough to say that a letter of credit is considered safe because payment is essentially secured. Aside from the quality of the issuing or confirming bank and any especially complex conditions with which to comply, the degree of remaining risk is determined by the time frame in which the letter of credit is supposed to, and indeed does, arrive. This is important relative to the exporter's necessary investment in the transaction prior to the credit's arrival in order to meet the shipping deadline. However much protection it provides an exporter, an ILC raises its own difficulties in terms of costs and responsibilities. Letters of credit are discussed as three different concepts: first, as a means of getting paid, with reference to their mechanical and operational aspects (see Chapters 20 and 21); second, as a means of securing open terms or specific performance on your part or by your customer (see Chapter 22); and third, as a financing tool (see Chapter 36).

Documentary Collection Against Payment or Acceptance

Shipment on "collection" terms is the closest equivalent in international trade to COD or cash on delivery, which is not really part of the international lexicon. Because it is expensive to open a letter of credit, the overseas buyer may request the much-less-expensive documentary collection term. Under these terms, the seller must ship before getting paid, but in the case of the more frequently used documents against payment (D/P) variety, the buyer does not receive the negotiable documents and therefore does not gain possession of the goods until payment is made to the collecting bank. In the case of documents against acceptance (D/A), the buyer receives the goods after signing a time draft promising to pay in a certain period of time after receiving the documents. Although it sounds very much like an open account, the seller on D/A terms has a potentially negotiable financial instrument in place of an account receivable, which can always be open to dispute. One of the seller's first risks in either case is the possibility that the overseas buyer will not contact the collecting bank to acknowledge either presentation or acceptance, and the collecting bank is under no obligation to force such acknowledgment. See Chapter 23 for a complete understanding of this useful credit tool.

Open Account

Open account is an unsecured extension of credit with no distinction between domestic and overseas operations. This payment term should only be used with well-established overseas customers that have good-to-excellent credit ratings. Open account terms should state the number of days from a specific date on which payment is due to be made. Normally this is measured from invoice or shipping date, even though it is a frequent practice for the importer to wait until the goods arrive before paying, regardless of the due date. Sometimes the agreement is for a certain number of days from receipt of goods (ROG), in which case, transit time makes a big difference in terms of due date. Because the ROG condition can leave the exact due date of all invoices in question, it is a much better practice to take transit time into account and base the due date on a set number of days from date of invoice or date of shipment. To minimize your risks under open account, just as with documentary collection terms, foreign credit insurance is available. This increases the cost factor but diminishes the risk factors. (See Chapter 25.)

Minimum Guarantee

As another method of payment for market-dominated products or those with a very elastic price, the minimum guarantee can be a satisfactory arrangement for firms that have a long-established relationship and a good sales record. The overseas customer agrees to pay the exporter a certain minimum, which may only cover freight charges or some percentage of the FOB value of the product or some combination of these. Both parties share in a specified profit ratio above that minimum once the product is sold and all sales figures are recorded. The exporter has the right to inspect the records of the overseas customer and to receive proper verification of all sales. The cautions and practices are essentially the same as under consignment (discussed next). The advantage, however, is that the exporter does have a firm order and therefore knows that all the goods are sold at some predetermined price, however modest. The exporter may even be assured this minimum payment in the form of a letter of credit covering the floor price. This adds a safety factor, but perhaps more important, it gives the exporter the opportunity to finance a portion of the export sale to the extent of the minimum value stated.

Consignment

Consignment terms, or floor plans, should only be granted to reputable customers with good credit ratings, customers with whom you have a good credit history and who are doing business in countries that enjoy economic and political stability. The term implies that shipment is made to an overseas customer who will receive and sell the goods and thereafter pay the exporter—who should have a very clear understanding of the overseas market and the sales potential of the product in that market. Sales on consignments are usually restricted to market-dominated commodities, such as produce, or to floor plans to high-ticket items, such as autos or equipment. You are essentially entrusting your money to the abilities and qualifications of your overseas buyer.

Balancing Costs, Risks, and Alternatives

As you consider these various sales terms, be sure to also consider a country or region of the world in light of its customs, practices, and political or environmental risks, rather than merely assessing the commercial risk that the buyer's credit standing represents. Each form of payment has associated transactional costs. These costs must be added to the exporter's past experience with losses incurred on less-secured or unsecured terms and be factored by the payment habits or customs of the destination country before the true cost can be approximated. For instance, if your firm has been taking losses of .05 percent on its open account sales throughout the past several years and does not plan to change its practices, the cost of open account terms becomes .05 percent plus the monthly cost of money for however many days credit is extended. If the export accounts are covered by foreign accounts receivable insurance, another .05 to 1 percent may need to be added for the cost of insurance over and above the first loss deductible required under the policy. On the other hand, negotiating a letter of credit for smaller transactions could cost as much as 3 percent or more—far more than open account.

In any case, be sure the customer understands the terms. If open account is involved, state, besides the number of days to pay, just when the clock starts running (e.g., on receipt of goods, date of invoice, date of shipment). If the terms are letter of credit, mention precisely the conditions that must be included or omitted in the letter of credit specifications. (See Chapter 21, Figure 21-1.)

Two factors need to be considered with all terms: method of payment transmission and time or "usance" allowed before payment is due. Monitor how long it takes the bank to credit remittances to your account and especially the delay associated with your wire transfer receipts (a common problem). Remember, banks like float just as much as your financial officer does. Consider electronic fund transfers (EFT) and courier services as a possibility. These costs can be very low compared to interest on large transactions. Check in advance to see if any given usance letter of credit can really be discounted and at what price. Every kind of sales transaction has a price. Be sure you are aware of what it is. For a broad overview of the circumstances and factors to consider when offering payment terms study Table 19-1.

Table 19-1. Factors to Consider Before Setting Payment Terms

Factor	Require a Letter of Credit	Consider Documentary Collection Presentation	Consider Documentary Collection Acceptance	Consider Open Account
CUSTOMER QUALITY	Uncertain	Acceptable	Good	Good Credit & History
RELATIONSHIP	New	Established	Established	Established
NATURE OF ORDER	Custom	Regular Production		In Stock
POLITICAL STATUS —Buyer's Country	Unstable	Stable		Strong
ECONOMIC STATUS —Country paying	Unstable	Stable	Strong	Strong
TRANSACTION SIZE	Large to Moderate*	Moderate	Moderate	Moderate to Small†
PRICE VOLATILITY	—A letter of credit protects against pressures to re-negotiate underlying agreement and pricing			
CASH FLOW NEEDS	—A letter of credit provides the most positive and practical control over timing of payment			
COMPETITION	—Shades above considerations to a more, or less, conservative response.			

*To $5,000 and L/C costs too much to open and negotiate unless buyer willing to pay all costs both sides. $5,000 to $10,000 is questionable for L/C costs. See comments in preceding paragraphs.

†"Large," "Moderate," and "Small" are relative terms in relation to seller's financial strength and buyer's credit rating as used here, except in terms of dollar transaction size compared to negotiation and fee costs.

20

Elements of
Letters of Credit

The letter of credit is the most commonly used and universally accepted form of secured payment, especially in international trade. It requires the utmost care, both by the buyer on issuance and by the seller when collecting (negotiating). A letter of credit is a document issued by a bank or other financial institution at the buyer's/importer's request and according to the buyer's specific instructions. It spells out the agreement to pay the named seller/exporter a certain sum after the seller supplies the bank with documents exactly in accordance with the terms specified in the letter of credit. Insofar as these documentary conditions are met, the buyer's creditworthiness is replaced by that of the issuing bank.

Modern letters of credit tend to follow standard formats and wording, especially those that are now issued by teletransmission. The fewer conditions the better, especially from the bank's and the exporter's point of view. Banks also dislike references to preliminary documents of agreement, such as purchase orders or contracts, and nondocumentary conditions incorporated within the letter of credit are ignored when negotiating it. Therefore, if such a condition is crucial, it must be incorporated into the documents by means of requiring a specific statement certifying compliance by the exporter or third parties, such as inspection, forwarding advice of some event, and so forth. Negotiating banks have usually insisted on being blind to everything but the letter of credit itself and the documents it calls for, which primarily represent acts of completed performance. These are typically transport documents, invoices, packing lists, insurance policies, and inspection certificates. But what is required must be presented precisely as stated, with all the t's crossed and the i's dotted. Banks do not take responsibility for the accuracy of such information as the counts provided them or for fraudulent statements. In such instances, the buyer must seek remedies under the law.

Aside from the financial security a letter of credit offers the seller, it provides commerce with a codified standard of language and performance, the latest of which is the revision of the Uniform Customs and Practice for Documentary Credits, effective January 1, 1994. The revision was designated Number 500 and accomplished under the auspices of the International Chamber of Commerce. It is commonly referred to as the UCP 500. The current version was written to take into account the rapid changes and technology developments in the communication and transportation industries, including document design and reproduction, as well as common practice and the recent increase in litigation since the 1983 version known as UCP 400 and the 1974 version prior to that.

The UCP is the basis of a common international understanding among the banks and financial institutions of more than 160 countries. The Bank of China in the PRC only began referring to the UCP in its letters of credit early in this decade, which represented one more step in China's growing international role. While virtually all banks accept the UCP 500, each letter of credit must specifically state that it is subject to the UCP 500 for those customs and practices to apply. The UCP 500's predecessor, the UCP 400, instituted some radical, although somewhat ambiguous, revisions and the result was a sharp increase in discrepancies. This was another reason for the new code. Your bank or freight forwarder can probably provide you with a copy of the UCP 500, or it can be ordered from the ICC Publishing Corp. in New York, New York. (See Appendix J.) It is a relatively short and concise document, and even though you will miss some of its finer points on first inspection, you will know the right questions to ask.

In spite of the stylized language, a skillfully drawn letter of credit can perform many functions, and constitute a most flexible document for many different applications. By virtue of the documents required, or not required, the letter of credit can function as a very simple means of payment or a very difficult and restrictive means of payment.

Prime Parties to a Letter of Credit

Various names are used to refer to the same parties to the letter of credit, depending on circumstances. The primary parties to a letter of credit and their most important alternative names, depending on circumstances and the transaction, are: the buyer, the opening bank, the paying bank, the advising bank, the confirming bank if there is to be one, and the seller.

The Buyer

The buyer opens the letter of credit. This party might also be referred to as the account party, accountee, or applicant, and is usually the importer.

The Opening Bank

The opening bank normally issues the letter of credit. This party substitutes its credit for that of the buyer, to whom it looks for reimbursement for payments made under the letter. It is most commonly known as the issuing bank, except in the case of a small bank, which might request its international correspondent bank to actually issue the international credit.

The Advising Bank

The advising bank relays the issuing bank's undertaking stating that "this advice conveys no engagement on our part." It is, however, an agent of the issuing bank, usually a correspondent of the issuer, and by the act of advising, it also implies that it is aware of the issuing bank's authenticity. It may agree to take on the responsibilities of the negotiating and/or paying bank, depending on the terms of its nomination by the issuing bank, whatever credit arrangements it may have with the bank, and its past relationship.

The Confirming Bank

The bank that advises the letter of credit may also confirm it and thereby substitute its credit for that of the issuing bank as far as the beneficiary is concerned. It can then negotiate the documents and will be obliged to pay or accept the letter of credit even if the issuing bank cannot or will not pay. Thus, if it exists, it is clearly a principal party to the credit.

The Paying Bank

The paying bank (nominated bank) is the bank on which the drafts (also known as bills of exchange) are to be drawn under the credit. The paying bank is also called the drawee or drawee bank. The paying bank may act as the advising bank, negotiating bank, confirming bank, or all of these, depending on its responsibilities. In fact, the paying bank and the issuing or opening bank can be the same.

The Seller

The seller is the party to whom the credit is issued. This party is mostly referred to as the beneficiary, is usually the exporter or shipper, and is also the drawer after the draft is drawn and ready for acceptance or payment under the letter of credit.

There are other roles as well, such as transferee and assignee, but they would not be called primary roles. The meaning of these ancillary functions is explained in the following pages.

Key Phrases and Conditions

Revocable Versus Irrevocable

An exporter should always insist and make sure that the letter of credit is irrevocable (ILC). This ensures that once the letter of credit is opened, it cannot be changed or altered in any way without the express permission of all parties involved, especially the exporter. A revocable letter of credit would be very suspicious in normal trade and has little value because it can be amended or canceled by the issuing bank at the request of the account party at any time prior to negotiation, with or without notifying the beneficiary. Its principal use might be between related companies or as a method of obtaining currency under certain foreign exchange regulations. The UCP 500 states that unless the letter of credit specifically states that it is revocable, it is deemed to be irrevocable, which eliminates the possibility of an easily made oversight.

Confirmed Versus Advised

A second and crucial aspect of the letter of credit is whether it is to be confirmed or advised by a second bank, which in either case is usually a bank in the country of the seller. Confirmation by an American bank is usually preferable, because you then have the American bank's promise to pay, based on its own examination of documents in place of both the buyer and the overseas issuing bank, although it will cost your customer additional fees unless you elect to be responsible for that part of the fee. The confirming bank will then negotiate the letter of credit and pay at sight in about three days. However, in the case of a strong bank in a stable, commercial country, such as Germany or Canada, confirmation may be an unnecessary, naive, or perhaps even an offensive demand. Your banker can advise you as to the general creditworthiness of both the foreign bank and the country.

If the letter of credit is advised, the advising bank in the United States clearly states that it is acting as an advising bank and that the credit "conveys no engagement on our part," meaning that it is not confirmed. The UCP 500 places a new obligation on the nominated advising bank to check the "apparent authenticity" of the letter of credit it advises. If it cannot do so and elects nonetheless to advise the credit, it must so inform the beneficiary.

When the beneficiary desires to draw on the credit, the advising bank will review the documents and verify that they are in order, but the advising bank's future role depends on its relationship with the issuing bank and other elements of the credit. At the least, the advising bank will send the documents to the issuing bank, which will confirm the advising bank's examination for compliance under the letter and thereafter receive funds from the issuer to pay. The issuing bank, usually on instructions or with permission from the buyer, may designate the advising bank to also serve as the negotiating and paying bank. In that event, the advising bank's instructions usually state that drafts are to be drawn on the advising bank. If the advising bank chooses to accept the responsibility of becoming the paying bank, even though it is not confirming the letter of credit, it also becomes the negotiating bank. The letter of credit continues to convey no engagement on the bank's part, and payment of the draft under such circumstances is done only with recourse. Even though not confirmed, payment by an advising bank in this country is a major advantage to the beneficiary for two reasons:

1. It eliminates transmittal time to the foreign bank, saving time and the cost of telex and cable communication in the event of a discrepancy, and often eliminates the time required for the transmittal of funds.

2. Minor technical errors on the beneficiary's part may be spotted by a local bank that will give the beneficiary an opportunity to correct what would otherwise be a discrepancy. Also, the beneficiary's own bank may be able to negotiate, or at least review, the documents. In any case, the beneficiary must be sure to submit the documents to the designated bank's *counters* early enough so that the inflexible time frames can be met, allowing time for problems and/or corrections. Keep in mind that statistically discrepancies occur on first presentation in almost 50 percent of letter of credit negotiations, but a skilled documentary clerk should achieve for better initial results.

Even though permitted to do so, advising/negotiating banks will not usually pay until funds are transferred from the foreign bank unless the issuing bank is a correspondent of the advising bank, has its funds on deposit, and has been authorized to pay on its behalf. The safest course is to call the bank to which you intend to present documents and check its position as to payments, especially if your cash flow is tight. Remember that a paying bank must also be the negotiating bank, but a negotiating bank need not necessarily be a paying bank.

Straight Credit Versus Negotiation Credit

Whether the letter of credit is confirmed or not, payable at an advising bank or not, it may be issued as a straight letter or as a negotiation letter. A straight letter of credit can be paid only at the counters of the paying bank (the bank the credit states drafts should be drawn on), which in the case of straight letters of credit will usually be the issuing bank or its American branch or prime correspondent. You can, however, request a bank of your own choosing to act for you, but this bank will be acting purely as your agent in your name.

A negotiation letter of credit can be presented at any bank, even though a different advising bank is involved. Depending on a negotiating bank's relationship with the confirming or issuing bank (including the possibility that the issuing bank keeps a transfer account with the negotiating bank), the negotiating bank may, in effect, purchase the draft that accompanied the letter of credit to become a "holder in due course" and pay the beneficiary. The payment is normally made with recourse, and possibly only after you sign a letter of guarantee or your own bank provides a letter of indemnity for you. These documents are based on your credit, and are a promise to repay the bank if the issuing, paying, or confirming bank does not pay the negotiating bank as it is obliged to do.

Sight Versus Usance

An important component of the letter of credit is the date on which payment is due. This is most often at sight, meaning that the exporter is paid as soon as the paying bank has determined that all documents are in order according to the letter of credit and that funds are available or have been transmitted. If the buyer has asked for extended terms, the letter of credit will be a usance credit (sometimes called an acceptance credit) and will state that the draft is to be drawn at a certain number of days after sight, or some related time such as shipping date, meaning that the exporter will be paid in that many days after negotiation and acceptance, or other named date. (See Figure 20-4.)

The usance time is usually provided in 30-day increments up to 180 days. The number of usance days can be tied to the bill of lading date, date of draft, or a day's date certain. The latter "day's date" bill of lading date term is better for the exporter if discrepancies are discovered when negotiating the letter of credit, which may cause delays in acceptance by the drawee and therefore further extend the time before funds are received. The acceptance can normally be turned over to the accepting bank for cash, discounted for the term of the pre-payment at the acceptance rate, plus a fee charge. This is the bank's lowest lending rate, usually below the prime rate, an important element if you feel that the usance feature is a selling tool for you. The interest, or discount fees, are usually a cost to the beneficiary but, by agreement with the buyer, the credit can state that one or both are for the account of the applicant/buyer.

Another form of usance serving somewhat the same purpose is deferred payment. The letter of credit will clearly state that payment is to be deferred and does not call for a draft to be drawn for negotiation and presentation of the documents. Therefore, no instrument is created for acceptance. The effect may be nearly the same—you can present the letter of credit to the paying bank for discount—but it is much less certain that the bank will prepay the deferral. The legal reasons are complicated. If you are counting on the money, it's a good idea to discuss the matter with the paying bank in advance. Deferred payment credits are often used in Europe to save the cost of revenue stamps on the draft instrument, and in the United States to permit credit extensions beyond the 180-day maximum allowed by the Federal Reserve Bank.

Bills of Lading and Other Transport Documents

A transport document of some kind is a key item in the negotiation of most operating letters of credit. When arranging for the shipment, you must use great care to receive a document that is acceptable under the credit. More latitude has been permitted as to acceptable transport documents in the newest version of the UCP in 1994 to accommodate the many new forms of intermodal transportation and documentation. The UCP 500 further clarifies some prior ambiguities, such as provisions as to what can be an "original," which were broadened to include documents appearing to be reproduced by reprographic, automated, or computerized systems, or even carbon copies with facsimile or stamped signatures, so long as they are marked "original."

Until you have gained some firsthand experience in dealing with acceptable transport documents, check in advance with the documentary department of your international bank or your freight forwarder, especially if you contemplate negotiating the credit with anything other than an onboard marine bill of lading from a regularly scheduled ocean vessel, or, in the case of air shipments, an air waybill issued by a regularly scheduled airline or its agent. If, for cost or logistical reasons, there is good reason to do otherwise, check with your international banker or forwarder as to the appropriate wording for the document you need to use and state the required wording in the pro forma invoice or instructions to the buyer for inclusion in the letter of credit. Different banks and their individual negotiators have slightly different views as to what is acceptable, and if a bank does not handle many international letters of credit, it can be particularly unpredictable.

For the first time, the UCP 500 deals with each type of transport document in a positive fashion, with definitions for each as to what is and what is not acceptable. It is expected that this approach will give rise to fewer questions and inadvertent discrepancies. There are specific articles, beginning with Article 23, setting forth requirements for each of the following: marine/ocean bill of lading (negotiable); sea waybill (a non-negotiable document new to the UCP but having increasing use in some regions and intended to expedite the discharge of the goods on arrival); charter party bill of lading (a party chartering a vessel in its own name and thereafter contracting to carry other cargo); multimodal transport document; air transport document (air waybill); road, rail, or inland waterway transport document; courier and post receipts; and transport documents issued by freight forwarders, provided that they are acting as agent for a carrier or as a multimodal transport operator. This last document by freight forwarders is an exception, in that it is stated as a negative condition that, *unless* the freight forwarder is indicated on the face of the document as acting as an agent for a carrier or as a multimodal transport operator (and is signed and authenticated as such), the transport documents will not be acceptable.

However, there are still certain conditions in bills of lading or transport documents that are unacceptable unless specifically allowed in the credit, such as bill of lading for vessels propelled by sail only; or bills of lading stating that the goods are being loaded on deck (a statement that they *may* be loaded on deck is acceptable). In all cases, the transport document must not contain notations as to an observable defective condition of the goods or packaging; in other words,"clean." Also, look for these four key statements or conditions to be present or in place:

1. An original signature on the bill of lading as agent for the carrier or as master or responsible employee of the named carrier, preferably on the carrier's own form.

2. The bill of lading indicates: that goods are dispatched or taken in charge or loaded on board, or when a marine bill of lading is required; and that the goods have been loaded on board or shipped on a named vessel. (Note here that the only, but vital, difference in requirements between ocean or marine bills of lading and other transport documents is the difference concerning laden on board and the named vessel.)

3. A full set of originals (usually three) has been issued, if more than one original was issued or is required.

4. The transport documents meet all other stipulations in the letter of credit.

To determine whether the transport document is issued by a carrier or its agent, look to see if a vessel is named on the document, or better yet, if the carrier's own form is used. Look for the words "agent for carrier" or "agent for master" together with a named carrier or master in connection with an "original" signature. Also observe the conditions of carriage, which are in the fine print on the back of the document. Lacking such fine print, or merely stating references to other documentation or sources, is now acceptable according to the UCP 500 if properly worded, but it indicates that a short-form bill of lading has been used. Many letters of credit specifically prohibit short forms. Even though not prohibited under the letter of credit, some banks have hesitated in the past to accept short-form bills of lading despite the fact that the UCP 500 does not reject them.

If the letter-of-credit language specifies only an onboard bill of lading, "onboard" will be understood to include onboard any kind of carrier, ocean or otherwise. If it is required to be laden onboard, this is taken to mean physically onboard an ocean vessel—in other words, a marine bill of lading. If the letter of credit intends for the goods to be shipped by air, the documents will call for an air waybill or an air transport document in the words of the current UCP. In the case of insurance documents, check the credit to be certain as to whether a certificate or policy is required, the number of originals, type of cover, and all other details. Insurance documents are the basis for numerous discrepancies.

Multimodals, NonVessel Operating Common Carriers (NVOCCs), freight forwarders, or airfreight consolidators often stretch a point when stating that they are acting as an agent for a carrier, but it is regularly done and accepted where the freight forwarder or the NVOCC so states on the document's face. Nevertheless, many banks are complaining that freight forwarders are going too far in issuing their own transport documents. If there is any doubt, request that in resulting documents required, the credit be specific—stating, for example, that an "NVOCC bill of lading is acceptable" or that a "house air waybill is acceptable."

Not all banks are comfortable with some of the recent changes, however, so check with your negotiator first. The ability to consult directly with the negotiating bank illustrates one good reason for insisting that the letter of credit be negotiable and payable in this country, and preferably in your city.

For a complete explanation and expansion of the underlying principles of transport documents, study the UCP 500 statement concerning these issues. They are addressed in the UCP document section, articles 20 through 38.

Shipping and Expiry Dates

A letter of credit with requirements you cannot meet is worse than no letter of credit at all. The exporter may request an amendment to extend the deadline for shipping or expiry dates, but the buyer is not obligated to provide them. It is important to note in the credit not only when, but also where the credit expires. The place stipulated is usually the counters of the paying or negotiating bank. In the case of straight credits, expiry is often at the overseas issuing bank, so check carefully. Whatever the date and place, the complete set of documents called for in the credit, without discrepancies, must be physically at that location by that business day or sooner. If the bank is closed that day, the following business day applies.

This automatic deadline extension does not apply in the case of an equally important date in the letter of credit, the shipping date. Latest shipping dates are not always stated in the letter of credit, but when they are, the latest shipping date typically precedes the expiry date by 10 to 14 days. If not specified, the goods can be shipped at any time, provided that: the transport documents required are dated prior to the expiry date; the documents are presented to the bank before that date; and the transport documents are less than 21 days old, based on the date of issuance.

Regardless of a defined shipping date, the exporter must be sure to have sufficient time prior to the expiry date to get all required documents to the bank. This includes time for the steamship line to issue bills of lading, time for all paperwork and deliveries, and especially time to get invoices and other documents notarized and/or certified, which could involve various government agencies and offices of foreign representatives in distant American cities. It can take the steamship line up to ten days to issue the bills of lading after loading, although three days is closer to normal. The discrepancy of late shipping or late presentation of documents is one of several discrepancies that cannot be corrected. The letter of credit is subsequently valid only if the buyer accepts the discrepancy, or amends and extends the credit. Again, irrespective of the expiry date, any bill of lading over 21 days old is considered invalid (stale) unless the letter of credit specifies otherwise.

Clean and Onboard

Clean and onboard are terms that are so much a part of documentary and shipping terminology that they are often overlooked in explanations. *Clean* in shipping terminology refers to bills of lading or other documents accepted by the receiver, agent, or shipper without notations of taking exception to the condition. A bill of lading, airway bill, or even a dock receipt is clean if there are no specific notations to indicate merchandise damage at the time of taking in charge or receiving onboard. Note that a similar, but different, definition of *clean* is used in banking and documentary terminology to indicate that no complicating conditions exist. Thus, a clean drawing would be a sight draft drawn against a letter of credit, where no supporting documents were required as proof, such as invoices, bills of lading, packing lists, or other special documents. In practice, however, the credit usually calls for some sort of statement or certification at a minimum.

Onboard occurs when the merchandise literally crosses over the ship's rails and the tackle is released. For air cargo shipments, a clean receipt is obtained when the merchandise is put into the hands of the appropriate carrier or agent at the airport. This definition also applies to most inland carriers.

Partial Shipments Allowed

Partial shipments are allowed if not stipulated otherwise. Virtually all letters of credit, however, specifically state that partial shipments are, or are not, allowed. It is a good idea for the beneficiary to request that the letter of credit allow for partial shipment even if both parties agree that only one or two or some other stated number of shipments will be made and this is so specified in the letter of credit. In this case, expect the importer to specify in terms of units or percentage the minimum size for a partial shipment. This permits the exporter to collect for what is shipped against the letter of credit even if, for any reason, it is less than the total order covered by the letter of credit. If partial shipments are not allowed, the letter of credit is valid only when the total shipment is complete. In some industries, such as textile and apparel, it can be very difficult to safely bet on receiving a totally complete shipment, so the issue becomes vital and dangerous. If the buyer insists on no partial shipments, the trade intermediary's only defense is to organize similar terms within a letter of credit with the supplier.

There is an automatic 5 percent allowance over or under the order amount in terms of weight and measure, unless the credit specifically states that the quantities must not be exceeded or reduced. This allowance does not apply to individual unit counts such as items or cartons, but only to bulk measures such as weight or length. Use of the word *over* applies only to quantity, because this still does not permit collection of more than the value indicated in the letter of credit.

"About" or "Approximately"

If "about," "approximately," "circa," or other similar expressions are stated in the letter of credit when referring to the amount of the credit, the quantity, or unit price, there is then an allowable variance not to exceed 10 percent of that respective specified amount, quantity, or unit price to which the expression refers. Do not apply the variance to any measure not specifically so referenced. In the case of specified installment shipments under a partial shipment clause, if any one installment shipment is missed, the entire letter of credit becomes invalid, not just for that shipment, but for *all* future shipments, unless stated otherwise. Many types of variances can be specified in the letter of credit, which, as indicated before, can be a very adaptable instrument if so desired.

Transshipment

Transshipment occurs when goods are off-loaded from one carrier and placed on another carrier, vessel, or conveyance. If the transport document indicates transport from origin to destination, it is accepted in the normal course of events, although it should be avoided if possible, because of the increased chance of damage and pilferage. Transshipment is usually specified as either allowed or not allowed, but if *not* so specified, transshipment is allowed. Unless specifically prohibited, so long as the entire ocean carriage is covered by a single bill of lading, transshipment is allowed, as in land-bridge arrangements. Furthermore, under the UCP 500, in the case of a credit calling for a marine bill of lading and prohibiting transshipment, the bill of lading will be accepted if the entire carriage is covered by the one bill of lading, *provided* it is a containerized or similarly unitized shipment. Nevertheless, if shipment is to be made to a port not serviced directly by carriers sailing from a port you are required to ship from in the letter of credit, it is much safer to be sure that the credit allows transshipment. This permits shipment to an intermediate port and from there to the port of disembarkation. Transshipment is usually a special concern when it involves discharge and reloading in the course of an ocean voyage because of scheduling, pilferage, and handling factors.

Amendments

An irrevocable letter of credit can only be amended with the approval of the issuing bank, and the confirming bank (if any), and the beneficiary. The buyer is under no obligation to initiate an amendment, and the seller need not accept any amendment provided. If any one amendment is to be accepted, however, it must be accepted in total, as stated by the issuing bank. If the amendment is to be rejected, the beneficiary should promptly notify the advising or issuing bank. Because it is increasingly expensive in terms of special fees for the buyer to amend a letter of credit and for the seller to receive it, the exporter should advise the buyer in advance of all appropriate details to avoid amendments. This is one reason a pro forma invoice can be very useful and save both parties extra banking fees. Since the UCP 500 change became effective, special care must be taken to avoid any implied acceptance by tendering documents for negotiation without having first rejected not-yet-accepted amendments.

A recommended approach is to provide your customer with a format of how the letter of credit should read. If you are planning on using such a format, consult first with your bank as to what provisions should be included or excluded in your particular case. This is bound to reduce the number of discrepancies and requests for amendments. (A checklist and suggested format for this purpose are provided at the end of Chapter 21.) Be sure to ask about common practices and courtesies, because some bankers will go overboard in suggesting one-sided provisions that can put the exporter in a bad light. For example, it is usually better to follow common practice, such as permitting banking fees in this country to be for the beneficiary's account. If the margins are that close, build an allowance for such expenditures into the price.

Transferable Letter of Credit

The right to transfer a letter of credit to a second beneficiary can be very useful in financing an export transaction, but that right must be specifically granted in the credit. The downside is that requesting transferability from your buyer will show some financial weakness on your part. It permits you to transfer the proceeds of the letter of credit, in total or in part, to your supplier or subcontractor. The transferee must then also take full responsibility for letter-of-credit performance conditions just as if it were the initial beneficiary. (See Chapter 36 for more details.) Transferring can ease financing problems and avoid overline borrowing or having to arrange a back-to-back letter of credit, which is usually difficult. If the letter of credit is drawn to be transferable, it can be transferred in whole or in part, in any practical number of fractions, so long as the total value is not exceeded. It can usually only be transferred once, however.

Even though a letter of credit is stated to be transferable, the transferring bank, which must be nominated by the issuing bank, is not obliged to perform the transfer, although banks customarily do. Recently, however, banks have started to resist a multiplicity of transfers. If a transfer is made, the first beneficiary has the right to substitute invoices, documents, and drafts for those of the second beneficiary or beneficiaries, so long as they do not exceed the credit and are acceptable documents.

Assignment

Unlike the other phrases explained in this chapter, assignment is not a phrase used within a letter of credit, because all letters of credit are assignable within the provisions of the applicable local law. It is mentioned here because so many exporters confuse assignment with a transferable letter of credit. Unlike transfers, letter-of-credit proceeds can be assigned regardless of any conditions in the letter of credit. The beneficiary gives the bank first rights to the proceeds of the letter of credit and the bank promises the assignee it will receive its stated share of the proceeds before the bank pays the balance to the beneficiary. It is a right of the beneficiary that is useful as long as the assignee is willing to accept an assignment of proceeds as a form of settlement. To do this, the supplier must have confidence in the letter of credit and the ability of the beneficiary to perform under its conditions. Some banks resist making more than one assignment of any given letter of credit because the assignment places the burden on the bank to pay all assignees before giving over any remaining proceeds to the beneficiary. (For further information, see Chapter 36.)

Revolving Letter of Credit

A revolving letter of credit can be drawn in many ways. It can be opened for a certain dollar amount for a given period of time and automatically replenished each time a payment is made. Such a credit can be accumulative or nonaccumulative for given time periods or quantities, and it can be limited in amount by time periods or in total. A revolving credit can also be amended by the buyer to be replenished at specific intervals. It implies a unique relationship between buyer and seller and may be used to aid a buying agent or be opened by a buyer who desires a steady flow of merchandise from a well-established supplier. It is also sometimes used between parent corporations and a foreign subsidiary.

Special Clauses

There are four commonly discussed special clauses, of which the red clause or its variant is most often mentioned:

1. *Red clause.* This clause effectively passes on to the seller the credit standing of the buyer, since it permits clean advances (no bills of lading need be presented) to finance the exporter's performance of the contract prior to shipping. A red clause is accompanied by a statement to the effect that appropriate shipping documents will be provided later. Needless to say, it is seldom seen.

2. *Green clause.* This is a variation of, and similar to, the red clause. It also permits drawing of clean drafts but requires the subject merchandise to be stored in the name of the paying bank until documents are received. Both the red and green clauses are a favorite subject of conversation and often mere wishful thinking, for lacking a very special relationship with the buyer or some other unusual circumstance, they are not readily offered, since they present the buyer who is opening the credit with substantially increased risks and liabilities depending on the performance of the beneficiary.

3. *Telegraphic transfer clause.* This is another often-mentioned dream clause for trade intermediaries. It requires the issuing bank to pay the invoice amount to the order of the negotiating bank on receipt of a tested telex indicating that the required documents have been received in good order and are being forwarded. The purpose is to speed payment if one is not located in a financial or shipping center.

4. *Evergreen clause.* This clause provides a periodic expiry date with an automatic extension unless advance notice is provided, and it usually states an ultimate, final date. It can be used in standby or revolving letters of credit, or in credits where a long validity is anticipated but the issuing bank and/or account party wishes to periodically assess its risk exposure.

Special Documents

Most regular or operational letters of credit ask for the basic documentation requirements of invoice, packing list, and air waybill or ocean bill of lading.

The terms of sale will dictate other types of documents. One very critical special document is the insurance certificate or policy, in the case of CIP or CIF terms. (See the section on insuring transit risks in Chapter 25, as well as the section on shipping documents in Chapter 26.)

Less regulated, loosely created documents must be accepted in the case of alternative inland terms. For FCA factory shipments it may be a postal receipt or a truck bill of lading; for other inland points, perhaps a warehouse or dock receipt. Apart from the buyer's difficulty in determining the final costs, terms of sale describing a transit process prior to FOB vessel are looked upon with disfavor because of the lack of controlled and traditional regulated documents. The combined transport bill of lading is increasingly being used to compromise this issue.

The buyer/importer may specify other documents required by the buyer's government or for the buyer's added protection. It is most important that the letter of credit be carefully examined on receipt to be sure that all such special documents can be obtained. If any of the terms of the letter of credit are not acceptable or as agreed, the exporter should telex the overseas customer immediately and request an amendment to the letter of credit. State the exact wording of the requested change or addition, as suggested by your bank's documentary department. If your position is strong enough and the wording is clearly contrary to your original understanding, you may want to insist that the buyer pay the amendment charges by both the issuing and advising bank.

If any special certifications, attestations, statements, or lists are required that seem to be telling you not to do certain things, or not to deal with certain parties, proceed with caution, especially in the case of Middle Eastern countries. These statements may relate to boycott attempts and should be discussed with your freight forwarder and banker or your attorney. (See the section in Chapter 32 on antiboycott regulations.) It is with these miscellaneous requirements or special documents that some of the most difficult problems can arise. They can drastically impact what may otherwise be an acceptable production or procurement time frame; they can even effectively negate what otherwise appears to be an irrevocable letter of credit.

While it would be nearly impossible to list all such documents here, a few are listed as illustrations:

Transit Insurance Taken Out on Behalf of Buyer.   In the case of CIP or CIF terms, the letter of credit calls for insurance documents, and if issued in more than one original, the UCP 500 requires that all originals be included in the document package. Many discrepancies have occurred in the past because a "certificate" was provided when a "policy" was called for, but today, unless otherwise stipulated, a certificate or declaration under an open cover policy is sufficient if signed by the insurance company or its underwriters, in lieu of a policy. Without a contract or instructions to the contrary, the insurance need only cover from loading onboard, dispatch, or taking in charge to discharge. The document must not bear a date of issuance later than the date of loading onboard or taking in charge. Unless stipulated the cover can be minimal, but most exporters will take warehouse-to-ware-house to be safe and for their own protection and cover from factory to the point of risk transfer. (See the section on insuring transit Risks in Chapter 25, as well as the section on shipping documents in Chapter 26.)

Copies of Telexes or Other Communication.   These documents provide certain advice, usually relative to shipping times, vessels, and so forth. The information can include a wide variety of items, all of which need to be carefully noted, because no matter how minor or insignificant they sound, they represent conditions your buyer wants, and the credit cannot be negotiated without them.

Consular or Embassy Certifications.   These certifications are not to be confused with the chamber of commerce or even Arab chamber of commerce certifications. Such certifications can force you to send the invoice and possibly the packing list to the embassy in Washington, D.C., or perhaps to a consulate in a major American city, where the time factor can be a problem. In some cases the process can take two to three weeks, which may have a bearing on which vessel you can ship or on your ability to perform within the time frame of the letter of credit. When you see such a requirement, check with your freight forwarder and with the embassy itself as to probable and worst-case time intervals. Your location, or your forwarder's location, also has a bearing on this.

Import/Export Licenses.   While the export license is not normally a condition for the letter of credit, occasionally a buyer will want a copy of the export license because the exporter cannot legally ship without it. In any event, the license must be obtained prior to your starting the shipping process, and adequate time must be allowed to obtain the license, based on your knowledge or information from the licensing agency or your export licensing consultant. (See Chapter 31.) On the other hand, a letter of credit is often the means for the buyer's government to control imports issue import licenses. This is especially true in Asia, a fact that sometimes accounts for the readiness of the Asian importer to offer a letter of credit which becomes, in effect, both an import license and a currency exchange permit.

Acceptance Certification or Statements.   These statements can take many forms, and in some situations they are to be expected. The point is to determine whether these statements are reasonable and fair and do not present you with excessive risk exposure. For example, in a turnkey situation, obviously the buyer must be satisfied that the plant or equipment meets specified standards. The keys are: the percentage of the letter of credit that has been left unpaid pending the acceptance; the clarity with which the performance standards are spelled out to avoid arbitrary and self-serving buyer decisions; and a specified time frame within which acceptance must be determined and procedures followed if there is a problem. These items are normally found in detail within an underlying contract, but the letter of credit would have to make specific reference to the percentage to be paid, and under what circumstances, if it is for less than 100 percent of the invoice.

Inspection Certificates.   These can be reasonable, fair, and acceptable or can virtually relieve you of all the security you thought you had as part of the letter of credit terms. *Use caution if the buyer or an agent under the buyer's control has this inspection right, because this requirement may render the letter of credit, in effect, inoperable!* Alternatively, if there are no time requirements as to when inspection must occur, the buyer or agent can simply fail to inspect and your letter of credit may not be negotiated. On the other hand, if prudently and correctly used, a preshipment inspection certificate can be a comfort to the seller by making it possible to avoid claims after arrival. It permits the exporter to deal with problems before the shipment leaves, when it is much cheaper to do something about problems. This is especially true in cases where a letter of credit calls for progressive payments as the project proceeds. Certainly it is preferable to on-site or foreign dock inspections. In any case, it is important to know that the inspector is at least a reasonably impartial third party and exactly what the parameters and objective of the inspection will be.

Mandated Preshipment Inspection or PSI Programs

Unfortunately, preshipment inspection (PSI) requirements in their present form continue to be a problem for the exporter, insofar as they are mandated by the buyer's government. The name is not entirely accurate. Ordinary preshipment inspections may be requested by any private, quasi-sovereign, or sovereign buyer and for no other purpose than to be sure the merchandise is what the invoice says it is and/or that it works. The objectives of PSI programs can go much further and can call for far-reaching inspections that involve, in addition to quantity and quality, comparable world prices regardless of previously negotiated prices, the exporter's fair profit margins, freight charges, and perhaps proper customs classification. PSI programs are in effect in about 24 countries, with another 40 countries considering them. These are Third-World countries with foreign exchange and debt problems, mostly in Africa and Latin America.

Three international inspection firms have most of the government inspection contracts. They are SGS Control Services (by far the largest), Bureau Veritas, and Intertek. If you wish to learn more about their services, whether you are inspecting or being inspected, check with SGS North America Inc., 42 Broadway, New York, New York 10004, or check your local directory for their closest office. These firms are also well known for the more conventional inspection services. Their defense for some of these onerous procedures is that countries with limited foreign exchange must be diligent in protecting against fraud and flight of capital. The countries requiring PSI programs claim that they lose capital through buyer/seller collusion in overinvoicing (inflating prices in collusion) and that they lose asset values by permitting import of obsolete or abused equipment as a substitute for the specified goods. These countries also claim that improper classification of imported goods costs them tax income in terms of tariff losses on undervalued imports, a situation that also arises through buyer/seller collusion.

Inspection requirements can create shipping delays, especially when the inspection firm has no constrictions as to how quickly after notification it must inspect. More important, the system can virtually destroy the value of a letter of credit and the sanctity of the underlying contract, including the price. In addition to quality and quantity, the inspector may have the right to verify that it is within 3 to 5 percent of a fair price on a worldwide basis, to examine the exporter's books to determine that not more than a fair profit was made, and so on. In recent years, inspectors have taken to comparing prices only to others from the same country of origin sold to the same class of customer, which makes the exercise of this right somewhat less threatening. The purpose of inspection is to see that the country receives full value and its full share of taxes. In the past there have been many reports that a very arbitrary and Third-World-government point of view has been taken by some of the inspectors, but complaints have diminished somewhat as the major inspection firms have made efforts to reduce the worst abuses.

In terms of export operations and the letter of credit, it is important to determine early in the negotiations if a PSI program will be involved, and then determine if you can meet its requirements. Possibly you can, or may have to, but it has proved expensive for those exporters who underestimated its impact and the broad and arbitrary authority the inspection firm wields. Usually the inspection firm is specified and you are entitled to call them to discuss exactly what they propose to examine and what they are using as standards. Some inspectors have come to realize that in the past they have perhaps been too arbitrary, excessively zealous, or slow to the point of being unfair, and have taken appropriate corrective steps. Nevertheless, be sure you understand the rules of the game.

Study Figures 20-1 through 20-6 for examples of a negotiation letter of credit and an acceptance letter of credit, together with a letter of credit application and the security agreement that is part of the application. The application and agreement shown in Figures 20-1 and 20-2 are, in effect, a credit agreement between the issuing bank and the importer or account party. The usance or acceptance letter of credit illustrated in Figure 20-4 is in the S.W.I.F.T. format, which has become increasingly the most common format as letters of credit are computerized and interfaced with the other export/import documentation exchanges.

Bank of America ① **Application for Commercial Letter of Credit**

Location	Date
SAN FRANCISCO, CA	June 6, 19XX

TO: Bank of America NT&SA ④ I request you to issue an irrevocable documentary letter of credit as shown on this application by:
☐ Full Text Teletransmission ☒ Airmail ☐ Airmail with Brief Preliminary Teletransmission Advice.

The opening of this credit is subject to the terms and conditions of the Security Agreement for Commercial Letter of Credit (the "Agreement") on the reverse. The words "I," "me," and "my" in this application and in the Agreement refer to each signer of the application "You" and "your" refer to Bank of America (the "Bank") If this application is signed by more than one person, the Agreement will be the contract of the signers both as individuals and as a group. I have read the Agreement and agree to its terms and conditions.

Name of Applicant	Signature	Title
ABC Toys Imports Inc.	X *Bill Block*	V.P. Finance
	X *Tina David*	Assistant Treasurer

1. Advising Bank (If blank Branch or Correspondent Bank)	4. For Account of (Applicant Name and Address)
Bank of America ⑤ Hong Kong Branch	ABC Toys Import Inc. ② 300 Main Street San Francisco, CA 94000

FOR BANK USE ONLY	5. In Favor of (Beneficiary Name and Address)
2. L/C No	XYZ Toys Export LTD ③ 8th Floor Stone Bldg. 45 Kowhan Road Kowloon, Hong Kong
3. Expiration Date Drafts to be drawn and presented to the negotiating or paying bank on or before August 15, 19XX ⑦	6. Amount U.S. $85,350.00 ⑥

7. Covering (Full invoice value unless otherwise specified)

⑧ full _____ % invoice value.

⑨ Available by drafts at (Tenor) ___sight___ on you, your branch or your correspondent at your option or you may waive draft requirement

9. Partial Shipment ⑩ ☒ Permitted ☐ Not Permitted	10. Transhipment (Not applicable to Air Shipments or Combined Transport Shipments) ☐ Permitted ☒ Not Permitted

11. Shipment/Dispatch/Taking in Charge from/At	Latest	For Transportation To
Hong Kong	August 10, 19XX	San Francisco / Bay Area

12. Merchandise to be described in invoice as (omit unnecessary details and specify price basis below)

⑪ Inflatable toys and toys:
Catalogue No. 1234 25,000 pcs. @ U.S. $3.00 each
Catalogue No. 6789 10,000 pcs. @ U.S. $1.035 each

13. Price Basis (Check one)
⑫ ☒ CIF ☐ C & F ☐ F O B ☐ Other

14. Documents Required (Check applicable boxes below)
☒ Signed Commercial Invoice in duplicate
☒ Marine and War Insurance Policy or Certificate for 110% invoice value in duplicate
Insurance to be effected by _____
☐ Original clean ☐ Air ☐ Truck ☐ Rail transport document
Consigned to _____
⑬ Notify (if different from consignee): _____

☒ * Sole original clean on board vessel Marine Bill of Lading, to order of Shipper, blank endorsed, marked: "Notify"
⑭ buyers/customers Clearing Agent, 100 Main St., San Francisco, CA 94000 – Freight prepaid
☐ * Sole original clean Combined Transport Bill of Lading, to order of shipper, blank endorsed, marked: "Notify"

If on board Bill of Lading is required, check ☐ on board vessel ☐ on board inland carrier

* If more than one original is required, please indicate number required
☐ Other documents Certificate of origin, Form A where applicable or Beneficiary's
certificate that none is required.
Packing list. ⑮

⑯ Documents must be presented to the negotiating or paying bank no later than ___5___ days after date of transport document (on board validation applicable for ocean shipment) but within the validity of the credit.
All documents to be forwarded in one cover, by airmail, unless otherwise stated under Special Instructions.

15. Special Instructions
_____
_____
_____   SPECIMEN
_____
_____

FX-156 5-86

(If more than one page is used, all pages must be signed.)
SUBMIT IN DUPLICATE

Bank of America NT&SA

Figure 20-1. Application for letter of credit. (*Reproduced with permission of Bank of America.*)

APPLICATION FOR
COMMERCIAL LETTER OF CREDIT

(1) This application from the buyer to the bank outlines information that will be included on the letter of credit form. By signing the application, the customer also is signing the security agreement on the reverse side.

(2) The applicant is the party on whose behalf a commercial letter of credit will be issued. In this trade situation, the commercial letter of credit will be issued by Bank of America-San Francisco on behalf of its customer, the applicant, who is the importer, for example, ABC Toys Import Inc. The applicant often is referred to as the "account party."

(3) This is the beneficiary (seller, exporter or shipper). The beneficiary is the party to whom the letter of credit is addressed and payment is made. The beneficiary also is the only party who can present documents to and claim payment from the issuing bank, negotiating bank, or collecting bank.

(4) Bank of America-San Francisco will send the letter of credit via airmail to the advising bank for forwarding to the beneficiary, XYZ Toys Export Ltd. Letters of credit can also be sent by full text teletransmission or Society for Worldwide Interbank Financial Telecommunications (S.W.I.F.T.) to a bank for forwarding to the beneficiary, or a brief teletransmission advice may be sent with full details to follow by airmail.

(5) Bank of America will designate the advising bank unless ABC Toys Import Inc. designates a particular bank requested by the beneficiary. The only responsibility of the advising bank is to verify the authenticity of the letter of credit through the signatures and then mail or deliver it to the beneficiary, XYZ Toys Export Ltd. In addition, advising banks might be requested to negotiate credits, but have no obligation to do so. (See page 29.)

(6) The amount refers to the total amount of the letter of credit. The applicant can specify that the amount be denominated in any currency, although in practice, only the major currencies are used.

(7) This is the date on which the letter of credit expires; hence it is the latest date that the beneficiary can present drafts and documents to the negotiating bank or to the paying or accepting bank.

(8) While letters of credit generally are issued for 100 percent of invoice value, they can be issued for less than the full amount if, for example, there has been an advance payment.

(9) According to the particular agreement between buyer and seller, the seller can draw drafts on the issuing bank or a named paying bank either "at sight" or on a time basis.

(10) In this space, the applicant must note whether or not partial shipments and transhipments are permitted. Transhipments apply only to ocean shipments and usually are not permitted unless direct shipments are not available or are very scarce.

(11) In the letter of credit application, a brief description of the merchandise is included; the detailed description of merchandise belongs in the contract between buyer and seller or in the purchase order.

(12) This indicates the price basis included in the letter of credit. International trade terms used in connection with specific prices should be understood thoroughly by both buyer and seller. The price terms determine which charges are paid by the buyer and which are paid by the seller, as well as outline the respective responsibilities of buyer and seller. (See Incoterms, pages 48-60.)

(13) The applicant will specify the documents he wants. Insurance may be effected by seller or buyer—these terms will have been previously agreed upon by the two parties. Check "Marine Bill of Lading" if port-to-port ocean shipment is required; check "Combined Transport Bill of Lading" if more than one mode of transport will be used. If "on board Combined Transport Bill of Lading" is checked, see if "on board vessel" or "on board inland carrier" are checked. If neither is checked, we will accept either an "on board vessel," an "on board inland carrier" or a "received for shipment" Combined Transport Bill of Lading.

(14) In this space, the applicant should enter the name and address of the party to whom the shipping company is to send a notice of arrival. The "notify" party can be the buyer, the buyer's freight forwarder, or the customs house broker. Also, the applicant should indicate whether the freight is to be prepaid (for C.I.F. or C. & F. shipments) or collect (for F.O.B. or F.A.S. shipments).

(15) The applicant can note any other documents that the beneficiary must present in order for the beneficiary to receive payment. Such additional documents might include a weight certificate, health certificate, or a consularized invoice.

(16) If this space is left blank, documents must be presented no later than 21 days after the date of shipment. Generally, the number of days is based on the mailing time for the bill of lading to proceed from the place of shipment to the place of destination. The latest date that documents can be presented is established to allow time for the bills of lading to be processed and delivered into the importer's hand before the merchandise arrives. Bills of lading that arrive after the merchandise are said to be "stale," and the unclaimed merchandise may incur storage charges.

Figure 20-1. (*Continued*)

Security Agreement for Commercial Letter of Credit

TO: BANK OF AMERICA NT&SA

In order that you may open a commercial letter of credit (the "Letter of Credit") for me, I agree to the following:

1.   The Letter of Credit will substantially agree with the terms in the Application for Commercial Letter of Credit shown on the reverse. In this Agreement, "Letter of Credit" includes any sight or time drafts drawn in connection with the Letter of Credit.

2.   I will pay you on demand in U.S. dollars all the money you pay in connection with the Letter of Credit. If the Letter of Credit is issued in a foreign currency, I will pay you on demand the U.S. dollar equivalent of the foreign currency amounts of all drawings under the Letter of Credit. The foreign currency amount of each drawing will be converted to U.S. Dollars at the rate of exchange you apply to that drawing. I will also pay you all related interest, commission, and customary charges. I authorize you to charge any of my accounts at the bank for all money due you, or for which I become liable, under the Letter of Credit.
   I will provide you enough money to meet all payments concerning the Letter of Credit at least one day before the payments are due.

3.   I grant you a security interest in the following:
   a.   All goods and documents that come into my possession or control, or in which I may acquire an interest, in connection with the Letter of Credit;
   b.   All goods and documents that come into your possession or control, or that of any of your correspondents, in connection with the Letter of Credit; and
   c.   All property of mine, including deposit accounts, that comes into your possession or control.

The security will protect payment of the following:
   a.   All payments by you or your correspondents under the Letter of Credit;
   b.   Any interest, commission or other customary charges relating to the Letter of Credit; and
   c.   Any other of my obligations to you.

4.   Any sum not paid when due under this agreement will bear interest from the due date until the date of payment at the annual rate of _____*_____ percent (__*__ %) of the sum of:
   a.   the interest rate that you publicly announce from time to time in San Francisco, California as your reference rate, plus
   b. _____*_____ percentage points. Any change in your reference rate will take effect at the opening of business on the day specified in your public announcement of a change in your reference rate. (The reference rate is set by you based on various factors, including your costs and desired return, general economic conditions and other factors, and is used as a reference point for pricing some loans. Loans may be priced at, above or below the reference rate.)
   Interest will be computed on the basis of:

   ■ a three hundred sixty-five (365) day year and actual days elapsed.

   □ a three hundred sixty (360) day year and actual days elapsed. (This results in more interest payable than if a three hundred sixty-five (365) day year were used.)

5.   If I default in any promise in this Security Agreement, you may sell any goods or documents covered by the security interest granted above. The sale of secured goods or documents will be governed by the California Uniform Commericial Code. If the sale does not pay for the whole amount due, I will pay the shortage to you immediately. If the sale results in more than the amount due, you will pay the surplus to me or those who have a right to it. If the value of the secured goods declines, I will deliver to you on your demand more collateral that is acceptable to you.

6.   I, or a third party, will obtain insurance on all goods described in the Letter of Credit. The insurance will cover fire and other usual risks, and any additional risks you may request. I authorize you to collect the proceeds of the insurance and apply it against any of my obligations to you under the Letter of Credit.

7.   I have obtained any import or export licenses required for the Letter of Credit.

8.   Neither you nor your correspondents will be in any way responsible for the beneficiary's performance of its obligations to me, nor for the form, sufficiency, correctness, genuineness, falsification or legal effect of, or authority of person signing, any documents called for under the Letter of Credit if these documents appear on their face to be in order.

9.   Subject to the laws, customs and practices of the trade in the area where the beneficiary is located, the Letter of Credit will be subject to, and performance under the Letter of Credit by you, your correspondents, and the beneficiary will be governed by, the "Uniform Customs and Practice for Documentary Credits (1983 Revision), International Chamber of Commerce, Publication No. 400," or by later Uniform Customs and Practice fixed by later Congresses of the international Chamber of Commerce as in effect on the date the Letter of Credit is issued.

10.   I agree that all directions and correspondence regarding the Letter of Credit will be sent at my risk. You are not responsible for any inaccuracy, interruption, error or delay in transmission or delivery by post, courier or teletransmission, or for any inaccuracy of translation.

11.   I agree to pay all costs and expenses you may incur because of any dispute in connection with the Letter of Credit, including attorneys' fees for independent counsel and for your in-house counsel.

12.   If the cost to you of issuing or maintaining the Letter of Credit increases because of any reserves, special deposits, FDIC assessments or similar requirements imposed on you, I agree to pay you on demand an additional amount sufficient to compensate you for the increased cost, as determined by you.

SPECIMEN

Administration Use

Consumer Financial Services
To: Regional Credit Administration # _____

World Banking Division
To: □ Division Credit Administration # _____
       □ Division Area Office # _____

Approved:
Date

Credit Administrator

X _____

Office Use

□ Recommended — CR-32/CR-115 in triplicate attached. Forward to Regional/Division Credit Administration.

☒ Approved — One copy of CR-32/CR-115 or CR-116 to Credit Review Center (Reporting Only)

FX-150 to: ☒ International Services — San Francisco #661
             □ International Services — Los Angeles #662

Commission	
☒ Per MISC-42	
□ Other _____	

☒ Credit

□ Prepayment (U.F.E. attached)

Financial Services Officer Name (type Or Print) | Bank Amernet No.
T. Jones

☒ Charge Branch

Signature

□ Charge directly   □ Commissions and charges only
                    □ Drawing, commissions and charges

X _____

Branch/AMG Name
San Francisco Main Office | No. 33

D.D.A. Customer A/C No.

Figure 20-2.   Security agreement. (*Reproduced with permission of Bank of America.*)

SECURITY AGREEMENT
(Commercial Letter of Credit)

This agreement is a contract between the applicant and the issuing bank. The agreement outlines the customer's obligation to reimburse the issuing bank for payments made in accordance with the terms and conditions established under the letter of credit. The form also grants to the bank a security interest in the goods and documents which come into the bank's possession or control, among other things (see paragraph 3C on agreement). It is the reverse of the letter of credit application on page 20.

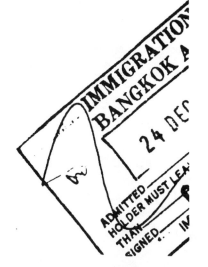

Figure 20-2. (*Continued*)

BANK OF AMERICA
TRADE FINANCE SERVICES #661
550 MONTGOMERY ST., SAN FRANCISCO, CA 94110
P.O. BOX 37020, SAN FRANCISCO, CA 94137

7

PLACE AND DATE OF ISSUE: SAN FRANCISCO JUNE 7, 19XX	**①** IRREVOCABLE DOCUMENTARY ● NUMBER CREDIT ● 078910

① IRREVOCABLE DOCUMENTARY • NUMBER
CREDIT • 078910

DATE AND PLACE OF EXPIRY:
AUGUST 15, 19XX IN HONG KONG

APPLICANT
ABC TOYS IMPORT INC.
300 MAIN STREET
SAN FRANCISCO, CA 94000

BENEFICIARY
XYZ TOYS EXPORT LTD
8TH FLOOR STONE BLDG.
45 KOWHAN ROAD
KOWLOON, HONG KONG

②

ADVISING BANK
BANK OF AMERICA
HONG KONG BRANCH

AMOUNT: U.S. 85,350.00 (EIGHTY FIVE
THOUSAND THREE HUNDRED FIFTY U.S. DOLLARS)

PARTIAL SHIPMENTS: PERMITTED
TRANSHIPMENTS: NOT PERMITTED

CREDIT AVAILABLE WITH ANY BANK

SHIPMENT
FROM HONG KONG
LATEST AUGUST 10, 19XX
FOR TRANSPORTATION TO
SAN FRANCISCO / BAY AREA

BY: NEGOTIATION
AGAINST DOCUMENTS DETAILED BELOW
AND BENEFICIARY'S DRAFTS
AT SIGHT ON US

③ THE LETTER OF CREDIT COVERS FULL INVOICE VALUE
DOCUMENTS REQUIRED:
1. SIGNED COMMERCIAL INVOICE IN DUPLICATE
2. MARINE AND WAR INSURANCE POLICY OR CERTIFICATE FOR 110% INVOICE VALUE IN
   DUPLICATE.
3. SOLE ORIGINAL CLEAN ON BOARD VESSEL MARINE BILL OF LADING, TO ORDER OF SHIPPER,
   BLANK ENDORSED, MARKED: "NOTIFY BUYERS AND S.F. CUSTOMERS CLEARING AGENT, 100
   MAIN STREET, SAN FRANCISCO, CA 94000 AND FREIGHT PREPAID".
4. CERTIFICATE OF ORIGIN, FORM A WHERE APPLICABLE OR BENEFICIARY'S CERTIFICATE
   THAT NONE IS REQUIRED.
5. PACKING LIST.

MERCHANDISE DESCRIPTION:
INFLATABLE TOYS AND TOYS, C.I.F. SAN FRANCISCO / BAY AREA
CATALOGUE NO. 1234 25,000 PCS. @ U.S. $3.00 EACH
CATALOGUE NO. 6789 10,000 PCS. @ U.S. $1.035 EACH

DOCUMENTS MUST BE PRESENTED WITHIN 5 DAYS AFTER THE DATE OF ISSUANCE OF THE
SHIPPING DOCUMENT(S) BUT WITHIN THE VALIDITY OF THE CREDIT.

④ WE HEREBY ISSUE THIS DOCUMENTARY CREDIT IN YOUR FAVOUR. IT IS SUBJECT TO THE
UNIFORM CUSTOMS AND PRACTICE FOR DOCUMENTARY CREDITS (1983 REVISION INTERNATIONAL
CHAMBER OF COMMERCE, PARIS, FRANCE PUBLICATION NO. 400) AND ENGAGES US IN
ACCORDANCE WITH THE TERMS THEREOF. THE NUMBER AND THE DATE OF THE CREDIT AND THE
NAME OF OUR BANK MUST BE QUOTED ON ALL DRAFTS REQUIRED. IF THE CREDIT IS AVAILABLE
BY NEGOTIATION, EACH PRESENTATION MUST BE NOTED ON THE REVERSE OF THIS ADVICE BY
THE BANK WHERE THE CREDIT IS AVAILABLE.

ALL DOCUMENTS TO BE FORWARDED IN ONE COVER, BY AIRMAIL.
NEGOTIATING BANK CHARGES, IF ANY, ARE FOR ACCOUNT OF BENEFICIARY.
THE ADVISING BANK IS REQUESTED TO NOTIFY THE BENEFICIARY WITHOUT ADDING THEIR
CONFIRMATION.

Authorized counter signature   Authorized signature

⑤ Please examine this instrument carefully. If you are unable to comply with the terms or conditions, please communicate with your buyer to arrange
for an amendment. This procedure will facilitate prompt handling when documents are presented.

Figure 20-3. Irrevocable negotiable letter of credit. (*Reproduced with permission of Bank of America.*)

IRREVOCABLE
NEGOTIATION LETTER OF CREDIT

(1) This shows how the information on the application, pictured on page 20, is converted into the actual letter of credit. An irrevocable letter of credit is one that cannot be canceled or revoked without the consent of all parties concerned and is the type of credit customarily used in international trade.

(2) A letter of credit can be available by payment with a designated bank, by acceptance with the drawee bank, by deferred payment or by negotiation. If available by negotiation, it can be with a designated bank or freely negotiable with any bank. In this case, XYZ Toys Exports Ltd. may present the draft and documents to the advising bank, Bank of America, Hong Kong branch or any bank in its locale. When the negotiating bank has examined the documents and determined that they are in order, the negotiating bank will pay the beneficiary and will claim reimbursement from the issuing bank.

(3) The terms presented here coincide with the precise conditions stipulated by the importer, ABC Toys Import Inc., in the application for the commercial letter of credit.

(4) This is the engagement clause. Bank of America agrees to honor a drawing in accordance with the provisions of the Uniform Customs and Practice for Documentary Credits. As is the case with most documentary credits, this credit is operated in accordance with the International Chamber of Commerce's Uniform Customs and Practice for Documentary Credits (1983 Revision International Chamber of Commerce Publication No. 400), which is recognized by banking communities in countries around the world.

(5) Easily overlooked, this section of the credit asks the beneficiary to examine the letter of credit to see if it conforms to his contract and that he is able to perform under the credit. If the beneficiary must request an amendment to the original terms and conditions, he should communicate with the account party directly and ask for an amendment covering the point or points to be changed. The account party then must make an application to the issuing bank for an amendment.

Figure 20-3. (*Continued*)

```
TYPE ADM
TEST 0 TESTED 06/10/XX IN CALIFORNIA
FROM:/SR-10 BQEI FRPP
      BANQUE EMETTRICE INTERNATIONALE
      PARIS, FRANCE


TO:  /SO 10BOFAUS6SYXXX30330
     BANK OF AMERICA
     SAN FRANCISCO, CALIFORNIA


DATE: XX0610


::700 ISSUE OF A DOCUMENTARY CREDIT          (1)


:27 PAGE NUMBER: 1 OF 1
:40A FORM OF DOC CREDIT:IRREVOCABLE
:20 DOC CREDIT NUMBER: 2264A
:31C ISSUE DATE: XX0610 10JUNXX
:31D EXPIRY DATE/LOCATION:
XX0905 05SEPXX
SAN FRANCISCO CAL
:50 APPLICANT/ACCOUNT PARTY:
COMPTOIR D'IMPORTATION DE PRODUITS ELECTRONIQUES
15 RUE GEORGES DUMAS (75009)
PARIS, FRANCE
:59 BENEFICIARY:
RANDALL COMPUTER INC.
350 10TH AVENUE, PALO ALTO, CALIF.
94303 U.S.A.
:32B AMOUNT
USD US DOLLARS 872,770.00
:39 DETAILS OF AMOUNT:
MAXIMUM
:41D AVAILABLE WITH/BY:
BANK OF AMERICA NT AND SA,
SAN FRANCISCO, CALIF.
BY ACCEPTANCE
:42 DRAFTS AT/DRAWN ON:               (2)
DRAFTS AT 90 DAYS SIGHT
DRAWN ON BANK OF AMERICA NT AND SA
SAN FRANCISCO CALIF.
:43P PARTIAL SHIPMENTS: PROHIBITED
:43T TRANSSHIPMENT: PROHIBITED
:44 SHIPMENT INSTRUCTIONS:
SHIPMENT FROM ANY AIRPORT IN U.S.A.
TO CHARLES DE GAULLE INTERNATIONAL AIRPORT, PARIS
DTD NOT LATER THAN AUGUST 25, 19XX
:45A COVERING SHIPMENT OF:
505 RANDALL MODEL 39 COMPUTERS
QUOTATION F.O.B. U.S.A. AIRPORT
ACCORDING TO PURCHASE ORDER NUMBER
6703 DATED 04/15/XX
:46A DOCUMENTS REQUIRED:
AIR WAYBILL, MARKED FREIGHT COLLECT CONSIGNED TO BANQUE EMETTRICE
INTERNATIONALE TO NOTIFY COMPTOIR D'IMPORTATION DE PRODUITS
ELECTRONIQUES, 15 RUE GEORGES DUMAS (75009)
PARIS, FRANCE
COMMERCIAL INVOICE IN ORIGINAL AND THREE COPIES,
PACKING LIST IN ORIGINAL AND THREE COPIES.
:47A ADD'L CONDITIONS:
BENEFICIARY MUST PRESENT THE DOCUMENTS LATEST 5
DAYS AFTER SHIPMENT DATE.
:49 CONFIRMATION INSTRUCTIONS: CONFIRM
:53D REIMBURSEMENT:
AT MATURITY DEBIT OUR ACCOUNT WITH YOU.
:78 INSTRUCTIONS TO PAY/ACCEPT/NEGOTIATING BK:

SEND DOCUMENTS IN ONE COVER BY COURRIER
:72 RECEIVER INFO:
BUYERS INSURE HERE, THIS CREDIT
DOES NOT REQUIRE IMPORT LICENCE.
ACKNOWLEDGE BY MAIL.
-AUT/7E5F
```

ORIGINAL

This letter of credit forms an integral part of our attached advice and is recorded under our reference N° 900000

BANK OF AMERICA
NATIONAL TRUST AND SAVINGS ASSOCIATION
Trade Finance Service #661
P. O. BOX 37020
San Francisco, CA 94137

AUTHORIZED SIGNATURE

Figure 20-4. Irrevocable acceptance (usuance) letter of credit. (*Reproduced with permission of Bank of America.*)

CORRESPONDENT'S IRREVOCABLE ACCEPTANCE LETTER OF CREDIT

(1) A correspondent bank is a commercial bank in one city or country which agrees to handle certain transactions for a bank in another city or country. In this case, Banque Emettrice Internationale, the correspondent bank, has issued its letter of credit on behalf of the importer, Comptoir d'Importation de Produits Electroniques, which is their customer. This is a copy of the incoming telex we received from the issuing bank. It is authenticated by Bank of America. The telex follows the S.W.I.F.T. (Society for Worldwide Interbank Financial Telecommunications) format.

(2) An acceptance credit, also called a usance credit, is a letter of credit that provides for time drafts. The drawee bank, Bank of America-San Francisco, will accept the draft on presentation of the documents from Randall Computer Inc. on or before the expiration date. At maturity, Bank of America will receive reimbursement from the issuing bank, Banque Emettrice Internationale.

(3) Under the conditions and terms of this letter of credit, drafts will be drawn on Bank of America-San Francisco, the confirming and accepting bank. This type of credit is known as a "time" or "usance" letter of credit. When the beneficiary presents the drafts and documents to the accepting bank, Bank of America-San Francisco, and the bank has determined that they are in order, that bank will stamp on the face of the draft the word "accepted" and will sign and date it (see page 30). The bank thus promises to pay the full amount of the draft at the determined future date and the accepted draft becomes a bankers' acceptance. If the beneficiary wants to receive payment earlier than 90 days after sight, the beneficiary can request the confirming/accepting bank to discount the U.S. dollar acceptance and pay the beneficiary an amount less than full face value. The discount equals the bank's market acceptance rate plus commission on the day of discount.

Figure 20-4. (*Continued*)

Bank of America

(1)

Date 6/11/XX

Our Ref.–0900000

Mail To

RANDALL COMPUTER INC.
350 10TH AVENUE
PALO ALTO CA. 94303
USA

Favor

YOURSELVES

WE HAVE BEEN REQUESTED BY BANQUE EMETTRICE INTERNATIONALE TO ADVISE YOU THAT THEY HAVE
ESTABLISHED THEIR LETTER OF CREDIT. ORIGINAL/AUTHENTICATED COPY IS ENCLOSED.

THE ENCLOSED COPY OF THE CABLE/LETTER OF CREDIT AUTHENTICATED BY US IS THE ORIGINAL
LETTER OF CREDIT.

AS REQUIRED BY THE CREDIT, YOUR TIME DRAFTS DRAWN ON US MUST BE PRESENTED TOGETHER
WITH THE DOCUMENTS. THE DRAFTS WILL BE RETURNED TO YOU PROMPTLY AFTER OUR ACCEPTANCE
UNLESS A WRITTEN INSTRUCTION IS GIVEN BY YOU TO HOLD OR DISCOUNT THE DRAFTS.

A DISCREPANCY FEE OF $45.00 WILL BE CHARGED TO YOU ON EACH SET OF DOCUMENTS THAT
CONTAIN DISCREPANCIES.
PRESENTATION OF DOCUMENTS: 550 MONTGOMERY ST., 7TH FL., SAN FRAN. CA 94111

DOCUMENTS REQUIRED UNDER THIS LETTER OF CREDIT MAY ALSO BE PRESENTED TO ANY BANK OF
AMERICA'S OFFICES WITH INTERNATIONAL BANKING SERVICES OR ANY BANKAMERICA INTERNATIONAL
OFFICE. THESE SERVICES ARE NOW AVAILABLE AT SAN FRANCISCO, LOS ANGELES, SAN DIEGO,
NEW YORK, MIAMI, CHICAGO, HOUSTON, ATLANTA. THE ORIGINAL LETTER OF CREDIT AND ALL
AMENDMENTS THERETO ARE REQUIRED FOR PRESENTATION OF YOUR DOCUMENTS.

PLEASE EXAMINE THIS INSTRUMENT CAREFULLY. IF YOU ARE UNABLE TO COMPLY WITH THE TERMS
OR CONDITIONS, PLEASE COMMUNICATE WITH YOUR BUYER TO ARRANGE FOR AN AMENDMENT. THIS
PROCEDURE WILL FACILITATE PROMPT HANDLING WHEN DOCUMENTS ARE PRESENTED. THIS CREDIT
IS SUBJECT TO THE UNIFORM CUSTOMS AND PRACTICE FOR DOCUMENTARY CREDIT, 1983 REVISION,
INTERNATIONAL CHAMBER OF COMMERCE, PUBLICATION NO. 400.

(2) WE CONFIRM THIS LETTER OF CREDIT AND THEREBY UNDERTAKE THAT ALL DRAFTS DRAWN UNDER AND
INCOMPLIANCE WITH THE TERMS THEREOF, WHEN ACCOMPANIED BY DOCUMENTS AS SPECIFIED, WILL
BE DULY HONORED.

Very Truly Yours

T. Jones

Authorized Signature(s)

THIS FORM PRINTS EIGHT (8) LINES PER INCH

COVER LETTER ACCOMPANYING CORRESPONDENT'S LETTER OF CREDIT

(1) This is the advice to the beneficiary which accompanies the authenticated copy of the telex. It lists various statements and conditions which apply to this letter of credit.

(2) A confirmed credit is a letter of credit in which the issuing bank's obligation to pay is backed by a second bank. The confirming bank agrees to pay if the terms of the letter of credit are met, regardless of whether the issuing bank pays. This is Bank of America-San Francisco's "confirmation clause" stating that all drafts in compliance with the terms of the credit will be accepted on presentation and paid at maturity.

If this were an advised credit instead of a confirmed credit, this clause would then be a "disclaimer clause" which would read: "This letter is solely an advice of credit opened by the above mentioned correspondent and conveys no engagement by us." This sentence would represent Bank of America's commitment only to verify the authenticity of the credit.

Figure 20-5. Cover letter for letter of credit. (*Reproduced with permission of Bank of America.*)

BANK OF AMERICA — (1) **BILL OF EXCHANGE**

Date July 13, 19XX No. B-210

Place of Drawing Kowloon, Hong Kong (2) At ------------- Sight Of This Bill Of Exchange

Pay To The Order Of XYZ Toys (3) Export Ltd.

EIGHTY FIVE THOUSAND THREE HUNDRED FIFTY U.S. DOLLARS — U.S. DOLLARS 85,350|00

(4) Value Received And Charge To Account Of Drawn under Bank of America, Credit No. 078910 Dtd June 7, 19XX

(5) To Bank of America NT & SA (6) XYZ Toys Export Ltd. Drawer

At San Francisco, California A. Smith Authorized Signature

SPECIMEN

FX-2006-83 Bank of America NT&SA

BANK OF AMERICA — **BILL OF EXCHANGE**

Date July 25, 19XX No. D-413

Place of Drawing Palo Alto, California (1) At 90 Days Sight Of This Bill Of Exchange

Pay To The Order Of (2) Randall Computer Inc.

EIGHT HUNDRED SEVENTY TWO THOUSAND SEVEN HUNDRED SEVENTY U.S. DOLLARS — U.S. DOLLARS 872,770|00

Value Received And Charge To Account Of Drawn under Banque Emettrice Internationale, Paris, France Credit No. 2764A Bank of America Ref. No. [illegible]

(3) To Bank of America NT & SA Randall Computer Inc. Drawer

At San Francisco, California Authorized Signature

SPECIMEN

The transaction which gives rise to this instrument is the Export of Computer from USA to France NO. 424156

ACCEPTED July 26, 19XX

BANK OF AMERICA NATIONAL TRUST AND SAVINGS ASSOCIATION SAN FRANCISCO, CALIFORNIA

AUTHORIZED SIGNATURE

AUTHORIZED SIGNATURE PAYABLE THROUGH BANK OF AMERICA SECURITIES SERVICES 55 BROADWAY, NEW YORK 10006, IF DESIRED

FX-2006-83 Bank of America NT&SA

BILL OF EXCHANGE

(1) A bill of exchange or draft is an instrument, much like an ordinary check in appearance, which is used as a formal demand for payment in a business transaction.

(2) This bill of exchange is a sight draft and is drawn in accordance with both the application for the commercial letter of credit of page 20 and the irrevocable negotiation letter of credit on page 24.

(3) XYZ Toys Export Ltd., the beneficiary, is the payee, or recipient of funds.

(4) As established by the irrevocable letter of credit on page 24, all drafts must be marked with Bank of America's credit number for identification purposes.

(5) Bank of America-San Francisco is the drawee, or bank to which this bill of exchange is presented for payment.

(6) The drawer is the party who signs an order directing the drawee, Bank of America-San Francisco, to pay a specified sum of money to the payee. In this situation, XYZ Toys Export Ltd. is both the drawer and the payee.

BILL OF EXCHANGE— BANKERS' ACCEPTANCE

(1) This "usance" bill of exchange is the demand for payment of the correspondent's irrevocable acceptance letter of credit on page 26.

(2) Randall Computer Inc., the beneficiary of the credit, is the drawer and payee of the bill of exchange. At maturity of the acceptance, Randall will receive payment for selling goods to Comptoir d'Importation de Produits Electroniques. Randall Computer can either retain the draft until maturity at 90 days sight or discount the draft through Bank of America-San Francisco or another bank and receive an amount less than its full face value. Randall Computer Inc. also would endorse the draft on the reverse side.

(3) Bank of America-San Francisco is the drawee and has accepted the draft on July 26, 19xx. The draft will mature 90 days from the acceptance date, October 24, 19xx. On October 24, 19xx Bank of America will charge the account of Banque Emettrice Internationale and pay Randall Computer Inc. or the presenter of the draft if it was discounted and sold in the secondary market.

Figure 20-6. Bills of exchange. *(Reproduced with permission of Bank of America.)*

21

Negotiating a
Letter of Credit

A crucial point in the letter-of-credit process comes when the shipment is made and the exporter is preparing to negotiate and receive payment against the draft under the letter of credit. If there are any discrepancies, the bank will reject the documents and refuse to pay until the discrepancies are corrected and/or accepted by the buyer. If the discrepancies are not correctable, or time does not permit correction, the exporter must rely on the good will and continued interest of the overseas buyer in obtaining the ordered goods to receive payment in a prompt and orderly fashion. This exposes the exporter to some special risks, since there is always the possibility that the overseas customer may capriciously refuse to amend the letter of credit, leaving the exporter with an open account transaction or something less, lacking any of the prior good faith and credit evidence usually implied when selling on open account.

A conscientious and knowledgeable forwarder is your first line of defense against these problems, depending on how much of your forwarding process is done in-house. If you are gearing up for substantial export volume, it is prudent to develop sufficient in-house expertise to function as a safety check. If discrepancies are discovered—whether they be the fault of the forwarder or the exporter—a good banking relationship, together with a resourceful forwarder, can be of enormous help. Even if your bank will not be negotiating the letter of credit, it can receive the negotiating documents, check them, and send them to the advising or negotiating bank. If you have developed a good relationship with your own bank, its help and advice may be available even though it is not the advising or negotiating bank.

These comments apply to discrepancies that are subject to correction before final presentation. Unfortunately, there are many kinds of discrepancies, some of which are not correctable. The International Chamber of Commerce and other experts state that over 50 percent of credit presentations have discrepancies. Most are correctable, and even those that cannot be corrected are usually ultimately accepted, albeit only after collection delays and additional expense. Fifty percent is a very high figure, and it is one of the reasons for the most recent UCP revision. If your discrepancy experience exceeds 20 or 25 percent, your documentation department is not doing its job. Analyze the source of the majority of these errors, which might have to do with a certain country or certain term. Once the source is found and corrected, many problems and discrepancies can be resolved.

About Discrepancies

The precise working definition of a discrepancy varies slightly from bank to bank, but is essentially defined in the UCP 500. Some cannot be fixed, like the following three primary discrepancies, which cannot be corrected under any circumstances:

1. Late shipment
2. Late presentation
3. Expired letter of credit

Three other major discrepancies that are quite difficult, and sometimes impossible, to correct are:

1. An incorrect bill of lading
2. A draft in excess of credit amount remaining
3. A freight insurance policy bearing a date later than the bill of lading

Some banks refuse commercial invoices in excess of the value of the credit even though the draft is drawn for the credit amount and the excess is stated as due and to be "settled outside the letter of credit." Also, the description of the goods on the invoice must comply exactly with what is described in the credit and must not be contradictory with any other documents, such as the packing list, which must almost always be presented with the credit. Consistency and accuracy are key conditions for avoiding discrepancies. The UCP 500 states that if documents appear on their face to be inconsistent with one another, they are presumed to be not in accordance with the credit. Thus, the packing list can be in greater detail than the invoice as long as the enlarged descriptions do not appear to be inconsistent with the invoice as to quantity, quality, or any other conceivable feature, including extraneous items such as freight or surcharges. It does not matter that the quantity or quality may be greater or superior.

Some discrepancies caused by typographical errors can be avoided these days because banks and the UCP accept photocopies or any type of copy as originals provided they are so marked and are "signed by handwriting, by facsimile signature, by perforated signature, by stamp, by symbol, or by any other mechanical or electronic means of authentication." This helps because a typographical error or misspelling on the letter of credit not duplicated in the documentation may be considered a discrepancy. Omitting an import license number that the letter of credit requires, or a similar omission is considered a discrepancy. The bank normally allows the exporter to take care of these discrepancies by correcting and resubmitting the documents, *if* the expiry date allows time for this to be done.

In respect to leeway time, as well as in terms of cash flow, the new UCP 500 improves the climate for exporters and places a greater burden on negotiating banks by now defining "reasonable time" as seven banking days following receipt of the documents. This is the maximum amount of time allotted to examine documents, to refuse them for discrepancies and give notice to the beneficiary, or to accept them. The notice must cite all the discrepancies and state whether the bank is holding the documents at the disposal of the presenter or is returning them to the presenter. If the issuing or confirming bank fails to act in seven days, it is precluded from dishonoring the credit. If the bank undertaking negotiation is any other nominated bank acting on behalf of the issuing or confirming bank, it does not have any obligation to pay, although some penalty may be imposed under local law. Although many beneficiaries believe the rule to be three days, this was never the case. The three-day limit applied only to payment *after* the documents were accepted, which was any "reasonable" time, and even this rule applied only to domestic credits under the United States Uniform Commercial Code (UCC), Article 5, not to the UCP international credits. Note that when the U.S. law, as codified in the UCC, conflicts with the UCP 500, the UCC law prevails in U.S. courts.

Common Errors in Dealing with Letters of Credit

In some cases, discrepancies prompt the overseas buyer to cancel orders. But in most instances, the discrepancies are corrected or waived and the sales completed. In all cases, however, the exporter does not get paid until the discrepancies are accepted or rectified, thus losing the use of the proceeds for a period of time. In addition, discrepancies usually entail further bank charges that can be substantial. In order of descending importance, here are the ten most-common errors as adapted from an article by Arthur Bardenhagen and Joseph Colleran of Irving Trust Company.[1]

1. Exporters present documents late, after the letter of credit has expired. Even if documents are only one day late, the letter of credit is no longer valid. Usually the exporter starts preparing documents too late and finds

out that items such as consular invoices take much longer to obtain than anticipated.

2. Exporters ship their goods later than the credit allows. Again, even if the shipment is made only one day later than specified in the letter of credit, the letter of credit is invalid.

3. Exporters try to draw more money than the letter of credit allows for. This often happens in cases where the letter of credit allows partial shipment and the final shipment is for more money than there is left in the letter of credit. Often this is done by mutual agreement between exporter and importer; however, the letter of credit must be amended accordingly.

4. Exporters delay presenting documents for an undue period. Even though a letter of credit may not be near expiration, many specify that documents must be presented to the bank within a certain number of days of shipment. If no cutoff is specified, the UCP rules apply. These rules stipulate that the exporter must present documents within 21 days after the goods are shipped (transport document date).

5. Exporters make unallowed partial shipments. Usually the exporters have not studied the letter of credit carefully enough and hope to receive early partial payment if part of the shipment is made early.

6. Exporters present invoices that do not describe the merchandise exactly as it is described in the credit. Since the bank does not inspect the merchandise but only the documents covering shipment of same, it must report any discrepancy between the wording on the invoice and the wording on the letter of credit. This applies even if it is very similar, such as "cartons" versus "boxes," or a partial description, such as "equipment" instead of a specific type of equipment.

7. Exporters do not supply all the documents called for in the letters of credit. This can simply result from an oversight or an inability to obtain the documents or certifications in time. Sometimes it also springs from a desire to avoid paying for these documents. While the documents can usually still be furnished, the exporters do not get paid and run the risk that the letter of credit will expire before the discrepancies are corrected.

8. Exporters do not have documents legalized. Sometimes documents must be either notarized or must be visaed or legalized by a consulate of a foreign nation. It takes time to correct this oversight and can be difficult if the consulate wants to see other related documents.

9. Exporters fail to obtain completed onboard bills of lading. Some bills of lading lack an onboard stamp or contain a stamp that is undated or unsigned. Sometimes this is caused by a last-minute switch of the shipment to another vessel, and this again takes time to correct.

10. Exporters fail to obtain insurance coverage soon enough. Even though many exporters have an open-ended arrangement with their insurance

company, allowing them to write their own policies, such policies may not be approved until a few days after the vessel has sailed. This violates the UCP. To correct this error, exporters need only take the policy back and have it altered. However, there is the possibility that the goods may be damaged before the insurance takes effect—or worse yet, that the vessel may sink.

Not included in this list, but also responsible for negotiating delays—which in turn can lead to late presentation and an expired letter of credit—are such minor items as:

- Errors in arithmetic and addition
- Misspellings, or failure to copy misspellings in the letter of credit
- Obvious corrections (the bank wants clean originals)
- Drafts drawn on the wrong party or not properly endorsed and signed
- Notify party not properly stated or omitted

Besides creating payment problems, simple errors can cause problems for the importer when trying to clear customs. Erroneous unit counts or values can raise the suspicion of the overseas customs official as to the possibility that your customer is avoiding tariff charges. Even if they do not raise suspicions, mistakes delay customs clearance, possibly adding demurrage costs and other charges, as well as importer penalties. Chinese and Japanese officials are especially noted for meticulous inspection for such errors.

When Discrepancies Cannot Be Corrected

If, despite all your care, a discrepancy is found that cannot be corrected, don't immediately let the bank cable for authorization, much less send the credit for collection. Insist that the discrepancy first be reported to you, then study it and the UCP 500. Taking the following steps with diplomacy and knowledge can sometimes save a good deal of time and money. First, discuss the discrepancy with a banker in another bank. Then discuss it with the documentary clerk who reported the discrepancy. You will rarely succeed in changing the discrepancy decision at this level, but if you are knowledgeable and have a well-reasoned argument, you stand a good chance with the documentary manager if it is a highly technical or minor discrepancy. Many situations are also not black-and-white, and many documentary clerks consider it a mark of their skill to find discrepancies, including questionable discrepancies.

When the discrepancy must stand, you have three choices:

1. Ask the negotiating bank to contact the issuing bank, which will then contact the buyer who opened the letter of credit for permission to waive the discrepancy. This is usually the best course and the fastest in the long run. It is advisable, however, to also contact the buyer directly to explain and urge rapid

acceptance of the necessary change or discrepancy. The buyer might have a stake in a speedy resolution in view of demurrage and customs charges.

2. Send the documents for collection. On arrival, the issuing bank will ask the buyer for approval. If possible, this should be avoided because of the increased time factor, among other reasons. Again, it is important to advise your customer. In some cases it is wise to first determine which of these first two procedures will be most expeditious in view of the need to avoid demurrage charges if the goods will be held up in the port of destination waiting for documents.

3. Sign an indemnity agreement or guarantee with your negotiating bank to pay, but with recourse to you. This naturally requires a decision by your bank in respect to your creditworthiness. Such an agreement may be prohibited in the event of discrepancies under the terms of the credit. If the negotiation is not ultimately accepted by the buyer and the issuing bank, the paying bank will ask you to reimburse it, with interest.

Obviously, all these options leave you without the protection of the letter of credit and somewhat at the mercy of the buyer. If the buyer still wants the merchandise, however, the discrepancy must be accepted before the bank turns the documents over to the buyer. This will not prevent the buyer from trying to negotiate a price reduction with you in return for accepting the discrepancy. If acceptance is refused, it is up to you to dispose of the goods abroad or sue the buyer for breach of contract or for payment. Do keep in mind that a letter of credit is a payment mechanism to protect both buyer and seller. It is not intended to be a weapon in the hands of an unscrupulous buyer, but it does give that party the upper hand. This is especially true if the buyer has become indifferent to the receipt of the merchandise.

Letter-of-Credit Checklists

To avoid most of the mistakes that lead to discrepancies and collection problems, you need to study the terms of the letter of credit carefully, allow time to fulfill the terms, and then pay attention to detail.

Check the items on the checklists below against those that you request from your customer when preparing a letter of credit, as well as when the letter of credit is received. Additional details and brochures are available at all major regional banks and money center banks.

Checklist to Use When Requesting a Letter of Credit

- State total value and quantities

- State that the letter of credit is irrevocable

- Ask for or suggest a strong and reputable issuing bank

- Determine whether letter of credit should be confirmed

FORMAT FOR REQUESTING A LETTER OF CREDIT FROM OVERSEAS BUYERS

TO: _____   DATE: _____

Dear Overseas Buyer:

Regarding your purchase order number _____ dated _____, please ask that your bank issue an irrevocable commercial letter of credit according to the following terms and conditions.

Beneficiary: (exporter's name & address) _____

Requested Advising Bank: (name & address) _____
                                    telex _____ cable _____ Swift _____

Please open via air mail _____ teletransmission _____

In the amount of $_____. Payment to be effected in U.S. Dollars

Shipment and price quotations are _____ (ICC 350 Incoterm FOB, CIF, etc.) Destination _____

Payment Terms: The letter of credit must be payable at the counters of (name of bank) _____
OR: Letter of credit must be negotiable and payable at the counters of a bank in (city) _____

Draft(s) to be drawn at sight, or _____ days sight, or _____ days after the date of bill of lading. In the case of time drafts, discount charges are for the account of the ____ buyer ____ seller.

___ Please have letter of credit confirmed by _____ (Bank), OR ___ confirmation is not requested.
___ Please have letter of credit allow transfer.
___ Please have letter of credit state that NVOCC or House Bills of Lading are acceptable.

Documentary Requirements: The letter of credit funds should be available upon presentation of the following documents:
1. Signed Commercial Invoices 2. _____ 3._____ 4. (etc)

Shipment from _____ to _____

Partial shipments are _____ permitted, or _____ not permitted

Latest shipment date _____ Latest expiration date _____

_____ days after the date of shipment must be allowed for presentation of documents to the negotiating bank.

All banking charges in the U.S. are for the account of ___ buyer or ___ seller, all other charges for buyer's account.

Please ensure that the letter of credit is received by us _____ days before our agreed upon shipment date.
OR: The shipment date will be based on _____ days after our receipt of an acceptable letter of credit.

PLEASE NOTE: If you are unable to meet any of these terms and conditions, please contact us immediately, and prior to having the letter of credit issued. Any deviation from the above terms and conditions without our agreement, may result in a delay of the shipment until the letter of credit can be amended.

Sincerely,

Exporter

Figure 21-1. Format to request letter of credit from your buyer.

- Propose a local and convenient paying bank
- Determine whether the terms are usance or at sight, and if usance, state number of days from date certain (i.e., bill of lading date)
- State as payable in American funds
- State latest shipping and expiry date
- State latest date for receipt of letter of credit, or, alternatively, number of days for delivery from receipt of credit
- Determine whether partial shipments must be allowed
- Determine whether house bills of lading or NVOCC bills of lading must be allowed
- State terms of sales [i.e., FCA, FOB (named port), CFR, CIF]
- State shipping port or suggest "any port," East Coast port, etc.
- Name documents that will be required
- Determine whether letter of credit should be transferable

See Figure 21-1 for a format to use when requesting a letter of credit from your customer. One ETC provides a very specific format to its overseas representatives with the admonition that any amendment charges incurred because of the representatives' failure to have customers provide correct letters of credit will be deducted from their commission. This would clearly require very loyal and steadfast representatives.

It is vital to consider the relative fees and charges among your possible choices of paying or confirming banks. It is equally important to check on the strength and reputation of the issuing and confirming bank. There are many letters of credit from African banks that do not even exist, especially in the case of Nigeria.

Checklist to Use on Receipt of a Letter of Credit

The following is a checklist for items to make sure of on receipt of a letter of credit from the overseas buyer in order to avoid later problems.

- Is the letter of credit irrevocable?
- Is the paying bank of good reputation and is the currency convertible in the event that bank is overseas?
- Does the letter of credit need to be confirmed in the United States?
- Is the seller's name and address spelled correctly and are there other misspellings that might create discrepancies?
- Are the dollar amounts and quantities per your quotation?
- Is the letter of credit at sight, or if a usance credit, is it as agreed?
- Are the shipping terms correct (e.g., FOB, CIF)?

- Are the documents required as agreed?
- Can you provide insurance as required?
- Are letter-of-credit fees and costs as agreed?
- Is there sufficient tolerance as to quantity (i.e., is the word "about" or an equivalent word necessary)?
- Is the merchandise correctly described?
- Are partial shipments allowed?
- Is transshipment allowed if necessary?
- Is there sufficient time to meet the latest shipping and negotiation timetable?
- Can you ship from the port of embarkation that is stated?
- Is the shipping destination as agreed and possible?
- Will the style and type of transport document you will receive from the carrier be acceptable (e.g., house bill of lading versus ocean onboard bills)?
- If a named vessel or carrier is stipulated, can you comply both as to availability and voyage timing?
- Do you have time to obtain the consular legalization and the other certificates required?
- Are there inspection or mandatory PSI problems?
- Can you provide a packing list by carton?
- Can you meet marking and labeling requirements?
- If you need to ship on-deck, is this allowed?

Checklist to Use When Presenting a Letter of Credit

The person responsible for the negotiation of the letter of credit should carefully consider the following in-depth checklist prior to presentation to the bank:

Letter of Credit (At time of receipt by beneficiary)	1. Do credit terms agree with terms of contract? 2. Can credit terms be met? 3. Is merchandise to be shipped subject to stowage limitations?
Documents (General, at time of presentation by beneficiary)	1. Are you sure that the credit is not overdrawn, either in terms of the amount or the quantity of merchandise? 2. Is presentation made in time, before expiry and other time limits indicated in the letter of credit—or within 21 days after date of shipping document or onboard clause if any, provided no time limits are indicated? 3. Are all documents accounted for? Do they relate to each other? Are they consistent? 4. Do all documents show import licenses, letter of credit number, or other identification if required by the letter of credit? 5. Does cover letter contain complete and clear instructions?

Drafts	1. Are drafts drawn at tenor indicated?
	2. Are amount (both figures and words) currency, date (within expiry), and interest clause (if any) in accordance with letter of credit terms?
	3. Are drafts drawn on proper drawee and signed by authorized parties?
	4. Are drafts endorsed if made out to order of drawee ("ourselves")?
	5. Is the letter of credit number and drawee bank properly referenced?
Commercial Invoices	1. Does the commercial invoice conform with credit terms?
	■ Total amount
	■ Unit prices and computations
	■ Description of merchandise and terms (e.g., FCA, CPT, FOB, CFR, etc.)
	■ Foreign language used for description if used in credit
	■ Description of packing
	■ Declarations of clauses properly worded
	2. Is commercial invoice made out in name of applicant for the letter of credit?
	3. Is commercial invoice signed?
	4. Is commercial invoice countersigned by other party if credit so requires?
	5. Do shipping marks on commercial invoice agree with those on bill of lading?
	6. Do shipping charges on commercial invoice agree with those on bill of lading?
	7. If partial shipments are prohibited, is all merchandise shipped? If partial shipments are permitted, is the merchandise invoiced in proportion with the shipment?
Consular Invoices (Customs invoices)	1. Does the consular invoice tally with the commercial invoice and bill of lading?
	2. Is the description of merchandise in foreign language, if credit so states?
	3. Is official form completed in all places indicated?
	4. Are there no alterations except by a letter of correction issued by consulate?
	5. If legalized commercial invoices are required, have sufficient copies been properly legalized?
Insurance Documents	1. Is it an insurance policy or a certificate? (A certificate or broker's declaration under an open cover policy is acceptable under the UCP 500, but the credit may expressly demand nothing less than a "policy," which must then be provided.)
	2. Is the insured amount sufficient?
	3. Is insurance coverage complete and in conformity with the credit?
	■ Are special risks covered where required?
	■ Is insurance carried through to proper destination and for entire period of shipment?
	■ Have proper warehouse clauses been observed?
	4. Is certificate countersigned?
	5. Is certificate or policy endorsed?
	6. Are shipping marks identical to those on commercial invoice and bill of landing?
	7. Are all corrections signed or initialed? Are riders or binders attached or cross-referenced?
	8. Is policy or certificate dated prior to shipping date?

Bills of Lading	1. Are bills of lading in negotiable form?
	2. Are all negotiable copies being presented to the bank? Are they properly endorsed?
	3. Are bills of lading "clean" (i.e., no notation showing defective conditions of goods or packaging)?
	4. Do bills of lading indicate that merchandise was loaded on board and within term specified in the credit? If this is not part of the text, but in the form of a notation, is this notation dated and signed or initialed?
	5. Are the bills of lading made out as prescribed by the credit, including names and addresses of beneficiary, applicant, notify parties, flag, and visa, if any?
	6. If freight was prepaid, is this clearly indicated with a "Freight Prepaid" or "Freight Paid" stamp?
	7. Are bills of lading issued from a regular line steamer? (If charter party, sailing vessel, on-deck, forwarder's or consolidator's bills of lading are presented, does the credit allow for these?)
	8. Are marks and numbers, quantities, general description of goods, as per commercial invoice and credit? Is no excess merchandise shipped?
	9. Does bill of lading show transshipment?
	10. Are all corrections initialed or signed by carrier?
	11. Do bills of lading signed by an agent also name carrier or master as now required under UCP 500?
Other Shipping Documents: Air Waybills, Parcel Post, or Courier Receipts	1. Are marks and numbers, quantities, and general description of goods as on invoice and credit? Is no excess merchandise shipped?
	2. Are air waybills or parcel post receipts made out as prescribed by the credit (i.e., names and addresses of beneficiary, applicant, notify parties, flag, and flight number, via, if any)?
	3. If freight or postage was prepaid, is this clearly indicated?
	4. Is the air waybill not a "forwarder's bill of lading"? Is it and all corrections signed or initialed by carrier or agent?
	5. Are air waybills, courier receipts, or parcel post receipts dated within terms specified by the credit?
Certificates of Origin, Weight, Inspection, and Analysis	1. Are names and addresses as per commercial invoice and per letter of credit? Is country of origin if required as per commercial invoice and per letter of credit?
	2. Are the certificates issued by the proper party and signed? Do they show a description relative to commercial invoice and credit?
	3. Are the certificates in exact compliance with letter of credit and dated reasonably current?
	4. Does letter of credit call for certificate of origin to be issued by Chamber of Commerce or merely certified or countersigned by a Chamber of Commerce? If the former, an amendment should be requested.
Packing and Weight List	1. Is packing type the same as stated in the commercial invoice?
	2. Do quantity and units tally with commercial invoice?
	3. Is the exact breakdown of merchandise per individual package shown? Has a final comparative check of all documents been made?[2]

When a Letter of Credit Is Not the Answer

Many exporters and exporting companies feel that all transactions should be done only under letter-of-credit terms. There are many situations, however, in which letters of credit might not be to your advantage or fit the nature of your product and your shipping patterns. One example is that of an apparel exporter who must make many small, partial shipments of relatively low value. The letter-of-credit negotiation costs of each shipment will represent a large expense, and many other conditions of the letter may be needlessly restrictive or cumbersome. This, in turn, forces many requests for amendments that are costly to both exporter and buyer and do nothing for a comfortable working relationship. Shipments of $5000 to $10,000 should be considered a minimum under letter-of-credit terms when negotiating expenses to the beneficiary are considered. In some situations and in the case of some banks, these amounts are still too small for profit.

A survey in the December 1989 issue of *Exporter* magazine revealed some astounding facts relevant to the average size of export shipments and the costs of negotiating an advised letter of credit. There are an average of 700,000 export shipments per month from the United States and 85 percent of them, or about 600,000, are under $25,000 in value. The same survey finds that of the letters of credit with a value of from $10,000 to $25,000, the costs associated with negotiating them, not counting extra costs for amendments, discrepancies, financing, or confirmation fees, ranged from $70 to $340. A mean average might be around $185, with an additional $50 for regions such as the Middle East (except Saudi Arabia), and a reduction of $50 for most of Asia.[3]

The result is a negotiation cost in the range of 1 percent on an $18,000 shipment. In addition, flat fees of $10 to $100 for items such as discrepancies and amendments add even more to the cost. On a typical negotiation fee of one-eighth of 1 percent, a minimum of $75 is not exceeded until the letter of credit reaches $60,000.[4]

If you are unfortunate enough to have to negotiate through one of the banks charging higher fees, or in the event that amendments are necessary or there are discrepancies, your costs could quickly jump to 3 percent. If you are dealing in a lower transaction range of around $10,000, your costs could even rise to 5 percent. For this reason, you must check your bank's charges, avoid amendments and discrepancies, and quite possibly avoid taking letters of credit for small transactions. Furthermore, the very specificity of a letter of credit can impose restraints that you would not have to contend with in a typical purchase order, assuming that you are dealing with a qualified and reputable buyer. Sometimes letters of credit can be used to delay payment by an importer who seizes on every technical discrepancy to defer your negotiation. Product and procedures aside, competition and a harmonious relationship with your steady customers or distributors may force you to consider alternatives. Generally, you will discover that it is easier to get letters of credit in the Pacific Rim trade, where they are often offered without being requested.

You will encounter the greatest resistance to letters of credit among European buyers, who largely trade among themselves without them; some will even be offended if asked for one. Apart from buyer creditworthiness, a common and valid reason for requesting a letter of credit is the political risk or currency inconvertibility. You can understand that in the major currencies of the world—the Deutsche mark, French franc, British pound, Japanese yen, and the U.S. dollar for example—this reason for requesting a letter of credit is not usually valid.

Endnotes

1. Arthur Bardenhagen and Joseph Colleran, "Marketing Mistakes: How Exporters Go Astray," *Business Marketing,* January 1985.

2. *Author's note:* This checklist is not original, but unfortunately came to us without the originator's name. We express our gratitude to whomever might have prepared this list and the liberties we have taken to update or expand its contents.

3. "Letter of Credit Survey," *The Exporter,* December 1989.

4. *The Exporter* magazine, ibid.

22

Standby Letters of Credit

Our discussion of letters of credit has focused so far on letters of credit requiring shipment of goods or provision of services. Another type of credit, normally nonoperating, is known as a standby letter of credit. Its use is expanding in both variety and frequency. The standby letter of credit is helpful, even essential, to buyers, sellers, and contracting parties as a means of guaranteeing future obligations and actions. It can be used to support a single transaction or be opened for a year or more to effectively create an open credit line for transactions that have not yet been determined between the two parties.

In Lieu of a Transactional Letter of Credit

Used as an account receivable standby letter of credit, the credit is a form of receivables insurance. Usually the exporter ships on open account and agrees only to use the letter of credit to collect against a statement or invoices attested to be a certain number of days past due. No other documentation is normally required, and it is therefore almost a clean drawing. Both shipper and importer are relieved of some of the costs and other burdens, such as the detailed paperwork imposed by a letter of credit requiring negotiation for each transaction or shipment. Used in this fashion, it is commonplace in domestic transactions as well.

The typical standby credit used in this fashion is of particular importance if both the accountee (buyer), and the beneficiary (seller) understand how the other intends to perform, especially if many small shipments are contemplated. Exporters enjoy the same ultimate credit protection as they would with a regular letter of credit, and know that the worst case scenario would be for payment to be delayed by the number of days past due specified in the letter of credit. Assuming that it is opened and confirmed by a reasonably reliable and strong bank, the exporter is protected not only from commercial risk, but from political risk as well, especially if the standby credit is confirmed by an American bank. All this is accomplished without the cost and trouble of negotiating individual letters of credit.

The standby credit can be a face-saving device for both parties if a good overseas customer feels entitled to open account terms that the exporter does not wish to extend. In some cases, the political risks really are the major obstacle to providing the terms requested, and by use of a standby credit, both parties' objectives can be satisfied at less cost to each. It can also be an excellent tool, permitting a young company or an EMC/ETC to work more conveniently with a domestic supplier while establishing the beginnings of a credit relationship in the process.

One caveat: If you are a beneficiary, be sure your standby credit is valid for sufficient time to allow for the last shipment in a series, plus transit time, invoice maturity, and communication time to the issuing bank with your draft and demand, all prior to the standby credit expiry date.

As a Performance Bond and In Lieu of a Surety Bond

Surety bonds are designed to ensure the buyer financial compensation if the exporter or contractor does not perform contractually as agreed. If such is the case, the surety company agrees to pay whatever is necessary up to the maximum amount of the bond to create equivalent performance for the buyer. Surety bonds are very difficult to obtain today, except by strong companies with a good performance track record, such as well-established and financially strong contractors. It is difficult for insurance companies to fully assess their risks. It is, therefore, also difficult for a firm to find a willing surety company if it lacks a strong balance sheet or is undertaking a new area of endeavor, no matter how well established otherwise. The answer might be the Small Business Administration's surety bond guarantee program. (See Chapter 39.) Should you be fortunate enough to have an insurance company that will underwrite a surety bond at a reasonable price, by all means use it. You will have less risk exposure because the insurance company will use its prerogative of demanding proof to verify the validity of the claim before paying. If the claim cannot be verified, the insurance company will deny the claim and undertake litigation if necessary. If the insured's failure to perform is proven, the insurance company must pay, and thereafter, of course, the company has recourse against the insured.

A standby letter of credit as a performance bond issued by a bank and a surety bond issued by an insurance or surety company are entirely different, but both serve a similar purpose. A bank must honor a drawing under a standby credit based entirely on compliance at face value with minimal documentation and authentication of the facts in the document. Payment is usually based on little more than the beneficiary's request, with the only recourse being litigation as to an "unfair calling." Standby letters of credit in lieu of surety bonds are, nevertheless, the most common solution and are being used in a variety of situations, usually representing 5 to 10 percent of the contract and valid until performance is complete and the project is working. This is not only because of the lack of availability of surety bonds, but also because of the increasing insistence by foreign project managers on getting standby letters of credit to provide them greater protection as their security or guarantee of performance. This is understandable from the buyer's point of view because, as indicated before, the buyer with a standby credit does not need to defend a claim of nonperformance. Since the standby credit represents a contingent extension of credit from the issuing bank to the exporter, once again, the SBA, Eximbank, or even your state's export finance office may be able to provide financial support through an export working capital loan guarantee program.

As a Bid or Tender Bond

Used in lieu of a bid bond, the standby credit tells the buyer that, should you, as the exporter, be the successful bidder but fail to accept and/or sign the contract on which you bid and thereafter immediately post the performance bond the contract normally requires, you will forfeit the amount specified in the bid bond. The bid bond is always a lesser amount than the performance bond—in the range of 2 to 5 percent of the contract, most often 3 percent, and typically valid for up to six months. Its purpose is to protect the buyer from losses in accepting an invalid bid, and thereby losing the opportunity to accept other valid bidders that might by then have withdrawn their bid for a variety of reasons.

Established contractors and regular pursuers of tender offers normally have surety companies that are willing to provide bid bonds even if the surety company does not intend to participate in the subsequently required performance bond. The bid bond is very commonplace in dealing with sovereign buyers in reference to tender offers. When offering a bid bond, be sure that some institution is prepared to follow up with support on the performance bond. If you do not, you will have built your own trap and lose the bid bond amount by default.

As an Advance Payment Guarantee

In this case the standby letter of credit is intended to protect the overseas buyer from losses in the event the contractor or exporter fails to provide the initial performance the advance payment is meant to assure. As a general rule, if an advance payment is demanded or offered, a standby credit will be required in an amount equal to the down payment. If you are ever faced with negotiating a down payment in exchange for an advance payment guarantee or a performance bond, you should seriously consider the possibility of foregoing the down payment. The reason is that unless you have unlimited credit and a proven ability to perform, the bank will ask you to provide collateral for the standby credit with cash or the equivalent—which is usually the same cash received as a down payment. Now you are back where you started, except that depending on the bank, the country, and how the standby credit is drawn, it may take on a life of its own beyond the validity shown on the face. It could even tie up your money beyond completion of the contract as they wait for the equipment or project to reach performance specification. It can also turn into a chicken-or-egg problem: the bank wants the cash down payment before it issues the standby letter of credit, and the buyer wants to receive the standby credit first. This dilemma, however, can usually be resolved with an "effective on receipt of funds" clause in the standby credit.

The advantage of the down payment, even with the offsetting standby-backed guarantee, is that the funds advanced can earn interest while on deposit with your bank to serve as collateral for the standby letter of credit. There is also the probability that a credit extension in the form of a standby credit will be less costly than the interest on the equivalent working capital loan. Standby letters of credit may state that they do not become operative until the underlying letter of credit is received by the issuing bank. Determine in advance that the issuing bank will accept your bank's standby credit rather than a bank letter of guarantee, described in the next section.

In addition to standbys as bid and performance bonds or advance payment guarantees, there are other variations that have a similar effect, but are intended for still other specific purposes. For example, maintenance bonds allow for early release of funds that would otherwise be held back during start-up periods, and retention bonds in the order of 5 to 10 percent are in lieu of a letter of credit percentage holdback in warranty clauses.

About Letters of Guarantee

Whether for an advance payment guarantee, bid bond, or performance bond, the letter of guarantee—the Middle Eastern counterpart of a standby letter of credit—is clearly the document of preference throughout the Middle East, including Turkey and Egypt. Although the same basic principles apply to both the letter of guarantee and the standby letter of credit, banks in the United States are not permitted to provide bank letters of guarantee. Yet many export contracts or purchase agreements, primarily in the Middle East, require letters of guarantee. American bank regulatory bodies (e.g., the FDIC, the Federal Reserve, and the Office of the Comptroller) do not permit such guarantees because of regulations written in the 1930s to cover the abuses of the preceding period. Their concern was focused on the uncertainty and negotiable aspect of the resulting contingent liability, and therefore, on the implied inaccuracy of bank statements of account. Most other countries in the world permit letters of guarantee, which are a gray area but often play an important role in project finance and other major purchases. As a result of a series of court decisions,

U.S. banks are allowed by the regulatory agencies to substitute standby letters of credit in lieu of letters of guarantee, mitigating what would otherwise be a serious shortcoming for U.S. exporters.

This understanding as to standby letters' potential to back up or counterguarantee letters of guarantee issued by a bank in the buyer's own country is now an accepted practice and provides similar results for both the buyer and seller, as well as essentially the same contingent liability for the banks. While the point remains debatable, most experts contend that because of technical differences, the letter of guarantee is less of a threat to the exporting applicant party than the standby credit is an advantage to the buyer. In part, this is because the letter of guarantee is still a bank's promise to pay, but without the strict structuring of a credit. Somewhat like a surety bond, the guarantee can be readily extended when a project is running behind schedule or while the nonperformance or other incident that created, or threatened to create, a *calling* (demand for payment) is being defended by the guarantor and perhaps being discussed or negotiated between the buyer and the bank. Because such negotiations are troublesome and time-consuming, U.S. banks welcome the fact that letters of guarantee are prohibited. In contrast, and to the advantage of the importer or beneficiary, remember that standby credit practices call for immediate payment as long as the required documents specifying nonperformance appear to be correct on their face at presentation.

When a letter of guarantee is required, the U.S. bank can ask its foreign subsidiary, branch, or correspondent bank to open a letter of guarantee on the U.S. bank's behalf to resolve the impasse. In that case, the U.S. bank backs up its request for a letter of guarantee from the foreign bank with its own standby letter of credit. Be prepared to pay more for a guarantee than for a standby credit because of the potential time and effort in negotiation costs that the surety aspect of the letter of guarantee can cause a bank. Another expense may result from the fact that the guarantee document is the one most subject to remaining valid until the beneficiary chooses to physically return the guarantee.

A Caveat Concerning Standby Letters of Credit as Bonds

A *Euromoney Trade Finance Report* article provides a very negative, but thorough, view of bonds in the April 1986 issue that any type of bond "can mean a step into the unknown for exporters, it also refers to them as "Hostages to Fortune,"[1] especially in the Middle East. Bonds can indeed be of a most arbitrary nature, especially where clean drawings are called for under the supporting letter of credit. Here is a recap of the special hazards to keep in mind, even though you may find it impossible to avoid exposure to them:

1. A bid bond can be extended against your wishes, as can a performance bond in some cases, by a maneuver called "extend or pay (call)." The party receiving bids may want more time to study the bids or, for other reasons, request an extension. If the extension is refused, the party then proceeds to

"call" on the standby credit, or advises that it intends to do so. Refusing or fighting such a request is not only hopeless, but fairly well eliminates the possibility that you will be awarded the bid in any case. A similar situation applies in the case of performance bonds, as a means of extending the warranty in a sense, or because of a construction delays, and there, the stakes are higher.

2. In spite of the existence of an expiry date on the standby letter bond, some countries have laws that state that the standby, like a letter of guarantee, nevertheless remains valid until physically returned by the beneficiary to the drawer's bank. Even without such laws, some banks continue to hold it as a contingent liability against the drawer (exporter) until its physical return. Court cases are divided, and of course expensive. The most arbitrary of these abuses have often been associated with a few Middle Eastern countries, such as Iran and Libya, and a few Third-World nations. One must also distinguish between sovereign versus private buyers and the probabilities for reliable and responsible behavior associated with each.

3. The possibility of an unfair or capricious calling of a standby letter of credit is present even if there has been no actual failure to perform or other breach of contract. Historically, the chance of an unfair calling is only one-fourth of 1 percent, which is a rate comparable to regular loan charge-offs. It is easy to overemphasize the risks, therefore, because for standby letters of credit overall, including usage in lieu of a bond, the final net loss ratio after recovery was a mere one twenty-fifth of 1 percent according to a 1979 Federal Reserve Board study—ten times *less* than regular loan charge-offs. On unfair callings by a private party, you have remedies by law; if committed by a sovereign buyer, it is a political risk, and your only source of protection is limited insurance from the Overseas Private Investment Corporation (OPIC), or through private facilities, primarily Lloyds of London in this particular field.

As with contract repudiation insurance, private sector cover is available to the smaller exporter only if the contract is with what is considered to be a sovereign buyer and therefore is categorized as political risk. In this case, private insurers will insure single transactions and the minimum premium can be as low as $1000 to $2000 (if Lloyds of London remains at their presently stated minimum premium). Other private insurers charge in the range of $2500, which is acceptable on a contract of $500,000 or so, but high for smaller transactions. On the other hand, if the buyer is a private party and the risk is therefore commercial, there is a problem because the of large annual minimum premium of $35,000 to $50,000 required for insurance from private sector providers on such specialized cover in the commercial risk category. (More information will be provided on this subject in Chapter 25.)

4. It is important to structure your contractual agreement so that the performance bond or advance payment guarantee does not become valid before the underlying contract or guarantees to repay advance payments that have not yet been received. The reason for this precaution is that the bank's standby credit does not, in itself, relate to the contract and will probably simply call for a

drawing on demand. At the most it may require a statement that the contractor is in some form of default. In that case, the bank is bound to make payment at your expense even though you did not yet have a contract under which you could perform or protest and had no funds in your bank to return. It has happened.

Banks will likely become even more conservative in terms of collateral requirements for standby letters of credit used as bid, performance, or advance payment guarantees. While standby credits always have been subject to a bank's individual lending limit, they are not presently chargeable to outstanding loans relative to lending reserves because of the contingent liability factor. The United States and most major trading national banking administrators came to a common agreement around 1990 that resulted in 50 percent of the standby credit monetary value being subject to capital reserve requirements. This rule was effective as of 1992. Currently, banks most often ask dollar-for-dollar cash collateral on standby letters from all but their most creditworthy customers.

Study Figures 22-1 and 22-2 (see pages 298–301) for an example of the bank application that must be signed before opening a standby letter of credit and an example of the standby letter of credit itself, courtesy of Bank of America. Figure 22-3 (see page 302) is the reverse side of the standby application and represents the loan agreement necessary to support the contingent extension of credit that a bank provides by virtue of the standby credit.

Endnotes

1. Sandy Troden, "Giving a Bond: Your life in Their Hands," *Euromoney Trade Finance Report,* April 1986.

Bank of America   (1)   **Application for Standby Letter of Credit**

LOCATION	DATE
San Francisco, CA	May 3, 19XX
	For Bank Use Only

To: Bank of America NT&SA   (5)   L/C No.

I request you to issue an irrevocable standby letter of credit as shown on this application by:

☐ Full text teletransmission   ☒ Airmail   ☐ Airmail with brief preliminary teletransmission advice

For Account of (Applicant, Name and Address)   (2)

Polyester Piping Corporation
35 Main Street
San Francisco, CA 94116

In Favor of (Beneficiary, Name and Address)   (3)

HongKong Water & Power Authority
GPO Box 333
Hong Kong, Hong Kong

Advising Bank (If blank, Branch or Correspondent Bank)   (4)

Bank of America
Hong Kong Main Office #6055

Amount   (6)

U.S. $3,500,000.00 (Three million five hundred thousand United States Dollars)

Expiration Date   (7)

Drafts to be drawn and presented to the negotiating or paying bank on or before: December 31, 19XX

(8)

Available by drafts at sight on you, your branch or your correspondent at your option or you may waive draft requirement.

Documents required (should clearly reflect beneficiary's right or reason for drawing):   (9)

A letter from HongKong Water & Power Authority certifying that Polyester Piping
Corporation has failed to perform as required under paragraph 15 of contract #78910
entered into between HongKong Water & Power Authority and Polyester Piping Corporation
for the supply of Reinforced Polyester Pipe couplings and that the amount drawn covers
50% of the contract price.

All documents will be sent in one cover by airmail unless stated otherwise under Special Instructions.   (10)

Special Instructions: This credit is to be automatically reduced by 50% of the contract
price of each invoice amount of the respective partial shipments under Bank of America,
Hong Kong L/C #6055-1234

The opening of this credit is subject to the terms and conditions of the Agreement for Standby Letter of Credit (the "Agreement") on the reverse. The words "I," "me," and "my" in this application and in the Agreement refer to each signer of the application. "You" and "your" refer to Bank of America (the "Bank"). If this application is signed by more than one person, the Agreement will be the contract of the signers both as individuals and as a group.

I have read the Agreement and agree to its terms and conditions.

NAME OF APPLICANT	SIGNATURE	TITLE	Controller
Polyester Piping Corporation	X	TITLE	Treasurer
	X		

FX-148 5-86   (If more than one page is used, all pages must be signed.)   Bank of America NT&SA

SUBMIT IN DUPLICATE   (Reproduced with permission of Bank of America)

Figure 22-1. Application for standby letter of credit. (*Reproduced with permission of Bank of America.*)

APPLICATION FOR
STANDBY LETTER OF CREDIT

1 Under certain circumstances, a party may want protection in the event that a business transaction is *not* performed. A standby letter of credit can be issued by a bank on behalf of its client to convey such protection to a third party/beneficiary. The bank is committed to pay against documents the amount stipulated in the standby letter of credit should its client fail to meet its contractual obligation to beneficiary. In this application, the issuing bank, Bank of America-San Francisco, is requested to make payment if the beneficiary, Hong Kong Water and Power Authority, states in writing that the issuing bank's client, Polyester Piping Corporation, has failed to perform in accordance with the terms and conditions of the contract.

2 The applicant is the party on whose behalf a standby letter of credit is issued. In this case, the standby letter of credit is issued by Bank of America-San Francisco on behalf of its customer (the applicant) Polyester Piping Corporation. The applicant is often referred to as the "account party."

3 The beneficiary is the party to whom the standby letter of credit is addressed and payment is made. In this example, the beneficiary is Hong Kong Water and Power Authority.

4 Bank of America will designate the advising bank unless Polyester Piping designates a particular bank at the request of Hong Kong Water and Power. The only responsibility of the advising bank is to verify the authenticity of the letter of credit through the signatures, and then to mail or deliver it to the beneficiary.

5 Bank of America-San Francisco will send the letter of credit via airmail to the advising bank for forwarding to the beneficiary, Hong Kong Water and Power. Standby letters of credit can also be sent by full text teletransmission to a bank for forwarding to the beneficiary or a brief teletransmission advice may be sent with full details to follow by airmail.

6 The amount refers to the total amount of the standby letter of credit. The applicant can specify that the amount be denominated in any currency, although only the major currencies are generally used.

7 This is the date on which the standby letter of credit expires.

8 According to the particular agreement between the buying and selling parties, the beneficiary can draw drafts "at sight" on the issuing bank or a named paying bank.

9 The standby letter of credit requires only the beneficiary's statement that the transaction was not completed properly in order to draw on the standby letter of credit. It is advisable to include the exact text of the required statement as an attachment to the letter of credit application.

10 This area allows for the stipulation of any special instructions by the applicant. In this application, the issuing bank is requested to agree to make payment if the beneficiary, Hong Kong Water and Power Authority, states in writing that the account party, Polyester Piping Corporation, has failed to perform in accordance with the terms and conditions of the contract. Because Bank of America-San Francisco is the paying bank (under a commercial letter of credit #1234 issued by Bank of America-Hong Kong Main), each time a drawing is made under the commercial letter of credit, Bank of America-San Francisco will automatically reduce the standby letter of credit by 50 percent of the invoice amount.

Figure 22-1. (*Continued*)

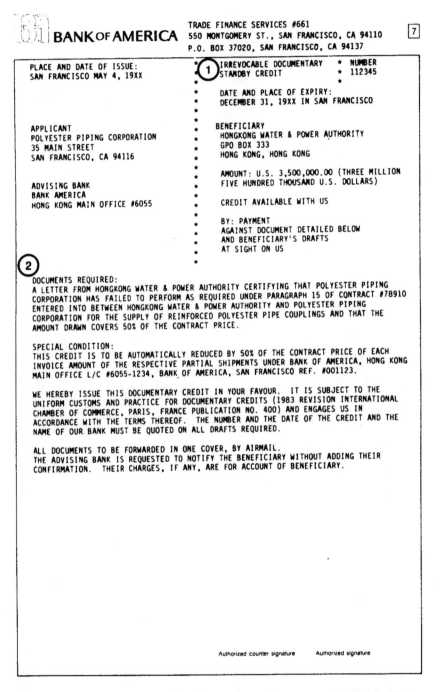

Figure 22-2. Irrevocable standby letter of credit. (*Reproduced with permission of Bank of America.*)

IRREVOCABLE STANDBY LETTER OF CREDIT

(1) An irrevocable standby letter of credit is a letter of credit that cannot be changed or modified without the consent of all parties involved.

(2) These are the particular terms and conditions of the credit, as outlined in the application for the standby letter of credit on page 32. Hong Kong Water and Power Authority, the beneficiary, can draw drafts on Bank of America-San Francisco only when these conditions are fulfilled. The required document in this case is a written statement certifying that Polyester Piping Corporation has failed to perform according to the established terms and conditions of its contract.

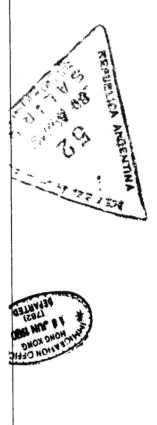

Figure 22-2. (*Continued*)

Agreement for Standby Letter of Credit

To: Bank of America NT&SA

I hereby apply to you for a loan to be made in connection with the letter of credit I am applying for on the other side (the "Letter of Credit"). This loan is to be (check one)

[X] in the principal amount of

Three million five hundred thousand U.S. Dollars

U.S. DOLLARS (U.S. $ 3,500,000.00).

[ ] (if the Letter of Credit is issued in a foreign currency) in the principal amount equal to the total of the U.S. dollar equivalents of the foreign currency amounts of all drawings under the Letter of Credit. To determine U.S. dollar equivalents, the foreign currency amount of each drawing will be converted to U.S. dollars at the rate of exchange you apply to that drawing.

This loan is subject to the following terms and conditions:

1. The loan will be disbursed only to pay drawings under the Letter of Credit. (Each disbursement is referred to as an "advance.")

2. Each advance will bear interest payable monthly at the annual rate of _____ * _____ percent (_____ * _____ %)

of the sum of (a) the interest rate that you publicly announce from time to time in San Francisco, California as your reference rate, plus (b) _____ * _____ percentage points. Any change in your reference rate will take effect at the opening of business on the day specified in your public announcement of a change in your reference rate. (The reference rate is set by you based on various factors, including your costs and desired return, general economic conditions and other factors, and is used as a reference point for pricing some loans. Loans may be priced at, above or below the reference rate.)

Interest will be computed on the basis of:

[ ] a three hundred sixty-five (365) day year and actual days elapsed.

[X] a three hundred sixty (360) day year and actual days elapsed. (This results in more interest payable than if a three hundred sixty-five (365) day year were used.)

Each advance will mature on the earlier of either

(a) _____ sixty _____ (60) days from the date it was disbursed, or (b) when any event specified in Paragraph 5 below occurs. Upon your request, following any advance I will execute and deliver to you a promissory note which includes these terms.

3. So long as any undisbursed portion of the loan remains available, I will pay you a commitment fee. This fee is payable (quarterly/semiannually/annually) in advance. It is computed from the date you issue the Letter of Credit on the undisbursed portion of the loan at the annual rate of _____ * _____ percent (_____ * _____ %) and on the basis of a three hundred sixty (360) day year and actual days elapsed. (The three hundred sixty (360) day year results in a larger fee than if a three hundred sixty-five (365) day year were used.) I agree that you will not refund any portion of the commitment fee paid for any quarter during which (a) the Letter of Credit expires or otherwise terminates, or (b) the undisbursed amount is reduced by drawings or by amendment.

4. If the cost to you of issuing or maintaining the Letter of Credit increases because of any reserves, special deposits, FDIC assessments or similar requirements imposed on you, I agree to pay you on demand an additional amount sufficient to compensate you for the increased cost, as determined by you.

5. You have the right to make all outstanding principal balances of advances and interest on advances immediately due and payable if any of the following events occurs:

(1) I default on any payment of principal, interest, or commitment fee under this agreement;
(2) I default on the payment of any other debt I owe;
(3) Any bankruptcy or similar proceeding is filed by or against me.

If at the time any such event occurs any portion of the loan is still undisbursed (that is, if the Letter of Credit is still in effect and has not been completely drawn against), I will, upon your demand, pay you for application to drawings under the Letter of Credit the entire undisbursed amount of the loan or, if the Letter of Credit is issued in a foreign currency, at your option the foreign currency amount not yet drawn under the Letter of Credit or the U.S. dollar equivalent of that foreign currency amount converted at your rate of exchange applicable at the time of your demand. If I have paid you that U.S. dollar equivalent and that payment, plus any further payments made pursuant to this sentence, becomes less than the U.S. dollar equivalent of the foreign currency amount not yet drawn because of exchange fluctuations, I will, upon your demand made from time to time, pay you such additional amounts of U.S. dollars as you require so that the total of the U.S. dollar amounts I have paid you is the U.S. dollar equivalent of that foreign currency amount, converted at your rate of exchange applicable at the time of the respective demand. Any amount so paid that has not been drawn on or before the expiration date of the Letter of Credit will be repaid to me without interest.

6. Neither you nor your correspondents will be in any way responsible for the beneficiary's performance of its obligations to me, nor for the form, sufficiency, correctness, genuineness, falsification or legal effect of or authority of person signing any documents called for under the Letter of Credit if these documents appear on their face to be in order.

I understand that the risk to me is greater if I request a clean Standby Letter of Credit rather than a documentary Standby Letter of Credit. With a clean Standby Letter of Credit, the beneficiary need not provide support documents to receive payments.

7. Subject to the laws, customs and practices of the trade in the area where the beneficiary is located, the Letter of Credit will be subject to, and performance under the Letter of Credit by you, your correspondents, and the beneficiary will be governed by, the "Uniform Customs and Practice for Documentary Credits (1983 Revision), International Chamber of Commerce, Publication No. 400," or by later Uniform Customs and Practice fixed by later Congresses of the International Chamber of Commerce as in effect on the date the Letter of Credit is issued.

8. I agree that all directions and correspondence regarding the Letter of Credit will be sent at my risk. You are not responsible for any inaccuracy, interruption, error or delay in transmission or delivery by post, courier or teletransmission or for any inaccuracy of translation.

9. I agree to pay all costs and expenses you may incur because of any dispute in connection with the Letter of Credit, including attorneys' fees for independent counsel and for your in-house counsel.

The foregoing is accepted and agreed to:

By (Authorized Signature and Title)

Bank of America NT&SA   X T. Jones   V.P.

Administration Use

Consumer Financial Services	Approved:
To: Regional Credit Administration # 3510	DATE May 3, 19XX
World Banking Division	CREDIT ADMINISTRATOR
To: [ ] Division Credit Administration # _____	
[ ] Division Area Office # _____	X

Office Use

		Check One	Check One	COMMITMENT FEE
[X] Recommended — CR-32/CR-115 in triplicate attached. Forward to Regional/Division Credit Administration.	[ ] Approved — One copy of CR-32/CR-115 or CR-116 to Credit Review Center (Reporting Only)	[ ] PREPAID / SOLD FOR CASH (UFE attached)	[ ] MONEY MARKET SUPPORT—TAXABLE	_____ * _____ %
FX-149 to: [X] International Services—San Francisco #661		[ ] SECURED BY CASH	[ ] MONEY MARKET SUPPORT—TAX EXEMPT	MINIMUM FEE
[ ] International Services—Los Angeles #662		[X] SECURED BY OTHER ASSETS (SPM 404.1(b) definition)	[ ] CONSTRUCT. / BID / PERFORM. BONDS	$ _____
FINANCIAL SERVICES OFFICER NAME (Type or Print) A. MacDonald	BANKAMERINET NO 622-4197	[ ] OTHER	[X] OTHER	
SIGNATURE X		[ ] Charge Branch		
		[X] Charge directly	[X] Commissions and charges only	
BRANCH / AMO NAME San Francisco Main Office	NO	D D A CUSTOMER A/C # 033-01234	[ ] Drawings, commissions and charges	

Figure 22-3. Agreement for standby letter of credit (*Reproduced with permission of Bank of America.*)

23

Documentary Collections

Just as the UCP 500 outlines the rules for letters of credit, so a code called the Uniform Rules for Collections (URC 322) outlines the regulations for banks and users of documentary collections, and the same institutional signatories generally agree to abide by them. URC 322, published by the International Chamber of Commerce, is much briefer than the letter of credit codes because it is a much simpler concept, with fewer responsibilities for all concerned.

Documentary collections are called many names, including the abbreviated title "collections." But using only the word "collections" implies that no documents are involved, a situation that would call for the term *clean drawing.* Sometimes, documentary collection is also referred to as selling on a sight draft basis, which is inaccurate. A draft, much like a check, is merely a demand for payment by the drawer, and when countersigned by the drawee and allowed to flow through the proper banking channels, accomplishes an exchange of money. When drawn at sight, the exchange is immediate; if it is a usance draft, the exchange is set for a certain number of days from acceptance. The key to documentary collection is that the buyer receives the documents only after the sight draft is paid or a usance draft accepted. Therefore, it is best to use the term *documentary collection,* or better yet, the more specific phrases *documents against payment* (D/P) or documents against acceptance (D/A). There is rare use of the term *cash against documents* (CAD) for a procedure in which demand is made against an invoice and shipping documents in place of a draft, which would be more likely to occur in the context of a nonbank third party's involvement. In any case, it is important to understand that, insofar as a bank is concerned, it is serving only as conduit, and takes no responsibility for collection.

Documents against Payment

Under these terms, the exporter draws a draft (also called a bill of exchange) on the buyer for the amount of the sale. In a document against payment (D/P) transaction, this amounts to a demand draft made out by the exporter (drawer) on the importer (drawee) through the foreign bank (collecting bank) that has received the collection from the exporter's remitting bank. It is much like a check, except that it is made out by the payee instead of the payor. It does not matter whether the collecting bank has an account for the importer, because the importer can simply pay the bank the amount of the draft on presentation. When the collecting bank is paid or is allowed to charge the draft to the importer's bank account, it endorses over to the buyer the ocean bill of lading, together with any other accompanying documents. On presentation of the bill of lading, the buyer can obtain the merchandise from the steamship line or otherwise have access to it for import clearance. Until the drafts are paid, the exporter retains title and control of the goods shipped, thus requiring the importer to pay before obtaining the goods.

There is nothing to prevent the importer from refusing to acknowledge the call for presentation (and therefore payment) made by the foreign bank, thus creating a nonacceptance. In this case, the shipment is considered abandoned and the exporter has the choice of having the merchandise returned for sale on the domestic market or selling it to another buyer in the region. If the importer fails to accept the draft, the banks involved have no further responsibility except for certain notification requirements. Most banks, however, feel some responsibility to take at least minimal action to protect the merchandise while making follow-up contact with the buyer or waiting for instructions from the seller.

It can be of some advantage to request that your bank present the draft through a collecting bank that is the importer's primary bank, rather than through the U.S. bank's correspondent, which is the normal procedure. Using the importer's bank might possibly result in some passive moral suasion on its part over your customer if it appears to the bank that its client is acting in an irresponsible or capricious manner concerning nonacceptance. Aside from nonacceptance, there is the further risk that somehow the merchandise may come into the possession of the importer before payment, or that the importer's financial situation may suddenly deteriorate, or even that the currency exchange availabilities in the country may change. Therefore, credit references must be obtained and country as well as commercial risks considered.

These procedures for documentary collections apply to ocean shipments only, and adjustments to these procedures must be made for air shipments. This is because of a fundamental difference in the documentary practices of the two transportation modes. In the case of air shipments, the shipping evidence and contract is an air waybill or air transport document, which is little more than a shipper's receipt and contract. It is not a negotiable title document, as in the case of an ocean bill of lading. On arrival, the importer or an agent need only ask for the shipment, which will be handed over if the importer's name is on the air waybill as the consignee. Provided someone has paid the freight, nothing more is needed to obtain the shipment for custom's clearance. Therefore, to achieve the purpose and gain the protection afforded by D/P, do not show the importer's name on the documents, but rather a third party as consignee. It is obviously necessary to obtain advance agreement from that party, which may be the collecting bank, a foreign customs broker, or the shipper's own agent. In fact, URC 322 specifies that advance agreement must be obtained. The importer's name should be mentioned as a notify party for easy identification of the shipment. It is understood among all parties, including the airline, that the goods will not be physically delivered to this third party. If you fail to note this procedure, air shipments sent for collection will have little more protection than an open account transaction, and the importer could easily obtain the goods before payment.

Documentary Collection Bank Procedures

Banks have a fairly standard form, called a collection instruction and receipt, that must be completed. The section of this form called Collection Instructions can be somewhat confusing, especially the boxes labeled Protest and No Protest. See Figure 23-1 for an example of the collection instruction and receipt.

Protest Versus No Protest

Protest means that in the event of nonpayment or nonacceptance, the bank must make formal presentation through a notary or similar official. If good customer relations are of interest, this is seldom requested in practice, since it could needlessly annoy buyers who may be delaying acceptance or payment of the draft until the shipment has actually arrived in port (a common practice). In some countries, it could seriously embarrass the buyer because of practices such as the advertising of protests.

The protest does not ensure payment and can be expensive and is of little value unless you have reason to feel you may have to take the collection to court. In that event, protest can be very helpful, and can also be a factor in foreign risk insurance claims. *No Protest* means that the collecting bank will not automatically protest, but you are not waiving any rights. It does mean, however, you will have to otherwise establish that proper procedures were followed should you subsequently go to court. It would be a good idea to discuss the options presented by these collection instructions with your bank's documentary advisor.

When the foreign bank (the collecting bank) receives the money from your buyer, it remits the funds to your bank (the remitting bank). If the foreign bank is unable to present the documents for collection or does not transfer funds within a reasonable time, your bank is expected to automatically trace the transaction to obtain an advice of fate. This does not relieve you of the responsibility

TO **Bank of America**
National Trust and Savings Association

(1) COLLECTION INSTRUCTIONS AND RECEIPT

TRADE FINANCE SERVICES #661
BOX 37020
550 MONTGOMERY STREET
SAN FRANCISCO, CA 94137

(2) [X] COLLECTION

March 4, 19XX
Date

WE ENCLOSE FOR   [ ] IMMEDIATE CREDIT   DRAFT(S) AND DOCUMENTS DESCRIBED BELOW:

COLLECTION INSTRUCTIONS ARE MARKED "X"	
X	Forward to YOUR CORRESPONDENT **(3)**
	Forward to:
X	Deliver documents against PAYMENT **(4)**
	Deliver documents against ACCEPTANCE
X	DO NOT PROTEST **(5)**
	PROTEST for non-payment and/or non-acceptance
	Collect interest from DRAWEE(S) @ %P.A. to approximate date proceeds arrive in
X	Your Correspondent's charges are to be paid by DRAWEE(S).
X	Your charges are to be paid by DRAWEE(S).
	All charges will be paid by us.
X	Waive all charges if refused by the DRAWEE(S) and charge them to us.

(7) DETAILS OF DRAFT NO. 1250

(8) DRAWN ON: East Africa Suppliers, Ltd.
P.O. Box 60032
Nairobi, Kenya

(9) TENOR Sight   **(10)** AMOUNT: $7,600

(11) [ ] ADDITIONAL DRAFT(S) ARE DESCRIBED ON REVERSE SIDE WITH THE DOCUMENTS WHICH ACCOMPANY EACH DRAFT. All other instructions remain the same for collection.

(12) INSTRUCT YOUR COLLECTING BANK TO:

ADVISE NON-ACCEPTANCE and/or NON-PAYMENT BY:	ADVISE PAYMENT BY:	REMIT FUNDS BY:
X CABLE	X CABLE	X CABLE TRANSFER
AIRMAIL	AIRMAIL	AIRMAIL

(6) (13) DISPOSITION OF FUNDS

	CREDIT our(my) Commercial Account at
X	Mail your Check to us(me).

IN CASE OF NEED REFER TO **(14)** _____
ADDRESS_____
WHO IS AUTHORIZED BY US to endeavor to obtain honoring of the draft as drawn without altering any of our instructions.

DOCUMENTS	BILL OF LADING	INSURANCE	CONSULAR INVOICE	CERTIF. ORIGIN	INVOICE	INSPEC. CERTIF.	QUALITY CERTIF.	WEIGHT CERTIF.	SANITARY CERTIF.	OTHER DOCUMENTS
No. Enclosed **(15)**	3/3	**(16)** 3			4			**(17)**		

COVERING SHIPMENTS OF Agricultural Tools   VIA S.S.Eventide   **(18)** B/L #3767

ALL DOCUMENTS TO BE FORWARDED IN ONE COVER, BY AIRMAIL, UNLESS OTHERWISE STATED UNDER SPECIAL INSTRUCTIONS.

SPECIAL INSTRUCTIONS If required by exchange regulations, release documents against provisional payment in local currency and drawee(s) written undertaking to remain responsible for any exchange fluctuation. Surrender draft when dollar remittance effected.

If immediate credit has been given for the drafts described hereon or on the reverse hereof, it is understood that such credit is conditional and is subject to collection and receipt by you of the requisite number of dollars; in the absence of such receipt and collection by you, the undersigned will, upon your demand, reimburse you for the amount so advanced plus the agreed rate of interest for the time outstanding. If the collection is returned unpaid, documents are to be returned by regular mail to the address below.

FOR BANK USE ONLY

In receiving items for deposit or collection, this Bank acts only as depositor's collecting agent and assumes no responsibility beyond the exercise of due care. All items are credited subject to final payment in cash or solvent credits. This Bank will not be liable for default or negligence of its duly selected correspondents nor for losses in transit, and each correspondent so selected shall not be liable except for its own negligence. This Bank or its correspondents may send items directly or indirectly to any Bank, including the payor, and accept its draft or credit as conditional payment in lieu of cash, it may charge back any item at any time before final payment, whether returned or not, also any item drawn on this Bank not good at close of business on day deposited. Unless otherwise specified, this collection is subject to the uniform rules for the collection of commercial paper, International Chamber of Commerce, Brochure No. 322.

(19) Transglobe Manufacturing Co.
Firm or Individual's Name

333 Van Ness Ave., S.F. CA/
Address   94127

C H Marlin
Authorized Signature

FX-5 12-80 ORIGINAL

Figure 23-1. Collection instruction and receipt. (*Reproduced with permission of Bank of America.*)

COLLECTION INSTRUCTIONS & RECEIPT

1 Bank of America, acting as the exporter's agent, forwards the documents and collection instructions to a bank in the buyer's location for presentation to the importer. Upon payment by the importer, the documents are delivered to him, and the funds are remitted to Bank of America and paid to the exporter.

2 In this case, the seller has checked the "collection" box, indicating that the exporter receives his money when the importer pays. If the seller checks the "immediate credit" box, this indicates the exporter receives an immediate credit under a previously established line of credit, at a rate of interest established by arrangement between the exporter and Bank of America. However, if the collection is unpaid, the exporter will be required to repay the bank.

3 If, according to the contract between buyer and seller, the buyer does not prefer that a particular collecting bank be used, Bank of America-San Francisco will send the collection to its nearest branch or correspondent bank. Had East Africa Suppliers Ltd. indicated its own bank, that bank's name and address would have been listed under the "forward to" section.

4 "Deliver documents against payment" applies to sight drafts and indicates that the buyer is to pay immediately for the collection in order to receive the documents. "Deliver documents against acceptance" applies to time or usance drafts and means that, in order to receive the documents, the buyer is to accept the drafts for future payment.

5 By checking the "do not protest" box, Transglobe Manufacturing Co. has determined that if the buyer, East Africa Suppliers Ltd., refuses to make payment, the collecting bank is not to make further legal presentations. A "protest" may arise when a buyer refuses payment of a draft he accepted previously. In the case of a protest, the collecting bank is directed to make a formal presentation through a notary or similar official. This establishes legal evidence that the collecting bank has presented the necessary drafts and documents to the buyer, which may be beneficial if court action is required to collect payment.

6 The arrangement between buyer and seller should specify which party will assume payment for the collection charges and should be indicated here.

7 This number must be identical to the number on the draft.

8 The seller must include the buyer's name and complete address.

9 The seller also must designate whether the draft is payable at sight or, in the case of a time or usance draft, if it is payable at a determined number of days after sight. For collections involving usance drafts, the collecting bank presents the usance draft to the importer for acceptance and, unless directed by the exporter to return the accepted draft to the exporter, will hold the accepted draft until the due date. On the due date, the accepted draft is presented

for collection with payment to be made by the importer. The exporter carries the costs of both the merchandise and the shipment until the acceptance matures and the importer pays. This transaction is known as a trade acceptance, for the bank has neither an obligation nor a commitment to pay a trade acceptance on maturity, should the importer fail to pay. Instead, the exporter assumes the risk of the importer's non-payment.

10 Here, the seller should indicate the particular currency of the draft and the amount.

11 If applicable, the seller should note that more than one draft and set of documents are being sent under one collection and should provide a description on the reverse side of this form.

12 While the seller can choose to have the collecting bank respond either by cable or by airmail, cable is a faster form of advice, albeit more expensive, and is recommended for international collections.

13 "Disposition of funds" is instructions the exporter gives to Bank of America-San Francisco and indicates how Bank of America-San Francisco is to remit to Transglobe Manufacturing Co.

14 "In case of need" is an agent in the vicinity of the buyer who represents the seller. If, for instance, the buyer fails to perform as expected, it may be necessary for the seller to rely on his agent.

15 In this section, the seller notes the number of all documents attached to the collection.

16 Here, the seller need include only a very brief description of the merchandise.

17 The name of the vessel carrying the goods should be mentioned here.

18 This is the bill of lading number.

19 This represents the name of the exporter and should include a complete address, as well as the signature of an authorized officer or individual.

Figure 23-1. (*Continued*)

to follow up with the bank and the consignee, but you do have the assurance, by virtue of standard banking practices, that efforts to present will continue to be made until the collecting or presenting bank is advised by your bank to abandon the effort. The bank will then ask what disposition you wish made of the documents and the merchandise. There is space on the instruction and receipt form to give the name of an agent or office that the collecting bank is to call in case of need to protect your interests and your shipment. Any special powers your agent may have on your behalf should be stated in the form.

Documents against Payment without Using Domestic Remitting Banks

Because of continuously increasing bank charges, some firms using D/P terms routinely shortcut the normal procedure for smaller transactions to which minimum fees apply. These firms send the documents directly to the foreign collecting bank without going through the exporter's remitting bank, thus saving part of the fee but losing the helpful assistance of the exporter's bank and the benefit of the interbank relationship and communication for follow-up. The overseas bank thus becomes both the remitting and collecting bank. It is best done only by prior arrangement with the consignee's bank.

If you are faced with the necessity of many small transactions for which letter of credit terms are too expensive but you want the protection of D/P terms, this procedure can offer worthwhile savings. With or without a domestic remitting bank, there are clear advantages to documentary collections, apart from the payment prior to receipt feature. The advantages include low costs to both parties in terms of fees and finance costs, and often faster payment than in the case of open account.

Documents against Acceptance

Documents against acceptance (D/A) is exactly like documents against payment except that, instead of sighting the sight draft and paying on presentation of documents to receive the bill(s) of lading, the importer signs a usance (time) draft that creates an obligation similar to a promissory note called a *trade acceptance.* This can be used for financing purposes under some conditions. This is a promise to pay in a certain number of days after accepting the documents, usually for a term of between 30 and 180 days (the normal maximum). The terms of documents against acceptance are more secure than those of open account because the transaction and receipt of goods are evidenced by a negotiable instrument. It is much easier to enforce a financial instrument than an account receivable, which must be proven to the courts. However, a sharp increase of risk in D/A over D/P occurs because the importer now has the goods, and the exporter only has a promise to pay. The bank has no responsibility to collect the funds on or after the due date. Both your bank and the foreign bank are purely conduits, or agents, for transmittal and collection.

It is very important not to confuse a banker's acceptance, which carries the credit of a bank, with a trade acceptance, which is the case being considered here. A trade acceptance is no better than the credit and integrity of the buyer in contrast to a bank's normally high credit rating.

Figure 23-1 which is a model collection instruction and receipt with accompanying line-by-line instructions will help provide an idea of the procedures for documentary collections.

24

Export Contracts

For many transactions, nothing more than a simple fax memo can serve as both the purchase order and a form of contractual agreement. In the July/August 1993 issue of *Exporter* magazine, Michael Forzley writes that the fax, or any other form of electronic transmission, now makes international transactions so fast and easy that businesspeople need some kind of format and structure guiding the exchange of communication to ensure that the end result is a prudent, mutually understood, and enforceable contract, or alternatively, a nonbinding offer to buy or sell. He suggests keeping in mind the basic four elements of a sales contract: (1) what to sell; (2) at what price; (3) in what quantity; (4) of what quality. With these elements offered and accepted by some kind of mark serving as a signature, you have a fax that represents a binding contract.[1]

But what about delivery? Does urgent, immediate delivery or delivery well into the future change the offer so materially as to void the understanding? If common sense tells you that either fast or extended delivery is extreme and well away from the industry's norm, there is no deal. If it is not that patently apparent, then there could be an open question that might create serious misunderstandings or litigation. The issue of delivery is but one of many factors that should be clarified so you can know you have a safe and comfortable deal, which is why an underlying and consistent structure needs to be part of your transaction pattern. Such opportunities for misunderstanding are much less likely within the measured and thoughtful pace of pro forma invoice preparation or contract negotiations.

If a letter of credit is involved, the credit itself may be the only, but very rigid, evidence of a contractual relationship. It is often a mistake to let the letter of credit function as a contract. Keep in mind that a letter of credit is strictly documentary and provides funds to the seller and protection for the buyer solely on a prima facie basis. The bank properly refuses to be in a position of interpreting an agreement or referring to other documents or conditions, even though reference may be made to them in the letter of credit. In the event of complicating issues, such as inspections, installation of service, deposits, guarantees, or progressive drawings on projects, a contract becomes necessary for both parties. Should a technical, even a nonmaterial, discrepancy result in your being unable to collect under the credit, a signed agreement or even just a detailed purchase order could be vital to collecting outside the credit by negotiation, arbitration, or litigation.

Another instance in which a contract is a wise precaution is when the transaction is governed by forces not entirely under the control of the seller (especially as a third-party exporter), and the normal rules or customs of the industry or situation contradict the conventional practices in that area of international trade. The case of the exporter selling textiles overseas illustrates the point. The American textile industry has many well-established rules within the industry (such as providing that the buyer must accept and pay for overruns up to a given percentage) and various rules on an allowable percentage of flaws and other specific situations, which to the foreign buyer are probably unacceptable.

So it can be seen that there may be good reasons of expediency to sell under conditions of a quick exchange of faxes and/or more prudent reasons to take the time for a more detailed contract or pro forma invoice. But both can and should result in a binding agreement that possibly may be governed by a United Nations international commercial code rather than that of the country of the buyer or seller, without any reference to governing law by either party to the agreement.

UN Convention on Contracts for International Sale of Goods

A treaty called the United Nations Convention on Contracts for the International Sale of Goods (CISG), also known as the Vienna Sale Convention, effective in January of 1988, is becoming more often a factor in interpreting what you assumed was a common understanding. This can potentially be helpful in minimizing disputes, and in speeding a fair settlement of those disputes that do occur. It can also present problems, especially to those unaware it would be the governing body of law. The negotiations leading to the CISG were conducted under the auspices of the United Nations Commission on International Trade Law (UNCITRAL) and, as of 1994, had 35 signatory countries with still more pending adoption of what is rapidly becoming a global uniform commercial code.

One slight cause of confusion, however, is the fact that each ratifying party can declare any one of five standard reservations to the convention, so contracting parties must ascertain how a given reservation selected by the country of either party will affect them. The United States has reserved that CISG will only apply to the U.S. party when the other party also has its place of business in a

CISG contracting country. So besides having a current list of signature nations, it is useful to know what reservations were declared by any particular country.

As a signatory to the convention, the United States now has in effect two sets of commercial law that can be applied to contracts: our own model Uniform Commercial Code (UCC), adapted by each state with slight variations for domestic transactions, and the Vienna Sales Convention, which applies to an international sales contract if the governments of all parties to the contract have signed the convention. Of course, this new body of law may be specified not to apply, and some other body of code or law may be substituted in whole or in part by the contracting parties themselves. American businesses are fortunate in that much of the CISG parallels articles of the U.S. UCC. Therefore, traders in this country should be more at home with this new law than traders in many other nations are. Even when the buyer and seller wish to have their contract interpreted under the laws of their own countries, CISG may supply some terms not specified in their agreement or by the laws of their countries.

In spite of the reference to the similarity with UCC, there are pronounced differences between CISG and UCC in some areas. Listed below are a few examples brought to light by various attorneys studying the CISG, including Mr. Forzley.[2]

- The U.S., but few other countries, requires "some writing" for a contract of $500 or more to be enforceable; CISG does not, nor does it have anything comparable to the Statute of Frauds.

- CISG requires that a "sale" is occurring—not a financing, license, franchise or joint venture agreement. Unless there is a buy-and-sell event, but not a sale at retail, the CISG does not apply.

- An offer is irrevocable if sufficiently definite (as in the basic four provisions); and if it is accepted without material change, a contract has been formed, unless a time limit for its validity has been stated and the acceptance is made after the limit. Unlike the UCC, under CISG no contract can be formed without specified prices. An offer may be withdrawn if the offer reaches the offeree before the offeree has accepted. Acceptance, coupled with material modifications, constitutes a counteroffer rather than acceptance. (Note that acceptance is formed as of when acceptance is received by the offeror, not when it was mailed or transmitted as in the UCC rules.)

- If you wish additional details to be incorporated into the contract beyond the basic provisions mentioned, it must be made clear that they are to be in writing, and that there will no contract until all points of the agreement are resolved by fax, telex, or in writing. Certain points of agreement, however, must be in writing. Two that have been highlighted are: (1) an election to arbitrate disputes rather than litigate; and (2) any waivers to be made of product liability.

- The buyer must notify the seller of any nonconformity and, if it is fundamental, the buyer can reject the goods unless the buyer can rectify the breach in reasonable time; otherwise, the goods must be accepted and a price adjustment made as damages.

- Maximum time for discovery of a defect by the buyer may be as long as two years, although notification is still required in a reasonable time after discovery. (In the UCC, time for discovery must not exceed three months.)

The convention deals only with sales contracts, acceptance by the buyer as in U.S. law, buyer/seller obligations, transfer of risk in the goods, breach of contract, and remedies. It does not cover transfer of ownership or criteria for validity, which are left to national laws, nor does it cover service contracts. It also does not cover payment procedures, such as letters of credit or collections, which are left to the ICC conventions. With reference to ICC conventions, there may be a difference between Incoterms and CISG which refers to transfer of risk of loss at the place of delivery. However, since both the UCC and CISG allow for supplementation of agreements with trade usages and established conventions, there should be no conflict. In transactions of substance it is a good idea to insert the word "Incoterms" in parentheses next to the shipping terms acronym as clarification. In fact, it is a very good idea to have printed transaction forms that specify or confirm shipping terms by printing "Incoterms" in the box on the form used for that purpose.

Any U.S. firm exporting to a signatory country should study the law to determine if it wishes to be bound, and if so bound, what reservations might be in effect and if there are specific terms it wishes to include in lieu of contractual agreement or domestic law. If not excluded, CISG will apply. If both buyer and seller are governed by countries that are party to the CISG, do not wish to be covered, and instead can agree on a jurisdiction whose law will govern the agreement (presumably this would be a U.S. jurisdiction, for otherwise it would seem wise to stick with CISG unless you were very familiar with the commercial code in the buyer's country), it is not sufficient to say "the laws of New York apply," because under some circumstances the CISG would be the law of the State of New York. It is suggested that a clause such as the following be added to the contract:

> The provisions of the Uniform Commercial Code as adopted by the State of New York, and not the United Nations Convention on Contracts for the International Sale of Goods (Vienna Convention), apply to this agreement.

You can study a complete copy of the code at your DOC district office, or you can find it on pages 6262–6280 in the *Federal Register* of March 2, 1987. Additional information is also available from the American Bar Association, Section of International Law and Practice in Chicago; or from the Treaty Section, Office of Legal Affairs, United Nations, United Nations Plaza, New York, New York 10017.

The Pro Forma Invoice as a Contract

There are several means of formalizing or expressing a sales agreement between the buyer and seller besides the purchase order, and the pro forma invoice is one of them. It is a useful document for many purposes and, if acknowledged by the buyer, it can have the effect of serving as a contract. It is also a commonly used method of providing the buyer the necessary information with which to open a letter of credit. In the body of the pro forma, a brief statement can be made of certain conditions, preferably with the suggestion of specific clauses to be inserted in the letter of credit if applicable. It is also advisable to link the delivery date to a certain number of days from receipt of the letter of credit if it is your intention not to start the procurement for the project, goods or services ordered until the letter of credit is in hand. If this clause goes beyond a few short paragraphs, you might consider the next step, which is a detailed acknowledgment form. (See the section on pro forma invoices in Chapter 18.)

The Order Acknowledgment as a Contract

A formal order acknowledgment, countersigned by the buyer, is a good format for a sales agreement and is used by many exporters. How practical and necessary it will prove to be is governed by the time available, the detail in the buyer's purchase order, and whether it is signed or the sale was entirely conducted via telecommunication.

The pro forma is more of an initiating document, while the acknowledgment is more of a reactive document. An acknowledgment can substitute for a hard copy of the signed purchase order or confirm additional terms and conditions that the seller has had to place on the transaction not covered in the buyer's purchase order.

The acknowledgment is especially valuable if your terms are other than a letter of credit, but even if a letter of credit is forthcoming, you may need the acknowledgment to place your supplier orders before the letter of credit arrives. While the increasing use of telex transmission of the operating letter of credit lessens this problem, many importers delay opening the letter of credit for financial or other reasons, including lack of confidence in the exporter's ability to perform.

A formal order acknowledgment accepts and identifies the purchase order without necessarily repeating all its details. It clarifies delivery schedules and other details that, if clearly stated, may improve the seller's position in the event of a dispute. It should always be drawn by the seller, and it is intended to be countersigned by the buyer. An acknowledgment form, with the reverse side reciting in detail the codified rules of several American industries in fine print, was used by one firm for years without a single objection—even though it stated that the buyer accepted the conditions printed on the reverse side. This form probably did not have the strength of a real contract, but it would have been helpful if a transaction had gone sour and required arbitration. Incidentally, the reverse side also specified settlement by American arbitration in the event of a dispute. If you propose to develop such a form, be sure to get the assistance of an attorney, and preferably one with some international experience. One would not normally use an acknowledgment, if a signed pro forma invoice had been, or was to be, provided and formally identified in the buyer's confirmation and acceptance.

Formal Contracts

When you are engaged in a transaction requiring a complete contractual agreement, it's a good idea to be its initiator, and at least for the first contract covering that particular subject, to obtain the assistance of an attorney. The fees you save by letting your buyer be the initiator of the language and details of your agreement can cost you dearly later on. If it is not practical for you to draw the contract, at least have your attorney review it. Keep in mind that it is the contract that should control the performance of all parties, not the letter of credit. A letter of credit is used only to see that the parties are paid on fulfillment of its conditions. Any sale or transaction is an implied contract to which you have rights in court even if, because of a discrepancy or for other nonessential reasons, you cannot obtain payment under the letter of credit that supported the transaction.

The contract formats for guideline purposes are mentioned in Appendices P, Q, and R. However, there are many more formal and authoritative sources that have been suggested to us for a variety of international agreements that might be researched.[3] In addition, the United Nations Industrial Development Organization (UNIDO) will often provide model form agreements that can be incorporated into the exporter's own international agreement.

Before signing a contract for an international transaction, whether for goods, services, or a project, pay particular attention to developing triggers that force certain things to happen and help prevent your transaction from being stalled by silence or inaction. With the language, time, and distance barriers that are still inherent in international trade, even with modern communications, it can be relatively easy for a buyer to delay receiving or accepting the goods and paying for them. Carefully crafted contracts and the letters of credit that go with them can minimize this problem. (One example is the automatic waiving of the right of inspection if, after proper advance notice as to time and place, the buyer is not present during the conduct of the required test.) Triggers can be built into letters of credit as well, but it is often more difficult.

Arbitration

One good reason for a written contract or agreement is that this is the best opportunity to spell out the use of arbitration in the event of a dispute. Controversies are not necessarily more likely in international trade than in domestic transactions, but they are usually more difficult to resolve. Gaining jurisdiction over a foreign party for the purpose of litigation is costly and time-consuming, and court judgments can prove difficult to execute. Furthermore, it is desirable to resolve the dispute in the friendliest and least-expensive manner, while overcoming the natural barriers created by differences in language, culture, and varying court procedures.

Some of the practical aspects of arbitration are as follows:

- The contracting parties can negotiate and select in advance the arbitration as well as the language, the country, the arbitration group, and the nationalities of its arbitrators in advance.

- No party need enjoy advantages or be disadvantaged relative to other parties because of this flexibility.

- Privacy is assured, since there are no court records.

- A party inclined to breach the contract has less of an advantage derived from uncertainty as to the effectiveness of the settlement process.

- Conversely, the lack of a discovery phase can work to one party's disadvantage if the other party has all the witnesses.

- There is no opportunity to gain interim relief.

- Experience has shown that, if the outcome depends primarily on a point of law rather than facts, you may be better off before a court of law.

- Decisions are final and binding on all parties and widely respected internationally, with 95 countries now acceding to the New York Convention by which a nation agrees to recognize and enforce arbitral awards, in addition to several other multilateral conventions to that effect. In fact, most international arbitral awards using recognized standards normally receive voluntary compliance.

Although there are surely many other pros and cons, on balance most international contracts call for settlement by arbitration. This is usually speedier and less expensive in the long run and thought to be more efficient and practical in the main. Arbitration is also more likely to be impartial in terms of nationalities, especially if a three-person arbitration panel includes one neutral nationality. Many buyers are quite satisfied to have arbitration in the United States, while others will insist it be in a neutral country. The UN Convention on Recognition and Enforcement of Foreign Arbitral Awards, adopted in 1970, (New York Convention) provides that each signatory recognize foreign arbitral awards as binding and enforceable so long as certain minimal requirements are met. There is also a similar Inter-American Convention on International Arbitration that the United States finally ratified in 1990, which is important in terms of helping to overcome Latin American reluctance in accepting arbitration.

The choice of which country to choose should be influenced by the choice of the international arbitration organization. Fees for administration and arbitration vary considerably and therefore should be considered when making this choice. The two best known to American companies are: the American Arbitration Association (AAA), 140 West 51st Street, New York, New York 10020; and the U.S. Council of the International Chamber of Commerce (ICC), 1212 Avenue of the Americas, New York, New York 10036. (While the latter is the United States contact, the headquarters of the ICC Court of Arbitration are in Paris.)

In addition, arbitration can be done under the UNCITRAL Arbitration Rules, but there is no existing institution that administrates them as is the case of those mentioned here. A more complete list is shown in Appendix G. Contracts drawn involving the People's Republic of China seem to lean to arbitration in Sweden by the Stockholm Chamber of Commerce arbitration group if they are unsuccessful in negotiating their first choice, which is the Arbitration Committee of the China Council for the Promotion of International Trade in Beijing.

For most companies, it is best that the arbitration clause specifies an international, institutionalized forum and, therefore, an established set of rules for arbitration. All the forums mentioned can provide further information. When drawing a contract, the arbitration clause is very important because if advance thought has been given to the arbitration organization and the country in which the arbitration is to take place, the arbitration rules of that organization can be covered more or less by reference to that organization's standard rules. The number of arbitrators and the method of choosing them, as well as the place of arbitration in most cases, must still be spelled out. The number of arbitrators is important because of its influence on cost. A fee is paid to each arbitrator, so that using one in place of three can be a major saving, especially in the case of disputes concerning small amounts. In fact, the ICC International Court of Arbitration reports a clear trend toward a sole arbitrator; as of 1993, 45 percent were handled in this fashion. The arbitration agreement can specify the use of one arbitrator up to some dollar limit, and thereafter up to three. The organization selected will provide its own model clause. For example, in the case of ICC the model clause is:

> All disputes arising in connection with the present contract shall be finally settled under the Rules of Conciliation and Arbitration of the International Chamber of Commerce by one or more arbitrators in accordance with the said Rules.

Experts recommend using the clause exactly as stated to avoid further arguments about the scope and meaning of the clause that can come into question by the arbitrators once any change is made.

Arbitration is further advanced by the U.S. adoption of UNCITRAL's Model Arbitration Law, which provides for a fair and neutral environment in which to settle disputes. It is anticipated that a number of states will in turn adopt the model law as part of their state codes, as California has done. This makes it increasingly certain that the results of arbitrated disputes will be equally effective abroad as in this country, and foreign parties to contracts arbitrated in the

United States can also have increased confidence in the process and execution.

Other organizations, such as the World Bank and various trade associations and chambers of commerce, also provide arbitration assistance. Costs of arbitration are fairly reasonable as legal costs go. Naturally, the percentage cost of arbitration is much higher for smaller amounts. ICC, whose fees are thought to be among the highest, estimates that a $1 million case settled by one arbitrator would require an advance of $45,475 (4.5 percent) from the two parties combined, with possible additional charges, depending on circumstances. A $25 million dispute might cost as little as 1.5 percent to settle, while disputes in the range of $25,000 would cost closer to 15 percent.

Endnotes

1. Michael Forzley, "Selling by FAX," *The Exporter,* July/August 1993.

2. Michael Forzley, "U.N. Convention on Contracts for International Sale of Goods," *The Exporter,* November 1993.

3. Among such sources are: Fox, *International Commercial Agreements,* Kluwer Law and Taxation Publishers, Norwell, Massachusetts; Nelson (ed.), *Digest of Commercial Laws of the World: Forms of Commercial Agreements,* Oceana Publications, Inc., Dobbs Ferry, New York, N.Y.; Ezer, *International Exporting Agreements,* Matthew Bender & Co., New York, N.Y.; Thomas E. Johnson, *Export/Import Procedures and Documentation,* 2nd edition, AMACOM, Saranac Lake, N.Y., 1995.

25

Managing Export Risks

Business cannot be done without some risks, and the businesses in greatest peril are those that do not take the time to perceive and analyze those risks. Their folly is only exceeded by that of the businesses that perceive the risks, but do nothing to mitigate them. Risks should be a controllable part of the firms' long-range expense structure. Of course, catastrophic or uninsurable events are an exception to this rule, but some risks are caused by premeditated management decisions, such as doing international business on credit terms as a competitive measure. Even letters of credit carry a degree of commercial and political risk, depending on the country, the bank, and the exporter's ability to meet the conditions, but most export businesses will eventually do some open-account business, if for nothing more than samples or replacement parts.

Transit risks, too, cannot be avoided entirely, even if shipment terms are Ex-Works. But sound decisions and prudent insurance coverage, combined with good management that leaves no doubt that the insurance you have is fully in effect and protecting you can take the gamble out of this risk. It is even possible to cover the transit risk that is implied, but often not recognized, when the buyer rather than the seller insures the shipment.

It is important to understand how to analyze and seek information about the degree and character of the risks involved and to consider the costs of protecting against those risks. They should be part of your day-to-day cost of doing business that gets budgeted into your direct cost or overhead when making export quotations.

Analyzing Foreign Credit Risks

Accurate and up-to-date credit information is even more essential in international trade than it is in domestic selling. Credit reports will help you make decisions in choosing your representative or other buyers. Even though your selling terms may be letters of credit, a good customer with excellent credit may still be forced to ask that the opening of the credit be deferred to a predetermined date prior to shipment but later than confirmation of the order because of cash-flow considerations. You, in turn, may have to make a partial investment relating to such an order before the letter of credit is scheduled to be received. Therefore, you certainly need to know the credit standing of the customer in terms of its ability to open a letter of credit.

Another reason to get credit reports is to have some assurance of the integrity of your customers in case there is a discrepancy when collecting against letters of credit. Acceptance of noncritical discrepancies without undue delay is often the mark of firms that are both pleasurable and profitable to do business with. Still another important reason for background information on your customers, quite apart from determining their ability to pay, is ascertaining their knowledge and skill relative to purchasing your product and being able to conclude the transaction competently. Dealing with unknowing or naive buyers is often the first step toward contract disputes or unjustified claims.

The prime tools for credit decisions and information on overseas customers are identical to those for domestic transactions. Your own ledger experience remains one of the best sources if you have a history with your customer. A valuable source that is commonly requested for domestic purposes, but often wrongly neglected in foreign business, is a balance sheet and operating statement, if a substantial sum is at stake. Accounting is a universal language, although rules for contents and preparation of a specific account are far from universal. This is evidenced by the fact that most of the big six accounting firms in this country have offices or branches in most of the industrialized or even newly industrialized countries (NICs) in the world to handle U.S. subsidiaries and joint venture activities by U.S. firms.

Although accounting is universal, credit evaluation and extension is not. The June 1992 issue of *Export Today* makes a specific analysis and comparison concerning the vastly different standards for financial evaluation and decision that exist among various developed countries, as well as making mention of many anecdotes concerning these practices in less-developed countries.[1] Of particular note are the standards in Southeast Asia. In that fast-paced growth area, companies come, go, and grow, with alarming rapidity. Since the business community is dominated by the Chinese, oriental standards are employed with respect to credit evaluation and credit practices. These involve strong reliance on verbal contracts, private but mutual compromises as to damages suffered, strong family ties and support, and a willingness to commence credit extension again immediately following a compromised bad debt write-off. Firms carry more marginal accounts requiring excessive collection efforts, which in turn also have marginal financial ratios and relatively high exposures.

All these factors affect the evaluation of Southeast Asian companies' accounts receivable and credit references. Their financial statements are further confused by virtue of the dominance of family-run businesses and the manner in which members mix family and business assets together. These factors together with the reluctance of Asian firms to provide statements, and the lack of governmental requirements to file such statements, sharply diminish the validity of standard credit evaluation methods. To complicate matters further, they also tend as a group to be highly leveraged and inclined to overexpansion. Many other world regions have their own idiosyncrasies, such as multiple versions of their financial statements. This is not to say that foreign financial statements are of no value, just that there is a need to be aware of practices in those countries in which you do a lot of business or have major investments. Their practices are not always according to what your accountant understands to be generally accepted accounting principles (GAAP).

Credit reports must be obtained as a precondition to obtain foreign credit insurance from Eximbank. Since it can take some time to get these reports, it is a good idea to request them soon after your initial sales contact and as soon as you feel there is a real possibility you will be doing business with a particular overseas firm.

Government Credit Information Sources

The *World Traders Data Reports* (*WTDR*), available through the DOC, are prepared by U.S. commercial officers abroad in answer to requests for information about a certain firm in a specific country. These reports contain information on the firm's business activities, its standing in the local business community, its general financial reputation, and its overall reliability and suitability as a trade contract, including its number of employees, products, ownership, and general operations. The *WTDR* is not specific as to trade references, amounts owing or overdue, and similar types of information you would expect to see in a domestic credit report, but you should study the codes and symbols of these reports carefully to get maximum value from them. Check with your local district DOC office for forms and the current best way to request *WTDR*s. To provide speedier service, they are now using both E-mail and fax to contact the foreign posts.

Eximbank maintains a large list of buyers whose credit it has checked, as well as records of its individual experience with particular buyers, and it will make this information available to its credit insurance customers (except for any privileged information it may have). If you use Eximbank insurance or work with Eximbank in any way, ask your Eximbank regional office to determine if it already has current information on your customer. For more information on Eximbank's Credit Information Service, call the Eximbank Hotline, 800/565-3946 if there is no regional office in your area. (See also Chapter 40.)

Domestic Private Credit Information Sources

Although there are a number of firms, some with very specific territorial focus, these are the six most-often-used domestic sources for credit information on foreign firms:

1. *Dun & Bradstreet.* This is the largest and best-known American credit reporting agency. Its international division provides reasonably fast and detailed credit reports on most overseas firms for its members, although some people question their accuracy. You need a fairly expensive annual contract for minimum usage to access D&B's international sources, regardless of any domestic contract or usage you may have. Prices decrease as you contract for more units. D&B also has an overseas bad-debt collection service. There are D&B offices in every major U.S. city, with headquarters in New York.

2. *Graydon America.* This is the U.S. subsidiary of the European firm, Graydon, which represents a merger of three leading European credit reporting firms and can provide credit reports for companies in most major trading nations. Graydon has a good reputation, and some regular users prefer its reports to those of other firms. Graydon offers the advantage of serving accounts on an individual-request basis without the necessity of a minimum contract, although its reports are less expensive with an annual contract. Graydon also has a bad-debt collections service. It can be accessed directly through its U.S. subsidiary, Graydon America Inc., 71 West 23rd Street, Suite 1629, New York, New York 10010.

3. *Owens OnLine, Inc.* This company tries to make up for its small size with fast service and reasonable fees, even for one-at-a-time credit reports, with further discounts for annual contracts. Its service is global, but has a special focus on Latin America. Owens is located at 4707 140th Avenue North, Suite 208, Clearwater, FL.

4. *Teikoku Databank America, Inc.* This is the U.S. subsidiary of the large Tokyo-based company by the same name. It was established in New York in 1992 and is the first Asia/Pacific credit firm in the U.S. Its reports are the most expensive, averaging about $350 to $400, but they go into much greater detail. Their address is 750 Lexington Avenue, 28th Floor, New York, New York 10022.

5. *TRW Credit Services.* Well known as a source for domestic and personal credit checks, TRW expanded its international division to provide worldwide, global commercial credit reporting in 1992. TRW also requires an annual contract for a minimum of $3100, but it can be used for domestic or international purposes interchangeably. Recent international prices ranged from $35 for Canada, $95 to $150 for Europe, $175 to $220 for Latin America, $205 to $250 for Asia/Pacific, and $230 for Africa.

6. *FCIB-NACM Corporation.* This is another U.S. organization that provides assistance in getting credit information on foreign companies. It is a trade association for executives in finance, credit, and international business. Its full name is the Finance, Credit, and International Business subsidiary of the National Association of Credit Management. It is located at 100 Wood Avenue South, Metro Center One, Iselin, New Jersey 08830. Its International Special Credit Report Service is compiled from a network of independent correspondents worldwide and provides very specific information about the company and the country in

question. You must become a member of the association to receive the report. Usage fees for service vary according to country and type of report. FCIB-NACM Corporation has excellent regional roundtable meetings for its members to discuss credit and collection experience on a country-by-country basis.

Foreign Credit Information Sources

There are other options that you might discuss with your banker, freight forwarder, and Eximbank insurance broker. If your firm is doing substantial business with a number of companies in a limited number of countries, by all means check into the possibility of local agencies within those countries as an alternative solution. This can be much less expensive, and in some cases may well be more accurate than domestic credit information services because of greater familiarity with the area.

The Exporter's Guide to Foreign Sources for Credit Information lists credit firms in 45 countries to help find an appropriate agency. It would probably be too costly for most exporters to deal with a number of these organizations, but depending on your situation, some of them could be well worth investigating.

Other Sources of Credit Information

It is always a good idea to find out if your contact has recently dealt with another American company. Most domestic companies will gladly report their experience if you request it in a typed letter where they only need to fill in a few blanks, such as, "Recent high credit," "Terms," "Prompt or days late," "Years selling," and enclose a self-addressed, stamped envelope. Often your own competition can be a source of valuable information. Most people in credit, and especially those doing business overseas, are happy to share their experiences, both good and bad, and particularly good.

If you have the name of your prospect's bank, ask your own bank to get a credit report through its regular banking channels, although it will not be in as much detail as a commercial credit report. The report will probably only contain a statement to the effect that the dollar amount inquired about "is within the normal range of the client's business" and/or that the client "does not normally engage in transactions it cannot properly complete." This would be a good report because it addresses both the amount relative to the company's ability to pay and its general reputation. You might get a response advising that the company's general reputation is satisfactory, but suggesting a secured transaction. This is "not as good" and means the sum mentioned seems large for its normal business. In this case, consider requesting a letter of credit or at least a documentary collection, depending on other input. If there is no response from the overseas buyer's bank, it is possibly a bad report, and you should be suspicious because a bank will usually not provide derogatory information. Ask your banker to follow up on the original request in the very possible event that it got lost or mishandled.

In some situations it may be prudent enough to offer foreign credit without insuring the account, depending on your knowledge and information who the customer you sell to, the relative size of any one account, and the credit costs as a percentage of sales and gross margin. Consider that while insurance may cost one-half of 1 percent of sales before factoring in the cost of annual and percentage deductibles, letters of credit will run about 1 percent of sales if there are no discrepancies and the orders exceed the $5000 to $10,000 range. If you plan to use your receivables for financing purposes, however, most lenders will require that the receivables be insured, and in order to get insurance, you need credit information. If you obtain an Eximbank credit insurance policy from an insurance broker qualified in foreign accounts receivable insurance, the broker might have good domestic and foreign sources for credit information and additional recommendations.

Bad Debt Collection Facilities

In addition to providing credit information, a few of the credit agencies such as Dun & Bradstreet and Graydon, have bad-debt collection divisions. There are also specialized collection agencies with overseas divisions serving 75 countries. The American Bureau of Collections, Inc. (ABC) of Buffalo, New York, was given an "E" award by President Bush and the DOC for export excellence. In its case, the award was for saving U.S. exporters from bad debts abroad, thereby making it easier for them to be competitive with open-account terms.

Insuring Credit Risks

Insured foreign accounts receivable can be a reliable form of working capital collateral, but your loan officer will not ordinarily consider financing your foreign accounts receivable without insurance, no matter how thoroughly you have checked your buyer's credit unless they are truly world class, AAA accounts. This is one compelling reason to consider insurance. The other, of course, is to protect your assets.

Public Sector Insurance

Eximbank is likely to be your best source for receivables insurance, which Eximbank created because of the difficulty all but the largest exporters were having in obtaining this kind of insurance. Today that situation is changing somewhat, especially relative to the more stable foreign markets. The exporter must first apply for an Eximbank policy, which can be done through almost any insurance broker but preferably through a broker specializing in international insurance. Insurance can be obtained directly through one of Eximbank's five regional offices in New York, Chicago, Houston, Miami, and Los Angeles. (See Appendix F.) Applicants must have a net equity in their business and present a financial condition that would indicate that they, too, have something to lose and that they will still be in business when the time comes to pursue a claim.

Chapter 40 contains a complete account of most of Eximbank's credit insurance policies, as well as its working capital program, which can help finance export receivables, and its guarantee and direct loan programs to support the credit of overseas customers. The details of each policy are explained and summed up in an analysis segment on choosing the right short-term policy. The insurance division of Eximbank has by far the most activity of any of the Eximbank programs and accounts for the second-largest capital exposure in terms of dollars. For small and midsize businesses, however, the insurance aspect completely dominates Eximbank's activity.

As noted earlier, at one time Eximbank was the only realistic source of foreign credit insurance cover for smaller business, and even though the private sector is once again offering some very attractive and practical policies, Eximbank remains the largest source for short-term (to 180 days, exceptionally 360 days) and medium-term cover (one to five years, exceptionally seven years). Each individual receivable is insured for from 90 percent to 100 percent of the shipment value, depending on the type of policy, various options, and the kind of buyer (sovereign, private, etc.). Agricultural products receive 98 percent cover, and short-term policies can be extended to 360 days for agricultural commodities. In the case of countries with a significant level of political risk, Eximbank will probably always remain the primary source of cover. The exception to this statement is those firms that cannot meet the following Eximbank rules:

1. All shipments covered must be at least 50 percent U.S. content

2. No coverage is provided on shipments originating outside the U.S.

3. Coverage is restricted to nonmilitary goods and services

In addition, in some cases, firms will have difficulty with restrictions on country eligibility, which can be affected by U.S. foreign policy.

In recent years Eximbank has restructured its program and its priorities with regard to small business assistance. It is now probably a better source for foreign receivable risk management than it ever was. It offers small business policies designed to encourage banks to lend against their foreign receivables by virtue of a "hold harmless" endorsement that assures the lender that no matter what oversight or mismanagement occurs on the part of the business in question relative to the handling of its responsibilities under the Eximbank policy, the lender will be repaid for any losses incurred that were collateralized by receivables so insured. Of course, the exporter continues to be liable for failure to perform. The bank is now also encouraging small business export efforts with policies that have no first-loss deductible, offer the higher percentage covers already mentioned, and have modest or zero annual premiums, and offer discretionary individual buyer coverage limits without the necessity of first obtaining specific Eximbank authorization. These are excellent policies, offering significant advantages for the new-to-export business that can be utilized until the export credit sales annual volume for the company exceeds $3 million.

In addition to Eximbank, there are other specialized federal entities offering assistance in managing export risks. The Overseas Private Investment Corporation (OPIC) specializes in insuring investments, contractors, and exporters in third-world countries, primarily from sovereign and political risks. (A complete description of OPIC's activities can be found in Chapter 41.) For agriculture, besides the Eximbank insurance mentioned, the Commodity Credit Corporation (CCC), provides 98 percent guarantees on foreign letters of credit to aid and promote commodity transactions abroad. And, finally, in Chapter 44 you will learn about many state programs that interface with the federal programs to facilitate and manage the risks of extending credit overseas.

Private Sector Credit Insurance

The alternative to insuring foreign accounts receivables with Eximbank is through the private sector insurance market. This market has been limited, especially in this country, but in the last few years there has been a marked improvement in availability for the smaller business. At this writing, several American companies are active and well-established providers of foreign credit insurance. Figure 25-1 is a chart comparing key details of the short-term policies of the five most active U.S. companies in this field, plus Lloyds of London, which is also very active in the American market. These companies are arrayed alongside Eximbank's short-term multibuyer policy. Notice that those offering comprehensive political and commercial cover are on one page and the three offering commercial cover only are on the following page. A sixth U.S. company that is a major player in the field, American Insurance Underwriters (AIU) in New York, is not compared because its target market is large companies fully staffed to make their own buyer credit decisions, and this focus is borne out by their annual minimum premium of $25,000.

Although Eximbank can service you directly in its regional offices or though one of its qualified brokers, all the private companies, including Lloyds of London, are also serviced by brokerage firms located throughout the United States. Should you care to address any question to them directly or ask for information about insurance agencies that could sell and service their policies, check with their headquarters. The insurers are: American Credit Indemnity in Baltimore; Continental Credit Insurance in Cranbury, New Jersey; Foreign Credit Insurance Association (FCIA) administering for Great American Insurance in New York; Trade Underwriters, administering sales for Reliance Insurance Company of New York; Fidelity & Deposit Company of Baltimore, Maryland; and American Insurance Underwriters in New York. Even though carrying an insurance policy other than Lloyds of London for general credit insurance, many exporters turn to Lloyds of London for their case-by-case needs for special political risk situations, such as contract repudiation cover.

For most firms, the best approach is to contact one of about 18 insurance brokers specializing in foreign country and commercial credit risk insurance. Four of them are very large and have headquarters in New York and multiple branch offices. They are: Intercredit Agency, a division of Frank B. Hall;

Alexander & Alexander; Johnson & Higgins; and Marsh & McClennan Credit International Associates (CIA), a division of Republic Hogg Robinson. A fifth firm is Sedgwick James, based in London but also having offices in New York.

The remainder are smaller firms that specialize in export credit and transportation insurance, including Eximbank insurance, which Richard Barovick, editor and publisher of the *Eximbank Letter,* refers to as boutique firms. A few well-known firms in this classification are International Insurance Associates, Downey (Los Angeles), California; Roth Insurance Agency, St. Louis, Missouri; Export Insurance Agency, Walpole, Massachusetts; and Export Insurance Service, Atlanta, Georgia.

As you will note from the chart, commercial coverage can now be obtained for as little as a $1000 annual minimum, going up to a high of $2500 for all but FCIA, at $10,000. Thus commercial credit insurance is a viable alternative to Eximbank, but factors other than minimum premiums need to be considered if much activity is to be covered. One important consideration arises with the possible need for political coverage in certain countries. Eximbank will provide cover in many countries that most private sector insurance companies do not cover. In other cases, Eximbank will deny cover in a particular country for foreign relations reasons. By contrast, many private companies, which are not affected by such factors, are quite willing to provide cover in such countries. Until recently, South Africa was a prime example. For some exporters, political cover does not matter if they only ship to Western Europe and Canada, for instance. But if you are shipping to Latin America, the Middle East, Africa, or Eastern Europe, it should be very important. While Eximbank will not provide you with commercial cover only, it will provide you with political cover only, although, as explained in Chapter 40, this does not always amount to much premium savings, and Eximbank does not encourage the practice. Private sector insurance companies that do not offer political cover usually do not offer any cover at all in those countries where political cover might be crucial. In connection with political risk cover, one should also review and factor in to the final decision the amount of business done with sovereign and quasisovereign entities, as compared to the amount of business done with commercial buyers.

Another major consideration in your decision about whether to use Eximbank or most private insurance companies is the premium assessment basis as it relates to your product and customer profile. Suppose, for example, that you make many shipments to customers so that their open account at any point in time covers several shipments, but that the account enjoys a good turnover as a result of regular payments and shipment. Most private insurers will assess your premiums on the basis of a high open-account balance, which may favor you. Eximbank and FCIA (now a private sector insuror but formerly the administrator for Eximbank insurance which now administers only for Great American Insurance) levy the premium per shipment, so that what you pay is based on total sales rather than on an open-account balance, which may be much less than the annual sales to an active account. Of course, their relative premium rates reflect this difference to some extent, but depending on how your firm's activity is weighted, using one or the other method can make a large difference.

COMPARISON CHART OF FOREIGN CREDIT INSURANCE PROGRAMS
COMPREHENSIVE COVERAGE (COMMERCIAL AND POLITICAL)

	FCIA (GREAT AMERICAN INSURANCE COMPANY)	EXPORT IMPORT BANK	TRADE UNDERWRITERS (RELIANCE INSURANCE CO.)	LLOYDS OF LONDON
RESTRICTIONS	No U.S. content restriction. Product may be 100% foreign content.	Products must be 51% U.S. content on cost basis. Military goods and/or services not eligible. Must be shipped from U.S.	No U.S. content restriction. Product may be 100% foreign content.	No U.S. content restriction. Product may be 100% foreign content.
COVERAGE	Commercial and Political Option 1: 95% for monthly reporting policy Option 2: 90% for country limits policy with a % refund for no claims bonus	Commercial and Political Option 1: 95% for both commercial and political. Option 2: 90% commercial and 100% political.	Commercial and Political 95% coverage a 5% refund for no claims bonus	Commercial and Political 90% coverage
COUNTRY ELIGIBILITY	All countries can be considered. Determined by each country's economic and political climate. Can include domestic sales Policy endorsed for countries covered	Dependent on U.S. government foreign policy. Specified by country limitation schedule.	All countries can be considered. Determined by each country's economic and political climate. Can include domestic sales Policy endorsed for countries covered	All countries can be considered except domestic sales. Determined by each country's economic and political climate. Policy endorsed for countries covered
CREDIT APPROVALS	Flexible Discretionary Credit Limits giving insured option to approve accounts to approved limits.	Discretionary Credit Limits giving insured option to approve accounts to approved limits.	Flexible Discretionary Credit Limits giving insured option to approve accounts to approved limits.	Flexible Discretionary Credit Limits giving insured option to approve accounts to approved limits.
DEDUCTIBLE	Policy year deductible, but one policy deductible can apply to shipments made to a buyer within 90 days of each other even if shipments were made in two policy years.	Per policy year deductible, based on date of shipment.	Policy year deductible, based on date of shipment.	Policy year deductible, based on date of shipment.
PREMIUM PAYMENT	Monthly or pre pay , determined as a percentage of insured sales. Requires spread of risk normally whole turnover	Monthly determined as a percentage of insured sales. Requires spread of risk normally whole turnover	Pre pay determined as a percentage of approved country limits. Requires spread of risk normally whole turnover. May be eligible for 5% refund.	Pre pay or quarterly installments, determined as a percentage of insured sales. Requires spread of risk or key accounts
MINIMUM PREMIUM	$10,000 per policy year. Minimum insured volume of $3,000,000.	$500 per policy year.	$10,000 per policy year. Minimum insured volume of $3,000,000.	$2,500 per policy year.
CLAIM FILING	90 days after due date.	90 days after due date	90–360 days after due date	180 days after due date

PLEASE NOTE THAT THIS CHART IS ONLY AN ADMINISTRATIVE GUIDE AND CONVEYS NO PERSONAL NOR AGENCY LIABILITY ON BEHALF OF INTERNATIONAL INSURANCE ASSOCIATES. (FCCOMP)
8202 FLORENCE AVENUE, SUITE 200
DOWNEY, CA 90240-3937

Figure 25-1. Comparison chart of foreign credit insurance programs. (*a*) Comprehensive coverage (commercial and political). (*b*) Commercial coverage only.

COMPARISON CHART OF FOREIGN CREDIT INSURANCE PROGRAMS
COMMERCIAL COVERAGE ONLY

	FIDELITY AND DEPOSIT	AMERICAN CREDIT INDEMNITY	CONTINENTAL INSURANCE COMPANY
RESTRICTIONS	Product may be 100% foreign content. No coverage to government buyers. Insolvency must occur while policy is in force	Product may be 100% foreign content. No coverage to government buyers. Insolvency must occur while policy is in force	Product may be 100% foreign content. No coverage to government buyers. Insolvency must occur while policy is in force
COVERAGE	Defined Insolvency and protracted default in eligible countries. Excludes insolvency due to war. Normally 85% coverage	Defined insolvency and protracted default in eligible countries. Excludes insolvency due to war. 100% insolvency coverage, 85% protracted default	Defined insolvency and protracted default in eligible countries. Excludes insolvency due to war. 100% insolvency coverage, 75% protracted default
COUNTRY ELIGIBILITY	List of eligible countries, primarily developed countries.	List of eligible countries, primarily developed countries.	List of eligible countries, primarily developed countries.
CREDIT APPROVALS	F&D gathers information and establishes credit limits for each buyer.	ACI gathers information and establishes credit limits for each buyer.	Continental gathers information and establishes credit limits for each buyer.
DEDUCTIBLE	No deductible.	Per policy year deductible.	Per policy year deductible.
PREMIUM PAYMENT	Prepayment, with year end adjustment. Determined as a percentage of insured sales.	Prepayment with adjustments for changes in buyer credit limits. Premium based on approved credit limits, endorsements, face value of policy. Premium charged per credit limit approved, based on quality of each buyer's credit rating	Prepayment with adjustments for changes in buyer credit limits. Premium based on approved credit limits, endorsements, face value of policy. Premium charged per credit limit approved, based on quality of each buyer's credit rating
MINIMUM PREMIUM	$1,250 per policy year.	$10,000.	$2,500
CLAIM FILING	Insolvency claims can be filed at any time during policy period as soon as practicable after acquiring knowledge. Protracted default 180 days after due date.	Insolvency claims can be filed at any time during policy period but must be within 2 0 days after acquiring knowledge or 90 days from date of insolvency, whichever date is earlier. Past due claims must be filed within 3 months after due date. May have collection charges. 1 year waiting period for past dues	Insolvency claims can be filed at any time during policy period but must be within 2 0 days after acquiring knowledge or 90 days from date of insolvency, whichever date is earlier. Past due claims must be filed within 3 months after due date. May have collection charges.

Figure 25-1. (*Continued*)

A knowledgeable broker handling both Eximbank and private insurance companies can help you select the insurance cover that best suits your needs.

Insuring Political/Country Risk

In managing your risks, don't forget the matter of country risk, irrespective of the creditworthiness and reputation of the buyer. If there is a coup, or war, or a lack of foreign exchange in your buyer's country, the buyer will probably be unable to pay, either temporarily or permanently. Your only hope then is the political risk coverage portion of your policy, unless there are funds in a bank outside the country, which is not altogether uncommon. Political, or country risk, whether in relation to commercial or sovereign buyers, is automatically covered if your insurance is with Eximbank. Reflecting on Mexico's 1995 disaster, there are obviously many countries who appear to be stable but have hidden weaknesses or underlying political currents that few people are aware of. There are more borderline cases than you might suspect and some for which it is impossible to obtain coverage.

Expropriation sounds like a remote possibility in most countries, but there have been a number of instances in recent years, from Iran to Iraq to Zaire, which took over U.S. oil company assets, and more. Consider the outbreaks of war recently experienced in Central Europe, the civil unrest in Algeria and in Central Africa, with many more possibilities looming ahead, some anticipated but some not. Even letters of credit are not without political risks unless they are confirmed in the United States. China executed nine bankers in 1993 for issuing letters of credit that were not authorized for foreign exchange funds and that were not honored. If any country freezes its foreign exchange by fiat, it does not matter how strong the issuing bank is.

To recognize potential country risk, watch for political unrest, high interest rates, high inflation, and major balance-of-trade deficits. There are a number of means of determining the level of country risk, beginning with the DOC or a call to the regional Eximbank office or a review of Eximbank's Country Limitation Schedule. FCIB-NACM, as an association, also provides country risk reports, but membership dues are required. Your own international bank subscribes to political risk services and may have their own independent and ongoing analysis of political risk. Some banks provide this analysis to businesses on a subscription basis for a fee, as does the Bank of America for example. All will provide their best information available to bank customers concerning any specific transaction. The magazine *Euromoney,* of Euromoney Publications, London, is noted for regular monthly focus on the political and foreign exchange outlook on specific countries or regions as well as an annual worldwide summary. Standard & Poor and Moody's, the well-known risk-rating firms in New York, also study international risks. There are several specialized sources for country information, a partial list of which includes:

- International Business Communications, Syracuse, NY, has a subsidiary called "Political Risk Services"

- Business International Corp., New York, NY offers: "Political and Economic Forecasts" and Currency Forecasts

- The Economist Intelligence Unit, Ltd., New York, NY offers: "Quarterly Economic Reports" and "EIU Outlooks"

Fortunately, some of these sources of information can be found in larger university libraries, because subscribing to these reports can be quite expensive. For only the occasional need, you probably will be able to get satisfactory advice informally through your international banker or from Eximbank. In the case of Eximbank, however, be again cautioned that U.S. politics and affairs of state are sometimes imposed in Eximbank's own risk analysis and underwriting policies. Therefore, Eximbank is occasionally forced to provide cover for policy reasons on countries for which it might be economically unsound, and conversely, refuse it for some countries that might merit coverage in terms of creditworthiness but not on ideological or political grounds.

Insuring Transit Risks

Open Cargo Policies

Transportation insurance, especially marine insurance, can be complicated, but with the open cargo insurance policies available in recent years, it has become relatively straightforward. Such policies typically provide all-risk, warehouse-to-warehouse insurance and comparable coverage for airfreight and parcel post shipments. An alternative to your own open marine policy is the policy held by your freight forwarder, especially if your export activity is limited. Except for special situations and for exporters of bulk products, there are few situations in which an exporter should accept other than warehouse-to-warehouse or door-to-door coverage for whatever specific risks are covered.

Alternative risk coverages include the less-comprehensive coverages, such as free as free of particular average (FPA) or with average (WA) coverages, and specified risk coverage, or even doing without coverage except for the carrier's liability for negligence. In the case of airfreight, there is the option of insurance purchased from the airline on a flight-by-flight basis. Warehouse-to-warehouse coverage provides considerable comfort to both exporter and banker at minimal additional cost. An open cargo policy can be custom-tailored to your needs and specific risk exposures. There is one other, still-broader form of policy and coverage called a blanket policy. A *blanket policy* is a negotiated policy and covers all shipping activity with no need for reports, and it usually has a substantial deductible. It tends to apply only to very large shippers.

Reliance on the freight forwarder's open policy is the simplest solution. If you are not a regular export shipper, you may find your own policy minimums to be too high, or the insurance company may decline to issue you a policy at any price because of an inadequate spread of risk or because of inexperience, which concerns the insurer in terms of perceived added exposure.

Other reasons for caution on the part of insurance companies are frequent shipments of hazardous cargo; identifiable, high-value cargo subject to pilferage; shipments to countries where pilferage rates are exceptionally high; and shipments to politically unstable areas. Under such circumstances, by all means use your freight forwarder's open policy if possible. The spread of risk and the forwarder's experience will absorb your extra exposures at a lower premium cost in the long run and offer you better coverage. An example of the opposite extreme is the exporter that regularly ships into the European market and specializes in the shipment of goods with a low value-to-volume ratio. You will probably obtain better rates than those your forwarder could offer and you will enjoy a better one-on-one relationship with the insurance company and its agents when the time comes for a claim. Your forwarder might still be willing to insure some of the out of the ordinary shipments to destinations that could not be covered under your own policy because of restrictive terms to which you might have agreed in order to qualify for a superior rate.

The Insurance Company of North American (a CIGNA company), one of several major insurance organizations in the United States specializing in marine insurance, distributes an excellent booklet in layman's language entitled *Marine Insurance*.[3] With the company's permission, much of the following information on marine insurance is based on that booklet for a better understanding of a rather arcane subject.

Transfer of Risk According to Shipping Terms

The Incoterm highlights described in Chapter 18 explain when the merchandise becomes the responsibility of the buyer. (Be sure to note the comments in Chapter 18 on this issue relative to shipping terms.) In a very general way, the risk transfer point for the most common shipping terms are:

- *Ex-Works*. The buyer assumes the risk from the time the goods have been placed at its disposal according to the time and place the buyer agreed to accept delivery. The seller may have certain interim risks but there is no transit risk.

- *FCA*. Risk transfer occurs when the goods have been handed over to the carrier requested at its terminal, or loaded on to the carrier's truck, rail car at a named point or, if none named, a point at which the carrier is willing to accept goods according to its general practice; or into the custody of a named person such as a freight forwarder. If no carrier or person is so named, then the seller may choose a carrier, or person which can reasonably carry out the wishes of the buyer as to carriage.

- *CPT, CIP*. Similar to FCA above, except that the goods must be handed over only to the custody of a carrier, its terminal, agent, or conveyance, or those of the first carrier named or selected in the case of multiple carriers.

- *FAS*. Risk transfers after proper delivery to the named port in a manner customary to that port.

- *FOB, CFR, CIF.* Risk transfers after the goods have crossed the ship's rails.

- *All "D" Terms.* Risk does not transfer until the goods have been placed at the disposal of the buyer in the condition and in the named place of delivery stated in the "D" term.

Note that even though the seller is obliged to obtain insurance on behalf of the buyer, that requirement does not change the point at which risk transfers. Only under the "D" terms is the risk transfer delayed the goods are necessarily at the buyer's disposal. It should also be noted that while warehouse-to-warehouse coverage is in most common use today, coverage called free of particular averages (FPA) coverage, explained later, is all that is legally required under Incoterms, unless specified otherwise.

FOB or FCA Sales Endorsement

An FOB sales endorsement to an open marine policy can cover transit risk from the point of origin until the risk transfers, at which point the seller provides or relies on the buyer having main carriage insurance. Otherwise, trip coverage or carriers' liability must be relied on, unless the buyer has adequate warehouse-to-warehouse insurance in force.

Contingency Insurance

Regardless of the shipping terms, and even though risk may have transferred so that technically the exporter has no risk in the goods, it is quite possible that you still have an important financial interest that is protected if the buyer is not insured as claimed. The reason for this is that you have not yet been paid, and the buyer will have little interest in paying you if the goods are damaged or lost. Even with a letter of credit, the terms probably will require a clean, onboard bill of lading that may not be available for negotiation. This is also true of documentary collections or open-account terms.

There are other, less-assessable exposures that the exporter faces in respect to the buyer's coverage. These involve questions such as: Did the buyer insure at all? How complete is the coverage in terms of door-to-door protection? How reliable and financially strong is the insurance policy? In what currency will a claim be paid? Can the foreign insurer transfer funds out of the country to pay the claim with reasonable promptness?

Apart from appropriate use of the FOB sales endorsement, the remainder of these problems can be solved by means of contingency insurance. The cost is a fraction of regular insurance and is intended to protect you in any situation in which the exporter responsibly relied on the buyer to insure but sustained a loss because of inadequate coverage from that source. The contingency insurance will cover situations in which the FOB sales endorsement would otherwise have served had that been in force. This is not to say that contingency insurance necessarily need be taken out in all situations. It will depend on your knowledge and the insurance of the buyer and how critical a potential loss might be.

Cargo Insurance Procedures

How to insure your cargo is a rather technical and arcane subject, but worth having at least a superficial understanding of, as well as knowing how much to insure it for.

How to Insure.   While specific marine insurance policies for individual shipments are available, for firms not regularly exporting, the forwarder's open policy may be the better choice if it is available. For regular exporters, the principal means of insurance is the open cargo policy with warehouse-to-warehouse coverage. It provides automatic protection within the limits of the policy from the time the shipment leaves the exporter's premises, or any other named point, until arrival at the buyer's premises. Shipments are to be declared as soon as practical, but an errors and omissions coverage included in the policy language protects against good-faith failure to report. It is relatively convenient and you know your precise insurance costs in advance.

When documenting insured shipments, a certificate can be used, but for letter-of-credit purposes, in some cases the exporter must prove to the buyer and/or a lender that the shipment was duly insured by filling out a separate form called a special policy. Although this form is part of your open cargo policy, it stands on its own merits in the eyes of the documentary clerks and the law. Either document must be signed (usually printed on the form) by the insurance company or its agent. The shipment must be identified by shipping marks or other means and the points of origin and destination declared. This is a critical point in many letters of credit, and a certificate will be rejected if a policy is called for in the credit. As previously noted, the UCP is more lenient on this point than it once was, but in any given credit, a special policy may be called for, so check this point carefully.

How Much to Insure.   While export insurance must be at a minimum of 110 percent of invoice value to comply with typical letter-of-credit provisions, as well as according to general custom, the importer can request more insurance because of anticipated profit on an increase in value of the shipment at the time of arrival, or for other special reasons. The value of the estimated insurance premium itself is included in calculating 110 percent of CIF value, along with all transportation and other costs. There is a probability that a higher percentage will have to be covered in cases where a letter of credit is transferred to a supplier. (See Chapter 36.)

Terms and Conditions of Coverage

The history of marine insurance goes back to Babylonian times. English maritime history of the seventeenth and eighteenth centuries, as well as English admiralty law, bear directly on it today, in terms of both words and concepts. Even the term *average,* as used in marine insurance, initially had its roots in the Arabic language (*awarijah:* merchandise damaged by seawater), which were blended with the present English meaning of *average.* There are two ways in which the term is used. *Particular average loss* is a partial one that affects specific interests only. A *general-average loss* is one that affects all cargo interests onboard the vessel as well as the ship itself.

General Average.   The term *general average* confuses many people. While it pertains mostly to recoveries and claims adjustment, it is in a real sense an additional risk to be considered and insured. This is because a general-average loss involves losses over and above your own direct marine losses (even if you had no direct loss at all), regardless of whether or not your goods are insured. General average would come about as a result of intentional sacrifice or expenditures incurred by the master of the vessel for the common good in time of peril to both ship and cargo. Examples would be the jettisoning of the ship's own equipment or the shipper's cargo to lighten a stranded vessel, or being towed into a port for repairs. The vessel owner then declares the ship under general average concerning equipment or towing or cargo being thrown overboard, with the intention that all will share in these costs proportionally.

General average adjusters are called in to determine what the average contribution of both vessel and cargo owners must be to equalize the loss. Therefore, even a shipper without losses must post a bond or provide security in order to obtain release of the cargo because the ship's owner then has a lien on the cargo pending the outcome of the lengthy general-average determination process. Once determined, the shipper must pay the general-average contribution or the cargo will be sold to obtain the contribution. If the cargo owner is insured to full value, the underwriter will post the bond and subsequently pay the contribution. If it is only partially insured, it will be shared pro rata. The 110 percent insurance custom is partially to provide leeway for just such situations.

Free of Particular Average.   Free of particular average (FPA) is the narrowest form of insurance in force today, and it is used primarily in special situations, such as bulk cargo, where any potential losses are likely to be a total loss. FPA intends to cover total loss only, plus partial losses resulting from perils of the sea, but only in the event that certain specified disasters occur to the ship (as in its being stranded, sunk, burnt, on fire, or in collision). A broader form, *with average* (WA) is more inclusive and covers the FPA losses, plus partial losses, without requiring a disaster, if the loss exceeds 3 percent of value. Additional named perils can be added to the WA clause. Unless specified otherwise, FPA is the degree of the risk coverage implied under CIF terms, even though few shippers take advantage of this fact, feeling that broader coverage is in everybody's interest.

In terms of claims, the words *particular average* as used in the term FPA refer to the means of determining a partial loss. If this refers to total damage or to damage of a portion of the goods, there is essentially an arithmetical solution. If the loss is because of damage, an agreement must be reached as to depreciation, or the goods must be repaired to full value. If neither of these approaches can be agreed on, the goods will be sold to establish value.

All-Risk Coverage.   Even when the *all-risks* phrase, providing maximum coverage, is stipulated, there are some types of losses not covered. War risks, as well as strikes, riots, and civil commotions are not covered under this clause. Loss of market because of delays and trade losses due to damage, deterioration, or decay arising out of delays are seldom covered. If they are, it is by special amendment at a very high price. This is considered an indirect or consequential damage, not physical loss or damage.

There is another broad class of loss known as *inherent vice,* which is excluded from every policy and is not insurable. This is loss because of external cause by virtue of causes such as faulty packing, age, or over-ripeness of fresh produce at the time of shipment. It also includes losses that are a certainty, such as losses from evaporation. There are occasional exceptions to the uninsurability of inherent vice, as in the case of Lloyd's all-risk insurance, for certain, specialized coverages.

Nevertheless, all-risk insurance today is broad and thorough coverage. It is also the most expensive, and is not necessary on all types of cargo, such as those that would be unlikely to sustain partial losses (as in the case of bulk ore or oil shipments). FPA coverage is more appropriate in these situations. Some losses may be so minor and noncatastrophic that it would make sense to self-insure, especially if the shipment is being sent to your own branch operation rather than a customer. Even though damage caused by the negligence of vessel operators (which is interpreted much more narrowly than might be expected) can be recovered directly, it is a long and trying process. Claim agents for carriers—whether air, ocean, or rail—are employed to not pay claims, and a lawyer is often required even in the most obvious cases of negligence. Therefore, most exporters want such negligence covered under their policy so they can deal with the insurance agent and let the insurance company deal with the carrier. Often, the cost differential for better coverage can be offset by the interest cost during the claim recovery process.

Strikes, Riots, and Civil Commotion Coverage.   Strikes, Riots, and Civil Commotion (SR&CC) coverage must be considered on a case-by-case basis, since its cost and its necessity fluctuate. It can be endorsed as part of the marine insurance, whether it is a specific or open cargo policy.

War Risk.   War risk is a different matter, since it cannot be endorsed onto the open cargo or specific marine policy, even though it is usually issued in conjunction with marine insurance. It is written and covered under a separate policy. Most shippers take it, but some CIF quotations specifically state that war risk will not be included in the case of shipments to hostile or unstable areas of the world. Since rates can change radically in 48 hours, it is a liability the exporter should not have to gamble on and is rightly a problem of the receiver. According to Incoterms, it is not part of a CIF quote, although exporters in practice often include it, except when the risks and resulting rates are high.

Extended Coverages.   The open cargo policies can extend coverage to your shipments by airfreight, parcel post, or mail, and offer excellent coverage. Very important is the warehouse-to-warehouse or door-to-door coverage that protects the shipper from the time the shipment leaves the plant until the consignee physically receives it. This has provided an outstanding improvement in transportation insurance and shipper comfort. The coverage applies even as the merchandise moves through multiple modes of transportation and interim warehousing.

Airfreight Insurance

Lacking the long history of marine insurance, the rules for airfreight insurance are quite different and more akin to inland transportation conditions. Air carriers can be held liable for losses because of their negligence, but only to the limit of their liability. This is currently just over $9 per pound, or $20 per kilogram of shipment. Additional liability can be had by addition of a valuation charge, which currently costs 45 cents per $100. An exporter can also request airfreight insurance from the carrier that will be reflected on the air waybill and charged with the airfreight costs. This covers all risks, with war risks as an option for an additional premium. It does not cover other modes of transportation involved before or after the insured flight. This approach is usually cheaper than paying the additional valuation charges, and liability does not have to be proven. If, however, an open cargo or marine policy is available, it will likely be the best overall insurance buy and should be utilized for air as well. (See Chapter 28.)

General Casualty and Liability Risks Overseas

Beyond risks in the extension of credit and the movement of goods, a firm doing business overseas faces the same risks relative to its investment in assets and its business-related activities as that firm would face in its domestic operations. In some cases and with some policies, these risks would be covered through existing business policies, but often they are not. Every business with international interests should review each kind of coverage it feels is important to its interests in the United States and determine what, if any, further coverage is needed for the overseas operations. This will naturally vary with the country and its political and civil climate.

Consider first the physical property and equipment investment and the key issue of the competency of the insurer to cover it and to settle future claims. In the case of shipments to Third-World countries, it may be necessary to discuss this problem with OPIC, especially if concerns such as expropriation are warranted. Although product liability is not the issue overseas that it is in the United States, it is a liability that does exist to a greater or lesser degree depending on the region. Liability will also be more difficult to defend abroad and it may be impacted by activities from parties over which the firm has less control and supervision than is the case at home in this country.

Next, look at personnel liability for employees traveling or living abroad. What is their health insurance coverage in case they become ill thousands of miles away from their own doctor or HMO? There may be personal injury liability relative to sales offices or warehouses overseas. Exporters' workmen's compensation claims may or may not be valid if originating from activities while overseas. What about auto liability coverage on employees driving automobiles in other countries?

It's important to gain knowledgeable help to resolve such questions or exposures. As little as possible should be left to chance in international situations where potential costs can escalate rapidly, even in what would have been a minor event at home in the United States.

Foreign Currency Exchange Risk

Currency exchange risk refers to the risk associated with quotations in other than U.S. dollars. The long-term trend of the dollar has been downward. It lost 35 percent of its value from 1985 to 1992, and the sharp decline in early 1995 was so severe as to make some experts question the degree to which it can continue to be the single dominant world currency even though later in the year it enjoyed a partial recovery. One wonders now if it may not be undervalued, if the United States begins to treat the budget and trade deficits with the seriousness they deserve. In any case, the U.S. dollar is no longer "almighty." It may at times be necessary—or even to your advantage as during this period of decline—to quote your product in pounds sterling, yen, marks, francs or other strong foreign currencies. This is bound to become an issue if you are in a buyer's market. It is especially noteworthy in the flourishing Pacific Rim trade, where the yen is challenging the dollar as the prime international currency. The unknown factor in this challenge, and a vital ingredient if it is to materialize, is the extent to which Japan's future international policies will permit open foreign investment in that country. The day could yet come when the yen may be called the "coin of the Pacific Rim realm." The deutsche mark is clearly the dominate currency of Europe. Dealing with payments in a currency other than the U.S. dollar is something that we may have to get used to, and something that exporters of other nations have long accepted as a matter of course, just as the more aggressive midsize and large American international marketeers already have.

While everyone, especially the smaller business, will probably always prefer to be paid in dollars, the overriding objective is to realize a fair price for your goods or services and achieve your company's fair market share. To that end, you should not rule out the possibility of accepting a currency for which a ready market is available. This naturally excludes currencies under restrictive control by their governments—those with nonliquid currencies that are held unnaturally steady until periodically forced to make or allow very large and sudden value adjustments. The Mexican debacle in 1995 is the most recent, all too excellent, example.

Hedging

In the context of currency, hedging is a means of protecting against major downside losses by making a counterbet in the opposite direction. It will offset all or most of a possible gain but at the same time avoid or minimize possible losses. It is the opposite of what is known as "taking a position." If a company does not hedge its future foreign currency receipts or obligations, it accepts the full downside risk and upside gain for any foreign currency it cannot use or of which it already has a surplus, in the case of obligations. In that posture it must make a spot sale or purchase at the current market price. The alternative is to hedge foreign exchange risk, which is done with four financial instruments plus one trading scheme: (1) forward contracts and forward window contracts; (2) options; (3) swaps; and (4) futures contracts. Forward contracts and forward window contracts are probably of the most use to the largest number of exporters, but all techniques, including internal pairing of exposures or matching of assets and liabilities held in foreign currencies, should be discussed with your banker and accountant within the framework of a firm's total import and export activities and the existence of foreign subsidiaries, branches, or joint ventures.

The easiest and safest method for smaller companies with a good credit standing is to deal with *forward contracts* through their international bank's foreign exchange department, or through the bank's money center correspondent bank. The foreign exchange department can usually arrange a forward contract, even in lesser currencies, to sell the anticipated foreign receipts at the planned forward date, thus fixing the dollars to be realized. If it is for only a few days ahead, it merely becomes a spot sale instead of a forward contract. If the bank is consulted in advance, an accurate calculation can be made of what the offering price should be in the foreign currency. The bank's commission or fee is normally built into the price quotation. The premium or discount in the futures price has to do with the stability, trend, or volatility of the currency, the volume of trading, and the term. It is important to understand that before engaging in this activity, the bank must be prepared to extend a line of credit to ensure that the exporter will fulfill the contract at maturity, because it really is a contract and the foreign currency must be delivered on that date. The credit line need not be for the full value of the contract, just for enough to protect the bank if the exporter fails to deliver the foreign exchange. This depends on the currency's market size and volatility, usually in the range of 10 to 25 percent of the transaction value.

The *forward window contract* is a variation on the forward contract that may serve your purpose better when there is a need for flexibility because of uncertainty as to the date of settlement. However, there should still be no doubt that the transaction will occur and be settled in the anticipated general time frame or window. A forward window contract guarantees constant pricing throughout the window of time, at a somewhat higher cost, of course. That cost may be more than offset by the costs associated with shifting foreign currency settlement positions from one date to another.

Options are the second alternative and are very similar to puts and calls in stock option trading. This method is relatively new, but it more closely resembles insurance than hedging because the option must be purchased up-front and carries with it the right to purchase or sell a foreign currency at a certain price, though there is no an obligation to do so. If it is not used, part or all of the cost may be made up in currency gain; if it is used, it converts what may have been a serious loss into a budgeted cost for the transaction, or the reverse, depending on the direction of the transaction.

The third method of hedging mentioned consists of buying futures contracts. It is similar to a forward contract, but unlike forward contracts, futures contracts are fixed and have a limited number of maturity dates each year. Typically, those are at the end of each calendar quarter: March, June, September, and December. The contracts are bought on the exchange through brokers, and in reality it is commodity trading, which is a highly leveraged, volatile proposition. The advantage is that a bank credit line is not necessary, but the exchange requires that a margin account be maintained with a cash balance equal to a small percentage of the contract value—typically 1 or 2 percent of the contract values. Just as with stock margin accounts, if the market starts declining on the contracts a firm owns, it must increase the margin account to cover. Of course decreases in the contract value should be offset by the increasing value of the exporter's underlying transaction, but in the interim, the cash demands could be a problem. A disadvantage of this method is also that the exchanges trade in only a limited number of currencies. Most of such trading, besides that done in U.S. dollars, is in the Deutsche mark, Swiss franc, British pound, and Japanese yen. Depending on the exchange, of course, one should include the French franc and the Canadian and Australian dollars. Generally, the parameters for currency hedging are thought to be for transactions of more than $50,000 (perhaps as much as $100,000) and when the forward period is in the range of 30 days to 6 months.

Finally, *swaps* contracts are a more recent product of the 1980s and "amount to a series of forward contracts pieced together," in the words of Margaret E. Osius, a consultant in financial risk management, in the August 1989 issue of *Export Today*. Osius gives an excellent description of swaps in her article and states: "The two parties agree to exchange or 'swap' cash flows in specified currencies at specified dates and prices. Usually one of the parties is a bank." From that point on it becomes a bit more complicated, but "it is a versatile method of hedging of complex exposures in amounts and maturities tailored to the exporter's specific requirements."[4] However, the documentation requirements are extensive and the cost, therefore, may be higher than the other alternatives. Swaps should probably be reserved for the larger, more experienced FX operations.

If you are in a solid financial condition, an interesting alternate option to all of the above you may wish to discuss with your banker is making a working capital loan in the amount required for the transaction in the currency proposed for payment. This can be done through your bank's correspondent in the buyer's country. If it is a major low-interest-rate currency, you can also convert the borrowing to dollars and gain by the differential of the lower interest plus equalizing the foreign currency's gain or loss when paid by using dollars to repay the foreign loan.

In the case of much weaker Third-World currencies not regularly traded, it is possible to look for a relationship with the weak country and a strong currency country. This most likely will be the Third-World country's former colonial power that maintains an official government rate for the weak currency. An example is France, for their former African colonies. Under these circumstances, hedging the major currency can accomplish almost the same objective.

Endnotes

1. Paul Ragan, "Foreign Financials: Reading Between the Lines," *Export Today,* June 1992.

2. Edited by World Trade Consultants, *The Exporter* magazine, First Washington Associates, *The Exporter's Guide to Foreign Sources for Credit Information,* Trade Data Reports, New York, NY, 1989.

3. *Marine Insurance: Notes and Comments on Ocean Cargo Insurance,* used by permission of the publisher Insurance Company of North America (CIGNA), 1986.

4. Margaret E. Osius, "Dealing with Foreign Currencies," *Export Today,* August 1989.

26

Shipping Documents and Electronic Data Interchange

The accuracy and conformity of shipping documents often determines whether the exporter gets paid on time—or at all. For this reason, they require very careful attention to detail. Improper documentation may prevent the shipment from clearing customs on arrival, thereby incurring a number of charges, penalties, and fines and possibly even seizure of the goods. (See Chapter 21.) Other consequences range from having to bring the goods back, to losing the goodwill of your customer. The requirements for shipping documents vary, depending on the country of destination and the commodity being shipped. What follows is a summary of general information about each of the most-commonly-used shipping documents. (A more detailed study is necessary, however, if you plan to prepare your own shipping documentation.)

Shipping Documents

Shipper's Export Declaration

The shipper's export declaration (SED) is required by the U.S. government for all export shipments valued in excess of $2500 or for a shipment of any size requiring a validated export license. The declaration serves a dual purpose, since it first must state the license under which you are shipping if one is required. The SED must also show the proper Schedule B Number, quantities shipped, FOB value of the shipment, and the destination. The latter information is used by the Bureau of the Census for the statistical reports we have described, which are available to both government and nongovernment users and are so important to export marketing research. The SED information is also used by U.S. Customs and the Bureau of Export Administration (BXA) for certain monitoring and enforcement purposes relative to licensing and destination. The exporter is subject to civil and criminal penalties if you or your forwarder falsify or fail to complete this form. (See Figure 26-1 for a sample form.)

Validated License

An export license is essential if required. See Chapter 31 for more information on this critical subject.

Commercial Invoice

The commercial invoice includes a "Sold To" and a "Shipped To" heading and must be completed according to the terms and conditions under which the shipment is made. It should also include the order date and number, shipping date, method of shipment, terms of sale, payment terms, a description of the merchandise, unit and total price, and actual shipping charges or as agreed upon. The invoice should very closely resemble the pro forma invoice if one was initially provided. If payment is to be against a letter of credit, the letter-of-credit number must be shown on the invoice. In the case of air shipments, refer to an air waybill number; for ocean shipments, indicate the steamship line, voyage number, ocean-bill-of-lading number, and if applicable, container and seal number. The invoice should not only be free of errors but also be free of apparent corrections.

The invoice should always be signed and may contain a statement similar to the following: "We certify that the above merchandise is in accordance with buyer's order, that it is of United States of America origin and manufacture (or whatever third-party country might be involved) and that the invoice is true and correct in all particulars," unless a separate certificate of origin is called for. The commercial invoice is essential for customs clearance at destination and is often used by foreign governments to determine the true value of goods for assessment of customs duties. Some countries require that the commercial invoice (and possibly other documents as well) be certified or legalized by one of their U.S. trade consulates, their embassy, or a third party such as the U.S. Arab Chamber of Commerce. Without an invoice, your customer can be placed in a very difficult position by having to post a bond until the documents arrive, pay additional fees, sustain fines, and possibly have the goods seized.

U.S. DEPARTMENT OF COMMERCE — BUREAU OF THE CENSUS — INTERNATIONAL TRADE ADMINISTRATION

FORM **7525-V** (1-1-88)   **SHIPPER'S EXPORT DECLARATION**   OMB No. 0607-0018

1a. EXPORTER *(Name and address including ZIP code)*		
	ZIP CODE	2. DATE OF EXPORTATION / 3. BILL OF LADING/AIR WAYBILL NO.

b. EXPORTER'S EIN (IRS) NO.   **c.** PARTIES TO TRANSACTION
☐ Related   ☐ Non-related

4a. ULTIMATE CONSIGNEE

b. INTERMEDIATE CONSIGNEE

5. FORWARDING AGENT

6. POINT (STATE) OF ORIGIN OR FTZ NO.   **7.** COUNTRY OF ULTIMATE DESTINATION

8. LOADING PIER *(Vessel only)*   **9.** MODE OF TRANSPORT *(Specify)*

10. EXPORTING CARRIER   **11.** PORT OF EXPORT

12. PORT OF UNLOADING *(Vessel and air only)*   **13.** CONTAINERIZED *(Vessel only)*
☐ Yes   ☐ No

14. SCHEDULE B DESCRIPTION OF COMMODITIES,   *(Use columns 17–19)*
15. MARKS, NOS., AND KINDS OF PACKAGES

VALUE (U.S. dollars, omit cents)
(Selling price or cost if not sold)

D/F (16)	SCHEDULE B NUMBER (17)	CHECK DIGIT	QUANTITY — SCHEDULE B UNIT(S) (18)	SHIPPING WEIGHT (Kilos) (19)	(20)

21. VALIDATED LICENSE NO./GENERAL LICENSE SYMBOL   **22.** ECCN *(When required)*

23. Duly authorized officer or employee | The exporter authorizes the forwarder named above to act as forwarding agent for export control and customs purposes.

24. I certify that all statements made and all information contained herein are true and correct and that I have read and understand the instructions for preparation of this document, set forth in the "Correct Way to Fill Out the Shipper's Export Declaration." I understand that civil and criminal penalties, including forfeiture and sale, may be imposed for making false or fraudulent statements herein, failing to provide the requested information or for violation of U.S. laws on exportation (13 U.S.C. Sec. 306; 22 U.S.C. Sec. 401; 18 U.S.C. Sec. 1001; 50 U.S.C. App. 2410).

Signature   Confidential - For use solely for official purposes authorized by the Secretary of Commerce (13 U.S.C. 301 (g)).

Title   Export shipments are subject to inspection by U.S. Customs Service and/or Office of Export Enforcement.

Date   **25.** AUTHENTICATION *(When required)*

This form may be printed by private parties provided it conforms to the official form. For sale by the Superintendent of Documents, Government Printing Office, Washington, D.C. 20402, and local Customs District Directors. The "Correct Way to Fill Out the Shipper's Export Declaration" is available from the Bureau of the Census, Washington, D.C. 20233.

Figure 26-1. Shipper's export declaration.

Packing List

The packing list is an extremely important document because, aside from your customer's requirements, it is often used by customs officials on both sides to check and verify a shipment, and should, therefore, contain complete details of the shipment. With the packing list, the merchandise can be physically located by individual carton or container. This list is a document many consider optional in domestic transactions; however, in international trade, it is an absolute necessity for customs clearance procedures, especially if the shipment consists of two or more packing units. The packing list must show the type of package, weight, and dimension of each unit and their total, both in U.S. measure and metric. Shipping marks (which usually consist of an abbreviation of the consignee's name and underneath it the name of the port city) also should be shown on the packing list, together with the shipper's and buyer's reference numbers. If the shipment consists of several cartons, each carton must be numbered and the packing list must refer to that number with details of the contents of each carton. For shipments against a letter of credit, the packing list should be without visible corrections and must be consistent with the invoice and letter of credit. It should be signed and refer to the letter-of-credit number. A copy of the packing list should be attached to the lead (No. 1) carton.

Consular Invoice

Some countries require that invoices be made out on their special forms, sometimes in the language of the importing country. These forms can usually be purchased from the respective consulate or embassy. They too, must be free of errors.

Certificate of Origin

Even though the invoice may already state that the goods are of U.S. manufacture or origin, many countries require a separate certificate of origin. This must usually be countersigned by the local chamber of commerce, and in certain cases, must be visaed by the resident consul of the foreign country.

Insurance Certificate (Special Policy)

If the terms of sale are CIF, the exporter has to provide proof of insurance by means of an insurance certificate; or often a special policy is required according to the terms of sale or the letter of credit. If the exporter does not have an insurance policy, coverage sometimes can be obtained through the forwarder. The policy must be made available in however many originals and specify the shipment, points of origin, and destination, and whichever document is called for. Some form of signature must appear (usually preprinted) on behalf of the insurer or its agent. (See Chapter 20 on letters of credit.) Indicate by date or statement that it is effective at the latest by date of loading on board. It must be in the same currency as the credit itself unless otherwise indicated and for a minimum of 110 percent of the CIF value, covering all specified risks called for in the credit. An all-risk policy that does not clearly name such specified risks may not be acceptable as covering all specified risks under some circumstances. (See Chapter 25 for more information.)

Ocean Bill of Lading

The ocean bill of lading is a negotiable instrument and as such is an especially important document that serves several purposes. It can be used as proof that the goods were received by the steamship line and, if dated and marked clean onboard, indicates that the carrier has taken no exception to the condition of the shipment or its packing and that the merchandise has actually been laden onboard the vessel. The bill of lading also represents the contract between the shipper and the carrier, subject to the provisions of the United States Carriage of Goods Sea Act, detailed on the reverse side of the bill of lading. Because it is negotiable, the bill of lading serves as a means of transferring title by endorsement from one party to another. If shipment is made under a letter of credit, the forwarder must have a copy of the letter of credit to make sure that the transport documents meet its requirements.

There are two basic types of ocean bills of lading. One is the straight bill of lading, not normally negotiable, that indicates the name and address of the consignee and is mostly used for shipments on open account. The other type is a shipper's order or negotiable bill of lading that is always used for shipments against a letter of credit or documentary collection. The shipper endorses the original bill of lading before presenting it with the other documents to the bank. The letter of credit will stipulate if the bills of lading should be endorsed in blank or to the order of a third party, such as the paying bank.

The steamship company issues the bill of lading after the vessel has sailed, traditionally—and in keeping with ancient practices—in three originals, each signed and stamped onboard as of a specified date by the master's agent, with several additional copies. For clearing a shipment that was sold on open account terms, the importer will receive two originals and the exporter will retain the third original in case of loss of the first two. When shipment is made against a letter of credit, it often calls for a full set of bills of lading, consisting of three originals and at least four copies.

The exporter should be prepared to pay freight charges in order to receive the bills of lading if no prior credit arrangements have been made with the steamship line or the forwarder. It can take as much as ten days—but three days is normal—for the steamship line to provide the bills of lading. Messenger service or some kind of express service is frequently used, since the bill of lading is often the last document to complete the set of documents necessary to present to the bank for collection. Time and money can be saved by speeding up its receipt.

Sea Waybill

The sea waybill is not a common document in U.S. shipping but it is finding increased usage and is addressed for the first time in the UCP 500 as mentioned in Chapter 20. It is a non-negotiable document that permits the consignee to go directly to the terminal to claim the goods without waiting for processing delays that might occur while waiting a negotiable bill of lading to be endorsed over. Some say it finds more use in Europe, others in Asia.

Air Waybill

The air waybill is prepared or cut by the airfreight forwarder, usually with information from the shipper's invoice and packing list. In contrast to the ocean bill of lading, the air waybill is a non-negotiable instrument and serves as a shipping contract and receipt to the shipper, evidencing that the airline has accepted the goods as listed on the air waybill and agrees to carry the consignment to the airport of destination according to the conditions of its carrier contract. If the shipment is to be prepaid, the forwarder bills the shipper and pays the airline for the freight costs. Collect airfreight shipments are not accepted for all countries or for all commodities, so verify with the airline or the forwarder before agreeing to this method of shipment.

Other Documents

Following are other documents not so consistently required, depending on the type of shipment or the foreign country:

- *Phytosanitary inspection certificate.* This certificate is a form of preshipment inspection conducted by inspectors of the U.S. Department of Agriculture. It is a necessary document for shipments of plants, plant material, fruits, and vegetables to most countries. It certifies that the products shipped conform with the quarantine import regulations of the foreign country.

- *Inspection certificate.* An inspection certificate is an added protection that the buyer may request to certify that the goods conform to the order in quantity and quality. The importer can request this inspection certificate from an independent inspector, or simply use an affidavit by the shipper or exporter. (See Chapter 20 for complete details.)

- *Dock or warehouse receipts.* These receipts are used in circumstances such as might occur when shipments are made on an FAS basis, or when the exporter otherwise needs to prove that goods have been delivered or taken in charge by a warehouse or pier for further disposition by the importer or the importer's consolidator.

Electronic Data Interchange

Electronic Data Interchange (EDI) was once considered cutting edge because of its cost and rarity. Today, the combined cost of software and hardware is easily within the reach of most exporters and no more is needed than what millions of computer buffs have in their homes. With so many considering E-mail a part of life and so many surfing the Internet and using on-line, EDI has simply become another variation on a daily theme.

The Bureau of Census's Automated Export System intends to make electronic submission of the SED mandatory sometime in 1996, with voluntary submission encouraged as of July 1, 1995. Furthermore, the SED filing by the carrier, a consistent past practice, is no longer allowed; it must be taken care of by the exporter or the exporter's agent, such as a freight forwarder, for which a fee would surely be charged. This development will speed up the automation of export documentation and SDI at a much faster pace than formerly anticipated. There is an incredible amount of regulatory, procedural, and research information readily available to exporters at any time of day or night, not only from Internet but also on CD-ROM from the National Trade Data Base, NAFTA, GATT, the National Technical Information Service and any number of federal agency-sponsored databases.

Earlier, Electronic Data Interchange was briefly mentioned in connection with computers as a basic tool of exporters because most documents used in export today can be created on computers for transfer to another computer. Seen as a basic export procedure, EDI is the final evidence needed to understand the dependency of international trade on electronics. What is common for research and general office use now will soon be equally commonplace for the movement of funds, documents, and the coordination of shipments. EDI capability is also what is needed for many major improvements in operations management and quality control as well as Just-in-Time inventory management, which demands this kind of automation. Indicative of the broadening influence of EDI is the name change of its principal trade organization, from Transportation Data Coordinating Committee to Electronic Data Interchange Association (EDIA). It involves everyone from exporters to freight forwarders, banks, and carriers to government procurement. Wherever there is information to be exchanged or transmitted in a prescribed order and form via computer modem, EDI is a prime subject of interest. Electronic Fund Transfer (EFT) is also of growing importance and part of the EDI story. In developing EDI capability, the first step is to achieve the ability to transmit and receive data in a formatted transmission. The next step permits interconnections between the freight forwarder, the banks involved, and the merchandise carriers.

Because of the obvious interest of the Bureau of Census in improving its own job performance and cost containment—to say nothing of the exporter advantage in speed and convenience—the Census Bureau has created a National Clearinghouse for Exporter Data Processing Services. This service provides information on software companies with programs that will do all or part of the

EDI job. For details, contact the Program Manager for Automated Reporting, Foreign Trade Division, DOC, Bureau of the Census, Washington, D.C.; 301/457-2220. For other compilations of software sources and new developments, contact either *Export Today* or the *The Exporter* magazine, whose addresses are listed among other leading export publications in Appendix L. *Export Today* published a large and detailed listing in their June 1993 issue and the *Exporter* has repeatedly published articles and reference lists of software developments. Major sources of EDI information are: Electronic Data Interchange Association (EDIA), 225 Reineckers Lane, Suite 550, Alexandria, Virginia 22314; Pan American EDIFACT Board, 1800 Diagonal Road, Suite 355, Alexandria, Virginia 22314; and EDI Yellow Pages, P.O. Box 811366, Dallas, Texas 75381.

27

The Freight Forwarders

Freight forwarders are an integral part of the exporting business. As a liaison between the exporter, the transportation company, the banker, and an assortment of parties in between, freight forwarders can do much to smooth the path of exporting. On the other hand, an inefficient or careless forwarder can create major problems. Virtually all exporters depend on forwarders to varying degrees. Your dependence on the forwarder will be determined by the size and experience of your export staff, as well as by the level of control you wish to retain over the shipping and documentary side of your export operations. In theory, you don't need a forwarder at all, but only a limited number of firms could consider this a possibility. A good forwarder employs a number of highly skilled people who, in a sense, work for you. Therefore, it is wiser to let your staff, at least in part, simply double-check and support the forwarder's efforts rather than rely entirely on your own. Some firms, including some of substantial size and extensive import/export activities, are going one step further and contracting with logistics management firms to oversee all the problems and functions of moving goods, including selection and oversight of their freight forwarder and customhouse broker.

The Functions of a Forwarder

Freight forwarders are regulated and certified by the Federal Maritime Commission, which regularly audits forwarders to make sure they qualify and follow the rules established for being licensed and bonded. Some might be acting as Nonvessel Operating Common Carriers (NVOCC), which is the ocean version of airfreight consolidators. Airfreight forwarders are licensed by the International Air Transportation Association (IATA) and most are also licensed as airfreight consolidators. Some forwarders handle either air or ocean shipments exclusively, but the majority regularly handle both, although in separate departments.

Forwarders can act as your agent or representative, and can provide many valuable services, from the point at which you receive your first order and need help in making your quotation, to the preparation of documents necessary for collecting the payment for your export sale. To be of maximum assistance in handling your shipment, the forwarder should receive a copy of the letter of credit, if one is involved, together with your shipper's letter of instructions (SLI) (see Figure 27-1). See the section on shipping rates in Chapter 18 on how to use the services of a forwarder most effectively. The forwarder can perform the following services during the export transaction. They are listed more or less in chronological order:

- Advise on the various means of transportation and routes.

- Do research for the most favorable rates. Today, this can often be facilitated through computer software programs.

- Advise the shipper, both from direct experience and by use of sometimes costly reference works, of special conditions in the country of destination concerning port and airport facilities, regulations for clearing goods through foreign customs, and other arcane facts that can save a great many future headaches.

- Act as the shipper's agent in moving cargo overseas after being authorized to do so with a power of attorney.

- Arrange for inland freight and warehousing, if necessary.

- Receive and consolidate the merchandise for shipment and make delivery to the appropriate carrier.

- Advise on and arrange for special crating and packing.

- Make the booking on a carrier for the desired flight or voyage, and reserve the required containers.

- Supervise the on-loading of the shipment.

- Arrange for receipt of a clean bill of lading or air waybill according to the terms and conditions of the SLI, the order itself, and/or the letter of credit.

- Prepare the shipper's export declaration (SED) for the Bureau of the Census statistics and for customs clearance of the shipment. (See the comments as to new requirements for electronic filing of the SED by the exporter or the exporter's agent in Chapter 26.)

- Obtain the necessary consular invoices, certifications, legalizations, and any of the many other special documents that may be required.

ABF-5 WHSE CONTROL #0623   TO REORDER CALL: (800) 438-0182

SHIPPER'S LETTER OF INSTRUCTIONS

1a. EXPORTER (Name and address including ZIP code)	**SHIPPER: PLEASE BE SURE TO COMPLETE ALL BLUE SHADED AREAS.**

ZIP CODE

b. EXPORTER'S EIN (IRS) NO.

c. PARTIES TO TRANSACTION
☐ Related   ☐ Non-related

4a. ULTIMATE CONSIGNEE

b. INTERMEDIATE CONSIGNEE

5. FORWARDING AGENT

8. LOADING PIER (Vessel only)

9. MODE OF TRANSPORT (Specify)

10. EXPORTING CARRIER

11. PORT OF EXPORT

12. PORT OF UNLOADING (Vessel and air only)

13. CONTAINERIZED (Vessel only)
☐ Yes   ☐ No

SHIPPER REQUESTS INSURANCE   ☐ No   ☐ Yes $

SHIPPER MUST CHECK

☐ PREPAID ☐ COLLECT C.O.D. $_____

☐ AIR   ☐ OCEAN   ☐ CONSOLIDATE   ☐ DIRECT

SHIPPER'S INSTRUCTIONS IN CASE OF INABILITY TO DELIVER CONSIGNMENT

AS ASSIGNED ☐ ABANDON ☐ RETURN TO SHIPPER

☐ DELIVER TO

14. SCHEDULE B DESCRIPTION OF COMMODITIES,
15. MARKS, NOS., AND KINDS OF PACKAGES

(Use columns 17 – 19)

SHIPPER'S REF. NO.   DATE

VALUE (U.S. dollars, omit cents)
(Selling price or cost if not sold)

D/F (16)	SCHEDULE B NUMBER (17)	CHECK DIGIT	QUANTITY – SCHEDULE B UNIT(S) (18)	SHIPPING WEIGHT (Kilos) (19)		(20)

SHIPPER NOTE:

IF YOU ARE UNCERTAIN OF THE SCHEDULE B COMMODITY NO. DO NOT TYPE IT IN – WE WILL COMPLETE WHEN PROCESSING THE 7525V.

WE HAVE FORWARDED TO YOU, THE SHIPMENT DESCRIBED BELOW VIA:
☐ YOUR TRUCK, OR
☐ OTHER CARRIER (LISTED BELOW)
TRUCK LINE NAME _____
RECEIPT (PRO) NUMBER ___

DECLARED VALUE FOR CARRIAGE
$

21. VALIDATED LICENSE NO./GENERAL LICENSE SYMBOL

22. ECCN (When required)

PLEASE SIGN THE FIRST EXPORT DECLARATION IN BOX 23 WITH PEN AND INK

23. Duly authorized officer or employee

The exporter authorizes the forwarder named above to act as forwarding agent for export control and customs purposes.

DOCUMENTS ENCLOSED:

24. I certify that all statements made and all information contained herein are true and correct and that I have read and understand the instructions for preparation of this document, set forth in the "Correct Way to Fill Out the Shipper's Export Declaration." I understand that civil and criminal penalties, including forfeiture and sale, may be imposed for making false or fraudulent statements herein, failing to provide the requested information or for violation of U.S. laws on exportation (13 U.S.C. Sec. 305; 22 U.S.C. Sec. 401; 18 U.S.C. Sec. 1001; 50 U.S.C. App. 2410).

Signature

Confidential - For use solely for official purposes authorized by the Secretary of Commerce (13 USC 301 (g)

SPECIAL INSTRUCTIONS:

Title

Export shipments are subject to inspection by US Customs Service and/or Office of Export Enforcement.

Date

25. AUTHENTICATION (When required)

NOTE: The Shipper or his Authorized Agent hereby authorizes the above named Company, of his name and on his behalf, to prepare any export documents, to sign and accept any documents relating to said shipment and forward this shipment in accordance with the conditions of carriage and the tariffs of the carriers employed. The shipper guarantees payment of all collect charges in the event the consignee refuses payment. Hereunder the sole responsibility of the Company is to use reasonable care in the selection of carriers, forwarders, agents and others to whom it may entrust the shipment.

Figure 27-1. Shipper's letter of instructions.

- Arrange for the appropriate transit insurance, possibly under the forwarder's own master policy if the exporter does not have one.

- Prepare the documentation for presentation to the bank for collection against documents or under a letter of credit.

- Deliver all documents to the shipper's office at any point in the shipping process that the exporter wishes to assume control and responsibility for documentation.

- Follow up on the fate of the shipment at the foreign destination or at any of the transfer points in between.

- File any transportation claims that arise with the airlines or steamship lines. This is an area in which a forwarder can be of particular help.

- Send telexes or FAX communications and provide messenger service during the course of the entire export shipping and collection.

Most forwarders are capable of performing all of these duties, but because they involve so much detail and so many exceptions, few can perform perfectly in all roles on all occasions without error and direction. Any shipper is advised to keep track of the export transaction, and many exporters are better equipped to handle certain portions of the shipping process themselves, with export license application and processing being foremost among the details probably better handled by the exporter.

Forwarding charges are in addition to what the forwarder receives in commission from the carriers or, in the case of air shipments, included as profit margin in the freight rate quoted or received as a consolidator's discount. This keeps airfreight forwarding fees to a very modest level if the shipment is of reasonable value. Naturally, many of the items on the list are out-of-pocket costs or direct overhead and will be charged for separately; among these are documentation fees, messenger costs, and telexes. In the case of air shipments, air freight forwarders often share part of the substantial special volume discount they receive for being very active on a particular route with their regular customers in the form of reduced rates.

Between deregulation and the fact that airfreight today is a seller's market, your shipments must be considered in the light of at least two factors. First, of course, is the rate, but second is the reliability that the freight will move on schedule rather than being bumped for a higher-priority shipper or shipment. While the forwarder's combined volume is of great help in obtaining priority, even this does not always provide definite assurance that the shipment won't get bumped.

Except for larger shipments—usually more than 2200 pounds—you must rely on the forwarder to have good consolidation facilities for your primary routes and to give you a fair quote based on its consolidation rate or its negotiated rate if consolidation is not involved. Keep in mind that the forwarder's margin over the consolidation rate or negotiated rate is the forwarder's airfreight division's primary source of profit. Once you have located a suitable airfreight forwarder, it is best to work closely with the staff and let them handle your easy shipments, as well as those requiring hard work. It is the overall relationship of costs, service, and rates that must be considered in the case of your airfreight forwarder. On the other hand, you might need more than one forwarder to get favorable rate structures to all your destinations. The forwarder's speed in handling documents and the special necessity for such speed in the case of airfreight, is another consideration you must keep in mind as a shipper.

Surface shipments are a somewhat different matter. Marine rates can be studied more on a case-by-case basis because the forwarder has less at stake in terms of rate structure. Ocean freight forwarders do not upcharge on ocean rates. They provide a rated bill of lading to assure you that the rate you were charged is the same as the ocean carrier billed. Again, deregulation has changed the rules, such as diminished control by steamship line conferences, and directly negotiated rates. NVOCCs have also changed the ocean shipping competition picture.

The ocean forwarder receives a much smaller commission from the steamship line, and therefore must rely much more on the freight forwarding fees and handling charges. Many forwarders have their own NVOCC operation, and there are independent NVOCCs through whom you can ship directly or access through your own forwarder. Bargains on ocean rates are much more difficult to find with today's upsurge in export activities, and there has been much discounting. Also, there may be less differential in NVOCC rates than there once was now that the industry has stabilized after the weaker operations were forced out. The greatest savings in surface shipping today can be found by experimenting with combinations of routes to various ports and with intermodal arrangements (see Chapter 18).

In most cases, the forwarder will bill the exporter for the freight charges, as well as for handling and any special charges, if the exporter's good credit is established. For new customers, or on very large shipments, however, the forwarder may request that freight be paid before the bill of lading is released.

Working with Your Forwarder

Exporters should not rely solely on the forwarder for freight quotations. Because of deregulation, stiff competition, constant changes in conference statuses, and frequent changes in rates both for air or ocean shipments, it is an extremely time-consuming task to get the best rates. Even though forwarders offer to find the best freight rates available and must try do so to remain competitive themselves, remember that while the new computer programs help, their employees are under time pressures just as much as yours are, and there are economic limitations to the forwarders' staff research time. It is in your best interests to check with the carriers directly, especially in the case of large shipments or new situations. It is wise to keep informed of any changes in the industry through trade papers and shipping magazines, since it is an area that can mean the difference between being fully competitive and something less. The prime publications for tracking ocean vessels are the *Pacific Shipper,* the *American Shipper,* and the *Journal of Commerce,* as well as the *Shipping Digest* to some extent for the East Coast shippers. (See Appendix L.)

Those exporters who prefer to remain in control of their documentary collections and try to minimize documentary discrepancies themselves can request that the forwarder send all documents to the exporter for verification before presentation and forward the documents to the bank themselves. This is a recommended practice if you have the staff and the skills. The best possible relationship is one in which the shipper's staff and the forwarder's staff are each addressing themselves to those tasks that they are best equipped to do in terms of facilities, skills, and time.

Finding the Right Forwarder

In view of the key role forwarders play, it is best to go to some lengths to find the right one for your needs. Some lean more to the import work of the custom house broker, others more to air or ocean, or to particular commodities such as produce. Some forwarders have better consolidation and storage control facilities than others; some are advantageous because they are small, while others offer the benefits of a worldwide network. Reliability is key. There are many forwarders, so it is best to ask for recommendations from carriers you are likely to use, as well as from a particular forwarder's present customers. Plan on going to their place of business for an interview. Explain your needs and ask questions, because this is one more support area that will determine your success. Once you have found a good forwarder for your purposes, or a set of forwarders if necessary, work with them closely and give them enough business so that it is a valuable partnership for both parties.

28

Dealing with Claims

Under the best of circumstances, dealing with claims is an unpleasant subject. After the satisfaction of getting the order, the care in filling it, the organizing and shipping of it, comes the unpleasant notice of bad arrival, damaged or spoiled goods, or pilfered or short shipments. With new customers, and possibly with some old ones as well, the first reaction is invariably one of suspicion. As with all bad news, it is best to confront it immediately because claims never improve with age. The variety and uniqueness of transit claims boggles the imagination as most of us believe that if the plane doesn't crash or the ship doesn't sink we are home free. Barry M. Tarnef, director of marine loss control services at the CIGNA Companies, writing in the May 1993 issue of *Export Today,* recites a litany of weird claims.[1] They include the story of a yacht shipped on the deck of a vessel next to a large crane that had been welded to the same deck for transport. When welders removed the crane, sparks landed on the flammable tarp covering the yacht, which was totally destroyed. Then there was the large air shipment of women's sportswear made in Turkey for a famous designer name manufacturer in New York, whose name was prominently displayed on the external packaging. The routing required a stopover in Paris with surface transit from Orly Airport to DeGaulle Airport. During the course of the transfer, more of the sportswear was transferred to the backs of Parisians than to the waiting hands of New Yorkers. In another case, a leaky 20-foot container of antiques was shipped during winter across the Atlantic and arrived as a 20-foot-long block of solid ice. Tarnef goes on to point out that simple care and common sense would readily have prevented all these losses, but that somewhere, somehow, claims are always waiting to happen. His experience leads him to believe that 75 percent of cargo losses could be avoided if the shipper took the trouble to adhere to the most basic principles of export packing and transportation. From 1988 to 1991 a total of 43 percent of CIGNA's cargo losses were attributed to improper handling and/or stowage and only 21 percent to accidents such as sinking, stranding, collision, fire, or heavy weather.[2]

Steps in Claim Procedures

There are several steps that are clearly vital to the successful and fair settlement of a potential or pending claim. As described by Barry Tarnef in his article they are:

- *Step 1.* Depending on the nature of the loss, the overseas consignee (or the shipper's agent in the case of air shipments) should have instructions to take exception on the air waybill or carrier's delivery receipt by noting any shortage or apparent damage prior to signing it as a receipt for the merchandise. Once the carrier has a clean receipt from the consignee, it is increasingly difficult to get settlement of a claim. In the case of ocean shipments, the insurance agent and the insurance representative in the foreign port should be notified immediately and advised of the location of the claimed goods so that inspection can be made.

- *Step 2.* All possible steps should be taken by the shipper and consignee to prevent further damage and minimize the loss. These are the same sort of steps you would take if the shipment were not insured and the loss was to be all at your account. This is a matter of law as well as good judgment.

- *Step 3.* For both ocean and air shipments, an independent survey should be arranged at the earliest moment after notification of a problem and the carrier or the carrier's agent advised of the loss and the forthcoming survey. This step can be used to substantiate the findings of the insurance inspector or to have separate recourse against the carrier or other responsible party.

- *Step 4.* A substantiation of your claim should be prepared with: (a) the original and duplicate of a Special Marine Policy; (b) the ocean bill of lading or air waybill or other applicable bill of lading or carrier's receipt; (c) an original of the shipper's invoice; (d) the packing list and any evidence of the condition of the goods at the time of shipment; (e) the survey report if done by an independent surveyor; and (f) a copy of the claim letter to the carrier and the carrier's reply.[3]

The most important instruction to your customer in respect to transportation claims is to make timely reports—that is, as soon as possible following arrival! Write a preliminary notice-of-claim letter to the carrier involved and to the insurance company to give all parties concerned an opportunity to inspect the cargo. A telephone call might help to get things moving but is not a substitute for timely written notice. "Put it in writing" is a cardinal rule in handling claims.

Because of the remaining insurable interest you have in the merchandise, and depending on the size of the shipment and possible loss involved, it could be a very wise investment to be personally present for the formal claim inspection and appraisal and to get the claim process started. It is an all-too-often-observed contradiction of best-interest judgment for an exporter facing a substantial loss to be unwilling to invest a few days and a few thousand dollars to minimize the loss by such an on-site inspection. Yet, that same person might board a plane at a moment's notice to close a deal that would net a much smaller bottom-line dollar contribution than the claim loss might represent. A similar situation exists in the case of legal expenses. A letter from a good admiralty or claims lawyer can often settle or reduce a claim and save months of aggravation.

As mentioned in the basic steps above, when the extent of the damage is determined, present a formal claim to the appropriate party. Many times the forwarder will take care of these details; however, since *your* money is at stake, it is best to work closely with the forwarder when preparing the actual report of loss or damage. Once a transportation claim is submitted, it can be very difficult to increase the claim if all the damages were not initially considered. These costs should, of course, include the basic value of the cargo, inland freight, ocean- or airfreight, customs duty, documentation and handling charges, and any other costs incurred, on a prorated basis. If there is any salvage on the damaged goods, proceeds are deducted from the total amount claimed. Insurance companies may allow additional losses of up to 10 percent of the value of the goods if an increase in the value or incurment of additional expenses can be evidenced, provided your insurance was for the international trade standard of 110 percent of CIF value.

If the shipment is insured and the claim is properly documented and proven, the insurance company will pay the insured and then present its claim to the carrier for redress. If the shipment was not insured, there is a certain liability for loss or damage that each carrier assumes by law and in accordance with its published tariffs. This liability is normally limited to a specific dollar amount per pound, hundred weight, or package. In some instances, this liability can be increased if an additional valuation charge was taken out with the carrier. The carrier may not accept any, or very limited, liability for certain cargo and generally will not accept liability whatsoever if there is any indication that the loss can be attributed to the shipper's negligence. Because there are any number of casualties beyond the control of the carrier, such as fire on board a vessel, mechanical malfunctions on airplanes, delays because of strikes or weather conditions, and even navigational errors by the crew, there is substantial risk of loss for which the carrier can and will decline all responsibility.

Often there is more than one carrier involved in an export shipment, such as a trucking line and a steamship company, which makes it difficult to pinpoint blame for a claim, especially in the case of concealed shortage or damage. This exposes the shipper/exporter to additional risks and can best be overcome with an insurance policy that includes coverage on all portions of transportation— that is, warehouse-to-warehouse or door-to-door coverage that is typical of the modern open-cargo policy. This type of insurance is usually not only less expensive than the cost of increasing the carrier's liability, it is also easier to collect. It is particularly important to obtain this type of coverage for high-value cargo. (See the section on insuring transit risks in Chapter 25.)

There are very definite rules concerning the validity period for claims. The general rule is two years from the date of arrival—in the case of air shipments—and one year for ocean shipments. Thereafter, the claim is extinguished unless legal action has been taken. One exporter pursued a claim vigorously with an air cargo carrier claims manager for two years. All replies were of a delaying and mitigating nature. At the end of the two years, the claim manager advised that "the claim is now invalid due to expiry of the allowed claim period." (P.S. The shipper won that one in small claims court.) Remember, the carrier's claim agents are paid not to pay claims!

Minimizing Claims

Many claims easily could be avoided with more emphasis on quality control and proper care when first planning the overseas shipment. Too often no consideration is given to heat or cold during transit, causing accidents such as cosmetics arriving melted in the Middle East or onions freezing en route to Scandinavia. Such claims are often denied on the basis of "inherent vice." Another major factor is proper packaging of the product and intelligent loading plans for containers. Many pallets are not strapped well enough to withstand the rolling motion of ocean shipments or the movement of the container from truck to vessel to truck. Even the best-strapped pallets need to be properly braced in the container itself to avoid tilting. Remember that a ship moves in six different ways: it rolls, pitches, heaves, surges, sways, and yaws. It is said to be not unusual for cargo to travel in a 70-foot arc several times in one minute. Many steamship lines spot-check containers delivered to their dock to make sure the cargo is correctly loaded and braced in order to avoid damage in transit claims or bad public relations as a result of claim disputes.

Avoiding claims is crucial for the exporter, not only because of the merchandise sales loss and the administrative and legal costs of a claim, but because of the greater long-run potential loss of importer/customer satisfaction and goodwill. Even without blaming the exporter, many an importer has decided that it was simply too much trouble to import that particular product because of the high-loss ratio. No matter that all claims were satisfactorily settled; if the importer contracted to import 100 widgits and 50 were damaged, destroyed, lost, or stolen, everyone lost. The importer had the accrued costs of selling 100, financed a letter of credit for 100, and anticipated the per unit gross profit on 100. Instead, only half the gross profit materialized, while the other costs remained fixed. The importer's customers were unhappy, and the importer faced expensive administrative, and possibly legal, costs to settle the claim. The exporter faced similar problems, but the worst was the loss of the customer's interest in ordering any more of that product, despite all the travel, time, and trouble the exporter had put into the arrangement in the first place. In other words, the hidden costs were by far the greatest. This is not an exaggeration or an isolated incident but an all-too-common fact in many exporter's lives.

Both breakage and pilferage are controllable, even though they probably cannot be eliminated. Often pilferage is the greater villain, and the harder one of the two to control. However, when you look at the cost of better packing, properly loaded containers, possibly even airfreight versus ocean freight, and other means of minimizing claims, keep in mind the cost of the losses you might be risking. Whatever losses do occur should be reported and documented to the people in your firm who may be able to help avoid a similar problem in the future. That would include: the financial staff whose concern is for the profit contributions the export sale is expected to produce; the people making and shipping the product, including the plant foreman, the shipping supervisor and logistics people in the export department; and the marketing people who control to whom and where you sell.

Resolving Product Claims

A critical problem arises when the importer receives a claim from the foreign distributor or the overseas retailer after the duty has been paid and there is no recourse against the carrier. If an end user finds the product wanting or faulty, the wholesale cost of the claim is by then far above the original manufacturer's selling price, even removing the exporter, importer, wholesaler, and retailer profits in turn. Duty, freight, financing, and miscellaneous costs have all been paid, and no one is willing to share in the drastically increased costs of the claim. If you are a third-party exporter, you will probably find the manufacturer less than enthusiastic about accepting responsibility for the faulty product at this point and at these costs, which is a problem to keep in mind during the original EMC/ETC negotiations. Worse yet, the matter of verification and inspection of end-user complaints is not as easily accomplished as it is in domestic business. It is impractical to ask that all faulty goods be returned, because of freight and packing costs. In fact, whenever possible, it should be stipulated that nothing can be returned without written permission, regardless of all other rights the claimant might have.

It should be noted here, however, that it is fairly easy to have import duties waived on returned merchandise so long as it can be proven that the same goods were previously exported and are of U.S. origin. In that case, it is not difficult to have them classified "American Goods Returned (AGR)" and no duty will be levied, except on any value added to them. The process for the importer to retrieve import duties already paid abroad may be much more difficult—possibly not even worth the trouble.

To verify a claim overseas, someone must be involved who can be trusted to examine the goods abroad, or certain percentage rules for sampling must be established. Also remember that, at least in some countries, quality standards are as high or higher than those of American consumers. The best example of this is Japan, whose consumers are the fussiest in the world and among the most pampered by their retailers and suppliers.

In view of these considerations, the cooperation of the overseas importer in dealing with claims of all kinds is of vital importance, especially if it is not practical for the exporter to be on hand to assess the damage or validity of the claim, arrange for surveys, inspections, or repairs, properly store and handle the undamaged goods, and salvage whatever possible of the claimed merchandise.

The best way to deal with claims is to do everything possible to avoid having them in the first place. When claims do occur, speed and thoroughness in reporting them to all parties involved and then as expeditious a settlement as possible are essential. As soon as you can, calculate the dollar figure of the total claim value so that everyone is aware of the extent of the damage or problem. And, just as with your personal automobile insurance, it may be beneficial in the long run to settle some nuisance claims without invoking all seller's rights or involving the insurance company, just to keep a clean record and a satisfied customer.

Endnotes

1. Barry M. Tarnef, "A Loss Control Primer for Today's Exporters: How to Protect Your Goods in Transit Without Going Along for the Ride," *Export Today,* May 1993.

2. Tarnef, ibid.

3. Tarnef, ibid.

29

Foreign Trade Zones and Duty Drawback

On occasion, an exporting manufacturer has to pay duties on imported goods or components that are subsequently reexported for a variety of reasons, some pre-planned, others by virtue of an unexpected sales opportunity. In other cases the exporter may have to handle or process the imported goods as part of the routine manufacturing process of a product, part of which is then exported. In either case, U.S tariff laws apply, and duty must be paid. If this is routine or a frequent problem involving meaningful sums of money, there is a means of accommodating it through the duty drawback process or indefinitely deferring the need to pay duty through the use of an existing foreign trade zone (FTZ) or establishment of a new specific zone or facility until the product enters the United States officially or the duty is waived as it is exported overseas from the FTZ.

U.S. Foreign Trade Zones

Foreign trade zones are domestic sites that are legally construed to be outside U.S. customs territory. They provide facilities for operations involving storage, repacking, inspection, exhibition, assembly, remanufacturing, and other processing. For export operations, FTZs provide export status for the purpose of excise tax rebates and customs drawback. For import and reexport activities, no duties or federal excise taxes are charged on foreign goods until the goods, or products made from them, are moved into customs territory. Also, no quota restrictions ordinarily apply. Therefore, FTZs offer an opportunity to blend American manufacture for export with foreign-made goods, without the necessity of paying duties that would otherwise be assessed. Such processing can even occur in relation to imported goods that are in excess of allowed import quotas.

These features should be of particular interest to an exporting manufacturer, possibly as a subzone FTZ. The latter is a special-purpose facility set up by a manufacturer whose operations cannot function effectively in a public FTZ, and so therefore an FTZ is permitted on the manufacturer's own premises.

There are readily apparent advantages to the regular or subzone FTZ concept to avoid the heavy paperwork load to process duty drawbacks. Most of the necessity for these is avoided by FTZs because no duty is paid in the first place. In 1994 there were over 200 approved FTZs throughout the United States (up from 165 in 1970) and their uses and applications for other areas are growing rapidly. Observers say the program is still greatly underutilized and a well-kept secret. About one-third of the total value of goods handled by FTZs is for export and two-thirds for import. Promoters of FTZs explain that merchandise can be moved from zone to zone under customs bond and even to a portion of the manufacturer's plant designated as a subzone. One advantage of public FTZs is that the operators and tenants are often experts in international trade who offer added knowledge and skills that helps increase the export expertise of newcomers. Merchandise can also be held in an FTZ, pending the reopening of a quota.

Information about existing zones or the establishment of a new zone or subzone is available from your nearest US&FCS district office, local chamber of commerce, port authority, or from the Executive Secretary, Foreign Trade Zones Board, Room 1529, International Trade Administration, Department of Commerce, Washington, D.C. 20230.

Bonded Warehouses

Bonded warehouses are available in many locations where goods can be warehoused without duties being assessed until they are released from the bonded warehouse. Again, the nearest port authorities for air or ocean can advise you as to the location of such bonded warehouses, and they can also be found in the Yellow Pages. Bonded warehouses can be government-owned or -operated, private, or commercial. Private bonded warehouses can be a designated area of a company's regular storage facility, and merchandise can be stored in bonded warehouses for up to five years. Unlike an FTZ facility, no manufacturing can take place in a bonded warehouse, but it can still serve as a tool for eliminating the necessity of accounting for drawback in some circumstances. Bonded warehouses are also useful for deferring duty, holding goods pending the reopening of quotas or anticipated lowered duties. They also serve as a place for cleaning or repacking goods, even though manufacturing or processing is not allowed, thus maintaining flexibility in serving both American and export markets from the same inventory.

Drawback of Custom Duties

Regardless of the circumstances of entry, there are rules that allow recovery of most of the duties paid. There are a number of steps to follow, and a lot of paperwork is usually involved. If the merchandise entered the country from overseas, custom duties presumably will have been paid on the merchandise. When the goods are reexported, the exporter can obtain relief through the U.S. Customs Service, an agency of the United States Department of the Treasury. This relief is called *drawback,* in reference to obtaining a return of duty paid on imports that are subsequently reexported. Only 99 percent of the duty is refunded, and 1 percent is withheld to cover costs. The Tariff and Trade Act of 1984 authorizes several types of drawback, but the two following forms are those of primary interest to exporting manufacturers:

1. If articles manufactured in the United States with the use of imported merchandise are exported, the duties paid on the imported merchandise that was utilized can be refunded, less 1 percent. To obtain this type of drawback, you must file a proposal with the Regional Commissioner of Customs.

2. If both imported and domestic merchandise of the same kind and quality (fungible) are used to manufacture articles, some of which are exported, then duties that were paid on the imported merchandise are refundable as drawback on the exported portion whether or not that particular merchandise was used in the exported articles. This is referred to as substitution. It need not even be the identical merchandise that was imported, and could have previously been imported as many as three years earlier if the goods are *fungible* (freely substitutable and interchangeable).

To obtain the drawback, file a proposal with the Drawback and Bond Branch, Customs Headquarters, 1301 Constitution Avenue NW, Washington, D.C. 20229. You must be able to establish that the articles on which the drawback is being claimed were exported within five years after importation of the merchandise in question. In the case of substitution of domestic items, fungible with previously imported merchandise, the time limit is three years. Once the request for drawback is approved, the proposal and approval together constitute the manufacturer's drawback rate.

A word of caution: This is very much a "red tape" process that should be avoided if possible through advance planning or accomplished by means of the use of foreign trade zones or bonded warehouses. The government states that of the estimated $4.8 billion in duties paid which were eligible for drawback, only $480 million was reclaimed in 1992. In part this was due to the substantial paperwork entailed, although now there are software programs for PCs that reduce the cost of recovery to only about 10 percent of the anticipated returns. The alternative means of avoiding red tape is to use a drawback specialist to do this process in the name of the company, with the specialist keeping a percentage of the recovery.

5

Staying Out of Trouble

30

Intellectual Property Rights

An often overlooked, but very important, consideration is which trademarks and patents should be obtained before marketing in target countries. This is of special concern if good opportunities to license the design or technology or develop consumer brand consciousness in a particular country can be identified. Protection is not only important against piracy and infringement in the foreign markets, but can also have a bearing on duplication of your product overseas for sale back into the U.S. domestic market. Trademark protection provides identification of your firm's product and services on which a sales or advertising campaign can focus, even in circumstances where a patent cannot be obtained.

The umbrella term describing patents, trademarks, copyrights, and know-how or trade secrets is Intellectual Property Rights (IPR). To maximize the value of these rights, first seek protection for your intellectual property rights under applicable U.S. laws, and then be aware of the calendar. Many foreign countries grant priority based on *when* a patent or trademark was applied for in the United States, and a timely corresponding application then being filed in the foreign country. There are several international treaties aimed at protecting intellectual property rights, including protection from counterfeiting.

Copyrights

Copyrights presently have the most convenient arrangements to obtain ready coverage in many countries with a single application. The Universal Copyright Convention automatically protects works by U.S. authors in about 75 member countries as long as they post a copyright notice on the work by indicating the following:

- The symbol "c" in a circle (in some countries the word *copyright* or the symbol *c* in a circle is equally acceptable)
- Author's name
- Year of publication

The Buenos Aires Copyright Convention specifies that authors from the United States and 17 Latin American nations who have obtained copyrights in their own country have protection in each of the member nations if the work has a statement indicating the reservation of the property rights, typically "all rights reserved." The cost of foreign copyright coverage is therefore, virtually nil. Indeed, one need not even file in the United States to obtain protection, although United States filing is desirable to preserve certain statutory remedies in the United States. Copyright protection in the United States lasts for the life of the author plus 50 years after death.

The United States is now a member of the other major international copyright convention, the Berne Convention for the Protection of Literary and Artistic Works, which the United States joined in 1989. American authors no longer have to publish their works in one of the member countries simultaneously with their first publication in the United States to be eligible to obtain automatic protection in all member countries.

Computer software is eligible for protection under U.S. copyright laws, but in many foreign countries, protection is not currently available. On the other hand, most of the industrialized countries do permit copyright protection for software. For further up-to-date information on protection through international conventions, contact the U.S. Copyright Office, Library of Congress, Washington, D.C. 20559.

Trademarks

The United States and about 88 other countries belong to the most important international treaty in this field, the Paris Union International Convention for the Protection of Industrial Properties, which covers protection of both patents and trademarks. An important provision is that filings made within six months of the U.S. filing will date back to that filing. The United States also belongs to the General Inter-American Convention for Trademark and Commercial Protection of 1929 and to several other bilateral treaty arrangements and conventions. Most of these adhere to the national treatment concept, meaning that foreign firms receive the same treatment under their patent and trademark laws as they extend to their own citizens. Contrary to the impression of many exporters, however, there is no means by which a trademark can be registered in one of these convention nations or through some central authority in order to receive protection from all the signatory nations. Firms are advised to seek competent legal counsel in order to secure and protect their foreign rights in this area, which is so essential to a global marketing plan.

In many countries, it is not uncommon for a company to find that someone else has registered its trademark. This can be done because in most countries prior use is not a prerequisite for registration—the only restrictions are on names that sound similar to merely descriptive common words, geographic names, or brand names already registered or in use in that country. Sometimes the registrant will be a local distributor, or even a complete stranger who learns of, or speculates on, future importation. The risk is that when a company with a trademark that has been registered by other than the rightful owner starts to sell or operate in the foreign country, or desires to terminate its local distributor, it discovers it must negotiate to buy its name back for a substantial sum. Many firms are led into this trap because, in the United States, a company can have exclusive rights to a trademark by being first to use it under common law. Registration can occur later, but the trademark must remain in use. Once registered in the United States, a trademark is good for ten years.

Overseas you do not have to be currently using a trademark to protect it (contrary to the practice in the United States). Therefore, it is wise to consider registering your company's trademark in the major countries that appear to be the best and most obvious prospects for your product, even though an export sales undertaking is not part of your present plans. One factor that keeps this strategy from becoming too burdensome is that, at least initially, registering a trademark is not very costly. In most countries it is a step-by-step charge over a period of as much as two, three, or even more years. The initial charge can range from $150 to $500 per country.

Make a decision about the number of countries in which you want to register. This is a decision in which your budget plays a controlling part. The first step is to list the primary target countries. If this seems too broad, consider countries that are most likely to imitate your product and name. A prime criterion is the country that has the production capacity and demand but lacks creativity in your product area. You may want to omit countries that, although having the expertise and production facilities, lack a sufficient home market for the product unless they can sell into the more populous neighboring countries where you have registered your trademark.

One further factor to consider is your trademark and/or company name relative to a licensing or distributorship agreement. If the license grants use of the trademark or logo, determine if that action and the agreement itself must be recorded in the host country. In some countries, especially the British Commonwealth countries, a trademark license or distributorship comes under the registered-user provisions of the Trademark Law and failure to record the license or distributorship, coupled with the use of the trademark by the licensee or distributor, may invalidate the foreign trademark registration owned by the U.S. company. The result can be a situation in which, even when the agreement expires, your former licensee's or distributor's rights to your name and logo do not. In addition, in some countries trademarks can be canceled through nonuse, usually over a three- to five-year period. If the licensee is not specially recorded as a registered user, that licensee's use will not count as "use" for this purpose.

Note that use of *TM* to indicate the trademark is claimed, while *R* in a circle indicates it has been registered. In many countries, including the United States, use of the circled R is prohibited if the mark has not been registered in that country. In such cases, *TM* is used.

Most American attorneys who specialize in intellectual property rights have working agreements with their counterparts in most of the important industrial countries who can provide expertise on complying with local laws. For further information on foreign trademark protection, laws, and conventions, contact the Foreign Business Practices Division, Office of International Finance and Investment, Bureau of International Economic Policy, in the International Trade Administration, Department of Commerce. Official journals of foreign patent offices providing trademark information are maintained by the U.S. Patent and Trademark Office, Crystal Plaza, 2021 Jefferson Davis Highway, Arlington, Virginia 22202.

Patents

Filing patents is by far the most difficult and expensive procedure in the intellectual property rights protection process. Foreign patent applications are costly, and it is probably not economical to file in each country to which you wish to export. The country elimination process is similar to the one mentioned for trademarks, except that the emphasis shifts to facilities and techniques available to practice the technology as opposed to the market in which you desire to sell your product. The patent infringer can approach your target market directly. Unless you have a patent in a particular country, the only protection is to enjoin importation into the United States under your U.S. patent. The validity period for U.S. patents was changed in 1994 to generally run for a period of 20 years from the filing date, to conform with prevailing international standards.

There is no way to have the U.S. patent automatically recognized and protected in a foreign country, but there continues to be some progress in easing the foreign patenting process. The United States and 35 other countries belong to the Patent Cooperation Treaty that became effective in 1978. This treaty serves to simplify filing procedures by allowing one patent application to be filed with the U.S. Patent and Trademark Office as a central source, with the effect of filing in each member country that is requested. Thereafter, each country proceeds under its own unique set of procedures, but some substantial costs can be saved.

Still more streamlined is the European Patent Convention, under which U.S. nationals can file a single application at the European Patent Office in Munich and designate the European countries in which this European patent is desired. It is granted as a national patent in the designated country. The United States belongs to a number of other treaties, conventions, and bilateral agreements, most notably the Paris Union International Convention of 88 countries and the Inter-American Convention of 12 countries. Primarily, these allow U.S. nationals treatment equal to nationals of the host country. To maintain the priority you are entitled to under the Paris Union International Convention, you must file your foreign patent within 12 months of the U.S. patent filing date. This gives you priority in other countries dating back to your first U.S. filing and gives you the maximum foreign protection.

How quickly you file your U.S. patent before any public use or publication of the process or invention can enhance the validity of your foreign application even though in the United States you have one year to file after earliest publication or use. Use, sales, or advertising activities concerning the patented product in the United States or any other country before filing may weaken the foreign patents obtained subsequent to the American patent. Keep in mind that in most countries, patents are issued on the basis of "first to file," contrary to the U.S. standard of "first to invent."

If, for whatever reason, you cannot file for the foreign patents within 12 months from filing the U.S. patent, it is still possible to file, under some circumstances, up to the time the U.S. patent is issued, as long as there has been no publication (or sale, in some cases) of the invention. You are not, however, entitled to the special priorities discussed in the two preceeding paragraphs. Most industrial countries will not issue a patent after the U.S. patent has been issued. A few countries will issue confirmation or importation patents, but they must be filed before any use of the product in that country. For further sources on patent information, contact the same organizations mentioned in the discussion of trademarks.

It is important that you consult a competent attorney for patent filing procedures. The cost of obtaining a patent in foreign countries is typically about $2000 per country for English-speaking countries, $4000 for initial filing in the European Union, and $6000 to $7000 for Japan and Brazil, together with increased costs for translation in almost any non-English speaking country. In practice, there is little patent registration done in Latin America on the part of smaller firms except in Brazil and Argentina. In the European Union, besides the "front door" joint EU filing fee, upon completion of the patent process there will be final registration costs of $1000 to $2000 per country, but it is not necessary to register in each of the 15 EU countries for some will probably not be critical to the product's patent protection. For most countries, achieving a patent is at least a two-year process that can extend up to three or four years in Japan. Thereafter, in almost all countries there will be maintenance fees of $200 to $500, typically required every other year.

Trade Secrets

According to U.S. common law, trade secrets are any "formula, pattern, device or compilation of information which is used in one's business, and which gives an opportunity to obtain an advantage over competitors who do not know or use it." Such proprietary information has protection in the United States of unlimited duration so long as it is kept secret. Many states will enforce noncompetition agreements against exemployees and make misappropriation of trade secrets a criminal offense. Trade secret protection abroad is both rare and limited. Even in the case of well-drawn licensing agreements or contracts, there is often no effective legal remedy to prevent or punish misappropriation of trade secrets.

The GATT Uruguay Round and IPR

The lengthy Uruguay Round of international trade negotiations finally concluded in 1994 and resulted in the creation of the World Trade Organization (WTO) to replace the GATT framework, effective January 1995. One of the major achievements of the negotiations is an agreement on Trade-Related Aspects of Intellectual Property Rights (TRIPS).

Under this agreement, the countries that are members of the WTO commit to greatly strengthen enforcement of intellectual property rights. The Berne Convention (copyrights) and the Paris Convention (patents and trademarks) became the general minimum standards, even for countries that are not actually signatories to those treaties. Member countries agree to extend copyright protection to computer programs and improve protection for audiovisual works. For trademarks, the minimum terms for registration are seven years, renewable indefinitely. Cancellation for nonuse can only be done after three years of unjustified nonuse. Use by another person is recognized as valid use if the use is controlled by the owner of the trademark, as in the case of an authorized distributor or dealer. The scope of available patent protection is broadened to include pharmaceutical and biological technologies. The opportunity to require compulsory licensing of patents is sharply limited. All members agreed to adopt measures to establish legal status for trade secrets and protect them from misappropriation. In addition, extensive border control procedures are to be established so the customs officials of each country can detain, inspect, and seize infringing goods.

In January 1996, the industrialized country members of the WTO will begin enforcing the TRIPS regime. Developing countries will have an extra four-year grace period to establish procedures called for under the agreements, while the least-developed countries may delay full implementation for a maximum of ten years. During the next few years, the laws and practices of many countries will be extensively changed in favor of owners of intellectual property. Hopefully, China will be among them, even though it is not currently a member of the WTO. The Office of the U.S. Trade Representative (USTR) has conducted several difficult negotiations with China to change what had been very loose and disorderly practices concerning intellectual property rights, and particularly copyrights, with software and films being the special focus. With the apparently successful conclusion of the February 1995 negotiations, which nearly resulted in a major trade war, it is hoped that the worst of China's practices have been dealt with, but it appears there are plenty more to come.

Conclusion

While it is important to get all possible protection for intellectual property rights insofar as practical, it is also important to recognize that enforcement of this protection will always vary from country to country and that some countries are not, and will never be, party to any treaty. Violations of American intellectual property rights, mainly through sales of counterfeit and pirated goods, pose a serious problem to consumers worldwide and have become extremely costly to the United States in terms of lost revenues and jobs. Protection of intellectual property rights remains a high-priority matter with the USTR. The office has achieved major success in recent years in persuading many countries to adopt modern laws protecting international property rights. The best-known examples are Brazil, Hong Kong, and Singapore. Efforts concerning China, India, Indonesia, and other countries are expected to require a number of years more. For basic information on foreign copyright, trademark, and patent protection, obtain a copy of International Business Practices, 1993 edition, a DOC publication.

There are four government offices that can answer questions concerning intellectual property rights overseas. They are:

1. Patent and Trademark Office 703/557-3341

2. International Trade Administration (ITA) 202/482-4501

3. U.S. Customs Service 202/566-5765

4. Copyright Office, Library of Congress, Subcommittee on Intellectual Property 202/395-6161

31

Export Licensing

Those new to export often think of an export License as a "business license" similar to that which is often required by local city governments in order to legally do business. This is not the case regarding export Licenses. Rather, an export License is a U.S. Government authorization to export concerning a specific transaction that one of the U.S. agencies responsible for export licensing administration has ruled requires an export license because of the nature, end-use, end-user, and/or destination of the product. You do not need an "export license" just to be in the business of exporting.

The National Export Strategy and Export Controls

The United States Government's National Export Strategy developed in recent years has been referred to in several places in this book because it represents an effort to pursue and promote a realistic and updated approach to America's export deficiencies, particularly as related to export controls. Thus, the U.S. exporter is clearly a beneficiary of this strategy and the end of the Cold War, because it has resulted in significantly reduced U.S. Government control of exports.

In recent years the total value of goods for which U.S. Government Licensing approval prior to export is required has fallen sharply. For example, these types of exports have fallen from $6.1 billion per quarter in the fourth quarter of 1993 to less than $1.5 billion per quarter as of early 1995, and it is expected to continue to decline because the U.S. Department of Commerce's Bureau of Export Administration (BXA) has recently revised and streamlined the export Licensing requirements and procedure of the Export Administration Regulations (EAR).

These changes are the result of the many significant political and technological changes that have taken place in the world in recent years. U.S. Government export controls were originally based on keeping certain types of technology and materials out of the hands of our Cold War enemies and other "less than friendly governments and individuals," who were fairly well defined. The recent changes in export controls are based on the more difficult task of keeping certain types of technology and materials out of the hands of international terrorists, or mischief makers and certain unfriendly governments.

The control of nuclear weapons and materials, chemical and biological weapons and materials, missile delivery systems, and various crime and terrorism materials is a very difficult and complex task. It requires the cooperation of all U.S. exporters and those of the other nations of the world that want to keep the world free from international violence and destruction. Until the end of the Cold War, many of the "Western" nations joined in a concerted effort to control technology and material transfers by means of an organization called COCOM. However, with the present world situation and new focus on the items mentioned above, COCOM was terminated and has been replaced with a less formal organization consisting of many of the countries of world who desire to reduce the threat of international violence and destruction.

Two primary members of this new organization are the United States and the European Union. There has been very close cooperation between these two influential parties and the other participating countries to define a more-or-less uniform set of Licensing controls. The U.S. Government in turn, has established its export controls based on these agreed upon limits defined by the new organization (often referred to as "multilateral controls"), as well as additional more restrictive requirements desired by the U.S. Government (referred to as "unilateral controls").

Thus, for some items, the exporter will find that for similar products, the U.S. Government Licensing controls exceed those of the other cooperating nations and therefore places the U.S. exporter at a competitive disadvantage in the international market place.

It is important for the U.S. exporter to keep in mind that these Governmental regulations are "living documents" and thus change from time-to-time as the political and technological world changes. It is the responsibility of the exporter to be knowledgeable regarding these regulations and the changes that take place.

This can be accomplished by a review of the Federal Register, or more readily through specialized subscriptions or on the computer by means of FEDWORLD, a free service of the NTIS, or the NTDB. More details on this are provided at the end of this chapter.

With all of the recent changes in the regulations, the authors decided to turn to someone still working with BXA export regulations on a day-to-day basis and consequently asked Mr. William Filbert of International Diversified Technologies, Inc., who had previously counseled us on this subject, to write all that follows for this third edition. Mr. Filbert regularly consults, lectures and arranges seminars on the subject of export Licensing and marketing, and we thank him for this important contribution to *Exporting: From Start to Finance*.

Overview of Export Controls

The U.S. Government's Export Administration Act is the basis for governmental control of designated U.S. exports, covering certain commodities, technology, and software (hereinafter referred to as "items"), where technology also includes all forms of information transfer: i.e., verbal, written, fax, computer data transfers, etc. The U.S. Government not only controls the initial export of items, but their reexport from the original consignee to another consignee. Therefore, keep in mind that all regulations for controlled exports also apply to reexports, with few exceptions. The U.S. Government also controls exports regardless of the method of export: i.e., air, ocean, truck, hand carry, baggage, mail, fax, etc.

Various U.S. Government agencies have established their own specific and detailed regulations that define what U.S. exporters are required to do. Each of these agencies have placed specific restrictions on the export of certain items, and to certain countries and individuals.

It is important to understand that exporting is considered to be a privilege by the U.S. Government and it is the responsibility of the exporter to understand and adhere to the export regulations should they apply to all or part of any entity's exporting activities. Ignorance of these laws is not an acceptable excuse or defense if the U.S. Government determines that a violation has been committed. Thus, it is important to note that the summary presented here is not intended to be comprehensive or a substitute for the actual regulations.

The exporter of record is responsible for ensuring that each of its exports is in compliance with the export Licensing requirements of the U.S. Government agency that has jurisdiction for that particular item.

Agencies Involved in Export Control and Licensing

Since most of the items exported from the United States are of a non-military nature and are in the form of commonly available consumer or industrial items, the greater part of which do not require governmental approval prior to exporting, and those which do, most often fall under the jurisdiction of the Bureau of Export Administration (BXA) within the U.S. Department of Commerce (DOC). In turn, the BXA has established and maintains the Export Administration Regulations (EAR), which defines all of the License rules and regulations that must be adhered to by the exporter when exporting these items. These regulations are covered in the U.S. Government's Code of Federal Regulations CFR 15.

However, depending on the item being exported, its intended use, and the country of destination, other U.S. Government agencies may have jurisdiction over the export. Some of these commodities and the related government agency are:

- Defense services and defense articles (including the U.S. Munitions List as defined and governed by the Arms Export Control Act)—controlled by the

U.S. Department of State, Office of Defense Trade Controls (DTC), covered under CFR 22.

- Foreign assets and transactions—controlled by the Department of Treasury, Office of Foreign Assets Control under CFR 31.

- Narcotics, dangerous drugs, and their processing equipment—controlled by the Drug Enforcement Administration, CFR 21.

- Natural gas and electric power—controlled by the Department of Energy, CFR 10 and 18.

- Nuclear equipment, materials, reactor vessels, and other specifically designated commodities; and nucelar technical data for nuclear weapons/special nuclear materials—controlled by the Nuclear Regulatory Commossion, CFR 10.

- Patent filing data sent abroad—Patent and Trademark Office, CFR 37 and 15.

- Watercraft (U.S. Coast Guard documented watercraft of 5 net tons or more, for export or transfer to a foreign interest)—U.S. Maritime Administration, App. U.S.C. 808, 839.

- Various agricultrual plants and products—U.S. Department of Agriculture.

- Endangered fish and wildlife, dead or alive—U.S. Fish and Wildlife Service

It is extremely important to keep in mind that it is the exporter's responsibility to determine which Government agency has jurisdiction for the items to be exported. The exporter must be knowledgeable of the applicable regulations, and request and receive Licensing authorization from the appropriate governmental authority. Specialists at the various agencies may be able to assist you with your Licensing questions, as described later in this chapter. Keep in mind that their verbal opinions are not binding on that agency or on the other agencies mentioned above. Only opinions in writing can be depended upon in which case it is important to ensure that the written opinion is based on a clear presentation and understanding of your specific situation.

The Exporter's Responsibility and the EAR

Since a majority of the exports requiring prior governmental approval fall under the jurisdiction of the BXA, the remainder of this chapter is an orientation to the Export Administration Regulations (EAR) administered by the BXA and applies only to exports under its jurisdiction.

It describes the overall procedure and approach in some detail. Exporters whose products might require special treatment through one of the agencies listed above should contact that agency and obtain full details to fit their special circumstances. Unfortunately, no description can help you determine the licensing required for your specific item without your direct participation. Neither can it teach you the details and procedural exceptions required to protect yourself and minimize delays if BXA prior written License approval is required for the export of a specific item.

There is no substitute for having experience in dealing with the EAR. The best advice is to read the applicable portions of the EAR yourself with your products and destinations in mind; contact the BXA for clarification or assistance in understanding any issues that arise; and should your products or world areas of export activity indicate special problems or considerations, retain a qualified Licensing consultant. Depending on the destination, product, and intended use, outside assistance can be a time and profit saving investment, at least while you are acquiring personal experience. But, as with most other export related procedures, if you are the responsible exporter and in charge, you should understand the principles of the Licensing process for prudent decision making and to export within the provisions of the law.

It is also true that some freight forwarders are familiar with certain aspects of the licensing regulations and procedures, and may be able to make suggestions regarding your export licensing requirements. It is very important, however, to keep in mind that the freight forwarders are not ultimately responsible, and often do not have the technical knowledge required to determine the correct type of License a given export shipment requires. The time frames required for Governmental approval are often such that a forwarder normally would not be involved in a transaction at the time when application for Licensing approval should be made.

If you depend on the freight forwarder or other person to assist you in the licensing determination and process, you as the exporter of record are ultimately responsible since this responsibility cannot be transferred.

The New Regulations

The following comments concerning specific procedures and policies are based on recently proposed new BXA policies and Export Administration Regulations as set forth in May 1995. The final approved version is expected shortly after this book's publication date. While few changes are anticipated, it will be incumbent on the reader to confirm this fact. If you have had some familiarity with the old EAR, keep in mind that the new regulations implement many major changes in procedures, License designations, and forms. For example:

1. No License or other authorization is required for any transaction unless the regulations "affirmatively" state the requirement. The previous regulations stated that all exports were prohibited unless a general license was applicable, or a validated license or other authorization had been established by the BXA.

2. The term "License" is now used only to refer to authorization issued by the BXA upon application. In addition, there are several "exceptions" to the obligation to seek a License when the Commerce Control List indicates that the particular item going to the stated country generally requires a License. These "exceptions" may be covered by a series of designations called

"License Exceptions," discussed subsequently in further detail. The previously used terms of "general" license and "validated" license are no longer used.

3. The chapters of the EAR are arranged to give the exporter and reexporter a logical path to follow.

4. The affirmative statements of the need to obtain a License are consolidated into ten general prohibitions.

5. There is a new Country List that defines four country groups (A, B, D, and E) and is referenced when determining the applicability of the Licensing Exceptions.

6. The Commerce Control List has been redesigned to more clearly state the reasons for controls for each Export Control Classification Number.

7. There is a Commerce Country Chart that is used in tandem with the redesigned Commerce Control List to assist in defining export limitations to specific countries.

Using the EAR

The EAR defines all of the BXA licensing requirements and includes a list of commodities the U.S. Government wants to control.

Since it is not possible to summarize in a few brief sentences, a technique for determining the licensing requirements for a specific export because of the multitude of variables involved, suffice it to say that in most cases the best place to start is with the Commerce Control List (CCL) in EAR Supplement No. 1 to Part 774. Its organization and usefulness is discussed later in this chapter.

Keep in mind that it is particularly important to always check your proposed export transaction against a screening procedure that takes into account the chemical & biological, nuclear nonproliferation, and missile technology regulations, in particular. This is very important because, if for example, you desire to export paper clips, which ordinarily you could export without a License, and you know or should have reason to know that they are going to be used in the assembly of a nuclear weapon in a country for which the U.S. Government has imposed nuclear weapon export controls, your proposed export may be in violation of the EAR.

If you ship a variety of products to multiple destinations, it is best to have on hand the EAR, available from the U.S. Superintendent of Documents for a fee, to determine if a License is required for your products. Orders for the EAR can be placed by calling the Government Printing Office order desk at (202) 783-3238.

The annual subscription to the EAR includes all supplementary bulletins issued during the year until the next issue. In addition, the BXA publishes several free pamphlets that can be very useful, but are no substitute for the EAR. If you find there is any possibility that export licensing will apply to you, consider attending an appropriate export Licensing seminar presented by various organizations to help you become familiar with its requirements.

Policies and Administration of the EAR

While the BXA is responsible for the administration of the EAR, U.S. Customs assists in the enforcement, through its review of the document called the Shipper's Export Declaration (SED) and through its authority to review all records and inspect all exports, as it deems necessary.

In the course of its administration of the EAR, the BXA may confer with other U.S. government agencies, some of which have their own set of regulations restricting exports as previously described. Two agencies regularly involved on an inter-governmental agency basis for review of EAR decisions with BXA are the Department of Defense (DOD) and Department of State. It is the DOD review that often gives exporters special problems concerning proposed shipments of items that can or might be used in military applications. They tend to be very deliberate in their review, take considerable time to reach a decision, and when there is the slightest question regarding the proposed export, they reject the application. The Department of State makes recommendations to the BXA concerning controls relative to foreign policy and terrorism and are much easier to deal with as compared with the DOD.

Steps for Determining License Requirements

So that you have an idea of the License determination process, following is an outline of the fourteen steps recommended in the EAR Part 736:

1. Determine if your technology or software is publicly available as defined in the EAR Part 732.7. If it is, then you may proceed with your export. If it is not publicly available, as defined within the scope of the EAR, then you must comply with the rest of the prohibitions defined in the EAR.

   Publicly available information is information that is generally accessible to the interested public in any form and, therefore, not subject to the EAR. A complete definition is covered in EAR Part 732.7.

2. Determine the country of ultimate destination. If the country is an embargoed country, whatever the product, or other country listed in EAR Part 746, then you must apply for a License to export and/or reexport.

3. Determine whether your transferee, ultimate end-user, any intermediate consignee, and any other party to the transaction is a person denied export privileges as defined in the "Denied Persons List," which is later explained. If they are on the list, you cannot perform the export without BXA approval.

4. Review the end-uses and end-users prohibited under the General Prohibitions of the EAR Part 734 and 744.

5. Determine the Export Commodity Control Number (ECCN) classification of your export item as defined in the Commerce Control List (CCL). This step is the key in helping you determine if you need a License and under what conditions and/or restrictions.

6. Determine the reason for control within the ECCN for your particular commodity. This reason, when referenced with the Commerce Country Chart, will indicate the export and reexport limitations.

7. If your foreign-made item incorporating U.S.-origin items is described in an entry on the CCL, and the Commerce Country Chart requires a License to your export or reexport destination, you may require a License.

8. If your foreign-produced item is described in an entry on the CCL, and the Commerce Country Chart requires a License to your export or reexport destination, you may require a License.

9. Be sure you "know your customer" as defined in the EAR Part 744 Supplement No. 3, so that you do not export to a prohibited party.

10. Be sure you do not export to someone involved in a "Proliferation Activity" (such as chemical & biological weapons, nuclear weapons, and missile technology) as defined in the EAR Parts 734 and 744.

11. Review the terms and conditions of your order to ensure they are not in violation of the EAR, some of which are defined in EAR Parts 734 and 740.

12. Review the "in-transit" conditions to ensure that the items are not "unladened" or shipped "in-transit" to prohibited countries.

13. After completion of the twelve steps listed above, review all ten of the general prohibitions listed in EAR Part 734 to determine if any of them apply to your contemplated transaction. If none of the ten general prohibitions apply to your export, you can probably proceed without a License. On the other hand, if one or more of the ten general prohibitions do apply, then you probably need a License prior to exporting.

14. Review the miscellaneous additional duties defined throughout the EAR that may apply to your export transaction to ensure the export is proper.

Commerce Control List and Export Control Classification Number

As soon as you know the item and the country to which you would like to make an export, determine the Licensing requirements by referring to the CCL found in the EAR Part 774, Supplement No. 1. This list provides an Export Control Classification Number (ECCN) for each item the BXA wants to control, as well as the conditions for Licensing for each country of destination.

The CCL is divided into the following ten categories as defined in EAR Part 738.2:

1. Materials

2. Materials Processing

3. Electronics

4. Computers

5. Telecommunications and Information Security

6. Sensors

7. Avionics and Navigation

8. Marine Technology

9. Propulsion Systems and Transportation Equipment

10. Miscellaneous

Each category is divided into the following five groups, each identified with a letter:

A. Equipment, Assemblies, and Components

B. Test, Inspection, and Production Equipment

C. Materials

D. Software

E. Technology

Within each CCL category are ECCNs, each of which relate to specific items. An example of an ECCN format is: 4A03. The first digit identifies the general category with which the entry falls. The letter immediately following this first digit identifies which of the five groups the item is listed under. The final two digits differentiate the individual entries and identify the type of controls that affect the item. The following list identifies the numbers associated with each reason for control:

01-19 National Security, Regional Stability, Supercomputers

20-39 Missile Technology, Regional Stability

40-59 Nuclear Non-proliferation

60-79 Chemical & Biological Weapons

80-99 Other Controls, including Crime Control, Antiterrorism, UN Sanctions, Short Supply, etc.

Your task is to determine the correct ECCN for each item you wish to export. After determining the proper ECCN, the ECCN entry will list the specific Licensing controls to which you must adhere. The reason(s) for control may be based on:

1. Anti-Terrorism

2. Chemical and Biological Weapons

3. Crime Control

4. Missile Technology

5. National Security

6. Nuclear Non-proliferation

7. Regional Stability

8. Supercomputers

9. Short Supply

10. UN Sanctions

Commerce Country Chart

The Commerce Country Chart shown in EAR Part 738 Supplement No. 1, used in conjunction with the ECCN reason(s) for control, allows you to determine if you need a License to export your item to a particular destination.

Country Groups

The Country Group charts shown in EAR Part 740 Supplement No. 1, are used in association with various EAR Parts which specify Licensing restrictions for the countries listed in the charts.

Types of Transactions Regulated

There are five general types of transactions regulated by the BXA:

- Direct exports of American goods and technical data.

- Reexports of American goods and technical data from the original export destination to another destination.

- Foreign use of American goods as parts and components of foreign-made products and the disposition of those products.

- The disposition abroad of foreign-made products that are a direct result of American technical data.

- Exports of purely foreign products by foreign companies controlled by Americans.

It is apparent that much more than the export of physical items from the United States to foreign countries is involved. Verbal communication of technology possessed by you or your company, spoken to a foreign customer seated in your own office in the U.S. is an export and can be a violation of the Licensing regulations and subject to major penalties.

Classifying Items

The most important step when dealing with the subject of Licensing is to properly classify each item you wish to export. It is critical because proper classification will give you an understanding of all of the restrictions and controls for the item and the assurance that you will be exporting in accordance with the EAR.

You must very carefully search through all of the CCL categories and individual ECCNs, in combination with the Country Chart, until you find the ECCN that describes or incorporates the parameters of the item and its destination in question. The ECCN will list the Licensing Requirements and License Alternatives for you to implement. Also listed will be the reason(s) for control which will give you an indication of the time and difficulty you might experience in obtaining your License.

At this point, keep in mind that if, after a complete and thorough search of the CCL, you are absolutely certain that the item is not described or covered, then by exception, the item does not require a License (except for export to the imbargoed countries and other possible EAR exceptions in affect at that time).

Before arriving at the conclusion that no License is required, beware of what gets many exporters in trouble, especially those dealing in equipment with complex subassemblies and components. The equipment itself might be exportable without a License, but the accessories, subassemblies or components may require a License. This situation is often overlooked because the subassembly or component might represent a very minor part of the total technical or dollar value.

Unless you are very familiar with your product, and in many cases have the necessary technical knowledge of it as well, determining its proper ECCN can sometimes be very difficult. This is because the control specifications for each ECCN are usually defined in terms of technical performance parameters. Therefore, in order to determine the correct ECCN for a specific item, you must be very familiar with the technical characteristics of the item and also know the organization of the CCL.

If there is any doubt regarding the proper ECCN classification of a particular item, you should prepare a written request to the BXA in Washington, D.C., asking for their classification and advisory opinion, in writing. The procedure for making this request is described in the EAR Part 750.2. It requires that you describe the product and its intended application, state your opinion as to the proper ECCN classification, and provide descriptive technical data sheets for their review. A response is usually provided within two weeks. Keep in mind that BXA opinions are official only if they are in writing, and all verbal opinions are not official.

It is recommended that you not depend on the trade officer in the DOC district office to provide commodity classifications of a technical nature since it is unlikely the officer would have the technical product knowledge and EAR familiarity to provide a correct classification except in the broadest terms. You may want to consider using an export Licensing consultant who can bridge the gap between the technical characteristics of the item and the CCL and ECCN formats if there is any question in your mind or if the BXA response appears to be less than definitive.

License Exceptions

The EAR defines several "License Exceptions" that can be used in place of a License when the export of the item meets certain specific requirements as specified in the item's ECCN. Specifically, a "License Exception" is an authorization defined in EAR Part 740 that allows you to export or reexport, under stated conditions, items subject to the EAR that otherwise require a License under one or more of the ECCNs in the CCL. An example of such a License Exception designation is the symbol "TMP" which is established authorizing the export and reexport of items for temporary use abroad subject to the conditions and exclusions described in EAR Part 740.8.

Following are examples of several of the other License Exception designations that may be of use to the exporter. It should be kept in mind that there are many detailed restrictions on the use of each of the designations and thus the exporter must first refer to the EAR Part 740 before using any designation.

LVS   Shipments of Limited Value: Within each ECCN, there is an entry indicating the dollar value, if any, below which an item can be exported as a single shipment using this designation without applying for a License.

GFT   Gift Parcels: Is established to authorize exports and reexports of gift parcels by an individual addressed to an individual.

TUS   Exports of Items Temporarily in the United States: Is established to authorize, under certain conditions; Items temporarily in the United States; Items moving in transit through the United States; Items imported for display at U.S. exhibitions or trade fairs; Return of unwanted shipments; and return of shipments refused entry.

Keep in mind that if your export requires a License, you should carefully read the provisions of each of the License Exceptions to determine if your export qualifies for its use. If it does, then you need not apply for a License, but rather, you can export using the appropriate License Exception designation.

Export Designations if No License Is Required

If you export without a License issued by the BXA, you are responsible for determining that the transaction is outside of the scope of the EAR, or the export is designated as "No License Required" or "Not on List," as defined in EAR Part 758.

The "NLR" (No License Required) designation is to be used on the shipping documents for items listed on the CCL but that do not require a license by reason of the Commerce Country Chart. The "NOL" (Not On List) designation is to be used on the shipping documents for items not listed on the CCL.

Exports to Canada

The United States relations with Canada are such that no License is required for most exports to Canada provided the item is to be used and retained in Canada.

However, this Licensing exception does not pertain to exports to Canada that are going to be reexported to another country.

Applying for a License

Preferably as you plan your export strategies and products, but surely as soon as you obtain a request for quotation or an order, which ever comes first, immediately start the process of determining the need for a License. In general, you can submit an application for a License if you have a firm order or have a reasonable chance of obtaining an order from a specific customer. The application should be based on more than a mere inquiry. As you "plan" your License application, remember that a License is issued for a specific item(s), for a specific consignee in a specific country, and for a specific quantity. Licenses are not "open ended."

The BXA License processing time can take anywhere from one or two weeks to indefinitely, depending on the item, end use, individuals involved, and countries involved. While most Licenses may be issued within two or three weeks, there is always a possibility that the BXA will never authorize the export. Thus, you do not want to trap yourself in the position of having a signed contract with penalties for non-performance and at the same time, not be allowed to export under the provisions of the EAR.

To apply for a License, use Form BXA-748P which can be obtained from the BXA Headquarters in Washington, D.C. and at the BXA regional offices, and follow the procedure described in EAR Part 750.

Following are a few hints relative to completing the License application Form BXA-748P:

1. In Box 21, be specific about the buyer-seller relationship, end use, and the user (keep relative to the consignee in Box 19), and specify if reexport authorization to other specific countries is needed.

2. In Box 22 and 23, the "shipping tolerance" allowed, as defined in EAR Part 750.11, is dependent on how the item is Licensed: i.e., by dollar value, number, or by area, weight, or measure.

3. Attach sufficient specifications, data sheets, and information about the item to permit a final decision by the BXA during their first review. Otherwise, the application will be returned to you, creating delays. Remember, you are dealing with a bureaucracy, so it is more natural for them to deny or return the application rather than ponder or inquire.

4. Vagueness as to the types of items, lack of information pertaining to the end use and user, an incomplete detailed description of each item, and failing to sign the application are the most common errors leading to its rejection or return. It is important to submit a complete and correct application so that there will no processing delays.

Supporting Documents for License Applications

Depending on the country of destination, you may need to provide a "supporting document" from the consignee as described in EAR Part 748.9, along with your License application. In certain situations you will need an "International Import Certificate" provided by the Government of the importing country, or a document called a "Statement by Ultimate Consignee and Purchaser" (Form BXA-711). This is a statement signed by the foreign purchaser and consignee certifying that they will not resell or dispose of the goods in a manner contrary to the EAR, or the U.S. License under which the items were originally exported. The ECCN classification and the country of destination will determine the type of supporting documentation required as defined in EAR Part 748.

Using Your License

Having been granted your License, it is now yours to use responsibly according to the regulations, and, among other things, to see that: the License number is recorded on the Shipper's Export Declaration; it is used before its expiration, which is usually two years from the date of issue; and you do not export more than the authorized amount (including the tolerance that may be applicable as defined in EAR Part 750.11). The License need not be returned to the BXA unless specifically requested by the BXA.

Denied Persons List

One illegal use of a license would be to permit your export to be involved with someone on the Denied Persons List. The Denied Persons List identifies those persons in the U.S. and worldwide, denied export privileges by the BXA pursuant to the terms of an order issued under the Enforcement provisions of the EAR as defined in Part 764.

Consult the Denied Persons List currently in effect (see EAR Part 764 Supplement No. 2) to be sure your proposed export does not involve a party currently denied export privileges as a result of past violations. Alternatively, it can be found on the NTDB CD-ROM or through access to FEDWORLD. You must not deal with anyone on this list regarding your export transaction unless specifically authorized by the BXA.

Special Comprehensive License (SCL)

If you are going to be exporting one or more items to one or more consignees for which multiple Licenses will be required over a short period of time, you may want to consider applying for a Special Comprehensive License (SCL). The SCL, if granted by the BXA, will allow you to export preapproved items to preapproved consignees located in preapproved countries. This, of course, will simplify the actual exporting process and more importantly, give you assurance that you will be able to perform the export at the time you receive the consignee's order.

However, since the SCL gives you a certain amount of flexibility not available with a License, your responsibilities and recordkeeping requirements are significantly increased regarding the assurances required by the BXA that each export will be in accordance with the SCL and the overall EAR requirements. In addition, you and your consignees are subject to periodic formal on-site comprehensive inspections by the BXA.

To apply for a SCL involves a special application procedure that justifies your need for the SCL and requires that you and each of your consignees develop and implement a comprehensive "Internal Control Program" (ICP). The ICP is a formal procedure tailored to your specific export items, consignees, and activities. The SCL is granted only after extensive evaluation by the BXA.

Destination Control Statements

Although there are a few allowable exceptions, it is required that for all exports, one of four "Destination Control Statements" (as defined in EAR Part 758.5 and 758.6) must be shown on all copies of the bill of lading or air waybill, and the related commercial invoice. The most generally used statement (No. 1) reads: "These commodities, technology or software were exported from the United States in accordance with the Export Administration Regulations for ultimate destination (name of country). Diversion contrary to U.S. law is prohibited." Refer to EAR Part 758.6 for a description of the other three statement versions and their intended usage.

Shipper's Export Declaration (SED)

Both the Foreign Trade Statistics Regulations of the Census Bureau and the EAR require that Shipper's Export Declarations be submitted to the U.S. Government for exports. There are a few exceptions to this rule, all of which are covered in detail in EAR Part 758.1 and 758.3. One of the exceptions often used when applicable is where any shipment, other than a shipment made under a License issued by the BXA, to any country in Country Group B (see Supplement No. 1 to EAR Part 740) or to the People's Republic of China if the shipment is valued at $2,500 ($500 in the case of mail) or less per Schedule B Number. The Schedule B Number of an item is that shown in the current edition of the Schedule B document, "Statistical Classification of Domestic and Foreign Commodities Exported from the United States."

In Box 21 of the SED, you are required to indicate the criteria under which the export is being made: i.e., "NOR" (No License Required), "NOL" (Not on List), the License number and expiration date, or the License Exception symbol, all of which are described in EAR Part 758.1 and 758.3.

In Box 22 of the SED, you are required to indicate the ECCN for the items being exported under a License or a License Exception symbol.

Keep in mind that exports by mail have their own set of SED documentation requirements.

Know Your Overseas Customer

As you review the provisions of the EAR, you will note that it is very important that you know your overseas customer and ensure that they will not violate any of the EAR rules because of the liabilities concerning end use and reexport. In certain situations you can be held responsible for violations made by your customer.

Missile, Nuclear and Chemical/Biological Weapons Control

You should be knowledgeable regarding the BXA's major focus on Nuclear Weapons and Missile Systems nonproliferation, Chemical and Biological Weapons nonproliferation, and conventional arms nonproliferation and unilateral controls.

This requirement is part of the BXA's "Enhanced Proliferation Control Initiative" (EPCI) and "Know Your Customer" requirement as defined in EAR Part 744. Included are certain provisions requiring an exporter to obtain an individual license if the exporter "knows" that any export otherwise eligible for license exception is for end-uses involving nuclear, chemical, or biological weapons, or related missile delivery systems, in named destinations listed in the EAR.

Thus, a requirement imposed on all exporters is to ensure that no export of any item be used in violation of these "EPCI" regulations. In some cases, depending on the consignee, the item's intended use, the item's possible use, and the country of destination, a License may be required even though under normal circumstances, the commodity could be exported without a License. Thus, the BXA recommends that all exporters have in place a procedure or system that ensures compliance with the EPCI nonproliferation requirements, as defined in EAR Part 744.

Recordkeeping

Recordkeeping is a very important aspect of conforming to the EAR since it requires that complete and accurate records be maintained by the exporter for a period of at least five years from the date of export, for all export transactions regardless of whether or not a License is used. To summarize what is described in detail in EAR Part 762, the exporter is required to maintain for each export transaction complete documentation, including, but not limited to: the commercial invoice, bill of lading or air waybill, and shipper's export declaration.

Sanctions and Violations

For both practical and legal reasons, the exporter must realize that he or she is responsible for obtaining and using the correct License and is also the party subject to criminal and civil penalties, and the possible denial of export privileges in the case of EAR violations as defined in EAR Part 764.3. Willful violations can involve penalties of up to $250,000 in fines and 10 years imprisonment for individuals, and for companies the fines go up to $1 million or up to five times the value of the export involved, whichever is greater, together with the loss of the export privileges. Exporters found guilty can also be placed on the Denied Persons List. Criminal penalties are usually invoked only in instances of deliberate violation or evasion, but administrative penalties for failure to observe the regulations are nevertheless stiff, even in cases of the most innocent of violations or omissions. As a minimum, the shipment might be detained by U.S. Customs, and even seized in the more serious situations.

Keeping Up with Changes in the EAR

Keep in mind that the BXA (as well as the other Government agencies regarding their respective jurisdictions) is continually issuing changes and administrative rulings to the EAR and it is your responsibility to keep informed of these changes because they may affect your Licensing requirements. Thus, it is recommended that you keep up with the latest changes in the U.S. Government export rules and regulations as published in the "Federal Register." This can be accomplished by subscribing to the "Federal Register" itself, following changes through the monthly updates on the NTDB disks, instant updating by downloading from FEDWORLD to your computer, supplementing your knowledge by subscribing to the BXA Quarterly Newsletter or other organizations that offer frequent summary updates to the EAR. FEDWORLD is a free service (other than long distance costs) that can be accessed by direct dial to 703/321-3339, or via the Internet.

If you have questions or problems contact a BXA office, or FEDWORLD staff for voice questions at 703/487-4608.

Suggestions and Cautions

As you can see, for each item you contemplate exporting, it is very important that you determine its ECCN and note the applicable export restrictions, if any. You cannot simply rationalize or conclude that a License is not required for any item, no matter how readily available it may be domestically or internationally, since the U.S. Government may still have imposed export restrictions and Licensing requirements. The ECCN will give you guidance regarding what countries are approved for export of the item, if any.

It is also prudent to provide an escape clause in your contract or pro forma invoice in the event you cannot fulfill its terms because of your inability to obtain a License from the U.S. Government, particularly if you have to depend on first receiving the buyer's import certificate or other supporting documentation to apply and/or obtain your License.

While the BXA offers valuable assistance regarding the EAR, as with any Government agency, the reliability of the verbal information received can vary, depending on the person to whom you are talking. That is why it is suggested that for any critical questions, you obtain an answer in writing from the Government agency and/or your export licensing consultant.

Help and Hotlines

As confusing or difficult as the export Licensing process may seem, if you study and become familiar with the EAR, seek help when it is really needed, and exercise a combination of diligence, curiosity, and patience, export Licensing can be a very straightforward exercise. It is important to determine when you need help, and then obtain assistance from the variety of Governmental offices and private consulting sources available.

Some of the electronic aids for exporters available from the BXA include:

ELAIN—Export License Application and Information Network. ELAIN is an on-line computer service with the acronym standing for Export License Application and Information Network, that can be used to submit License applications to the BXA. Keep in mind that there is a fee involved since you must communicate through a facility such as Compuserve. It should be considered if you expect to submit many License applications. Otherwise, submitting your applications using the mail or an express delivery service is probably more cost effective. To obtain more information regarding ELAIN, contact the BXA's Exporter Assistance Staff at 202-482-4811.

STELA—System for Tracking Export License Applications. STELA is an automated voice response system with the purpose of providing exporters easy access to the status of their License applications. If the application already has been approved without conditions, STELA can provide authority to ship even before you receive the hard copy of the License. STELA can be reached at (202) 377-2752 by any touch tone telephone. If additional information or clarification on how to use the system is needed, call the BXA at (202) 482-4811.

In addition to the BXA headquarter's office in at the U.S. Department of Commerce, 14th Street and Pennsylvania Ave., N.W., Washington, D.C., 20230, (202) 428-4811, the BXA has two western regional offices located at: 3300 Irvine Ave., Suite 345, Newport Beach, CA 92660, (714) 660-0144; and 5201 Great American Parkway, Suite 226, Santa Clara, CA 95054, (408) 748-7450. The regional offices can provide field assistance but they cannot issue Licenses or provide written classification determinations.

Restrictive Trade Practices or Boycotts

The antiboycott provisions of the Export Administration Act are contained in EAR Part 760, which defines who is covered by the antiboycott rules; what actions in response to boycott requests are prohibited; what exceptions to the prohibitions are permitted; and what the reporting requirements are, but the subject is so apart from export licensing that it is addressed separately in Chapter 32. It is important for you to be familiar with these rules and conform to their requirements since the U.S. Government actively enforces the antiboycott provisions.

32

Antiboycott Regulations

Antiboycott regulations incorporated into Export Administration Regulations are under the title "Restrictive Trade Practices or Boycotts," Part 760 of 15 CFR within the newly revised regulations. The initiating legislation, however, has nothing in common with the balance of the Export Administration Act in terms of time frame, purpose, or application. What it does have in common is that this, too, represents an administrative problem to the exporter and a potential threat in terms of both civil and criminal penalties.

While the antiboycott regulations prohibit various actions, they also require that the exporter report certain boycott requests—even though the exporter has no intention of accepting, much less complying with, the proposed boycott terms. The act was put into effect in 1965 in response to the practice of the Arab League that was blacklisting firms that had dealings with Israel. These regulations were intended not only to prevent such secondary and tertiary boycotts, but also to learn which Arab firms and countries were attempting such activities and thus to do whatever possible to forestall them through the reporting feature of the act.

Violations of the boycott regulations are much less frequent today than they were in the 1960s and 1970s (although apparently not substantially different from their frequency in 1989), because the portion of the Arab League that wants to do business with the United States has learned to sidestep or omit provisions in their contracts, letters of credit, and orders that run contrary to the regulations. Whether through error or intent, thousands of reportable violations continue to occur, although the bulk of them are amended to be permissible or have been approved as exceptions. In 1993, for example, 2859 prohibited requests were reported, in addition to 1414 permissible requests. The demand concerning "origin of goods" took first place, accounting for about 40 percent of the violations; restrictions in financial arrangements, mostly relative to letters of credit came second, accounting for 19 percent of the violations; and restrictions as to specific parties not being involved came third. Less than 1000 exporters, plus 100 to 200 banks, report the majority of the boycott request. Although there have not been a great many companies fined or criminal penalties assessed under this law, what fines there have been have been substantial, and there has also been at least one criminal sentence. This being the case, it would be well to remain vigilant in looking for prohibited or reportable requests.

If you familiarize yourself with the general nature of the illegal actions described later in this chapter, you will learn to check further when you sense there might be exposure to violations. In such an event, any bank with an experienced international department or your forwarder can advise you as to illegal clauses contained within a letter of credit of shipping and insurance instructions or the like. If, however, the Middle East is your target marketing area, become acquainted with the regulations firsthand. Also, keep in mind that while it was the Arab League's efforts to boycott Israel that created the regulations, the Arab League could choose to apply the boycott provisions against other nations at some future date.

If an audit of your books by U.S. Customs or the International Trade Administration (ITA) in respect to any part of the Export Administration Regulations is possible, the antiboycott area might easily be audited for good measure. Furthermore, U.S. Customs has authority to make random surveys of U.S. firms to determine the scope of reportable boycott requests.

It is essential to understand the difference between a primary boycott and a secondary or tertiary boycott action; and also the difference between a negative and a positive request. The United States does not and could not object to any nation refusing to do business with Israel. This is a primary boycott, and we have some of our own in effect. Everything else is a secondary or tertiary boycott, and it does not matter which of the two it is—the intent is to prohibit both. A positive request, which is likely to be acceptable, would ask you to certify that the merchandise is of U.S. origin. A negative request or order, usually unacceptable, would request certification that it is not made in a boycotted country.

The essence of the secondary and tertiary boycott is the blacklist onto which a person or firm, often without their knowledge, is placed. The prospective Arab buyer advises the exporter that he cannot do business with the blacklisted party relative to a given transaction, or possibly, that he cannot do business with the party whatsoever. To do so could mean being blacklisted in turn. Such advice can be made in any form: verbally or through correspondence, purchase order, letter of credit, or shipping and insurance instructions.

The distinction between positive and negative can be misleading, and therefore the intent and purpose must be considered. A so-called whitelist, for example, which lists those firms or persons with whom you *can* do business, is in effect advising you with whom not to do business and can therefore be just as illegal as the blacklist.

Antiboycott Prohibitions

The specific conducts prohibited by law are:

- Refusing to do business with a boycotted country, firm, or person when "such a refusal is pursuant to an agreement, requirement, or request from, or on behalf of, the boycotting country."
- Taking discriminatory actions against any U.S. citizen based on race, religion, sex, or national origin.
- Furnishing information about race, religion, sex, or national origin.
- Furnishing information about business relationships with boycotted countries or blacklisted persons and firms.
- Furnishing information about associations with charitable and fraternal organizations.
- Implementing letters of credit containing prohibited conditions and requirements.

The regulations state that inadvertent compliance with a boycott request is not culpable; however, the prohibitions cover so many forms of behavior—some very oblique—that it is not wise to use ignorance as a defense in order to evade the regulations or comply with any boycott action. Furthermore, the enforcement procedures relative to the regulations do not hesitate to "look behind the curtain" and clearly make every effort to stop any form of discrimination, including hiring practices. Enforcement is especially strict concerning letters of credit.

Exceptions to the Prohibitions

These specific exceptions to the prohibitions are listed in a very abbreviated form. In addition, there are many administrative rulings to clarify the regulations. It is acceptable for the U.S. exporter to:

1. Comply or agree to comply with import requirements of a boycotting country. When components of an exporter's product normally come from a country boycotted by the buyer's country, for example, the exporter can agree to substitute parts.
2. Agree to comply with requirements regarding the shipment of goods to a boycotting country. This includes agreeing not to ship on carriers of a boycotted country or via a specific route, or not pass through specific ports.
3. Comply with import and shipping document requirements of the boycotting country in terms of origin, carrier, route, supplier, or provider of services.

However, the regulations demand that relevant certifications or requirements be phrased in positive rather than negative terms (i.e., "the goods were made in X country"—not "the goods did not originate in Y country").

4. Comply or agree to comply with unilateral, specific selections by the buyer in a boycotting country of carriers, insurers, or suppliers of services to be performed within the boycotting country. Treat this exception carefully because it involves shaded meanings and degrees. To meet the exception concerning services, "a not insignificant part" must be necessarily performed within the boycotting country. Goods must be identifiable in terms of origin on entry into the boycotting country by uniqueness of trademark, packaging, and so forth.

5. Comply with the export requirements of a boycotting country in terms of shipping from that country to a second or third country, or transshipping. (This is primarily meant for the petroleum industry.)

6. Comply or agree to comply with immigration, passport, visa, employment requirements, and local law insofar as the exporter or his or her family is concerned, but the exporter cannot so agree or comply concerning employees or others.

Reportable Actions and Requests

The actions described as being prohibited are also all reportable. In addition, some actions, though permitted, nevertheless might be reportable. The regulations regarding reporting are especially vague. The six prohibited provisions are expanded to what is simply referred to as restrictive trade practices. This is given a very broad interpretation, to the effect that any person who "has reason to know" that the purpose of the request (not necessarily the action) is to implement or support a foreign boycott, must file a report. Negative requests are especially suspect.

Again, the demand to report is modified by certain exceptions. These exceptions apply to actions or certifications (in some cases even negative certifications) specifically pertaining to the following requests:

1. To refrain from shipping on vessels of a certain flag or vessels owned or operated in a certain country, or a request to certify to that effect.

2. To ship on a prescribed route or refrain from a route, or to so certify.

3. To supply affirmative certification as to the origin of the goods and the name of the supplier, manufacturer, or service provider.

4. To comply with the laws of another country, except a request to comply with that country's boycott laws.

5. To supply information about one's self or family (but not others) for immigration, visa, or employment purposes.

6. To provide affirmative certification indicating destination or port of unloading.

7. To provide certification by owner, charter party, or employee of same that the vessel or aircraft is eligible or permitted to enter, or not restricted from entry, of a certain port, country, or group of countries, pursuant to their laws. (Note: It remains illegal for the exporter to certify this.)

8. To supply an insurance company certificate stating that the insurer has a duly-authorized agent or representative within a boycotting country and/or name and address. (Note: It remains illegal for the export to certify this.)

9. To comply with a condition that provides that the vendor bear the risk of loss and indemnify the buyer if the vendor's goods are denied entry into a country for any reason if the buyer was using such a clause prior to January 18, 1978.

A perfect example of the lack of logic of the many administrative rulings to this act can be found in Interpretations, Supplement 2, Part 769, page 1, regarding items 7 and 8. Here is an administrative interpretation of the rule that otherwise provides that only a carrier or shipping company can provide a certificate that a vessel is eligible to enter into the ports of a boycotting country, and that only the insurer must certify that he has a duly-qualified agent in the boycotting country. The exporter is not permitted to make such certifications, except in the case of Saudi Arabia, on the basis of certain explanations the Saudis have provided. There are several similar exceptions made on behalf of both Saudi Arabia and Egypt. Such exceptions based on administrative interpretation are not exclusive to the United States. The boycotting countries in certain instances have made gross exceptions to boycott rules based on the "greater good" of the league.

In the event the exporter does receive a reportable request in any form, including verbal, it must be reported to the Office of Antiboycott Compliance on form DIB-630P (see Figure 32-1). These forms are usually available either at your forwarder or your bank.

Legal Status of Specific Requests

The book by Liebman and Root entitled *United States Export Controls,* has been of great assistance in our legal summary of the antiboycott provisions of the Export Administration Act and is thankfully acknowledged.[1] In addition, a summary table of boycott-related requests in specific, export-related languages, relative to their status as to prohibition and reportability, was prepared by John F. McKenzie, of Baker & McKenzie of San Francisco. An adapted version of this table is provided here, courtesy of McKenzie.[2]

Requested Boycott Actions: Not Reportable and Permitted

- Provision of a positive certificate of origin
- Provision of a war risk certificate regarding an Israeli flag vessel

OMB No. 0625-0028

FORM ITA-621P
(REV 12-83)

U.S. DEPARTMENT OF COMMERCE
INTERNATIONAL TRADE ADMINISTRATION

THIS SPACE FOR ITA USE

865962

REPORT OF REQUEST FOR RESTRICTIVE TRADE PRACTICE OR BOYCOTT
SINGLE TRANSACTION

(For reporting requests described in Part 369 of the Export Administration Regulations)

Pursuant to section 4A (b) (2) of the Export Administration Act of 1969, as amended (50 U.S.C. App. 2401 et seq.), information regarding the quantity, description, and value of any articles, materials and supplies, including technical data and other information, to which this report relates will be kept confidential when the reporting person certifies that disclosure would place a United States person involved at a competitive disadvantage, unless the Secretary of Commerce determines that disclosure thereof would not place such United States person at a competitive disadvantage or that it would be contrary to the national interest to withhold the information.

A	BATCH			

MONTH/YEAR

RSN

SUBSET

RTP

CLASS   FILING   TAG

This report is required by law (50 U.S.C. App. §2407 (b) (2) P.L. 96-72; E.O. 12214; 15 C.F.R. Part (369). Failure to report can result both in criminal penalties, including fines or imprisonment, and administrative sanctions.

INSTRUCTIONS Complete all items that apply. Assemble original report form and accompanying document(s) as a unit, and submit intact and unaltered. Assemble and submit a duplicate copy of report form and documents, marked with the legend "PUBLIC INSPECTION COPY" If the reporting firm certifies that disclosure of certain information specified in item 10 below would result in competitive disadvantage, the public inspection copy (report form and accompanying documents) must be edited accordingly.

1a. Identify firm submitting this report:

Name:

Address:

City, State and ZIP:

Country (if other than USA):

Telephone:

Firm Identification No. (if known):

29-34

Specify firm type:

☐ Exporter
☐ Bank
☐ Forwarder
☐ Carrier
☐ Insurer
☐ Other

35

1b. Check any applicable box:

☐ Revision of a previous report (attach two copies of the previously submitted report)

☐ Resubmission of a deficient report returned by BTR (attach form letter that was returned with deficient report)

☐ Report on behalf of the person identified in Item 2

☐ Dual report on behalf of self and the person identified in Item 2

2. If you are authorized to report and are reporting on behalf of another U.S. person, identify that person (e.g., domestic subsidiary, controlled foreign subsidiary, exporter, beneficiary):

Name:

Address:

City, State and ZIP:

Country (if other than U.S.A.):

Type of firm (see list in Item 1a):

Firm Identification No. (if known):

3. Identify exporting firm, unless same as Item 1a or 2:

Name:

Address:

City, State and ZIP:

Country (if other than U.S.A.):

Firm Identification No. (if known):

36-41   42

4. (a) Name of boycotting country from which request originated:

(b) Name of country directing inclusion of request, if different from (a) above

43-44

5. Name of country or countries against which request is directed:

45-46

6. Reporting firm's reference number (e.g., letter of credit, customer order, invoice):

71-77

7. Date firm received request (use digits for month/day/year):

47-52

8. Specify type(s) of document conveying the request:

— Request to carrier for blacklist certificate (submit two copies of blacklist certificate or transcript of request)

— Unwritten, not otherwise provided for (make transcript of request and submit two copies)

53-54

— Letter of credit

— Requisition/purchase order/accepted contract/shipping instruction

— Bid invitation/tender/proposal/trade opportunity

— Questionnaire (not related to a particular dollar value transaction)

— Other written (specify) _____

Submit two copies of each document or relevant page in which the request appears

9. Decision on request (Check one)

— Have not taken and will not take the action requested

— Have taken or will take the action requested

— Have taken or will take the action requested and claim it is subject to a grace period (attach detailed explanation).

56-57

— Have taken or will take the action requested but in a modified form (attach detailed explanation).

— Unable to report ultimate decision on the request at this time and will inform the Bureau of Trade Regulation of the decision within ten days after decision is made

Additional information The firm submitting this report may, if it so desires, state on a separate sheet any additional information relating to the request reported or the response to that request. This statement will constitute a part of the report and will be made available for public inspection and copying.

10. Unless indicated otherwise by checkmark in the box below, I (we) certify that disclosure to the public of the information regarding quantity, description, and value of the commodities or technical data contained in Item 11 below would place a United States person involved at a competitive disadvantage, and I (we) request that it be kept confidential. I (We) certify that all statements and information contained in this report are true and correct to the best of my (our) knowledge and belief.

Sign here in ink _____
Signature of person completing report

Type or print _____
(Name and title of person whose signature appears on line to left)

Date _____

I (We) authorize public release of all information contained in this report
(Remove stub from public inspection copy at perforation if confidentiality is requested in Item 10)

11. Describe the commodities or technical data involved, and specify quantity and value

Description

Quantity

Value to nearest whole dollar $

58-69

ORIGINAL Submit to Report Processing Staff, Office of Antiboycott Compliance, ITA, U.S. Department of Commerce, Room 2096, Washington D.C. 20230

Figure 32-1. Report of boycott request.

- Provision of a war risk certificate regarding a vessel owned by, or chartered to, an Israeli person or firm

- Provision of a war risk certificate regarding a vessel not scheduled to call at Israeli port prior to arrival at port of destination

- Provision of vessel eligible certificate (Egypt and Saudi Arabia only)

- Provision of vessel eligible certificate, to be made by the vessel owner*

- Provision of insurer's resident agent certificate (Egypt and Saudi Arabia only)

- Provision of insurer's resident agent certificate, to be made by the insurer*

- Certification as to identity of supplier, shipping company, insurance carrier, and so forth

- Compliance with unilateral selection of supplier, shipping company, and so forth by Arab customer (unless the selection is known to be boycott-based and other limitation; see number 4 under "Exceptions to the Prohibitions."

- Agreement to comply with the laws of boycotting country (stated generally)*

- Negotiation of a Saudi letter of credit prohibiting shipment of goods or packaging bearing any symbols prohibited in Saudi Arabia

- Agreement of risk of loss provision (provided that the requesting firm adopted such a policy prior to January 18, 1978)

Requested Boycott Actions: Reportable and Permitted

- Agreement not to obtain goods covered by specific order from Israel or from an Israeli firm

- Negotiation of a letter of credit prohibiting shipment of Israeli goods (providing no certification is made)

- Provision of a no blacklisted supplier certificate (self-certification)*

Requested Boycott Actions: Reportable and Prohibited

- Provision of a no blacklisted supplier certificate (certification as to third parties)

- Provision of vessel eligible certificate, to be made by the exporter (countries other than Egypt and Saudi Arabia)

- Provision of insurer's resident agent certificate, to be made by the exporter (countries other than Egypt and Saudi Arabia)

---

*Your attention should be directed to the Internal Revenue Code (IRC), section 999, which also concerns itself with antiboycott provisions. The penalties in the tax section essentially concern nondeductibility of certain expenses or tax penalties rather than civil or criminal penalties. While the two codes are different, it would seem that compliance with Part 760 of the EAR boycott provisions discussed here, will usually satisfy IRC, Section 999, except for four phrases, which the table prepared by McKenzie brings to your attention. An asterisk has been placed by those which EAR regulations permit, but which IRC, Section 999, would prohibit.

- Agreement to comply with boycotting country's boycott laws
- Agreement not to do business with or in Israel
- Negotiation of a letter of credit prohibiting shipment of goods or packaging bearing a six-pointed star
- Agreement not to do business with a blacklisted American person or firm
- Agreement not to obtain goods covered by a specific order from a blacklisted American
- Provision of a no blacklisted vessel certificate

Endnotes

1. By permission of John R. Liebman and William Root, *United States Export Controls*, Aspen Law & Business, Gaithersburg, Maryland, 1991.

2. By permission of author John F. McKenzie, "The United States Program of Anti-boycott Regulations: An Overview," a paper prepared by the law firm of Baker and McKenzie, San Francisco, California, 1994.

33

Foreign Corrupt Practices Act

The Foreign Corrupt Practices Act (FCPA), 15 USC Section 78, might have been more carefully and fairly drafted in today's export environment. However, when the FCPA became law, it was a different world, and the United States was the largest creditor nation in history with a trade surplus. Consequently, when congressional hearings revealed that more than 400 American companies were regularly engaging in bribery, Congress felt something had to be done to maintain the ethical image of the United States abroad; never mind that the United States was not alone in that practice or what the competitive consequences might be.

Always inherently unfair for its ambiguous definitions of what is illegal and the degree of vicarious liability imposed, the FCPA is clearly seen today as another export disincentive, even though some improvements have been made as to fairness and clarity. While aimed primarily at the multinationals, it excludes no one and no form of business, individuals, or associations. Employees are made liable as well as the company, and it provides that the company cannot directly or indirectly pay fines on behalf of the guilty employee.

The Omnibus Trade Bill of 1988 limited unknowing liability and better defined certain accounting standards, as well as clarified certain illegal acts. It also, however, increased penalties. Plainly, the FCPA will not be repealed and every exporter should understand its fundamentals. Nevertheless, the government recognizes that it is asking firms doing business overseas to carry the FCPA burden largely alone among our competitor nations. Consequently, part of the National Export Strategy calls on the United States to pursue efforts in conjunction with international institutions such as the Organization for Economic Cooperation (OECD) to prevent companies in other countries from making the type of illicit payments the FCPA prohibits U.S. business from making. The OECD is a good place to begin, because one of its primary functions is to restrain nations from undue competition in concessional lending (as explained in Chapters 37 and 40). In May of 1994 the U.S. State Department convinced OECD to adopt a recommendation calling on all its members to take effective measures to combat bribery through both domestic action and international cooperation.

The FCPA deals with three areas. The first covers certain accounting requirements and applies only to issuers, which are public corporations whose stock has been registered under the Securities Exchange Act of 1934. These provisions are not solely aimed at bribery prevention but, obviously, compliance with the accounting standard facilitates enforcement investigations. We are making the assumption here that any such public corporation is already well aware of the act, and if not, will immediately consult its attorneys. We mention these requirements, therefore, only to briefly acquaint the reader, because the accounting issue is often a point of concern when the FCPA is discussed. The second area is the definition of bribery and illegal payments. The problem is that in both these areas the law is ambiguous and therefore difficult to apply. The third area provides for the penalties.

Accounting Requirements

The accounting requirements set standards of accounting, which make management accountable for assets and the use of funds. Therefore, the books and records must be kept in reasonable detail to trace transactions and the disposition of assets. Under the Omnibus Trade Bill, reasonable detail is defined and liability limited to "knowingly falsified or circumvented," which is an improvement.

The FCPA demands that the system of internal controls provide reasonable assurance that:

1. "Transactions are executed in accordance with management's general or specific authorization."

2. Transactions are recorded in conformity with "generally accepted accounting principles" and "to maintain accountability for assets."

3. "Access to assets is permitted only in accordance with management's general or specific authorization."

4. "The recorded accountability for assets is compared with the existing assets at reasonable intervals and appropriate action is taken with respect to any differences."

While these standards sound straightforward, they are not, because there is no definition of what internal accounting controls are necessary. The Omnibus Trade Bill has proposed Justice Department guidelines that might help. Small businesses complain that they cannot afford the level of accounting sophistication necessary to comply with the law. This is something each firm should discuss with its accountant. Several of the big six accounting firms have published pamphlets on the subject.

Definitions of Bribery

Bribery applies to both issuers and domestic concerns. The domestic concern definition is all-inclusive, covering individuals, proprietorships, associations, partnerships, and corporations whose place of business is in the United States. In the definition of the bribery portion of the law, foreign corrupt practices are expressed as offering, paying, promising, or authorizing the giving of "anything of value" to:

1. "any foreign official" to influence his act or decision or another official's act or decision to perform or fail to perform or induce him or another official to in turn use his influence with a government or instrumentality to help the export to obtain, retain, or to direct certain business.

2. "any foreign political party or official thereof" or political candidate, to influence or induce another party to influence, regarding business as stated above.

3. "any person, while knowing or having reason to know that all or a portion of such money or thing of value will be offered, given, or promised, directly or indirectly, to any foreign official, to any foreign political party or official thereof, or to any candidate for foreign political office, for purposes of" influencing or inducing as stated above. The Omnibus Trade Bill changes "knowing or having reason to know" to simply "knowing," including the Justice Department definitions of "knowing."

The law then defines *foreign official* as "any officer or employee of a foreign government or any department, agency, or instrumentality thereof, or any person acting in an official capacity for or on behalf of such government or department, agency, or instrumentality. The term [*foreign official*] does not include any employee of a foreign government or any department, agency, or instrumentality thereof whose duties are essentially ministerial or clerical."

The maximum penalties specified are $1 million for corporations and $10,000 and/or five years in prison for officers, directors, stockholders, and employees of businesses found guilty under the law. Note the direct application of criminal and civil penalties to the employee, as mentioned in the introduction.

The section concerning unlawful payments is important for four reasons:

1. Knowing which of the payments made really are "corrupt."

2. The possibility that your foreign sales agent might be making illegal payments without your knowledge. (The trade bill eases this provision.)

3. Which foreign government employees have duties that are essentially "ministerial or clerical," since payments to them are legal no matter how large. But what if that person has "discretionary authority" and you are not aware of it?

4. The real need in some countries and in some situations to become involved in small-scale bribery as a matter of both self-preservation and competition. Under the Omnibus Trade Bill, payments made for routine governmental actions, such as processing paper or unloading goods, are clearly not covered offenses.

Smaller exporters are primarily concerned with the exclusion for foreign government employees whose duties are essentially ministerial or clerical. The catch is, you might have no idea of that person's real responsibilities or place in the hierarchy. Another concern is that conceivably a competitor in your country or in the buyer's country could report activities you thought were legal to the U.S. Attorney General or the SEC, which are the enforcing agencies for this law.

Overall, the most distressing problem has been the vicarious liability incurred under the "knowing or having reason to know" standard for American executives and companies in determining their responsibilities for what their foreign sales agents do. This was one of the primary revisions in the Omnibus Trade Bill that modified FCPA in terms of culpability under this standard. This was done largely by changing that phrase to "knowing" only and then clarifying the definition of knowing. Criminal penalties are eliminated when "knowledge" is not proven and only civil penalties apply even in cases of "reckless disregard" of risk that third parties might be bribing.

Preventive Measures

The following are steps you can and should take to protect yourself:

1. Carefully research the background of anyone being considered for retention as a sales consultant, agent, representative, or similar position however described.

2. Draw up a written contract, including a job description and a clear mention of any "legal" bribes that the agent may be permitted to undertake.

3. Include a clause that if "illegal" bribes are required for the agent to perform agreed-upon obligations, the contract is null and void.

4. Request that your sales intermediaries in those territories where the FCPA is a potential problem provide you with an annual certificate to the effect that no bribes have been paid.

5. If there is a question as to what is legal or illegal, it is possible to submit a request to the Department of Justice for a Review Release. Attorneys who suggest the above measures, however, hesitate to recommend this choice. The department's advice is very conservative on the one hand, and on the

other, if you do get a favorable ruling, it can readily be set aside if they decide you omitted any relevant fact.

In terms of prevention, the "reason to know" standard (and even the new "knowing" standard) is why M. Haskins and R. Holt, in an article in *Export Today*[1], recommend dealing with distributors instead of agents under the theory that, in most cases, money is not paid to distributors, thus reducing the possibility of "vicarious liability." The authors add that you should nonetheless be suspicious if the distributor has requested an unusually large discount in light of a large sale being negotiated with a government. You should also be alert for exceptional commission requests and payments to third-country banks.

In summary, the absolute minimum in terms of precautions you should pursue are:

1. Maintain good records.

2. Know your agents or distributors.

3. Determine the capacity of government officials as to their "ministerial or clerical" duties if and when you pay the commonplace, everyday bribes or tips that are necessary to do business in some countries.

Endnotes

1. Mark E. Haskins and Robert N. Holt, "Why Exporters Should Learn These Two Four-Letter Words: FCPA and RICO," *Export Today*, August 1987.

34

Antitrust Laws

If most small businesspeople were asked about their principal concerns, antitrust complications would probably not even be on their list. This would apply even more to the entrepreneurial export trader or management company. Yet both can run afoul of antitrust regulations, and in some ways, are much more likely to do so in the case of foreign antitrust regulations than our own.

U.S. Antitrust Regulations

The Sherman Antitrust Act and the Federal Trade Act, the two main pieces of antitrust legislation, list broad principles rather than specific acts that violate the antitrust purpose. There are certain trade restraints known as per se violations. That is, they are illegal on the face of the situation, and would include such things as price-fixing agreements and conspiracies, market-division agreements among competitors, and group boycotts. A second legal standard is called the rule of reason. This requires a showing that certain acts occurred and that such acts had an anticompetitive effect. Under the rule of reason, a variety of factors are considered, including business justification, the impact on prices and output in the market, barriers to entry, and market shares of the parties.

For most individuals or small companies, there is little likelihood of an opportunity to impede commerce or control prices. However, a determining issue is market share, and in today's high-tech and specialized world, some markets can be very small but significant, as well as controllable by a very small firm with a patent or even a trade secret.

When considering technology licensing agreements or joint ventures, keep in mind that unreasonable restraints to prevent competition by importation into the United States of a new technology or product are an antitrust violation, no matter how small the market. As a practical matter, with a small issue of minor importance, it would probably not come to the attention of the U.S. Department of Justice for investigation unless a complaint were filed, which could be done by a competitor. The same situation, however, might be quite a different matter in a small foreign country.

The Export Trading Companies Act removes many export activities from antitrust review that might formerly have been susceptible. Now, under Title IV of that act, there must be a "direct, substantial, and reasonably foreseeable" effect on the domestic or import commerce of the United States or on the export commerce of a U.S. citizen before any activity can be challenged. If there is any doubt, or if certain per se actions are planned for marketing or bidding abroad, an Export Trade Certificate of Review granting certain exemptions can be obtained under Title III of the act. Some call this an antitrust insurance policy. Many benefits can accrue from this approach, including economies of scale in areas such as shipping and advertising, risk diversification, and negotiating strength. It is done through DOC with the concurrence of the Department of Justice. (For more information, contact the Office of Export Trading Company Affairs at DOC.)

A certificate of review provides immunity from government suits within the stated realm of activities by you and your associate companies, plus a presumption of legality and a limit to damage awards to third-party plaintiffs of single damages. Legal expenses and attorney fees are awarded to you as defendant if you win, in the event of such a third-party suit. Certificates of review may include such areas as joint agreements on prices, joint bidding, joint negotiations on shipping costs with carriers, licensing agreements, and exclusive dealerships. Common generic advertising and promotion are facilitated. Be sure to include all the relevant facts so that the review is not voided by failure to fully inform.

If you have further concerns about antitrust matters or the possible need to obtain a certificate of review, consider ordering two pertinent publications from the Department of Justice. They are the *Antitrust Guide for International Operations* (1977) and the *Antitrust Guide Concerning Research Joint Ventures* (1980).

Foreign Antitrust Regulations

Because of relative market size, especially when a small but important bit of technology is concerned, and because of the multiplicity of national borders in other parts of the world, there are many ways in which the American exporter, technology transferor, or service provider can have difficulties with foreign versions of antitrust laws and regulations. The following are highlights of problems with such laws in two of our most important export markets, based on a paper written by Jacqueline A. Daunt of Fenwick, Davis & West, in Palo Alto, California, and summarized here with her permission.[1] It will give you some idea of what to look for in other countries.

The European Union

One of our largest trading partners, the European Community (EC) strongly enforces its antitrust laws. These laws were derived from two provisions of the Treaty of Rome, which created what has become the EU. Articles 85 and 86 of that treaty broadly prohibit agreements in restraint of trade and abuses of dominant position. In breadth and effect, they are similar to the Sherman Act, with one major difference—the importance placed on eliminating trade barriers among the EU member states. In fact, the majority of the actions brought by the commission and those that have resulted in the heaviest fines, have occurred in cases where firms have attempted to restrict the free export of goods and services among EU member states. This has an immediate and direct bearing on attempts to divide up the Common Market with multiple-distribution agreements having defined territorial limits.

Besides exclusive distributorships with absolute territorial protection, other prohibited practices mentioned in article 85(1) include horizontal price fixing, resale price maintenance, restrictions on trading conditions, limitations on production and markets, horizontal market sharing, price discrimination, and tying.

If the products covered by an agreement are of minor importance—that is, if they do not represent more than 5 percent of relevant product market and if the annual revenue of the firms that are party to the agreement does not exceed 50 million European Currency Units (ECU)—Article 85(1) does not apply. However, the phrase *5 percent of relevant product market* deserves careful attention, because a new product for which there is no substitute, might have a 100 percent market share, and fines have been imposed under just such circumstances. Also, *revenue* refers to consolidated revenues of parent and subsidiary firms, and bears watching for a rapidly growing firm as well. Another circumstance that could lead to problems is a highly specialized trading company representing two or three American suppliers with no direct competition in Europe, which could easily exceed the exemption limits. A small company should therefore not dismiss this rule as being altogether irrelevant.

The commission is empowered to interpret and enforce Treaty of Rome provisions and to impose fines as high as U.S. $10 million for violations of Articles 85 and 86. The treaty has provided exemptions to Article 85(1) through article 85(3) where official notification has been provided and specified conditions apply. The commission has also provided block exemptions from Article 85(1) in its regulation 83/83 concerning exclusive distribution agreements. This exempts certain agreements to which only two firms are a party and allows the supplier to enter into an agreement to supply only the other party to the agreement with the contract goods in the contract territory. It also allows the supplier to prohibit the distributor from obtaining the contract goods from anyone else, from manufacturing or distributing competing goods during the term of the contract, and from soliciting customers, establishing branches, or maintaining distribution centers outside its territory. In addition, the supplier can require that the distributor buy a complete range of goods or minimum quantities, sell the contract goods under a certain trademark, or require that the goods be packed and presented as specified and that the distributor take measures for promotion of sales.

It is important to note that these exemptions to Article 85(1) do not apply if an agreement restricts a distributor's choice of customers, or if it restricts its freedom to set prices and conditions of sale, or if it in any way restricts parallel imports between member states. In addition, there are other exceptions and conditions for withdrawals of exception waivers on Article 85(1) that should be understood. Therefore, before undertaking efforts to establish a series of distribution agreements in the EU, you should obtain counsel or at least obtain Articles 85 and 86 from the treaty, together with the commission's rulings and regulations on the subject. You will also find potential distributors and representatives using it as a negotiating tool in situations that do not really apply. The only defense against them is knowing that your proposal is legal, and being armed with information to support your position.

Even though your selected distribution system may be acceptable to the commission, several EU members have their own competition and pricing laws prohibiting conduct not prohibited by the Treaty of Rome. EU antitrust law does not preclude the application of these sometimes stricter national laws, which may subject a firm to criminal sanctions in a particular member state.

Japan

Another major trading partner, Japan, has very specific prohibitions relevant to licensing agreements in which technology is licensed by a foreign licensor to a Japanese licensee. This is a somewhat different approach to antitrust law in that it seems to be more concerned with protecting the Japanese licensee from the foreign licensor than the public from monopolistic prices. However, it falls into the same category. The Japan Antimonopoly Act requires that within 30 days after execution of any "international know-how licensing agreement" by a Japanese firm, the contract must be submitted to the Japan Fair Trade Commission for review of compliance with the act.

Specifically, a foreign licensor is not permitted to restrict the area to which the Japanese licensee can export, except that the foreign licensor can restrict the Japanese licensee from territories where the foreign licensor has patents or where the licensor is actively engaged in selling the licensed product or where the licensor has granted rights to third parties, such as other distributors of the licensor. Except for these permissible restrictions, the foreign licensor cannot otherwise restrict the export activities of the Japanese licensee.

In addition, a foreign licensor is not permitted to:

- Restrict the Japanese licensee from purchasing competing products or technology, unless the license is exclusive
- Require the licensee to purchase, from the licensor or any designated third party, raw materials or components for use in connection with the licensed technology

- Restrict distribution channels within Japan

- Restrict the licensee's resale prices

- Require a grant back from technology developed by the licensee unless the licensor bears similar obligations

- Require the licensee to pay royalties on products not using the licensed technology, except where it is difficult to separate the licensed technology from other products

- Require the licensee's use of any minimal quality of materials or components except to the extent necessary to protect the licensor's trademarks

These are important, but by no means exclusive, examples of antitrust issues that must be considered. Before an agreement is concluded that could be illegal in these or other countries, it is worth checking on the country regulations. The more commercially sophisticated countries are naturally the most likely to present difficulties in the antitrust area. The Canadian version of antitrust is now called the Competition Act and is very similar to U.S. law. Australia has its own antimonopoly law. The few countries specifically mentioned in this chapter probably cover the greater part of those with antitrust legislation around the world.

Endnote

1. Jacqueline A. Daunt, "Avoiding Legal Pitfalls in High Tech International Distribution," Fenwick, Davis & West, Attorneys at Law, Palo Alto, California, 1986.

6

Financing an Export Business

35

Money—And How
to Get It

Before discussing banks and business lending, the distinctions between a start-up business and a small business need to be clearly understood. With a start-up business, especially one that intends to be involved in international trade, a banking relationship must be established. It is virtually impossible to obtain any kind of business loan from a bank or any other type of financial institution, public or private unless the firm has highly liquid collateral to offer in return.

Whatever your cash savings lack, in terms of providing sufficient equity for initial investment and working capital, you will have to make up through personal borrowing. This can mean borrowing from friends, relatives, or financial institutions, using personal assets, like a second mortgage on your home, as collateral. The reason is simple. Your lender has no performance or profit history on which to base any judgment, even if it can be proven that you have the administrative knowledge. This may mean starting on a small scale so that your operation does not require borrowing to accommodate your transactions. While it isn't easy, many have done it.

Working with Your Banker

Your choice of bank or bankers will be one of the keys to your success in exporting. As a small business, you probably will find the larger banks a cold environment. While banks may have excellent package services for depositors and consumer credit, they are seldom interested in the customized lending arrangements and services you will need for international trade unless you require credit lines in excess of $250,000, and some banks prefer to deal with even much larger credit lines. Although there are always exceptions, this is as true of the branches of larger banks as of their headquarters, with the added complication that your branch loan officer is not as likely to have the special knowledge necessary to help in financing your exports and export business.

Consider first the smaller banks that have international departments, or at least officers oriented and skilled in international banking, even if they use one of the larger regional banks as a correspondent bank for documentary transactions and their international information network. If you have sufficient capital or an active domestic business, you might want to establish a second banking relationship to provide banking alternatives. If you are planning on, or see developing, a fair amount of need for transactional export financing, consider as your second bank one that specializes in trade finance. Many of these are agency or representative banks of large foreign banks that cannot take regular deposits but have considerable skills in trade finance and can be very aggressive. In general, banks withdrew from trade finance, as well as foreign risk, in the 1980s, but there is now a clear trend by banks to get back into trade finance, and with diligence you can find an interested banker with appropriate skills.

We use the word *diligence* here because by no means are all, or even most, banks involved in trade finance. To help, the Bankers Association for Foreign Trade (BAFT) has developed an outstanding program to link exporters with appropriate banks. Called Access to Export Capital (AXCAP), it is a free service established in 1993 and based on a nationwide bank database, including over 215 banking organizations having thousands of branches. AXCAP receives 30 to 40 calls per week asking for matchmaker help from exporters seeking international banking services. The banks in the database all have trade finance services that are categorized along with all the other services the bank may offer, including its areas of special interest by world region, transaction size, and customer profile in the interests of a lasting relationship. Call the AXCAP administrator on the AXCAP hotline 800/49AXCAP (492-9227). AXCAP will fax the names and contact of banks in your area and will also advise the bank they refer you to of your interest, which serves as an introduction.

International Business (one of the publications in Appendix L) prepared a global banking special report in its midyear 1994 issue highlighting banks' newly found interest in trade finance and in serving international trade needs. The report includes a list of such banks, including the many foreign banks with U.S. offices aggressively pursuing American firms.[1] Still earlier, *Export Today* reported that some of the most aggressive banks with strong trade finance departments had strong and very active bases in Hong Kong, regardless of where the headquarters might be. Included, besides The Hong Kong and Shanghai Banking Corporation, were First Interstate Bank and Standard Chartered Bank (making it noteworthy that First Interstate subsequently made a joint agreement with Standard Chartered Bank to handle its trade finance business); also Chase Manhattan Bank and Chemical Bank (and it is also noteworthy that these two are merging in the Fall of 1995). All of these banks are, or were, some of the more active international banks in the United States, and at least some of them also serve midsize and even smaller firms.[2] But at the same time *International Business* explained how many smaller firms that could not find adequate general working capital financing from qualified international banks worked out their problem by turning to merchant bankers for transaction based financing and to some extent, asset based financing.[3] As of today, however, more and more banks are offering trade financial facilities.

Talk at some length with your account or loan officer. Rapport is extremely important because of the judgment factor involved. This individual, in many respects, *is* the bank as far as you are concerned. Don't wait for the banker to take you to lunch. Take your banker to lunch (literally or figuratively). Your account officer and the other people in the bank who will be important to you—international department vice presidents, your documentary officers, perhaps the officer in charge of state and federal financing programs, even the person in charge of the telex remittance room—all these people can have an impact on the success and profitability of your export efforts.

Your loan officer should be personally acquainted with international trade and trade finance. The loan officer, as part of a profit center in the bank, may actually give (and get) more attention where your problems are concerned. If the bank of your choice is organized so that its international division is simply regular staff, rather than being part of its profit center, be sure your loan officer is interested and eager to work both with you and with the bank's international staff. Some loan officers clearly tend to avoid international trade and international staff altogether.

If you can find a financial institution that suits you and your needs, it's important to get started on the right foot. When you request a loan, request something possible; don't expect the lender to take an equity position in your company. You must provide the basic equity and collateral to support your financial needs. The lender's job is to assist you with supplemental and peak-funding needs. No bank is interested in venture capital; banks don't like risks, and it is quite true that banks prefer lending money to companies that don't need to borrow. Therefore, it is axiomatic that you should always make arrangements for the loan *before* you need the money, or at least arrange the borrowing facility before the immediate necessity arises. This is especially important in the case of transaction financing. Discuss the deal with your banker before, not after, signing the contract.

It's important to recognize that banks don't like to see static conditions on general working-capital loans. Banks want to see the loan paid down, even if only in relatively small amounts, despite the fact that you may borrow again in the near future; this is the nature of working capital. Working capital requirements change almost daily; therefore, the bank doesn't expect to see a general working-capital loan become a fixed, long-term loan. Also, don't be surprised if the bank requires that such a facility be paid off in full at least once a year and possibly more often. If this will be difficult or impossible for you, it may be best to check first with the Small Business Administration regarding a loan guarantee.

Most lenders and most borrowers prefer structured working-capital loans, frequently based on accounts receivable. This usually removes some of the burden for paying the loan off in full periodically and provides both parties with a clear guideline based on a mutually agreed-upon formula as to an acceptable maximum outstanding credit secured by a fluctuating value asset, such as receivables. The open general assets working-capital line is fine if you can get one, but you must have substantial assets available to support it. If you do have such a facility, handle this valuable credit line with care and save it for emergencies or unusual situations of short duration if possible.

If your bank has the knowledge and interest in terms of international trade expertise, an accounts receivable loan, based on insured foreign receivables, may be an ideal working-capital loan collateral for both you and your bank. If possible, consider developing several trade finance credit lines within your overall banking relationship, divided among several specific purposes, as opposed to a single credit line. Examples include an Eximbank insured accounts receivable line, a line supported by export letters of credit for the purpose of opening domestic or standby letters of credit, and perhaps a much-smaller general working-capital line. The advantage is usually a larger total line, the disadvantage resides in miscalculating your needs within each separate category.

If you are a third-party exporter—an export management company (EMC) or an export trading company (ETC)—it's important to find a bank that has other such customers and understands that an export company requires, and can support, more leverage in its lending facility than most businesses need or can justify. One reason for this is the lack of standing inventory that is therefore not in danger of aging, and the lack of other tangible assets, such as capital equipment that isn't necessary in a business that consists of such a large service element.

The EMC/ETC business normally undertakes relatively large sales against fairly small margins or perhaps only commissions. This is possible because of its potential for substantial sales volume while employing a minimum amount of staff and equipment. If you can find a banker who understands this, you are fortunate indeed. Your biggest asset and borrowing leverage will probably be your receivables, which can be secured by letters of credit and accounts receivable insurance. A second opportunity for collateral borrowing is on inventory that is already clearly committed to export channels over which your banker can exercise considerable fiscal control by means of liens, including the revenues arising from the sale of that inventory. (See Chapter 37.)

SBA and Other Guarantors

For your working capital financing, there are alternatives to banks both in the public and the private sector. Banks, however, remain a necessary element and prime choice. In any event, you must use bank facilities for their international financial and documentary services. Also, banks are usually the fastest and least-expensive source. If a bank will not support you on your own, investigate whether it would consider a working capital loan with a Small Business

Administration (SBA) guarantee. (See Chapter 39 for a detailed discussion of SBA, its export support system, its international trade loan and export working-capital loan guarantees, and its domestic programs that can provide other than financial support for your export activities.

In addition to the SBA, there are various public sector avenues for financial support at almost every level of government, including some at the state, county, and city levels, besides the federal agencies. The latter include the U.S. Export-Import Bank (Eximbank) and the Overseas Private Investment Corporation (OPIC). (See Chapters 39–44.) Check with your state's department of commerce and possibly even with your DOC district office; they may be able to direct you to the appropriate state agency. (You will also find further information regarding state trade and finance export agencies in Chapter 44.) Don't overlook the possibility that your state may be one of the eight to ten states with an active export finance program for small businesses; many more states have legislation to that effect that has not yet been activated. In considering the various support options, keep in mind that these programs vary widely as to financial purpose and terms, and try to determine in advance which will best suit your needs. Some are very specific as to purpose or focus on a specific type of borrower, such as minorities, while others are meant for more general working-capital needs or longer-term investments, such as commercial buildings or equipment.

Nonbank Lenders

As an alternative to financing through a bank, look into the possibility of nonbank lenders (merchant banks primarily), although their fees are generally higher. Proven leaders among nonbank lenders with an export specialty are such firms as World Trade Finance in Los Angeles, which specializes in taking on difficult cases guaranteed by the California Export Finance Office, but finances other firms as well. It and others like it can be lifesavers in helping with the extra big deal or with general transaction-based financing until a firm's balance sheet permits it to approach a conventional bank. Also noted for trade finance deals for any size firm are Bristol Trade Finance, Inc., in Dallas and Trading Alliance Corp. in New York. The field continues to grow. In some states with active export support programs, the state offices are in a position to know of nonbank lenders in the region.

Altress Financial's, based in Honolulu but serving the western United States, specializes in several forms of export assistance. It offers the Eximbank Umbrella policy to help its clients borrow against their foreign receivables under *Altress Financial's* own receivables financing program. It also offers participation in its shared foreign sales corporation. A firm called Trade Guaranty Insurance Services in Irvine, California, is offering a program designed especially for trade intermediaries like ETCs. Through Great American Insurance, they provide a surety bond that guarantees the suppliers in a given export transaction that they will be paid, allowing the trade intermediary to obtain favorable payment terms from the supplier to limit or eliminate the need for working-capital financing. All of this relates to a trend reported in the June 28, 1993, issue of *Time* magazine on the increasing share of all business borrowing being done with nonbank lenders, including insurance companies. As of 1992, the banks' share had fallen to 22 percent according to the *Time* article.

Don't overlook two SBA-related lenders: the small business investment centers (SBIC), which are public/private ventures that have SBA backing and the certified development companies that package and share fixed-asset-based loans for improving plant and equipment with other lenders to provide longer-term loans with SBA support. (Both these programs are mentioned in Chapter 39 on the SBA.) There are also a few new or experimental approaches being developed for small business lending, often utilizing SBA guarantees and replenishing available limited funds by selling the loans in the secondary markets. One of these is the concept of the business and industrial development company (BIDCO) pioneered in California. Michigan has followed California's lead and expanded it to include loans with equity features. BIDCOs are intended to fill a gap by financing businesses too risky for banks but not attractive enough in terms of return on investment opportunities for venture capitalists. BIDCO loans are typically guaranteed by SBA and then sold to private investors. Several other states are anticipating legislation to permit and encourage BIDCOs. Although there is not yet a very high level of activity in this area, you should check to see if this interesting entrepreneurial tool may have become available in your state.

Still other new types of private sector business lenders, not necessarily specializing in international trade, can be a great help to the small business and entrepreneur because they aggressively seek the type of business many banks try to avoid. An example of these lenders, many of which operate nationwide, is The Money Store. In addition to providing money against second mortgages on homes, these lenders become SBA-certified and specialize in business lending in conjunction with SBA guarantees. As a result of a positive attitude toward SBA guarantees and specialization, they can often dramatically expedite the guarantee and loan process for eligible borrowers.

The top six nonbank providers of qualified SBA loans in 1994, according to the SBA, were: The Money Store Investment Corp., Heller First Capital Corp., ITT Small Business Finance (being sold to General Electric Finance at this writing), AT&T Small Business Lending Corporation, Government Funding CALBIDCO (California only), and Emergent Business Capital, Inc. Your nearest SBA office can help refer you to other reliable organizations of this type. They are usually listed under Lending Institutions in the Yellow Pages. Note, however, that while useful for general working-capital borrowing, only a limited number of these lenders are interested in lending that is oriented toward export transactions.

Sources of Funding Defined

While not directly related to exporting, financial management is of vital importance to any business, and every exporter should be familiar with as many aspects of general financing as possible. This applies to the individual going into business for the purpose of exporting goods manufactured by others, as well as to small, established manufacturing firms starting to export their own product. Think of your sources of funding in terms of permanency, duration, and source. These priorities can be stated in the following order:

1. Equity, which is the basic investment.

2. Private party loans or funding in any form, based on faith in you and your ability. These loans usually have a fairly advance maturity date and perhaps no immediate installments due.

3. Capital loans for real estate, buildings, and major equipment, secured by land, improvements, or the equipment itself (medium- to long-term).

4. Working-capital loans from banks or other financial institutions, which include:
   - General working-capital loans secured by the company and your personal signature. Such loans, if available, usually require a collateral of tangible and liquid assets, often from outside the business.
   - Accounts receivable loans secured by the company's receivables. These have various conditions imposed by the bank to ensure its enforceable rights in this form of collateral. This is probably one of the most common-place forms of working-capital loans, even for export companies if the receivables are insured.
   - Other asset-based working-capital loans are secured by assets like inventory or equipment. This would not apply to most EMCs/ETCs because of the transitory nature of their inventories.

5. Transaction-based loans, or trade finance, are based on individual transactions and the supporting documents evidencing an international transaction. (See Chapter 37.)

6. Self-financing, for firms with established trade credit, can be gained between the time of collections under letters of credit and the due date on the account payable relative to that transaction. Unfortunately, if yours is a new company, this is also more likely to be a negative factor because your domestic terms might be COD or cash in advance. As you develop a good credit reputation and can obtain open 30-day terms or better from your suppliers, cash flow advantages, thanks to creditor terms, can be a major source of funding, especially if you are exporting under letter-of-credit terms. Abuse of this source of funding by stretching terms can backfire quickly and add negative leverage to an already difficult problem. Protect this source of funding at all costs, and in the worst-case scenarios, sit down to discuss the problem with your creditors before they feel forced to contact you.

7. Bank float as a source of funding has virtually been eliminated by modern electronic banking. In any case, when combined with the ever-tougher rules regarding the waiting period for crediting deposited checks to your account,

float through your bank account is most likely to be negative. Said in reverse, this means that banks are today often beneficiaries of float as a result of the slow transmittal of funds to the exporter's account and the almost-instant recording of checks drawn. This is especially true of foreign checks. Without the U.S. banking system's microencoding, they can take four to eight weeks to be credited, which is a burden to the exporter.

Financial Planning and Assistance

There are many sources of assistance for both your initial and ongoing financial planning. You may need this assistance to properly prepare and present the plans suggested here in a convincing and professional manner to those from whom you seek financing. Having the appropriate financial plans and tools at hand will help you find a bank with knowledgeable and understanding loan officers. Knowing what is reasonable for you to request and having evidence of sound financial planning in the form of business plans and cash flow projections, will take you a long way in gaining the lender's confidence. The best business plans are straightforward statements prepared by an informed party who knows what is needed and what it will take to obtain it in terms of money, equipment, experience, and staff.

This principle can be applied both to the strategy to be followed by the entrepreneurial exporter who is attempting to establish a sound banking relationship, or to the established smaller company seeking new financing for a major export drive or a large export project. In either case, what you claim and project must be realistic, even if understated in your own mind. To do otherwise invites a credibility gap. Some of the crucial elements of a business plan are:

- Your experience with the product or project
- Your marketing plans and marketplace experience
- Your anticipated gross margins and net profit
- Your calendar of events and development or your project timetable and production cycle
- Your advance or up-front costs and borrowing needs
- The security or assurance of payment of the underlying transaction, if one exists
- Your cash flow projections

An objective analysis by the potential borrower or his advisers should identify areas of strength and weakness and pinpoint details that one might otherwise overlook. A good plan will not only show how you propose to achieve your goals, but also demonstrate how you would solve some problems before they arise. Such advance thinking will make your prospective or present lender much more comfortable.

A cash flow projection is vital, not only in a business plan, but in many borrowing situations as well. If it is properly prepared, it will show the lender that you are borrowing the right amount for the purpose you have stated. Too little can be as dangerous as too much. It also helps the lender understand how and when repayment can be expected in the natural course of events. This projection becomes part of the business plan and is often the portion studied most carefully by your lender.

A cash flow projection is not nearly as mysterious as it sounds, and to be really helpful, needs as much direct input from management as possible. Try putting down some figures along these lines, using mostly common sense:

- List cash and equivalent liquid assets at the beginning of the projection period.

- Project your sales or income over the cash flow projection term—usually six months to two years. If a major export project is involved, you may isolate the project sales volume and gross margin on separate lines.

- Use your historical percentages for gross margin and expenses to bring down the gross revenue line to operating income. If something about the project or business growth plan is going to make a major change in gross margins or expenses, make an estimated adjustment to reflect this.

- Adjust profit to cash flow (decrease/increase in working capital) by deducting expenses and other items that do not actually reduce cash, primarily depreciation, but possibly accruals and deferrals, if substantial. Don't forget the month that income taxes are due.

- Estimate changes in the level of accounts receivable, accounts payable, and inventory over the projection period and adjust for those changes as they might increase or decrease cash available.

- Reflect the cash infusion from the borrowing you are applying for, plus any new investment, less principal payments necessary on existing debt and the proposed new debt.

The bottom line indicates your cash shortfall—or increase by period—and impact on working capital, as well as total cash available at the end of each period. A Lotus 1-2-3 spreadsheet on a personal computer makes this whole process much easier and lets you do more experimenting with various scenarios. Your accountant or bookkeeper should help, but working on it yourself first is probably a better plan. It costs less, and enjoys a better chance of success. Once done, you will have learned a lot, and what you have learned will become a key to achieving your objectives. Your local SBA office can also help in preparation of cash flow projections through SBA's SCORE counselors as discussed in Chapter 39. SBA distributes a pamphlet called *Understanding Cash Flow* and they also developed in cooperation with the National Business Association a cash flow software program you should inquire about. (See Appendix K for a further look at the subject of cash flow.)

If you don't have an accountant, consider obtaining the assistance of a reputable loan packager. The SBA office is an excellent place to obtain references for such people. The loan packager's function is to help you prepare a report that will give you the best chance of receiving a serious and sympathetic hearing from a financial institution. The packager's function does not normally include accounting, but he or she will advise you if your accounting statements do not seem to be in proper order. "Proper order" includes omitting personal or frivolous assets such as valuable pets or other items of a personal and perishable nature that are difficult to appraise. It also means avoiding highly optimistic estimates of homes or property and other entries that tend to make your lender feel that the whole statement is inflated or too heavily represented by assets that would be difficult to liquidate.

If your statement is not in order, the packager will advise you on what to discuss further with your accountant or bookkeeper, or will work with you directly. The packager also should help you think out and articulate your business plan as well as the cash flow projections. A word of caution in selecting your packager: If the fee seems exorbitant or promises are made such as "I guarantee that you will get the loan," beware! References can usually be obtained from the SBA or your bank. If you wish to become more familiar with any of the important accounting and planning tools, almost any one of the major accounting firms will have a manual written in layman's language that you will find helpful. A variety of manuals are available at your SBA district office (call 800-U-ASK-SBA for its location) and through your banker.

There are other, less-expensive ways of better understanding how to articulate your plan and present your finances for the purpose of making your most favorable financial arrangements. One is through SBA's own counseling programs, including its local SCORE (Service Corps of Retired Executives) unit. This is a fine program utilizing dedicated men and women who take a lot of enjoyment and satisfaction from assisting other businesspeople in fields similar to those from which they have retired after their own successful careers.

Another source of help is the Minority Business Development Agency, associated with SBA, or the Minority Resource Center of AID (see Chapter 13). Their objectives include programs to promote and improve minority enterprises, provide financial assistance to both public and private organizations, render technical and management assistance to minority businesses, and establish centers for information dissemination. As a result of the Gray Amendment, women-owned businesses are eligible for this assistance. (See Chapter 13 in the section on the Agency for International Development.) Included among a large array of programs is the Export Development Program, specifically formulated to provide technical assistance to minority businesses thought to have potential to enter the international marketplace. Under certain circumstances, this program provides for underwriting half the cost of outside consulting in addition to the free services offered by the center. This is as true of small business corporations owned by minorities as it is of an individual proprietor. The quality of assistance will naturally vary from center to center, depending on the contractor, but it is definitely worth looking into as a source of help. The definition of minorities is very broad, and it is astounding how many people are eligible for what can be very valuable, inexpensive—even free—assistance.

Endnotes

1. Lori Ioannou, "Global Banking Special Report," *International Business,* July 1994.

2. Beverly Wolpert, "Hong Kong Banks Take Lead in Financing Asia-Pacific Transactions," *Export Today,* June 1992.

3. Lori Ioannou, "Getting Credit in a Crunch," *International Business,* July 1992.

36

Letter of Credit as an Export Financing Tool

The letter of credit is such a basic instrument of international trade that, for many exporters, it represents the primary means of payment for a large percentage of their dollar volume, possibly even for their unit transaction volume. Using letters of credit to finance purchases for export or to support export-related borrowing to your best advantage is extremely important. Letters of credit can serve to minimize the borrowing problems that are discussed in Chapter 35. The techniques discussed in this chapter are more accurately referred to as *export finance,* rather than as trade finance, and they represent the best use of your letters of credit for working capital to support specific export activities.

A letter of credit from an overseas buyer can be used for financing export purchases through your banker, your supplier, or a combination of both. This is accomplished by transferring or assigning a portion of your benefits under the letter of credit to the supplier or using it to support bank borrowing. The ease of doing this depends on how clearly and simply the letter of credit is drawn and how strong it is. A simple letter of credit is one that keeps complications and special conditions, such as inspections, consular legalization, and so forth, to a minimum. A strong letter of credit is issued or confirmed by a bank of known financial strength and reliability. If the letter of credit is not confirmed in this country, you must consider the political stability and foreign-exchange or transfer risks of the country in which it was issued or confirmed. Your banker will have this information available.

Transferable Letters of Credit

See Chapter 20 for an explanation of transferability in the overall context of letter of credit terminology. You must specifically ask your buyer to make the letter of credit transferable, which the buyer may or may not be willing to do. Unless the credit states that it is transferable, it is not. A request to transfer indicates that you are not the original supplier, that you lack the financial strength to fulfill the order on your own, and that you desire to substitute the buyer's financial strength for your own. In many buyer/seller relationships this arrangement is understood and is quite acceptable to all parties. Only you can judge your buyer's willingness to provide the clause in the letter of credit and the effect your request will have on your relationship.

If, and only if, the credit is transferable, you can transfer the letter of credit once to one or more suppliers, providing the transferring bank is willing to perform the transfer. In most cases, they are willing. All terms and conditions of the letter of credit must be transferred by the transferring bank to the second beneficiary, who becomes entirely responsible for performance under the credit. It should therefore have no effect, nor need reliance on, the transferor's credit or credit facilities. Because the increasing use of transfers has caused numerous problems around the world, however, the newest version of the UCP 500 sets forth a step-by-step outline on how transferable credits are to be handled:

> The credit can be transferred only according to the terms and conditions specified in the original credit, with the exception of: the amount of the credit, any unit price stated therein, the expiry date, the last date for presentation of documents…,[and] the period for shipment, any or all of which may be reduced or curtailed.

Note that the time periods for shipment, expiry, and presentation can be shortened to allow for substitution of shipping and other documents prior to the expiration of the same named dates in the original letter. In addition, the UCP 500 states that the percentage for which insurance cover must be effective may be increased in such a way as to provide the amount of cover stipulated in the original credit. This is because the transferee (second beneficiary) is presumably selling at a discount to the first beneficiary, so that if the credit called for 110 percent insurance based on the buyer's price, a higher percentage would need to be applied by the transferee to comply with the original credit. Furthermore, the name of the first beneficiary may be substituted for that of the original applicant (buyer), unless the name of the applicant is specifically required by the original credit to appear in any or several documents other than the invoice, in which case those instructions must be followed. For the first time the UCP provides that an issuing bank must nominate a transferring bank, or banks.

You may experience some difficulty in persuading your supplier to accept the transferred letter of credit, because the supplier now must meet all requirements of the credit in terms of performance, documentation, and shipping. Without an export department, or if the firm is not familiar with export, the supplier may be unwilling to oblige or may feel that those should be your duties as the exporter. Still, if your supplier is motivated to make the sale, it can usually be persuaded.

If the letter of credit is transferable, partial transfers are permitted only if the original letter of credit allows for partial shipments. Note that banks will not make partial transfers if the original credit calls for either installment shipments or shipment schedules. You can limit the transfer to the dollar amount you owe the supplier and arrange for the transferring bank to substitute invoices, which is conventional practice. This act deletes the supplier's invoices and substitutes yours at the higher price. The transferring bank pays the supplier first and then pays you the difference. The standard transferable clause permits transfer only once, but on that single occasion permits multiple transfers to several suppliers if partial shipments are allowed in the credit. Banks will resist transferring to a number of suppliers, however, and the bank charges also place limits on this practice. The transferring bank will be much more cooperative if the transaction is structured for one transferee only and one shipment only.

Maintaining Buyer and/or Seller Anonymity

Besides the caution concerning increasing the percentage of insurance coverage in CIF or CIP shipments, there are several other problems with transfers if the exporter needs to conceal the ultimate supplier from the buyer and/or the buyer's name from the transferee supplier. This can often be done, but with some letter-of-credit terms or conditions it can be impossible. The following points should be noted:

- *Concealing the name of the buyer from the transferee.* The original credit must specify that the bill of lading calls for notification (notify party) of the first beneficiary, a freight forwarder, customhouse broker or the issuing bank; rather than the buyer (account party), which would be the normal requirement. Otherwise, the supplier would have to have the name of the buyer to have proper shipping documents prepared.

- *Concealing the actual supplier from the buyer.*
  1. The shipper of record on the bill of lading must be the first beneficiary, a freight forwarder, or some other third party. This can be organized without regard to the original letter of credit, but it is preferable if the original letter is requested to state "all shipping documents to be in the name of the first beneficiary."
  2. Care must be taken concerning identifying marks on crates, packages, wrappings, or the merchandise itself, as well as documents such as packing lists or certificates of origin if the latter are called for as separate documents which might move with the merchandise itself. The first beneficiary must work with the forwarder on these issues to be sure they are reproduced on the forwarder's or first beneficiary's letterhead or that of some other middleman. This can be difficult if the buyer's letter of credit calls for a beneficiary's certificate of origin rather than simply a certificate of origin.

■ *Handling problems with legalized documents or consular invoices.*   A problem most frequently associated with Middle Eastern transactions occurs when the credit calls for a legalized document. Requirements concerning consular invoices may reveal the first beneficiary's lower price from the supplier because legalized consular invoices cannot be substituted because since most consulates maintain that only one consular invoice can be obtained for any given shipment. We are advised that some consulates do not take this position. Careful checking in advance is needed in such cases. There is also a problem when legalized documents require considerable extra time if the exact and final quantities in the shipment cannot be ascertained until the transferee has completed its invoice and shipped.

Assignment of Proceeds of the Letter of Credit

Assignment of proceeds of a letter of credit is the simplest way of using it as leverage to finance your transaction purchases. Any letter of credit can be assigned because it does not require the assent of the buyer or the buyer's bank. No extension of bank credit is required to assign and it imposes no burdens on the supplier. The assignment is irrevocable and advises the bank to first pay the assigned party a certain percentage, or a fixed amount, of the collection under the letter of credit.

The supplier thus has the bank's promise to transfer all the assigned proceeds insofar as they are collected under the assigned letter of credit before any proceeds are remitted to the beneficiary. The supplier's risk is that you will fail to properly perform your duties as the shipper and negotiator of the letter of credit. The supplier is also entitled to know that you have a valid letter of credit with a solvent bank in a country that has available foreign exchange. That being the case, if the supplier knows you and knows you have the necessary experience, chances are that the assignment will be accepted.

Occasionally, the supplier will insist on verifying the strength of the letter of credit. If you do not wish to display the entire letter of credit to convince the supplier of its strength, perhaps a photocopy with the buyer's name obliterated will suffice or you may be able to enlist your banker to provide informal reassurance as to the validity of the letter of credit.

Back-to-Back Letters of Credit

Back-to-back letters of credit constitute a subject more discussed than executed. If the exporter does not wish to request a transferable letter of credit, the bank can be asked to use the export letter of credit to issue a back-to-back letter of credit that will assure payment to the domestic supplier. In theory, this can be accomplished without any need for the bank to rely on the exporter's credit standing. In fact, most banks are very shy about issuing such a back-to-back domestic letter of credit that largely relies on the bank's documentary skills to keep it risk-free. If you do not have an established credit line to assist you in this maneuver, most American banks will decline. You may find the smaller foreign bank more agreeable, and Asian banks especially seem to be more comfortable with back-to-back credits than most other banks.

For the bank issuing the second letter of credit, a perfect back-to-back letter of credit effectively eliminates the risk of nonperformance by the original beneficiary on the first letter of credit. This is because all duties and responsibilities placed on the original beneficiary, the exporter, are now also required of the supplier, including obtaining any necessary shipping documents, just as in a transferred letter of credit. Therefore, the bank issuing the second, or back-to-back letter, will only have to pay under its terms and conditions if all documents and conditions are in order to permit the exporter to collect under the initial export letter of credit. Thus, the bank is theoretically free of all contingent liabilities, especially if it is also the confirming and negotiating bank for the original letter. The bank then negotiates and pays the exporter under the initial letter, less its outlay of funds to the supplier made under the second domestic letter, and the remainder represents the exporter's gross profit. If the exporter's bank is not a confirming bank, it exposes itself to any foreign risk it perceives in the issuing bank or its country, plus any potential error on its part in negotiating the back-to-back credit.

In theory, using an export letter of credit to open a back-to-back letter of credit requires that only the following four items be changed if it is to be a perfect back-to-back transaction:

1. The name of the beneficiary (seller)

2. The name of the accountee (applicant or buyer)

3. The dollar amounts in total and per unit

4. The latest shipping and/or validity date, advanced to a few days earlier date to provide time for substitution of the documents for collection under the original letter

It is rare that no other conditions need to be changed to make the second letter work and make it a true back-to-back letter of credit. There are many situations that open the bank to losses in the event that the original beneficiary or the supplier fails to perform. A common finding is that the same consular invoice problem occurs as in the case of a transferred letter, when the original letter of credit calls for legalization of the invoice at the U.S. consulate of the buyer's country, such as in the case of Saudi Arabia and other countries in the Middle East. As previously mentioned, this is because at least at some consulates only one invoice can be legalized for a given shipment. The second letter cannot include that same condition and the bank must now rely on the beneficiary of the original letter to fulfill that condition of the letter of credit after the supplier has already drawn on it. The bank is then exposed to performance conditions after already having advanced funds.

Another frequent spoiler of an otherwise perfect back-to-back letter of credit occurs if the supplier is unable to adhere to the terms of the credit or refuses to accept and undertake the ocean shipping responsibilities and wants to draw on the letter of credit with a truck bill of lading or a dock receipt. In such an event, the bank must rely on the exporter, not only to get the goods safely to the port, but also to get a clean onboard bill of lading. In both cases, this understandably amounts to more risk than banks are willing to undertake if they cannot rely on your credit as a secondary means of repayment.

Banks also dislike the back-to-back concept because of the burden it places on their documentary officers who, they feel, could possibly overlook some discrepancy that might be discovered by the original bank. Even when all skills are in place and the other conditions are perfect, the larger banks are concerned about adequate communication between the loan officer and the documentary department, which is perhaps why some smaller banks with international trade orientation and up-close supervision are more amenable.

While all may agree that a particular letter of credit is as good as gold, until the product is exported and the proper documents are presented, it is of no value at all. Many new-to-export people find this very difficult to accept, but you will have a better rapport with your bankers if you understand and appreciate their point of view. Even without a back-to-back deal, your letter of credit remains a valuable document for facilitating and supporting a request for credit in the form of a domestic letter of credit for your supplier, or for obtaining some other form of credit extension.

A Letter of Credit in Support of a Credit Extension

Support means that, even though it is much less than a perfect back-to-back letter of credit, your lender may be prepared to accept your ability to perform according to the terms of the letter of credit and, because of that, be willing to extend you credit. However, the lender is relying first of all on your creditworthiness, and once the domestic letter of credit is issued, it will decrease your line of credit accordingly. The key difference is that, by acknowledging your ability to perform, the requirements concerning your balance sheet strength become less demanding as more emphasis is placed on your ability to perform according to the letter-of-credit terms. In the last and most practical analysis, this is how most of export financing is accomplished in an ongoing business when letters of credit are involved.

This reintroduces one of the reasons and advantages of distinguishing between your working capital lines of credit, secured by whatever means, and your specific trade finance lines of credit. If approached as a separate line and identified as a trade finance credit extension made to facilitate the execution of your export letters of credit transactions on a case-by-case basis, the odds are that you will increase your total borrowing power.

If the letter of credit is used to support domestic letters of credit instead of cash borrowing, you will save on bank interest, but you will have to pay letter of credit opening fees and any commitment fee the bank might require in lieu of interest on cash loans for advance payment purposes. Unless you do considerable business with your bank, commitment fees are likely to be necessary, because in opening the domestic letter of credit, the bank has made a form of credit extension, relying on your performance under the export credit. This means that the bank has accepted a contingency risk over the life of the credit, and under the new banking rules, has used part of its loan reserves. The letter of credit fees represent documentary department costs and overheads, while the commitment fee relates to the lending profit center. The commitment fee, however, will be much less per annum than the loan interest.

It is easier for the bank to justify extending this additional credit in the form of a domestic letter of credit to a supplier because the bank is assured of exactly how the advance will be utilized. In fact, through the documentary process, your banker can maintain a perfected security in the goods until shipped and collected. This can be done through documents such as UCC-1 Purchase Money Security filings and Trust Receipts.

37

Trade Finance

Trade finance refers to borrowing or lending based on specific import/export transactions, backed by various documents evidencing that each transaction is either in process or has been executed. Such documents may consist of warehouse receipts, accounts receivable, transport documents, bills of lading, drafts or bills of exchange, to name the most common. The term *export finance,* as used in Chapter 36, is a more inclusive term describing any form of financing exports, whether based on specific transaction documents or not, and frequently based on export letters of credit.

There is a worldwide network of public and private institutions established for the specific purpose of supporting international trade and for relieving the exporter of foreign risks that the exporter had limited means of evaluating or sustaining. The special nature of foreign risk is one of the reasons why some of these financing techniques are almost exclusive to international trade—or at least were first devised to finance international accounts, as opposed to domestic receivables.

Documentary procedures, which are nearly universally recognized, permit a lender to secure credit extensions by means of the merchandise being imported or exported, or by means of the documents that represent the transaction. Most countries have national banks or other special public institutions to help finance exports and provide guarantees or insurance on international trade accounts to both exporters and private banks. In this country, the leading institution for that purpose is the Export-Import Bank of the United States (Eximbank) for financing, guarantees and insurance on foreign accounts receivables. (See Chapter 40 for a summary of Eximbank's operations.)

Definitions

The following definitions will assist in understanding the financing programs offered by various export trade finance organizations, both public and private, including Eximbank. They are also the terms that should become part of your vocabulary when considering the possibility of seeking financing to support export or credit extension activities.

Supplier Credit

Supplier credit is trade credit extended by the seller or exporter, or by a financial institution on the exporter's behalf, to a foreign firm or government and is normally evidenced by some sort of acceptance of goods or services, implied or specific. This nomenclature applies even though the exporter (supplier) obtains financing based on buyer obligations, even if guaranteed by a bank or other entity in the buyer's country. Until paid, the obligation appears as an asset on the books of the exporter.

Buyer Credit

Buyer credit is credit extended to the buyer through a third party, with or without guarantors. While the seller may have made a proposal to the bank or provide an outline of the financing scheme at the time of proposal, or may even continue to cooperate in structuring the financing, the buyer becomes the lending institution's borrower and the primary arranger of the financing, even though it is through the seller's bank or the seller's national export finance agency. The seller receives cash and is completely taken out of the transaction.

Short-Term

For Eximbank purposes, *short-term* is any term up to six months (with a few exceptions), which is the normal limit for Eximbank's basic short-term policy. It is also the minimum term for eligible banker's acceptances in this country. Many lenders and programs, however, consider *short-term* to mean anything less than one year.

Medium-Term

Medium-term can mean more than six months or one year to three, four, or five years, depending on the nature of the item being financed. Some consider *medium-term* to mean as many as seven years. In reality, it is whatever falls between short-term and long-term within the framework of the programs or lenders involved.

Long-Term

Long-term implies terms from five years to as many as 20 or 30 years for government infrastructure projects. Eximbank's current definition for its guarantee or direct loan purposes is "anything over 7 years or $10 million," which indicates how arbitrary these definitions can be. However, *long-term* is used only for transactions or projects of substantial size.

Full Recourse

Full recourse refers to the transfer or sale of a document, note, or receivable to a second party or financing agent, by which the seller takes responsibility in the event of a debtor default.

Limited Recourse

In trade finance, *limited recourse* usually refers to the concept that the lender or purchaser of the credit instrument (holder in due course) has no recourse in the event of a default, but does have recourse if the underlying document, note, or receivable is flawed, fraudulent, or the transaction is otherwise illegal. This can become tricky, because the principle is impacted by legal systems of various countries and regions. For practical purposes, however, it is best to think in terms of no recourse as long as there is no fault or fraud on the part of the exporting seller or the export documentation. In the case of limited recourse financing, accounting rules often permit the offsetting contingent liability to be entirely removed from the seller's balance sheet, thus improving the exporter's liquidity, because no borrowing liabilities are reflected and the asset is cash rather than the much-less-liquid receivable.

Nonrecourse

Nonrecourse means exactly what it says. The seller or exporter has no further responsibilities relative to the indebtedness, which is then entirely off the balance sheet to the benefit of the seller's credit position and liquidity.

Documentary Banker's Acceptances

If your buyer resists opening a letter of credit because of inventory or receivables financing costs or other cash flow problems, you may be able to retain the advantage of a letter of credit and yet be of assistance to your buyer. This can be accomplished by means of a usance letter of credit, also known as an acceptance or time letter of credit. The usance credit does not necessarily solve your buyer's working capital problems, but it may reduce the buyer's cost of carrying inventory or receivables, and it improves the buyer's cash position. However, the outstanding accepted draft will reduce the buyer's available credit line from the time the credit is opened until the draft is settled. The letter of credit is drawn to include the provision that a draft be drawn on the paying bank for a certain number of days from sight. Other transaction dates or fixed dates may be used which are better for the seller's certainty of settlement date, as discussed in Chapter 20. Usance tenor does not customarily exceed 180 days, because this is the maximum time for an eligible *banker's acceptance* (BA) according to the Federal Reserve regulations concerning acceptances. An *accep-*

tance is what the seller will receive in place of cash when presenting documents under a usance letter of credit.

If you are willing to finance your buyer under these conditions, you will in turn have available the easiest and cheapest form of receivables financing possible. On negotiating your usance letter of credit, the paying bank will return your draft drawn under that letter of credit marked "accepted and signed by the bank," thus creating a BA. This means the bank has given you, or any other holder in due course, its promise to pay in the number of days specified, and the draft becomes a fully negotiable instrument. You now have two options. The first is to keep the draft and present it to the accepting bank at maturity in the stated number of days for a cash collection. The second option is to ask the accepting bank to discount its acceptance and give you the face value less the discounted interest as of whatever date you choose to present it. Interest is based on the bank discount rate, which is a very favorable rate and is why BAs provide financing at the lowest possible rate of interest available.

In addition to the bank's discount for interest, based on the number of days that you were paid prior to maturity, there will also be an acceptance fee, which is usually for the buyer's account. This is what the bank charges for lending its name and credit rating and for the trouble of performing the transaction. While not legally obliged to discount an acceptance, the paying bank is now dealing with its own instrument and therefore its own money, and customarily *will* do so. Other banks may be willing to discount as well, depending on the strength of the accepting bank. It is best to check with the banks involved first, to make sure as to costs and the certainty of discounting the draft, if so desired.

In the case of a reputable bank in a developed country, the acceptance fee will be in the range of .5 to 1 percent per annum, but, depending on risk, it could run as high as 2 percent. If too risky, the bank will simply refuse to discount the acceptance, in which case the bank does not disburse but still has the obligation to pay at maturity. The flat acceptance fee obviously becomes a higher percentage cost the shorter the discount term. Often the importer might agree to pay the acceptance fee and the exporter would pay the discount interest. If competition permits, in pricing your product you can take whatever acceptance financing costs you bear into account, so that your customer knowingly or unknowingly is paying for them. Your buyer may prefer paying the usance costs to avoid an increase in the price of the product. This is because the resulting higher duty (a factor of which you should be aware) would be more expensive than the financing costs. When dealing with usance or time letters of credit, knowledge of the issuing, paying, or confirming bank becomes still more important and your banker should be consulted on this, as well as on the country risks.

Clean Bankers' Acceptance Financing

Clean acceptances are those that are not supported by a letter of credit, but that do relate to a specific transaction or group of transactions and the related merchandise. The bank accepts a time draft, drawn on itself, that is similar to the one the exporter would have drawn to collect under a letter of credit. But in this case the support for the draft is a separate loan agreement for the BA line that the borrower first arranged with the accepting bank.

When the bank accepts the draft by stamping and signing it "accepted," it has created a negotiable document that can be sold and resold in the secondary market and that carries the credit rating of the accepting bank, not the borrower. If the document has met certain conditions under Federal Reserve regulations for acceptances (including a 180-day limit as to tenor), it has also created an eligible BA that may be discounted at the Federal Reserve window and consequently does not reduce the lending bank's loan reserves. Actually, most BAs are not discounted at that window, but following Federal Reserve rules, the bank avoids reserve requirements and therefore they still tend to govern the parameters of most banks' BA rules. This is also one of the reasons banks offer acceptance financing at lower rates. BA financing is available for five purposes or types of transactions:

1. Preexport financing
2. Preimport financing
3. Import financing
4. Storage financing
5. Domestic shipment financing

Even though BA financing may be requested for a transaction based on a solid underlying export sale, it is still only offered to companies with a strong balance sheet. It is not a practical tool for the young company with a less-than-robust balance sheet. This is because BAs are expected to be a very secure investment and are honored by the accepting bank without question at maturity. It is a practice primarily engaged in by the money center and large regional banks.

BAs are a relatively inexpensive form of financing because of their ready negotiability for banks and, to a lesser degree, their neutral impact on the bank's loan reserves. An excellent discourse on this technique is provided in *Export Financing—A Handbook of Sources and Techniques* by Business International Corporation.[1] It explains the borrower's rate is determined by a combination of the acceptance commission that reflects the risk and normally ranges from .75 to 2 percent (mostly 1 to 1.5 percent today) per annum on a $100,000 BA for a middle market company (sales under $50 million), and the discount interest rate. The total of the two is called the all-in rate, which is the manner in which acceptances are usually quoted. The typical 90-day discount rate is slightly less than the 90 day LIBOR (London Interbank Offer Rate) interest rate or the American prime rate, which is usually well over LIBOR. Even assuming that a relatively high acceptance rate is negotiated, it will still be considerably below the borrower's normal rate. The all-in rate can be calculated against the fixed term, the total dollar cost, or cost on a per annum basis and can be readily determined.

If you can interest your bank in this type of short-term financing, your borrowing rates can be substantially lowered. The all-in rate is probably more to your advantage during relatively high-interest-rate periods than in low-rate periods. It is considered the cheapest form of financing for firms that do not have access to the commercial paper market. Another advantage is that it can be more available when credit is tight because the bank can move it out of its portfolio. The fixed rate also is considered an advantage. The disadvantage is its inflexibility because it is tied to a transaction, the various Federal Reserve rules that apply to it, and the fact that it is not available for prepayment except with penalties.

Export Financing estimates that documentary and clean BAs collectively are used by 34 percent of large American exporters. The most popular size for resale is in lots of $500,000, but banks market BAs in batches and therefore can deal with the exporter in smaller denominations. Amounts of $100,000 are practical for individual transactions, and some banks say they will work with BAs as small as $50,000 for imports, or even for as little as $15,000 to $20,000 for exports, to accommodate their correspondent bank overseas.[2]

Unfortunately, bankers as a group tend to think of BA financing solely in terms of import financing, which seems to be its most common usage. Even those who look upon it as an export finance tool fail to consider that, unlike BA rules for domestic transactions, it is not necessary that the acceptance be tied to goods in storage or transit in which the bank can take the warehouse receipt or bill of lading. Few realize that it can be used to support preexport working-capital loans insofar as there is a firm export order to support it. The bank still has the safety of a short-term credit supported by a specific transaction of the same tenor, thus defining a means of repayment. The BA has become a very important tool for many exporters, especially those who can work with the larger regional or money center banks.

Trade Acceptances

An alternative to clean banker's acceptance financing is trade acceptance (TA) financing. In this case, it is the importer who accepts the usance draft or bill of exchange; the exporter subsequently sells the negotiable interest in the market at a discount, provided the importer has good credit. The buyer of the draft is more often a nonbank trade finance company than an international bank, and then only with recourse in most cases.

Borrowing Against Receivables

For purposes of accounts receivable financing, documentary collections and open account terms can be treated alike to a certain extent. (See Chapter 23 for the description and usage of documentary collections.) Foreign accounts receivable insurance is less expensive for documentary collections than open-term receivables, especially documents against payment (D/P) in which case, the time during which the receivable is outstanding is quite brief. Documentary collections in general offer more options in terms of financing receivables because of the underlying negotiable instrument, while open-account sales are represented at best only by an invoice, a transport document, and a ledger entry. Nevertheless, borrowing against a book of open-accounts receivables is the most basic form of supplier credit financing and is considered working-capital financing as well as a form of trade finance in the case of export receivables.

Borrowing against foreign receivables becomes an issue beyond the mere fact that they represent an asset to be used as collateral. They also tend to increase the need for working capital more than domestic receivables because many overseas firms pay more slowly, with those in Europe being among the worst offenders, assuming all are creditworthy accounts. Italians are the very worst offenders, with an average payment time of 90 days in 1993 according to a survey in the July 1994 issue of *International Business*. Spain is next at 80 days; France, 70; Belgium, 57; the United Kingdom, 49; and The Netherlands, 47.[3] Other surveys indicate less slowness, but Italy is always the slowest.

If you really intend to use your foreign receivables as revolving collateral for your financing purposes, you should plan on insuring them. Very few banks will consider loaning against foreign receivables unless they are insured. Some banks will not lend even against insured foreign accounts, but in that event you probably did not contact the right bank to begin with. If a bank were to lend against uninsured receivables, it would be for a much smaller percentage of your receivables. If insured, the bank might consider a figure as high as 80 to 85 percent. While the availability of private insurance has vastly improved depending on the countries and buyers, it would be wise to consider both commercial insurance, and one of the Eximbank policies. (See the discussion on insuring credit risks in Chapter 25 and Chapter 39 on Eximbank foreign credit insurance.) An Eximbank policy can be especially helpful in encouraging a bank to lend against the foreign receivables of a smaller business if a hold harmless agreement can be provided in conjunction with an assignment of insurance proceeds. The hold harmless agreement is available in two different Eximbank policies that are designed especially for new exporters or occasional exporters.

While almost any bank reserves its option to receive all payments and have each buyer notified that the payments are due to the lender, you may be able to negotiate an arrangement whereby you provide only a monthly detailed aging schedule as long as the credit line is performing well and the receivables schedule and backup can be made available on demand. This is not only operationally easier for the exporter, it is also a great deal easier for the bank and better in terms of customer relations. The advantages to accounts receivable financing are flexibility and a collateral base that rises and falls in close correlation with specific needs. Possible loss of customer contact and follow-up is a disadvantage if the lender insists on receiving payments directly.

Sale of Receivables

Customer relationships aside, there is little difference between borrowing against your receivables and selling your receivables except that the second option is less likely to work out. The primary difference is that you are much more likely to find a bank interested in lending than in buying. If you succeed in finding a bank willing to purchase receivables, the advantage is the possibility of getting both the receivables and the loan off your balance sheet in the event that your overall borrowing seems too leveraged. The disadvantage can be in terms of customer relationships.

Even though a bank is likely to insist on insurance, it may buy only the receivables with full, or at best limited, recourse; in which case you might consider factoring your receivables, subsequently discussed. Under the right circumstances, especially so long as the receivables sold to the lender are insured, you are still permitted the accounting practice of removing both entries from your balance sheet, even with the bank's recourse clause. At most, it is covered by an accounting footnote describing the contingent liability. In this approach, documentary evidence of the underlying transactions in the form of bills of lading, invoices, notes, and so forth must definitely be provided to the bank to back up each transaction. The costs are similar to accounts receivable financing, depending on the recourse details. To be considered at all, each of the receivables has to be of substantial size, with high-quality creditors.

Factoring

Factoring volume has quadrupled in the last ten years. On the face of it, factoring is more expensive than selling or borrowing on receivables because of the service involved and the risk level your foreign receivables represent to the factor. Factoring, however, is more accessible, and the variety of services provided offset part of the costs. In evaluating factoring costs, the exporter must consider the items the factor might absorb. Two up-front costs are credit investigation ($75 to $200 or more per account) and the cost of a possible need for export credit insurance otherwise, which could run from .5 to 1.5 percent alone, depending on policy type and risk. Factoring can also permit you to do business on a relatively normal basis, without insurance, in a country in which, for policy reasons, Eximbank may be offering no coverage at all (such as was true of South Africa until apartheid ceased).

A complete factoring service contract may provide that the factor will do all credit research and make all credit decisions, advancing without recourse typically 70 to 80 percent of your receivable. Other factoring services can require a certain amount of credit information and input from you, and a smaller percentage advance with recourse. The fee ranges from 2 to 4 percent of the sale and covers the factor's credit investigation, ledger recording, collecting and guaranteeing of the receivables. Of course, it does not include the cost of borrowing against the pending receivables. Obviously, the cost will vary widely between these two extremes, but in either event, the following services would be expected and could offset a fair portion of the factor's charges. These are:

- Credit investigation, often with better access to local knowledge.

- Collection, which has the advantage of in-person, on-site conduct. Because this service is so important, the exporter must be sure to investigate the countries in which the proposed factor has an active, manned office as opposed to more distantly related contractors.

- Bookkeeping, statements, and age analysis.

- Local knowledge and the ability to intervene or arbitrate buyer disputes.

- Usually no requirement for export credit insurance because of the factor's direct involvement in the country, or that of its associate company.

You may have the option of taking your money either on or after maturity or receiving percentage advances, which of course creates discounts. Some factoring plans pay you on maturity or after an agreed-upon fixed number of days up to 90 days past maturity, thereafter taking on themselves the burden of carrying the past due account during extended collection efforts. Advance payment is obviously a direct financing element. One of the major appeals of factoring is the possibility of gaining the cash from sale transactions without showing an offsetting liability on the books in the form of a loan. Depending on the levels of service provided, your cost of factoring will depend on what your firm offers in terms of volume and experience, including ledger history. It also depends on your company's financial strength, experience, and stability, as well as on the diversity or spread of risk and the rate of concentration in the higher-risk areas.

The world's largest international factor is an umbrella group called Factors Chain International (FCI) which now includes 95 independent factoring companies in 35 countries, including several in the United States. FCI is headquartered in Amsterdam and can be contacted directly by fax in Amsterdam at 31-20-625-7628. The following U.S. firms are currently members of FCI: BNY Financial Corp. in New York City, CIT Group/Commercial Services in New York City, and NationsBanc Commercial (a subsidiary of NationsBank Corp.) in Atlanta, Georgia. Heller Financial Inc. also operates on a worldwide basis from headquarters at 101 Park Avenue in New York City. Mergers and acquisitions force frequent changes in the names of the players. For a current listing of organizations offering factoring, contact the excellent AXCAP program conducted by BAFT (described in Chapter 35). Call 1-800/49AXCAP.

Forfaiting

Forfaiting is an increasingly popular form of private financing for individual sales transactions. It is considered classic trade finance and even though looked on as relatively new in this country, has been a major financial tool for financing East/West trade in Europe for about 40 years. Previously thought to be rather exotic, as it becomes better understood and with more American financial institutions offering the facility, it is today considered a useful alternative form of limited-recourse, medium-term financing that is still essentially supplier credit, even for small to midsize exporters.

The term *forfaiting* comes from the French term for the technique *à forfait*. The idea is the seller forfeits the right to future payment in return for immediate cash. It features fixed rate financing, usually for a medium term (three to five years), most often on capital goods and equipment, although it can be applied to commodities or other goods or services with an underlying transaction. Some call it nonrecourse financing because it is free from any recourse resulting from nonpayment. However, forfaiting is technically limited-recourse financing because the exporter guarantees that the notes are legal and enforceable and that the regulatory requirements of the importer's country have been met, including the documents' authenticity. Therefore, the exporter can be sued by the primary forfaiter for fraudulent representation.

The mechanics of forfaiting are interesting. The four parties to a typical forfait transaction are:

1. The forfaiting house
2. The guarantor (most often a bank in the country of the buyer), who usually provides a form of guarantee, called an aval in forfaiting, unless the buyer is of such unquestioned financial standing that an aval or other guarantees are not required
3. The exporter
4. The importer

Typically, the exporter and the buyer, who want medium-term trade credit, agree on terms that will permit a series of semiannual notes, drafts, or bills of exchange to be drawn to liquidate the balance due on the sale over the term. The forfait can be for the unpaid balance of a contract or for 100 percent of the sale (no down payment necessary), which can often be a critical point to closing a deal.

The exporter makes arrangements with a forfaiter who, together with the importer, finds a bank or other financial institution to provide a guarantee of the buyer's credit, preferably an aval. The *aval* constitutes an endorsement of the note itself, as opposed to a guarantee agreement, and a promissory note or bill of exchange, as opposed to a loan agreement. This capacity for dealing with uncomplicated, negotiable instruments instead of contracts is part of the appeal of forfaiting. The simpler documentation adds to the speed and ease of transfer in the secondary markets. This technique has special appeal in situations that could previously have only been supported by government export programs. Forfaiting is speedier, can cover 100 percent of the transaction, and the exporter can be given a firm advance commitment with a specified fixed interest rate for the buyer. A broad range of country risk is available if the right forfaiter can be found.

In general, forfaiting is used in minimum transactions of about $250,000 and most deals would not exceed $8 to $10 million. A typical "10×6" forfait would be ten six-month notes for a total five-year term. Terms normally range from one to ten years. All documents necessary to assure validity to the initial forfaiter must accompany the note and therefore may include shipping documents, foreign exchange approval, and an import license. The costs are the straight discount rate, usually expressed in a percentage over the London Interbank Offering Rate (LIBOR); a small cost allowance made for the number of days required to receive and collect the remittance, called grace days; and a commitment fee in the range of .5 to .75 percent per annum, if, as is usually the case, an advance commitment is required by the exporter. Decisions on forfaiting can be made quickly—in a matter of hours or days, assuming that a guarantor is available, or if a sovereign buyer is involved.

Forfaiting specialists are becoming more available in the United States, but the majority are still European firms, although with ample representation here. One of the appeals of forfaiting is its broad application and fast response to the exporter trying to cost out a transaction to determine whether it can be done. Another is the ability to finance 100 percent of the sale, whereas if a bank with an Eximbank guarantee or intermediary loan were to be used, a 15 percent down payment would be required. In addition, it overcomes the problem of Eximbank's U.S. origin requirements. The same is true of foreign versions of Eximbank. The countries in which forfaiting can be applied have become numerous, although naturally costs escalate rapidly in less-developed countries, where debt problems make 100 percent financing especially useful. Still, risk takers can usually be found in most areas of reasonable risk.

Because of forfaiting's popularity, new applications for it are constantly being developed. These include shorter and longer terms, application to the service industry, floating rates, government guarantees, and even forfaiting without guarantees. For more details, check with the large regional or money center banks in your area. Some well-established forfaiting names in this country include Midland Bank Aval Ltd. and Kaines (U.K.) Limited, both with offices in London and New York, plus A.I. Trade Finance (a subsidiary of AIG) in New York. It is not necessary to deal with money center banks or world financial capitals, however. A recent example brought to our attention is the British-American Forfaiting Company in St. Louis, Missouri, which specializes in brokering smaller deals. Many large regional or money center banks will handle forfait transactions for their clients. If, after you've discussed forfaiting possibilities with your international banker or consultant, your own bank doesn't seem interested, call the AXCAP program at 1-800/49AXCAP for lenders offering this and other international trade finance services in your area.

International Leasing

Always an important form of trade finance for medium- to long-term financing of capital goods, the use of international leasing is growing and will be further facilitated in this country by the support it is now getting through Eximbank's insurance in the form of an international lease insurance policy. (See Chapter 39.)

International leasing is referred to as either *cross-border leasing,* or *foreign leasing.* Cross-border leasing is of primary interest here and takes the place of an export transaction, with the capital goods to be leased originating in one country (in this case the United States) and then shipped to the foreign lessee. In the case of a foreign lease, the goods are of foreign origin, but the lessor is located in the same country as the lessee, even though the lessor may be a company wholly or partly owned in the country of product origin or elsewhere.

Leasing methods are categorized as operational or financial. In an operational lease there presumably is a real purpose for the lease other than as a means of financing. The value of the equipment at the end of the lease may still be substantial, with the lessor prepared to reclaim it; political risk is a primary concern. In a financial lease the principal function is financing, and the sum to be paid for the lessee to take final possession is rather nominal. Therefore, the commercial risk factors may be paramount.

The United States is a leader in international leasing, probably as a result of its dominance in the aviation and transportation industries and because the tax advantages to the lessor are substantial. Leasing is an important form of financing worldwide, with leasing centers developing for structuring deals to combine and take advantage of the tax laws of two countries without regard to origin of the product. As would be expected, Hong Kong is a center for Asian leasing, but Japan is rapidly becoming more active. The parties involved must shift quickly as changing tax laws close loopholes.

Leasing gives the lessee the advantage of little or no down payment and payments carefully tailored relative to use and return on investment. For these reasons, it is particularly useful in less-developed countries, where foreign exchange is tight and for companies that could not otherwise afford to show an equivalent obligation on their balance sheet. The key to the popularity of leasing is that it is off-balance-sheet financing. Many times leasing companies finance deals for which conventional lending institutions cannot be found.

The manufacturer and/or prospective exporter does not have to be the direct lessor. There are many international leasing firms that have a subsidiary in the country of the lessee, which creates a foreign lease. For the exporter, leasing also has competitive advantages and can facilitate a faster conclusion to the transaction. The disadvantages lie in the legal complications and conflicts between the legal system of the exporter's country and that of the lessee. This creates problems as to title retention, which is the basic premise that makes leasing practical. It must be thoroughly reviewed, giving careful consideration to both countries' laws and tax systems before the lease is concluded.

Because of the interest in leasing by American businesses, including the many involved in the maquiladora program in Mexico where plant equipment needs to be leased to the contract manufacturer, Eximbank's insurance program makes leasing much more practical for the smaller or less internationally oriented company. This is especially true because this policy also covers the political risks of expropriation or confiscation of the equipment, which is one of the primary risks of leasing.

Where to Find It

You may wonder why your banker has not suggested these or other banking facilities. See Chapter 35 for several suggestions and alternatives, and especially for discussion of BAFT's export capital program, AXCAP. For a brief summary of trade finance questions and answers and appropriate federal agencies to help you, pick up SBA's free booklet: *Bankable Deals.*

Endnotes

1. Louis J. Celi and I. James Czechowicz of Business International Corporation, *Export Financing—A Handbook of Sources and Techniques,* Financial Executives Research Foundation, Morristown, NJ, 1985.

2. Celi and Czechowicz of Business International Corporation, ibid.

3. Staff survey, "Europe's Worst Offenders," *International Business,* July 1994.

38

Countertrade

Countertrade can be seen as a way of financing the buyer, a marketing tool, a simple necessity, or a profession. In fact, it is all of these, but first of all it is a method, a technique. If you do not have solid knowledge and experience concerning the proposed exchange of goods and a channel for their distribution, or cannot afford a competent third party to complete the transaction on your behalf, you should avoid it.

Although, at its most basic, countertrade is the most ancient form of trade, modern countertrade grew out of the European East/West trade of the 1970s and mid-1980s. In this country a substantial amount of countertrade came about somewhat earlier through the defense and aviation industry in a specialized form known as offset. Apart from these two versions and locales, countertrade is a subject more often discussed than accomplished. Except for the defense industry, which largely handled its own offset deals, a few European trading firms were initially the major traders, and the products traded were largely in the area of commodities, especially oil.

Forms of countertrade remain an important element of the East/West trade, but have now spread well beyond Europe. Southeast Asia is very much involved, and there, as in Eastern Europe, countertrade is often a government requirement for approval on larger transactions, especially in Indonesia and Malaysia. India and the entire subcontinent have become active in countertrade. It has spread into Latin America, which is no surprise in view of its debt problems in the 1980s, with the governments of some countries demanding countertrade in certain cases and others strongly encouraging it by means of their exchange regulations. However, its use in Latin America has not developed as anticipated because of the rapid improvement in many of those economies and a reverse capital flight in the late 1980s and early 1990s. Unfortunately, with the advent of Mexico's problems afflicting all of Latin America to some degree, there may be some resurgence. Countertrade is expected to become an important feature of the sub-Sahara African trade, but it has not yet become commonplace there. China is another countertrade area, but even there, anticipation has been greater than reality—some say largely because the government has not been able to make up its mind on the rules.

There is wide disagreement as to the percentage of international trade conducted by means of countertrade. International organizations such as IMF, GATT, and OECD make estimates in the 5 to 10 percent range. Others, including the Department of Commerce, once stated figures well over 20 percent, but that is now very doubtful. Much of countertrade involves oil and still another very large portion of it is done within the major defense industries and their sovereign customers. Euromoney's publication *Trade Finance* (now simply entitled *Euromoney*) estimated in its September 1987 issue that "almost 80 percent of countertrade involving U.S. goods is for military supplies."[1] The same magazine, however, stated that more than 90 countries countertraded in 1987, as compared to 15 countries ten years prior. In a *Business America* article of November 1992, the Department of Commerce stated that over 100 countries were involved with a number of transactions peaking in the mid- to late 1980s.[2] *Trade Finance* thinks that relatively few firms are currently involved, and the most profitable deals tend to be concluded by the largest of the countertraders.[3] This is because much of today's countertrade is accomplished by a limited group of insiders and quasi-nationals. When you consider these factors, the remainder available for the not-so-inside private sector must be much less than 5 percent of world trade. However, 3 to 4 percent of well over $2 trillion is still a lot of business.

Since countertrade has not experienced the anticipated increase in the number of transactions or volume, many firms and consultants established to facilitate countertrade have changed or given up the claim to that specialty. The well-established countertrade firms in Europe, as well as some of the diminishing number of private trading companies in the United States, continue to be active. In Appendix C of the book *Export Financing* (see Appendix K), you will find a list of countertrading firms by country, although you can be assured some of them will no longer exist.[4] A money center bank also will put you in touch with countertrade firms, some of which are international banks and their trading companies, as well as established trading houses.

In spite of the recent decline in countertrade, civil unrest and political events in parts of the world may result in many exporters having to reckon with countertrade in the future. It should not, therefore, be dismissed as being for the giants only. There are four reasons why countertrade can be a vital part of overall international trade:

1. To develop hard currency

2. To acquire more advanced techniques

3. To enter new markets

4. To improve a negative balance of trade

Countertrade must be broken into classifications to be understood, but it can be difficult to recognize what is a classification and what is just another variant of the same thing. There is disagreement as to how many categories of countertrade there are, even as to their names and definitions. Taking most of the variants into account, the primary breakdown appears to be as follows:

- Barter
- Compensation
- Counterpurchase
- Buyback
- Offset

Barter

This is the earliest and most ancient form of trade. Barter is characterized as a direct exchange of goods of roughly equal value, so that little or no currency changes hands. Also, in a basic barter transaction, only one contract or agreement is involved. In this form, countertrade may be undertaken by the smaller company or exporter if sufficient knowledge and channels to move the exchange without undue delay or risk are available. Profit margins have to be adjusted to account for the double effort on the sale—that is, the resale.

There is also a form of barter at a much more sophisticated level, practiced between sovereign trading partners, called barter and switch, or *switch trading*. In this arrangement, two nations engaged in bilateral trade use a third party to act as a clearinghouse of imbalances following a series of transactions in order to maintain a prearranged balance of trade.

Compensation

Compensation is a more modern version of barter. In compensation, both of the exchanged products are valued in specific currencies and are invoiced in those same currencies. Compensation permits unbalanced transactions with payments partly in currency and partly in product, and permit the overall transaction or project to cover extended periods of time as in major industrial projects requiring technology transfer and resulting in manufacturing facilities that produce products which can help pay for the project as one source of repayment. The deliveries of the products involved are not scheduled to occur simultaneously but over a period of years, and a third party is often involved. The similarity of compensation to barter and the prime difference from other forms of countertrade is that both transactions are covered by a single contract. This makes compensation deals somewhat complex or unwieldy. In this format, payment in full is usually delayed until a sale for the compensated goods is concluded.

Counterpurchase

As practiced by multinational corporations and large established countertrade firms, counterpurchase is a primary form of countertrade in terms of volume. It is also known as *parallel trade* or *parallel barter*. This form of countertrade is often inappropriate for the smaller trader with a less-complicated deal for which barter or compensation might be more practical. In a *counterpurchase* deal, the exporter signs a separate, second contract to buy an agreed-upon amount of other products in return for concluding an export contract. Delivery, invoicing, and payment are carried out independently for each transaction, and a third-party countertrader is often involved to complete the counterpurchase. The contracts may be in the medium-term range, perhaps as long as five years. The initial export transaction is typically a large transaction, such as an infrastructure project or a basic commodity. The counterpurchase, in turn, probably has nothing to do with the first product or service. The signing of two separate agreements, even though they might be linked by a memo of understanding, is considered an essential element and a precaution.

Buyback

Buyback is similar to counterpurchase, and some authorities do not consider it a second category. It seems, however, quite different from the more sophisticated and wide ranging counterpurchase concept. Buyback is typically part of negotiations for turnkey projects, such as construction of a plant or facility, in which the foreign builder looks for entry into foreign markets to find a quick outlet for initial production.

Buyback is an agreement to purchase or distribute the end result of the project or supplies sold to the buyer. Although the sales contract for the supplies, machinery, equipment, or project may make reference to the buyback arrangement, it is important that this be a separate contract and not affect the payment for the initial transaction, particularly in the case of smaller exporters. To protect the buyer, there is often a retention amount specified in the primary contract, or a performance bond secured by a standby letter of credit, or both.

The DOC considers buyback an important form of countertrade today and in the future because of its use in financing construction of new production capacity in developing nations. The nature of the scheme also provides a legal mechanism in case of default, and it is therefore seen as a good long-term supplement to traditional finance and project finance.

Some relatively small companies are finding themselves engaged in buyback as a result of turnkey projects with countries such as the Peoples Republic of China (PRC). This is especially true in the high-tech industries, where many companies are negotiating major deals with the PRC, and it is a good example of small firms becoming involved in countertrade.

There are several important things to consider when making buyback agreements, including ensuring that the contract leaves adequate leeway in terms of allowable marketing territory, product varieties, quality specifications, and redress in the event of inferior quality. This is especially important, because one reason the buyer wants the buyback arrangement is that it places a burden on the turnkey provider to produce a good plant or process. On the other hand, the exporter wants the right to train operators and get other assurances that will make it possible for the exporter or its agent to receive a quality product to fulfill the buyback obligations.

Offset

Offset is closely linked to counterpurchase and is in the domain of what some Europeans refer to as cooperation. Offset developed after World War II, and is primarily used in sales of Western defense and aircraft systems and equipment to less developed countries and the Middle East. *Offset* typically involves transferring technology or arranging for joint ventures. The client customer is usually sovereign, and the primary objective is to add sources for acquiring foreign exchange and/or improving the country's gross national product (GNP) to better afford the high cost of today's military and space technology. In a growing number of countries, offset is mandatory and fixed at a certain minimum percentage of the military purchase. The U.S. share of world countertrade is largely focused on this form because of the large U.S. share of foreign military sales.

Countertrade Guidelines

Under whatever name, and however described, the opportunities for negotiation in countertrade are nearly limitless, which is probably what makes it so difficult and time-consuming. Your first point of negotiation should always be to minimize the percentage of the sale that is to be compensated for in some form of countertrade. Your leverage on this point will go from excellent, for goods the countertrading country really needs, to close to zero, or 100 percent countertrade, for nonessential consumer goods. Even though you are dealing with a private party, that party is often being controlled by its government because it is only through the government that import licenses and foreign exchange can be obtained.

Count on much higher costs than in conventional export transactions, even if you plan to handle the imported goods yourself. If you are planning to have a countertrade house or an ETC handle the resale, the cost could be as much as 20 percent. Even then, it would be very difficult to get third-party help for a deal of less than $1 million. Check the penalty clauses and determine what happens if the penalties should apply, and what the downside risk is. Even though the penalties seem vague, you can assume that any uncompensated infringement by you of your agreement will mean the end of your trading days with that country.

While countertrading can be a potent marketing tool and sales achiever, and in some situations, a profitable and wise thing to do for the bold trader, in most cases it is better to avoid countertrade if possible. In other words, don't go out looking for countertrade—let it find you. Apart from the obvious risks, it will have a tendency to slow your total pace of doing business because of the tedious negotiations involved and the relatively large number of proposed transactions that do not materialize. Mandated by the 1988 Omnibus Trade Bill, the Department of Commerce established a Finance and Countertrade Division as part of the Finance and Trade Information Office. They monitor and study the extent and impact of countertrade in the world, as well as the participating companies. (See Appendix K for additional reading on countertrade.)

Endnotes

1. "Countertrade," *Euromoney* (then called *Trade Finance*), September 1987, Euromoney Publications PLC, London, U.K.

2. Pompiliu Verzariu, "Trade and Developments in International Countertrade," *Business America,* November 2, 1992, U.S. Department of Commerce, U.S. Government Printing Office, Washington, DC.

3. *Euromoney (Trade Finance)*, op. cit.

4. Louis J. Celi and I. James Czechowicz of Business International Corporation, *Export Financing—A Handbook of Sources and Techniques,* Financial Executives Research Foundation, Morristown, NJ, 1985.

7

Government Programs for Export Assistance

Caveat and Update

As this book is going to press late in the Fall of 1995, the final decisions of the 104th Congress relative to the extent of budget measures to shrink U.S. budget deficits and reduce the role of the federal government are being made. These decisions will have an impact on the government export support and assistance programs described in Part 7, many of which have also been referenced in a number of chapters leading up to Part 7. Although the fiscal 1996 budget proposed by Congress for the International Trade Administration's (ITA) activities indicates strong underlying congressional support for exporters, it now appears the attempt to eliminate the Department of Commerce could be successful. In that event, it is anticipated most of the ITA activities, will survive as the "International Trade Office" and could function, at least temporarily, within the U.S. Trade Representative's Office (USTR). Ultimately, a consolidation of some of the international support organizations is possible under a future umbrella organization, which might include Eximbank, OPIC and the Trade Development Agency. Already, the name of the U.S. Foreign and Commercial Service (US&FCS) is in the process of changing to "the Commercial Service," symbolic of the effor to unify the overseas offices and functions with those of the district offices and trade specialists.

The Agency for International Development (AID) will likely be returned to the Department of State with a reduced budget and in all probability diminished activities. The U.S. Export-Import Bank (Eximbank) will survive intact but with a $40 million budget cust for fiscal 1996. The Overseas Private Investment Corporation (OPIC) should remain in fairlty good shape. The small Trade Development Agency (TDA) will take by far the largest percentage budget cut at nearly 35 percent. The Small Business Administration (SBA) took a severe hit in terms of the percentage it could guarantee of a small business loan, that now being 80 percent for loans under $100,000, and 75 percent for loans over that amount. Its highly subsidized fees were increased as expected, to 8 percent up to $250,000, and graduated increased to 3 percent for loans over $500,000. However, apparently an exception will be made in the case of SBA's Export Working Capital Program, for which the guarantee fee for loans of one year will be raised to a total of only 3/4 of 1 percent. The lower guarantee will have a damaging impact on SBA's new Export Working Capital Loan program that had been harmonized with Eximbank's at a 90 percent guarantee and a 25 percent total fee for a loan with a one-year term.

It is logical that many of the structural changes can only take place over a two to three year period. On finding a program or function no longer exits under the name or agency described in the following pages, it will be up to the reader to find where it has been moved and what it is now called. Most of the programs that follow will be salvaged in some form, for we are convinced that common sense will prevail as this nation, like every developed nation, considers the economic benefits of its export trade and the important role exports can play in the development of a small business as well as the resulting potential contribution small business should make to total exports and therefore to the overall economy.

39

Small Business Administration

The Small Business Administration (SBA) offers a variety of domestic and international programs, nearly all of which can be used to support the exporter. Like so many governmental organizations, SBA is both cursed and praised, often by the same parties and frequently at the same time. Both views are probably often enough deserved, but it's impossible to deny that there are many firms in business today that wouldn't be there without the help of the SBA. Some were started with SBA funds, others depended on SBA for expansion, and still others looked to SBA for funding to save them in a crisis, whether created by nature, calamity, or poor judgment.

As of this writing, however, SBA appears to be targeted for some sharp cutbacks by the 104th Congress, which will undoubtedly modify its recently enlarged international programs as well as some of its basic programs and infrastructure. The programs, at least in the past, have had little or no cost-recovery built into them, making them very inexpensive, but therefore also very vulnerable to budget cuts. For all but the very largest states there will be only one SBA office per state, which undoubtedly spells substantial personnel cutbacks. Additionally, the SBA budget for subsidized guarantee programs is scheduled for a substantial reduction that will force an increase in loan guarantee fees, which have been well below realistic costs.

SBA's first objective is to provide business development and financial assistance to the "small business," which for its purposes is defined as an entity (individual, partnership or corporation, including all affiliates) that is independently owned and operated, has been in business for not less than one year, is not dominant in its field, and falls within the employment or sales limits estab-

lished by SBA. There are a number of such standards, but the following definitions indicate that there is room for many U.S. businesses in the SBA program:

- *Manufacturing.* The maximum number of employees is 500, exceptionally
  1000 for specified industries.

- *Wholesaling.* Not to exceed 100 employees.

- *Services.* Annual gross receipts not to exceed $3.5 million to $12.5 million,
  depending on the industry.

- *Retailing.* Annual sales or gross receipts not to exceed $3.5 million to $13.5
  million, depending on the industry.

Beside the internationally oriented programs, there are many SBA domestic
loan programs that can be useful to export business. A few of those most likely
to help the exporter will be summarized here, in addition to a more detailed
review of SBA's export financial, counseling, and information programs. If
either the domestic or international finance programs are of interest to you, it
would be worth your time to visit the nearest office and discuss the programs
and their application in more detail.

SBA was not established to support foreign trade activities but, with the realization of the potential for increased exports by small business, it was mandated
to serve small business exporters through its present array of ten regional
offices across the United States and 107 regional, district, or branch offices in
major cities to say nothing of supporting 900 Small Business Development
Centers (SBDCs). Even though the number of these offices may be sharply
reduced, SBA hopefully will still be able to take an active role in supporting
and initiating export programs for the truly new-to-export entrepreneur or firm
that Commerce's U.S. Foreign & Commercial Service (US&FCS) is no longer prepared to handle.

In addition to providing financial assistance, SBA sponsors a number of no-
charge export seminars, conferences, and publications through its Office of
International Trade. For nonfinancial export programs, especially, there seems
to have developed an unstated assumption and synergistic policy in quiet collaboration with DOC that SBA would focus on the very small or new-to-export
firms and individuals without too much concern as to export-readiness. The
assistance offered comes with considerable start-up and general business advice
and help. Also, SBA's excellent volunteer Service Corps of Retired Executives
(SCORE) has about 850 individuals with international experience, and they will
no doubt be called upon to play a larger role in view of the proposed cutbacks.
In contrast, the DOC's more export-sophisticated ITA and US&FCS organizations, which are often shorthanded, can thereby have more time to spend with
export-ready firms or at least with those having more export potential in the
short run, while referring the rest to SBA for start-up. This approach is facilitated by the fact that the Trade Information Center, administered by DOC, is an
interagency unit well acquainted with all the federal international trade support

agencies and hopefully can be the starting point for most general inquiries, some of which would be well served by being directed to the SBA. In addition, SBA has its own Small Business Answer Desk.

On the financial side, SBA, after many false starts at export financing and transaction-based loan guarantees, took a page from California's very successful and active export working-capital loan guarantee program. If properly administered, this program will be a great help to smaller exporters through the local SBA offices which can add to the hands-on help available by using SCORE volunteers. Even if experienced international help can only be found via the larger offices' international departments and staff, they will be more accessible than Eximbank with its Washington headquarters and four regional offices for the entire country. This will be particularly true if the 15 planned USEACs materialize and prove to be as export loan–oriented as the USEAC in Long Beach, California, which recently gained delegated authority by SBA. Here again, SBA has formed a partnership with Eximbank. The SBA working-capital guarantee is harmonized with Eximbank's comparable program and organized to handle the smaller range of the Eximbank working-capital guarantees. To further secure and extend this partnership, which was strongly encouraged by the National Export Strategy and the Trade Promotion Coordinating Committee, SBA executed a cooperative guarantee program with California. This gives SBA a chance to become accustomed to transaction-based finance and keep the two programs reasonably parallel, while serving as a guideline for future partnerships with other state finance programs. It is still a test program and, if not successful, look for the program to be reinstated at Eximbank or conceivably some other agency.

SBA Export Assistance and Outreach Programs

Although most noted for its loan programs, SBA offers the following meaningful help in terms of export services and counseling though its Office of International Trade.

Small Business Answer Desk

As seems to be the style these days, the SBA has an all-purpose 800 number to call as a starting point. The Small Business Answer Desk is designed to provide information on specific issues and to refer inquiries to the SBA department or program officer who can best assist you. The answer desk can be reached at 1-800-U-ASK-SBA (800/827-5722).

Export Counseling, Training, and USEAC

Individual counseling by international trade specialists is offered in key SBA offices in your area, and it is likely they could be more readily available than the nearest DOC District Office with US&FCS services. The one-on-one counseling is supplemented by the excellent conferences and seminars already mentioned. All U.S. Export Assistance Centers (USEAC) include SBA international trade specialists as part of their standard staffing, so you will be able to obtain good information from all the agencies including SBA if a center is near you. To find out, call 1-800-U-ASK-SBA or 1-800/USA-TRADE.

Breaking into the Trade Game

Breaking into the Trade Game, a 287-page small business guide to exporting and co-sponsored by AT&T, is free. It considers many facets for the new-to-export business from budgeting and planning to telephone and address contacts and publications. New and updated versions are published every other year or so and it is distributed through the SBA offices, seminars, and USEAC. A second publication is a pamphlet called "Bankable Deals," which provides an excellent brief explanation of trade finance.

Export Legal Assistance Network

The Export Legal Assistance Network (ELAN) is a nationwide group of attorneys with experience in international trade who provide free initial consultations to small businesses on export-related matters. It is an excellent means of determining just what your problem is and what to do about it. The staff at ELAN may be willing to review a proposed agreement and point out the pitfalls, but don't expect them to draw new agreements or take on your legal problem. ELAN's attorneys are available for initial contact and can be very helpful, but they cannot be considered a substitute for legal assistance and counsel.

SCORE/ACE Programs

Individual assistance and training is available through the dedicated Service Corps of Retired Executives (SCORE) whose membership includes more than 850 persons with international experience. They are prepared to give advice in all areas of management, including financial and technical areas, as well as helping to evaluate export potential. The Active Corps of Executives (ACE) is a volunteer organization of more than 2500 still-active executives that provide a similar service but within a more limited time availability. Many of these executives have also had international trade experience and are pleased to impart their knowledge.

SBDC/SBI Programs

Individual business counseling and assistance are offered through over 900 Small Business Development Centers (SBDCs), usually in cooperation with the particular state government and local area associations or other participants. To a greater or lesser degree, many of the SBDCs are capable of providing export business information and counseling. Some SBDCs, however, have been organized specifically to an export orientation, depending on local needs and demand. The SBDCs also regularly provide training seminars and SBDC-sponsored export events.

The Small Business Institute (SBI) programs are conducted jointly by SBA and selected colleges or universities. They operate at some 450 learning centers and utilize business students who provide counseling, surveys, and strategic feasibility studies under faculty supervision, again according the local demand and need. Some provide export counseling and research based on such needs and program strength within the school. Unfortunately, this is another SBA program that may come under siege by the Office of Management and Budget (OMB). The principal loss will be experienced by the students and interns who will miss the opportunity to learn international research from their work on real business projects. The SBA Answer Desk can help you locate both of these entities nearest you.

Office of Minority Small Business and Capital Ownership Development

Through this office's 7(j) Management and Technical Assistance Program, SBA contracts for the services of professional management and others, as appropriate, to provide management and technical assistance to 8(a) firms, which must be certified as *both* economically and socially disadvantaged, and other eligible participants in the areas of accounting, marketing, proposal preparation, and industry-specific issues. The assistance can also include counseling for export projects.

This activity was first discussed in Chapter 13 relative to SBA's responsibility for monitoring Small Business and Disadvantaged Enterprises (Gray Amendment) set-asides to secure appropriate bid and contracting opportunities on AID-financed international bid projects. The program is typical of what the 104th Congress seeks to eliminate. The office activities are all relative to the SBA 8(a) program, which is intended to assist disadvantaged firms gain special concessions in seeking contracts from any federal agency offering opportunities for contracts for goods and services.

The 8(a) program permits the SBA to contract with any federal agency, including AID, on a noncompetitive basis to provide goods and services. SBA, in turn, subcontracts with approved 8(a) businesses for the performance of the contract and ensures that the selected firm has the capability and, in fact, does perform the specified job or project requirements.

Financial assistance to 8(a) contractors is available in the form of counseling and professional guidance in management, as well as in the form of loans for advance payments and business development expenses. Assistance is also provided under some circumstances for performance bonding when necessary to meet the conditions of government contracts. Participation in the program is limited to five years, with no more than one extension. Firms must submit a business plan showing adequate business experience and demonstrate sufficient potential for completing the program before they are accepted. Details of this program should be obtained through discussion with your nearest SBA office. As previously noted, however, considering the political uncertainty regarding affirmative action the future of set-asides for minority or disadvantaged businesses is in question.

SBA Loan Guarantee Programs

Export Working Capital Program, Section 7(a)14

SBA recognizes the critical need of small businesses for export working capital if they are to continue to generate their increase in exports as a percent of their total sales. The Export Working Capital Program (EWCP) replaces its little-used predecessor, the Export Revolving Line of Credit (ERLC). The new version not only borrows from the very successful California Export Finance Program (CEFP), but is also harmonized with the Eximbank Working Capital Program, which must be used for loans exceeding $833,333, which is SBA's program limit. It is intended to be transaction-based and therefore requires less emphasis on the value of current net worth and profits so long as both the exporter's ability to duly perform the transaction and a solid source of payment or a creditworthy by the buyer are assured. Note the collateral requirements in item 3 below, whereby SBA demands no more than 100 percent collateral and includes the assignment of proceeds as collateral from the sale or contract, completely changing the standard equity–based lending analysis procedure. The catch is to work with a lending officer who accepts this approach. But even with the most dedicated transaction-based lender, the paramount factor becomes the officer's complete comfort and conviction that the buyer can and will pay and that the exporter or contractor can and will perform.

Because the loan officers in SBA have historically concentrated on longer-term working-capital loans and fixed asset loans, it is not easy for them to adjust to the concept of trade finance and transaction-based collateral. We can therefore expect a fairly extended learning curve, even assuming continued strong support from the SBA administration, which is not yet assured. Adding to the transition problems, the EWCP is supposed to be processed faster than a conventional SBA loan guarantee. The key provisions are as follows:

1. The SBA will guarantee 90 percent of the loan amount.

2. The use of the proceeds may be for preexport purposes such as acquiring inventory, goods, or services and/or paying manufacturing costs for export transactions. It is important to note that, contrary to Eximbank's mandated policy, SBA export working-capital loan proceeds *may* support exports of less than 50 percent U.S. origin. The proceeds may also be used for postexport accounts receivable financing. In a complete reversal of past SBA policies, the loan may be used to support standby letters of credit serving as bid bonds, performance bonds, or payment guarantees as required to complete the export transaction according to the contract conditions offered by the foreign buyer.

3. The collateral must cover 100 percent of the loan disbursement, which should include a first-priority interest in the export inventory and receivables and an assignment of the contract and/or letter of credit proceeds. In the case of the foreign receivables, foreign credit insurance from Eximbank or equivalent may be required. In addition, personal guarantees will generally be required from principals with a 20 percent or more ownership in a closely held company.

4. The loan may support a single, identified export transaction or multiple transactions on a revolving loan basis.

5. The repayment term on identified transaction loans must not exceed one year. In the case of revolving loans the term may be up to three years. This is not recommended, however, because it dramatically increases the guarantee fee from 0.25 of one percent for one year loans to 2 percent for terms over one year. In either case, revolving loans will normally be renewed, barring an adverse change in the exporter's financial condition.

6. A bonus feature of the EWCP is that the exporter may apply directly to SBA and obtain a preliminary commitment valid for 60 days. This makes it easier to shop for a lender and for the lender to give a positive and fast answer because the exporter has the SBA commitment in hand.

7. There is an application fee of $100, plus the 0.25 of 1 percent guarantee fee for loan terms of one year or less (or 2 percent for loan terms longer than one year). This low-guarantee fee represents a subsidized or concessional fee and is considerably below the Eximbank fee on comparable programs, or most state programs. The EWCP is also unique for SBA because it has no ceilings on the lender's interest rate or initiation fees, leaving this to negotiation between lender and borrower. This provision has the advantage of making it easier to find a bank willing to accept the guarantee, but it obviously tends to increase the borrowing cost.

International Trade Loan Program

The International Trade Loan provides long-term financing to help small businesses compete more effectively and to expand or develop export markets. If the purpose of the loan can be shown to be for the acquisition or modernization of facilities for the production of goods or services for exports, the SBA's 7(a)16 program applies, with a maximum term of 25 years for the facilities and equipment portion of the loan. The Omnibus Trade Bill increased the maximum loan limit for this particular loan to $1 million, but the firm must prove the loan will help it expand exports, or that it is being adversely affected by imports. An additional $250,000 of eligibility under 7(a)16 program may be for working capital, in contrast to facilities. Thus, the international trade aspect of this program represents a meaningful bonus because, while SBA limits its total exposure from any one borrower on any of its guarantee programs to $750,000, the limit in this case may be $1.25 million if the International Trade Loan is combined with a regular working capital loan or the EWCP.

Regular Business Loan Program, Section 7(a)

The 7(a) guarantee is the foundation of the SBA financial program and covers a wide variety of specialized loans, including the international trade loan guarantees already mentioned. The 7(a) guarantee is available for medium- and long-term loans for working capital, general or export, or for acquisition of fixed assets. The SBA can guarantee up to 90 percent of the loan up to $155,000 and 85 percent of larger loans. Loan guarantees for fixed asset acquisitions have a maximum maturity of 25 years, and general purpose working capital loans have a maximum maturity of seven years.

For revolving credit needs, the 7(a) program has been given authority designated as *Greenline revolving credit,* which permits SBA to structure working-capital loans for one to five years (but more frequently on one-year-renewable terms) for which the level of funds advanced fluctuates according to the financing based on the current level of the inventory or accounts receivable used as collateral for the loan. The inventory build-up may be for an export project contract, for example.

Low-Documentation Loan Program

The SBA's low-documentation loan program (LowDoc) is a relatively new program that has become one of SBA's most popular. It is especially suited to young or growing small companies, including EMCs/ETCs, desiring to export and needing loans up to $100,000. It also is essentially a part of the 7(a) program, with similar borrower eligibility features and a similar guarantee, but with less emphasis on collateral and greater emphasis on character, management experience, and credit history. As implied, it also features minimum documentation for speedy approval.

Surety Bond Guarantee Program

SBA can guarantee contractor bonds for contracts up to $1.25 million. The application in the export context is that many overseas contracts involving advance payments or performance risks to the buyer require a performance bond secured by a standby letter of credit or a surety company. Often the buyer won't accept the bond of a surety company for reasons explained in Chapter 22, but there are many exceptions. There may be advantages to obtaining a surety bond, and it is possible to look to SBA for help through a surety bond guarantee, if that is the case. The SBA fee for the guarantee is $6 per $1000 of total contract value (plus the surety company's charge, of course). A standby letter of credit can be supported under the EWCP should that prove to be the better approach, but the surety bond guarantee program provides this alternative option.

The 504 Loan Program

Suppose your export activities create a need for an expansion of fixed assets requiring a long-term loan well in excess of the applicable SBA loan guarantee limit, and SBA can only guarantee $1 million in this case. To make up the rest, you might consider contacting a nearby SBA-designated Certified Development Company (CDC). The CDC itself may be sponsored by private interests, or by state or local governments. They handle the paperwork and SBA loan packaging. A 10 percent equity is required of the borrower. Typically, a private lender funds 50 percent of the loan and receives a first lien on the equivalent of at least 100 percent of the loan value. The CDC funds 40 percent of the loan, which is 100 percent guaranteed by SBA, permitting it to sell 40 percent of the loan, to the secondary market.

Small Business Investment Company Financing

Small business investment companies (SBICs) are limited partnerships or corporations that are approved, licensed, and regulated by SBA. They may provide financing in the form of equity investment, including investments in export trading companies. Less commonly, they provide financing as direct loans subject to certain SBA regulations or as convertible debentures or loans with warrants permitting future exercise of options to purchase at a fixed price up to prespecified amounts of the borrower's common stock. Such arrangements may exceed the SBA's $750,000 statutory guarantee limit on loan guarantees. SBICs can invest in export trading or management companies in which banks have equity participation, as long as the other SBIC requirements are met. Provided the company is a domestic company, with at least half its operations and assets in the U.S., portions of the funds may be used in overseas branch or subsidiary operations unlike SBA financing. A SBIC may invest up to 20 percent of its private capital in a single business, or several SBICs may participate to increase the maximum SBIC investment. This is another program that may be forced to change or further privatize as to the relationship between the SBIC and SBA in view of the political climate.

40

The Export-Import Bank of the United States

The Export-Import bank is known as Eximbank throughout the world and is the primary U.S. agency charged with providing support for American exports through credit risk protection and lending programs. Eximbank has nothing to do with imports, in spite of its name, but it plays a key role in determining the competitiveness of the United States among its major trading partners, because its buyer credit programs are often a major component of our overseas customers' ability to finance, and therefore to buy, American products. Eximbank's willingness and ability to insure foreign private or sovereign buyers in any corner of the world often determines whether you, the U.S. supplier, can offer competitive or acceptable terms to the foreign buyer.

Eximbank joins in co-financing large projects with other U.S. government financial agencies, the World Bank, the regional multilateral development banks (MDBs), and private sector financial institutions. Together with like agencies in other developed countries, Eximbank's lending guarantee and insuring policies conform with certain parameters jointly agreed on by an organization of 22 developed nations called the Organization for Economic Cooperation and Development (OECD). Some of OECD's principal functions are to establish lending rates, repayment terms, and other conditions, including the use of tied aid (concessionary financing terms to developing countries tied to the purchase of goods and services from that country) in conjunction with such credits to finance purchases and projects by less-developed nations. The purpose is to prevent developed nations from engaging in unfair and unrestricted competition with each other. They are not always successful in achieving this end.

Eximbank states that its responsibilities are to: assume most of the risks inherent in financing the production and sale of exports when the private sector is unwilling to assume such risks; provide financing to foreign buyers of U.S. goods and services when such financing is not available from the private sector; and help U.S. exporters meet officially supported and/or subsidized foreign credit competition. These roles fit into four functional categories:

1. Export credit insurance
2. Foreign loan guarantees
3. Supplier credit working-capital guarantees
4. Direct loans to foreign buyers

Eximbank, along with the other federal support programs for export finance and promotion, can be looked on as a competitive weapon provided by the United States to help match your export marketing advantages with those extended by foreign governments on behalf of their exporters and your foreign competition.

In 1986–1987 Eximbank engaged in a major restructuring to make its programs more accessible to small businesses, easier to use, and more competitive with the export credit agencies of other countries. This effort was only partly successful, and so the restructuring continued, until finally it claims to have "reinvented" itself in 1994, with its "final" reforms to be completed in 1995. Currently, overall support through guarantees, loan, or insurance by region is as follows: Latin America, $5.2 billion; Asia, $4.6 billion (of which the Peoples Republic of China was the biggest recipient in 1994); Europe and Canada, $2.7 billion; Africa and the Middle East, $340 million.

Before we describe Eximbank's various programs, it should be pointed out that Eximbank has a wealth of information on foreign buyers as a result of its insurance, guarantee, and lending activities. Whatever it has been given in confidence it will not divulge, along with certain other credit specific or country specific information, but general information about the repayment habits of buyers insured or financed by Eximbank is available. Call or fax Credit Services at Eximbank for further information.

Eximbank's Washington headquarters are at 811 Vermont Avenue NW, Washington D.C. 20571, and its toll-free hotline number for general information and specific contacts is 800/565-EXIM (1-800/565-3946); fax 202/565-3380. There are five regional offices—in New York, Miami, Chicago, Houston, and Los Angeles. (For their addresses, see Appendix D.)

Foreign Credit Insurance

Eximbank's credit insurance programs are by far the most active and widely used portion of Eximbank's programs in terms of transactions. They account for the second-largest portion of its support to exporters in authorized dollar activity ($4.2 billion, out of a record-high total activity of $14.6 billion in 1994). Insurance is also the principal area in which small businesses use Eximbank. A few years ago there were very limited alternatives for the smaller business to obtain foreign credit insurance except through Eximbank. Today, private sector insurance alternatives, at least in the case of the friendlier and more stable countries, are at last becoming more available, as well as more practical from an expense standpoint. For these alternatives and the functional aspects of using Eximbank insurance, see Chapter 25.

Eximbank insurance is now both sold and underwritten by Eximbank itself, but until 1993 a quasi-governmental insurance organization, the Foreign Credit Insurance Association (FCIA), marketed and underwrote the Eximbank insurance program. Even though Eximbank bore most of the risk, it shared that risk to some degree with the private sector. Many people still associate FCIA with Eximbank, but the FCIA organization is now entirely privatized and functions as the administrator and underwriter for a private foreign credit insurance group. Its majority owner is Great American Insurance, and it is primarily focused on large exporting businesses.

You can learn more about Eximbank's credit insurance programs directly through one of Eximbank's five regional offices or through an insurance agent active in the marine and international trade area. If you cannot find a specialized broker familiar and qualified to handle Eximbank and alternative foreign credit insurance plans, it may be better for you to work with a regional Eximbank office in any case, because foreign credit insurance is highly specialized. The cost of Eximbank insurance is the same either way. Eximbank must determine that you are creditworthy before it will issue a policy. While the general requirements for acceptance of your firm are modest, your export experience, customer list, and target countries, transaction size, past credit losses, and proposed annual insurable volume will all have something to do with your eligibility as well as with the type of policy you select.

General Eximbank Precepts

There are four Eximbank principles that hold true in all its programs, insurance policies, guarantees, and loans (with minor exceptions as noted). These principles are as follows:

1. The goods and services must be exported from the United States and the U.S. content must be at least 50 percent.

2. Eximbank does not support sales of military goods or service except for drug interdiction or humanitarian purposes and some items which could be put to dual use (civilian or military).

3. There must be a reasonable assurance of payment.

4. Eximbank's intention is not to compete with the private sector.

In addition, there are definitions relative to maturity terms and risk descriptions that are, in part, unique to Eximbank, but which are also consistent throughout all its programs:

- *Short-term.* Usually means credit terms of 180 days or less, or, in the case of agriculture and occasional other exceptions, terms of 360 days.

- *Medium-term.* Usually means repayment or insurance terms of one to five years (or, occasionally, seven years) for capital goods and related services, offered when the financing, guarantee, or insurance value is for less than $10 million.

- *Long-term.* Usually means repayment terms of more than five years, offered when the guaranteed or financed value is greater than $10 million.

- *Commercial risk.* A buyer's inability to pay, due to financial difficulty or bankruptcy, when an obligation is due.

- *Political risk.* Adverse events beyond the control of the buyer usually caused by government action or failure. Such events may include: (1) political violence; (2) government expropriation; (3) cancellation of export or import licenses; and (4) transfer or inconvertibility (exchange risk), i.e., inability to purchase U.S. dollars in a legal market or refusal of the central bank to release funds going out of the country.

Short-Term Multibuyer Policy

The Short-Term Multibuyer Master Policy is the heart of the Eximbank insurance program, and is the most used of all Eximbank facilities. This policy is the basic policy against which all other short-term insurance policies will be compared for our purposes here. It is designed to cover most of the risks in extending credit to overseas buyers for terms of 180 days or less and serves to insure credit for the general range of goods and services except where high value capital goods are concerned. In the case of most agricultural goods and certain consumer durable goods, the term can be extended to 360 days with a special endorsement. This policy is renewable annually to cover all short-term credit sales, or at least all credit sales within a given world region, with an option as to reporting and covering unconfirmed letter of credit sales. It is intended for established businesses with reasonable skills in export and extending and evaluating foreign credit.

Policy Highlights

- *Coverage.* One of two options can be selected:
  1. 100 percent of the political risk—no first-loss deductible/90 percent of the commercial risk (sovereign buyers 100 percent)—after annual first-loss deductible

2. 95 percent political risk/95 percent commercial risk—after annual first-loss deductible—(sovereign buyers 100 percent) (98 percent coverage in either option available for bulk agricultural sales)

- The interest is covered to a maximum of prime rate minus 0.5 percent.

- The maximum terms are 180 days (360 days for agricultural commodities, consumer durables, capital equipment).

- The minimum annual premium is $500.

- The monthly premium billed is based on a single flat rate applied against all shipments in a given month. The rate is determined for each policyholder on the basis of the exporter's sales profile, loss history, spread of country risk, and the mix of credit payment terms extended. This rate is adjusted annually as the profile shifts.

- Discretionary credit limits (DCL), available for experienced exporters, will permit insurance on most sales without prior approval.

- Political risk coverage alone is available at a reduced premium.

Annual first-loss deductible refers to a sum stated in the policy representing losses to be accepted with insurance cover in a policy year before coverage applies. Subsequent losses are reimbursed to whatever the stated percentage of cover happens to be. *First-loss deductible* is an arbitrary amount set for each policyholder based on credit volume and past credit loss experience, typically in the general range of .5 percent to 1 percent of insured credit sales volume, the idea being, that the objective of the insurance is to protect against unforeseen and unusual losses, not to replace the losses one should budget for as a part of the routine cost of doing business.

Discretionary credit limit (DCL) refers to the amount of the total outstanding balance for any one buyer that the policyholder may consider to be insured, provided that certain minimum acceptable credit information has been accessed and filed. If the buyer account exceeds the DCL, to maintain full coverage it is necessary to first obtain Eximbank's approval in the form of a special buyer credit limit (SBCL). The appropriate credit information normally required by Eximbank for a sound credit decision must be in the exporter's possession at the time of shipment for the insurance to be valid. The size of the discretionary credit limit will depend on a number of factors, including experience, number and size of foreign accounts, average transaction size, countries being exported to, and the length and quality of the exporter's past credit extension history. Eximbank has become more like private credit insurers in preferring to grant insured discretion to cover up to 90 percent of an insured firm's transactions, depending on experience and history.

Your choice of coverage depends on two factors. If most of your sales will be to politically stable countries, such as those in Western Europe, consider taking the 95/95 option to increase your coverage under commercial risks to 95 percent. If you will be selling to weaker countries with foreign exchange problems, choose 100/90 coverage. One advantage of the 95/95 option is that it eliminates arguments and delays with Eximbank over whether the loss was commercial or political, which can be debatable. Even though commercial risk coverage is not available when you are shipping to an affiliate or subsidiary, remember you can still have coverage for political risk alone. Where foreign credit insurance is at issue, be keenly aware of just how real is the added political risk factor relative to your domestic account risks. For example, all your accounts in a given foreign country could be frozen because of a currency collapse or various other government actions. The political risk factor is one of the chief reasons why foreign credit insurance is so much more common than domestic credit insurance; political risk is also a major component of the cost of foreign credit insurance, especially in all but the most stable countries. The sudden and unexpected impact of the risk must never be underestimated. For some exporters, buying only political risk insurance may be a viable possibility from both a cost and a safety standpoint.

As with all Eximbank account-receivable policies, there are certain rules regarding the possession of current credit information that you must either follow before you can exercise your DCL authority or that you must provide to Eximbank in order to apply for an SBCL. An SBCL is necessary if the sale, or the highest outstanding value of the receivable, exceeds your discretionary authority, or if the buyer is in a country in which Eximbank currently has restrictions on discretionary coverage. Discretionary authority allows qualification of buyers based on either (1) your own ledger history on the customer, or (2) having two current and favorable summary type credit reports on the foreign buyer prior to shipment. More detailed information, including financial statements, is often needed on larger sales. Typical credit reports might be a *World Trade Directory Report* (*WTDR*) from the DOC, a Dun & Bradstreet International or similar agency credit report, and a bank report. Your firm's ledger experience with the account is always a very important and desirable qualifier. There is an uplift provision that permits you to increase a buyer's high limit by 25 percent increments of the current high credit if you have experienced prompt payment (considered to be within 60 days of due date). Some countries may be ineligible for Eximbank coverage. For others in marginal situations an SBCL application may be required to qualify any buyer at all in the questionable country.

Eximbank's credit policies can sometimes seem demanding, and an inexperienced exporter may feel that Eximbank is unreasonable regarding the information it requires, especially considering that it is more difficult to obtain reliable credit reports from overseas, and that it is also more difficult to obtain good trade references unless the buyer happens to be dealing with a number of U.S. firms. Often what is being asked is no more than what a good, hard-nosed credit manager in charge of the domestic business for the same firm might demand. Since 1994 Eximbank has tried to reorganize its budget so that more funding is set aside for risk taking and supporting small business. Part of this is done at the expense of reducing the subsidization of interest rates for foreign buyer credit extensions. This has led to higher discretionary credit limits and to faster and more lenient acceptance at higher credit limits of buyers where SBCLs are still necessary.

In addition to obtaining the credit information on your buyer and requesting and receiving the SBCL if the required high credit makes that necessary, you must provide Eximbank with a monthly report of all sales in those categories you and Eximbank have agreed will constitute a spread of risk for the purposes of your policy contract. Your report is the basis for Eximbank's monthly billing. In addition, Eximbank requests a monthly report on items 90 days past due. Otherwise, the only paperwork involved is the normal forms you would expect in the event of a claim.

The terms *whole turnover* and *spread of risk* refer to the concept that you must give an insurer all, or most, of your exposure to protect it from insuring only the riskiest accounts. To do otherwise, it is argued, makes it difficult or impossible for the insurer to calculate the risks, and therefore, your insurance rate. At one time Eximbank would only permit omitting the sales made under letters of credit in the monthly report. Today, however, the issue is somewhat negotiable and sales reports from certain countries in which you are already well established may be omitted with Eximbank's permission. In any event, however, Eximbank will want to be assured of obtaining a reasonable spread of risk.

The cost of this short-term coverage currently runs from approximately $.35 to $1 per $100, depending on the type of selling terms (e.g., open account, documents against payment or acceptance and letters of credit). For multibuyer policies, a composite rate is calculated based on terms of sale, country risk, past bad debt and payment experience, and whether the export buyers are in the private sector or the public sector. The established rates then apply to all sales for the policy year. The premium is paid monthly based on the dollar value of that month's shipments times the rate per $100. The minimum annual premium for Eximbank's Short-Term, Multibuyer Policy is $500.

For most exporters, Eximbank used to be the only option, because in the alternative, private insurance market, the nonrefundable advance premium typically ran from $20,000 to $35,000 for similar coverage if your policy was intended to cover commercial risk, as opposed to political risk coverage only. With some insurers, this continues to be the case because they only want to write large-volume and large-transaction business with highly qualified credit departments of large firms. But there are some excellent private sector policies competing for Eximbank's business, depending on the circumstances and the countries involved. (Refer to Chapter 25 for more information on managing export risks.)

There is always the option of not insuring at all, or of considering alternative policies from Eximbank. When considering these policies, consider the cost of the first-loss deductible, which for some companies with many accounts and small individual sales may even exceed what could be expected for total losses with prudent credit management and a limited concentration of risk. The latter cost factor becomes especially severe when added to the cost of maintaining current credit information, if there are a number of accounts. Extending the validity of SBCLs to two years, assuming there is satisfactory ledger experience, is a substantial help. In any event, most of the credit information called for should be obtained. Be sure you discuss and understand exactly what Eximbank requires and what constitutes current information, depending on how active your ledger experience is. It is important that Eximbank insurance coverage be structured to meet the needs and goals of the individual exporter. The time and effort you invest in the determination of these as well as in the application process are often rewarded with substantial future administrative savings. You, as the exporter, and Eximbank both benefit when coverage for most foreign buyers can be based on the discretionary authority delegated to you by Eximbank. This authority is extended on the basis of demonstrated prudent credit management.

The Small Business Policy

The Small Business Policy (formerly the New-to-Export Policy) is intended for the company or exporter with little or no history in export but adequate office staff and skills to manage and track the policy stipulations and clerical procedures. It is limited to firms with average annual export credit sales of less than $3 million (excluding sales under confirmed letters of credit or cash in advance). It is designed to ease entry into exporting by providing more complete protection in the form of 95 percent coverage on commercial losses, while still offering 100 percent coverage on political losses. It has the very substantial cost advantage of having a no-annual-deductible feature, which definitely lowers the effective rate of your insurance, assuming that you do have some losses.

Policy Highlights

- 100 percent political risks protection.

- 95 percent commercial risks protection (bulk agricultural 98 percent).

- The interest is covered to a maximum of prime rate minus 0.5 percent.

- Short-term coverage is for up to 180 days (360 days for bulk agricultural commodities, consumer durable goods, and capital equipment).

- The minimum annual premium is $500.

- A standard rate schedule applies to all small business policies. The premium charged for individual sales depends on the length of the trade terms involved and whether payment is by a private buyer, letter of credit, or from the public sector. The country of the buyer (country risk) does not affect rates in the case of either small business policy.

- There is no annual first-loss deductible.

- The policy proceeds are assignable to the lender, with a "hold harmless" assignment clause to the benefit of the lender.

If bank financing of receivables is important to you, undoubtedly the most advantageous feature of this policy is the hold harmless assignment agreement that Eximbank provides to the exporter's lender with any of the small business policies. This agreement protects the lender against loss, provided the documentation furnished by the exporter at the time of financing indicates that the transaction(s) is (are) insured, regardless of any subsequent failures or misrepresentations of the exporter. Of course, Eximbank retains recourse against the exporter if the loss is a result of exporter nonperformance. This agreement provides substantial comfort to the lender and increases the exporter's chances of financing the insured receivables.

Remarkably, the "new" Eximbank not only permits exporters to stay with one of the small business policies indefinitely—as long as they meet the Small Business Administration's eligibility requirement and have annual export sales volume, excluding confirmed letters of credit, of under $3 million (which is not *that* small)—it also provides discretionary credit limits (DCLs) to a limited degree. Here too, Eximbank has reduced the time and expense of renewing credit reports and investigation on the SBCL accounts up to $50,000 by extending validity from one year to two years. The need to obtain new annual credit reports on a number of accounts can quickly become a major expense at about $150 for the average report, to say nothing of clerical time. All in all, it is a very attractive policy, but when export credit sales exceed $3 million, the exporter must graduate to the standard Short-Term Multibuyer Master Policy, unless it is one of the special environmental policies.

Umbrella Policy

The Umbrella Policy is also intended for small, new, or infrequent exporters, and provides special support for exporters who need or want help in properly administering their policy. It must be obtained through an *administrator,* who can be any party qualified by Eximbank, such as a bank, an export trading company, a state agency, or an insurance broker. So far this role has been occupied primarily by specialized insurance brokers or state agencies. States or related public sector bodies holding umbrella policies as of early 1995 include Arkansas, California, Indiana, Maine, Maryland, Massachusetts, New Jersey, New York Xport Port Authority, Oklahoma, Virginia, and Washington, D.C. (The City/State Eximbank program is discussed in Chapter 44, and all relevant addresses are noted in Appendix E.) It might be a good idea to contact the Eximbank City/State coordinator for the most current status of your state relative to Eximbank in general and especially in regard to the umbrella Policy.

The eligibility requirements as well as benefits for this policy are similar to those of the Small Business Policy. The policy is for a small business as defined by SBA criteria. The firm's annual export credit sales must be less than $3 million, and the firm must be acceptable to Eximbank. Coverage and benefits are identical to those under the Small Business Policy, including the hold harmless agreement for assignment and financing; and there is no annual first-loss deductible. Infrequent exporters are those best able to use this policy to advantage, because of its higher cost, and also because of the extra time and expense involved in getting a special buyer credit limit (SBCL) approval from Eximbank on each and every proposed buyer.

Policy Highlights

The same as the Small Business Policy but distinguished by the following key differences:

- There is no minimum annual premium.

- The policy administrator relieves the exporter of administrative responsibilities by providing all the required reporting to/from Eximbank, including premium payments.

- There is no discretionary credit; Eximbank must provide SBCL for all buyers.

- The administrator's add-on fee for services is added on top of the same short-term rate structure per $100 of export sale, as in the Small Business Policy.

The base premium charged by Eximbank for the Umbrella Policy is identical to that for the Small Business Policy, but the final cost to the exporter is substantially higher because of the administrator's costs. The administrator in this case must pay the $500 minimum annual premium for the master policy, and, in addition, must be compensated for preparing reports, conducting the credit investigation, reviewing the documents sent to the lender for funding, accounting for the exporter's premium remittance, and carrying out the follow-up on the exporter's performance under the policy. The administrator must also commonly carry its own insurance protection against administrator errors and omissions. The total cost varies from administrator to administrator, but normally adds $.20 to $.30 per $100 to the insurance premium rate.

Thus, although it substantially increases the effective rate, some broker/administrators state that much of the added cost is offset by what can be saved on credit reporting fees by utilizing contracts the administrator may have with foreign credit reporting agencies plus savings in management time. This is very possibly true. The exporter must apply for an Umbrella Policy, just as for all other policies, and both the administrator and Eximbank must agree to accept the exporter under the Umbrella Policy before insurance is available. Eximbank's exporter acceptance criteria for this application is somewhat more lenient because of the administrator's role, but it still usually includes the stipulation that the exporter have a positive net worth. The exporter should carefully consider the prospective administrator who essentially takes responsibility for the paperwork and supervision of the policy. Coverage could conceivably be invalidated on a given transaction or receivable due to negligence on the part of the administrator, even though that might be recovered by the errors and omission insurance policy the administrator presumably has.

Small Business Environmental Policy

This policy is designed to encourage the export of products and services to control pollution or protect against toxic substances. It is identical to the regular Small Business Policy except for two factors:

- The policy can only be used by a small business for the export of environmental goods and services.

- As long as the exporter can qualify for the policy, it can be retained regardless of export credit sales volume, even though that be in excess of $3 million.

Short-Term Single-Buyer Policy

The Short-Term Single-Buyer Policy makes it possible to insure a relatively large single-credit sale on an individual basis or a series of sales to a single buyer over the course of one year, even though the exporter might not routinely insure overseas credit or is carrying political coverage only.

Policy Highlights

- There is equal coverage for political and commercial risks, based on buyer category.
  1. Sovereign buyers, 100 percent
  2. Private sector and nonsovereign public sector, 90 percent
  3. Letter of credit transactions, 95 percent
  4. Bulk agricultural sales, 98 percent

- The interest is covered to a maximum of prime rate minus 0.5 percent.

- The maximum term is 180 days (360 days for bulk agricultural goods, consumer durable goods, and capital goods).

- Political-risk-only coverage is available at a lower cost.

- Policy proceeds are assignable for financing purposes.

- There are significant minimum premiums, but with a major break for small businesses:

	Small Businesses	All Others
Sovereign buyers	$1000	$ 2,500
L/Cs, nonsovereign public buyer	$1000	$ 5,000
Private sector buyers	$1000	$10,000

Minimum premiums aside, for each single buyer the policy rate per $100 is individually determined according to risk, based on the terms of sale, country risk, and whether a public buyer, private buyer, or bank-guaranteed buyer is involved. There is no deductible and, of course, no spread of risk or whole turnover consideration. However, since Eximbank has returned to individually rating countries as to political risk, lower premiums in the stable countries are being offset by higher rates in the high-risk countries. This underwriting approach permits coverage in some countries that could not previously be insured.

Choosing the Right Short-Term Policy

The choice between the Short-Term Multibuyer Policy, the Umbrella Policy, the Small Business Policy, and possibly even the Single-Buyer Policy is a question of strategy that depends on your perception of the exposures and your export plans. As between the two small business policies, Eximbank enhancements to both policies have eliminated several differences that once existed as a result of its differing levels of maximum export sales permitted. The former restrictions on switching policies have also been eliminated. The considerations involved in choosing the right policy are best illustrated by using four prototype companies, all having export credit sales of less than $3 million and all therefore eligible for the small business policies: They are:

Company ONE.   A very small, new-to-export business. ONE takes a passive approach to export opportunities.

Company TWO X.   A small business lacking export experience. TWO X has decided to pursue an aggressive export strategy, but its office staff is limited in numbers, time, and experience.

Company TWO Z.   A business just like TWO X, but TWO Z has an experienced office manager and clerical staff.

Company THREE.   A small to midsize business. THREE wishes to expand its exports and one of its strategies is to offer more competitive selling terms.

ONE should probably obtain an Umbrella Policy if there is an Umbrella administrator in the area that can service its business. The cost per shipment will be greater because of the higher rate, but possibly ONE will not export enough to incur charges over the $500 minimum premium, so the Umbrella will be a saving. In addition, it avoids burdening a small staff with administration and reports. Obtaining an SBCL for the export customers may delay the initial shipment to new customers somewhat and it will also be a nuisance, but ONE does not expect a large number export accounts. Also, the administrator can save ONE money on the cost of obtaining credit reports because the administrator may have bulk-use contracts with foreign credit agencies.

TWO X has more to consider because it is going to actively seek export sales and wants to do so in the safest and most profitable fashion. It has a limited staff, however, with no experience in export credit, so the Umbrella would be one less worry in getting the export process started, and the company could change over to the Small Business Policy later. On the other hand, it could save some money with the cheaper rate and, optimistically, it expects to exceed the $500 minimum premium in any case. The coverage is the same, as is the absence of a loss deductible, which provides TWO X comfort in the case of both policies. Since the firm anticipates finding a number of new export customers during the year, having even a little discretionary authority to cover new accounts while making relatively small, trial shipments, the Small Business policy seems tempting when compared to the Umbrella, which has no discretionary policy. The issue should probably be decided on the availability of the Umbrella, a realistic estimate as to volume of export credit sales, and a decision as to who, if anyone other than the boss, could be found to properly administer the policy.

TWO Z has a good enough staff to take care of things without jeopardizing the policy's coverage or neglecting other duties, so the decision can more readily be reduced to one of time and insurance expense. Like TWO X, there is real appeal to TWO Z in its ability to finance the working capital required to finance the new export accounts with an assignment of the receivables and the hold harmless clause which provides the lender a lot of extra protection. In fact, if TWO Z already had some export volume and its management had some previous export experience, combined with optimism for potential sales because of its product's export appeal, TWO Z might even be tempted to consider the Multibuyer Policy, provided that it had a good balance sheet and a corporate history that would make the firm acceptable to Eximbank for the policy at a competitive rate. However, since its exports previously have been too minimal to give its staff a real feel for what the norm would be on export credit write-offs, conservatism makes TWO Z decide to go with the Small Business Policy, for the first year anyway.

THREE has experience and a qualified staff and wants to maximize its profits with the lowest possible insurance costs. It has previously done well enough with its exports that Eximbank can offer it an advantageous initial rate, with a chance to bring it even lower in future years if its experience continues to be good. Also, since THREE intends to expand exports through competitive terms, it wants to be able to respond as fast as possible to initial orders and does not fear writing off a fraction of 1 percent of its export accounts due to bad debts before the insurance coverage begins. This, after all, is similar to its domestic credit experience and its past limited export sales experience, which its profit margins readily cover. THREE wants insurance to avoid the unpredictable disaster not predictable and ordinary credit extension costs.

Furthermore, while the hold harmless clause feature of the Small Business loan is nice, it is not so critical to THREE, because it has a substantial book of domestic accounts that are not being fully used for working capital loans. It can use those domestic accounts or inventory instead of the new export accounts themselves to finance the increased receivables. THREE's bank adds the assurance that it will consider accepting some of THREE's best overseas accounts for collateral after the company has acquired a ledger experience with the new customers. THREE will probably decide on the Multibuyer Policy unless it decides to acquire one more year's export experience under the Small Business Policy while acquiring or improving its track record for export credit to achieve the best possible premium rate Eximbank has to offer on a Multibuyer Policy next year. This delay will also give THREE a chance to be sure the cost analysis of the lower insurance premium costs plus first-loss deductible expense adds up to less premium on average than the higher cost of the Small Business Policy with no first-loss deductible.

In contrast, if THREE were willing to *go without* insurance because it had successfully developed enough small overseas accounts over the years so that no probable combination of single-account losses would pose a financial problem, it might want to continue to go without credit insurance and only insure the exceptionally large transactions or a single big and steady buyer regularly running an open account of significant size, perhaps in a less-than-stable country. In this scenario, the right decision would probably be Single-Buyer insurance policies on a case-by-case basis. Alternatively, even though THREE may have been very comfortable with its well-established European business, it now wants to expand to Asia, where it lacks experience. There's a good chance THREE could arrange with Eximbank to insure all of THREE's Asian business without insuring its European business. This is probably a good compromise between safety and cost.

Medium-Term Single-Buyer Policy

Medium-term refers to contracts or receivables in excess of 180 days up to a term of five years (exceptionally seven years) in amounts under $10 million. This new and improved version of Eximbank's medium-term policy can be accessed directly by the exporter or by the exporter's financial institution and is applicable to exports of capital equipment and project-related services. The policy can cover single or repetitive sales to a single buyer, but the policy must define such details and be issued in the appropriate usage format.

Policy Highlights

- A 15 percent cash payment is required of the buyer.
- The remaining 85 percent due is treated as a 100 percent insured loan, with cover available for both political and commercial risks.
- The premium is assessed on the basis of commercial and political risks.
- There is no first-loss deductible.
- Political-risk-only coverage is available.
- Product disputes are covered for financial institutions only.
- Policy proceeds due to exporters may be assigned to the exporter's financial institution.
- The interest is covered at the rate stated in the note and may extend to the lesser of date of claim payment or 270 days.

Even though called *medium-term,* within that time framework maximum repayment terms are established, depending on the contract price. Briefly, the maximum terms are: two years to $75,000; three years to $150,000; four years to $300,000; and up to five years over $300,000.

Normally, capital equipment sales to dealers are limited to three years regardless of size. The policy is issued in one of two ways:

1. To the exporter; this is called a *nondocumentary* policy, but it may be assigned to a lender by means of a documentary assignment that protects the lender against fraud, disputes, or other defects relative to the underlying transaction

2. To a lender in the form of a documentary policy, with the same result in terms of the lender's protection.

In most other ways, the general policies of Eximbank relative to its Multibuyer Short-Term export policy apply to the medium-term policies, including the special provision for bulk agricultural crops. One exception pertains to foreign content, where the medium- and long-term rules are somewhat stricter. Eximbank insists that any foreign content be insured or financed outside Eximbank's programs. There are exceptions and special circumstances, but that is the rule of thumb.

This new policy is considered a major improvement for the export industry because of its 100 percent cover on commercial risks (as compared to its former 90 percent cover); and because of its hold harmless assignment protection feature for lenders, which is similar to that for the small business policies; that is, exporter's failure to perform or fraud. The new policy also promises much faster issuance (within days), as compared to the unconditional medium-term loan guarantee. It is therefore being used much more than the former medium-term insurance policy; it is also frequently used in place of the medium-term loan guarantee.

Special Policies

Bank-to-Bank Letter-of-Credit Policy.   While issued to banks rather than to exporters, bank-to-bank letter-of-credit-policies are useful to know about if you are trying to get your bank's support when you are holding an unconfirmed letter of credit from a relatively weak country. This type of policy was designed and intended to encourage and permit banks to provide support and should be a selling point for a bank seeking the exporter as a customer. There is no deductible, and the coverage is 100 percent for sovereign financial institutions, but commercial coverage is limited to 95 percent (banks are allowed to pass the 5 percent on to the exporter), and in this area banks do not want any risk. Therefore, most banks want to feel they have a good correspondent relationship with the issuing bank, and their primary concern relates to country risk, although the bank remains responsible for meeting all documentary requirements.

Financial Institution Buyer Credit Policy.   The Financial Institution Buyer Credit Policy can serve in special situations where a direct relationship exists between a U.S. lender and a foreign buyer. Typically, this would be the U.S. office or agency of a foreign bank, which is more likely to assume the risk or responsibility for the 10 percent uninsured buyer risk than a U.S. bank would be. There are substantial minimum premiums involved, however, ranging from $2500 for sovereign buyers to $10,000 for the private sector. Each single or multiple transaction policy issued is individually risk-assessed. There is no first-loss deductible, just as with the Short-Term Single Buyer Policy, but only 90 percent of the risk is insured.

Financing or Operating Lease Policy. A financing or operating lease policy is designed to support the increasing use of leasing as an international trade tool. The coverage is 100 percent on sovereign leases and 90 percent on all others, and there is no first-loss deductible. It can be used for both cross-border leases, in which the lessor and lessee are in different countries, and international leases involving two parties in the same country (other than the United States), so long as it is 90 percent U.S. content. The insured has the option of choosing either the financing lease, which covers total payment under the lease, or the operating lease type of policy, which typically covers a five month's stream of payments. The operating lease presumes that the lessor will undertake repossession efforts if payment problems exist. The coverage is divided into two parts: the stream of payments, and the host government's refusal to permit repossession. The insured specifies a separate value for each risk, and the premiums are calculated accordingly. The financing lease policy is viewed as medium-term coverage and Eximbank insists on 15 percent down, as in its medium-term insurance. As an alternative, the lease can be covered under a guarantee rather than by insurance. (See the discussion of international leasing in Chapter 37.)

Political Risk Policies. Virtually all the political risks covered deductible previously, described policies that can be covered without carrying commercial risk coverage as a variation on each of the policies by specifying "political risks only," which allows for coverage at considerably lower rates. This option can be especially appropriate in the case of sales to subsidiary or affiliated companies for which commercial risks cannot be insured in any event. In general, however, it does not reduce premiums as much as one would expect, and Eximbank does not encourage deleting commercial risk coverage.

Special Endorsements for Eximbank Policies

Preshipment Coverage. Preshipment coverage protects against losses sustained by virtue of the insolvency of the contracting buyer, or for political reasons, such as war, cancellation of the export or import license after shipment, and similar events. It does not cover contract repudiation by the buyer. Preshipment coverage is available by request on a case-by-case basis under any of the short-term policies.

Nonacceptance Coverage. Nonacceptance coverage is also available by request on a case-by-case basis when there is a written contract or agreement to purchase and the buyer refuses to accept the goods, as long as it can be clearly demonstrated that the refusal is not part of a buyer claim and there is no fault of the insured as to compliance with the sale contract. Nonacceptance coverage is often used in connection with sales made under documentary collection terms in which this represents the primary credit risk and it can easily be demonstrated that there is no buyer claim since the buyer would not be able to obtain the goods without documents.

Consignment Coverage.   Consignment coverage is applicable when the seller is to retain title for a substantial or indefinite period of time, as in consignment sales. The coverage provides against losses sustained because of political or administrative events that might prevent the goods from legally remaining in the consignee's country or such events prohibiting payment for the goods subsequent to sale by the consignee.

Foreign Exchange Endorsement.   Eximbank now permits a transaction to be payable in Canadian dollars, Japanese yen, German marks, English pounds, Swiss francs, or French francs without special endorsements. Contracts utilizing other transferable currencies may be admitted for coverage by application for a specific endorsement in advance. When a currency other than U.S. dollars is to be used, Eximbank retains the right to pay claims either in that currency or in U.S. dollars. This makes it clear that the foreign exchange endorsement does not cover losses because of exchange rate fluctuations.

Caveat

Keep in mind that whatever policy is being dealt with, there is no insurance coverage unless the buyer is eligible, either by virtue of discretionary authority or according to the terms and conditions spelled out by Eximbank in a special buyer credit limit. Also, the coverage is invalid if conditions or limitations that Eximbank has imposed concerning the country of the buyer are not observed, or if Eximbank does not offer coverage in that country. The country risk issue comes first, regardless of the buyer's strength.

Eximbank Loan Guarantees

Just as with Eximbank's short-term insurance programs, which are usually the earliest, and often the only, point of contact with Eximbank; so the working-capital guarantee for small business is an anomaly, and more often than not is the only Eximbank guarantee the average exporter will have occasion to use. All of the other guarantee and loan programs support foreign buyer credit instead of supplier credit, and buyer credit is most often involved with longer-term and larger transactions. The basic principles for Eximbank involvement recited at the beginning of this chapter relative to the insurance division also apply in the case of the direct loan and guarantee programs.

Exporters Working Capital Guarantee Program

To put the programs in perspective, in 1994 of $14.6 billion in export authorizations, guarantees accounted for $7.4 billion (of which $5.8 billion was for long-term); insurance accounted for $4.2 billion (of which $3.6 billion was for short-term); and $3 billion was for direct loans. Eximbank's working-capital guarantee program (EWCP) is a relatively minor part of the overall Eximbank program in dollar terms, accounting for a mere $181 million of the $14.6 billion of export authorizations. Nevertheless, the EWCP is the keystone of Eximbank's response to congressional mandates to provide better service to small businesses which actually receive most of their support through the short-term insurance program. Although Eximbank's working capital-guarantee program has been in place in some form well over ten years, as presently structured it is a pilot program that has been harmonized with the harmonized SBA Export Working Capital Program (EWCP) (described in Chapter 39). The purpose is to share the concept by having each agency do what it knows best. SBA, as a small business and small loan specialist, is authorized to process export working capital loan guarantee requests up to SBA's statutory limit of $750,000 (a 90 percent guarantee on a $833,000 loan). Eximbank will handle all small business export working-capital guarantees larger than $750,000, with no limit as to maximum size. There is an exception to this division of responsibility in that, if a lender having Eximbank's delegated authority chooses to use it for the Eximbank program, it may do so regardless of the guarantee size. The SBA/Eximbank harmonized EWCP helps the smaller firms falling within the SBA guarantee limit to have hands-on help closer to the business than Eximbank's headquarters or regional offices are likely to be. The program is unique because all others are meant to finance exports *after* shipment or the payment of a service contract, whereas this program can also address the needs of a business for working capital *before* the export occurs to allow it to undertake the export commitment.

Under the working-capital program, when lenders feel the need for additional security to make an export loan, Eximbank can guarantee the lender against the exporter's default on the loan. This is a common problem for exporting companies because of bank reluctance to lend on export transactions. Only the bank is guaranteed against default by the exporter for whatever cause. The program does not cover the exporter should the foreign buyer default. To the extent that this is a risk, as it so often is, it must be covered by Eximbank's foreign credit insurance or private sector insurance, and it is most likely that—except for the very strongest buyers or when the terms are letter of credit—the lender would make insurance a condition of the guarantee or the loan.

Guarantee Highlights

- The loan amount must be in excess of $833,333 unless the lender has Eximbank's delegated authority.

- 90 percent guarantee of principal and interest to lender.

- 100 percent collateral required, including an assignment of proceeds of the letter of credit and/or the receivables.

- Maximum maturity of one year.

- The loan may be used for a specific transaction(s) or specified as a revolving credit supported by export accounts receivables.

- 1.5 percent guarantee facility fee per annum, plus $100 application fee.

- The exporter must demonstrate its ability to perform with a minimum of at least one year's successful operating experience.

- The guarantee is available to support standby letters of credit necessary to the export contract, in which case only 50 percent, rather than 100 percent, of standby letter value will be required as collateral.

- A number of banks have substantial delegated authority with special incentives, making it more likely for the Eximbank Working Capital Program to be offered as support to the exporter. The lender is also allowed to make separate collateral arrangements for the unguaranteed 10 percent, giving it further incentive to utilize the program.

- The Private Export Funding Corporation (PEFCO) can be used by Eximbank as a lender of last resort if a conventional lender cannot be found. (For information about PEFCO, see page 486.)

The collateral required can include inventory, even the inventory to be exported, as well as foreign accounts receivables if they are of very good quality, or if they are insured. In the case of smaller firms, a personal guarantee from the borrower's principals is usually required because of the importance of exporter performance in preshipment export credits. Documents supporting the receivable or letter of credit collection are usually substituted for other collateral after the shipment takes place.

Exporters can approach Eximbank directly or through their bank for a working-capital guarantee. This is now possible with almost all Eximbank programs, but it is especially important in the context of this program. When a preliminary commitment (expressing willingness to provide the guarantee to a qualified lender) is given, it is valid for 180 days, by which time a banking arrangement must have been made and the 1.5 percent per annum facility fee paid in full by, or prior to, loan disbursement. A number of incentives, liberalizing concessions, and operating conveniences were incorporated into the program in 1994 to assure greater acceptance by the lending industry and better utilization of the program generally.

Buyer Credit Guarantee Programs

Buyer credit-risk protection comprises the third Eximbank function after foreign credit insurance and exporter working-capital export loan guarantees. Eximbank medium- and long-term loan guarantees cover the risks of nonpayment by the foreign buyer or country due to political and economic problems. Even in this area the exporter may approach Eximbank directly, and if the Eximbank is favorably inclined to deal with the proposition, it will provide the exporter a letter of interest. The letter of interest can be used for all guarantee and direct loan programs. It is not a financing commitment as the preliminary commitment in the Working Capital Program is, but it is an indication of Eximbank's support and therefore can be used as a selling tool. Letters of interest are supposed to be available in seven days, if the exporter's documentation of the proposal is adequate.

Financial Guarantee Program. This guarantee is designed to support capital equipment, services and projects for either medium- or long-term export transaction contracts. It guarantees the lender repayment of fixed or floating interest rate export loans made by financial institutions or large exporters financing their own transactions. There are no limits to the amount of the loan, but its size does dictate the maximum repayment terms, as in the case of insurance and as noted under "Eximbank General Criteria" (see pages 483–485).

Guarantee Highlights

- A minimum 15 percent cash payment by buyer required.

- 100 percent of the principal and interest guaranteed for both political and commercial risks.

- An up-front exposure fee based on repayment term, type of buyer (sovereign, private, etc.) and country risk rating paid at the time of each disbursement, and a commitment fee of 0.125 percent per annum on the undisbursed balance of the guaranteed loan.

- The guarantee is unconditional and transferable and may be used to cover multiple sales financed by a line of credit from a U.S. bank to a foreign bank.

- Guarantees under $10 million do not have restrictions as to shipping on U.S. vessels.

- Special enhancements for environmental goods and services.

Credit Guarantee Facility. This facility largely pertains to the currently popular, and very effective, concept of *bundling*—that is, taking a number of smaller transactions and putting them together to take advantage of large-scale trade finance techniques and lower interest rates. The facility was first used intensively in Latin America, and its use has since been expanded into Eastern Europe and Asia. Its purpose is to facilitate the sale of U.S. capital goods and service within a medium-term timeframe (one to five years), by guaranteeing repayment to U.S. or foreign lenders on lines of credit to foreign banks or large foreign buyers. The guarantee recipients can be large, creditworthy individual entities, with large amounts of ongoing medium-term procurement, but more often will be strong foreign commercial banks for on-lending on equivalent tenor to many small businesses so they can buy directly from U.S. firms. The program is not available for agricultural commodities, spare parts, raw materials, or other products regularly sold on short-term repayment conditions.

Program Highlights

- A mandatory 15 percent cash payment by foreign buyer and a 100 percent guarantee on the 85 percent account balance for commercial and political risks.

- A facility fee of a flat 0.0625 percent plus an up-front exposure fee on each subloan disbursed, based on repayment term and country risk rating; the minimum facility is $10 million.

- The foreign bank makes the credit judgment and accepts the risks relative to its customers.

- Standard documentation permits use for small facilities and rapid response.

- Individual disbursements can be consolidated and sold in the secondary market (bundling).

Engineering Multiplier Program

This is a program designed to stimulate the export of architectural, industrial design, and engineering services. Eximbank will extend loans or guarantees for up to 85 percent of the total value of such services if they involve future projects with the potential of $10 million, or double the original service contract, whichever is greater. Included in its guarantee or loan can be approved-project related costs within the host country of up to 15 percent of the U.S. export value. It is not a widely used program.

Eximbank Direct Loans

Direct loans comprise Eximbank's fourth function. The direct loan programs were once Eximbank's major activity, but in recent years use of these programs has declined significantly, and they are now the least important, at $3 billion in 1994 compared to guarantees and insurance of $11.6 billion. The loans are at a fixed interest rate set by Eximbank based on the repayment term, country, and foreign buyer for capital equipment and on projects for either medium- and long-term tenor. The financed portion of the goods, projects, or services usually exceeds $10 million.

Direct Loan Highlights

- A 15 percent cash payment minimum and a loan of up to 85 percent of contract amount.

- A commitment fee of 0.5 percent per annum on any undisbursed balance of the loan; with an up-front exposure fee based on repayment terms and country risk rating to be paid at each disbursement, which may be financed.

- The lending rates are the lowest permitted under OECD international agreement guidelines, which is the appropriate Treasury rate plus an agreed-upon spread.

Project Finance Loans and Guarantees

Although Eximbank has done a great deal of project financing, it considers this to be a new area because in the past such financing has not been done on the basis of traditional project finance criteria. Eximbank is now willing to base the credit decision on the revenue stream and cash flow of the project, rather than on sovereign, financial institution, corporate, or other guarantees. The essence of repayment lies in the successful completion of the infrastructure project within its budget, plus any allowances for overages and its subsequent profitable operation. (It is typical of the projects financed by the MDBs discussed in Chapter 13 and OPIC in Chapter 41.) This approach permits credit extensions that could not otherwise be issued on the basis of the guarantor's liquid assets alone. Eximbank established Project Finance as a new division in 1994.

Within the rules of the Organization for Economic Cooperation and Development (OECD), Eximbank proposes to offer maximum support for major projects in the interest of providing the best opportunity for participation by major U.S. suppliers and their subcontractors and suppliers. Included in the Eximbank project finance team's agenda is:

- Financing of interest accrued during construction.

- Permitting 15 percent foreign content in the U.S. package and including another 15 percent of host country local costs in the U.S. contract value. The latter point is a key issue, competitively speaking.

- No maximum or minimum size limitations, but typically in excess of $50 million.

- Flexible, negotiated arrangements as to combinations of direct loans and guarantees or equity structure so long as sponsor equity cannot be transferred without Eximbank's permission.

- Special considerations given to environmentally positive projects.

- Most details negotiable but the 15 percent cash payment rule remains in effect because of the flexible nature of this type of financing.

- Political-risk-only coverage is available during construction.

General Eximbank Criteria for Loan and Guarantee Programs

In addition to Eximbank's general precepts for all programs, it also has additional specific criteria that a transaction must meet regarding terms and products before a related loan can be made or a guarantee issued. The working capital guarantee is an exception to all other loans or guarantees in this regard, and its criteria have already been discussed.

Repayment Terms

For capital goods, the maximum repayment terms by contract value are as follows:

- Up to $75,000—two years
- $75,000 to $150,000—three years
- $150,000 to $300,000—four years
- More than $300,000—five to ten years

Some products or projects, such as aircraft, ships, and power plants, may have longer terms and lower-unit-value items may be assigned shorter terms. In exceptional circumstances, the maximum length of long-term loans can be extended beyond ten years, depending on the nature of the product or project and OECD rules. The Eximbank distinction between medium- and long-term is important because it changes certain loan or guarantee conditions. *Long-term* is now defined as a repayment period longer than five years or is arbitrarily classified as long-term whenever the loan value exceeds $10 million, whatever the term. It is also a question of purpose; *medium-term* is used for trucks and equipment, and so forth, and *long-term* is used for heavy industrial equipment or projects.

Where international competitive bidding is involved, repayment terms or maturities are controlled by OECD agreement, on the basis of one of two country categories. Category I refers to the wealthier nations of the world, including all the developed nations. Category II includes all nations not on the Category I list. For Category I the maximum repayment term is five years unless OECD is notified otherwise, in which case eight-and-a-half years is permitted. For Category II countries, ten-year repayment terms without OECD notification are permitted. OECD also has special rules for ships, planes, and power projects.

Interest Rates

Government-supported loans or credits are also controlled by the minimum consensus interest rates and maximum maturity terms set by OECD agreement, which is reviewed every six months. As with repayment terms, these rates are equalized for each of the two OECD country categories. Eximbank consistently utilizes the lowest allowable OECD rate for its direct loans, which is the comparable Treasury rate plus the OECD allowed spread. Direct loans and long-term loans are almost always negotiated at fixed rates, which is typically the most sought-after condition for long-term financing. In the case of the guarantee programs, the lender sets the rate, which can be fixed or floating. Eximbank, besides guaranteeing the principal to the lender, will guarantee the accrued interest in case of default at the lesser of the loan agreement rate or near the Treasury borrowing rate, or similar benchmarks.

Eligible Markets

Eximbank is now willing to support exports to many foreign countries it would not have considered before. The reason is its new risk-rating procedures that compensate Eximbank for the risk assumed in place of the prior policy of considering most foreign risks as equal for fee establishment purposes—an obvious contrivance adopted for reasons of state and politics, as opposed to sound underwriting policies. However, there will always be some countries that are ineligible for credit reasons or for national interest reasons.

Eligible Exports

The eligibility of exports is primarily a question of U.S. content. Loans or guarantees are available for 100 percent of the financed value of the American content. Consequently, the coverage usually is 100 percent, but with the required 15 percent cash payment, the value to be financed is usually 85 percent of the export price. There are some technical exceptions and definitions relative to foreign content, including foreign components installed in the United States. Also, there are special rules for project finance as noted. Anything near a borderline case is worth discussing with the program administrator. Classified as ineligible are exports of military goods and services, just as in the case of Eximbank insurance.

Shipping

In the case of long-term financing programs, Eximbank-supported sales are subject to the U.S.-flag shipping requirements in "P.R. 17" (i.e., they must be shipped in a vessel of U.S. registry unless the foreign buyer obtains a waiver from the U.S. Maritime Administration). In most cases, however, this requirement is waived for loan or guarantee facilities under $10 million.

Foreign Versions of Eximbank

Keep in mind when considering possible uses of Eximbank facilities and the limitations that are imposed on you by the foreign content rules that many other nations have similar programs. Just as Eximbank makes direct loans to foreign buyers, you may utilize another country's facility in the course of your own overall international trade activities. Such foreign organizations can support you if you have an overseas subsidiary, a joint venture, or are using a substantial amount of that country's manufacture in a product you are producing for a third country.

Some countries running a serious trade deficit with the United States are using their export-import bank facilities to help correct this serious geopolitical problem. The major examples are Japan, Taiwan, and Korea. Only certain products are eligible, but they represent broad and important export areas, (except in the case of Korea, where only raw materials are currently emphasized).

Very favorable interest rates and repayment terms are offered by these countries. The Export-Import Bank of Japan (JEXIM) structures its terms as a buyer credit using a combination of a direct loan and a loan through a Japanese bank to the buyer. Taiwan's "C-Eximbank" has an excellent program providing fixed-rate supplier credit on a bank-to-bank basis, permitting the American exporter to offer very favorable terms on a transaction-by-transaction basis to the Taiwanese buyer. Korea's more limited program, called KEXIM is structured in the form of advantageous terms for buyer credit when purchasing from U.S. firms. Therefore, if there appears to be problems in arranging financing through commercial banks or through Eximbank, check with the export-import bank version of the buyer's country in appropriate situations, especially in the case of Japan, Taiwan, and Korea. There are also many unique and special programs offered by the United States and other governments throughout the world. These are briefly listed and described in William Delphos's book, *Inside Washington.*[1]

Private Export Funding Corporation

Although a separate organization, the Private Export Funding Corporation (PEFCO) is closely related to Eximbank and is mentioned here to round out the Eximbank picture and to cover all the facilities. PEFCO serves as a supplemental source of long-term financing for foreign buyers of American exports. It also has a new note purchase facility to assure liquidity for Eximbank guaranteed medium-term promissory notes. PEFCO is a private corporation owned by a number of banks and seven industrial corporations. PEFCO obtains the money it lends by selling debt obligations that are guaranteed by Eximbank. PEFCO supplements fixed-rate financing funds for a project only when its participation exceeds $1 million and the term exceeds five years. Typically, PEFCO would be involved in combination with private banks and Eximbank, accepting middle maturities longer than the bank's and shorter than Eximbank's. Because it is a private organization and fairly unstructured, it can help develop unique packages involving special interest rate pricing techniques that would not be possible for Eximbank, and would be undesirable to the private banks.

The newest arrangement with PEFCO came with the announcement in 1994 that it would serve as the "lender of last resort" for Eximbank's Working Capital Program by assuring access to a commercial lender under contract with PEFCO for this purpose. To be eligible, the exporter must have been referred to PEFCO by Eximbank after having first been issued a preliminary commitment for which a lender could not be found even with the guarantee (this facility does not apply to guarantees issued under SBA's working-capital program). Alternatively, to provide an assured source of liquidity and overline funding support for lenders extending export-related working-capital loans to their clients, PEFCO may purchase participations from lenders. Under this format PEFCO will purchase the participation, provided that investigation shows that the lender is sound, has had prior experience with the Eximbank working-capital program, and has an experienced trade finance officer on board who is responsible for managing the loan and the relationship with PEFCO.

These new developments bring PEFCO into the vision range of small- and medium-sized businesses for the first time. Eximbank considers these key features in its efforts to make the Eximbank programs as appealing as possible to the banking community and to encourage bank participation in trade finance to the benefit of smaller business and the competitiveness of all U.S. exporters, whatever their size.

Endnote

1. Delphos, William A., *Inside Washington: Government Resources for International Business,* Venture Publishing, Washington, DC, 1992.

41

Overseas Private Investment Corporation

The Overseas Private Investment Corporation (OPIC) is a key resource for those interested in investing in developing countries and new emerging markets. It is unlike any other federal agency in its entrepreneurial approach, and it is exciting to discover what this unique and rapidly expanding quasi-governmental organization has accomplished for both U.S. business and Third-World development while making a profit (or operating on a negative budget, if you will). In 1971 it was felt that, since the Agency for International Development (AID) operates mostly on a government-to-government basis, a separate, business-oriented organization should be created to assist American businesspeople and investors interested in investing or contracting in friendly emerging democracies and developing nations. OPIC now operates in 142 countries. Neither China nor Mexico are OPIC-eligible countries, but the entire territory of the former USSR is eligible, so that the better part of the less than fully developed world is OPIC territory.

Organized as a self-sustaining corporation, OPIC received only start-up funding. That has been repaid and, with a positive net income in every year of operation, OPIC has now accumulated reserves of more than $2 billion. Its purpose and mission is to promote economic growth in developing countries and newly emerging democracies by encouraging American private investment in the infrastructure and development projects of those nations. It accomplishes this by:

1. Financing businesses through loan and loan guarantees
2. Insuring investments against a broad range of political risks
3. Providing a variety of investor services

As in the case of Eximbank, it enjoys the "full faith and credit" backing of the U.S. government. Recently its maximum exposure per project was lifted from $50 million to $200 million, further facilitating OPIC's recent expansion. OPIC's primary functions are new-project-related medium- to long-term financing and political risk insurance or, in some cases, expansion of an existing investment. Although by the nature of its activities, the majority of OPIC's activities revolve around larger businesses, it also assists small businesses with some special programs and engages in educational and informational undertakings, notably through its investment missions and its contractor and exporter guarantee program.

The OPIC eligibility requirements for financing or insuring a project are that it must have a positive effect on U.S. employment, be financially sound, and promise significant benefits to the host country. There are also requirements of the countries eligible for OPIC operations, the first being that the host country must choose to have OPIC operate within the country. The second is that the host country must agree to be bound by certain rules—especially concerning neutral arbitration—as laid down in a government-to-government agreement. The agreement includes certain conditions that are not always acceptable to a particular country. For example, Mexico, a nation that could have greatly benefited from OPIC operations, has refused to agree to the arbitration conditions and is therefore ineligible for OPIC involvement. Because some countries may soon emerge from developing-nation or newly democratized status, while others may become so destabilized that OPIC cannot accept the risks any longer, OPIC's list of client countries is fluid. It is best, therefore, to check with OPIC if you are uncertain about the status of a program or country. OPIC can be contacted directly for prerecorded information, or you can speak with an information officer on the OPIC info line at 202/336-8779; fax 202/408-5155. There is a special fax line for obtaining specified program information, forms, and other documents. The general telephone number is 202/336-8400.

OPIC's programs are subject to frequent change in terms of emphasis or current availability, depending on existing budget and demand characteristics, although the essential content rarely changes.

Insurance

Investment Insurance

OPIC's largest program is its investment insurance program that covers against the risks of:

- *Currency inconvertibility.*   This includes the inability to transfer local currency into U.S. dollars as a result of lack of foreign exchange or adverse discriminatory exchange rates or laws. It does not protect against devaluation or exchange rate fluctuations.

- *Expropriation.*   This includes confiscation or nationalization, plus the more difficult situation of dealing with a set of actions whose cumulative effect is to deprive investors of their fundamental rights associated with the investment.

- *Political violence.*   This includes physical damage to tangible assets as well as lost income resulting from interruption of operations resulting from war, revolution, insurrection, or civil strife.

Coverage is available for two types of losses: business income losses and damage or loss of tangible property. The investor may purchase one or both coverages. Insurance premiums are based on two rates—the rate for the current amount selected by the insured, or the effective insurance and the standby rate that is similar to a commitment for available coverage as the project progresses. The sum of the current and standby coverage equal the maximum insured amount available. The current insured amount equals the insurance in force for any contract year. Standby is assessed at a lower rate, but is still part of the annual overall total cost. Only 90 percent of the total investment can be insured. OPIC will insure retained earnings and interest that may accrue on the insured investment. Typically, this is for 90 percent of the initial investment, plus an additional 180 percent standby commitment for future interest or earnings for a period of up to 20 years.

The insured's eligibility requirements are that investors must be American citizens; or corporations, partnerships, or other associations organized under U.S. laws and 50 percent beneficially owned by U.S. citizens; or foreign businesses at least 95 percent owned by investors who meet the preceding criteria. The project itself need not be owned or controlled by U.S. investors. But if it is not, OPIC will insure only the value of the American investor's interest in a foreign-controlled project, not the entire project. Special policies are designed for banks, cross-border leasing transactions, debt for equity investments, projects involving minerals, oil, gas, and alternative energy, or plans that offer significant development or trade benefits. Such endeavors may take many forms, including contracts for goods and services, such as licensing and technical assistance agreements, construction and service contracts, production-sharing agreements, and international financial or operating leases.

Please note: *To preserve eligibility for OPIC support, the American business must apply for and receive an OPIC registration letter before that business is irrevocably committed to the investment.* There is no charge for this provision.

Contractor and Exporter Insurance Program

Contractor and exporter insurance is a specialized coverage program to help protect an American contractor or exporter from wrongful action by government agencies and to a lesser degree private buyers in the developing world. The program represents an exception to OPIC's usual emphasis on medium- to long-term commitments, and coverage can be had for the appropriately much shorter term. It is intended to cover:

- Disputes pertaining to the underlying contract and unresolved conflicts over payment for goods or services, including change orders and cost overruns
- Wrongful calling of standby letters of credit supporting bid, performance, and advance payment guarantees
- Loss of physical assets and bank accounts because of inconvertibility, confiscation, or political violence

OPIC's coverage is for 90 percent of the financial loss in all three cases. In wrongful callings or arbitrary drawings and disputes coverage, there must be a decisional procedure described in the underlying contract that OPIC relies on to determine if there is a valid claim. The exception to this is bid bonds for which there is not yet a contract in existence. The injured exporter or contractor must invoke this decisional process. OPIC determines the extent of the insured's loss, based on failure of this procedure to function, impracticality or danger in pursuing the procedure, nonpayment of the award, or an award in favor of the buyer in which it can be shown the decision was influenced by fraud, corruption, duress, or which was unsupported by evidence.

This OPIC policy is primarily conceived as insurance against problems with the host government, which is the entity most often in charge of projects or contracts. The contractor or exporter can be covered for contracts with non-government entities. This is very limited, however, because compensation would only be made if nonpayment or noncompliance with the decisional procedures previously mentioned is caused by the host government. In the case of asset losses, the coverage is restricted to political risk, and evidence of a claim must be clear-cut: currency inconvertibility of proceeds from the sale of assets, government confiscation, or physical damage from political violence.

There is no minimum premium for this policy, and it can be obtained on a case-by-case basis. Since this insurance is available for many countries in which today's exporter or contractor may face these concerns, coverage can be vital, even though specialized, since it is not available in most cases through Eximbank or the private insurance market. Eximbank does not offer unfair calling insurance in any country, and for all practical purposes, unless the buyer is sovereign, it is not available in the private foreign insurance market. Contract disputes can be very arbitrary or bureaucratic in developing countries, and arbitration agreements can be one-sided. Again, it is important to understand the OPIC policy concerning application for insurance which requires registration (at no cost) prior to the investment or contract having been made or irrevocably committed. On receipt of such registration, OPIC will send a confirmation letter and the regular Application Form 52. Registration Form 50 may be obtained by fax and submitted by fax.

This coverage can only assist in achieving your rights under the contract you sign. OPIC can be of help in the negotiation process so that your contract is insurable by OPIC and so that you do not cede all of your rights to the arbitration process. This is one reason why OPIC wants to become involved before a contract is drawn.

Investment Financing

OPIC provides medium- to long-term loan guarantees, or direct loans to ventures that involve significant equity and management participation by American business, assuming that adequate financing for the project cannot be secured from commercial sources. There is no real distinction between direct and guaranteed loans in terms of eligibility. The loans or guarantees are available principally for project financing which, by definition, looks to the cash flow generated by the project for repayment rather than to sovereign or individual sponsor guarantees. An exception to this position involves a completion agreement with the principal sponsors (borrowers) that guarantees payment of debt service to OPIC prior to project completion, with an indication of their financial ability to perform those obligations. The purpose is to assure that, despite possible cost overruns, early operating problems or other unforeseen events, the project will be completed. OPIC's participation is based primarily on the economic, technical, marketing, and financial soundness inherent in the project, since it is nonrecourse financing. Therefore, OPIC must be assured that there is adequate cash flow to pay all construction, startup, and operational costs, to absorb initial losses, to service the debt, and ultimately to provide the owners with an adequate return on investment. OPIC must satisfy itself that the plan is financially sound, with a well-developed and favorable feasibility study, together with the financial and project management capability to perform under the agreement. A successful operating and management track record on similar projects is very helpful. When project financing is not practical, OPIC may consider more conventional secured lending techniques.

Unlike Eximbank, OPIC does not offer concessional financing or OECD interest rates, because it is oriented to the private sector and to projects that amortize themselves on an economic basis. OPIC does, however, sometimes consider creative financing to permit repayment terms scheduled to fit cash flow projections or similar flexibilities. OPIC will also assist in structuring and coordinating its loan with other lenders, including coordination with private banks, Eximbank, and multilateral development banks.

Aside from a sound plan, there are several other eligibility factors that cannot always be stated categorically. While the financing may be for a wholly owned American investor project, OPIC encourages joint ventures with local citizens or corporations. On a new project, OPIC may participate up to a maximum of 50 percent. For the expansion of a successful business, OPIC may consider a 75 percent participation. The U.S. investor is expected to assume a meaningful share of the risk, generally through the purchase of at least 25 percent of the equity in the project. OPIC prefers that at least 51 percent of the ownership comes from the private sector, and projects wholly owned by governments are definitely not eligible.

Sound debt-to-equity ratios are required. Typically, OPIC likes 60/40 or better debt-to-equity ratios, and although there is some flexibility on this point, OPIC avoids excessively leveraged situations. The same host country and American national considerations described for the insurance programs apply.

Direct Loans

OPIC's direct loan program is limited to projects sponsored by small businesses or cooperatives and generally ranges in amounts from $2 million to $10 million drawn from OPIC's own funds. While OPIC cannot normally invest in equity shares of a venture, it does at times loan through convertible debt instruments with profit participation features. This financial structure strengthens the venture's equity base. It may also assist in achieving some local ownership by sale of the instruments to host country citizens, and it increases OPIC's yield to compensate for the risks in its own portfolio.

Guaranteed Loans

Guaranteed loans are typically used for large projects with major corporations that would not be eligible for direct loans under the OPIC charter. They may, however, be utilized by small businesses taking part in a large project. Typically the OPIC guarantee is in the range of $10 to $75 million to a U.S. financial institution for loans at a fixed or floating interest rate consistent with other medium-long-term loans from, or guaranteed by, other U.S. agencies. Maturity is typically in the 5- to 15-year range. OPIC guarantee fees average 2 to 4 percent per annum on the outstanding amount.

Investment Funds

To provide indirect backing for U.S. companies that cannot allocate or raise sufficient equity capital to start or expand their businesses overseas, OPIC can provide financing to support a number of privately owned direct investment funds that have the capability to facilitate business formation or expansion. Such an OPIC-supported fund may invest in 5 to 40 percent of the equity capital of each company in its portfolio, which may ultimately number 10 to 30 companies. There are currently OPIC-supported funds in most countries in East Asia, sub-Saharan Africa, Israel, Poland, Russia, and among the Newly Independent States. There are other such funds specializing in environmentally oriented companies.

Investor Services

Investment Mission Program

Investment missions are five- to seven-day business development trips to target countries or key developing nations. OPIC usually plans four or five missions per year, well in advance, that represent an opportunity for an organized and informed visit in the appropriate situation. Missions include detailed briefings on the country's investment, economic, and political climate. The core of the mission, however, is individual business appointments arranged in advance according to the investor's interest.

Outreach

OPIC sponsors or participates in seminars and conferences around the United States to help make firms more aware of opportunities in less-developed countries and OPIC's role in taking advantage of them. OPIC also coordinates with the other federal export-support agencies and is part of the Trade Promotion Coordinating Committee (TPCC) and the National Export Strategy's Trade Information Center (TIC). You can obtain more information by calling 800/USA-TRADE.

42

U.S. Department of Commerce

The U.S. Department of Commerce (DOC) addresses both the domestic and international commercial activities of the United States and is a very large and complex organization. The purpose of this chapter is to help you understand the organizational structure of the DOC as it impacts international trade and to briefly describe the individual programs and publications offered by the various units. (The use and function of the DOC's key functions are discussed individually in the context of the chapters involving those functions.)

The International Trade Administration (ITA) of the DOC is responsible for the largest share of international trade promotion and export support for U.S. business, so ITA will be our primary focus. It is interesting to note that, due in part to agriculture's greater political influence in recent years, the Department of Agriculture's (USDA) export promotion and support budget is much larger, both in total dollars and as a percentage of exports, than the DOC's. (Agricultural exports represent about 10 percent of total U.S. exports.) Both departments have experienced staff reductions and spending restrictions due to budget measures and will almost surely be subject to more after the conservative 104th Congress finishes its first budget. This will undoubtedly impact some of the programs discussed here. Because of the numerous shifts in organizational charts, office locations, and telephone numbers, these will be omitted in most cases. Instead, we suggest you check first the most recent DOC guides or phone books in the district office or, easiest of all, call the Trade Information Center (TIC) number for the most direct telephone or fax contact. It is very easy to remember: 800/USA-TRADE (800/872-8723). TIC can help you contact many numbers throughout the government related to export assistance programs—not just the DOC, but also Agriculture, Eximbank, OPIC, SBA, TDA, AID, and others. In addition, TIC has general market information and can assist you in accessing reports and statistics from a variety of sources for specific questions. (The Department of Agriculture is discussed in Chapter 43.)

It is an interesting time for the International Trade Administration of DOC, for in the face of the problems mentioned above, the National Export Strategy, which began to take shape under the Bush Administration and came into full bloom as a comprehensive statement under Commerce Secretary Ronald Brown, increased the demands on ITA to make a greater impact on U.S. exports and global market share while at the same time improving its efficiency and productivity. Since ITA contained at least as much of an entrenched bureaucracy as any other part of government, this is a challenge. The *Washington Export Letter,* in its September and December 1994 issues, explained the focus of some of the most pronounced changes.[1] The U.S. Foreign and Commercial Service (US&FCS) was "reinvented," with the revamping falling into three clusters of activity:

1. Some shifts in organization structures at home and in the foreign posts, including a sharper focus on small and midsize firms

2. A refinement of the traditional US&FCS products—market research and information (including more interagency cooperation in its preparation)

3. The development of country and industry sector strategies

The results of this activity will be explained in the appropriate section as this chapter develops. The unit is also developing a new series of working facilities in key countries or important emerging markets, called commercial centers or American business centers, to encourage U.S. firms to take a more professional approach in business development, conferences, and product demonstrations, together with appropriate business facilities such as fax and computers. Although not mentioned specifically, because they are still in the experimental stage, US&FCS is also attempting to round out its formal products with interim reports called *Industry Subsector Analyses* and *International Market Insights.* There is a growing speedup in communications via E-mail and fax and supplemental distribution of current information through computer networks such as CompuServe and Internet, besides the main distribution medium, the National Trade Data Base (NTDB). There is also an increase in the privatization of traditional events such as trade shows and missions. In terms of country strategy, priorities are being assigned based on strategic thinking regarding regions of greatest opportunity and/or interest to U.S. business, in areas such as the ASEAN group in Southeast Asia and parts of Latin America. By industry, the focus is on auto parts, telecommunication, and computers, airport infrastructure equipment, and medical equipment. Part of the industry strategy is devoted to key functional areas, such as environmental exports and the Department of Energy's clean-coal technologies exports. The key to two other broad strategies is the Trade Promotion Coordinating Committee (TPCC). Its first role is to create and implement interagency cooperation opportunities. Its second role is to promote *advocacy*—the use of whatever influence key U.S government leaders can bring to bear on major overseas projects to help U.S. businesses seeking specific project opportunities abroad.

International Trade Administration (ITA)

The International Trade Administration (ITA) is a vital instrument of commerce. As an exporter, your primary contact relative to government affairs as they apply directly to your business will be the ITA. Its policies are developed and governed by the under secretary for international trade. The DOC and this administrator, therefore, have a major impact on exporters and influence our trade policies. ITA arranges for programs to assist your export promotion efforts, develops information and statistics that aid your market research, determines the availability and effectiveness of our domestic trade specialists and overseas officers, and participates in formulating and implementing part of our foreign trade and economic policies in cooperation with the U.S. trade representative (USTR) and the Department of State. The ITA is a primary player on the relatively new Trade Promotion Coordinating Committee (TPCC), an interagency group charged with developing and guiding our National Export Strategy and coordinating the activities of the many other agencies involved in U.S. support for international trade to increase each agency's overall efficiency, ease of access, and value to the export industry.

ITA prepares many reports and publications with the help of, and for use by, its four service units. Each unit is administered by an assistant secretary and deputy assistant secretaries, but the U.S. and Foreign Commercial Service (US&FCS) assistant secretary is known as the director general. The other three units are International Economic Policy, Trade Development, and Import Administration. The Bureau of Export Administration (BXA), formerly part of ITA, is now a separate bureau. (BXA is described in Chapter 31, which covers export licensing.) The sweeping Omnibus Trade Act of 1988 demanded that DOC, through ITA, step up market development and trade promotions and supported enhanced export promotion data systems, but the funds have been added to its budget rather slowly. The US&FCS was one of the ITA units chiefly responsible for carrying out the Trade Act's mandates, but for budgetary reasons, some of the results have been limited beyond ITA's most notable role in the development of the National Trade Data Bank and the placing of US&FCS officers in each multilateral development bank. The latter is intended to help American businesses achieve a more representative share of the export business opportunities offered by the multilateral development banks. (See Chapter 13.) Another constructive development evolving from the 1992 trade legislation has been the Trade Promotion Coordinating Committee (TPCC), which itself bred in turn a number of effective and creative ideas. Among them was the U.S. Export Assistance Center (USEAC) concept for the purpose of providing exporter interagency access to staff assigned from, or at least fully informed about, each agency directly responsible for export support from promotion to financing. USEACs are still quite experimental, and they are confined to major U.S. cities, but so far seem to be a worthwhile effort.

U.S. and Foreign Commercial Service

The U.S. and Foreign Commercial Service (US&FCS) is the first of the four basic ITA units of concern to international traders. It is responsible for recruiting and training the overseas commercial officers in 69 U.S. embassies and consulates in major export markets, plus maintaining close contact with commercial attaches in another 96 embassies and 36 consulates not covered by US&FCS staff. The US&FCS, in turn, is accessible to exporters through its U.S. staff of trade specialists in 47 DOC district office locations, plus 22 branches located in 69 U.S. cities.

The trade specialist's objectives are: (1) assist and inform both new-to-export firms and experienced exporters desiring to expand their overseas markets by assisting in their planning and research activities; and (2) to help them access the various statistics, reports, and databases available and gain the input of the overseas offices and US&FCS foreign staff. Sometimes the foreign trade officers overseas, or the trade specialists in the district offices, do an outstanding job; and sometimes their efforts leave much to be desired. It is people that make each office work or not work, although budgetary considerations often impose constraints on acquiring the staff to do the job right. Don't let a less-than-satisfactory individual experience prevent you from trying again.

Many of the US&FCS activities, as well as other ITA programs closely associated with the US&FCS, are emphasized and detailed individually in various chapters relative to each stage of the export process. (See Chapters 7, 8, 9, 11, and 12 for discussion of topics ranging from product and target determination, to country assessment and prospect search, to prospect credibility and qualification.) US&FCS activities also include primary responsibility for overseas trade fairs and missions under ITA, as well as for customized market research and consultation. US&FCS research and reporting services combine the resources of all ITA units and foreign posts, as well as calling on the Washington desk officers in the International Economic Policy unit and the industrial sector offices in Trade Development. As an interagency effort led by ITA, US&FCS provides the new annual Country Commercial Guides covering most countries. Much of this wealth of information can be accessed independently by exporters through the National Trade Data Bank (NTDB), which was mandated in the 1988 Omnibus Trade Act, or through the National Technical Information Service (NTIS), part of DOC, and to a diminishing extent from the Government Printing Office (GPO).

The US&FCS is for all exporters and should be used by all to one degree or another. However, for emerging businesses and new-to-export independent exporters, the Small Business Administration may be the more helpful initial route for individual attention, as explained in Chapter 39. The larger SBA offices also have international trade specialists and advisors designed for such new businesses. SBA is therefore one of the participants in the interagency USEAC offices with an interest in export trade as well as export finance. SBA's international specialists work with the US&FCS personnel by way of balancing the workload, and both attempt to achieve the most satisfactory results for all concerned. You can contact US&FCS officers within the nearest DOC district office. Call 800/USA-TRADE for more information or locations.

International Economic Policy Unit

The International Economic Policy Unit is organized according to five geographic regions, giving Japan a special designation in view of its economic importance. These are the five regions as ITA divides up the world:

1. Office of Africa, the Near East, and South Asia

2. Office of Europe, including the Office of European Community Affairs, and the Office of East Europe and Soviet Affairs

3. Office of Western Hemisphere, including South America, Mexico, the Caribbean Basin, and Canada

4. Office of East Asia and the Pacific, including China (PRC), Hong Kong, and the Pacific Basin

5. Office of Japan

Within each region or group are the country desks, covering all trading partner countries in the world. The specialists on these desks can provide volumes of information on such topics as:

- Legal and governmental environment—including import restrictions; bureaucratic and red-tape delays; laws on agency agreements, licensing, and joint ventures; type of legal system in use; commercial treaties; unwritten or ad hoc nontariff barriers; exchange controls; and tax regulations

- Product categories offering the best export potential and country statistics, by product, in sufficient detail to aid in market forecasting

- Methods of advertising, market research firms and their limitations, distribution channels and the degree of development, and service facilities and infrastructure

- Planned marketing events, such as trade missions and trade shows

Country desks are a key source of information for an intelligent and efficient marketing effort and are underused by most exporters. The country desk specialists work closely with the US&FCS officers. When planning an overseas trip to unfamiliar markets, it is wise to contact each country desk on your itinerary and obtain that person's viewpoint on the potential for your product and the problems you can expect to encounter. All of the offices and services are located at the DOC building in Washington, D.C. (See Appendix A for the telephone numbers of some of the most important country desks.) For the current phone number of any specific region or country desk in the International Economic Policy unit, call the Trade Information Center (TIC) at 800/USA-TRADE.

Trade Development Unit

The Trade Development Unit is organized to identify obstacles and opportunities on an industry-specific basis through the industry desk officers. It monitors foreign competition and develops programs to improve trade performance in each industry sector. This includes trade shows, seminars, trade missions, and group foreign buyer visits. Industry experts can provide market intelligence and direct assistance in developing a market strategy. They can also provide assistance relative to a particular product, and you should have a personal contact within this unit from your industry area.

The functional offices of Trade Development were recently reorganized. It is now divided into five industry sector groups, each administered by a deputy assistant secretary. There are also two offices to provide cross-sector export services. The sector groups are in turn divided into divisions, and some are further divided into branches. The current five industry sectors, each with divisions concentrating on specific industries, are:

1. *Technology and Aerospace.*   Includes offices for Computers and Business Development; Microelectronics; and Medical Equipment, Instrumentation, and Telecommunication.

2. *Basic Industries.*   Includes offices for Automotive Affairs; Materials, Machinery, and Chemicals; and Energy, Environment, and Infrastructure (the latter includes a Power and Construction unit).

3. *Textiles, Apparel and Consumer Goods Industries.*

4. *Service Industries and Finance.*   Includes offices of Service Industries; Finance; and Export Trading Company Affairs.

5. *Environmental Technology Exports.*   Specializes in matters relative to the current emphasis on environmental product exports.

The Infrastructure Division has assumed the role of the former Office of International Major Projects for oversight of major project opportunities and assistance to primary contractors and firms that engage in major overseas infrastructure and industrial projects. Its job is to identify and track such projects and alert a network of firms qualified for the particular project. The office has been downsized because it overlaps with the expanded Office of Multilateral Bank Operations for projects that involve MDB financing, and presumably to a lesser extent overlaps with the National Export Strategy's newly formed, but powerful, Advocacy Center. This is housed in Trade Development, but works on an interagency basis all the way up to White House cabinet-level strength.

ODA was moved to the Office of Finance and provides information on how to access Japan's untied foreign aid program to developing countries, of which about 5 to 6 percent, or $500 million, was utilized in 1994 for procurement by

U.S. suppliers and other foreign suppliers. (See Chapter 13 on international bid opportunities.)

In addition, there are two cross-sectoral units to help Trade Development provide overall statistical data and analyses for market research and export promotion. They are:

1. *Office of Trade and Economic Analysis.* This office deals with matters that cut across industry sector lines, such as economic, trade, and industry analyses; investment and finance data; and U.S. and international statistics. The purpose of this office is to assist U.S. businesses in their market planning and trade policy. They work with some individual firms, but the emphasis is on industrywide efforts through trade and industry associations.

2. *Office of Export Promotion Coordination.* This office operates for the primary purpose of industrywide promotion.

Import Administration Unit

The Import Administration unit provides the mechanism through which manufacturers or workers can request a determination as to whether they are victims of unfair trade practices, such as foreign subsidies or dumping. Should this be the case, and the International Trade Commission of the United States agrees, the U.S. government instructs the U.S. Customs Service to assess countervailing duties or other appropriate remedies. The Import Administration's duties include administering bilateral trade restraint agreements and similar arrangements. It also administers the Foreign Trade Zone program that is discussed in Chapter 29. Call TIC at 800/USA-TRADE for more information on the function of any of these units.

Advocacy Center

This unique unit is the hub of an interagency advocacy network for the 19 member agencies of the Trade Promotion Coordinating Committee (TPCC). Its mandate is a key element of the National Export Strategy's effort to make government, with DOC as the lead agency, more effective on vital issues selected on an ad hoc and as-needed basis, so it apparently has a very diverse agenda. The center is expected to quickly assess the range of government resources and develop a quick response strategy. The focus of its efforts relates to tracking about 160 pending major international projects where government assistance through advocacy might make the difference. Key government officials are recruited from any appropriate government department or agency, all the way up to cabinet rank plus the President himself. All may act as ambassadors and facilitators on behalf of major U.S. bidders or suppliers to be sure they have the attention of both the public and private sector decision makers in the project's host country. In the first year there were about ten multimillion dollar projects in which DOC feels that the Advocacy Center made the difference.

Other DOC Units of Special Interest

There are many functions within the DOC that are important to an exporter and that involve the ITA but may or may not be directly under its control or administration. (A large share of these are mentioned in Chapters 8 and 9.) Here are some of those units that could be of greatest interest, but in some cases only to very specialized export activities.

Office of Export Trading Company Affairs

An office within the Trade Development unit of the ITA, the Office of Export Trading Company Affairs was originally intended to foster the formation and use of entrepreneurial trading and management companies, as well as to offer counseling to business and trade associations regarding the export intermediary industry. But its duties have become primarily housekeeping duties largely consisting of issuing or keeping current the Export Trade Certificate of Review program under the Export Trading Company Act of 1982. A certificate of review provides exporting associations and groups or joint ventures protection from antitrust charges that would otherwise be considered collusion between competitors to foster joint export activities in which economies of scale and risk diversification might be achieved by that means. However, since the initial interest in the act, when over 150 groups were certified (representing about 5000 firms), now few, if any, new groups are certified each year. Most of the office activity involves recertifying new members added to the existing certified organizations. (See Chapter 6 for greater detail on the Export Trading Company Act.)

Multilateral Development Bank Operations

The Multilateral Development Bank Operations (MDBO) is an ITA group that was moved in late 1994 from the Trade Development unit to the US&FCS unit as part of the National Export Strategy to increase its impact on U.S. exporters by promoting easier access and better outreach. MDBO has added a counseling center to assist firms in working with MDBO, tracking the upcoming projects of the various MDBs, and gaining timely international project information on MDB-financed projects, including the World Bank's. The MDBO staff also facilitates information gathering for a new section of the National Trade Data Base discs on international financing assistance. This entire area is one in which U.S. firms have failed to gain their fair share of the $45 billion loaned by the multilateral development banks each year as they create opportunities in this area of world competition. The US&FCS liaison officers in the various banks are charged with troubleshooting for exporters facing problems relative to procurement, early identification and in-depth counseling. The MDBO is responsible for coordinating the flow of information from the various banks and the US&FCS liaison officers assigned to each major MDB as it is posted on the Economic Bulletin Board and the NTDB disks. The office will provide guidance in pursuing this business and help you decide which MDB publications you might want to subscribe to if you are interested. An initial inquiry can be made directly to the MDBO Office in Commerce, but after you are focused you should also speak to the appropriate MDB liaison officer directly. Call TIC for the most current contacts and phone numbers.

The Office of Multilateral Affairs

The Office of Multilateral Affairs (OMA) is an ITA office for firms already deeply involved in international trade. This office can help with matters such as rights or benefits relative to the Organization for Economic Cooperation and Development (OECD), the General Agreement on Tariffs and Trade (GATT), the General System of Preferences (GSP), or Multilateral Trade Negotiations (MTN). It is responsible for coordinating with and serving an interagency policy role with the U.S. Trade Representative (USTR) for multilateral trade negotiations and is an active participant in GATT affairs.

Market Development Cooperator Program

The Market Development Cooperator Program (MDCP) provides funding through cooperative agreements to assist in implementing creative private sector market development ideas. Exporters are expected to work in partnership with DOC and nonprofit organizations such as trade associations, world trade centers and state international trade departments. The applicant prepares a proposal and a strategic plan designed to increase or maintain market share for overseas market(s) over a one- to three-year period. Applicants are expected to supply two-thirds of the project costs. This is a new program and one that might be marked for funding difficulties in the tightened budget environment.

Bureau of Census

The maintaining of a census is one of the major functions of the DOC as a prime gatherer of statistics—not only of population, but of trade, domestic as well as export/import statistics. The primary source for export statistics is the Shipper's Export Declaration. Most of the statistics that apply to exporting are utilized for trade analysis by the ITA, as well as other areas of Commerce.

The key office for the exporter within the Census Bureau is the Center for International Research (CIR). This organization gathers useful data for international marketing purposes including:

- *International Data Base.* A compilation of overseas demographic trends, divided into broad geographic areas: China, USSR, Europe, Asia, Oceania, Latin America, and Africa. The categories for data are numerous and include such statistics as infant mortality, migrations, marital status and family planning, literacy, and housing indicators. More information on this service may be obtained from the Assistant Director for International Programs, Bureau of Census, Washington, D.C. 20233.

■ *Export/Import Trade Data Base.*   A compilation of worldwide U.S. import/export statistics tracked by mode of transportation and port of entry or exit, based on various levels or modes of classification, including the Harmonized System, SITC, SIC, and end-use classifications. This is the root source for much international trade statistical research. Most of these statistics are now available only on CD-ROM, with the NTDB disks containing the key import/export statistics. Customized tabulations and reports for the user can be obtained for a fee. Contact the Trade Data Services Branch at 301/763-7754. (See Chapter 7 for more details.)

National Institute for Standards and Technology

The National Institute for Standards and Technology (NIST) is part of the Technology Administration within the DOC that provides information for both domestic and foreign standards–related information. U.S. exports must conform to foreign national requirements, standards, testing, and certification requirements. They also have a special program to assist in matters relating to transition to, or use of, the metric system. The NIST maintains special hotlines with recorded messages that may affect your international business. For GATT's latest technical notifications for foreign regulations, call (301) 975-2128. For information about the European Union's ISO 9000 standards, call 301/921-4164. For additional information, contact the National Center for Standards and Certification Information through TIC or see details on the NTDB disk.

National Technical Information Service

The National Technical Information Service (NTIS) is also part of the DOC, under the Technology Administration, and is a self-supporting clearinghouse and archive for thousands of government research documents—some of which can be found no place else—on broad areas, both domestic and foreign. NTIS can be accessed by fax or modem by dialing FedWorld at 703/321-8020, or via the Internet to fedworld.gov. NTIS seems to be the information-age version of the venerable Government Printing Office. It can be difficult to work with unless you know what you are looking for, or a least have a very specific subject. NTIS can provide you with a free catalog of publications, databases, and services for a start. While much of NTIS's export data can be accessed through the DOC District Office, it can be contacted directly concerning further research details and specific requests at: National Technical Information Service, U.S. Department of Commerce, Springfield, Virginia 22161; 703/487-4650.

The U.S. Travel and Tourism Administration

The U.S. Travel and Tourism Administration (USTTA) promotes U.S. exports of goods and services in tourism, assists new-to-market travel agencies relative to export, encourages promotion in international travel markets, and provides research and training in international travel marketing. (See Chapter 10.)

The National Oceanic and Atmospheric Administration

The National Oceanic and Atmospheric Administration (NOAA) assists the seafood industry by improving access to markets in other countries. It also assists exporters in a variety of promotional ways. Its National Marine Fisheries Service addresses worldwide trade barrier problems affecting U.S. fishery exports.

Bureau of Export Administration

The Bureau of Export Administration (BXA) is included here only because it is an important and hotly debated part of the DOC. It is responsible for control and administration of most of the Export Administration Regulations for both export licensing and antiboycott regulations. (These subjects are discussed in detail in Chapters 31 and 32.) The NTDB disk includes current licensing regulations and changes and its annual report.

Technology Sharing and Grant Programs

Somewhat out of order, but worth mentioning here, are special programs for manufacturing technique and technology sharing within the U.S. Department of Transportation and the Environmental Protection Agency (EPA) and a wide array of grant and assistance programs in many departments and agencies. A TIC trade specialist should be able to provide you with the appropriate contacts for your special purposes. For technology sharing, as well as for the many and varied grant programs, capital sources, research and development programs, and technology transfer opportunities, many of which are related to export, and especially if you manufacture high-tech products, consult William Delphos's book *Capitol Capital: Government Resources for High-Technology Companies.*[2]

International Trade Administration Services

This concerns ITA services in terms of those activities which are carried out in person by a US&FCS Trade Specialist or foreign post staffer or some other individual on a customized or selective basis relative to a specific inquiry. In some way all serve the purpose of gaining or checking overseas sales contacts.

Export Counseling

Trade Information Center.   The Trade Information Center (TIC) is an interagency center that provides advice and directions for locating the appropriate office or agency. Call 800/USA-TRADE for a starting point to determine the address, and fax or phone number of a desired office or desk and, in some cases, for preliminary questions or procedures.

U.S. Export Assistance Centers. As explained in earlier chapters on research and initial contacts, the interagency U.S. export assistance centers, or USEAC, attempt to be a one-stop-shop for exporters. Created by the TPCC, they facilitate access to all the government can offer by combining in a single office personnel from the primary government agencies that provide export assistance or support. Always included are DOC trade specialists, Eximbank staff or a representative, SBA personnel, and sometimes staff from the Agency for International Development (or at least personnel familiar with AID procedures and opportunities). The first centers were located in Baltimore, Long Beach, Chicago, and Miami; about 11 more are scheduled to be added during 1995. Check with the DOC office in your area.

DOC District Offices. Individual counseling is available with trade specialists at any one of the DOC district offices or branches, which until recently have been the primary source for such help. They are now augmented by the Trade Information Center and the new USEACs and, with proper advance arrangements, at the US&FCS overseas offices.

District Export Councils. Although DOC states that counseling can be obtained from the private sector members of the 51 district export councils (DECs) that serve as advisory boards to the district directors, the availability of this potentially excellent source varies widely according to the current makeup of the nearest council, the exporter's subject and background, and the ability of an appropriate council member to find the time for such a one-on-one meeting. Much may depend on the inventiveness and personality of the person seeking such voluntary help.

Export Counseling and Assistance from Regional Business Centers

These centers are for counseling, information and assistance of a highly focused nature and are administered by ITA. In some cases they have parallel fax information retrieval systems to offer quick and easy access. The centers are established on an ad hoc basis, and will, or should be, added to or deleted from time to time. Call the Trade Information Center at 800/USA-TRADE for the telephone or fax retrieval hotline. The current list includes:

United States–Asia Environmental Partnership. The United States–Asia Environmental Partnership (US-AEP) is a comprehensive service to help U.S. environmental exporters enter markets in the Asia/Pacific region. The program is a coalition of public, private and nongovernmental organizations that promote environmental protection and sustainable development in 34 nations in the Asia/Pacific region. The partnership attempts to mobilize technology, financial resources, businesses, communities, and governments across the Pacific in public and private sector partnerships to this end. For more information on US–AEP, its projects, and its events, call TIC at 800/USA-TRADE.

Business Information Service for the Newly Independent States. The Business Information Service for the Newly Independent States (BISNIS) is one-stop-shopping for firms interested in doing business with republics of the former Soviet Union. BISNIS staff can provide advice, contact names, joint venture interests, upcoming promotional events and information on special support or grants available. In addition, the office maintains a 24-hour fax information line with varied menus for specific information. (See Appendix A.) This group can also be contacted about the American business centers (ABCs) in the former Soviet states. The ABCs are being established by a nonfederal entity with a cooperative agreement with DOC to provide good working space and essential services in seven cities throughout the region, plus five within US&FC posts in the area. In respect to an interest in the region and in BISNIS, learn about the Consortia of American Business in the NIS (CABNIS). CABNIS is a DOC-initiated grant program to stimulate U.S. business in the region and promote privatization by helping nonprofit organizations, industry groups, and trade associations open offices and provide a venue to U.S. business people that would otherwise have difficulty working in such an evolving and complex market. Grants have been awarded in such diverse fields as commercial and home building, management schools, technology associations, food processing, semiconductors, telecommunications, world trade centers in Alaska and in Orange County, California, and port authorities. TIC can advise or help to contact them if interested.

Eastern Europe Business Information Center. The Eastern Europe Business Information Center (EEBIC) has a function similar to that of BISNIS, but for Eastern Europe and the Baltic States. EEBIC has the names of potential partners, trade regulations, publications and a monthly newsletter. It also has a fax service with multiple menus. The Consortia of American Businesses in Eastern Europe (CABEE), formed for purposes similar to those of BISNIS and EEBIC, provides grants to groups in agribusiness, construction, environment, and telecommunications.

Japan Export Information Center. The Japan Export Information Center (JEIC) offers special help for exporting to Japan in the form of information, product-testing procedures, tariff and nontariff barriers, and some focused publications. JEIC also maintains close contact with the Japanese government's import promotion plans and advises on how to participate. It also has a hotline with various menus.

Agent/Distributor Service

The Agent/Distributor Service (ADS) is a customized service through US&FCS staff research to help identify up to six reputable prospects for agents, distributors, and foreign representatives that have reviewed the requesting U.S. firm's product literature and expressed an interest. The current price (subject to change) is $250 per country. (See Chapter 9.)

Customized Sales Survey

Formerly known as the Comparison Shopping Service, the Customized Sales Survey is a micro market research service conducted by US&FCS overseas staff to provide information relative to a specific product in a given country. The information provide the best distribution strategies, representation, pricing, competition, trade practices, trade barriers, and the most applicable trade events. It is not available for all countries. The current price ranges from $800 to $3500 per country. (See Chapter 9.)

World Traders Data Report

The World Traders Data Report (WTDR) is a service through the US&FCS for checking the buyer credibility, reputation, reliability, and financial status of a prospective trading partner. It includes information about size, employees, and products, as well as an appraisal by the overseas field officer of the candidate's suitability as a trading partner. The current price is $100 (see Chapter 9).

Export Contact List Service

The Export Contact List Service is a database retrieval of buyer contacts with names, addresses, products, and other relevant information on the foreign buyers. The names are screened and collected by the US&FCS personnel in the district offices from the Foreign Traders Index and by commercial officers in the overseas posts (see Chapter 9).

Gold Key Service

Available in a limited number of US&FCS overseas offices, the Gold Key Service is custom-tailored for a firm's travel and product promotion in a country. It combines market research, strategic planning assistance, orientation briefings, introduction to potential partners, interpreters and follow-up planning. This is a service that you would need to sit down and discuss with the trade specialists and foreign officers as to objectives, scope, capabilities, and the fee.

ITA Trade Fair and Exhibit Activities

Assistance in organizing initial contacts in the targeted region or in trade shows in this country is accomplished through these International Trade Administration activities. They help keep the costs down but are not necessarily better planned or more productive than the key events you might find most suitable for your product and objectives. Should an ITA-sponsored or certified event offer some special cost savings, shared booths, or compatible USA Pavilions and also happens to be an event you believe you should attend, then ITA involvement can be of great help. The NTDB disk always contains a current listing of these planned events about one year in advance. (There is more on this subject in Chapter 12.)

Foreign Buyer Program

This program involves quality trade shows in the United States with a high level of foreign buyer attendance, indicating good export potential. US&FCS is asked to publicize the event overseas with direct mailings and through foreign trade associations. An international business center is then established at the U.S. show, with US&FCS staff to facilitate direct contact and meetings with the foreign buyers attending. (See Chapter 9.)

Catalog and Video Exhibitions

These events offer the lowest-cost overseas contact, organized by industry experts, who present your sales literature through a third party to foreign audiences in several countries. This can often be a case of getting what you pay for—i.e., not very much. Contact ITA's Export Promotion Services office or TIC at 800/USA-TRADE. (See Chapter 12.)

Trade Missions

Sponsored trade missions are business development events focusing on a single industry or service sector for the purpose of introducing the overseas market to U.S. firms to let them organize well-conceived market entry strategies, gain advance publicity, and meet potential buyers, agents, and government officials. Individual appointments are arranged as well. The costs vary from $2500 to $5000, depending on the destination's and number of countries to be visited.

ITA is now also engaged in a certified concept involving a cooperative effort between industry trade associations, state trade promotion groups, and other regional or export-oriented groups for participation in trade missions. Consult your trade specialist for the events planned in the coming year.

Matchmaker Trade Delegations

Matchmakers are travel events similar to missions, but they may include a broader array of businesses, perhaps more new-to-export businesses, and are at a lower cost. Discuss your plans in detail with the ITA officials in charge and make sure that they will fit your objectives in terms of the others attending, trip focus, and the countries to be visited.

Trade Fairs and Exhibitions

Sponsored trade fairs and exhibitions are the prestigious means of presenting a product and making new sales contacts. They are also sure to be the most expensive means. DOC selects about 80 to 100 trade fairs worldwide each year in which to include a USA Pavilion that ITA helps organize and recruit U.S. exhibitors for. These arrangements are only attempted for shows that meet fairly high standards in terms of size, catalogs, and services available. ITA gives priority to events in viable markets suitable for new-to-export or new-to-market but export-ready firms and makes sure that there are as many US&FCS staff on hand as possible. Fees are in the range of $2500 to $12,000. For a list of planned events, contact TIC. Major fairs should be prepared for well in advance, preferably one year and no less than six months, so consult with your district office for its calendar early.

The term *Certified Trade Fairs* refers to about 50 events certified each year by ITA as good opportunities for U.S. exporters. Although endorsed by ITA, the recruitment and organization is left entirely to the private sector promoters. The US&FCS overseas staff is available to publicize and to help in these shows as well.

ITA Computerized Databases or Retrieval Systems

The floppy disk, CD-ROM, and computer networks such as FEDWORLD have finally almost completely taken over the job of disseminating information, statistics, and new developments to the international trader. And why not? These same PC tools are used to check for the exporter's compliance, file export and import reports and documents, and promote international export sales. Here are some of the systems and databases offered by DOC. There are many, many more from the federal government and the private sector. As already explained, NTIS has many databases besides its publications, and the most detailed of all export/import statistics are available on CD-ROM from the Bureau of Census. (See Chapter 7.)

National Trade Data Bank

The National Trade Data Bank (NTDB) (see Figure 42-1) has largely taken the place of the Commercial Information Management System (CIMS), which now serves primarily as an effective personal computer link between the domestic trade specialists, Washington, D.C., the US&FCS and agriculture's FAS foreign posts for customized information retrieval and communication. However, the NTDB database makes much of the information available to the public on CD-ROMs and combines statistics, market research reports, publications, and updated information, as supplied by 17 federal agencies, in its database. Two software programs are furnished that permit pyramid-style search from general menus to subtopics or systemwide searches for specifics. The database contains over 49 programs covering everything from how to guides to the most current information and statistics from the CIA's *World Factbook*. Among its many offerings are:

- The interagency Country Commercial Guides
- The *Foreign Traders Index, Export Promotion, and Trade Event Calendar*
- The USTR's *Foreign Trade Barriers Report*
- NAFTA information

U.S. Department of Commerce
Office of Business Analysis
HCHB Room 4885
Washington, D.C. 20230

Tel (202) 482-1986
Fax (202) 482-2164

☐ **Board of Governors of the Federal Reserve**
Foreign Spot Exchange Rates
Foreign Three-Month Interest Rates
Stock Price Indices for the G-10 Countries
U.S. Three-month CD Interest Rates
Weighted Average Exchange Value of the Dollar

☐ **Central Intelligence Agency**
Handbook of Economic Statistics
The World Factbook

☐ **Export-Import Bank of the United States**
Export-Import Bank of the United States, Quarterly Report

☐ **Office of the U.S. Trade Representative**
National Trade Estimates Report on Foreign Trade Barriers
North American Free Trade Agreement
Trade Projections Report to the Congress

☐ **Overseas Private Investment Corporation**
OPIC Program Summaries

☐ **Department of State**
Background Notes
Key Officers of Foreign Service Posts
Resource Guide to Doing Business in Central and
   Eastern Europe
Country Reports on Economic Policy and Trade Practices

☐ **U.S. International Trade Commission**
Trade Between the U.S. & Non-Market Economy Countries

☐ **U.S. Small Business Administration**
Small Business and Export Information System

☐ **University of Massachusetts (MISER)**
State of Origin of Exports

☐ **Department of Agriculture, Foreign
Agricultural Service**
Foreign Production, Supply & Distribution of Agricultural
   Commodities

☐ **Department of Commerce/ Economics &
Statistics Administration (ESA), Bureau of
Economic Analysis**
Fixed Reproducible Tangible Wealth Estimates
Foreign Direct Investment in the U.S.: Balance of
   Payments Basis
International Services
National Income & Product Accounts, Annual Series
National Income & Product Accounts, Quarterly Series
Operations of U.S. Affiliates of Foreign Companies
Operations of U.S. Parent Companies &Their Foreign Affiliates
U.S. Assets Abroad & Foreign Assets in the U.S.
U.S. Businesses Acquired & Established by Foreign Direct
   Investors
U.S. Direct Investment Abroad: Position, Capital, Income
U.S. Expenditure for Pollution Abatement & Control (PAC)
U.S. International Transactions (Balance of Payments basis)
U.S. Merchandise Trade (Balance of Payments basis)

☐ **Department of Commerce/Bureau of Export
Administration (BXA)**
BXA Today
Bureau of Export Administration Annual Report
Export Licensing Information

☐ **Department of Commerce/ ESA, Bureau of
the Census**
Exports from Manufacturing Establishments
Merchandise Trade-Imports by Commodity
Merchandise Trade-Exports by Commodity
Merchandise Trade-Imports by Country
Merchandise Trade-Exports by Country
Total Mid-Year Populations & Projections through 2050
Trade and Employment

☐ **Department of Commerce/International
Trade Administration**
Business America
A Basic Guide to Exporting
Domestic & International Coal Issues and Markets
Eastern Europe Looks for Partners
EC 1992: A Commerce Department Analysis of EC Directives
Europe Now: A Report
Export Programs: A Business Directory of U.S.
   Government Resources
Export Promotion Calendar
Export Yellow Pages
Foreign Direct Investment in the U.S. - Annual Transactions
Foreign Traders Index
Investment Guides
Market Research Reports: Country Marketing Plans; Industry
   Subsector Analyses; Foreign Economic Trends
North American Free Trade Agreement (NAFTA) Information
Trade Promotion Coordinating Committee Calendar of Events
Understanding U.S. Foreign Trade Data
U.S. Foreign Trade Update - Monthly Analysis
U.S. Industrial Outlook
U.S. Manufacturers Trade Performance - Quarterly Report

☐ **Department of Commerce/National Institute
of Standards & Technology**
GATT Standards Code Activities of NIST
Organizations Conducting Standards-Related Activities
National Standards & Metric Information Programs

☐ **Department of Commerce/ESA, Office of
Business Analysis**
NTDB BROWSE Manual
Sources of Information and Contacts

☐ **Department of Energy/Energy Information
Administration**
International Energy Annual

☐ **Department of Labor/Bureau of
Labor Statistics**
International Labor Statistics
International Price Indices

(Contents are listed as they appear in the NTDB and are subject to change)

Figure 42-1. The National Trade Data Bank.

- FAS information on agricultural production, supply, and distribution
- The Census Bureau's export/import statistics by commodity and by country
- The Federal Reserve's international stock market and currency statistics
- The Department of State's country and region reports
- The Bureau of Export Administration's current export licensing information
- GATT Standards and National Standards and Metric information
- The Department of Commerce's *Business America Magazine* and *A Basic Guide to Exporting*

In fact, the NTDB's database contains all this and so much more information that help should be sought first on the NTDB disks. Only when this source has been tried should a determination be made to look elsewhere, although some of the information will be disseminated only through the NTDB.

The database is offered only on CD-ROM and is sent monthly on two disks containing more than 100,000 updated and current documents. Each issue replaces all earlier issues, eliminating the need for updating records. It can be viewed on screen or downloaded to spreadsheets or printouts. The current price is $40 per monthly issue, or $360 annually. Alternatively, the CD-ROMs may be viewed at any of the nearly 900 federal depository libraries around the country, as well as at various trade centers, such as USEACs, US&FCS offices, or SBDC offices.

Country Commercial Guides

As much database as report, each of the *Country Commercial Guides* replaces eight former, overlapping commercial documents generated overseas by the DOC, Department of Agriculture, or the State Department. (The best-known of these former reports were *Foreign Economic Trends, Overseas Business Reports,* and *Market Share Reports.*) The multiagency guides, which each consist of from 100 to 200 pages, are a major improvement in foreign market information availability and came about as a result of the Trade Promotion and Coordinating Council's 1993/1994 National Export Strategy, which included the objectives of eliminating duplicate efforts, providing better in-depth information, and stepping up timeliness. They are now available for use with a personal computer CD-ROM reader to anyone possessing a current set of two NTDB disks or access to one of the over 900 federal depository libraries, or the many export support agencies. They are available only on NTDB CD-ROMs, which also increases the likelihood of their staying on an annual update schedule. The guides cover about 160 countries, certainly including all our regular trading partners, although some smaller countries will no doubt be combined into regions. At this time there are well over 100 country guides available, which truly represents a breakthrough and should be an excellent and up-to-date tool for country market research. To give you an idea of just how comprehensive they are, below is a list of the typical table of contents and appendices:

Table of Contents

Commercial Overview

Leading Trade Prospects for U.S. Business

Economic Trends and Outlook

Political Environment

Marketing U.S. Products and Services

Trade Regulations and Standards

Investment Climate

Trade and Project Financing

Business Travel

Appendices

Country Data

Best Prospects

U.S. and Local Business Contacts

Market Research

Trade Events

More information on the guides can be found by calling TIC at 800/USA-TRADE or Trade Data Services. (See Chapter 8.)

Foreign Traders Index

While already mentioned as one of the numerous items in the NTDB, the Foreign Traders Index (FTI) is sufficiently germaine to the start-up export process of contacts and research, it deserves special mention. It also serves as the prime underlying database for preparation of the Export Contact List Service. The FTI is categorized by commodity and by country and provides the company contact name, address and telephone, year established, number of employees and relative size, the date the firm requested information on U.S. resources and its products handled listed by name and harmonized code. The FTI contains over 55,000 names worldwide, any group of which can be downloaded and/or printed out. (See Chapter 9.)

If you need only the top trade leads portion of EEB and a monthly update of the leads is adequate for your purposes, it is available on the monthly NTDB disks. It can also be found in the *Journal of Commerce* and other commercial newspapers. For the best source for your purposes, talk to your trade specialist or call TIC at 800/USA-TRADE.

Single Internal Market 1992 Information Service

The Single Internal Market 1992 Information Service (SIMIS) is designed as a major contact point for the developmental process of the European Union (EU) in its continuing effort to achieve the equivalent of a single, unified market, for which they once had a goal of completion in 1992. SIMIS maintains a comprehensive database of EC directives and regulations, current legislation, and other information plus *limited counseling*. Call TIC at 800/USA-TRADE.

Regional Fax Retrieval Systems

The Newly Independent States, Eastern Europe, and Japan fax retrieval systems have already been mentioned relative to their business centers under "counseling." These and the unstaffed fax retrieval systems for certain other regions do provide excellent databases for a sharp focus on these particular regions. The current list, in addition to those of the business center mentioned, are:

GATT Uruguay Round Hotline.   This fax retrieval system hotline was established to keep the public abreast of GATT negotiations, but with the signing of GATT, the line is now maintained at TIC to provide information on the final agreement and any subsequent developments. Document #1000 provides the menu of available information packets.

Office of NAFTA and the Office of Latin America and the Caribbean Business Development Center (Amerifax).   This center promotes and facilitates business development in the Western Hemisphere by means of a variety of services and publications. Check with TIC (800/USA-TRADE) for the current phone and fax and the menus currently available. Known broadly as Amerifax, option #1 of Amerifax provides NAFTA information on Canada and Mexico and the NAFTA agreement. The main menu is #0101. Document #5000 contains information on making the NAFTA Rule of Origin Determination, #6000 is the Mexican tariff schedule; #7000 is the Canadian tariff schedule. Option #2 provides the Latin American and Caribbean information with a listing of the documents available on #0100.

Office of the Pacific Basin.   This office also offers a multi-menu fax system, including data on Vietnam, menu #8600. The main menu is #1000.

Office of Africa, Near East, and South Asia.   As with those mentioned above, this is another fax information retrieval system by ITA. The main menus are #3000, #0100, and #4000, respectively.

Trade Data Services for Bureau of Census Statistics

Trade Data Services (TDS) is the contact for obtaining the Census export/import statistics by commodity and by country that go beyond the detail available in the NTDB disks. Census provides these statistics on CD-ROM and in the CDIM and CDEX series discussed in Chapter 7. However, if you need only a limited amount of information, it can be extracted and sent to you by fax for a modest fee. If only a detail is required, it may be provided over the phone. Call TDS at 301/457-3484, or check the current number at TIC. Since most statistics can only be found with the Harmonized System ten-digit commodity code number (Schedule B for exports and HTSUSA for imports), it is essential to have the correct commodity code. If you are in doubt about the code, call the classification assistance number at Census, 301/457-3484.

National Technical Information Service

The National Technical Information Service (NTIS) has already been described under "Other DOC Units," but it is repeated here to call attention to the fact that its range of products includes many computerized databases.

DOC International Trade Publications

Commercial News USA

Commercial News USA is a sales catalog published ten times a year. It promotes the services and products of U.S. firms to more than 125,000 business readers and government officials in 155 countries and to 134,000 active bulletin board subscribers through cooperative arrangements with the private sector in 19 countries. In each issue there are sections devoted to three categories: (1) new products; (2) selected industry promotions; and (3) services. It can provide outstanding sales results at times with a minimal expenditure. Contact TIC at 800/USA-TRADE. (See also chapters 9 and 12.)

Business America

Business America is a monthly magazine for the exporter. It provides information on trade policies and government actions, the trade show calendar, and country or regional trade opportunity assessments. It can be useful, although it follows the DOC party line, as you would imagine. It can be found on the current NTDB disk and is also available from the Government Printing Office (GPO), currently priced at $32 annually.

Export Yellow Pages

The Export Yellow Pages is a directory of 18,000 U.S. manufacturing firms, banks, service providers and export trading companies published annually. It is distributed to 275 embassies, consulates and overseas posts and redistributed by those overseas entities to qualified buyers in the country. Free copies are available from your DOC District Office and are also included on the NTDB. See Chapter 9.

Other Publications from the Government Printing Office

Although not part of DOC, the GPO prints for DOC and many other government agencies besides the International Trade Administration, offering publications of immediate interest to exporters. The GPO may be contacted by writing to the Superintendent of Documents, Washington, DC 20402; or by calling 202/512-1800; or by calling TIC at 800/USA-TRADE. The GPO will provide a list of its publications pertaining to international trade. It also offers two free catalogs: *U.S. Government Books,* listing more than 1000 best-selling titles, and *Government Subscriptions,* a catalog of government periodicals. A sampling of publications of interest for the exporter includes:

- *A Basic Guide to Exporting* (also NTDB)
- *Exporter's Guide to Federal Resources for Small Business*
- *Standard Industrial Classification Manual*
- *The Export Trading Company Guidebook* (on starting and operating an ETC)
- *U.S. Export Administration Manual* (also NTDB)
- *Official U.S. and International Financing Institutions: A Guide for Exporters and Investors*
- *NTDB World Factbook*   A factbook that lists country-by-country data and maps and organization charts prepared by the CIA (also NTDB)
- *The Diplomatic List* and *Foreign Consular Offices in the U.S.*
- *Key Officers of Foreign Service Posts*
- *Commerce Business Daily*   A daily newspaper listing government procurement invitations and foreign business opportunities through the multilateral development banks (see Chapter 13)

Endnotes

1. *Washington Export Letter* (September 1994; December 1994). Available from International Business Affairs Corp., 4938 Hampden Lane, #346, Bethesda, Maryland 20814.

2. Delphos, William A., *Capitol Capital: Government Resources for High-Technology Companies,* Venture Publishing, Washington, DC, 1994.

43

U.S. Department of Agriculture

The U.S. Department of Agriculture (USDA) has an aggressive export program and a budget that is generous compared to the DOC budget. Both, however, have faced some budget tightening and will undoubtedly face still more. As with the Department of Commerce (DOC), the USDA is divided into a number of functional units, one of which is the Foreign Agricultural Service (FAS). Although FAS is a lesser part of the USDA than ITA is of the DOC, both carry similar responsibilities relative to commerce, manufacturing, and services in the case of ITA and agricultural products in the case of FAS. Overall, the USDA export programs are the responsibility of the under secretary for farm and foreign agricultural services. While agricultural exports, at $43 billion in fiscal 1994, are a fraction of manufactured goods exports, as an export classification they have represented a positive trade balance for 35 straight years, a record well worth the effort it requires to maintain that balance.

Foreign Agricultural Service

The Foreign Agricultural Service (FAS) has been called the "farmer's export arm," and is responsible for the administration and operation of USDA's overseas programs, including market intelligence, market access, and market development. FAS responsibilities also include administration of programs with grant or aid elements and financial guarantees to supplement Eximbank and OPIC programs with specialized buyer credit trade finance programs for agricultural commodities. FAS cooperates closely with ITA, and the overlap of some of their programs is now being minimized and replaced by joint efforts, thanks to the coordinating efforts of the Trade Promotion and Coordinating Committee (TPCC). The agricultural exporter will nevertheless do well to be informed of both structures. Knowing how the FAS is organized will help in understanding its part within the overall functions of the USDA as well as understanding its relationship to the overall U.S. national export strategy.

The FAS is presided over by an administrator, a general sales manager, and an associate administrator, who in turn oversee five areas conducted by deputy administrators. Those areas are: International Trade Policy, Foreign Agricultural Affairs, Commodity and Marketing Programs, International Cooperation and Development, and Export Credits.

International Trade Policy

This office encompasses USDA's input into the General Agreement on Tariffs and Trade (GATT) and general policy issues as well as the General System of Preferences (GSP) and subsidy issues. The first responsibility of the office is to make the position of USDA known relative to international policies. Regional officers are charged with the responsibility of knowing and reacting to the policies and trade practices of the other nations in their region, conducting trade and economic analysis, and establishing import policy recommendations and programs.

Foreign Agricultural Affairs

The Foreign Agricultural Affairs office coordinates agricultural activities between the USDA and its overseas posts by means of six world region officers located in Washington, D.C. FAS has approximately 100 agricultural economists and trade specialists who are posted at about 80 U.S. embassies, consulates, and trade offices covering 100 countries geographically. These overseas offices are similar to the Foreign Commercial Service officers in the DOC. Their job includes global reporting, market development and expansion, detection of trade barriers, monitoring other nation's trade practices, and providing agricultural advice to the U.S. ambassador in the area.

International Cooperation and Development

The office of International Cooperation and Development (ICD) is responsible for international organization affairs, research and scientific exchange, and technical assistance worldwide. The ICD objective is to enhance U.S. agricultural competitiveness by providing links to world resources and to serve as a bridge between U.S. technical expertise and developing nation needs in particular.

Export Credits

Among the several major divisions of the USDA is the federal financing corporation known as the Commodity Credit Corporation (CCC), a wholly owned government financing corporation, part of whose activities relate to exports, most notably the GSM-102 and GSM-103 programs. It also has many major domestic financial responsibilities. The Export Credits Office is responsible for the administration of the financial export support programs and operations of CCC and the PL 480 food aid program. This office will be considered separately at the end of the chapter.

Commodity and Marketing Programs

The Commodity and Marketing Programs (C&MP) are foreign market development, promotion, and reporting programs focused on specific commodities. They all include some degree of subsidized support intended to aid market penetration and/or to offset foreign subsidized competition. C&MP is divided into six product divisions, each with its own director. The divisions are:

- Grain and Feed
- Oilseeds and Products
- Tobacco, Cotton, and Seeds
- Horticultural and Tropical Products
- Dairy, Livestock, Poultry, Seafood
- Forest Products

FAS Exporter Programs

Trade Assistance and Promotion Office

The Trade Assistance and Promotion Office (TAPO) is the initial contact point within FAS for exporters seeking information and research on foreign markets. The office is staffed by knowledgeable personnel who provide export counseling and assistance, supply food market reports on over 50 countries, and can refer you to an appropriate desk for further details. While all of the offices and desks mentioned have direct phones, the best advice is to start with TAPO by calling 202/720-7420 or send a fax to 202/690-4374 and ask for the specific phone or fax number you need. If you have a problem with this number call the interagency TIC number, 800/USA-TRADE, for the correct reference.

AgExport Connections

AgExport offers four key contact services for exporters:

1. *Trade Leads.* Inquiries from foreign buyers are received daily at FAS for U.S. food and agricultural products (excluding equipment and chemicals). These leads can be accessed daily on the DOC *Economic Bulletin Board* (*EBB*), in the *Journal of Commerce,* or weekly on the AgExport fax polling system.

2. *Buyer Alert.* This is a weekly overseas newsletter designed to introduce food products to foreign buyers with a small fee charged to the exporter. Exporters

can submit their announcement or advertisement to AgExport, where it will be edited, compiled, and transmitted overseas, and then forwarded as a bulletin or newsletter by mail, fax, or courier to known overseas buyers.

3. *Foreign Buyer Lists.* These are lists of over 20,000 known foreign importers of food products that are updated annually in an FAS database. The list of company and buyer names, including company details may be ordered for a specific commodity worldwide, or for buyers by a specific country at $15 for each list. Agricultural commodities and buyers are also part of the Foreign Traders Index to be found on the NTDB disks.

4. *U.S. Supplier Contact Lists.* These are lists of over 6500 names from which to source food and agricultural products. The lists are available, by commodity, at $15 each.

Market Research Programs, Databases, and Publications

Among the numerous research programs, databases, and publications available to exporters are the following:

- National Trade Data Bank (NTDB). This is part of the same CD-ROM system described in earlier chapters on general market research and in Chapter 42. It may be accessed through your computer with a CD-ROM disk or at one of the federal depository libraries. Many FAS reports are on the NTDB under the AgWorld listing, and other NTDB listings have information on the foreign production, supply, and distribution of agricultural commodities. There are also export/import statistics by HS commodity code.

- Agriculture Trade and Marketing Center. This center is part of the National Agricultural Library and its AGRICOLA database, including on-line systems. Assistance can be obtained for its use.

- Economic Research Service (ERS). This service provides in-depth economic analysis on agricultural economies, foreign trade policies, and issues and their linkage with the U.S. food and fiber economy. This and much more is available on demand for very reasonable fees.

- Food Market Briefs. This is a newly revised information source that replaces the former Country Market Profiles. Each brief is a country-specific description of one of over 50 primary overseas markets for consumer food products. Market overviews and trends, U.S. market positions, competition, and general labeling and licensing requirements are mentioned. The briefs are a focused version of the more comprehensive 100- to 200-page Country Commercial Guides, which are produced jointly by the USDA, DOC, the Department of State, and others. The briefs, like the guides, are scheduled to be available soon through the NTDB disks.

- AgExporter. This is a monthly magazine for the food and agricultural export industry.

- National Technical Information Service (NTIS). This central information distribution facility can be used to subscribe to the *AgExporter* magazine plus a host of more specialized reports, including monthly circulares, fact sheets, and the *Agricultural Trade Highlights.* You may contact NTIS directly at its current number, 703/487-4630, for the NTIS subscription list of FAS publications. Alternatively, should the number be changed or more general information be necessary, contact TAPO for up-to-date details.

Marketing and Commodity Programs

Market Promotion Program.   The Market Promotion Program (MPP) promotes a wide variety of U.S. commodities and food products in almost every region of the world. Commodity Credit Corporation cash payments or, quite rarely, CCC generic commodity certificates are used to partially reimburse agricultural firms, associations, or state groups for the related specific project advertising and promotion expenses. The proposals are developed in the private sector or through the state groups and submitted to FAS for the program announcement and deadlines specified in the *Federal Register.* These relatively short-term promotion efforts have caused considerable controversy because, although small groups or businesses can make use of the program, large businesses promoting their own brand name consume substantial portions of the program budget.

Foreign Market Development Program (FMD).   A second promotional program is the Foreign Market Development Program (FMD), which is also known as the Cooperator Program. FAS, as the administrator of the program for USDA, enters into longer-term agreements with nonprofit trade organizations as well as individual businesses to share the cost of specified overseas marketing and promotional activities for generic and, to a lesser extent, brand-name products and commodities, with the objective of long-term market share development or expansion. The program includes trade fairs, advertising and allied market research, consumer and technical education, and promotional activities. Surplus stocks or funds from the USDA and CCC are used to partially reimburse organizations or businesses for projects on eligible products in specified countries. The plans are proposed by interested organizations and businesses and submitted to USDA for approval. Check with FAS's Commodity and Marketing Operations staff for a fact sheet and more information.

Export Enhancement Program.   A subsidy program formerly known as the Targeted Export Assistance Program, the Export Enhancement Program (EEP) is funded through CCC but administered through the Commodity and Marketing Programs office. In Section 1124 of the 1985 Food Security Act (reauthorized in 1990), the USDA was directed to provide export assistance for agricultural products that were suffering from unfair trade practices or subsidies. Commodities currently eligible include wheat, wheat flour, semolina, rice, frozen poultry, barley and malt, eggs, and vegetable oil. Similar programs are developed specifically for the dairy, sunflower, and cottonseed oil industries.

Support is given in the form of cash bonuses (formerly, and possibly again, by CCC-negotiable generic certificates redeemable for a like value in the designated surplus commodity stock). All sales are made by the private sector. An invitation is issued by FAS specifying the commodities and eligible countries. The exporter needs to contact prospective buyers and negotiate a sale contract that includes a performance bond requirement, contingent on USDA's acceptance of the bonus or subsidy, that allows the negotiated sale to take place. Subject to those events, the USDA and the exporter enter into a contract concerning the amount of the bonus and sale details, with the bonus payable after the commodities are exported.

Eligible exporters must meet certain standards and qualifications, including:

1. Documented exporting experience, within the last three years of the EEP commodity in question

2. A legal U.S. address where the exporter can be addressed for service of legal process

3. Details of the exporter's business structure

4. A certified statement of participation, if any, during the last three years in government programs or contracts

5. Evidence of the financial ability to put up a performance bond to assure CCC that it is dealing with a responsible exporter capable of the necessary performance to earn the bonus.

Invitations for bids are issued to qualified exporters by an automated fax system. A monthly history of EEP activity is available. Contact the Office of General Sales Manager at FAS for details about the EEP regulations and procedures.

Trade Shows and Overseas Activities

Exporters can profit from a wide variety of trade shows and overseas activities:

- International food shows. FAS regularly participates in food and beverage expositions in leading foreign markets. A special U.S. pavilion is usually established for the booths of participating firms. In the major markets, USDA/FAS also organizes its own American food shows.

- Sales missions. These missions target emerging markets for consumer-ready foods, and include market-orientation tours and briefings followed by previously arranged sales appointments with potential buyers.

- Agricultural trade offices. FAS maintains approximately 20 specialized offices in major markets to help exporters of farm and forest products. Most have facilities for conferences and seminars, as well as being prepared with kitchens for sample preparation, office space, and trade libraries to help individual agricultural exporters begin exploring particular markets.

Technical Support

Exporters will find technical support available through several sources:

- Food Safety and Technical Services, USDA. This office coordinates activities and provides exporters with information pertaining to food safety regulations, such as allowable pesticide residues, additives, labeling, and similar issues that may serve as barriers to trade.

- Transportation and Marketing Division, USDA. This division provides guidance to help exporters efficiently use transportation resources and protect product quality en route.

- Inspection certificates for food and agricultural exports. Issued by various agencies within USDA and DOC, these documents are necessary to clear imports of animals, plants, grains, meat, poultry, and seafood through foreign customs.

Commodity Credit Corporation Export Financing Programs

USDA operates two kinds of export assistance programs. The first type of program is commercial, and the terms of the export sale are within prevailing world market prices, terms, and interest rates. The second type of program is concessional, featuring long repayment terms and low interest rates, combined with reduced prices or even conditional gifts. The two primary CCC commercial programs are the Export Credit Guarantee Programs GSM-102 and GSM-103. The only concessional CCC program of real interest to the exporter and also the best known, is the Public Law 480 (P.L. 480) program.

The export credits area of the FAS organization chart is the entity for administration and operation of these export-related programs of the Commodity Credit Corporation and the administration of the Title I portion of Public Law 480. Just as with Eximbank, the international finance programs of CCC are buyer credit programs. Even though the commercial programs, GSM-102 and GSM-103, are conducted entirely within the private sector, with real opportunities for exporters, the CCC trade finance programs all have a government-to-government tilt, involving determinations of country need and financial condition, as well as U.S. marketing objectives. As with all government programs, there is a tendency for them to evolve because of competition, budgetary restrictions, and reasons of state. While often buyer-originated, the programs can be utilized with exporter initiative, but this generally requires knowledge of the players and good advance planning.

GSM-102 (Export Credit Guarantee Program)

The Export Credit Guarantee Program, or GSM-102, is currently the largest and principal program of the CCC. The allocations for fiscal 1995 were $2.92 billion, clearly involving substantial export opportunities. GSM-102 provides the exporter, through a bank, with a full-faith-and-credit guarantee of the Commodity Credit Corporation on the foreign letter of credit, for 98 percent of the FAS or FOB value of the commodity. The terms of the letter of credit may call for deferred payment from six months to three years. The aim is to facilitate 100 percent U.S. agricultural commodity exports to countries experiencing hard-currency restraints that may prevent them from purchasing U.S. commodities without credit. It is nevertheless considered commercial because its financing is at prevailing market rates.

The GSM-102 program is structured entirely for letters of credit and antici-pates that the exporter will assign or sell the letter of credit to a bank to permit immediate exporter payment. To facilitate this, the form of assignment of the guarantee provides the bank a virtual hold harmless agreement against the faults or omissions of the exporter. This makes the program much more attrac-tive to the bank and allows the program to accomplish its goal of providing financing to meet competition and maintain agricultural exports.

The question naturally arises as to why a guarantee is necessary, since the seller receives a letter of credit. Apart from the possibilities of foreign bank fail-ure, foreign exchange controls, and other political risks, the guarantee permits the exporter to sell the negotiated draft because it allows the bank to exceed its own country risk limitations or to be involved with countries to which it might not normally extend credit. In fact, if the CCC is not wholly satisfied with the strength of the opening bank, it can insist that the central bank of the buyer's country insures the obligation of the opening bank. In addition, a bank does not normally consider such long terms for agricultural commodities considering the anticipated storage life and cost of the product. The sum of these reasons, combined with the strength of the guarantee assignment and the guarantor, is a lower, more internationally competitive interest rate.

In order to further ensure U.S. agriculture's competitiveness, CCC also keeps the guarantee fee as modest as possible: about 1 percent for as much as a three-year term. The quoted shipping terms are generally FAS or FOB because the CCC will not guarantee ocean freight costs, except under extremely limited cir-cumstances. In the event that the exporter plans to be the initiator, advance application and approval of the transaction as to commodity, country, and buyer is necessary. Since the fee is payable with the application and is not refundable, it is incumbent on the exporter to first ascertain the financial ability of the buyer to open the necessary letter of credit.

Actually, in most cases, the importer (often the foreign government itself) will indicate in the bid invitation that it reserves the right to use GSM-102 and is fully aware of the amount of the commodity credit lines approved for the importer's country. The bidder needs only to find out the cost factors, such as guarantee fees, letter-of-credit costs, the name of the bank the bidder will be working with (the importer's bank most likely will already have arranged financing with a U.S. bank), and what other rules and regulations apply. Importers are usually very familiar with the rules of GSM-102, so the exporter is advised to seek information from the bank or the USDA concerning the operation. In these situations, the exporter has very little control over the operation and financing.

The program is supposed to be flexible, with no minimum transaction size, and accessible to any exporter. CCC maintains that if everything is in place, the exporter's application may be processed in as little as one week. This may be true, but typically it is merely a pro forma exercise if the commodity is already on the list of those that the CCC commonly works with (mostly basic crops) and is going to a country for which allocations are already established. A given country may make application to the CCC to request that the country and the commodities it requires be announced or listed. On the other hand, new country and new commodity requests will cause delays of several months.

GSM-103 (Intermediate Credit Guarantee Program)

The Intermediate Credit Guarantee Program, or GSM-103, was established in 1986 and is meant to replace former direct loan programs. It is now essentially a twin of GSM-102 except that it provides for terms of three to seven years, but with substantially higher guarantee fees because of the longer terms and because it covers sales to less stable countries. It is anticipated to have less than 10 percent of the activity of GSM-102, and overlaps the recipient eligibility parameters of the PL 480, Title I program. In contrast to the nearly $3 billion allocated purchases in GSM-102, GSM-103 has an allocation of only $167 million. GSM-103 is intended for friendly countries with major economic problems.

Public Law 480 (Agricultural Trade Development and Assistance Act of 1954— Food for Peace)

Public Law 480 (PL 480) is food aid on concessional terms to needy countries or even on a gift basis for emergency aid or starving nations in the case of Titles II and III. This is why the Agency for International Development (AID) is now charged with administration of Titles II and III, leaving FAS in charge of Title I. PL 480–donated food may be shipped from CCC surplus commodity inventories or procured by the U.S. government on a competitive bid basis from the private sector.

PL 480 is a government-to-government program over which the exporter has no control, but an exporter or agricultural enterprise can participate in the sales and export function. Sales are made by private business on a bid basis in response to public tenders in the United States. The prospective export supplier must obtain details of the program from FAS and apply to the PL 480 Operations Office to be named an eligible supplier. The exporter will then be advised in a timely fashion of such tender offers.

44

State and Other Organizations Offering Export Assistance

States across the nation are implementing the variety of export-support programs, realizing that their exporters and industries need more help than the federal government can provide. U.S. export support programs are still not all they might be, although many are better today thanks to the Trade Promotion Coordinating Committee, the National Export Strategy, and the information age. Of the major industrialized nations, the United States budgets the fewest dollars per capita to promote exports. The United Kingdom spent .28 cents per $1000 of GDP in 1992, an amount more than nine times the United States figure of .03 per $1000. France spent .18 cents; Germany, .04 cents; and Canada, .10 cents. Whether analyzed in gross national product (GNP) on exports in dollars, or by figures based on the population, the answer is the same. A more dramatic means of comparison was drawn in an article describing the overseas offices of the various states in the newsletter, *Clearinghouse on State International Policies*. It is stated that in Jakarta the US&FCS had but a few bookshelves serving as a product reference library for foreign buyers and distributors while Japan's commercial library in Jakarta was reported to be three stories high.[1] We should add this might also be true, in part, to U.S. suppliers' reluctance to part with as many catalogs and product literature as the Japanese firms, to say nothing of translating some of the product literature into a variety of languages.

There is no question that there have been serious budget problems, but budgets are balanced by economic growth and new jobs, and nothing has more leverage on these criteria than export sales. The problems become more acute as the budget becomes more restricted and the cost of the overseas posts grows as the relative value of the dollar falls. Higher priorities for integrated interagency export support set in 1993, at least in terms of planning, coordinating, and strategy, have helped even in the face of staff cuts. But it is not realistic today to expect that a significant dollar increase in federal funding can occur in this era of budget restraints, and a much worse scenario can be envisioned considering the mood in Congress. Perhaps they will eliminate the Department of Commerce and send the states a block grant!

As states construct their own programs to offset these problems, many of them are entering into the City/State partnership with Eximbank in Washington, D.C., as one means of leveraging the federal effort. Participation in the City/State Program varies widely as the abbreviated descriptions of activity for each of the 26 participating states listed in Appendix E would indicate. States should at least be able to expect the U.S. government to halt its real dollar decline on the best of the existing structures and programs. There are many signs that this expectation may not be justified, and states should be alert to see that their congressmen and senators are aware of the export-generated job creation factors and of proposed budget cuts that threaten to neutralize state level expenditures and efforts. In the last analysis, state efforts can be very helpful in bringing export support to the local level with a local product focus. But local support should always be viewed as a supplement to what is a federal responsibility in the face of international competition. It remains to be seen what the bottom line will be with the 104th Congress, for even though the Congress is very business-oriented, it has also shown some skill in "throwing out the baby with the bath water" in its haste to cut taxes and programs as it seeks to balance the budget. It bears watching by exporters and state administrators alike. The appropriation sub-committee was rather kind to the International Trade Administration of DOC, but other committees are insisting on dismantling it.

Current State Programs

In view of present conditions, it is fortunate that the states and lesser units of government have stepped in to help their local and regional industries in spite of budget problems of their own. Virtually all the states report some level of export support and a fair number have substantial and wide-ranging programs. In fact, a statistic developed around 1990 indicated that the combined state budgets for export promotion now exceed that of the DOC, and they may be forced to grow bigger still.

How-To and Trade Lead Support

In the area of general how-to export training, information, and proliferating export trade leads, almost every state has some sort of program. States have found that with a relatively modest budget they can act as cheerleaders in encouraging firms to export, provide start-up information and counseling, disseminate trade leads, and engage in low-cost trade promotion. Trade promotion is a key activity and includes a variety of undertakings, such as hosting overseas missions, presenting catalog shows, and facilitating arrangements for visiting foreign buyer delegations, especially at industry-specific trade events in the state. Another popular and helpful form of promotion is in joint trade show pavilions to keep costs to a minimum and make it easier to undertake a first overseas showing. Virtually all states shown as participating in Eximbank's City/State Program have some form of export consulting for new-to-export firms and many not so listed as well.

A survey by the *Clearinghouse on State International Policies* in 1994 found that among smaller businesses basic information and buyer contacts were the most used of state services and that 60 to 80 percent of the users found they had a positive impact. State agencies provided 38 percent of all export training to small exporters and were the source of 30 percent of all trade missions, according to the midsize businesses reporting. The survey conclusion was that the smaller the exporter, the more likely it was to respond to state programs.[2]

State Overseas Offices

A survey in 1992 by the same publication indicated that 40 states had significant permanent office representation totaling 137 offices in 18 countries. A 1993 survey by Mentor International indicated that 30 states have a total of 37 offices in Europe alone, with staffs ranging as high as ten. Not surprisingly, the greatest number were in Germany, followed by the United Kingdom, although the offices in the latter had by far the greatest average annual number of U.S. commercial visitors, at 300 per office.[3] Interestingly enough, many of the states that instituted overseas offices for "reverse investment" purposes soon found that the majority of their activity was related to export support and promotion. Unfortunately, state budgets and expenditures as well as attitudes in this area fluctuate with the legislative mood even more than with the federal budget roller coaster.

State Export Finance Programs

California's overall international program is often noted for being one of the most ambitious of the state international programs. It includes the Office of Export Development and the Export Finance Office (CEFO), both of which are now housed in the Trade and Commerce Agency, in addition to the state's overseas trade offices. At this time there are California offshore offices in seven countries, with an eighth planned for South Africa. There is yet another export program for California agriculture. The star of the state's program, however, seems to be the Export Finance Office (CEFO), which enjoys great popularity with the commerce, banking, and state government hierarchy. There is a noticeable tendency to emphasize the expanding Overseas Trade Offices and the Export Finance Office at the expense of the Office of Export Development. The Export Finance Office had its capital doubled in 1994 to $10 million, and further additions are being considered. This is somewhat understandable in view of CEFO passing the $1 billion mark in direct export sales support in 1994, as its activity rate continues to grow rapidly with 900 guarantees securing $215 million in working capital loans provided over the past nine years. CEFO is now authorized to, and regularly does, guarantee loans up to $750,000.

It may be true that few states have the potential for export volume that California enjoys (especially for export volume generated by relatively small high-tech companies). Nonetheless, there is an important lesson to be learned from California. If any given state's export finance program has sufficient capital, combined with adequate lending or guarantee authority, to interest the banking community, and it can also put together a small staff with transaction-based lending skills, *meaningful export sales can be generated for the state, which translates into jobs!*

A second lesson is that, given relatively equal funding and staff, export finance can probably account for as many or more export-related jobs as trade promotion is capable of creating. One advantage export finance programs have in terms of acceptance is that their results are more readily quantified than most other forms of export support.

Many of the smaller states are also very active. Maryland, for instance, offers export promotions, export finance, and foreign offices. Reviewing states with finance programs such as Maryland, there appears to be little or no correlation between an active program and the state's ranking in terms of export dollars. Although as many as 28 states claimed some form of finance program in 1991, many did not go forward for lack of funding or appropriate staffing. Other states stayed with the counseling function plus packaging for the Eximbank working-capital program, or simply settled for carrying the Eximbank Umbrella Policy for its small exporters. Besides California, there are several states with similar, active programs although on a smaller scale, including Florida, Kansas, Maryland, Minnesota, the Port of New York/New Jersey's XPort Trading Company. The states of Alaska, Connecticut, Georgia, Illinois, Utah, Virginia, and Wisconsin, as well as some we are not aware of, have a desire or plans to start or re-start a finance program in the foreseeable future; and still others can do so in a limited way as part of a domestic oriented small business guarantee or lending authority.

Support for export financing is still one of the newest and most aggressive of the programs that state governments are undertaking to enhance their regional international trade posture. Finance programs run from merely financial counseling and interfacing with the financial community, to aggressive transaction-based leveraged guarantees to direct loans. Between these extremes are programs for access to foreign credit insurance coverage through a state-administered Eximbank Umbrella Policy and loan packaging for Eximbank's Working-Capital Loan Guarantee program. Some of these programs are tied into state or local economic development funds, and some have special funding or collateral set-asides for the single purpose of supporting exporters. Since 1988, Eximbank has aggressively established outreach programs through the City/State program (see Appendix E). This program has been successful and has given some of the smaller participating states or cities an opportunity to become involved and to start financial support programs on a very low budget.

The present high level of interest on the part of most states in international trade is typically centered in the state department of commerce, often with considerable support from the executive branch. However, expect to find it located almost anywhere, as indicated by the list of participants in the City/State program and state activities in Appendix E. Your search should not end with this list, however, because almost any level of government potentially houses help for exporting. This includes counties, cities, port authorities, and free-trade zones in the area.

Begin by calling your state's commerce department for contacts. That agency will very likely know of other state agencies that may be involved and also perhaps of nonstate government agencies that may have programs.

City, County, Academic, and Port Authority Programs

After exploring what the state has to offer, you might still take the time to check with the cities or counties within which you operate. The help available from a wide variety of these agencies is too extensive to list, but here are some ideas to help you make sure you have investigated all possibilities. First, try the mayor's office, which will probably not only know about what the city has to offer but about most of the other government entities as well. If there is a world trade center near you, investigate its activities. The staff will also be knowledgeable about other programs in your area, which may include Centers for International Trade Development (CITDs), often situated in colleges or universities. Check also for local Small Business Development Centers (SBDCs) and Small Business Investment Companies that may include personnel with international skills.

In the case of counties, the help is most often related to agriculture or an especially vital industry in that area. Check with the county agriculture extension office and the county seat. Don't forget to ask one of the most obvious sources—your local international trade or export associations and organizations. Also check with the port authorities in the region. Some of these have extremely interesting programs. Mississippi's Port of Pascagoula offers free trade zones (FTZs) and matching funds for export marketing. Other ports have export management and trading operations to help you get started. Among these is XPORT, a trading company for smaller and new-to-export firms in the Port of New York/New Jersey. These two ports also sponsor trade missions and a wide variety of other export support and counseling activities. MASSPORT in Massachusetts provides selling aid to exporters through promotional assistance and its own foreign offices. PACRIMEX in Washington's Port of Bellingham is starting similar activities, as is the Detroit/Wayne County Port Authority.

The Future of State Programs

Overall, this level of state interest has not come too soon. The Small Business Administration (SBA) reported that 90,000 firms were exporting at the start of the decade and the number was expected to have doubled by the end of 1995.

According to a survey by Arthur Anderson's Enterprise Group and National Small Business United, of all medium- and small-sized businesses, 26 percent now export, compared to 20 percent in 1994 and 16 percent in 1993. Many of these new-to-export firms will be disappointed by unanticipated problems caused by a lack of advance research and/or not even knowing where to look for reliable answers. These firms will likely need help at the local level if they are to succeed in their ventures into international trade. It makes sense that states contribute to our national export effort by focusing on the special needs of their particular geographical, industrial, and economic communities. Some states have, or are looking into, opportunities for regional cooperation among themselves. The New England Governors' Conference approved creation of a Regional Export Trade Strategy in 1990 that resulted in the Tri-State Northeastern Regional Group, made up of Maine, New Hampshire, and Vermont. Several other regions are considering such a move. This makes sense, especially for smaller states and for specialized programs such as export financing, in which competition among states would not strain relationships since it applies to business already captured.

The National Association of State Development Agencies (NASDA), the Department of Commerce, Eximbank, the Small Business Administration, and others have cooperated to encourage state activity. NASDA is to be applauded for interest in international trade and for maintaining updated information on the activities of the various states.

In addition to the federal programs, it is apparent that the various states, counties, cities, world trade centers, trade associations, ports, universities, and colleges all have something to offer in the quest for sources of information and methods of assisting the expansion of profits and jobs through exports. And there are still more sources, as yet unmentioned, that the aggressive exporter will discover in the pursuit of a difficult solution. The contacts for many of these sources may be found in the appendices or in the specific programs described elsewhere in this book.

Beyond the less-than-obvious entities, with their varied sources of information only partly detailed in this book, such as AID, the numerous multilateral development banks, including the World Bank, and the UN, there are still more. Consider even the Organization of Economic Cooperation and Development (OECD) whose primary function is the task of governing interest rates and lending operations by the 24-member countries whose export credit agencies, similar to our Eximbank, extend or guarantee loans to other nations: They too, offer a wealth of publications covering foreign trade statistics and economic surveys that are available to the research-minded exporter at very modest costs. For more information on the OECD Catalog of Publications, call 202/785-6323.

With this much information available, one of your problems is to determine what is really necessary for good planning so that not too much time is wasted in research or in burdening oneself with too much help. It is our good fortune that the NTDB has brought so many of these sources together and is making them more accessible and timely. However, sometimes an adviser or consultant, whether public or private, may be of the greatest service to the prospective exporter by saving its client from too much help or information.

Endnotes

1. "State Overseas Offices," February–March 1994, *Clearinghouse on State International Policies,* Southern Policies Growth Board, Research Triangle Park, NC.

2. Kenan Institute of Private Enterprise, University of North Carolina, "Where Exporters Go for Advice," *Clearinghouse on State International Policies,* November–December 1994 issue, Southern Policies Growth Board, Research Triangle Park, NC.

3. "1992 State Overseas Offices Survey," *Clearinghouse on State International Policies,* February–March 1994 issue, Southern Policies Growth Board, Research Triangle Park, NC.

4. Levine, Jerry: *American States in Europe: A Summary of Findings,* 1993, Mentor International, 442 Post Street, San Francisco, CA.

Appendix A
Export 1-800 and DOC Country Desk Numbers

1-800 Numbers for Export Assistance

DOC Trade Information Center (TIC)

800-USA-TRADE. Operated by the U.S. Department of Commerce for information on export assistance offered by the 19 federal agencies comprising the Trade Promotion Coordinating Committee. Trade specialists advise exporters on how to locate and use government programs and guide them through the export process.

Small Business Foundation of America Export Opportunity Hotline

800/243-7232. Answers questions about getting started in exporting. Offers advice on product distribution; licensing and insurance; export financing; distribution options; export management firms; customs; currency exchange systems and travel requirements.

Small Business Administration (SBA)

800-U-ASK-SBA. The SBA answer desk is available for information on SBA export and financial assistance, as well as for minority programs.

Agency for International Development (AID)

800-USAID-4-U. This number at the Center of Trade and Investment Services provides country-specific information.

Export-Import Bank of the United States

800/424-5201. Provides information on Eximbank's financing programs, including the export credit insurance and working capital guarantee programs for small and midsize firms.

Overseas Private Investment Corporation (OPIC)

800-424-OPIC. OPIC has information on its programs to promote economic growth in developing countries through U.S. private investment in those countries.

Export Hotline

800-USA-XPORT. A corporate-sponsored, nationwide fax retrieval system providing international trade information for U.S. business.

Country Desk Numbers at the DOC International Economic Policy Unit

For countries not shown, call 800-USA-TRADE.

Argentina	482-1548
Australia	482-3647
Belgium	482-5373
Brazil	482-3871
Canada	482-3101
Chile	482-1548
China	482-3583
Denmark	482-3254
Egypt	482-4441
Finland	482-3254
France	482-8008
Germany	482-2841
Greece	482-3945
Guatemala	482-2527
Hong Kong	482-2462
India	482-2954
Indonesia	482-3875
Israel	482-4652
Italy	482-2177

Japan	482-2425
Jordan	482-1860
Korea	482-4957
Kuwait	482-1860
Malaysia	482-3875
Mexico	482-4464
Netherlands	482-5401
New Zealand	482-3647
NIS	482-4655
Norway	482-4414
Oman	482-5545
Pakistan	482-2954
Panama	482-2527
Portugal	482-3945
Qatar	482-5545
Russia	482-4655
Saudi Arabia	482-4652
Singapore	482-3875
South Africa	482-5148
Spain	482-4508
Sweden	482-4414
Switzerland	482-2920
Taiwan	482-4957
Thailand	482-3875
United Kingdom	482-3748
United Arab Emirates	482-5545
Venezuela	482-4303

Appendix B
American Chambers of Commerce Abroad

The following is a list of American chambers of commerce abroad. Address mail to The American Chamber of Commerce in [country].

Argentina
Avenida Leandro North Alem 1110,
  Piso 13
1101 Buenos Aires

Australia
Level 2, 41 Lower Fort Street
Sydney, New South Wales 2000
Level 1, 123 Lonsdale
Melbourne, Victoria 3000

Austria
Porzellangasse 35
A-1090 Vienna

Belgium
Avenue des Arts 50, Boite 5
B-1040 Brussels

Brazil
C.P. 916, Praca Pio X-15
20,040 Rio de Janeiro, RJ

Chile
Avenida Americo Vespucio Sur 80
9 Piso, 82 Correo 34
Santiago

China
G/F Great Wall Sheraton Hotel
North Donghuan Road
Beijing

Colombia
Calle 35, No. 6-16,
Apto. Aereo 8008
Bogota

Costa Rica
Aerocasilla, P.O. Box 025216
Dept. 1576
Miami, FL 33102

Czech & Slovak Republics
Karlovo Namesti 24
12080 Prague 2

Dominican Republic
P.O. Box 95-2
Santa Domingo

Ecuador
Edificio Multicentra 4P
La Nina Y Avda 6 de Diciembre
Quito

Egypt
P.O. Box 33
Zamalek, Cairo

El Salvador
87 Avenue North, #720
Apt. A, Col. Escalon
San Salvador

France
21, Avenue George V
F-75008 Paris

Germany
Rossmarkt 12, Postfach 100162
D-6000 Frankfurt

Greece
16 Kanari Street 3rd Floor
Athens 10674

Guam
P.O. Box 283
Agana 96910

Guatemala
12 Calle I-25, Zona 10
Edif. Giminis 10, Torre Norte
12 Nivel, Of. 1206
Guatemala

Honduras
Hotel Honduras Maya, Apto. 1838
Tegucigalpa

Hong Kong
1030 Swire House, Chater Road
Hong Kong

Hungary
Dozza Gyorgy ut. 84/A Rm 406
H-1064 Budapest

India
American Business Council
U-50 Hotel Hyatt Regency
New Dehli 110 066

Indonesia
The Landmark Center, Suite 2204
Jalan Jendral Sudirman I
Jakarta

Ireland
20 College Green
Dublin 2

Israel
35 Shaul Hamelech Boulevard
64927 Tel Aviv

Italy
Via Cantu 1
20123 Milano

Ivory Coast
01 B.P. 3394
Abidjan 01

Jamaica
The Wyndham Hotel
77 Knutsford Boulevard
Kingston 5

Japan
4-1-21 Toranomon
Minato-ku
Tokyo 105

Korea
Chosun Hotel, Room 307
Seoul

Malaysia
15.01 Lev 15th, Amoda
22 Jalan Imbi
55100 Kuala Lumpur

Mexico
P.O. Box 60326, Apdo. 113
Houston, Texas 77205

Morocco
18, Rue Colbert
Casablanca 01

Netherlands
Carnegieplein 5
2517KJ The Hague

New Zealand
P.O. Box 3408
Wellington

Nicaragua
Apdo. 202
Managua

Pakistan
GPO Box 1322
Karachi 74000

Panama
Apdo. 168, Estafa Balboa
Panama 1

Paraguay
Edif. El Faro Int'l P. #4
Asuncion

Peru
Av. Ricardo Palma 836
Miraflores, Lima 18

Philippines
P.O. Box 1578, MCC
Manila

Poland
Pac Powstancow Warszawy 1
PL 00950 Warsaw

Portugal
Rua de D. Estafania 155
Lisbon 1200

Saudi Arabia
American Businessmen's Group of Ryadh
P.O. Box 3050
Riyadh 11471

Singapore
Scotts Rd., #16-07 Shaw Centre
Singapore 0922

South Africa
P.O. Box 62280
Johannesburg

Spain
Padre Damian 23
28036 Madrid

Sri Lanka
210 Galle Road
Colombo 3

Sweden
Box 5512
114 85 Stockholm

Switzerland
Talacker 41
CH-8001 Zurich

Taiwan
P.O. Box 17-277
Taipei 104

Thailand
P.O. Box 11-1095
140 Wireless Rd.
Bangkok

Turkey
Fahri Gizdem Sokak 22/5
80280 Gayrettepe, Istanbul

United Arab Emirates
P.O. Box 9281
Dubai

United Kingdom
75 Brook Street
London W1Y 2EB

Uruguay
Casilla de Correo 809
Montevideo

Venezuela
Apartado 5181
1010-A Caracas

Appendix C
World Trade Centers at Home and Abroad

World Trade Centers in the United States

Arizona

World Trade Center Phoenix
201 North Central Avenue, #2700
Phoenix, AZ 85073
Tel 602/495-6480
Fax 602/253-9488

California

World Trade Center Irvine
1 Park Plaza, #150
Irvine, CA 92714
Tel 714/724-9822
Fax 714/752-8723

Greater Los Angeles World Trade Center
One World Trade Center, #295
Long Beach, CA 90831
Tel 310/495-7070
Fax 310/495-7071

Los Angeles World Trade Center
350 Figueroa Street, #172
Los Angeles, CA 90071
Tel 213/680-1888
Fax 213/680-1878

World Trade Center of Oxnard
300 Esplanade Drive, #1010
Oxnard, CA 93030
Tel 805/988-1406
Fax 805/988-1862

World Trade Center San Diego
1250 6th Avenue, #100
San Diego, CA 92101
Tel 619/685-1453
Fax 619/685-1460

World Trade Center of
  San Francisco
345 California Street, 7th Floor
San Francisco, CA 94104
Tel 415/392-2705
Fax 415/392-1710

Colorado

World Trade Center Denver
1625 Broadway, #680
Denver, CO 80202
Tel 303/592-5760
Fax 303/592-5228

Connecticut
World Trade Center Bridgeport
177 State Street, 4th Floor
Bridgeport, CT 06604
Tel 203/336-5353
Fax 203/331-9959

Delaware
World Trade Center Delaware
1207 King Street, P.O. Box 709
Wilmington, DE 19899
Tel 302/656-7905
Fax 302/656-1620

Florida
World Trade Center Fort Lauderdale
200 East Las Olas Boulevard, #100
Fort Lauderdale, FL 33301
Tel 305/761-9797
Fax 305/761-9990

Jacksonville World Trade Center
3 Independent Drive
Jacksonville, FL 32202
Tel 904/366-6658
Fax 904/353-5343

World Trade Center Miami
One World Trade Plaza
80 Southwest 8th Street, #1800
Miami, FL 33130
Tel 305/579-0064
Fax 305/536-7701

World Trade Center Orlando
105 East Robinson Street, #200
Orlando, FL 32801
Tel 407/649-1899
Fax 407/649-1486

World Trade Center Tampa Bay
800 Second Avenue South #340
St. Petersburg, FL 33701
Tel 813/822-2492
Fax 813/823-8128

Georgia
World Trade Center Atlanta
303 Peachtree Street Northeast #100
Atlanta, GA 30308
Tel 404/880-1550
Fax 404/880-1555

Hawaii
State of Hawaii World Trade Center
201 Merchant Street, #1510
Honolulu, HI 96804
Tel 808/587-2797
Fax 808/587-2790

Illinois
World Trade Center Chicago
The Merchandise Mart #929
200 World Trade Center
Chicago, IL 60654
Tel 312/467-0550
Fax 312/467-0615

Iowa
Iowa World Trade Center
3200 Ruan Center
666 Grand Avenue
Des Moines, IA 50309
Tel 515/245-2555
Fax 515/245-3878

Kansas
World Trade Center Wichita
350 West Douglas Avenue
Wichita, KS 67202
Tel 316/262-3232
Fax 316/262-3585

Kentucky
Kentucky World Trade Center
410 West Vine Street, #290
Lexington, KY 40507
Tel 606/258-3139
Fax 606/233-0658

Louisiana
World Trade Center of New Orleans
2 Canal Street, #2900
New Orleans, LA 70130
Tel 504/529-1601
Fax 504/529-1691

Maryland
World Trade Center Baltimore
The World Trade Center #1355
Baltimore, MD 21202
Tel 410/576-0022
Fax 410/576-0751

Michigan
World Trade Center Detroit/Windsor
1251 Fort Street
Trenton, MI 48183
Tel 313/965-6500
Fax 313/965-1525

Missouri
Greater Kansas City World Trade Center
2600 Commerce Tower
911 Main Street
Kansas City, MO 64105
Tel 816/221-2424
Fax 816/221-7440

World Trade Center St. Louis
121 South Meramec, #1111
St. Louis, MO 63105
Tel 314/854-6141
Fax 314/862-0102

New York
World Trade Center New York
Port Authority of New York and
 New Jersey
One World Trade Center #35 E
New York, NY 10048
Tel 212/435-8385
Fax 212/435-2810

World Trade Center Capital District
One Broadway Center, #750
Schenectady, NY 12305
Tel 518/393-7252
Fax 518/393-8687

Nevada
Nevada World Trade Center
P.O. Box 71961
Las Vegas, NV 89170
Tel 702/387-5581
Fax 702/386-4821

North Carolina
Research Triangle World Trade Center
2525 Meridian Parkway, #50
Durham, NC 27713
Tel 919/544-8969
Fax 919/544-8970

World Trade Center Wilmington
P.O. Box 330
Wilmington, NC 28402
Tel 910/762-2611
Fax 910/762-9765

Ohio
World Trade Center Cleveland
200 Tower City Center
50 Public Square
Cleveland, OH 44113
Tel 216/621-3300
Fax 216/621-4616

World Trade Center Columbus
37 North High Street
Columbus, OH 43215
Tel 614/225-6907
Fax 614/469-8250

Oregon
World Trade Center Portland
121 Southwest Salmon Street, #250
Portland, OR 97204
Tel 503/464-8888
Fax 503/464-8880

Rhode Island
World Trade Center Rhode Island
1 West Exchange Street
Providence, RI 02903
Tel 401/351-2701
Fax 401/421-8510

South Carolina
South Carolina World Trade Center
81 Mary Street, P.O. Box 975
Charleston, SC 29402
Tel 803/577-2510
Fax 803/723-4853

Greenville World Trade Center
315 Old Boiling Springs Road
Greer, SC 29650
Tel 803/297-8600
Fax 803/297-8606

Tennessee
World Trade Center Chattanooga
1001 Market Street
Chattanooga, TN 37327
Tel 615/752-4316
Fax 615/265-9751

World Trade Center Memphis
67 Madison Avenue, #1004
Memphis, TN 38103
Tel 901/521-0142
Fax 901/521-0143

Texas
Houston World Trade Assoc.
1200 Smith, #700
Houston, TX 77002
Tel 713/651-2229
Fax 713/651-2299

World Trade Center Rio Grande Valley
Neuhaus Tower, Suite 510
200 South Tenth Street
McAllen, TX 78501
Tel 210/686-1982
Fax 210/618-1982

World Trade Center San Antonio
118 Broadway
San Antonio, TX 78205
Tel 210/978-7600
Fax 210/978-7610

Virginia
World Trade Center Norfolk
600 World Trade Center
Norfolk, VA 23510
Tel 804/683-8000
Fax 804/683-8500

Washington
World Trade Center Seattle
1301 5th Avenue, #2400
Seattle, WA 98101
Tel 206/389-7301
Fax 206/624-5689

World Trade Center Tacoma
3600 Port of Tacoma Road, #309
Tacoma, WA 98424
Tel 206/383-9474
Fax 206/926-0384

Washington, D.C.
World Trade Center Washington DC
6801 Oxon Hill Road at PortAmerica
Oxon Hill, MD 20745
Tel 301/839-2477
Fax 301/839-7868

Wisconsin
Wisconsin World Trade Center
8401 Greenway Boulevard
Middleton, WI 53562
Tel 608/831-0666
FAx 608/831-6982

Wisconsin World Trade Center
424 E. Wisconsin Avenue
Milwaukee, WI 53202
Tel 414/274-3840
Fax 414/274-3846

World Trade Centers Abroad

Argentina	Buenos Aires
Aruba	Oranjestad
Australia	Brisbane, Melbourne, Sydney
Austria	Salzburg, Vienna
Bahrain	Manama
Belgium	Antwerp, Brussels, Ghent
Brazil	Rio de Janeiro, São Paulo
Bulgaria	Sofia
Canada	Edmonton, Halifax, Montreal, Ottawa, Quebec-Beauport, Vancouver
Chile	Santiago
China (PRC)	Beijing, Chengdu, Chongqing, Guangzhou, Nanjing, Shanghai, Shenyang, Shenzhen, Tianjin, Wuhan, Xian
Colombia	Bogota, Cali

Croatia	Rijeka, Split, Zagreb
Cuba	Havana
Cyprus	Nicosia
Czech Republic	Brno, Prague
Egypt	Cairo
Ecuador	Quito
Finland	Turku
France	Aix-les-Bains, Grenoble, Le Havre, Lille, Lyon, Marseille, Metz, Nantes, Paris, Strasbourg
Germany	Bremen, Cologne, Hamburg, Hannover, Leipzig, Rostock, Gelsenkirchen-Ruhr
Hong Kong	Kowloon
Hungary	Budapest
India	Bombay, Calcutta, New Dehli
Indonesia	Jakarta, Surabaya
Israel	Tel Aviv
Italy	Bari, Genoa, Milan
Ivory Coast	Abidjan
Japan	Osaka, Tokyo
Jordan	Amman
Korea	Seoul
Latvia	Riga
Malaysia	Kuala Lumpur
Mexico	Guadalajara, Mexico City
Morocco	Casablanca
The Netherlands	Amsterdam, Eindhoven, Rotterdam, Schiphol
Netherland Antilles	Curaçao
Nigeria	Lagos
Norway	Oslo
Pakistan	Karachi
Panama	Panama City
Peru	Lima
Philippines	Manila
Poland	Szczecin
Portugal	Lisbon, Porto
Russia	Moscow, Novosibirsk, St. Petersburg
Saudi Arabia	Jeddah
Singapore	Singapore
Slovenia	Ljubljana

South Africa	Johannesburg, Sandton
Spain	Barcelona, Bilbao, Madrid, Sevilla, Valencia
Sweden	Gothenburg, Jonkoping, Stockholm
Switzerland	Basel, Geneva, Lausanne, Lugano, Zurich
Taiwan	Taichung, Taipei
Thailand	Bangkok
Tunisia	Tunis
Turkey	Ankara, Istanbul
United Kingdom	Cardiff
United Arab Emirates	Dubai
Venezuela	Caracas
West Indies	Martinique, Guadeloupe

Appendix D
Eximbank Offices

Export-Import Bank of the United States
811 Vermont Avenue NW
Washington D.C. 20571
Export Financing Hotline: 800/424-5201

Contact the following divisions at above address or FAX 202/566-7524.

Public Affairs and Publications	Tel 202/566-4490
Marketing and Programs Development Division	Tel 202/566-8860
Export Insurance Division	Tel 202/566-8197

Eximbank Regional Offices

Chicago
19 South LaSalle Street, Suite 902
Chicago, IL 60603
Tel 312/641-1915
FAX 312/641-2292

Houston
88050 Dairy Ashford, Suite 585
Houston, TX 77077
Tel 713/589-8182
FAX 713/589-8184

Los Angeles
One World Trade Center, Suite 1670
Long Beach, CA 90831
Tel 310/980-4550
FAX 310/980-4561

Miami	80 Southwest 8th Street, Suite 1800 Miami, FL 33130 Tel 305/372-8540 FAX 305/372-5114
New York	6 World Trade Center New York, NY 10048 Tel 212/513-4292 FAX 212/513-4277

Appendix E
Eximbank City/State Programs

Contacts	Programs
Arkansas	
Development Finance Authority P.O. Box 8023 100 Main Street, Suite 200 Little Rock, AR 72203 Tel 501/682-5909 FAX 501/682-5939	Export trade finance counseling. Packaging of federal assistance program and EWCP
California	
Export Finance Office 6 Centerpointe Drive, Suite 760 La Palma, CA 90623 Tel 714/562-5519 FAX 714/562-5530	Umbrella Policy, pre- & post-shipment loan guarantees SBA packaging
Florida	
Department of Commerce 107 West Gaines, Suite 366 Tallahassee, FL 32399 Tel 904/922-8830 FAX 904/487-1407	EWCP packaging and insurance counseling
Georgia	
Dept of Industry, Trade and Tourism Trade Division 285 Peachtree Center Avenue, Suite 1100 Atlanta, GA 30303 Tel 404/656-4504 FAX 404/656-3567	Six-city network for counseling & packaging of EWCP, Eximbank insurance and SBA

Contacts	Programs
Hawaii	
International Business Center City Financial Tower 201 Merchant Street, Suite 1510 Honolulu, HI 96813 Tel 808/587-2797 FAX 808/587-2790	Export trade finance counseling. Packaging of Federal assistance programs & EWCP
Illinois	
Development Finance Authority 2 North LaSalle, Suite 980 Chicago, IL 60602 Tel 312/793-5586 FAX 312/793-6347	Trade finance structuring, fixed asset financing, EWCP packaging
Indiana	
Department of Commerce Indiana Finance Authority/Trade Division One North Cal Street, Suite 700 Indianapolis, IN 46204 Tel 317/233-4337 FAX 317/232-4146	Trade finance structuring, insurance counseling, EWCP packaging
Louisiana	
Economic Development Corporation 101 France Street Baton Rouge, LA 70802 Tel 504/342-5675 FAX 504/432-5389	Trade finance structuring, fixed asset financing, EWCP packaging
Maine	
Office of Business Development International Commerce Division State House Station 59 Augusta, ME 04333 Tel 207/287-2656 FAX 207/287-5701	EWCP packaging, insurance, and counseling
Maryland	
Industrial Development Bank Financing Authority The World Trade Center, 7th Floor 401 East Pratt Street Baltimore, MD 21202 Tel 410/333-8189 FAX 410/333-4302	Trade finance structuring, Eximbank Umbrella Policy, preparation of applications for all Eximbank programs
Massachusetts	
Industrial Finance Agency 75 Federal Street Boston, MA 02110 Tel 617/451-2477 FAX 617/451-3429	EWCP packaging
Michigan	
International Trade Authority Keesee & Associates 540 South Glenhurst Birmingham, MI 48009 Tel 313/540-8476 FAX 313/540-2250	Trade finance structuring, insurance, and EWCP packaging

Contacts	Programs
Nebraska Department of Economic Development Office of International Trade 301 Centennial Mall South Lincoln, NE 68509 Tel 402/471-4668 FAX 402/471-3778	Counseling, technical assistance, and financial packaging
Nevada Commission on Economic Development Howard Hughes Parkway, Suite 295 Las Vegas, NV 89158 Tel 702/486-7282 FAX 702/486-7284	Counseling, loan packaging, referral service for Eximbank programs
New Mexico Border Authority 505 South Main, Suite 145 Las Cruces, NM 88001 Tel 505/525-5622 FAX 505/525-5623	Counseling, loan packaging, referral service for Eximbank programs
New Hampshire Office of International Commerce 601 Spaulding Turnpike, Suite 29 Portsmouth, NH 03801 Tel 603/334-6074 FAX 603/334-6110	EWCP packaging, insurance, and counseling
Ohio Department of Development International Trade Division P.O. Box 1001 Columbus, OH 43266 Tel 614/466-5017 FAX 614/463-1540	Technical assistance agent/distributor searches, marketing information, EWCP packaging
Oklahoma Department of Commerce Export Finance Program 6601 Broadway, P.O. Box 26980 Oklahoma City, OK 73126 Tel 405/841-5259 FAX 405/841-5142	Trade financing, EWCP packing, Eximbank Umbrella Policy; foreign accounts receivable financing
Pennsylvania Department of Commerce Office of International Development 486 Forum Building Harrisburg, PA 17120 Tel 717/787-7190 FAX 717/234-4560	EWCP packaging
South Dakota Export Trade Administration Governor's Office of Economic Development 711 East Wells Avenue Pierre, SD 57501 Tel 605/773-5735 FAX 605/773-3256	Full-service export support; EWCP packaging and insurance counseling

Contracts	Programs
Texas	
Department of Commerce P.O. Box 12728 Austin, TX 78711 Tel 512/320-9662 FAX 512/320-9452	EWCP packaging
Vermont	
Department of Economic Development 109 State Street, Suite 200 Montpelier, VT 05609 Tel 802/828-3221 FAX 802/828-3258	EWCP packaging, counseling for export trade structuring
Virginia	
Small Business Fin. Authority 1021 East Cary Street, P.O. Box 798 Richmond, VA 23206 Tel 804/371-8255 FAX 804/225-3384	EWCP packaging, Eximbank Umbrella Policy, trade finance structuring
Washington	
Export Assistance Center 2001 6th Avenue, Suite 2100 Seattle, WA 98121 Tel 206/464-7123 FAX 206/587-4224	EWCP packaging, SBA packaging, trade finance structuring
West Virginia	
Economic Development Authority Building 6, Room 525, Capitol Complex Charleston, WV 25305 Tel: 304/558-3650 FAX 304/558-0206	EWCP packaging, Eximbank Umbrella Policy, trade finance counseling services
Puerto Rico	
Economic Development Bank Credit Analysis Division 437 Ponce de Leon Avenue, 15th Floor Hato Rey, Puerto Rico 00919-5009 Tel 809/766-4300 FAX 809/756-7875	EWCP packaging, SBA loans, insurance, trade finance counseling, consulting services

Appendix F
Umbrella Export Credit Insurance Policy Administrators

Public Sector

Arkansas
Development Finance Authority
1000 Main Street, #200
Little Rock, AR 72203
Tel 501/682-5900
Fax 501/682-5939

California
Export Finance Office
6 Centerpointe Drive #760
La Palma, CA 90623
Tel 714/562-5519
Fax 714/562-5530

Indiana
Development Finance Authority
One North Capital #320
Indianapolis, IN 46204
Tel 317/233-4337
Fax 317/232-4146

Maine
Finance Authority
83 Western Avenue
P.O. Box 949
Augusta, ME 04332
Tel 207/623-3263
Fax 207/623-0095

Maryland
Industrial Development Financing
  Authority
401 East Pratt Street
Baltimore, MD 21202
Tel 410/333-8189
Fax 410/333-4302

Massachusetts
Industrial Finance Agency
75 Federal Street
Boston, MA 02110
Tel 617/451-2477
Fax 617/451-3429

New Jersey
Economic Development Authority
Capital Place One - CN990
200 South Warren Street
Trenton, NJ 08625
Tel 609/292-0187
Fax 609/292-0368

New York
Xport Port
Authority Trading Co.
One World Trade Center
34th Floor
New York, NY 10048
Tel 212/435-3248
Fax 212/432-0297

Oklahoma
Department of Commerce
6601 Broadway
P.O. 26980
Oklahoma City, OK 73116
Tel 405/841-5146
Fax 405/841-5142

Virginia
Small Business Financing Authority
1201 East Carey Street
Richmond, VA 23206
Tel 804/371-8255
Fax 804/371-8185

Washington, D.C.
Office of International Development
District of Colombia Government
717 14th Street NW, Box 4, Suite 1100
Washington, DC 20005
Tel 202/727-1576
Fax 202/727-1588

Private Sector

California Factors and Finance
1609 West Magnolia Blvd.
Burbank, CA 91506
Tel 818/842-4891
Fax 818/842-8731

ICQ Network Inc.
1675 Broadway #2325
Denver, CO 80202
Tel 303/592-8990
Fax 303/592-8995

Commerce Bank of Kansas City
1000 Walnut Street
P.O. Box 419248
Kansas City, MO 64141
Tel 816/234-2608
Fax 816/234-2799

Altres Financial L.P.
1164 South Main Street
Salt Lake City, UT 84101
Tel 801/531-1116
Fax 801/531-1215

International Insurance Assoc.
8202 Florence Avenue, #200
Downey, CA 90240
Tel 213/771-2000
Fax 310/923-6354

Export Insurance Services
  P.O. Box 11602
  Atlanta, GA 30355
  Tel 404/237-3979
  Fax 404/237-9933

Boatmans First National
  Bank of Kansas City
  14 West 10th Street
  Kansas City, MO 64105
  Tel 816/691-7460
  Fax 816/691-7930

Appendix G
International Arbitration Organizations

American Arbitration Association
140 W. 51st Street
New York, NY 10020

London Court of International Arbitration
International Arbitration Centre
75 Cannon Street
London EC4N 5BH, England

Swiss Arbitration Association
P.O. Box 4182
CH-4002 Basel, Switzerland

Arbitration Institute of Stockholm
Chamber of Commerce
P.O. Box 16050
S-10322 Stockholm 16, Sweden

Hong Kong General Chamber of Commerce
Arbitration Committee
Swire House, 9th Floor
Charter Road
Hong Kong

Inter-American Commercial Arbitration Committee
1889 F Street, NW
Washington, D.C. 20006

International Chamber of Commerce
The ICC International Court of Arbitration
38, Cours Albert, 1er
75008 Paris, France

U.S. Council of the International Chamber of Commerce
1212 Avenue of the Americas
New York, NY 10036

Japan Commercial Arbitration Association
2-2 Marunouchi 3-chome, Chiyoda-ku
Tokyo, Japan

Netherlands Arbitration Institute
P.O. Box 22105
3003 DC Rotterdam, The Netherlands

Cairo Regional Centre for Commercial Arbitration
16 Ramses Street
Cairo, Egypt

Appendix H
Japanese Trading Companies and JETRO Offices

Major Japanese Trading Companies in Japan

Chori Co., Ltd
  2-4-7, Kawara-machi
  Chuo-ku, Osaka 541

Itochu Corp.
  4-1-3, Kyutaro-machi
  Chuo-ku, Oskaka 541

Kanematsu Corporation
  Seavans No., 1-2-1, Shibaura
  Minato-ku, Tokyo 105-05

Marubeni Corporation
  2-5-7, Honmachi
  Chuo-ku, Osaka 541-88

Mitsubishi Corporation
  2-6-3, Marunouchi, 2-chome
  Chiyoda-ku, Tokyo 100-86

Mitsui & Co. Ltd.
  1-2-1, Ote-machi
  Chiyoda-ku, Tokyo 100

Nichimen Co., Ltd.
  1-13-1, Kyobashi
  Chuo-ku, Tokyo 104

Nissho Iwai Corporation
  2-5-8, Imabashi
  Chuo-ku, Osaka 541

Okura & Co., Ltd.
  2-3-6, Ginza
  Chuo-ku, Tokyo 104

Sumitomo Corporation
  4-5-33, Kitahama
  Chuo-ku, Osaka 541

Tomen Corp.
  1-6-7, Kawara-machi
  Chuo-ku, Osaka 541

Toshoku Ltd.
  2-4-3, Nihombashi
  Muro-machi
  Chuo-ku, Tokyo 103

Toyota Tsusho Corp.
  4-7-23, Meieki
  Nakamura-ku, Nagoya 450

Sogo Shosha Committee of the Japan
  Foreign Trade Council Inc.
  World Trade Center Building, 2-4-1,
  Hamamatsucho
  Minato-ku, Tokyo 105

Major Japanese Trading Companies with Offices in the United States

Chori America Inc.
 One Penn Plaza
 New York, NY 10118

Itochu International Inc.
 335 Madison Avenue
 New York, NY 10017

Kanematsu (USA) Inc.
 114 West 47th Street
 New York, NY 10036

Marubeni America Corp.
 450 Lexington Avenue, 35th Floor
 New York, NY 10017

Mitsubishi International Corp.
 520 Madison Avenue
 New York, NY 10022

Mitsui & Co. (USA) Inc.
 200 Park Avenue
 New York, NY 10166

Nichimen America, Inc.
 1185 Avenue of the Americas
 New York, NY 10036

Nissho-Iwai America Corp.
 1211 Avenue of the Americas
 New York, NY 10036

Okura & Co. (America) Inc.
 101 East 52nd Street
 New York, NY 10022

Sumitomo Corp. of America
 345 Park Avenue
 New York, NY 10154

Tomen America Inc.
 1285 Avenue of the Americas
 New York, NY 10019

Toshoku America, Inc.
 780 Third Avenue
 New York, NY 10017

Toyota Tsusho America, Inc.
 350 Park Avenue
 New York, NY 10022

Japanese External Trade Organization (JETRO) Offices in the United States

JETRO New York
 1221 Avenue of the Americas
 44th Floor
 New York, NY 10020
 (212) 997-0400

JETRO San Francisco
 235 Pine Street, #1700
 San Francisco, CA 94104
 (415) 392-1333

JETRO Chicago
 401 N. Michigan Avenue, #660
 Chicago, IL 60611
 (312) 527-9000

JETRO Los Angeles
 725 S. Figueroa Street, #1890
 Los Angeles, CA 90017
 (213) 624-8855

JETRO Houston
 1221 McKinney
 One Houston Center, #2360
 Houston, TX 77010
 (713) 759-9595

JETRO Atlanta
 245 Peachtree Center Avenue, #2208
 Atlanta, GA 30303
 (404) 681-0600

JETRO Denver
 1200 17th Street, #1110
 Denver, CO 80202
 (303) 629-0404

Appendix I
Multilateral Development Banks

The World Bank
1818 H Street NW
Washington, D.C. 20434

Divisions:

International Bank for Reconstruction and Development (IBRD)
(project lending to creditworthy developing countries)

International Development Association (IDA)
(concessional terms to poor and less developed countries)

International Finance Corporation (IFC)
(support for private sector investment in developing countries)

European Bank for Reconstruction and Development
One Exchange Square, London EC2A 2EH, United Kingdom

Asian Development Bank
P.O. Box 789, 1099 Manila, Philippines

Japan Development Bank
9-1, Otemachi 1-chome, Chiyoda-ku, Tokyo 100, Japan

African Development Bank
P.O. Box 1387, Abidjan 01, Ivory Coast

Caribbean Development Bank
Wildey, P.O. Box 408, St. Michel, Barbados

Inter-American Development Bank
1300 New York Avenue NW, Washington, DC 20577

Appendix J
Public and Private Export-Related Organizations

U.S. Government and Quasi-Government Agencies

Agency for International Development
Center for Trade and Investment
Services
320 21st Street NW
Washington, DC 20523

Bureau of Export Administration (BXA)
Office of Export Licensing
HCH Building, Room 1099
Washington, DC 20230

Customs Service
1201 Constitution Avenue NW
Washington, DC 20229

Department of Agriculture
Foreign Agricultural Service
14th Street and Independence Avenue SW
Washington, DC 20250

Department of Commerce
14th Street and Constitution Avenue NW
Washington, DC 20230

Eastern European Business & Information
Center
Department of Commerce
ITA Room 5341 HCHB
Washington, DC 20230

Export Import Bank of the United States
811 Vermont Avenue NW
Washington, DC 20571

International Executive Service Corps
333 Ludlow
Stamford, CT 06902

Overseas Private Investment Corporation
1100 New York Avenue NW
Washington, DC 20527

Private Export Funding Corp. (PEFCO)
747 Third Avenue
New York, NY 10017

Small Business Administration
409 Third Street SW
Washington, DC 20416

Superintendent of Documents
U.S. Government Printing Office
Washington, DC 20402

U.S. Patent and Trademark Office
International Affairs
Box 4
Washington, DC 20231

U.S. Trade Representative
600 17th Street NW
Washington, DC 20506

International Trade Related Organizations

American Association of Exporters &
 Importers
11 West 42nd Street
New York, NY 10036

American Society of International Law
2223 Massachusetts Avenue NW
Washington, DC 20008

Bankers Association for Foreign Trade
1600 M Street NW, #7F
Washington, DC 20036

Chamber of Commerce of the United
 States
1615 H Street NW
Washington, DC 20062

Export Managers Association of Southern
 California
110 East 9th Street, #A-761
Los Angeles, CA 90079

FCIB-NACM Corporation
100 Wood Ave. So.
Metro Center One
Iselin, NJ 00830

Federation of International Trade
 Associations
1851 Alexander Bell Drive
Reston, VA 22091

FSC/DISC Association Inc.
FDR Station, P.O. Box 0748
New York, NY 10150

ICC Publishing Corp.
156 Fifth Avenue
New York, NY 10010

National Association of Export
 Companies (NEXCO)
P.O. Box 1330, Murray Hill Station
New York, NY 10156

National Association of State
 Development Agencies
444 Capitol Street NW, #345
Washington, DC 20001

National Council on International Trade
 & Documentation
350 Broadway, #205
New York, NY 10013

National Foreign Trade Council
1625 K Street NW
Washington, DC 20006

OECD Publications & Information Center
1750 Pennsylvania Avenue NW
Washington, DC 20006

Organization of Economic
 Cooperation & Development (OECD)
2001 L Street NW, #700
Washington, DC 20036

Small Business Foundation of America
1155 15th Street NW
Washington, DC 20005

U.S. Council of International Business
1212 Avenue of the Americas
New York, NY 10036

World Trade Centers Association
1 World Trade Center, 55th Floor
New York, NY 10048

World Trade Institute
1 World Trade Center, 55 West
New York, NY 10048

International Chamber of Commerce
38, Cours Albert
75008 Paris, France

Appendix K
Export Reference Books

Books on Export Marketing and International Trade

The Arthur Young International Business Guide, by Charles F. Valentine, John Wiley & Sons, New York, NY.

A Basic Guide to Exporting, Superintendent of Documents, U.S. Government Printing Office, Washington, DC 20402 (Stock No. 003-009-00315-6).

Building an Import/Export Business, by Kenneth D. Weiss, John Wiley & Sons, New York, NY.

Capitol Capital: Government Resources for High-Technology Companies, by William A. Delphos, Venture Publishing, 3000 K St. NW, #690, Washington, DC 20007.

Chase World Guide for Exporters, One World Trade Center, #4533, New York, NY 10048.

Developing Skills for International Trade, by JuDee Benton, TEAM Export, 3544 No. G Street, #222, Merced, CA 95340

Elements of Export Marketing, by John Stapleton, Woodhead-Faulkner, Dover, NH.

Expanding Markets Internationally: A Dynamic and Practical Approach, by William E. Drees, Instrument Society of America, P.O. Box 12277, Research Triangle Park, NC 27709.

Expanding Your Business Overseas, Deloitte Haskins & Sells, 1001 Pennsylvania Ave., NW, Washington, DC 20004.

The Export Operation: Putting the Pieces Together, Unz & Compnay, 190 Baldwin Ave., Jersey City, NJ 07306

Export Sales and Marketing Manual, by John R. Jagoe, Export USA Publications, 4141 Parklawn Ave., Minneapolis, MN 55435.

A Guide to Export Marketing, International Trade Institute, Inc., 5055 N. Main St., #270, Dayton, OH 45415.

A Guide to Expanding in the Global Market, By Ernst & Young, John Wiley & Sons, New York, NY.

The Export Advisor, International Business Publishers, 330 E. 71st St., New York, NY 10021.

Exporters' Guide to Federal Resources for Small Business, U.S. Government Printing Office, Superintendent of Documents, Washington, DC 20402.

Exportise (No. 2), The Small Business Foundation of America, 20 Park Plaza, #438, Boston, MA 02116.

Export Trading Company Guidebook, U.S. Government Printing Office Superintendent of Documents, Washington, DC 20402.

Foreign Commerce Handbook, Chamber of Commerce of the United States, 1615 H St. NW, Washington, DC 20062

Going Global: Strategies and Techniques for New Multinations, by Business International Corp., 215 Park Ave. S., New York, NY 10003

Getting to Yes, by Fisher and Ury, Houghton-Mifflin, New York, NY.

The Global Edge: How Your Company Can Win in the International Marketplace, by Sondra Snowdon, Simon & Schuster, New York, NY.

Going International, by Lewis Griggs and Lennie Copeland, Random House and New American Library, available from Copeland & Griggs Productions, 411 15th Ave., San Francisco, CA 94118.

Inside Washington: Government Resources for International Business, by William A. Delphos, Venture Publishing, 3000 K St. NW, #690, Washington, DC 20007.

The International Business Woman: A Guide to Success in the Global Marketplace, by Marlene L. Rossman, Greenwood Press, 88 Post Rd. W., Westport, CT 06881.

International Marketing Handbook, Gale Research Inc., Penobscot Bldg., Detroit, MI 48226.

Management Export Information Manual, Southern California District Export Counsel, 11777 San Vicente Blvd., Rm. 800, Los Angeles, CA 90040

Profitable Exporting: A Complete Guide to Marketing Your Products Abroad, by John S. Gordon and J. R. Arnold, John Wiley & Sons, New York, NY.

Books on Cultures, Customs, and Negotiations

The Art of Negotiation, by Gerald Nierenberg, Cornerstone Books, Division of Simon and Schuster, New York, NY.

Asian Markets, Washington Researchers Publishing, 2612 P St. NW, Washington, DC.

Big Business Blunders: Mistakes in Multinational Marketing, by David A. Ricks, Irwin Professional Publications, 1333 Burr Ridge Parkway, Burr Ridge, IL 60251.

Culture Grams, Center for International Studies, Brigham Young University Publications, 280 HRCB, Provo, UT 84602.

The Cultural Environment of International Business, by Vern Terpstra, South-Western Publishing, 7625 Empire Drive, Florence, KY 41042.

Do's and Taboos Around the World, by Roger Axtell, John Wiley & Sons, New York, NY (also available in video format).

Doing Business in and with Latin America: An Information Sourcebook, by E. Willard and Ruby Miller, Oryx Press, 2214 N. Central, Phoenix, AZ 85004.

Doing Business in...Series, Matthew Bender and Co., International Division, 1275 Broadway, Albany, NY 12204.

European Markets, Washington Researchers Publishing, 2612 P St. NW, Washington, DC.

Funding for Research, Study and Travel: Latin America and the Caribbean, by Karen Cantrell and Denise Wallen, The Oryx Press, 2214 N. Central, #103, Phoenix, AZ 85004.

Getting Your Yen's Worth: How to Negotiate with Japan, Inc., by Robert T. Moran, Gulf Publishing Co., P.O. Box 2608, Houston, TX.

How to Do Business with Russians, by Misha G. Knight, Greenwood Press, 88 Post Rd. W., Westport, CT 06881.

How to Do Business with the Japanese, by Mark Zimmerman, Random House, New York, NY 10022.

International Business Practices, U.S. Department of Commerce, International Trade Administration, U.S. Government Printing Office, Washington, DC 20402.

International Exporting Agreements, Matthew Bender & Co., 1275 Broadway, Albany, NY 12204.

National Negotiating Styles, edited by Binnendijk, Foreign Service Institute, U.S. Department of State, Washington, DC.

Negotiation, by Roy Lewicki and Joseph Litterer, Irwin Professional Publications, 1333 Burr Ridge Parkway, Burr Ridge, IL 60251.

Non-Manupulative Selling, by A. J. Allessandra, Prentice-Hall, Englewood Cliffs, NJ.

OPIC Country Information Kits, 1100 New York Ave., Washington, DC.

International Negotiation: A Cross-Cultural Perspective, by Glen Fisher, Intercultural Press, Yarmouth, ME.

Japanese Business Etiquette: A Practical Guide to Success with the Japanese, by Diana Rowland, Warner Books, New York, NY.

Managing Cultural Differences, by Philip R. Harris and Robert T. Moran, Gulf Publishing Company, P.O. Box 2608, Houston, TX.

Single European Market Reporter, by Baker and McKenzie, 1 Prudential Plaza, 130 E. Randolph Dr., Chicago, IL 60601.

The Traveler's Guide to Asian Customs and Manners, by Kevin Chambers, Simon & Schuster, New York, NY.

The Traveler's Guide to European Customs and Manners, by Elizabeth Devine & Nancy Braganti, Simon & Schuster, New York, NY.

The Traveler's Guide to Latin American Customs and Manners, by Elizabeth Devine & Nancy Braganti, St. Martin's Press, New York, NY.

Understanding Cultural Difference: German, French, and American, by Edward T. Hall and Mildred Reed Hall, Intercultural Press, Yarmouth, ME.

World-Class Negotiating: Dealmaking in the Global Marketplace, by Rebecca A. and Donald W. Hendon, John Wiley & Sons, New York, NY.

Books on Letters of Credit, Documentation, and Shipping

Export Documentation, International Trade Institute Inc., 5055 N. Main St., Dayton, OH 45415.

Export Documentation Handbook, Dun & Bradstreet International, 40 Old Bloomfield Ave., Mt. Lakes, NJ 07046.

Export Documentation and Procedures, Unz & Co., 190 Baldwin Ave., Jersey City, NJ 07306.

Export/Import Procedures and Documentation, by Thomas E. Johnson, AMACOM, Saranac Lake, NY.

Export Letters of Credit and Drafts, International Trade Institute Inc., 5055 N. Main St., Dayton, OH 45415.

Export Shipping Manual, Bureau of National Affairs, Distribution Center, 9435 Key West Ave., Rockville, MD 20850.

A Guide to Export Documentation, by Donald E. Ewert, International Trade Institute, 5055 N. Main St., Dayton, OH 45415.

Guide to Incoterms, International Chamber of Commerce, ICC Publishing Corp. 156 Fifth Ave., #820, New York, NY 10010.

Harmonized System Reference Library, Unz & Co., 190 Baldwin Ave., Jersey City, NJ 07306.

Incoterms 1990, ICC Publishing Inc., 156 Fifth Ave., New York, NY 10010.

Incoterms for Americans by Frank Reynolds, Int'l Projects Inc. Box 397, Holland, OH 45528.

Letters of Credit, Methods of Payment and Export Finance, Center for International Trade & Development, 4840 River Bend Rd., Boulder, CO 80301.

Ports of the World: A Guide to Cargo Loss Control, CIGNA, P.O. Box 7728, Philadelphia, PA 19101.

Treaties and International Documents Used in International Trade Law, ICC Publishing Inc., 156 Fifth Ave., New York, NY 10010.

Books on Trade Finance, Insurance, and Countertrade

Countertrade Guide for Exporters, Project and Export Policy Division, Department of Trade and Industry, 1-19, Victoria St., London SW10ET, England.

The Countertrade Handbook, by Dick Francis, Greenwood Press 88 Post Rd. W., Westport, CT 06881.

Countertrade: Practices, Strategies and Tactics, by C. G. Alexandaides and Barbara L. Bowers, John Wiley & Sons, New York, NY.

Export Financing: A Handbook of Sources and Techniques, Financial Executive Research Foundation, 10 Madison Ave., P.O. Box 1938, Morristown, NJ 07960.

Financing and Insuring Exports: A User's Guide to Eximbank and FCIA Programs, Export-Import Bank of the United States, User's Guide, 811 Vermont Ave., N.W., Washington, DC 20571.

The FMS Financial Management Manual, Publication No. DOD 7290.3M, DISAM, Bldg. 125, Area B, Wright Patterson Air Force Base, OH 45433.

Forfaiting: An Alternative Approach to Export Trade Finance, by Ian Guild and Rhodri Harris, Universe Books, 381 Park Ave. S., New York, NY 10016.

International Countertrade: A Guide for Managers and Executives, S/N 003-009-001309 Superintendent of Documents, P.O. Box 371954, Pittsburgh, PA 15250-7954

International Countertrade: Individual Country Practices, S/N 003-009-00614-7, Superintendent of Documents, P.O. Box 371954, Pittsburgh, PA 15250-7954.

The Fundamentals of Trade Finance: The Ins and Outs of Import-Export Financing, by Jane Kingman-Brundage and Susan A. Schulz, John Wiley & Sons, New York, NY.

Guide to Documentary Credit Operations, ICC Publishing Corp., 156 Fifth Ave., #820, New York, NY 10010.

International Finance Library, Unz & Co., 190 Baldwin Ave., Jersey City, NJ 07306.

Up Your Cash Flow, by Harvey Goldstein, Granville Publications, 10960 Wilshire Blvd., #826, Los Angeles, CA 90024.

Books on Research and Statistics

Demographic Yearbook, United Nations Publications, Room DC2-0853, New York, NY 10017.

Economic Outlook, Organization of Economic Cooperation and Development Publication, 2001 L St. NW, #700, Washington, DC 20036.

Findex: The Directory of Market Research Reports, Studies & Surveys, Cambridge Information Group, 7200 Wisconsin Ave., Bethesda, MD 20814.

Guide to Foreign Trade Statistics, U.S. Department of Commerce, Superintendent of Documents, U.S. Government Printing Office, Washington, DC 20402.

High-Tech Exporter's Sourcebook, by Land Grant, LGC Publishing, 11 Garden Place, Brooklyn, NY 11201.

How to Find Information on Foreign Firms, Washington Researchers Publishing, 2612 P St. NW, Washington, DC.

Inside Washington: The International Executive's Guide to Government Resources, by William A. Delphos, Venture Marketing Corp., 600 Watergate NW, #630, Dept. W, Washington, DC 20037.

International Trade Statistics Yearbook, United Nations Publications, Room DC2-0853, New York, NY 10017.

Security Assistance Management Manual, Publication No. DOD 5105.38M, DISAM, Bldg. 125, Area B, Wright Patterson Air Force Base, OH 45433.

UN Statistical Yearbook, 37th Edition, United Nations Publications, Room DC2-0853, New York, NY 10017.

UNESCO Statistical Yearbook, Unipub, 4611-F Assembly Dr., Lanham, MD 20706.

World Bank Atlas, The World Bank Publications Dept., 1818 H Street NW, Washington, DC 20433.

World Factbook, U.S. Government Printing Office, Superintendent of Documents, Washington, DC 20402.

World Trade Resources Guide, Gale Research Inc., Penoscot Blvd., Detroit, MI 48226.

Dictionaries, Directories, and Encyclopedias

Bergano's Register of International Importers, Bergano Book Co., P.O. Box 190, Fairfield, CT 06430.

Dictionary of International Finance, by Julian Walmsley, John Wiley & Sons, New York, NY.

Directory of European Retailers, Newman Books, 33 Vauxhall Bridge Road, London SW1 V2SS, England.

Directory of Leading U.S. Export Management Companies, Bergano Book Co., P.O. Box 190, Fairfield, CT 06430.

Dun & Bradstreet Exporter's Encyclopedia, 1 World Trade Center, #9069, New York, NY 10048.

The Export Yellow Pages, Delphos International, 3000 K Street NW, #690, Washington, DC 20007.

Exporters' Directory/U.S. Buying Guide, The Journal of Commerce, 445 Marshall St., Phillipsburg, NJ 08865-9984.

Exporters' Encyclopedia, Duns Marketing Service, 3 Sylvan Way, Parsippany, NJ 07054.

Foreign Sales Corporation Annual Directory, FSC/DISC-Tax Assoc., Inc., FDR Station, P.O. Box 0748, New York, NY 10150.

Manufacturers' Agents National Association, European Distributors, P.O. Box 3467, Laguna Hills, CA 92654.

Partners in Export Trade Directory, Superintendent of Documents, U.S. Government Printing Office, Washington, DC 20402.

Reference Book for World Traders, Croner Publications, Inc.,

Registry of Export Intermediaries, National Association of Export Companies, SPC Marketing Co., P.O. Box 364, Northport, NY 11768.

Trade Directories of the World, Croner Publications, Inc., 211-03 Jamaica Avenue, Queens Village, NY 11428.

Trade Shows Worldwide, Gale Research Inc., Penoscot Blvd., Detroit, MI 48226.

Trading Company Sourcebook, International Business Affairs Corp., 4938 Hampden Lane, Suite 364, Bethesda, MD 20814.

Appendix L
Export Periodicals, Magazines, and Publications

American Shipper
P.O. Box 4728
Jacksonville, FL 32201

Business America
Government Printing Office
Washington, DC 20402

Business International
Business International Corp.
215 Park Avenue South
New York, NY 10003

Countertrade Outlook
P.O. Box 7188
Fairfax Station, VA 22039

Eximbank Letter
International Business Affairs Corp.
4938 Hampden Lane, #364
Bethesda, MD 20814

The Exporter
Trade Data Reports, Inc.
34 West 37th Street
New York, NY 10018

Export Today
733 15th Street NW
Washington, DC 20005

Foreign Trade Magazine
6849 Old Dominion Drive, #200
McLean, VA 22101

Global Trade Magazine
North American Publishing Company
401 N. Broad Street
Philadelphia, PA 19108

International Business
P.O. Box 50286
Boulder, CO 80323

The International Economy
1050 Connecticut Avenue NW #1220
Washington, DC 20036

International Trade Reporter
Export Shipping Manual
The Bureau of National Affairs
1231 25th Street NW
Washington, DC 20037

Journal of Commerce
Two World Trade Center, 27th Floor
New York, NY 10048

Pacific Shipper
560 Mission, #601
San Francisco, CA 94105

Semiconductor International Magazine
1350 East Towhy Avenue
Des Plaines, IL 60018

Shipping Digest
Geyer-McAllister Publications
51 Madison Avenue
New York, NY 10010

Trade & Culture
7127 Hartford Road
Baltimore, MD 21234

Washington Export Letter
(Reports on Federal Export Programs)
International Business Affairs Corp.
4938 Hampden Lane, #364
Bethesda, MD 20814

World Trade
30 Broad Street
Denville, NJ 07834

Appendix M
Table of Measurement Conversion

Metric and English Equivalents

LINEAR MEASURE

English Unit	Metric Unit
1 inch =	25.4 millimeters
	2.54 centimeters
1 foot =	30.48 centimeters
	3.048 decimeters
	0.3048 meter
1 yard =	0.9144 meter
1 mile =	1609.3 meters
	1.6093 kilometers
0.03937 inch	= 1 millimeter
0.3937 inch	= 1 centimeter
3.937 inches	= 1 decimeter
39.37 inches	
3.2808 feet	= 1 meter
1.0936 yards	
3280.8 feet	
1093.6 yards	= 1 kilometer
0.62137 mile	

LIQUID MEASURE

English Unit	Metric Unit
1 fluid ounce =	29.573 milliliters
1 quart =	9.4635 deciliters
	0.94635 liter
1 gallon =	3.7854 liters
0.033814 fluid ounce	= 1 milliliter
3.3814 fluid ounces	= 1 deciliter
33.814 fluid ounces	
1.0567 quarts	= 1 liter
0.26417 gallon	

SQUARE MEASURE

English Unit	Metric Unit
1 square inch =	645.16 square millimeters
	6.4516 square centimeters
1 square foot =	929.03 square centimeters
	9.2903 square decimeters
	0.092903 square meter
1 square yard =	0.83613 square meter
1 square mile =	2.5900 square kilometers
0.0015500 square inch	= 1 square millimeter
0.15500 square inch	= 1 square centimeter
15.500 square inches	
0.10764 square foot	= 1 square decimeter
1.1960 square yards	= 1 square meter
0.38608 square mile	= 1 square kilometer

CUBIC MEASURE

English Unit	Metric Unit
1 cubic inch =	16.387 cubic centimeters
	0.016387 liter
1 cubic foot =	0.028317 cubic meter
1 cubic yard =	0.76455 cubic meter
1 cubic mile =	4.16818 cubic kilometers
0.061023 cubic inch	= 1 cubic centimeter
61.023 cubic inches	= 1 cubic decimeter
35.315 cubic feet	
1.3079 cubic yards	= 1 cubic meter
0.23990 cubic mile	= 1 cubic kilometer

WEIGHTS

English Unit	Metric Unit
1 grain	= 0.064799 gram
1 avoirdupois ounce	= 28.350 grams
1 troy ounce	= 31.103 grams
1 avoirdupois pound	= 0.45359 kilogram
1 troy pound	= 0.37324 kilogram
1 short ton (0.8929 long ton)	= 907.18 kilograms
	0.90718 metric ton
1 long ton (1.1200 short tons)	= 1016.0 kilograms
	1.0160 metric tons
15.432 grains	
0.035274 avoirdupois ounce	= 1 gram
0.032151 troy ounce	
2.2046 avoirdupois pounds	= 1 kilogram
0.98421 long ton	= 1 metric ton
1.1023 short tons	

Appendix N

Acronyms of Export Transactions and Documents

AWB	Air Waybill
B/A	Bankers' Acceptance
B/E	Bill of Exchange
B/L	Ocean bill of Lading
CBM	Cubic Meter
CAD	Cash against Documents
C&F	Cost & Freight
CFR	Cost & Freight
CIF	Cost, Insurance and Freight
CIP	Carriage and Insurance Paid To
CPT	Carriage Paid To
CWT	Hundred Weight
DAF	Delivered at Frontier
D/A	Documents against Acceptance
D/P	Documents against Presentation
DCL	Discretionary Credit Limit
DDU	Delivered Duty Unpaid
DDP	Delivered Duty Paid

DES	Delivered Ex Ship
DEQ	Delivered Ex Quay
ECCN	Export Control Commodity Number
EXW	Ex Works
ECU	European Currency Unit
E&OE	Errors & Omissions Excepted
FAS	Free Alongside
FCA	Free Carrier
FOB	Free on Board
FPA	Free of Particular Average
FTZ	Free Trade Zone
GSP	General System of Preferences
GA	General Average
HS	Harmonized System
HTSUSA	Harmonized Tariff Schedule of the United States
IVL	Individual Validated License
L/C	Letter of Credit
LCL	Less than Car (Container) Load
NTB	Non-Tariff Barrier
OCP	Overland Common Points
PHYTO	Phytosanitary Inspection Certificate
ROG	Receipt of Goods
S/D	Sight Draft
SBCL	Special Buyer Credit Limit
SED	Shipper's Export Declaration
SIC	Standard Industrial Classification
SLI	Shipper's Letter of Instruction
SITC	Standard Industrial Trade Classification
SL&C	Shipper's Load and Count
SR&CC	Strikes, Riots, and Civil Commotion
SS	Steamship
TSUSA	Tariff Schedules of the U.S. Annotated
T/T	Telegraphic Transfer
TIB	Temporary Import Under Bond
TRC	Terminal Receiving Charges
VAT	Value Added Tax

Appendix O

Acronyms of Export Organizations and Programs

AAA	American Arbitration Association
ABC	American Business Center
ACE	Active Corps of Executives (SBA)
ADB	Asian Development Bank
ADS	Agent/Distributor Service (DOC)
AFDB	African Development Bank
AID	Agency for International Development
ALADI	Latin American Integration Association
AmCham	American Chamber of Commerce
ANCOM	Andean Common Market
ANSI	American National Standards Institute
ASEAN	Association of South-East Asian Nations
BIDCO	Business and Industrial Development Company
BISNIS	Business Information Service for the Newly Independent States (DOC)
BXA	Bureau of Export Administration
C&MP	Commodity & Marketing Programs (FAS)

CACM	Central American Common Market
CARICOM	Carribbean Common Market
CBERA	Carribbean Basin Economic Recovery Act
CCC	Commodity Control Corporation (USDA)
CCL	Commodity Control List (BXA)
CDB	Caribbean Development Bank
CEN	European Committee for Standardization
DEC	District Export Council (DOC)
DOC	Department of Commerce
DOD	Department of Defense
EAR	Export Administration Regulations (BXA)
EBB	Economic Bulletin Board (DOC)
ECU	European Currency Unit
EU	European Union
EEBIC	Eastern Europe Business Information Center (DOC)
EFTA	European Free Trade Association
ELAN	Export Legal Assistance Network
EMC	Export Management Company
EMS	European Monetary System
EPA	Environmental Protection Administration
ETC	Export Trading Company
EXIM	Export-Import Bank of the U.S. (Eximbank)
FAS	Foreign Agricultural Service (USDA)
FCPA	Foreign Corrupt Practices Act
FDA	Food and Drug Administration
FSC	Foreign Sales Corporation
FTI	Foreign Traders Index (DOC)
GATT	General Agreement on Tariffs & Trade
GPO	Government Printing Office
GSP	General System of Preferences
IATA	International Air Transport Association
IBRD	International Bank for Reconstruction & Development
ICD	International Cooperation and Development
IDA	International Development Agency
IDB	Inter-American Development Bank
IFC	International Finance Corporation
IMF	International Monetary Fund
ISO	International Organization for Standardization

ITA	International Trade Administration (DOC)
JEIC	Japan Export Information Center
JETRO	Japanese External Trade Organization
LAFTA	Latin American Free Trade Association
LDC	Less Developed Country
LIBOR	London Interbank Offer Rate
MDB	Multilateral Development Bank
MDBO	Multilateral Development Bank Operations (DOC)
MDCP	Market Development Cooperator Program (DOC, FAS)
MFN	Most-Favored Nation Tariff Status
MTN	Multilateral Trade Negotiations
NASDA	National Association of State Development Agencies
NATO	North Atlantic Treaty Organization
NTDB	National Trade Data Bank
NTIS	National Technical Information Service
OAS	Organization of American States
OECD	Organization for Economic Cooperation & Development
OIMP	Office of International Major Projects (DOC)
OMA	Office of Multilateral Affairs (DOC)
OPIC	Overseas Private Investment Corporation
PEFCO	Private Export Funding Corp.
SBA	Small Business Administration
SBDC	Small Business Development Center
SBIC	Small Business Investment Company
SCORE	Service Corps of Retired Executives
SWIFT	Society for Worldwide Interbank Financial Transactions
TAPO	Trade Assistance & Promotion Office (FAS)
TDA	Trade and Development Agency
TDS	Trade Data Services (Census)
TPCC	Trade Promotion Coordinating Committee
TOP	Trade Opportunities Program
UN	United Nations
UNCITRAL	UN Commission on International Trade Law
UNCLOS	UN Conference on the Law of the Sea
UNCTAD	UN Conference on Trade and Development
UNESCO	UN Educational, Scientific & Cultural Organization
UNIDO	UN Industrial Development Organization
US&FCS	U.S. & Foreign Commercial Service (DOC)

USEAC	U.S. Export Assistance Center
USDA	U.S. Department of Agriculture
USTR	U.S. Trade Representative
USTTA	U.S. Travel & Tourism Administration
WTC	World Trade Center
WTDR	World Trade Directory Report (DOC)

Sample Agreement between Manufacturer/ Supplier and EMC/ETC*

The following is a sample agreement made between the manufacturer/supplier and the EMC/ETC.

THIS AGREEMENT, entered into this _____ day of _____, 19____, by and between _____, hereinafter called SUPPLIER, and _____, hereinafter called EMC (Export Management Co.).

WITNESSETH:
WHEREAS, EMC believes it can adequately sell and distribute the products of the SUPPLIER in the territories of the world hereinafter set forth, these PRODUCTS at the present time specifically include: _____

---

*Wells, L. Fargo, and Karin Dulat, *Exporting: From Start to Finance,* 2d ed. (New York: Liberty/McGraw-Hill, 1991). Wells International P.O. Box 189, Pearblossom, CA 93553; Tel 805/944-2146; FAX: 805/944-0449.

as detailed in the current Supplier catalog/price list attached to this agreement as Appendix A, and;

WHEREAS, the SUPPLIER desires to sell its products in the territories hereinafter set forth and represents itself to be capable of delivery to the EMC quantities of the products according to terms, delivery times, conditions and prices set forth on the current price sheets and/or catalogs attached hereto, dated ——————, being subject to change as described in paragraph 8 below.

NOW, THEREFORE, in consideration of the above and each and all of the terms and provisions hereinafter contained, it is agreed as follows:

1. EMC shall have the exclusive right to sell above specified PRODUCTS of the SUPPLIER in the following areas: ————————————————————
——
——

   hereinafter referred to as the foreign TERRITORY. Merchandise sold to military posts in these same areas shall [shall not] be included as part of said foreign TERRITORY.

2. SUPPLIER grants EMC authority to appoint representatives or distributors for the sale of the PRODUCTS in the TERRITORY, but such representatives or distributors shall be subject to all limitations of the EMC set forth herein.

3. SUPPLIER agrees that all inquiries, orders, communications, and leads of any kind, referring to sales to be made directly or indirectly, to or for the foreign TERRITORY, shall be immediately referred by the SUPPLIER to the EMC.

4. SUPPLIER agrees to supply EMC with sufficient samples, catalogs, price lists, technical data, etc. which are required to suitably promote the PRODUCTS in the TERRITORY, and subject only to the discretion of the SUPPLIER, will also provide reasonable advertising support to promote the PRODUCT. This shall include an advertising rebate of ——% of a given export customer's net purchase, provided the customer supplies verified media billing and tear sheets. All literature hereinafter published by the SUPPLIER intended for overseas distribution in the foreign TERRITORIES shall display the following ——————(EMC)——————, Exclusive Distributor.

5. SUPPLIER's selling price to EMC will be the lowest price given to wholesalers, that price being presently retail less ——%, less ——%, and in addition EMC will receive a proportionate percentage of any present or future quantity and special promotion discounts. Sales samples will be furnished at the lowest regular wholesale price less ——%. EMC will keep special price structures as confidential information. Export selling prices shall be established at the discretion of EMC, and said selling prices will be regularly disclosed to the supplier by EMC.

[ALTERNATIVELY: EMC shall be compensated on the basis of a percentage commission of _____% of the negotiated exfactory price of the PRODUCT. The EMC commission shall be due and payable _____ days following SUPPLIER's receipt of clean shipping documents.]

6. EMC assumes full credit responsibility on all orders submitted by EMC to SUPPLIER or on orders received by the SUPPLIER and approved by EMC in writing. EMC may extend to the customers whatever terms of payment, which at EMC's discretion, are necessary and advisable to obtain orders. SUPPLIER shall not be at risk for such accounts, nor bear any of the costs of financing or granting of extended terms of payment to any such customers. EMC shall pay SUPPLIER in accordance with SUPPLIER's terms of _____ , plus _____ extra days.

    [ALTERNATIVELY: SUPPLIER assumes full credit responsibility and risk for all orders submitted by the EMC to the SUPPLIER subject to written approval given to the EMC by the SUPPLIER after appropriate analysis of the customer's creditworthiness. EMC shall cooperate by providing whatever customer information might be available directly from the customer or associates. It shall be the responsibility of the SUPPLIER to request and pay for any third-party credit information desired, such as credit reports or credit ratings. In the case of letters of credit, the EMC shall lend its best efforts to assist the SUPPLIER in successful handling and negotiation of same.]

7. In addition to active Independent Export Management, EMC will be responsible for the preparation of all export documentation, including consular papers, customs declarations, ocean bills of lading, airway bills of lading, pro forma invoices, and similar documents. EMC will also be responsible for airfreight and marine insurance, overseas billing and collection, staff travel, overseas postage, communication charges, and any other routine matters related to foreign trade not otherwise agreed upon herein.

8. SUPPLIER shall have the right to increase base prices at its own discretion, so long as consistent with the price changes in the domestic market. However, SUPPLIER shall, before such increased prices become effective, give to EMC a minimum of __90__ days notice of proposed price increase, or when applicable, notice of availability of new products or modifications of existing products and prices. Such notices shall be sent by registered mail, return receipt requested. Where firm quotations have been given by EMC and accepted by EMC's customers subject to the above, and where EMC has firm order but the necessary export formalities (such as obtaining of the import license, opening of letter credit, etc.) have not been completed, the order will be honored at quoted price for a period up to __90__ days from date of quotation.

9. SUPPLIER agrees within reasonable limits to extend to export sales the same warranty covering their merchandise as is extended in the domestic market. Details of the current warranty, return or exchange understandings; together with any necessary modifications recognizing the practical complications of foreign sales, such as transportation, customs procedures and duties; are made apart of this agreement by attached Appendix B.

10. SUPPLIER agrees that EMC has exclusive power to represent the SUPPLIER in all licensing agreements in the areas covered by this agreement and agrees to refer all inquiries regarding such licensing agreements to EMC. The term *license* is understood to include—but not necessarily be limited to—manufacturing, patent, or other franchise rights in the foreign territory or territories. SUPPLIER shall pay EMC an amount equal to _15%_ of the payment made to SUPPLIER within 30 days after SUPPLIER has received payment from the foreign licensee, patentee of franchise holder. It is understood EMC shall not initiate or conclude licensing agreements without the express written consent of SUPPLIER.

11. SUPPLIER agrees to indemnify and hold EMC and its customers harmless against any losses, expenses, or damages incurred or suffered by reason of any infringement or alleged infringement by SUPPLIER of patent or trademark rights of others. In addition, the SUPPLIER agrees to hold EMC harmless against any losses, expenses, or damages brought about by any third-party suits for products or other liability.

12. This agreement shall supersede all prior agreements, may not be modified except in writing, and shall be construed under the laws of the State of California.

13. This agreement shall remain in effect for an initial period of _____ year(s) from date of signing, and unless cancelled in accordance with the provisions set forth in paragraph 14, shall continue in full force and effect for a period of _____ year(s), and thereafter shall renew automatically on a year-to-year basis until cancelled or renegotiated in accordance with paragraph 14.

14. Cancellation may be accomplished by either party giving written notice to the other no less than 90 days prior to the next termination date, to be effective as of said termination date. In that event, SUPPLIER agrees to fill all orders from EMC which might be forwarded for 90 days following termination of this agreement. Following termination by SUPPLIER, EMC shall continue to receive commission for the remaining term of any license then in effect or subsequently consummated for which EMC was in negotiation at time of cancellation. However, in this event, EMC is obliged to continue to perform all its responsibilities relative to servicing such licenses at the option of licensor.

15. This agreement shall be binding on all successors to the principals named herein, subject only to the written consent of the SUPPLIER in the case of a sale of the majority of the EMC firm to a third party.

16. In the event of any dispute hereunder, both parties agree to arbitration in _____ under the rules and auspices of the American Arbitration Association.

17. The spirit of this agreement is that the two parties are to cooperate to the fullest extent in furthering their mutual interest.

18. Whenever, by this agreement, any notice shall be required to be given to either party, such notice shall be addressed to such party at the following address, or at such other address as may be provided in the future.

IN WITNESS WHEREOF, the parties hereto have set their hands and seals, executing this document in duplicate this _____ day of _____, 19_____ .

By _____ By _____

Appendix Q
Sample Distribution Agreement*

The following is a sample of a distribution agreement between a U.S. Manufacturer or EMC and a foreign distributor. (This format was used for nontechnical consumer goods that did not require post sales service.)

THIS AGREEMENT, made this _____ day of _____, 199 _____, between _____ _____, hereinafter referred to as the Company, and _____, hereinafter referred to as the Distributor.

WITNESSETH: In consideration of the mutual covenants hereinafter contained and for the purpose of promoting the sale within _____, hereinafter referred to as the Territory, of (general description and/or brand name of product), _____

_____

hereinafter referred to as the Product as detailed in the price lists and catalogs issued by the Company and attached hereto as Appendix A, it is agreed:

SECTION 1. The Company will, during the term of this agreement, sell to the Distributor and the Distributor will purchase from the Company the product to be resold by the Distributor in the Territory. The Distributor shall devote its best

*Wells, L. Fargo, and Karin Dulat, *Exporting: From Start to Finance,* 2d ed. (New York: McGraw-Hill, 1991). Wells International, P.O. Box 189, Pearblossom, CA 93553; Tel 805/944-2146; FAX: 805/944-0449.

efforts for the adequate exploitation and sale of the Product within the Territory and shall maintain an organization sufficient therefor. It is understood that during the term of this agreement, the Distributor is to be the sole distributor for the Product in the Territory and all inquiries received by the Company for the Product will be promptly referred to the Distributor.

SECTION 2. The Distributor shall not buy, sell, or negotiate for the sale of (1) the Product for use outside of the territory,

[NOTE: Obtain legal advice on above if an EC country.]

nor (2) the product of other manufacturers that may directly compete with that of the Company without first obtaining the teletransmitted or written consent of the Company.

SECTION 3. The Company shall sell the Product to the Distributor at the prices listed on the product price sheets and catalogs currently distributed by the Company from time to time, less the trade discounts as indicated and authorized therein.

[From the resulting net Ex Works price an additional basic distributor discount of _____% shall be applied.]

Said trade discounts are indicated in Appendix A of this agreement. Samples will be provided at discounts from the wholesale cost as further indicated in Appendix A of this agreement. Any Product not included in said price sheets or catalogs shall be the subject of special written or teletransmitted quotation by the Company, on request.

SECTION 4. The Distributor shall promptly advise the Company whenever special prices, shipping promises, terms, or other conditions are required to secure business not otherwise obtainable. In such cases, all elements relating thereto shall be agreed to in writing or by teletransmission by the Company and Distributor before the final closing of the order and shall not be used to establish a precedent.

SECTION 5. Unless otherwise authorized by the Company, all prices to the Distributor shall be based on the ICC Incoterms (1990), FCA (Free Carrier)...[named freight forwarder or other carrier agent acceptable to Distributor and/or Company].

[ALTERNATIVELY, if shipment by ocean is the norm, consider FOB...(named port), which would normally imply using Company's own freight forwarder to place the goods on board at the Company's expense.]

Shipments requiring air freight handling may be surcharged to the Distributor for the cost in excess of normal overland freight costs. CIF quotations and pro forma invoices for special circumstances are available upon request when indications of order quantities are received from the Distributor. For regular operations, the Distributor will provide accurate cube and weight specifications for standard product packs.

SECTION 6. The Company may change or withdraw its prices and/or trade discounts consistent with its domestic price changes at any time by teletransmission or written notice. If prior to the receipt of notice of any such change or withdrawal, the Distributor shall have made offerings based on the former price lists, then the Company will accept orders from the Distributor in fulfillment of such tenders, provided such orders are for immediate shipment as available and are received by the Company within _60_ days (1) after the date of any special quotations, or (2) after the date of any notice of a change or withdrawal of any such listed prices or discounts; except that the Company reserves the right to make special quotations binding for a period less than _60_ days, but in such event will so advise the Distributor at the time of making said special quotations.

[NOTE: In the event that this is a distribution agreement between an EMC and the foreign Distributor, the following paragraph #7 may require modification.]

SECTION 7. The Company guarantees the product to have the quality, capacity, ingredients, performance, [etc.] and serve the purposes stated in the Company price lists and catalogs, or as submitted in special written quotations, but the Distributor shall assume all responsibility with regard to the sufficiency and suitability of said Product for actual requirements in each instance. The Company assumes no contingent liability for failure of the Product to meet any such Distributor guarantees or assurances, stated or implied. All products are carefully inspected and tested during or upon completion of manufacture, but any special tests required by the Distributor may be charged for by the Company at cost.

[NOTE: In the event that this is a distribution agreement entered into by an EMC, it may be necessary to add the following Section 8 for the protection of the EMC.]

SECTION 8. The EMC hereby states that all rights extended by the EMC under this agreement are subject to its continuing appointment by the Company herein stated as exclusive export manager for the described Territory and, in the event of cancellation of such appointment by the producer, the obligations of the EMC relative to that product will terminate effective with the date of such termination, and that portion of this agreement will become null and void except as to any sums then owed by either party to the other. However, it is understood that to the extent this clause invalidates any portion of this agreement, the surviving portion will remain in full force and effect.

SECTION 9. All orders shall be payable in U.S. currency under irrevocable, sight letter of credit payment terms payable at the counters of a United States bank; or alternative terms mutually agreed upon by the Company and the Distributor.

SECTION 10. The Company may take such steps as it considers desirable to promote the sale of the Product in the Territory, including the right at its option to send Company representatives to spend time in the Territory in cooperation with the Distributor and the Distributor's representatives. Adequate advance notice of such actions will be provided by the Company to the Distributor.

SECTION 11. The Company shall not be responsible or liable for any loss, damage, detention, or delay caused by fire, strike, civil or military authority, insurrection or riot, common carrier embargoes, lockout, tempest, accident, delay in delivery of the Product by other parties, or by any other cause that is unavoidable or beyond its reasonable control; nor in any event for consequential damages.

SECTION 12. If the Distributor delays the shipment of any order that the Company has completed for or on its behalf, payment shall be made therefore by the Distributor as though shipment had been made, whereupon the Product will be marked as the property of the Distributor who shall pay to the Company from time to time all storage and insurance charges thereon, while such product is in the Company's possession.

SECTION 13. The Distributor shall not act as the agent for the Company under this agreement, nor shall the Distributor have any right or power hereunder to act for or to bind the Company in any respect or to pledge its credit.

SECTION 14. No licenses are granted or implied by this agreement under any patents or trademarks owned or controlled by the Company or under which the Company has any rights, except the right to sell and use the Product furnished by the Company. No rights to manufacture are granted by this agreement.

SECTION 15. It is understood by both parties that maintaining certain minimum levels of valid order activity is of the essence to this agreement and that these minimum standards are set forth in detail in Appendix B of this agreement. Therefore, it is one of the conditions for the renewal of this agreement that acceptable orders for the Product for the first term or the second term, as may be applicable, of the agreement have been tendered to the Company in sufficient unit quantity to meet those standards set forth in Appendix B of this agreement. Thereafter, in respect to future agreement renewals, minimum acceptable volumes will be mutually agreed upon, based on sales history and reasonable growth projections, but under no circumstance shall they be less than 75 percent of sales for the preceding one-year term.

SECTION 16. This agreement shall be in full force and effect from the _____ day of _____, 199 _____,

> [or, if not already in the hands of the Company, then from receipt of the agreed upon, valid opening order for the Product of no less than US$ _____ accompanied by an acceptable, irrevocable letter of credit at sight according to terms of the initial purchase order and confirmed by the company as payment in full for said order,]

until the _____ day of _____, 199_____, and thereafter may be renewed by mutual consent under the same terms and conditions, unless alternate conditions are set forth according to Appendix B, for _____ additional term(s) of_____ year(s) each, continuing until the _____ day of _____, 199_____; providing all the conditions of this agreement are met, including satisfaction in full of all accounts due and payable. The Distributor must give written notice of the request for renewal ninety (90) days in advance of any given term or forfeit the right to renewal under the same terms and conditions.

SECTION 17. If either party shall become insolvent, or if any petition in bankruptcy shall be filed by or against it, or if a receiver or trustee shall be appointed for any part or all of its property, then this agreement may be terminated by the other party upon written notice of its intention to terminate the same on a day to be specified not less than 5 days after the date when said notice is given.

SECTION 18. The rights conferred on the Distributor by this agreement are not assignable or transferable without the written consent of the Company.

SECTION 19. In the event of any dispute between the parties hereto in any way arising or growing out of this agreement, the same shall be referred to three arbitrators, one to be appointed by the Distributor, one to be appointed by the Company, and a third to be mutually agreed upon by the two arbitrators so appointed.

> [NOTE: As a cost consideration explained in Chapter 24, this clause might also state that: "*In the case of disputes involving less than $_____, a sole arbitrator will be appointed by the   (arbitration group)   which arbitrator must be acceptable to both parties.*"]

The arbitration will be conducted under the rules of the <u>American Arbitration Association (AAA) of New York.</u> The decision of a majority of the three arbitrators, including the apportionment of the expenses of the arbitration, shall be final and binding upon the parties hereto. The meeting of arbitrators shall be held in the City of _____ unless it shall be mutually agreed to hold such meeting elsewhere.

> [The arbitration group selected will provide its own model clause to replace the above sample.]

SECTION 20. This agreement shall be construed as having been made in and under the laws of the State of _____ in the United States of America, and shall be subject to the construction placed upon it by the courts of _____.

> [In the event the distributor is also in a country that is a signatory to the Vienna Convention (CISG), as explained in Chapter 24, the Convention code shall become the law governing the contract in any state and jurisdiction. In the event the parties should prefer to avoid having the laws set forth by the Convention apply, they can opt out of the Convention by a statement such as the following: "*The provisions of the Uniform Commercial Code as adopted by the State of New York, and not the United Nations Convention on*

Contracts for the International Sale of Goods (Vienna Convention), shall apply to this agreement."]

SECTION 21. All notices herein provided for may be given by personal delivery, by registered mail, or by teletransmission addressed to the Distributor at

_____

or FAX _____; or to the Company at _____,

_____ U.S.A., FAX _____

IN WITNESS WHEREOF, the parties hereto have caused this agreement to be duly executed this _____ day of _____, 199_____.

(Company) _____   (Distributor) _____

_____   _____

By: By:

[NOTE: Should the agreement require minimum inventories or substantial post sale servicing obligations, it is clear that additional sections would need to be added, spelling out the parameters of those obligations.]

Appendix R
Sample Design and Trademark Licensing Agreement

The following is a sample design and trademark licensing agreement between a U.S. manufacturer and a foreign licensee. It contains a design or consumer goods orientation rather than a technology emphasis, with minimal conditions.

THIS AGREEMENT, this _____ day of _____, 19___, and between _____, hereinafter referred to as Licensor and _____, hereinafter referred to as Licensee.

WITNESSETH:

WHEREAS, Licensor is engaged in business in the State of _____, United States of America, as a manufacturer under various names and in design and distribution of various products bearing the label an illustration of which is attached to Appendix _____, and

WHEREAS, Licensor has spent substantial time, money, and talent creating and making known said trade names and the various products to which it is applied, and is owner of all right, title, and interest in and to the trademark or trade name _____, as used in connection with various consumer products, and

WHEREAS, Licensee desires to acquire certain rights for the manufacture and sale of Licensor's product, hereinafter called 'said product' and to receive logo, artwork, samples, and designs of said product as the same is distributed or proposed to be distributed by Licensor, together with information, advice, and data with regard to the manufacture and sale thereof, and

WHEREAS, Licensor desires to grant such rights upon the terms, convenants, and conditions as hereinafter set forth.

NOW, THEREFORE, it is agreed by and between the parties hereto as follows:

LICENSOR SERVICES AND SERVICE CHARGES

1. During the continuation of this agreement, Licensor shall provide the following services to Licensee:
   a. Provide samples, designs, patterns, and other data together with complete specifications for the manufacture of said product.
   b. Upon request, supply a complete description of machinery, equipment, and attachments for the manufacture of said product.
   c. Keep Licensee informed of improvements in design, manufacturing techniques, and innovations to the said product, which may come to the knowledge of the Licensor.
   d. Exclusive use of the U.S. Trademark Application Serial Number _____ _____ and rights to any further trademark applications, copyrights, or copyright applications that may be allowed as they pertain to the product specified herein.

TERRITORY

2. The territory covered by this agreement shall be _____ (hereinafter called the 'Territory') and such other areas as shall be mutually agreed upon and accepted by each party in writing to the other by registered letter.

DESIGNS AND TRADEMARKS GRANTED

3. Licensor hereby grants Licensee the right to use all designs or trade names, as detailed in Appendix ____ of this agreement, which are now or at any time during the terms hereof owned by Licensor under the terms of this agreement, and to appoint Licensee registered user in its territory of the trade name and trademark on said product. Title to all such designs, trademarks, and trade names shall at all times be vested in Licensor.

PRODUCT IMPROVEMENTS

4. Licensee shall advise Licensor in writing of any improvements, proposed or made, to the design construction or packaging of the product, and such improvements will be assigned to the Licensor and will be included as part of this agreement.

TRADEMARK VALIDITY

5. Licensee agrees not to raise or cause to be raised any questions concerning, or objections to, the validity of the licensed trademarks or the right of the Licensor thereto, on any grounds whatever.

ROYALTY

6. The consideration for the service to be rendered by Licensor and for the License hereby granted shall be an amount equal to ____% of the said product net merchandise sales, as actually invoiced by the Licensee under this agreement to any category of customer, and shall be payable on or before thirty (30) days following the end of each quarter of the term hereof to Licensor in U.S. currency (hereinafter referred to as 'royalty payments').

ACCOUNTING FOR ROYALTY PAYMENTS

7. Licensee agrees to accompany all royalty payments as above set forth by a statement showing the details concerning the said products sold and the sales prices thereof. Said statement to be certified by Licensee's external auditor at least once during each year of this agreement and in connection with final termination statement. Licensor shall have the privilege of examining the books and records of the Licensee at any time during usual business hours and shall have the right to appoint auditors or agents to inspect the books and records of the Licensee concerning the manufacture and sales of the said product in order to verify the accuracy of the figures submitted. This privilege extends for one year beyond termination of this agreement.

MINIMUM ROYALTY PAYMENTS DUE

8. It is understood and agreed that Licensee shall pay the Licensor a minimum royalty payment of U.S. $_____ in advance of the signing of this agreement. During the second and third year of this agreement, Licensee shall pay the Licensor a minimum royalty payment of U.S. $_____ on the first day of each contract year.

TERMS AND RENEWAL

9. With regard to this agreement's terms and renewal:
   a. This agreement shall be effective for three years, said term to commence the ____ day of _____, 19____, and expire at midnight on the ____ day of _____, 19____.
   b. This agreement may be renewed by the Licensee under the same terms and conditions herein for one additional three (3) year period on the expiration of the term of this initial agreement, provided the Licensor is not in default of any terms of this agreement, including the timely accounting and pay-

ment of royalties due, and providing earned royalties for the last twelve (12) months of the initial term of this agreement exceed U.S. $_____. The Licensee shall give written notice of intention to exercise this option at least six (6) months prior to the expiration of the initial terms of this agreement.

LICENSEE CONDUCT

10. Licensee agrees to conduct its business according to the highest business ethics and to manufacture the said product to the same standard and specifications as manufactured and produced by Licensor.

TRADEMARK AND COPYRIGHT PROTECTION

11. Licensee shall extend its cooperation to protect all trade names, trademarks, and copyrights registered in Licensor's name in the Territory against infringement by others and may, upon permission by Licensor, institute and maintain such legal action as may be necessary to protect such registered trade names, trademarks, and copyrights. The expense thereof shall be borne equally by Licensor and Licensee, and any recovery had by reason of the said lawsuit shall be equally divided between them. It is understood, however, that Licensor's share shall be payable only out of royalties that may become due under this agreement.

LICENSEE ADVERTISING

12. Licensee shall properly advertise the said product at Licensee's expense and furnish to Licensor copies of all advertising and publicity of said articles during the term of this agreement. Licensee shall expend a minimum of U.S. $_____ in advertising said product in the first year and ____% of projected annual sales each year thereafter and provide on request copies of all media billing to permit such expenditures to be verified.

TERRITORIAL LIMITATIONS

13. This License pertains solely to the Territory and is an exclusive right to manufacture and sell the said product solely with the Territory. Licensee shall not sell or allow to be transshipped or redistributed to customers for use or resale outside of the Territory, and shall take all steps necessary to avoid such occurrences. Any agreements to the contrary shall be in writing between the parties.

LICENSEE's OWN CREDIT RISK

14. It is further understood and agreed that as to all sales, regardless of whether or not money for said products is collected by Licensee, all risk or loss and credit shall be borne by Licensee.

NONAGENCY

15. It is further agreed that Licensee shall purchase all materials and incur all expenses in connection with said business in its own name and shall not use the name of Licensor as a means of obtaining credit, and no authority is granted to Licensee to incur any indebtedness on the part of Licensor. It is understood that Licensee shall conduct an independent business of its own, separate and apart from Licensor's business, and that no agency or partnership or joint venture is contemplated by the parties.

GOVERNMENT APPROVAL

16. Licensee shall upon execution of this agreement use its best efforts to obtain any and all government approvals required relating to this agreement.

QUALITY STANDARDS

17. Licensor may, on written notice, advise Licensee of any reasonable dissatisfaction regarding the use by the Licensee of inferior quality or workmanship so as to depreciate the value of the trademark or name, and in the event that the condition so specified shall not be remedied within sixty (60) days thereafter, this agreement may be terminated by Licensor at its option upon written notice.

TRADEMARKS

18. Licensor agrees to immediately make all possible efforts at Licensor's sole expense to obtain registration of appropriate trademarks not in place on date of execution in _____, it being understood that any deficiencies or legal barriers to such trademarks will not otherwise render this agreement invalid.

BANKRUPTCY

19. Licensor may terminate this agreement in the event that either Licensee is adjudged bankrupt or a receiver or custodian of its business is appointed, or in the event that there is an assignment for the benefit of creditors, or in the event that Licensee avails itself of any law for the benefit or relief of debtors.

NONASSIGNMENT

20. It is understood that Licensee may not assign its rights under this agreement without prior written permission from Licensor.

LICENSEE DEFAULT

21. In the event that Licensee defaults or breaches any of this provisions of the license agreement, or fails to account for or pay Licensor hereunder,

Licensor reserves the right to cancel the License here granted upon thirty (30) days written notice to Licensee, provided however, that if Licensee within said thirty (30) day period cures the said default, breach, or nonpayment, the License herein granted shall continue in full force and effect. In the event of termination by Licensor of the License herein granted, Licensee shall not be relieved of any of the duties and obligations under this agreement or to pay royalties accrued and due and payable at the effective date of termination.

PROVISION FOR LICENSEE QUALITY SAMPLES

22. Licensee shall provide to Licensor without cost a sample of each item manufactured and sold by Licensee so that Licensor may have the opportunity to examine the quality of such product and to make suggestions and give advice to Licensee for the purpose of improving said product in such manner as the Licensor deems advisable.

NONWAIVER

23. The failure of the Licensor at any time to enforce any provision of this agreement shall not be deemed a waiver of any such provisions herein or of Licensor's right thereafter to enforce such provisions or any other provisions herein.

TERMINATION RIGHTS AND PROVISIONS

24. Upon termination of this license agreement, by either party for any reason, Licensee shall cease the manufacture of the said product and shall cease the use of all trademarks and all trade names belonging to Licensor, provided that Licensee shall be entitled to dispose of any stocks of the said product during the period of six (6) months after the date of such termination, provided all sums then due Licensor have been paid, and Licensee will continue to pay Licensor royalties of 5 percent of the new wholesale price of all such sales during the final sell-off period. Licensee shall provide Licensor within ten (10) days of termination of this agreement an inventory of licensed product on hand, and the Licensor shall have the right to conduct a physical inventory to verify said inventory.

HOLD HARMLESS

25. Licensee agrees to hold harmless and indemnify Licensor against all cost and expenses and all judgments and decrees resulting from any defect in manufacturing of said product.

JURISDICTION AND ARBITRATION

26. All disputes or differences of interpretation that may arise between the parties, out of or in relation to this agreement, or for the breach thereof, shall be finally settled by arbitration in _____, U.S.A., in

accordance with the Commercial Arbitration Rules of the American Commercial Arbitration Association. The award rendered by the arbitrator(s) shall be final and binding upon the parties hereto.

PARTIAL INVALIDITY

27. Should any of the provisions herein be contrary or repugnant to the laws of the United States or the Territory of any laws hereafter promulgated and, by virtue thereof, should any of the provisions herein become invalid, this fact shall not invalidate this agreement, and the remainder of this agreement shall remain the intent and purpose of the surviving portions.

NOTIFICATION

28. All notices referred to in this agreement shall be sent by registered mail addressed to the party for whom such notice is intended at its last known place of business, the current proper address for each party being: _____

_____

INCLUSIVENESS

29. This document contains all the undertakings and agreements of the parties hereto and shall not be altered, changed, or amended in any manner whatsoever except in writing, signed by both parties hereto.

IN WITNESS WHEREOF, the parties hereto have caused this agreement to be executed this ____ day of _____, 19___.

Index

About the Authors

L. Fargo Wells is one of America's most sought-after advisors on export. As director of the California Export Finance Office, he pioneered state support for selling abroad. He now serves as a consultant to both the private and government sectors and as a director of several corporations.

Karin B. Dulat is an experienced international trader who for many years has operated a respected and successful export management company in Southern California.